To our children

Peter

William

Benjamin

and Zoë Mae

About the Authors

Frances Howard-Snyder is Professor of Philosophy at Western Washington University, where she has taught since 1993. She has a PhD in philosophy from Syracuse University and an MA from the University of Cape Town. She has published articles on topics in normative ethics, philosophy of religion, and metaphysics in *The Journal of Philosophy*, *American Philosophical Quarterly*, and *Philosophical Studies*, among other places. When she is not doing philosophy, she most especially enjoys spending time with her husband, Dan, and her twins, Peter and William.

Daniel Howard-Snyder is Professor of Philosophy at Western Washington University, where he has taught since 2000. He has a PhD from Syracuse University and a BA from Seattle Pacific University. He is editor or co-editor of four books, *The Evidential Argument from Evil* (Indiana University Press, 1996), *Faith, Freedom, and Rationality* (Rowman & Littlefield, 1996), *Divine Hiddenness* (Cambridge, 2002), and *The Blackwell Companion to the Problem of Evil* (Blackwell 2013). He has published articles in, among other places, *Philosophy and Phenomenological Research*, *American Philosophical Quarterly*, and *Faith and Philosophy*. His chief love is his family—Frances, William, and Peter—without whom his life would be bereft of all joy.

Ryan Wasserman is Associate Professor and Chair of Philosophy at Western Washington University, where he has taught since 2005. He has a PhD from Rutgers University and a BA from Western. His main philosophical interests are in metaphysics, ethics, and the philosophy of language. He has published articles in many journals, including *Mind*, *Noûs*, and *Philosophical Quarterly*. He is also co-editor of *Metametaphysics* (Oxford University Press, 2008). Apart from philosophy, Ryan spends most of his time playing with his son, Benjamin, and his daughter, Zoë Mae.

Brief Contents

Contents

CHAPTER 5   *Categorical Logic: Statements*   197

CHAPTER 6   *Categorical Logic: Syllogisms*   225

CHAPTER 7 *Statement Logic: Truth Tables*   279

Preface

Critical thinking skills are some of the most prized commodities in today's knowledge-based economy, and the study of logic is one of the best ways to develop these skills. With its emphasis on presenting, understanding, and evaluating arguments, logic has the power to make us quicker, clearer, and more creative thinkers. It can help us to articulate and support our own views, and to analyze the views of others.

In short, there are many benefits to the study of logic. But there are also potential obstacles. Logic can be intimidating. It can be frustrating. It can even be *boring*.

The Power of Logic is written with the hopes of removing these kinds of obstacles. The book features a simple and direct writing style that helps makes even the most technical matters approachable. It features a wealth of helpful tips and on-line resources to combat common frustrations. And it includes hundreds of examples and exercises that give readers the opportunity to apply their critical thinking skills to interesting arguments from philosophy, politics, and religion. Our hope is that these features help to make logic accessible and interesting, and that they enable you to put the power of logic to work in your own life.

New Features

We have made many improvements in light of critical reviews and our classroom experience with previous editions. We have also made some very specific improvements as follows:

- The book has been heavily rewritten, with a focus on eliminating excess verbiage, repetitive passages, and outdated material.
- There are dozens of new definition boxes, which emphasize key concepts and important distinctions.
- There are over a dozen new summary boxes, including summaries of the abbreviated truth-table method and the finite universe method. These boxes contain simple, clear descriptions for quick reference and study.
- Chapter 2, Identifying Arguments, provides a clearer explanation of how to reconstruct an argument.
- Chapter 3, Logic and Language, expands the discussion of propositions, sentences, and truth.
- Chapter 4, Informal Fallacies, now emphasizes how sound or cogent arguments can resemble fallacies and explains how to avoid identifying them as fallacies. It also includes a new discussion of some purported fallacies

such as the "Intentional fallacy" and the "is-ought fallacy" that are sometimes invoked to avoid a more substantive discussion.

- Chapter 9, Predicate Logic, contains a revised definition of a WFF for the language of predicate logic. Section 9.3 includes five new sets of exercises, which allows students to master the quantifier rules one at a time.
- Chapter 10, Induction, has been reorganized and refocused. It includes a new discussion of arguments from authority, and a greater emphasis on the connection between probability and inductive logic.

Enduring Features

We have retained many of the features that have made *The Power of Logic* successful in the past.

- Early chapters focus on relatively informal methods. More technical material is introduced gradually, with symbolic logic receiving thorough treatment in Chapters 7 to 9.
- The writing is concise and lively throughout the text. The chapter on truth tables includes a discussion of the material conditional and its relation to the English "if-then" and emphasizes abbreviated truth tables.
- The system of natural deduction for statement logic is entirely standard, consisting of 8 implicational rules, 10 equivalence rules, conditional proof, and *reductio ad absurdum*.
- The chapter on inductive logic includes standard material on statistical syllogisms, induction by enumeration, arguments from authority, Mill's methods, scientific reasoning, and arguments from analogy. It also includes an accessible introduction to the probability calculus.
- The exercises on arguments from analogy require students to evaluate a stated criticism of each argument, which makes the exercises relatively easy to grade.

As in previous editions, various paths through this book are possible, depending on the time available, the needs of the students, and the interests of the instructor. Here are three possibilities:

- A course emphasizing traditional and informal logic, covering Chapters 1 to 6 and 10: Basic Concepts, Identifying Arguments, Logic and Language, Informal Fallacies, Categorical Logic: Statements, Categorical Logic: Syllogisms, and Inductive Logic
- A course giving roughly equal emphasis to informal and symbolic logic, covering Chapters 1 to 4, 7, and 8: Basic Concepts, Identifying Arguments, Logic and Language, Informal Fallacies, Statement Logic: Truth Tables, and Statement Logic: Proofs
- A course emphasizing symbolic methods, covering Chapters 1 and 2, 7 to 9, and 10.4: Basic Concepts, Identifying Arguments, Statement Logic: Truth Tables, Statement Logic: Proofs, Predicate Logic, and Probability

Supplements

An *Online Learning Center* accompanies this text at www.mhhe.com/howardsnyder5e. For instructors the site includes an updated solutions manual, a test bank, computerized test bank, and a complete chapter on modal logic for those who wish to cover this material. For students, the site offers learning objectives, and chapter summaries.

The site also provides accessibility to an online *Logic Tutor*, allowing students to do the vast majority of the book's exercises online with feedback. This includes creating Venn diagrams, truth tables, and proofs. Additionally, instructors can build proof, truth, and symbolization questions of their own that can also be graded by the *Logic Tutor*.

 Craft your teaching resources to match the way you teach! With McGraw-Hill Create™, www.mcgrawhillcreate.com, you can easily rearrange chapters, combine material from other content sources, and quickly upload content you have written like your course syllabus or teaching notes. Find the content you need in Create by searching through thousands of leading McGraw-Hill textbooks. Arrange your book to fit your teaching style. Create even allows you to personalize your book's appearance by selecting the cover and adding your name, school, and course information. Order a Create book and you'll receive a complimentary print review copy in three to five business days or a complimentary electronic review copy (eComp) via email in minutes. Go to www.mcgrawhillcreate.com today and register to experience how McGraw-Hill Create™ empowers you to teach *your* students *your* way.

Acknowledgments

Many people have helped improve this text throughout the years. Our greatest debt is to C. Stephen Layman, who authored the first three editions of *The Power of Logic* and is responsible for many of its best features. We also thank Allison Rona, Anne L. Bezuidenhout, Benjamin Schaeffer, Bernard F. Keating, Charles R. Carr, Charles Seymour, Cynthia B. Bryson, Darian C. De Bolt, Eric Kraemer, Eric Saidel, George A. Spangler, Greg Oakes, Gulten Ilhan, James K. Derden, Jr., Jason Turner, Jeffrey Roland, Jen Mills, John Casey, Jon-David Hague, Jordan J. Lindberg, Joseph Le Fevre, Keith W. Krasemann, Ken Akiba, Ken King, Maria Cimitile, Mark Storey, Martin Frické, Michael F. Wagner, Michael Rooney, Mitchell Gabhart, Nancy Slonneger Hancock, Neal Hogan, Ned Markosian, Nils Rauhut, Otávio Bueno, Patricia A. Ross, Paul Draper, Paul M. Jurczak, Peter Dlugos, Phil Schneider, Phillip Goggans, Rachel Hollenberg, Richard McClelland, Rico Vitz, Robert Boyd Skipper, Ron Jackson, Sander Lee, Sandra Johanson, Ted Sider, Terence Cuneo, Tom Downing, Ty Barnes, William J. Doulan, and Xinmin Zhu.

For the fifth edition, we thank our project team at McGraw-Hill Higher Education: Jessica Cannavo, Sponsoring Editor; Robin Reed, Developmental Editor; Angela FitzPatrick, Marketing Campaign Coordinator; Jane Mohr, Lead

Project Manager; and Margarite Reynolds, Design Coordinator. We are also very grateful to the following reviewers for their time, effort, and expertise:

Benjamin Arah, Bowie State University
Stewart Barr Pima, Community College
Joseph Campbell, Washington State University
Darron Chapman, University of Louisville
Paul Eckstein, Bergen Community College
Kevin Klement, University of Massachusetts–Amherst
Eric Kraemer, University of Wisconsin–La Crosse
Alex Levine, University of South Florida
Erik Meade, Southern Illinois University–Edwardsville
Gerald Mozur, Lewis & Clark Community College
Basil Smith, Saddleback College
Kiriake Xerohemona, Florida International University

Finally, we thank our families—especially our children—for their patience and understanding throughout the writing process. It is to them that we dedicate this book.

Frances Howard-Snyder
Daniel Howard-Snyder
Ryan Wasserman

CHAPTER 1

Basic Concepts

*E*veryone thinks. Everyone reasons. Everyone argues. And everyone is subjected to the reasoning and arguing of others. We are bombarded daily with reasoning from many sources: books, speeches, radio, TV, newspapers, employers, friends, and family.

Some people think well, reason well, and argue well. Some do not. The ability to think, reason, and argue well is partly a matter of natural gifts. But whatever our natural gifts, they can be refined and sharpened. And the study of logic is one of the best ways to refine one's natural ability to reason and argue. Through the study of logic, one learns strategies for thinking well, common errors in reasoning to avoid, and effective techniques for evaluating arguments.

But what is logic? Roughly speaking, logic is the study of methods for evaluating arguments. More precisely, **logic** is the study of methods for evaluating whether the premises of an argument adequately support (or provide good evidence for) its conclusion.

Logic is the study of methods for evaluating whether the premises of an argument adequately support its conclusion.

To get a better grasp of what logic is, then, we need to understand the key concepts involved in this definition: argument, conclusion, premise, and support. This chapter will give you an initial understanding of these basic concepts.

An **argument** is a set of statements where some of the statements are intended to support another. The **conclusion** is the claim to be supported. The **premises** are the statements offered in support. In some arguments, the conclusion is *adequately supported* by the premises; in other cases it is not. But a set of

1

statements counts as an argument as long as some of the statements are intended to support another. Here is an example:

> **1.** Every logic book contains at least one silly example. *The Power of Logic* is a logic book. So, *The Power of Logic* contains at least one silly example.

The word "so" indicates that the conclusion of this argument is "*The Power of Logic* contains at least one silly example." The argument has two premises— "Every logic book contains at least one silly example" and "*The Power of Logic* is a logic book." Of course, many arguments deal with very serious matters. Here are two examples:

> **2.** If something would have a future of value if it weren't killed, then it is wrong to kill it. Most fetuses would have a future of value if they weren't killed. So, it is wrong to kill most fetuses.
>
> **3.** If fetuses are not persons, then abortion is not wrong. Fetuses are not persons. So, abortion is not wrong.

As with argument (1), the sentences that precede the word "so" in arguments (2) and (3) are the premises and the sentence that follows the word "so" is the conclusion.

> An **argument** is a set of statements where some of the statements, called the *premises,* are intended to support another, called the *conclusion*.

What is a statement? A **statement** is a declarative sentence that is either true or false. For example:

> **4.** Some dogs are collies.
> **5.** No dogs are collies.
> **6.** Some dogs weigh exactly 124.379 pounds.

(4) is true because it describes things as they are. (5) is false because it describes things as other than they are. Truth and falsehood are the two possible **truth values.** So, we can say that a statement is a declarative sentence that has a truth value. The truth value of (4) is true while the truth value of (5) is false, but (4) and (5) are both statements. Is (6) a statement? Yes. No one may know its truth value, but (6) is either true or false, and hence it is a statement.

> A **statement** is a declarative sentence that is either true or false.

Are any of the following items statements?

7. Get your dog off my lawn!

8. How many dogs do you own?

9. Let's get a dog.

No. (7) is a *command*, which could be obeyed or disobeyed. But it makes no sense to say that a command is true or false, so it is not a statement. (8) is a *question*, which could be answered or unanswered. But a question cannot be true or false, so it is not a statement. Finally, (9) is a *proposal*, which could be accepted or rejected. But a proposal cannot be true or false, so it also fails to be a statement.

We have said that an argument is a set of statements, where some of the statements (the premises) are intended to support another (the conclusion).[1] We must now distinguish two ways the premises can be intended to support the conclusion, and hence two different kinds of arguments. A **deductive argument** is one in which the premises are intended to *guarantee* the conclusion. An **inductive argument** is one in which the premises are intended to make the conclusion *probable*, without guaranteeing it. The following two examples illustrate this distinction:

10. All philosophers like logic. Ned is a philosopher. So, Ned likes logic.

11. Most philosophers like logic. Ned is a philosopher. So, Ned likes logic.

The premises of argument (10) are intended to support the conclusion in this sense: It is *guaranteed* that, if they are true, then the conclusion is true as well. (10) is an example of a deductive argument. The premises of argument (11) do *not* support the conclusion in this same sense. Even if Ned is a philosopher and even if the majority of philosophers enjoy logic, it is not guaranteed that Ned enjoys logic; he might be among the minority who do not care for logic at all. The premises of (11) support the conclusion in a different sense, however: It is *probable* that if they are true, then the conclusion is true as well. (11) is an example of an inductive argument.

A **deductive argument** is one in which the premises are intended to *guarantee* the conclusion. An **inductive argument** is one in which the premises are intended to make the conclusion *probable,* without guaranteeing it.

Earlier, we said that logic is the study of methods to evaluate arguments. Since there are two kinds of arguments, there are also two areas of logic. **Deductive logic** is the study of methods for evaluating whether the premises of an argument guarantee its conclusion. **Inductive logic** is the study of methods for evaluating whether the premises of an argument make its conclusion probable, without guaranteeing it.[2] The first three sections of this chapter introduce some of the key elements of deductive logic. The fourth section focuses on inductive logic.

1.1   Validity and Soundness

A deductive argument is one in which the premises are intended to guarantee the conclusion. Of course, one can *intend* to do something without *actually* doing it—just as the best-laid plans of mice and men often go awry, so deductive arguments often go wrong. A **valid argument** is a deductive argument in which the premises *succeed* in guaranteeing the conclusion. An *invalid* argument is a deductive argument in which the premises *fail* to guarantee the conclusion. More formally, a valid argument is one in which it is necessary that, if the premises are true, then the conclusion is true.

> A **valid argument** is one in which it is necessary that, if the premises are true, then the conclusion is true.

Two key aspects of this definition should be noted immediately. First, note the important word "necessary." In a valid argument, there is a *necessary connection* between the premises and the conclusion. The conclusion doesn't just happen to be true given the premises; rather, the truth of the conclusion is absolutely guaranteed given the truth of the premises. That is, a valid argument is one in which it is absolutely *impossible* for the premises to be true while the conclusion is false. Second, note the conditional (if-then) aspect of the definition. It does not say that the premises and conclusion of a valid argument are in fact true. Rather, the definition says that, necessarily, *if* the premises are true, then the conclusion is true. In other words, if an argument is valid, then it is necessary that, *on the assumption that* its premises are true, its conclusion is true also. Each of the following arguments is valid:

12. All biologists are scientists. John is not a scientist. So, John is not a biologist.
13. If Alice stole the diamonds, then she is a thief. And Alice did steal the diamonds. Hence, Alice is a thief.
14. Either Bill has a poor memory or he is lying. Bill does not have a poor memory. Therefore, Bill is lying.

In each case, it is necessary that if the premises are true, then the conclusion is true. Thus, in each case, the argument is valid.

In everyday English, the word "valid" is often used simply to indicate one's overall approval of an argument. But the methods logicians develop for assessing arguments focus on the link between the premises and the conclusion rather than on the actual truth or falsity of the statements composing the argument.

The following observations about validity may help prevent some common misunderstandings. First, notice that an argument can have one or more false premises and still be valid. For instance:

> **15.** All birds are animals. Some cats are birds. So, some cats are animals.

Here, the second premise is plainly false, and yet the argument is valid, for it is necessary that if the premises are true, the conclusion is true also. And in the following argument, both premises are false, but the argument is still valid:

> **16.** All sharks are birds. All birds are predators. So, all sharks are predators.

Although the premises of this argument are in fact false, it is impossible for the conclusion to be false while the premises are true. So, it is valid.

Second, we cannot rightly conclude that an argument is valid simply on the grounds that its premises are all true. For example:

> **17.** Some Americans are women. Ashton Kutcher is an American. Therefore, Ashton Kutcher is a woman.

The premises here are true, but the conclusion is false. So, obviously, it is possible that the conclusion is false while the premises are true; hence, (17) is not valid. Is the following argument valid?

> **18.** Some Americans work in the television industry. Ellen DeGeneres is an American. Hence, Ellen DeGeneres works in the television industry.

Here, we have true premises and a true conclusion. But it is not necessary that, if the premises are true, then the conclusion is true. (Ms. DeGeneres could switch to another line of work while remaining an American.) So, even if an argument has true premises and a true conclusion, it might not be valid. Thus, the question "Are the premises and the conclusion actually true?" is distinct from the question "Is the argument valid?"

Third, suppose an argument is valid and has a false conclusion. Must it then have at least one false premise? Yes. If it had true premises, then it would have to have a true conclusion because it is valid. *Validity preserves truth*; that is, if we start with truth and reason in a valid fashion, we will always wind up with truth.

Fourth, does validity also preserve falsehood? In other words, if we start with false premises and reason validly, are we bound to wind up with a false conclusion? No. Consider the following argument:

> **19.** All Martians are Republicans. All Republicans are extraterrestrials. So, all Martians are extraterrestrials.

Is this argument valid? Yes. It is impossible for the conclusion to be false *assuming that* its premises are true. However, the premises here are false while the conclusion is true. So, *validity does not preserve falsehood*. In fact, false premises plus valid reasoning may lead to either truth or falsity, depending on the case. Here is a valid argument with false premises and a false conclusion:

> **20.** All highly intelligent beings are from outer space. Some armadillos are highly intelligent beings. So, some armadillos are from outer space.

The lesson here is that although valid reasoning guarantees that we will end up with truth if we start with it, valid reasoning does not guarantee that we will end up with falsehood if we start with it.

Fifth, notice that we can know whether an argument is valid or invalid even if we do not know the truth value of the conclusion and all of the premises. Consider this example:

> **21.** All Schnitzers are BMWs. Emily Larson owns a Schnitzer. So, Emily Larson owns a BMW.

Chances are that you have no idea whether the conclusion and all of the premises are true, but this argument is obviously valid; it is not possible for Emily not to own a BMW on the assumption that she owns a Schnitzer and all Schnitzers are BMWs. Here is another example:

> **22.** All reliabilists are foundationalists. William Alston is a foundationalist. Thus, William Alston is a reliabilist.

You probably haven't the foggiest idea what the truth values of these statements are; indeed, you might not even know what they mean. Nevertheless, you can tell that this argument is invalid because the premises do not rule out the possibility that Alston is a foundationalist of a nonreliabilist stripe.

Earlier, we said that an invalid argument is a deductive argument in which the premises fail to guarantee the conclusion. More formally, an **invalid argument** is one in which it is *not* necessary that, if the premises are true, then the conclusion is true.

> An **invalid argument** is one in which it is *not* necessary that, if the premises are true, then the conclusion is true.

In other words, an invalid argument is one in which it is *possible* for the premises to be true while the conclusion is false. Even on the assumption that the premises are true, the conclusion could still be false. Each of the following arguments is invalid:

23. All dogs are animals. All cats are animals. Hence, all dogs are cats.
24. If Pat is a wife, then Pat is a woman. But Pat is not a wife. So, Pat is not a woman.
25. Phil likes Margo. Therefore, Margo likes Phil.

Since the premises of argument (23) are in fact true but its conclusion is false, it is obviously possible for its premises to be true while its conclusion is false; so, it is invalid. Argument (24) is invalid because its premises leave open the possibility that Pat is an unmarried woman. And (25) is invalid because even if Phil does like Margo, it remains open whether she feels the same way toward him. In each of these cases, then, the conclusion could be false while the premises are true.

The foregoing five points about validity, invalidity, and truth are summarized by the following table:

	Valid argument	Invalid argument
True premises True conclusion	If Harry loved Dumbledore, then Harry was sad when Dumbledore died. Harry loved Dumbledore. So, Harry was sad when Dumbledore died. [1]	Some Americans work in business. Donald Trump is an American. So, Donald Trump works in business. [6]
False premises False conclusion	All sharks are birds. All birds are politicians. So, all sharks are politicians. [2]	Every genius is a philosopher. Forrest Gump is a philosopher. So, Forrest Gump is a genius. [7]
False premises True conclusion	All dogs are ants. All ants are mammals. So, all dogs are mammals. [3]	Everything colored is red. Stephen Colbert is a mortician. So, Stephen Colbert is hilarious. [8]
True premises False conclusion	[4]	All dogs are animals. All cats are animals. Hence, all dogs are cats. [9]
Unknown truth value	All of the Cappadocians accepted perichoresis. Basil was a Cappadocian. So, Basil accepted perichoresis. [5]	Some hylidae are heterophoric. Maggie is heterophoric. So, Maggie is a hylidae. [10]

Notice that validity is not enough all by itself for a *good* deductive argument. A valid argument with false premises can lead to a false conclusion (box 2). Moreover, truth is not enough all by itself for a *good* deductive argument. An invalid argument with all true premises can lead to a false conclusion (box 9). We want our deductive arguments to be valid and to have all true premises. An argument that has both is a *sound argument.* In other words, a valid argument in which all of the premises are true is a **sound argument.**

 A **sound argument** is a valid argument in which all of the premises are true.

Because a sound argument is valid and has only true premises, its conclusion will also be true. Validity preserves truth. That's why there is nothing in box 4. The argument in box 1 is sound; here are two more sound arguments:

26. All collies are dogs. All dogs are animals. So, all collies are animals.

27. If Mozart was a composer, then he understood music. Mozart was a composer. Hence, Mozart understood music.

In each case, it is necessary that, if the premises are true, then the conclusion is true; moreover, in each case, all of the premises are true. Thus, each argument is sound.

Valid + All Premises True = Sound

By way of contrast, an *unsound argument* falls into one of the following three categories:

Category 1: It is valid, but it has at least one false premise.

Category 2: It is invalid, but all of its premises are true.

Category 3: It is invalid and it has at least one false premise.

In other words, an **unsound argument** is one that either is invalid or has at least one false premise.

 An **unsound argument** is one that either is invalid or has at least one false premise.

For example, these three arguments are unsound:

28. All birds are animals. Some grizzly bears are not animals. Therefore, some grizzly bears are not birds.

29. All birds are animals. All grizzly bears are animals. So, all grizzly bears are birds.

30. All trees are animals. All bears are animals. So, all bears are trees.

Argument (28) is unsound because, although it is valid, it has a false (second) premise. It is in Category 1. Argument (29) is unsound because, although it has all true premises, it is invalid. It is in Category 2. Argument (30) is unsound because it has a false (first) premise and it is invalid. It is in Category 3. (Which boxes in the previous table contain unsound arguments? To which of the three categories does each unsound argument in the table belong?)

Here is a map of the main concepts we've discussed so far:

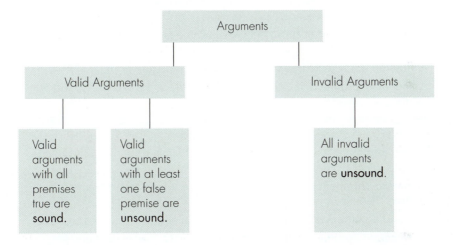

We said earlier that we want a deductive argument to be valid and have all true premises. That is, we want a deductive argument to be sound. That is *not* to say, however, that if an argument is sound, it leaves nothing to be desired. A sound argument that had its conclusion as a premise would be use-less (see section 4.3 on begging the question). Moreover, a sound argument whose premises were not reasonable for us to accept given our total evidence would hardly be a satisfying, compelling, and useful basis for believing the conclusion. To say the least, then, we want more from a deductive argument than its being sound.

Nevertheless, we want a deductive argument to be sound, and deductive logic plays an indispensable role in assessing whether an argument is sound. For an argument is sound only if it is valid, and as we said earlier, deductive logic is the study of methods for evaluating whether the premises of an argument guarantee its conclusion; that is, deductive logic is the study of methods of evaluating whether or not an argument is valid. In the next two sections we will display some initial methods for determining whether or not an argument is valid, and in the process we will get a better handle on the basic concepts that we have introduced thus far. But first, a note on terminology is in order. Given our definitions, arguments are neither true nor false, but each statement is either true or false. On the other hand, arguments can be valid, invalid, sound, or unsound, but statements cannot be valid, invalid, sound, or unsound. Therefore, a given premise (or conclusion) is either true or false, but it cannot be valid, invalid, sound, or unsound.

Summary of Definitions

Logic is the study of methods for evaluating whether the premises of an argument adequately support its conclusion.

An **argument** is a set of statements where some of the statements, called the *premises,* are intended to support another, called the *conclusion.*

A **statement** is a sentence that is either true or false.

A **deductive argument** is one in which the premises are intended to *guarantee* the conclusion.

An **inductive argument** is one in which the premises are intended to make the conclusion *probable,* without guaranteeing it.

A **valid argument** is one in which it is necessary that, if the premises are true, then the conclusion is true.

An **invalid argument** is one in which it is *not* necessary that, if the premises are true, then the conclusion is true.

A **sound argument** is a valid argument in which all of the premises are true.

An **unsound argument** is one that either is invalid or has at least one false premise.

EXERCISE 1.1

Note: For each exercise item preceded by an asterisk, the answer appears in the Answer Key at the end of the book.

PART A: Recognizing Statements Write "statement" if the item is a statement. Write "sentence only" if the item is a sentence but not a statement. Write "neither" if the item is neither a sentence nor a statement.

* **1.** The sky is blue.
  2. Let's paint the table red.
  3. Please close the window!
* **4.** Murder is illegal.

   5. Abraham Lincoln was born in 1983.

   6. If San Francisco is in California, then San Francisco is in the U.S.A.

* **7.** It is not the case that Ben Franklin.

   8. "Why?" asked Socrates.

   9. Table not yes if.

***10.** Either humans evolved from apes or apes evolved from humans.

 11. Davy Crockett died at the Alamo.

 12. How are you?

***13.** If seven is greater than six, then six is greater than seven.

 14. Let's have lunch.

 15. Go!

***16.** Shall we dance?

 17. Patrick Henry said, "Give me liberty or give me death."

 18. If punishment deters crime.

***19.** "Stand at attention!" ordered General Bradley.

 20. Despite the weather.

 21. The longest shark in the Pacific Ocean.

 22. Either Heather or Cheri.

 23. If there is only one human.

 24. Either shut the door or turn off the radio.

 25. Do you swear to tell the truth?

 26. Having seen all the suffering.

 27. Let's stop griping and get to work.

 28. Fame is a drug.

 29. By faith and love.

 30. Either Laura is angry or Edith is depressed.

PART B: True or False? Which of the following statements are true? Which are false?

* **1.** All valid arguments have at least one false premise.

   2. An argument is a set of statements where some of the statements, called the *premises*, are intended to support another, called the *conclusion*.

   3. Every valid argument has true premises and only true premises.

* **4.** Logic is the study of methods for evaluating whether the premises of an argument adequately support its conclusion.

   5. Some statements are invalid.

   6. Every valid argument has true premises and a true conclusion.

 * **7.** A sound argument can have a false conclusion.

   8. Deductive logic is the part of logic that is concerned with tests for validity and invalidity.

   9. If a valid argument has only true premises, then it must have a true conclusion.

 * **10.** Some arguments are true.

  11. If a valid argument has only false premises, then it must have a false conclusion.

  12. Some invalid arguments have false conclusions but (all) true premises.

 * **13.** Every sound argument is valid.

  14. Every valid argument with a true conclusion is sound.

  15. Every valid argument with a false conclusion has at least one false premise.

 * **16.** Every unsound argument is invalid.

  17. Some premises are valid.

  18. If all of the premises of an argument are true, then it is sound.

 * **19.** If an argument has (all) true premises and a false conclusion, then it is invalid.

  20. If an argument has one false premise, then it is unsound.

  21. Every unsound argument has at least one false premise.

 * **22.** Some statements are sound.

  23. Every valid argument has a true conclusion.

  24. Every invalid argument is unsound.

 * **25.** Some arguments are false.

  26. If an argument is invalid, then it must have true premises and a false conclusion.

  27. Every valid argument has this feature: Necessarily, if its premises are true, then its conclusion is true.

 * **28.** Every invalid argument has this feature: It is possibly false that if its premises are true, then its conclusion is true.

  29. Every sound argument has a true conclusion.

  30. Every valid argument has this feature: Necessarily, if its premises are false, then its conclusion is false.

  31. A deductive argument is one in which the premises are intended to make the conclusion probable, without guaranteeing it.

  32. An inductive argument is one in which the premises are intended to guarantee the conclusion.

  33. Inductive logic is the study of methods for evaluating whether the premises of an argument make its conclusion probable, without guaranteeing it.

  34. "It's raining outside, so the ground is wet" is best regarded as a deductive argument.

  35. "It must be raining outside. After all, if it weren't, then the ground would be dry, but it's soaking wet" is best regarded as an inductive argument.

PART C: Valid or Invalid? Much of this text concerns methods of testing arguments for validity. Although we have not yet discussed any particular methods of testing arguments for validity, we do have definitions of "valid argument" and "invalid argument." Based on your current understanding, which of the following arguments are valid? Which are invalid? (*Hint:* Use the definitions that have been provided.)

* **1.** If Lincoln was killed in an automobile accident, then Lincoln is dead. Lincoln was killed in an automobile accident. Hence, Lincoln is dead.

  2. If Lincoln was killed in an automobile accident, then Lincoln is dead. Lincoln was not killed in an automobile accident. Therefore, Lincoln is not dead.

  3. If Lincoln was killed in an automobile accident, then Lincoln is dead. Lincoln is dead. So, Lincoln was killed in an automobile accident.

* **4.** If Lincoln was killed in an automobile accident, then Lincoln is dead. Lincoln is not dead. Hence, Lincoln was not killed in an automobile accident.

  5. Either 2 plus 2 equals 22 or Santa Claus is real. But 2 plus 2 does not equal 22. Therefore, Santa Claus is real.

  6. Either we use nuclear power or we reduce our consumption of energy. If we use nuclear power, then we place our lives at great risk. If we reduce our consumption of energy, then we place ourselves under extensive governmental control. So, either we place our lives at great risk or we place ourselves under extensive governmental control.

* **7.** All birds are animals. No tree is a bird. Therefore, no tree is an animal.

  8. Some humans are comatose. But no comatose being is rational. So, not every human is rational.

  9. All animals are living things. At least one cabbage is a living thing. So, at least one cabbage is an animal.

* **10.** Alvin likes Jane. Jane likes Chris. So, Alvin likes Chris.

  11. All murderers are criminals. Therefore, all nonmurderers are noncriminals.

  12. David is shorter than Saul. Saul is shorter than Goliath. It follows that David is shorter than Goliath.

* **13.** It is possible that McGraw will win the next presidential election. It is possible that Lambert will win the next presidential election. Thus, it is possible that both McGraw and Lambert will win the next presidential election.

  14. All physicians are singers. Lady Gaga is a physician. Therefore, Lady Gaga is a singer.

  15. Samuel Morse invented the telegraph. Alexander Graham Bell did not invent the telegraph. Consequently, Morse is not identical with Bell.

PART D: Soundness Which of the following arguments are sound? Which are unsound? If an argument is unsound, explain why.

* **1.** All cats are mammals. All mammals are animals. So, all cats are animals.

  2. All collies are dogs. Some animals are not dogs. So, some animals are not collies.

3. All citizens of Nebraska are Americans. All citizens of Montana are Americans. So, all citizens of Nebraska are citizens of Montana.

* **4.** "Let's party!" is either a sentence or a statement (or both). "Let's party!" is a sentence. So, "Let's party!" is not a statement.

5. No diamonds are emeralds. The Hope Diamond is a diamond. So, the Hope Diamond is not an emerald.

6. All planets are round. The earth is round. So, the earth is a planet.

* **7.** If the Taj Mahal is in Kentucky, then the Taj Mahal is in the U.S.A. But the Taj Mahal is not in the U.S.A. So, the Taj Mahal is not in Kentucky.

8. All women are married. Some executives are not married. So, some executives are not women.

9. All mammals are animals. No reptiles are mammals. So, no reptiles are animals.

* **10.** All mammals are cats. All cats are animals. So, all mammals are animals.

11. Wilbur Wright invented the airplane. Therefore, Orville Wright did not invent the airplane.

12. All collies are dogs. Hence, all dogs are collies.

* **13.** William Shakespeare wrote *Hamlet*. Leo Tolstoy is identical with William Shakespeare. It follows that Leo Tolstoy wrote *Hamlet*.

14. If San Francisco is in Saskatchewan, then San Francisco is in Canada. But it is not true that San Francisco is in Saskatchewan. Hence, it is not true that San Francisco is in Canada.

15. Either Thomas Jefferson was the first president of the U.S.A. or George Washington was the first president of the U.S.A., but not both. George Washington was the first president of the U.S.A. So, Thomas Jefferson was not the first president of the U.S.A.

1.2 Forms and Validity

Deductive logic is the study of methods for determining whether or not an argument is valid. This section introduces the concept of an argument form and explains how an understanding of argument forms can help establish the validity of an argument.

Argument Forms

Consider the following two arguments:

31. 1. If Pepé is a Chihuahua, then Pepé is a dog.

2. Pepé is a Chihuahua.

So, 3. Pepé is a dog.

32. 1. If Obama is a U.S. president, then Obama is a U.S. citizen.

2. Obama is a U.S. president.

So, 3. Obama is a U.S. citizen.

In each case, lines 1 and 2 are the premises and line 3 is the conclusion. Both of these arguments are valid: It is necessary that, if the premises are true, then the conclusion is true. Moreover, both of these arguments have the same *argument form*, where an **argument form** is simply a pattern of reasoning.

> An **argument form** is a pattern of reasoning.

The particular form of reasoning exhibited by arguments (31) and (32) is so common that logicians have given it a special name: ***modus ponens,*** which means "the mode or way of positing." (Notice that, in each of them, the second premise posits or affirms the if-part of the first premise.) This pattern of reasoning can be represented as follows:

Modus Ponens

1. If A, then B.

2. A.

So, 3. B.

Here, the letters A and B are **variables** that stand in for statements. To illustrate how these variables work, suppose that we erase each appearance of A in the form above and write the same statement in both blanks (any statement will do). Next, suppose that we erase each appearance of B and write down the same statement in both blanks. We will then have a *substitution instance* of the argument form *modus ponens*. For example, if we replace each appearance of A with the statement "Pepé is a Chihuahua" and we replace each appearance of B with the statement "Pepé is a dog," we arrive at (31). Similarly, if we substitute "Obama is a U.S. president" for A and "Obama is a U.S. citizen" for B, we are left with (32). Thus, both arguments are substitution instances of the argument form *modus ponens*. Generalizing, we can say that a **substitution instance** of an argument form is an argument that results from uniformly replacing the variables in that form with statements (or terms).*

> A **substitution instance** of an argument form is an argument that results from uniformly replacing the variables in that form with statements (or terms).

---

*The reader should ignore the parenthetical comment at this point. We will discuss forms that result from replacing terms, rather than statements, in section 1.3.

We will look at further examples of argument forms and substitution instances in a moment. But let's first use the concepts to understand how an argument's validity can be entirely due to its form.

Consider the following argument:

33. 1. If A.J. Ayer is an emotivist, then A.J. Ayer is a noncognitivist.

2. A.J. Ayer is an emotivist.

So, 3. A.J. Ayer is a noncognitivist.

Argument (33), like (31) and (32), is an instance of *modus ponens* (it results from replacing A with "A.J. Ayer is an emotivist" and B with "A.J. Ayer is a noncognitivist"). Moreover, (33), like (31) and (32), is a valid argument. This much should be clear, even if some of the words in (33) are unfamiliar and even if one has no idea who A.J. Ayer is. Suppose it's true that A.J. Ayer is an emotivist (whatever that is). And suppose it's also true that, if A.J. Ayer is an emotivist, then he is a noncognitivist (whatever that is). Given those assumptions, it must follow that A.J. Ayer is a noncognitivist as well. That is just to say that it is impossible for the premises of (33) to be true while the conclusion is false. So, it is valid.

Arguments (31), (32), and (33) illustrate the fact that the validity of an argument that has the form of *modus ponens* is guaranteed by that form alone; its validity does not depend on its subject matter (or content). Hence, every substitution instance of *modus ponens* will be a valid argument no matter what its content happens to be. In this sense, *modus ponens* is a *valid argument form*. More generally, we can say that a **valid argument form** is one in which every substitution instance is a valid argument.

A **valid argument form** is one in which every substitution instance is a valid argument.

(Note that this is a definition of a valid *argument form*, which should not be confused with the definition of a valid *argument* from section 1.1.) The crucial point is this: It is no coincidence that all of the arguments we have looked at so far in section 1.2 are valid. They are valid because each of them is an instance of a valid argument form, namely *modus ponens*. In this sense, each of the arguments we have looked at is a *formally valid argument*, where a **formally valid argument** is one that is valid in virtue of its form.

A **formally valid argument** is one that is valid in virtue of its form.

While most valid arguments in ordinary life are formally valid, not every valid argument is formally valid. That is, some arguments are valid, but they are not valid in virtue of their form. For example, consider the following argument:

34. All philosophers are nerds. So, no squares are circles.

The conclusion of this argument is an example of what philosophers call a "necessary truth," because it *must* be true; that is, it is impossible for anything to be both a square and a circle at once. But if it is impossible for the conclusion to be false, then it is also impossible for the premise to be true while the conclusion is false. That is to say, it is impossible for all philosophers to be nerds while some squares are circles. Argument (34) is, therefore, valid. Its validity, however, has nothing to do with its form and everything to do with the content of its conclusion. Although (34) is unusual, it highlights the fact that an argument can be valid without being formally valid.

Even though an argument can be valid without being formally valid, the crucial point to grasp is that *if an argument is a substitution instance of a valid form, then the argument is valid.* Thus, if we determine an argument's form and tell that the form is valid, we can establish that the argument is valid.

In the remainder of section 1.2, we will begin the task of learning to recognize argument forms, which we will continue in later chapters. For now, we will present five "famous" valid forms and then use them to provide an initial method for determining the validity of arguments. But before we get started, we must pause to make an important observation. If-then statements play an important role in many of the arguments and argument forms we will be looking at in this chapter and beyond. Consequently, it is worthwhile to discuss them in some detail before going on.

Understanding Conditional Statements

Each of the following is a **conditional statement** (an if-then statement, often simply called a "conditional" by logicians):

35. If it is snowing, then the mail will be late.
36. If Abraham Lincoln was born in 1709, then he was born before the American Civil War.
37. If Abraham Lincoln was born in 1947, then he was born after World War II.

Conditionals have several important characteristics. First, note their components. The if-clause of a conditional is called its **antecedent;** the then-clause is called the **consequent.** But the antecedent does not include the word "if." Hence, the antecedent of conditional (35) is "it is snowing," not "If it is snowing." Similarly, the consequent is the statement following the word "then," but it does not include that word. So, the consequent of (35) is "the mail will be late," not "then the mail will be late."

> A **conditional statement** is an if-then statement—for example, "If A, the B"—often called a "conditional"; the if-part is the **antecedent** and the then-part is the **consequent**.

Second, conditionals are hypothetical in nature. Thus, in asserting a conditional, one does not assert that its antecedent is true. Nor does one assert that its consequent is true. Rather, one asserts that *if* the antecedent is true, *then* the consequent is true. Thus, (36) is true even though its antecedent is false (Lincoln was born in 1809, not 1709). If Lincoln was born in 1709, then, of course, his birth preceded the American Civil War, which began in 1861. And (37) is true even though its consequent is false. If Lincoln was in fact born in 1809, then he certainly was not born *after* World War II.

Third, there are many ways to express a conditional in ordinary English. Consider the following conditional statement:

   38. If it is raining, then the ground is wet.

Statements (a) through (f) below are all **stylistic variants** of (38), that is, alternate ways of saying the very same thing[3]:

   a. *Given that* it is raining, the ground is wet.
   b. *Assuming that* it is raining, the ground is wet.
   c. The ground is wet *if* it is raining.
   d. The ground is wet *given that* it is raining.
   e. The ground is wet *assuming that* it is raining.
   f. It is raining *only if* the ground is wet.

Each of (a) through (f) says the very same thing as (38), so (38) can be substituted for each of them in an argument. And as we will see, making such substitutions is an aid to identifying argument forms. Accordingly, a close look at these stylistic variants is warranted. Consider (c). Note that "if" comes not at the beginning but in the middle of the statement. Yet, (c) has the same meaning as (38). And the phrase "given that" in (d) plays a role exactly analogous to the "if" in (c). We might generalize from these examples by saying that "if" and its stylistic variants (e.g., "given that" and "assuming that") *introduce an antecedent*. But we must hasten to add that this generalization does not apply when "if" is combined with other words, notably "only." When combined with "only," as in (f), the situation alters dramatically. Statement (f) has the same meaning as (38), but the phrase "only if" is confusing to many people and bears closer examination.

To clarify the meaning of "only if," it is helpful to consider very simple conditionals, such as the following:

39. Rex is a dog *only if* Rex is an animal.

40. Rex is an animal *only if* Rex is a dog.

Obviously, (39) and (40) say different things. (40) says, in effect, that if Rex is an animal, Rex is a dog. But (39) says something entirely different—namely, that if Rex is a dog, then Rex is an animal. In general, statements of the form *A only if B* say the same thing as statements of the form *If A, then B*. They do *not* say the same thing as statements of the form *If B, then A*. Another way to generalize the point is to say that "only if" (unlike "if") *introduces a consequent*.

To discern the form of an argument more easily, it is best to convert stylistic variants of conditionals into the standard *if-then* form. This will be our practice as we develop our methods for discerning the validity and invalidity of arguments.

We will have more to say about conditionals in later chapters. But what we have said here is enough to facilitate our discussion of famous valid argument forms and the method they provide for assessing the validity of arguments.

Famous Valid Forms

We have already been introduced to the first of our famous valid forms, *modus ponens*. We must now meet its sibling, *modus tollens*. Consider the following pair of arguments:

41. 1. If it is raining, then the ground is wet.
    2. The ground is not wet.
So, 3. It is not raining.

42. 1. If there is fire in the room, then there is air in the room.
    2. There is no air in the room.
So, 3. There is no fire in the room.

In each case, lines 1 and 2 are the premises and line 3 is the conclusion. Both arguments are clearly valid: It is necessary that, if the premises are true, the conclusion is true also. Moreover, each argument is formally valid: It is valid because it is an instance of the argument form *modus tollens*, which means "the mode or way of removing." (Notice that, in arguments (41) and (42), the second premise removes or denies the truth of the consequent of the first premise.) We can represent ***modus tollens*** as follows:

Modus Tollens

1. If A, then B.
2. Not B.

So, 3. Not A.

No matter what A and B are, the result will be a valid argument.

Modus tollens is related to *modus ponens*. They both have a premise that is a conditional statement. The key difference lies in the negative nature of the last two lines. "Not A" and "Not B" stand for *negations*. The **negation** of a statement is its denial. For example, in (41), "The ground is not wet" plays the role of Not B and "It is not raining" plays the role of Not A, while in (42), "There is no air in the room" plays the role of Not B and "There is no fire in the room" plays the role of Not A.

The **negation** of a statement is its denial—for example, "It is not the case that A."

The negation of a statement can be formed in various ways. For example, each of the following is a negation of the statement "The ground is wet":

a. *It is not the case that* the ground is wet.
b. *It's false that* the ground is wet.
c. *It is not true that* the ground is wet.
d. The ground is *not* wet.

Three general points can be illustrated with *modus ponens* and *modus tollens*. First, whether an argument is an instance of an argument form is not affected by the order of the premises. For example, both of the following count as *modus tollens*:

43. If Shakespeare was a physicist, then he was a scientist. Shakespeare was not a scientist. So, Shakespeare was not a physicist.

44. Shakespeare was not a scientist. If Shakespeare was a physicist, then he was a scientist. So, Shakespeare was not a physicist.

In other words, arguments of the form *Not A; if A, then B; so, Not B* count as instances of *modus tollens*. Similarly, arguments of the form *A; if A, then B; so, B* count as instances of *modus ponens*. In the remainder of this chapter, keep in mind that the general point here—that the order of the premises does not matter—applies to all of the argument forms that we will discuss.

Second, the conditionals involved in an argument can be rather long and complex. For example:

> **45.** If every right can be waived in the interests of those who have those rights, then euthanasia is permitted in those cases in which the person to be "euthanized" waives his or her right to life. Moreover, every right can be waived in the interests of those who have those rights. Hence, euthanasia is permitted in those cases in which the person to be "euthanized" waives his or her right to life.

The conditional premise in this argument is relatively long and complex, but the form is still *modus ponens*. "Every right can be waived in the interests of those who have those rights" replaces A; "euthanasia is permitted in those cases in which the person to be euthanized waives his or her right to life" replaces B.

Third, putting an argument into explicit form helps to focus attention on the key issues. For example, according to some physicists who endorse the Big Bang theory, the universe cannot be infinitely old. The second law of thermodynamics tells us that in a closed physical system entropy always tends to increase; that is, energy gets diffused over time. (For instance, the radiant energy of a star will gradually become spread out evenly into the space surrounding it.) According to these physicists, if the physical universe has existed for an infinite period, there are now no concentrations of energy (e.g., no stars or planets). But obviously, there are stars and planets, so the physical universe has not existed for an infinite period. We can put this reasoning explicitly into the *modus tollens* form as follows:

> **46.** 1. If the physical universe has existed for an infinite period, then all the energy in the universe is spread out evenly (as opposed to being concentrated in such bodies as planets and stars).
> 2. It is not true that all the energy in the universe is spread out evenly (as opposed to being concentrated in such bodies as planets and stars).
> So, 3. It is not true that the physical universe has existed for an infinite period.

By putting the argument into explicit form, we are better able to focus our attention on the key issue. There is no debate whatsoever about the second premise of this argument. Stars and planets exist, so energy is not in fact spread out evenly throughout the physical universe. Nor is there any debate about the validity of the argument. Every argument having the form *modus tollens* is valid. The focus of the debate, therefore, must be on the first premise, and that is just where physicists have placed it. For example, some physicists think that the universe oscillates, that is, goes through a cycle of "Big Bangs" and "Big Crunches." And if the universe can oscillate, then its diffuse energy can be reconcentrated into usable forms, in which case the first premise is doubtful.[4]

Our third famous valid form is *hypothetical syllogism*. Consider the following argument:

47. 1. If tuition continues to increase, then only the wealthy will be able to afford a college education.
    2. If only the wealthy will be able to afford a college education, then class divisions will be strengthened.
So, 3. If tuition continues to increase, then class divisions will be strengthened.

This is an instance of **hypothetical syllogism,** which we can represent as follows:

Hypothetical Syllogism
    1. If A, then B.
    2. If B, then C.
So, 3. If A, then C.

The argument form is called *hypothetical syllogism* because it involves only hypothetical (i.e., conditional) statements. *Syllogism* comes from the Greek roots meaning "to reason together" or to put statements together into a pattern of reasoning. Every argument that exemplifies this form is valid. For example:

48. If I am morally responsible, then I can choose between good and evil. If I can choose between good and evil, then some of my actions are free. Therefore, if I am morally responsible, then some of my actions are free.

Note that the conclusion of a hypothetical syllogism is a conditional statement.

Thus far in this section, we have focused on argument forms that involve conditional statements. Not all argument forms are like this. Some use **disjunctions,** that is, statements of the form *Either A or B*, whose parts are called "**disjuncts.**" (For example, the disjuncts of "Either the Second Temple of Jerusalem was destroyed in 70 CE or my memory is failing me" are "the Second Temple of Jerusalem was destroyed in 70 CE" and "my memory is failing me.")

A **disjunction** is an either-or statement—for example, "Either A or B": the parts are **disjuncts**.

Now consider this pair of arguments:

49. 1. Either Pablo Picasso painted *Woman with a Guitar* or Georges Braque painted it.
    2. Pablo Picasso did not paint *Woman with a Guitar*.
So, 3. Georges Braque painted *Woman with a Guitar.*

50. 1. Either experimentation on live animals should be banned or experimentation on humans should be permitted (e.g., the terminally ill).

2. Experimentation on humans should not be permitted.

So, 3. Experimentation on live animals should be banned.

Each of these arguments is valid. Each affirms a disjunction, denies one of the disjuncts, and then concludes that the remaining disjunct is true. They are each an instance of **disjunctive syllogism,** which comes in two versions:

Disjunctive Syllogism (in two versions)

1. Either A or B.	1. Either A or B.
2. Not A.	2. Not B.
So, 3. B.	So, 3. A.

Argument (49) is an instance of the first version; argument (50) is an instance of the second. All arguments of either version of disjunctive syllogism are valid.

Some brief remarks about disjunctions are in order here. First, we will take statements of the form *Either A or B* to mean *Either A or B (or both)*. This is called the **inclusive** sense of "or." For instance, suppose a job announcement reads: "Either applicants must have work experience or they must have a bachelor's degree in the field." Obviously, an applicant with *both* work experience *and* a bachelor's degree is not excluded from applying.

Second, some authors speak of an **exclusive** sense of "or," claiming that statements of the form *Either A or B* sometimes mean *Either A or B (but not both)*. For example, in commenting on a presidential election, one might say, "Either Smith will win the election or Jones will win," the assumption being that not both will win. However, it is a matter of controversy whether there really are two different meanings of the word "or" *as opposed to* there simply being cases in which the context indicates that A and B are not both true. Rather than let this controversy sidetrack us, let us simply assume with most logicians that statements of the form *Either A or B* mean *Either A or B (or both)*.

Third, having made this assumption, however, we must immediately add that arguers are free to use statements of the form *Either A or B (but not both)*. This is equivalent to the combination of two statements: *Either A or B, and not both A and B*. Consider the following argument:

51. Either Millard Fillmore was the thirteenth president of the United States or Zachary Taylor was the thirteenth president of the United States (but not both). Millard Fillmore was the thirteenth president. So, Zachary Taylor was not the thirteenth president.

We can represent the form of this argument as *Either A or B; not both A and B; A; so, not B*. This form is valid, but notice that it differs from disjunctive syllogism.

Fourth, note that disjunctive syllogism differs from the following form of argument:

52. Either Hitler was a Nazi or Himmler was a Nazi. Hitler was a Nazi. Therefore, it is not the case that Himmler was a Nazi.

The form of this argument can be best represented as *Either A or B; A; therefore, not B.* As a matter of historical fact, the premises of (52) are true, but its conclusion is false; therefore, this argument form is invalid, unlike disjunctive syllogism.

Let's look at one more famous valid argument form: **constructive dilemma.** It combines both conditional and disjunctive statements. Here is an example:

53. 1. Either Donna knew the information on her tax returns was inaccurate or her tax preparer made a mistake.
2. If Donna knew the information was inaccurate, she should pay the fine.
3. If her tax preparer made a mistake, then he should pay the fine.
So, 4. Either Donna should pay the fine or her tax preparer should pay the fine.

The form of this argument is as follows:

Constructive Dilemma

1. Either A or B.
2. If A, then C.
3. If B, then D.
So, 4. Either C or D.

Arguments of this form are always valid. The age-old problem of evil can be put in the form of a constructive dilemma:

54. Either God cannot prevent some suffering or God does not want to prevent any of it. If God cannot prevent some suffering, then God is weak. If God does not want to prevent any suffering, then God is not good. So, either God is weak or God is not good.

This dilemma nicely illustrates how logic can be used to formulate a problem in a revealing way. Because argument (54) is valid, it is not possible for all of the premises to be true and the conclusion false. Theists, against whom the argument is directed, can hardly deny the first (disjunctive) premise. (If God can prevent some suffering, then God must not want to do so for some reason.) And the second premise seems undeniable. (After all, even we can prevent some suffering.) Historically, the third premise has been the focus of debate, with theists suggesting that God does not want to eliminate any suffering because permitting it is the necessary means to certain good ends (e.g., the personal growth of free creatures).

The Famous Forms Method

At this point, we have introduced five famous valid argument forms, which are summarized in the following table:

> ### Summary of Famous Valid Forms
>
> ***Modus ponens:*** If A, then B. A. So, B.
>
> ***Modus tollens:*** If A, then B. Not B. So, Not A.
>
> **Hypothetical syllogism:** If A, then B. If B, then C. So, if A, then C.
>
> **Disjunctive syllogism** (in two versions): Either A or B. Not A. So, B.
> Either A or B. Not B. So, A.
>
> **Constructive dilemma:** Either A or B. If A, then C. If B, then D. So, either C or D.

We can now use these forms to determine the validity of many arguments, by employing the following method. Here's how.

Consider the following argument:

> **55.** Tom is old *only if* he is over 80. But Tom is not over 80, and so he is not old.

First, we identify the component statements in the argument, uniformly labeling them with capital letters as we have throughout this section. To avoid errors, write the capital letter by each instance of the statement it stands for, taking negations into account, like this:

      A   *B*   *not B*   *not A*

> **55.** Tom is old *only if* he is over 80. But Tom is not over 80, and so he is not old.

Second, we rewrite the argument using capital letters instead of English statements and eliminate any stylistic variants (in this case, we replace "only if" with the standard "if . . . , then . . ." construction). The result is this:

> 1. If A, then B.
> 2. Not B.
>
> So, 3. Not A.

Third, we check to see whether the form is taken from our list of famous valid forms. In this case, it is *modus tollens*, so we conclude that argument (55) is valid.

Let's call the method just indicated the **famous forms method.** Here it is in action again. Consider the following argument:

> **56.** If Andrew knows he has a piano, then he knows he is outside the Matrix.
> Andrew knows he has a piano. So, Andrew knows he is outside the Matrix.

First, we identify and label the component statements in the argument, uniformly labeling them as follows:

A   *B*
56. If Andrew knows he has a piano, then he knows he is outside the Matrix.
        Andrew knows he has a piano. So, Andrew knows he is outside the Matrix.
        A   *B*

Next, we rewrite the argument using capital letters instead of English statements and eliminate any stylistic variants, arriving at this form:

> 1. If A, then B.
> 2. A.
>
> So, 3. B.

Finally, we ask whether this form is one of our famous valid forms. In this case, it is *modus ponens*. Thus, argument (56) is valid.

The Famous Forms Method

Step 1. Identify the component statements in the argument, uniformly labeling each with a capital letter.

Step 2. Rewrite the argument using capital letters instead of English statements and eliminate any stylistic variants.

Step 3. Check to see whether the pattern of reasoning is taken from our list of famous forms. If it is, then the argument is valid.

It will be helpful at this time to highlight a complication of the famous forms method. It can be seen by considering the following argument:

A   *B*
57. Frances is a fast runner *if* she can run the mile in under four minutes. Frances
        can run the mile in under four minutes. Therefore, Frances is a fast runner.
        B   *A*

When we rewrite the argument using capital letters and eliminate stylistic variants, we get this form:

> 1. If B, then A.
> 2. B.
>
> So, 3. A.

Our labeling results in *If B, then A* rather than *If A, then B*. But this is not a problem. There is no need to try to make the letters appear in alphabetical order.

The important thing is that the second premise affirms the antecedent of the conditional premise, while the conclusion affirms the consequent. Thus, we have an instance of *modus ponens*, and the argument is valid.

It is now time to acknowledge two limitations of the famous forms method. The first one can be seen through arguments like this:

58. Fred likes neckerchiefs. Daphne likes neckerchiefs. So, Fred likes neckerchiefs and Daphne likes neckerchiefs.

Even though this argument is trivial, it is formally valid. It is an instance of this valid argument form:

Form 1

    1. A.

    2. B.

So, 3. A and B.

It is not possible for the conclusion, A and B, to be false while the premises, A and B, are true. The problem is that this valid form is not a famous form from our list, so the famous forms method does not tell us that (58) is valid. Similarly, in our discussion of disjunctions, we noted that the form of argument (51) was this:

Form 2

    1. Either A or B.

    2. Not both A and B.

    3. A.

So, 4. Not B.

Form 2 is valid, but it is not on our list. This is a genuine limitation of the famous forms method. Although it is true that *many* valid arguments are instances of our five famous valid forms, there are also many other formally valid arguments, like arguments (51) and (58), that are not. Hence, the fact that the famous forms method does not show that an argument is formally valid does not mean that it is not formally valid. Of course, we could deal with this problem by adding Forms 1 and 2 to our list. While this solution contains a grain of wisdom (in essence, the proof systems we develop later are built on this insight), we would have to add infinitely many forms to cover all the possible valid forms, a daunting task indeed.

A second limitation of the famous forms method is that it does *nothing* to help us show that any invalid argument is invalid. It is concerned only with showing the validity of arguments.

If the famous forms method suffers from these limitations, why bother learning it? Well, despite its limitations, we should not lose sight of the fact that the famous forms method is simple, straightforward, and all that is needed

Summary of Definitions

An **argument form** is a pattern of reasoning.

A **substitution instance** of an argument form is an argument that results from uniformly replacing the variables in that form with statements (or terms).

A **valid argument form** is one in which every substitution instance is a valid argument.

A **formally valid argument** is one that is valid in virtue of its form.

The **negation** of a statement is its denial.

A **conditional statement** is an if-then statement, often simply called a "conditional."

The if-clause of a conditional is its **antecedent.**

The then-clause of a conditional is its **consequent.**

A **disjunction** is an either-or statement.

The statements comprising a disjunction are its **disjuncts.**

in many cases. Moreover, understanding it and its limitations constitutes an important first step toward grasping some basic logical concepts and appreciating more complete methods for assessing arguments.

EXERCISE 1.2

PART A: True or False? Which of the following statements are true? Which are false?

* **1.** A substitution instance of an argument form is an argument that results from uniformly replacing the variables in that form with statements (or terms).

 2. A conditional is an "if-then" statement.

 3. The parts of a disjunction are disjuncts.

* **4.** In logic, we treat statements of the form "Either A or B" as saying the same thing as "Either A or B, but not both A and B."

 5. The if-part of a conditional is the antecedent.

 6. A valid argument form is one in which every substitution instance is a valid argument.

* **7.** The consequent of "If it was reported in the *Daily Prophet*, then it's true" is "It was reported in the *Daily Prophet*."

 8. In logic, we treat statements of the form "Either A or B" as saying the same thing as "Either A or B, or both A and B."

 9. "Either Hermione gets Ron or she gets Harry" is a conditional.

*10. The inclusive sense of "or" means "Either A or B, or both."

11. "Either Fritz is a philosopher or he is a gambler" is a disjunction.

12. An argument form is a pattern of reasoning.

*13. The then-part of a conditional is the consequent.

14. If the successful candidate has a PhD in English literature or at least five years of university teaching experience, it follows that the successful candidate does not have both a PhD in English literature and at least five years of university teaching experience.

15. The antecedent of "If Professor Dumbledore died in Book Six, then he won't make an appearance in Book Seven" is "Professor Dumbledore died in Book Six."

*16. The negation of a statement is its denial.

17. A formally valid argument is one that is valid in virtue of its form.

18. The antecedent of "If Professor Snape was a disciple of Voldemort, then he should be imprisoned in Azkaban" is "He should be imprisoned in Azkaban."

*19. The consequent of "If Dolores Umbrage despises Harry, then she's a disciple of he-who-shall-not-be-named" is "She's a disciple of he-who-shall-not-be-named."

20. A disjunction is an "either-or" statement.

21. "There is no God" is the denial of "There is a God."

*22. The exclusive sense of "or" means "Either A or B, but not both."

23. In determining whether an argument is a substitution instance of an argument form, we must be careful to take the order of the premises into account.

24. The antecedent of "Either humans evolved from amoebas or humans were specially created by God" is "Humans evolved from amoebas."

*25. The antecedent of "The Sonics will move to Oklahoma only if the league permits it" is "The Sonics will move to Oklahoma."

26. The antecedent of "Bill will behave better in the future if Hillary forgives Bill" is "Bill will behave better in the future."

27. The consequent of "There is air in the room if there is fire in the room" is "There is air in the room."

*28. The following argument is a substitution instance of disjunctive syllogism: "Jill is in love with Sam or Henry; she is in love with Henry; so Jill is not in love with Sam."

29. Although the famous forms method does not allow us to show that an argument is invalid, it does allow us to show the validity of every valid argument.

30. The consequent of "There is fire in the room *only if* there is air in the room" is "There is air in the room."

PART B: Identify the Forms Identify the forms of the following arguments, using capital letters to stand for statements and eliminating any stylistic variants. If the argument form is one of the "famous" valid forms, give its name. If the argument form is not one of the "famous" valid forms, write "none."

* **1.** If the solution turns blue litmus paper red, then the solution contains acid. The solution turns blue litmus paper red. So, the solution contains acid.

  2. If the solution turns blue litmus paper red, then the solution contains acid. The solution does not contain acid. So, the solution does not turn blue litmus paper red.

  3. Lewis is a famous author only if he knows how to write. But Lewis is not a famous author. Hence, Lewis does not know how to write.

* **4.** If Susan is a famous author, then she knows how to write. Moreover, Susan knows how to write. So, she is a famous author.

  5. Souls transmigrate. But it is wrong to eat animals if souls transmigrate. Hence, it is wrong to eat animals.

  6. Either Jones is an innocent bystander or Jones fired a shot at the mayor. Jones is not an innocent bystander. Therefore, Jones fired a shot at the mayor.

* **7.** Rilke is a dreamer if he is a poet. Therefore, Rilke is a poet.

  8. Either you marry young or you wait. If you marry young, you incur a high risk of divorce. If you wait, the field of available partners grows ever smaller. So, either you incur a high risk of divorce or the field of available partners grows ever smaller.

  9. It is not wrong to kill spiders. But if spiders have eternal souls, then it is wrong to kill them. Thus, it is false that spiders have eternal souls.

* **10.** If you study hard, you refine your communication skills. If you refine your communication skills, then your job opportunities increase. Hence, if you study hard, your job opportunities increase.

  11. If Mubarak is from Egypt, then he is from Africa. Therefore, if Mubarak is not from Egypt, then he is not from Africa.

  12. Ben is a rat. Ben is a rat only if Ben is a mammal. So, Ben is a mammal.

* **13.** Sam is wealthy if he has more than a billion dollars. But Sam does not have more than a billion dollars. Therefore, Sam is not wealthy.

  14. There is life on Mars given that there is life on Earth. Hence, there is life on Mars.

  15. It is true that corrupt institutions are hard to reform. It is false that individuals are totally depraved. Therefore, if corrupt institutions are hard to reform, then individuals are totally depraved.

PART C: More Forms to Identify Identify the forms of the following arguments, using capital letters to stand for statements and eliminating any stylistic variants. If the argument form is one of the "famous" valid forms, give its name. If the argument form is not one of the "famous" valid forms, write "none."

* **1.** The sky is blue. The sky is cobalt blue only if it is blue. Hence, the sky is cobalt blue.

2. Abortion in the case of ectopic pregnancy is not wrong. But if it is always wrong to kill an innocent human being, then abortion in the case of ectopic pregnancy is wrong. So, it is not always wrong to kill an innocent human.

3. Kidnapping is wrong if society disapproves of it. Kidnapping is wrong. So, society disapproves of kidnapping.

* **4.** Eating meat is unhealthy if meat contains a lot of cholesterol. Meat does contain a lot of cholesterol. Therefore, eating meat is unhealthy.

5. Either the "eye for an eye" principle is interpreted literally or it is interpreted figuratively. If it is interpreted literally, then the state should torture torturers, maim maimers, and rape rapists. If the "eye for an eye" principle is interpreted figuratively, then it does not necessarily demand death for murderers. So, either the state should torture torturers, maim maimers, and rape rapists, or the "eye for an eye" principle does not necessarily demand death for murderers.

6. Affirmative action is preferential treatment of disadvantaged groups, and preferential treatment of disadvantaged groups is reverse discrimination. If affirmative action is preferential treatment of disadvantaged groups and preferential treatment of disadvantaged groups is reverse discrimination, then affirmative action is wrong. Hence, affirmative action is wrong.

* **7.** If the zygote lacks a brain, then the zygote lacks a soul. If the zygote lacks a soul, then killing the zygote is permissible. So, if the zygote lacks a brain, then killing the zygote is permissible.

8. If Mary is a psychiatrist, then she is a physician. Mary is not a physician. Therefore, Mary is a psychiatrist.

9. If you want to ruin your life, you should take hard drugs. But you don't want to ruin your life. So, you should not take hard drugs.

* **10.** Lying causes social discord. Hence, lying is wrong.

11. It is not true that acts are right because God approves them. But either acts are right because God approves them, or God approves of acts because they are right. Therefore, God approves of acts because they are right.

12. If Dracula is a vampire, then he is dangerous. But Dracula is not a vampire. Hence, he is dangerous.

* **13.** Either the animals used in research are a lot like humans or they are not a lot like humans. If the animals are a lot like humans, then experimenting on them is morally questionable. If the animals are not a lot like humans, then experimenting on them is pointless. So, either experimenting on animals is morally questionable or it is pointless.

14. The state cannot uphold the value of life by taking it. And if the state cannot uphold the value of life by taking it, then the death penalty should be abolished. Therefore, the death penalty should be abolished.

15. If my society approves of genetic engineering, then genetic engineering is right. But my society does not approve of genetic engineering. Hence, genetic engineering is not right.

PART D: Still More Forms to Identify Identify the forms of the following arguments, using capital letters to stand for statements and eliminating any stylistic variants. If the argument form is one of the "famous" valid forms, give its name. If the argument form is not one of the "famous" valid forms, write "none."

* **1.** Overeating is foolish only if it causes disease. Overeating does not cause disease. So, overeating is not foolish.

   2. Either films depicting graphic violence have caused the increase in violent crime or bad parenting has caused it (or both). Movies depicting graphic violence have caused the increase in violent crime. Therefore, bad parenting has not caused the rise in violent crime.

   3. Corporations contribute huge sums of money to political campaigns. If that is so, then corporations exert undue influence on elections. So, corporations exert undue influence on elections.

* **4.** You will win the chess tournament if you are very good at chess. Unfortunately, you are not very good at chess. Hence, you will not win the chess tournament.

   5. Either virtue is good for its own sake or it is good as a means to an end. It is not the case that virtue is good for its own sake. So, virtue is good as a means to an end.

   6. You should be an optimist if pessimists are less likely to succeed than optimists. And it is a fact that pessimists are less likely to succeed than optimists. Therefore, you should be an optimist.

* **7.** If God can arbitrarily decide what is morally right, then God can make cruelty right. And if God cannot arbitrarily decide what is morally right, then morality is not entirely in God's control. But either God can arbitrarily decide what is morally right or God cannot arbitrarily decide what is morally right. Therefore, either God can make cruelty right or morality is not entirely in God's control.

   8. The dinosaurs vanished due to a sudden, extreme drop in temperature. The earth must have suffered some sort of cataclysm millions of years ago, assuming that the dinosaurs vanished due to a sudden, extreme drop in temperature. So, the earth must have suffered some sort of cataclysm millions of years ago.

   9. Assuming that you treat like cases alike, you are fair. Hence, you are fair only if you treat like cases alike.

***10.** The death penalty is inequitably applied to the poor and to minorities. And given that the death penalty is inequitably applied to the poor and to minorities, it is unjust. Therefore, the death penalty is unjust.

11. Philosophy is important if ideas are important. And assuming that ideas change lives, ideas are important. Hence, if philosophy is important, then ideas change lives.

12. If you join the military, you give up a lot of freedom. If you go to college, you incur enormous debts. However, either you join the military, or you go to college. Therefore, either you give up a lot of freedom or you incur enormous debts.

* **13.** Mercy killing is morally permissible only if it promotes a greater amount of happiness for everyone affected than the alternatives do. And mercy killing does promote a greater amount of happiness for everyone affected than the alternatives do. Therefore, mercy killing is morally permissible.

14. You must either love or hate. If you love, then you suffer when your loved ones suffer. If you hate, then you suffer when your enemies flourish. Hence, either you suffer when your loved ones suffer or you suffer when your enemies flourish.

15. A severe depression will occur given that the economy collapses. The economy collapses if inflation soars. So, inflation soars only if a severe depression will occur.

PART E: Constructing Arguments   Construct your own substitution instances for each of the following argument forms: *modus ponens, modus tollens,* hypothetical syllogism, disjunctive syllogism, and constructive dilemma. If the substitution instance is not a sound argument, explain why. If you think that it is a sound argument, do you find it satisfying, compelling, or useful? Defend your answer.

1.3   Counterexamples and Invalidity

We have seen that a basic understanding of argument forms can help us identify many valid arguments. Unfortunately, we have also seen that there are many valid arguments left unidentified by the famous forms method. Moreover, although our list of valid forms may help us identify some common valid arguments, it does not help us identify any *in*valid arguments. In this section, we explore a method for uncovering invalid reasoning.

Counterexamples

Consider the following argument:

59. 1. If Britney Spears is a philosopher, then Britney Spears is wise.

2. Britney Spears isn't a philosopher.

So, 3. Britney Spears isn't wise.

At first glance, this argument might look like an instance of *modus tollens:*

Modus Tollens
      1. If A, then B.

      2. Not B.

So, 3. Not A.

But initial appearances can be deceiving, and in this case they are. A *modus tollens* argument denies the *consequent* of its conditional premise, and the conclusion denies the *antecedent*. Argument (59) denies the *antecedent* of its conditional premise, and its conclusion denies the *consequent*. So it is *not* an instance of *modus tollens*. It is instead an instance of what is known as the **fallacy of denying the antecedent,** where a *fallacy* is simply an error in reasoning. We can represent its form as follows:

Fallacy of Denying the Antecedent
      1. If A, then B.

      2. Not A.

So, 3. Not B.

The fallacy of denying the antecedent is an example of an *invalid argument form*, where an **invalid argument form** is one that has *some* invalid substitution instances.

 An **invalid argument form** is one that has some invalid substitution instances.

Recall that a *substitution instance* of an argument form is an argument that results from uniformly replacing the variables in that form with statements. Argument (59) is a substitution instance of the fallacy of denying the antecedent because it results from substituting "Britney Spears is a philosopher" for A and "Britney Spears is wise" for B. But it is also *invalid* since it is *possible* for the premises to be true and the conclusion false. This fact is easy to miss, however, because many take its conclusion for granted. But consider the following argument:

  60. 1. If Britney Spears is an oil-tycoon, then Britney Spears is rich.

       2. Britney Spears isn't an oil-tycoon.

  So, 3. Britney Spears isn't rich.

Arguments (59) and (60) are instances of the same form—the fallacy of denying the antecedent—but (60) provides a crystal clear demonstration of the invalidity of that form because most readers will immediately recognize that its premises are true and its conclusion is false. It is *clearly* invalid.

We will say that a **counterexample** to an argument form is a substitution instance in which the premises are true and the conclusion is false. A counterexample to the form of an argument shows that the form is not valid by showing that the form does not preserve truth—that is, it shows that it can lead from true premises to a false conclusion.

> A **counterexample** to an argument form is a substitution instance in which the premises are true and the conclusion is false.

But not all counterexamples are equally effective. The more obvious it is that the premises are true and the conclusion is false, the more effective it will be. Thus, although argument (60) is a good counterexample to the fallacy of denying the antecedent, the following argument is not:

61. 1. If there are Beefsteaks in Dan's summer garden, then there are tomatoes in it.

    2. There are no Beefsteaks in Dan's summer garden.

So, 3. There are no tomatoes in Dan's summer garden.

This argument is not a good counterexample to the fallacy of denying the antecedent because, although it is a counterexample, its premises are not well-known truths and its conclusion is not a well-known falsehood. Argument (60) is a good counterexample, however; most readers will know that oil-tycoons are rich (so that *if* Britney Spears is an oil-tycoon, then she is rich) and that Britney Spears is *not* an oil-tycoon (she is an entertainer); moreover, they will know that Britney Spears *is* rich (by virtue of her singing and endorsements). We will say that a **good counterexample** to an argument form is a substitution instance in which the premises are *well-known* truths and the conclusion is a *well-known* falsehood.

> A **good counterexample** to an argument form is a substitution instance in which the premises are well-known truths and the conclusion is a well-known falsehood.

To further illustrate the idea of a counterexample, let's look at a second fallacy. Consider the following argument:

62. 1. If Ryan is a true pop-culture buff, then he reads *Entertainment Weekly* religiously.

    2. Ryan reads *Entertainment Weekly* religiously.

So, 3. Ryan is a true pop-culture buff.

One might be tempted to identify the form of this argument as *modus ponens:*

Modus Ponens
> 1. If A, then B.
> 2. A.
>
> So, 3. B.

But this would be a case of mistaken identity. A *modus ponens* argument affirms the *antecedent* of its conditional premise and its conclusion affirms the *consequent.* Argument (62) affirms the *consequent* of its conditional premise and the conclusion affirms the *antecedent.* So it is not an instance of *modus ponens.* It is instead an instance of what is called the **fallacy of affirming the consequent:**

Fallacy of Affirming the Consequent
> 1. If A, then B.
> 2. B.
>
> So, 3. A.

To show that this form of argument is fallacious, consider the following counterexample:

> **63.** 1. If lemons are red, then lemons have a color.
>   2. Lemons have a color.
>   So, 3. Lemons are red.

The first premise is obviously true: Anything that is red has a color. And it is common knowledge that lemons have a color. Moreover, everyone knows that red and yellow are different colors. So the premises are well-known truths and the conclusion is a well-known falsehood. Argument (63) is, therefore, a good counterexample to the fallacy of affirming the consequent.

The Counterexample Method

Thus far, we have focused on how counterexamples can be used to demonstrate the invalidity of argument *forms.* We will now look at how counterexamples can be used to identify invalid *arguments.*

In section 1.2, we noted that if an argument is an instance of a valid argument form, then it is valid. It is natural to assume that, likewise, if an argument is an instance of an *invalid* argument form, then it is invalid. *If* this assumption is correct, a method for identifying the invalidity of an argument suggests itself: First, we identify the argument's form, and then we construct a counterexample to that form. Let us call this method the *counterexample method.* Until further notice, we will grant that the just-mentioned assumption is correct because it will allow us to simplify our initial explanation of the counterexample method. Later, we will explain why the assumption is false and why, despite its falsity, the counterexample method remains a highly effective technique for discerning invalidity.

Let's begin with an argument:

64. 1. George W. Bush was a U.S. president and George W. Bush went to Harvard.
2. Barack Obama is a U.S. president.
So, 3. Barack Obama went to Harvard.

As we intimated in the last paragraph, the counterexample method involves two basic steps. The first step is to identify the form of the argument. To do that, we identify the component statements of the argument and replace them with variables just like we did in applying the famous forms method. In the first premise of (64), the component statements are "George W. Bush was a U.S. president" and "George W. Bush went to Harvard." The second premise is a completely different statement, as is the conclusion; thus, they will require different variables. With these points in mind, here is the form of the argument:

Form 3

1. A and B.
2. C.
So, 3. D.

With this form in hand, we can move to the second step: Construct a substitution instance whose premises are well-known truths and whose conclusion is a well-known falsehood. Here is an example:

65. 1. George Washington was a U.S. president and George Washington is long dead.
2. Barack Obama is a U.S. president.
So, 3. Barack Obama is long dead.

"George Washington was a U.S. president" replaces A in Form 3, "George Washington is long dead" replaces B, "Barack Obama is a U.S. president" replaces C, and "Barack Obama is long dead" replaces D. Most readers will know that George Washington was and Barack Obama is a U.S. president. Moreover, most readers will know that, while Washington is long dead, Obama is very much alive. Hence, we have a good counterexample to Form 3. Given our assumption that an argument is invalid if it is an instance of an invalid form, argument (64) is invalid.

Argument (65) involves some of the same things in argument (64): Barack Obama and the presidency. But that is not a requirement for a good counterexample. Here's a counterexample to Form 3 that involves completely different things from (65):

66. 1. John Lennon was a member of the Beatles and Fuji apples are red.

2. Not everyone likes escargots de Bourgogne.

So, 3. The moon is made of limburger.

"John Lennon was a member of the Beatles" replaces A, "Fuji apples are red" replaces B, "Not everyone likes escargots de Bourgogne" replaces C, and "The moon is made of limburger" replaces D. Argument (66) is ridiculous, of course— the conclusion is laughable and the premises have nothing to do with one another. But remember: All it takes to serve as a good counterexample is for the argument to be an instance of the form in question, and for its premises to be well-known truths and its conclusion to be a well-known falsehood. (66) meets these requirements.

Here is a second illustration of the counterexample method. Consider this argument:

67. 1. If stem-cell research causes harm, then stem-cell research is wrong.

2. If stem-cell research causes harm, then it should be outlawed.

So, 3. If stem-cell research is wrong, it should be outlawed.

First, we identify the component statements of the argument and replace them with capital letters. If we replace "stem-cell research causes harm" with A, "stem-cell research is wrong" with B, and "it is should be outlawed" with C, we arrive at this form:

Form 4

1. If A, then B.

2. If A, then C.

So, 3. If B, then C.

Second, we construct a substitution instance for Form 4 whose premises are well-known truths and whose conclusion is a well-known falsehood. To make the task easier, it is helpful to break the second step into two parts. As a general rule, it is useful to start with a well-known false conclusion and to work backwards from there. For example, we might begin with the following:

68. 1. If A, then B.

2. If A, then C.

So, 3. If Johnny Depp is a mammal, then he is a horse.

Here, "Johnny Depp is a mammal" replaces B in Form 4 and "he is a horse" replaces C. The resulting conclusion is a well-known falsehood because it is well known that Johnny Depp is a mammal but not a horse. We are constructing a substitution instance, so we must uniformly replace the same letters with the same statements elsewhere in the form. Thus, we have the following:

> **69.** 1. If A, then Johnny Depp is a mammal.
>
> 2. If A, then he is a horse.
>
> So, 3. If Johnny Depp is a mammal, then he is a horse.

Now we just need to answer this question: What can we substitute for A that will result in premises that are well-known truths? In other words, what sorts of things are such that it is well known that, *if* Johnny Depp was one of them, he would be a mammal? And, what sorts of things are such that it is well known that, *if* Johnny Depp was one of them, he would be a horse? Lots of things come to mind, for example, a thoroughbred and a Clydesdale. That is, it is a well-known truth that if Johnny Depp is a thoroughbred, then he is a mammal, and, it is a well-known truth that if he is a thoroughbred, then he is a horse. Thus, we arrive at the following:

> **70.** 1. If Johnny Depp is a thoroughbred, then he is a mammal.
>
> 2. If Johnny Depp is an thoroughbred, then he is a horse.
>
> So, 3. If Johnny Depp is a mammal, then he is a horse.

This argument is a substitution instance of Form 4; moreover, its premises are well-known truths and its conclusion is a well-known falsehood. Thus, Form 4 is invalid. Given our assumption that an argument is invalid if it is an instance of an invalid argument form, and since argument (67) is an instance of invalid Form 4, (67) is an invalid argument.

Categorical Statements and Arguments

At this point, a problem arises for the counterexample method as we have developed it thus far. The problem arises in connection with arguments that contain *categorical statements*. A **categorical statement** is a statement that relates two classes or categories, where a class is a set or collection of things.

 A **categorical statement** is a statement that relates two classes or categories, where a class is a set or collection of things.

The premises and the conclusion of the following argument are categorical statements:

> **71.** 1. All presidents are human beings.
>
> 2. All human beings are mammals.
>
> So, 3. All presidents are mammals.

The first premise of this argument relates the set of presidents to the class of human beings—it says that everything that belongs to the class of presidents belongs to the class of human beings as well. The second premise relates the class of human beings to the class of mammals—it says that everything that belongs to the class of human beings belongs to the class of mammals. The conclusion relates the class of presidents to the class of mammals—it says that everything in the class of presidents is in the class of mammals. Categorical statements are often signaled by terms like "all," "some," and "no" because they make claims about what all, some, or none of the members of a class are like. Thus, "All Amorites are Canaanites," "Some Canadians are French," and "No Frisians are Tasmanians" count as categorical statements.

We said that arguments that contain categorical statements pose a problem for the counterexample method as we have developed it to this point. To see the problem, notice that argument (71) is simply a series of three statements that, given the way we have identified an argument's form up to this point, should be replaced with capital letters like this:

Form 5

    1. A.

    2. B.

So, 3. C.

Form 5 is obviously invalid—to construct a good counterexample, simply replace A and B with any two well-known truths and C with a well-known falsehood. Thus, given our assumption that an argument is invalid if it is an instance of an invalid argument form, our counterexample method leads to the conclusion that argument (71) is invalid. But (71) is *obviously* valid. It isn't possible for all presidents to be human beings and for all human beings to be mammals while some presidents are not mammals. Moreover, (71) is valid in virtue of its form; it is formally valid. That is, as a matter of necessity, if all members of one class are members of a second class and all members of the second are members of a third, then all members of the first class are members of the third. What makes matters worse is that argument (71) is not alone. Our counterexample method will count many valid arguments that contain categorical statements as invalid. How can we solve this problem?

The solution involves two steps. First, we must expand our use of variables in our procedure for identifying an argument's form. Second, we must explain how an argument can be valid even if it is an instance of an invalid argument form. If we can do both of these things, then we can sensibly affirm the validity of valid argument (71) while acknowledging that Form 5 is invalid. We will take each step in turn.

So far we have been using variables to stand only for statements. Consequently, we identified the form of argument (71) as the invalid Form 5 even though it is obvious that (71) is formally valid. So let us now use variables to stand for *terms* as well as statements. For the purposes of this chapter, a **term** is a word or phrase that stands for a class of things, like the class of presidents, the class of human beings, or the class of mammals.

 A **term** is a word or phrase that stands for a class of things.

In argument (71), the words "presidents," "human beings," and "mammals" are all terms. If we replace them with A, B, and C, respectively, we have the following argument form:

Form 6

  1. All A are B.
  2. All B are C.
So, 3. All A are C.

Form 6 is importantly different from the forms that we have seen up to this point since its variables stand for terms, not statements. Nevertheless, Form 6 is an obviously valid form. Its validity is illustrated by the following diagram:

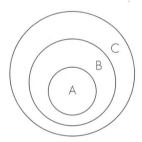

No matter what A and B and C stand for, it will still be the case that, if everything in the A-circle is in the B-circle and everything in the B-circle is in the C-circle, then everything in the A-circle is in the C-circle. For example, if all Autobots (A) are Transformers (B) and if all Transformers (B) are from Cybertron (C), then all Autobots (A) are from Cybertron (C). We can recognize that this conclusion follows from the premises even if we don't know the first thing about robots in disguise.

Earlier, on page 15, we defined a substitution instance of an argument form as "an argument that results from uniformly replacing the variables in that form with statements (or terms)" and, in a footnote, we counseled the reader to ignore the parenthetical remark until further notice. We can no longer ignore it. Since argument (71) results from uniformly replacing the variables in Form 6 with *terms,* (71) is a substitution instance of Form 6. Form 6 is valid, so argument (71) is valid too. It is valid in virtue of its form. Expanding our use of variables to include terms as well as statements helps us to recognize these facts.

Our first step toward a solution to our problem is complete: By allowing variables to stand for terms, we enrich our way of identifying an argument's form so that we can affirm that argument (71) is an instance of a valid argument form. Our solution would be incomplete if we stopped here, however. For, if we stopped here, we would be led to an absurdity. After all, as we just observed, argument (71) is an instance of a valid argument form, Form 6; thus, (71) is a valid argument. But (71) is an instance of an invalid argument form as well, Form 5; thus, (71) is an invalid argument, *given our assumption* that an argument is invalid if it is a substitution instance of an invalid form. Therefore, unless we take the second step and deny our assumption, we will have to conclude that argument (71) is both valid and invalid—an absurdity *par excellence*!

But can we sensibly deny our assumption? Yes. For virtually every argument can be an instance of more than one form, some valid and some invalid. Argument (71) is a case in point: It is an instance of Form 6, which is valid, as well as Form 5, which is invalid. So, obviously enough, contrary to our assumption, an argument can be valid even if it is a substitution instance of an invalid argument form. In that case, we do not have to say that argument (71) or any other argument is invalid simply because it is an instance of an invalid argument form. Hence, our counterexample method does not lead to absurdity.

Let us summarize our results. Our initial counterexample method faced the problem of counting many valid arguments that contain categorical statements as invalid. We solved the problem by first expanding our use of variables in the identification of an argument's form to include terms as well as statements, and then showing that an argument's being an instance of an invalid form is no guarantee of that argument's invalidity. Our solution is complete.

Although our problem has been solved, a minor concern remains. Suppose we have correctly identified one of the forms of an argument and we show that it is invalid by means of a counterexample. Since being an instance of an invalid form is no guarantee of an argument's invalidity, might it nevertheless, unbeknownst to us, have an additional form that is valid—at least in theory? Yes, that is a theoretical possibility. The counterexample method does not rule it out. Consequently, it yields only provisional results.

But if the counterexample method delivers only provisional results, what good is it then? Well, generally speaking, if we identify the form of an argument *with due sensitivity to its key logical words and phrases*—for example, "all," "some," "no," "if-then," "either-or," "not," "and," and others to be discussed later—and if the form thus identified is invalid, then the argument has no further valid form, and so it is formally invalid. This is why the counterexample method is a powerful tool for evaluating arguments even though, in theory, it cannot conclusively establish the invalidity of an argument. (It is important to understand that, even though the counterexample method for identifying invalid *arguments* yields provisional results, giving good counterexamples to an argument *form* conclusively establishes its invalidity.)

Let us return to arguments involving categorical statements. Here is one that is formally valid:

72. 1. All emeralds are gems.
    2. Some rocks are not gems.
So, 3. Some rocks are not emeralds.

This argument has the following form:

Form 7

    1. All A are B.
    2. Some C are not B.
So, 3. Some C are not A.

Here, A replaces "emeralds," B replaces "gems," and C replaces "rocks." We can diagram the logic as follows:

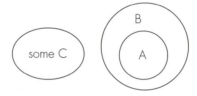

Clearly, if all members of class A are members of class B and some members of class C are not members of B, then some members of C are not members of A. This will be the case no matter what A, B, and C stand for. So every instance of Form 7 is valid; thus, Form 7 itself is valid.

Here is another example of a formally valid argument that contains categorical statements:

73. 1. Every sockeye is a member of *Oncorhynchus*.
    2. Some sockeye are natives of the Copper River (in south-central Alaska).
So, 3. Some members of *Oncorhynchus* are natives of the Copper River.

If we replace "sockeye" with A, "member of *Oncorhynchus*" with B, and "natives of the Copper River" with C, we have the following form:

Form 8

    1. Every A is a B.
    2. Some A are C.
So, 3. Some B are C.

We can diagram the logic as follows:

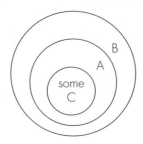

If every member of class A is a member of class B and some members of A are also members of class C, then some members of B are members of C. This will be the case no matter what A, B, and C stand for. So every instance of Form 8 is valid, as is Form 8 itself.

Of course, not all arguments involving categorical statements are valid. This can be shown by employing a slightly modified version of the counter-example method set out previously. To illustrate, consider the following argument:

74. 1. All logicians are smart people.

2. Some smart people are not stylish people.

So, 3. Some logicians are not stylish people.

First, we identify the pattern of reasoning by uniformly replacing terms in the argument with variables. If we substitute A for "logicians," B for "smart people," and C for "stylish people," we get the following:

Form 9

1. All A are B.

2. Some B are not C.

So, 3. Some A are not C.

Second, we construct a good counterexample to the argument form. As before, it is helpful to work from the conclusion backwards and to use terms whose interrelations are well understood—biological terms like "human beings," "mammals," "lions," and "felines" work particularly well, as do geometric terms like "square," "figure," "rectangle," and "circle." We might start with this:

75. 1. All A are B.

2. Some B are not C.

So, 3. Some lions are not felines.

Here, "lions" replaces A and "felines" replaces C. It is a well-known truth that all lions are felines; thus, the conclusion of (75)—some lions are not felines—is a well-known falsehood. We must use the same term for each occurrence of a variable, so we move to this:

76. 1. All lions are B.
2. Some B are not felines.
So, 3. Some lions are not felines.

Now we ask: What can we substitute for B to give us true premises? What category includes all lions, but also includes some things that are not feline? Several suggest themselves: carnassials, chordata, and atachyons, for example; but carnivores, mammals, and animals are more well-known and thus make for a good counterexample. Thus:

77. 1. All lions are animals.
2. Some animals are not felines.
So, 3. Some lions are not felines.

This is how the counterexample method can be modified to identify invalid categorical arguments.

Let's look at another example. Here's an argument:

78. 1. No movie stars are poor people.
2. Some bankers are not poor people.
So, 3. Some bankers are not movie stars.

Let A stand for "movie stars," B for "poor people," and C for "bankers." Thus, we have the following:

Form 10
1. No A are B.
2. Some C are not B.
So, 3. Some C are not A.

If we substitute "squares" for C and "closed plane figures" for A in the conclusion, our counterexample will begin to take shape like this:

79. 1. No A are B.
2. Some C are not B.
So, 3. Some squares are not closed plane figures.

Everyone knows that every square is a closed plane figure, so the conclusion is a well-known falsehood. Next, we uniformly replace C and A in the premises with "squares" and "closed plane figures" resulting in the following:

80. 1. No closed plane figures are B.

 2. Some squares are not B.

So, 3. Some squares are not closed plane figures.

Finally, we ask: What can replace B to result in two true premises? Well, what categories exclude some squares and all closed plane figures? Many categories fit that description: zebus, phenomenologists, and Amalekites, for example; but candidates more suitable for a good counterexample include walruses, Canadians, and Klingons. Hence, we have this counterexample:

81. 1. No closed plane figures are Klingons.

 2. Some squares are not Klingons.

So, 3. Some squares are not closed plane figures.

One might object that it is false that some squares are not Klingons. After all, *all* squares are not Klingons, or, to put it another way, *no* square is a Klingon. In logic, however, the word "some" means "at least one." Hence, the statement "Some squares are not Klingons" is true: At least one square is not a Klingon. And "Some squares are not Klingons" does *not* imply that some squares are Klingons. All of the following statements are true: "Some squares are not Klingons," "All squares are not Klingons," and "No square is a Klingon."

For easy reference, we summarize the counterexample method in the following box.

The Counterexample Method

1. Identify the most logically sensitive form of the argument. Use capital letters to stand for statements or terms.
2. Find English statements or terms that, if substituted for the capital letters in the conclusion of the argument form, produce a well-known falsehood.
3. Substitute these English statements or terms for the relevant capital letters uniformly throughout the argument form.
4. Find English statements or terms that, if substituted uniformly for the remaining capital letters in the argument form, produce premises that are well-known truths.
5. Check your work. If you have succeeded, you have shown the argument to be invalid.

We have already mentioned one limitation of the counterexample method: Its results are provisional because we might not identify the most logically sensitive form of the argument we are assessing. Another limitation is that, even if we do identify the most logically sensitive form, we might still be unable to construct a counterexample because sometimes it is difficult to think of one. When that happens, one of two things is the case. Either (a) the form is valid, and we cannot construct a counterexample because a valid form cannot have a counterexample, or (b) the form is invalid, and we simply need to be more creative in thinking of substitution instances. Unfortunately, for some argument forms, some of us might not be able to tell which of these alternatives we face. Thus, our inability to discern a counterexample does not guarantee that there is none. This is a second way in which the results of the counterexample method are provisional. To mitigate this limitation, we might combine the counterexample method with the famous forms method from section 1.2. In that case, if the form we have identified is one of our famous valid forms, then the argument under inspection is valid. But this helps to mitigate the difficulty only somewhat since our list of famous forms is limited.

In later chapters of this book, we will develop methods for discerning the validity and invalidity of arguments that improve on the two methods we have discussed in this chapter. However, the student of logic who has a firm grasp of these two methods will be in a much better position to understand and implement the more rigorous and complete methods to come.

Summary of Definitions

The **fallacy of denying the antecedent** is an invalid argument form: If A, then B; not A; so, not B.

An **invalid argument form** is one that has some invalid substitution instances.

A **counterexample** to an argument form is a substitution instance in which the premises are true and the conclusion is false.

A **good counterexample** to an argument form is a substitution instance in which the premises are well-known truths and the conclusion is a well-known falsehood.

The **fallacy of affirming the consequent** is an invalid argument form: If A, then B; B; so, A.

A **categorical statement** is a statement that relates two classes or categories, where a class is a set or collection of things.

A **term** is a word or phrase that stands for a class of things.

EXERCISE 1.3

PART A: Counterexamples Try to identify the most logically sensitive forms of the following arguments, using capital letters to stand for *statements* and eliminating any stylistic variants. Then, construct a good counterexample to the form to show that it is invalid. You might already have identified the forms in this part because these arguments are all of the invalid ones from Exercise 1.2, Parts B, C, and D.

1. Lewis is a famous author only if he knows how to write. But Lewis is not a famous author. Hence, Lewis does not know how to write.

* 2. If Susan is a famous author, then she knows how to write. Moreover, Susan knows how to write. So, she is a famous author.

* 3. Rilke is a dreamer if he is a poet. Therefore, Rilke is a poet.

4. If Mubarak is from Egypt, then he is from Africa. Therefore, if Mubarak is not from Egypt, then he is not from Africa.

* 5. Sam is wealthy if he has more than a billion dollars. But Sam does not have more than a billion dollars. Therefore, Sam is not wealthy.

6. There is life on Mars given that there is life on Earth. Hence, there is life on Mars.

7. It is true that corrupt institutions are hard to reform. It is false that individuals are totally depraved. Therefore, if corrupt institutions are hard to reform, then individuals are totally depraved.

* 8. The sky is blue. The sky is cobalt blue only if it is blue. Hence, the sky is cobalt blue.

9. Kidnapping is wrong if society disapproves of it. Kidnapping is wrong. So, society disapproves of kidnapping.

10. If Mary is a psychiatrist, then she is a physician. Mary is not a physician. Therefore, Mary is a psychiatrist.

11. If you want to ruin your life, you should take hard drugs. But you don't want to ruin your life. So, you should not take hard drugs.

* 12. Lying causes social discord. Hence, lying is wrong.

13. If Dracula is a vampire, then he is dangerous. But Dracula is not a vampire. Hence, he is dangerous.

14. If my society approves of genetic engineering, then genetic engineering is right. But my society does not approve of genetic engineering. Hence, genetic engineering is not right.

15. Either films depicting graphic violence have caused the increase in violent crime or bad parenting has caused it (or both). Movies depicting graphic violence have caused the increase in violent crime. Therefore, bad parenting has not caused the rise in violent crime.

*16. You will win the chess tournament if you are very good at chess. Unfortunately, you are not very good at chess. Hence, you will not win the chess tournament.

17. Assuming that you treat like cases alike, you are fair. Hence, you are fair only if you treat like cases alike.

18. Philosophy is important if ideas are important. And assuming that ideas change lives, ideas are important. Hence, if philosophy is important, then ideas change lives.

*19. Mercy killing is morally permissible only if it promotes a greater amount of happiness for everyone affected than the alternatives do. And mercy killing does promote a greater amount of happiness for everyone affected than the alternatives do. Therefore, mercy killing is morally permissible.

PART B: More Counterexamples Try to identify the most logically sensitive forms of the following arguments, using capital letters to stand for *terms*. Then, construct a good counterexample to the form to show that the form is invalid. Remember, it is usually best to employ terms whose interrelations are well known, such as "dog," "cat," "collie," "animal," and "mammal."

* 1. No genuine Americans are communist spies. Some Oregonians are not communist spies. Therefore, some Oregonians are genuine Americans.

2. All dogmatists are hypocrites. All dogmatists are bigots. So, all bigots are hypocrites.

3. All who seek public office are noble. Some who seek public office are not wise persons. So, some wise persons are not noble.

* 4. No rock is sentient. Some mammals are sentient. Hence, no mammal is a rock.

5. All fatalists are determinists. Some predestinarians are not fatalists. So, some predestinarians are not determinists.

6. All vegetarians who refuse to eat animal products are vegans. No vegetarians who refuse to eat animal products are cattle ranchers. Hence, no vegans are cattle ranchers.

* 7. Some intelligent people are highly immoral. All highly immoral people are unhappy. Therefore, some unhappy people are not intelligent.

8. No perfect geometrical figures are physical entities. No physical entities are circles. Therefore, no circles are perfect geometrical figures.

9. All Fabians are socialists. Some socialists are not communists. So, some Fabians are not communists.

*10. All trespassers are persons who will be prosecuted. Some trespassers are not criminals. So, some criminals are not persons who will be prosecuted.

11. All observable entities are physical entities. Some quarks are not observable entities. Therefore, some quarks are not physical entities.

12. No wines are distilled liquors. Some beers are not distilled liquors. So, some beers are not wines.

* **13.** All statements that can be falsified are scientific. All empirical data are scientific. Hence, all statements that can be falsified are empirical data.

14. All diligent persons are individuals who deserve praise. Some students are individuals who deserve praise. So, some students are diligent persons.

15. All black holes are stars that have collapsed in on themselves. All black holes are entities that produce a tremendous amount of gravity. So, every entity that produces a tremendous amount of gravity is a star that has collapsed in on itself.

* **16.** Every rock musician is cool. No nerd is a rock musician. Hence, no nerd is cool.

17. All miracles are highly improbable events. Some highly improbable events are cases of winning a lottery. So, some cases of winning a lottery are miracles.

18. No positrons are particles with a negative charge. No neutrons are particles with a negative charge. Therefore, some positrons are neutrons.

* **19.** All people who despise animals are neurotic. No veterinarian is a person who despises animals. Hence, no veterinarian is neurotic.

20. All destructive acts are evil. Some wars are evil. So, some wars are destructive acts.

1.4   Strength and Cogency

At the beginning of this chapter, we drew a distinction between deductive and inductive arguments: A deductive argument is one in which the premises are intended to *guarantee* the truth of the conclusion, while an inductive argument is one in which the premises are intended to make the conclusion *probable*, without guaranteeing its truth. So far we have focused on the first kind of argument; we now turn our attention to the second.

The goal of a deductive argument is for the premises to guarantee the truth of the conclusion, and a valid argument is one that succeeds in this sense—it is one in which it is necessary that, if the premises are true, then the conclusion is true. Since the goal of an inductive argument is for the premises to make the conclusion probable (without guaranteeing its truth), it will succeed if it is probable (but not necessary) that, if the premises are true, then the conclusion is true. A **strong argument** is one in which it is probable (but not necessary) that, if the premises are true, then the conclusion is true.

> A **strong argument** is one in which it is probable (but not necessary) that, if the premises are true, then the conclusion is true.

We could put the point negatively by saying that a strong argument is one in which it is possible, but improbable, that the conclusion is false, given the assumption that the premises are true.

We should immediately note the potential for terminological confusion: According to the definition of a strong argument, *no valid arguments are strong and no strong arguments are valid.* To say that no valid argument is strong is *not* to say that valid arguments are inferior to strong arguments. Rather, it is simply to note that a valid argument is one in which the conclusion follows *necessarily* from the premises whereas a strong argument lacks this feature by definition. Deductive and inductive arguments are different kinds of arguments, and it is helpful to have some terms that apply to one but not the other. "Valid" and "strong" are such terms.

A **weak argument** is one in which it is *not* probable that, if the premises are true, then the conclusion is true.

A **weak argument** is one in which it is not probable that, if the premises are true, then the conclusion is true.

To illustrate the difference between strong and weak inductive arguments, consider the following pair of arguments:

82. Ninety-eight percent of *Star Wars* fans hate Jar Jar Binks. Kris is a *Star Wars* fan. So, Kris hates Jar Jar Binks.

83. Fourteen percent of *Star Wars* fans prefer *Return of the Jedi* to *The Empire Strikes Back*. Nina is a *Star Wars* fan. So, Nina prefers *Return of the Jedi* to *The Empire Strikes Back*.

Argument (82) is not valid since it is possible for the premises to be true and the conclusion false—Kris might be a *Star Wars* fan and adore Jar Jar Binks, even if the vast majority of fans do not. However, if Kris is a fan and if 98 percent of fans hate Jar Jar Binks, then it is probably true that Kris does as well. Hence, (82) is a strong argument. Argument (83), by contrast, is neither valid nor strong. If only 14 percent of *Star Wars* fans prefer *Jedi* to *Empire* and Nina is a fan, it is not probable that she prefers the former to the latter (in fact, it is improbable). Hence, (83) is a weak inductive argument.

The distinction between strong and weak inductive arguments can be illustrated by types of inductive argument other than *statistical syllogism*, which is the type of argument that (82) and (83) are. For example, consider this pair of *arguments by authority:*

84. According to Boston University historian Howard Zinn, an expert in early twentieth-century American history, by 1933, the worst year of America's Great Depression, one-fourth to one-third of America's labor force was out of work. Therefore, one-fourth to one-third of American workers were unemployed in 1933.[5]

85. According to Fred D'Ignoratio, an incoming freshman at Bellevue Community College, the U.S. GNP will decrease by 4.67 percent next year. So, the GNP of the U.S.A. will go down nearly 5 percent next year.

Even widely recognized authorities like Howard Zinn can make mistakes, so it is *possible* that he did say that, by 1933, one-fourth to one-third of America's labor force was out of work, even though the figure was in fact closer to two-fifths. Thus, (84) is not valid. Nevertheless, when a historian with Zinn's admirable scholarly credentials sincerely asserts something in his field of expertise in a publication that has been reviewed by several similarly qualified experts, it is unlikely that what he says is false, even if it is possible. Thus, (84) is a strong argument by authority. By way of contrast, argument (85) is a weak argument by authority. While we might applaud Mr. D'Ignoratio's intelligence, self-confidence, and B+ in Introduction to Macroeconomics, his budding expertise hardly makes him a reliable authority regarding economic forecasts. Thus, it is not likely that the GNP will decrease nearly 5 percent next year, given that Mr. D'Ignoratio sincerely said so. Notice that it would be impossible to say with any numerical precision how strong or weak (84) and (85) are, respectively. Still, it is clear that the first is strong while the second is weak.

Like arguments from authority, *arguments from analogy* are very common, and they, too, can be strong or weak. Here is an example. Suppose Benjamin and Zoe are riding horseback. Zoe's horse jumps a fence, but Benjamin is unsure whether his horse can jump the fence. Zoe points out that his horse is very similar to hers in size, speed, strength, and training. She adds that because Benjamin is an experienced rider and weighs no more than she does, Benjamin's horse is not operating with a handicap. She concludes that Benjamin's horse can jump the fence, too. We could outline Zoe's reasoning as follows:

86. Benjamin's horse is similar in certain respects to Zoe's horse. Zoe's horse is able to jump the fence. Hence, Benjamin's horse is able to jump the fence also.

This argument is not valid because its conclusion can be false while its premises are true. For example, unknown to Zoe, Benjamin's horse may have been given a drug that renders it unable to jump well today. Still, the argument is strong. For, the respects in which Benjamin's horse is similar to Zoe's horse are *relevant* to the jumping ability of a horse. Thus, it is more probable than not that if the premises of (86) are true, then the conclusion is true. The argument is strong.

By way of contrast, suppose instead that the respects in which Benjamin's horse is similar to Zoe's horse are these: They have the same coat and eye color, they have the same length of mane and tail, they have the same number of nostrils, and both have riders wearing Levi's 501s. In that case, although Benjamin's horse is similar in certain respects to Zoe's horse, and Zoe's horse is able to jump the fence, it does not follow that it is likely that Benjamin's horse is able to jump the fence too, given those similarities. That's because they are *not relevant* to the jumping ability of a horse. Thus, it is not likely that, if the premises of (86) are true, then the conclusion is true. The argument is weak.

Thus far, we have seen that there are different types of inductive arguments and that they can be either strong or weak. We will explore the concept of strength and weakness more fully later, as well as the three types of inductive arguments we have mentioned and other types, too. For now, it will be useful to underscore an important difference between strength and weakness, on the one hand, and validity and invalidity, on the other.

The important difference is this: Strength and weakness come in degrees, but validity and invalidity do not. Either it is necessary that, if the premises of an argument are true, then so is its conclusion, or it is not necessary. Or, to put it another way, either it is possible for the premises of an argument to be true while the conclusion is false, or it is not possible. Thus, it makes no sense to speak of an argument being *more* valid or invalid than another, not in the sense of "valid" and "invalid" that the logician is interested in. In that sense, the only sense we are concerned with here, validity and invalidity do not come in degrees. Strength and weakness, however, are a different matter. Consider the statistical syllogisms that we used above to illustrate the difference between strong and weak inductive arguments. Here they are again:

82. Ninety-eight percent of *Star Wars* fans hate Jar Jar Binks. Kris is a *Star Wars* fan. So, Kris hates Jar Jar Binks.
83. Fourteen percent of *Star Wars* fans prefer *Return of the Jedi* to *The Empire Strikes Back*. Nina is a *Star Wars* fan. So, Nina prefers *Return* to *Empire*.

Argument (82) is very strong, but it would be even stronger if 99 percent of *Star Wars* fans hate Jar Jar Binks. Moreover, it would still be strong even if only 93 percent of *Star Wars* fans hate Jar Jar Binks. Argument (83) is very weak, but it would be even weaker if 11 percent of *Star Wars* fans prefer *Return* to *Empire*. Moreover, it would still be weak even if a higher percentage of *Star Wars* fans prefer *Return* to *Empire*, say 23 percent. Although it is easy to see that the strength and weakness of statistical syllogisms come in degrees (we simply raise and lower the numerical values of the percentages), it is important to also see that the strength and weakness of arguments by authority and analogy also come in degrees. In arguments by authority, the degree of strength and weakness will vary according to the reliability of the authority, while in arguments from analogy, the degree of strength and weakness will vary according to the relevance of the similarities of the items being compared.

Notice that we want more than strength from our inductive arguments. All else being equal, a strong inductive argument would be better if all of its premises were true. An inductive argument that has both is a *cogent argument*.

In other words, a strong argument in which all of the premises are true is a **cogent argument.**

 A **cogent argument** is a strong argument in which all of the premises are true.

Because a cogent argument is strong and has only true premises, its conclusion will probably be true. Argument (84) is a cogent argument. Here is another one:

87. All or nearly all lemons that have been tasted were sour. So, the next lemon you taste will be sour.

This argument is not valid because the conclusion concerns not merely the lemons that have been tasted but lemons in general, including those that have not been tasted. And the premise does not rule out the possibility that a large percentage of untasted lemons are not sour. Nevertheless, it is unlikely that the conclusion is false given that the premise is true. And the premise is true. So, the argument is cogent.

A cogent argument can have a false conclusion, for its premises do not absolutely guarantee the truth of its conclusion. In this respect, cogent arguments differ markedly from sound arguments. A sound argument cannot have a false conclusion because it is valid and all its premises are true. (And if a valid argument has only true premises, it must follow that its conclusion is true also.)

Strong + All Premises True = Cogent

As you might expect, just as the concept of a sound argument has its counterpart in the concept of an unsound argument, so the concept of a cogent argument has its counterpart in the concept of an uncogent argument. An *uncogent argument* falls into one of the following three categories:

Category 1: It is strong, but it has at least one false premise.

Category 2: It is weak, but all of its premises are true.

Category 3: It is weak and it has at least one false premise.

In other words, an **uncogent argument** is one that is either weak or strong with at least one false premise.

 An **uncogent argument** is one that is either weak or strong with at least one false premise.

For example, all of the following arguments are uncogent:

88. Most wizards are muggles. Hermione is a wizard. So, Hermione is a muggle.

89. According to a 2002 article in the *National Enquirer*, male members of Elizabeth Smart's family were involved in a gay sex ring. So, they probably were.

90. Hud's Ford Bronco 4x4 will get good gas mileage. After all, Dennis's Toyota Corolla gets good gas mileage, and like Dennis's Corolla, Hud's Bronco has velvet upholstery, tinted glass windows, and a six-disk CD player.

Argument (88) is uncogent, because although it is strong, it has a false (first) premise. It is in Category 1. Argument (89) is uncogent, because although it has a true premise, it is weak. It is in Category 2. Argument (90) is uncogent because it is weak and it has a false premise (Hud does not own a Bronco; he owns a Pathfinder). It is in Category 3.

Note that according to our definitions, no sound argument is cogent, for no valid argument is strong. Similarly, no cogent argument is sound, since no strong argument is valid. Note also that a valid argument with a false premise is unsound, but it is not uncogent because a valid argument is neither strong nor weak.

We said earlier that, all else being equal, we want an inductive argument to be strong and have all true premises. That is, we want an inductive argument to be cogent. That is not to say, however, that if an inductive argument is cogent, it cannot be improved. A cogent argument whose premises were not reasonable for us to accept given our total evidence would not be satisfying. Moreover, a cogent argument whose premises were not reasonable for us to accept independently of our acceptance of the conclusion would not be useful as a basis for believing the conclusion. So we want more from an inductive argument than mere cogency. Still, we want an inductive argument to be cogent, and inductive logic plays a critical role in evaluating whether an argument is cogent. For an argument is cogent only if it is strong, and, as we said earlier, inductive logic is the study of methods for evaluating whether the premises of an argument make its conclusion probable, without guaranteeing it; that is, inductive logic is the study of methods for evaluating whether or not an argument is strong.

We initially defined deductive logic as the part of logic that is concerned with the study of methods for evaluating whether the premises of an argument guarantee its conclusion. Later, we more precisely defined **deductive logic** as the part of logic that is concerned with the study of methods for evaluating arguments for validity and invalidity. We initially defined inductive logic as the part of logic that is concerned with the study of methods for evaluating whether the premises of an argument make its conclusion probable, without guaranteeing it. We shall now more precisely define **inductive logic** as the part of logic that is concerned with the study of methods for evaluating arguments for strength and weakness. Notice that we have defined deductive and inductive logic not in terms of the kinds of arguments they treat but in terms of the evaluative methods employed. And indeed, we might use methods from both branches of logic on the same argument. For example, we might use a method from deductive logic to determine that an argument is invalid and then use a method from inductive logic to determine that the same argument is strong (or that it is weak).

By definition, any argument that is either strong or weak is invalid, so we can draw a map of the main concepts discussed in this section as follows:

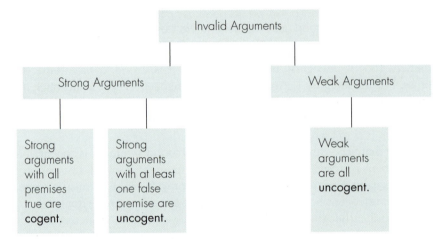

Note that strong arguments with at least one false premise are unsound (as well as uncogent). They are unsound for two reasons: (a) they are invalid and (b) they have a false premise. Of course, weak arguments are also unsound, for every weak argument is invalid. And if a weak argument has at least one false premise, then it is unsound both because it is invalid and because it has a false premise.

Summary of Definitions

A **strong argument** is one in which it is probable (but not necessary) that, if the premises are true, then the conclusion is true.

A **weak argument** is one in which it is not probable that, if the premises are true, then the conclusion is true.

A **cogent argument** is a strong argument in which all of the premises are true.

An **uncogent argument** is one that is either weak or strong with at least one false premise.

Deductive logic is the part of logic that is concerned with the study of methods of evaluating arguments for validity and invalidity.

Inductive logic is the part of logic that is concerned with the study of methods of evaluating arguments for strength and weakness.

Some general remarks on terminology are in order. Notice that given our definitions, arguments can be strong, weak, cogent, or uncogent. But arguments are never true and they are never false. Both premises and conclusions are either true or false. But neither premises nor conclusions are ever strong, weak, cogent, or uncogent.

EXERCISE 1.4

PART A: Matching In the space provided, write the letter of the item on the right that best characterizes the item on the left.

_____ **1.** Valid

_____ **2.** Invalid

_____ **3.** Strong

_____ **4.** Weak

_____ **5.** Sound

_____ **6.** Cogent

_____ **7.** Statement

_____ **8.** Unsound

_____ **9.** Uncogent

_____ **10.** Deductive logic

_____ **11.** Inductive logic

_____ **12.** Logic

_____ **13.** Argument

_____ **14.** An argument from analogy

_____ **15.** An argument from authority

A. A sentence that is either true or false.

B. An argument that is either invalid or has a false premise.

C. A strong argument with (all) true premises.

D. The part of logic concerned with the study of methods of evaluating arguments for validity and invalidity.

E. An argument in which it is not probable that, if the premises are true, then the conclusion is true.

F. A valid argument with (all) true premises.

G. The part of logic concerned with the study of methods for evaluating arguments for strength and weakness.

H. The study of methods for evaluating whether the premises of an argument adequately support its conclusion.

I. An argument in which it is necessary that, if the premises are true, then the conclusion is true.

J. A set of statements where some of the statements, called the premises, are intended to support another, called the conclusion.

K. Non-Hodgkins lymphoma is not as rare in the U.S.A. as one might have thought. For, according to the American Cancer Society, it is the fifth most common type of cancer in the U.S.A.

L. An argument in which it is not necessary that, if the premises are true, then the conclusion is true.

M. Many organs are like machines: They have parts that are interrelated in such a way as to serve a purpose. Machines are produced by intelligent design. So, many organs are produced by intelligent design too.

N. An argument in which it is probable (but not necessary) that, if the premises are true, then the conclusion is true.

O. An argument that is either weak or strong with at least one false premise.

PART B: True or False?

* **1.** All arguments having only true premises are cogent.

2. All strong arguments are cogent.

3. All weak arguments are uncogent.

* **4.** All arguments with a false premise are uncogent.

5. Some cogent arguments have a false conclusion.

6. Some sound arguments have a false conclusion.

* **7.** The following argument is true: "Over 90 percent of Americans speak English. Hank Williams is an American. So, Hank Williams speaks English."

8. The following argument is an argument from analogy: "According to Flew's *Dictionary of Philosophy*, the British philosopher Bertrand Russell died in 1970. So, Bertrand Russell died in 1970."

9. A strong argument is one in which it is impossible for its conclusion to be false while its premises are true.

***10.** Every uncogent argument has at least one false premise.

11. Every uncogent argument is weak.

12. Some arguments have valid premises, and some do not.

***13.** The following argument is an argument from authority: "Scholars are like the Roman emperor Nero. Nero, you'll recall, played his violin while Rome burned. Similarly, scholars play with ideas while civilization is threatened by the 'flames' of greed, poverty, racism, and violence. Now, plainly, Nero was morally irresponsible. Hence, scholars are morally irresponsible also."

14. A strong argument has these two features: (a) It is possible that if its premises are true, then its conclusion is false, and (b) it is probable that if its premises are true, then its conclusion is true.

15. A weak argument is one in which it is not likely that if its premises are true, then its conclusion is true.

PART C: Valid or Invalid? Strong or Weak? As best as you can determine, which of the following arguments are valid? Invalid? Which are strong? Weak?

* **1.** Fifty percent of serial killers were abused as children. Ted Bundy was a serial killer. Therefore, Bundy was abused as a child.

2. This lovely china plate is similar in size, weight, and composition to the one I just dropped. The one I just dropped broke. So, if I drop this lovely china plate, it will break.

3. According to Lillian Roxon's *Rock Encyclopedia* (New York: Grosset & Dunlap, 1969), Buddy Holly, who wrote "Peggy Sue," "That'll Be the Day," and other early rock hits, died in an airplane crash on February 3, 1959. So, Buddy Holly died in an airplane crash in 1959.

* **4.** One hundred percent of all the frogs that have ever been dissected had hearts. Therefore, 100 percent of the entire frog population have hearts.

5. It is always wrong to kill an innocent human intentionally. A fetus is an innocent human. So, it is always wrong to kill a fetus intentionally.

6. Research based on Gallup polls indicates that a random sample of 4000 is sufficient to support highly accurate conclusions about large populations—conclusions having a margin of error of only 2 percentage points. And according to a recent poll, 83 percent of a random sample of 4000 American voters favor Jones for president. Thus, approximately 83 percent of American voters favor Jones for president.

* **7.** A porpoise is similar to a human being. It has lungs rather than gills. It is warm-blooded rather than cold-blooded. And porpoises nurse their young with milk. Therefore, porpoises, like humans, are capable of speaking languages.

8. Every serial killer is a psychopath. Some criminals are not psychopaths. So, some criminals are not serial killers.

9. Ninety percent of the cars in the parking lot were vandalized, and your car was in the parking lot. Therefore, your car was vandalized.

* **10.** No spiders are humans. Dawn is a human. Thus, Dawn is not a spider.

11. All observed emeralds have been green. Therefore, the next emerald to be observed will be green.

12. Linda is younger than Maria. Hence, Maria is older than Linda.

* **13.** According to H. W. Janson, professor of fine arts at New York University, the Norwegian artist Edvard Munch painted *The Scream* in 1893. So, Munch painted *The Scream* prior to 1900. (See Janson's *History of Art* [New York: Abrams, 1971], p. 513.)

14. Sixty-five percent of the students at St. Ambrose College are Democrats. Joan is a student at St. Ambrose College. Therefore, Joan is a Democrat.

15. Mark Twain is identical with Samuel Clemens. Mark Twain wrote *Huckleberry Finn*. It follows that Samuel Clemens wrote Huckleberry Finn.

* **16.** No circles are squares. All circles are figures. So, no figures are squares.

17. According to Lewis Hopfe, a noted authority on world religions, the religion called Jainism originated in India in the sixth century BCE. It is the goal of Jainism to liberate the soul from matter. All life, but especially animal life, is sacred to the Jains. And the Jains hold that the gods cannot help humans attain salvation. Therefore, at least one religion holds that the gods cannot help humans attain salvation. (See Hopfe's *Religions of the World*, 4th ed. [New York: Macmillan, 1987], pp. 134–138.)

18. In a certain factory, there is a machine that produces tin cans. Quality-control inspectors examine (in a random fashion) one-tenth of all the tin cans produced by the machine. Of the tin cans examined by the inspectors, 5 percent are malformed. So, approximately 5 percent of all the tin cans produced by the machine are malformed.

*19. Computers are similar to humans in that both are capable of complex calculations. Humans generally feel ashamed if they make a mistake. Hence, computers generally feel ashamed if they make a mistake.

20. According to the *Encyclopedia Britannica*, the first use of poison gas as a weapon in modern warfare occurred on April 22, 1915, when the Germans launched a highly successful chlorine gas attack against the Allied positions at Ypres, Belgium. So, the first use of poison gas as a weapon in modern warfare occurred on April 22, 1915.

PART D: Cogency Which of the following are cogent? Which are uncogent? (If the argument is uncogent, explain why.) Which of the arguments are neither cogent nor uncogent?

* **1.** Most humans fear death. Woody Allen (the famous comedian and filmmaker) is a human. Therefore, Woody Allen fears death.

2. Fifty percent of the students at Seattle Pacific University are Republicans. Kathy is a student at Seattle Pacific University. So, Kathy is a Republican.

3. All humans are mortal. Socrates is a human. Hence, Socrates is mortal.

* **4.** All of the birds that have been observed (in the entire history of the world) can fly. Therefore, all birds can fly.

5. War is similar to playing a game of chess. For instance, in both war and chess, strategy is important. And in both war and chess, there is a struggle for victory. Now, when one is losing a game of chess, one should not attack one's opponent with lethal weapons. So, when a nation is losing a war, it should not attack its opponent with lethal weapons.

6. Ninety percent of Americans speak Chinese. Harrison Ford (the famous actor) is an American. Thus, Harrison Ford speaks Chinese.

* **7.** Sue is taller than Tom. Tom is taller than Fred. It follows that Sue is taller than Fred.

8. The vast majority of Americans are fluent speakers of English. The Queen of England is an American. So, the Queen of England is a fluent speaker of English.

9. Most Americans live in Nevada. Aretha Franklin (the famous singer) is an American. Hence, Aretha Franklin lives in Nevada.

*10. Forty percent of students at Reed College are from the Northwest. Sally is a student at Reed College. So, Sally is from the Northwest.

NOTES

1. We have said that arguments are composed of statements. Some logicians would prefer to say that arguments are composed of propositions. For more about this issue, see section 3.1.
2. Our characterizations of deductive and inductive logic are borrowed from Brian Skyrms, *Choice and Chance*, 3rd ed. (Belmont, CA: Wadsworth, 1986), p. 12.

3. A more complete list of stylistic variants for "if-then" is provided in Chapter 7. The intent here is to provide a short list of the more common ones.
4. For a useful discussion of these issues, see P. C. W. Davies, *The Physics of Time Asymmetry* (Berkeley: University of California Press, 1977), chap. 7, pp. 185–200.
5. Howard Zinn, *A People's History of the United States* (New York: HarperCollins, 1995), p. 378.

CHAPTER 2

Identifying Arguments

*I*n Chapter 1, we met arguments that looked like this:

> **1.** All philosophers like logic.
> Ned is a philosopher.
> So, Ned likes logic.

In real life, authors don't commonly state their arguments quite so straightforwardly. The conclusion may be given first or sandwiched between premises. A long argument may actually be a chain of shorter arguments. Authors sometimes add extra claims that play no role in the argument but add color or distract the listener. Instead of repeating statements or terms, they sometimes vary their language with synonyms. And they will often leave out claims they believe are too obvious to need stating explicitly. It is much more difficult to evaluate a real-life argument than a well-behaved textbook argument (which we will call "well-crafted arguments"), so it is useful to know how to convert the first kind into the second.

This chapter tells you how to identify arguments as they appear in ordinary language, how to convert them into well-crafted arguments, and how to identify the structure of the arguments.

2.1 Arguments and Nonarguments

We must first learn to distinguish arguments from nonarguments. Recall that an argument is a set of statements where some of the statements are intended to support another. One can do many things with language besides argue: extend greetings, tell a story, make a request, express one's feelings, provide information, tell a joke, pray, and so on. In this section, we will examine some nonargumentative uses of statements that are sometimes confused with arguments.

In general, it is important to distinguish between arguments and unsupported assertions. For example:

2. The U.S. unemployment rate was 9.1 percent in July 2011, down from its recent high of 10.1 percent in January 2010.

As it stands, this passage is not an argument but simply a statement about the unemployment rate. No supporting statements (i.e., premises) are provided here, and no inferences are drawn. Of course, supporting statements could be supplied, but because they do not appear in the quoted passage, it is not an argument in and of itself.

Unsupported assertions come in a variety of types, some of which may be confused with arguments. For example, a **report** is a set of statements intended to provide information about a situation, topic, or event. A report may contain many informational statements without containing any arguments. For instance:

3. Total global advertising expenditures multiplied nearly sevenfold from 1950 to 1990. They grew one-third faster than the world economy and three times faster than world population. In real terms, spending rose from $39 billion in 1950 to $256 billion in 1990—more than the gross national product of India or than all Third World governments spent on health and education.[1]

Again, these statements could be backed up with further statements, but the passage, as it stands, is a report and not an argument. No inferences are drawn—the passage merely contains a series of informational statements.

A **report** is a set of statements intended to provide information about a situation, topic, or event.

An **illustration** is a statement together with an explanatory or clarifying example:

4. Mammals are vertebrate animals that nourish their young with milk. For example, cats, horses, goats, monkeys, and humans are mammals.

One clue that can help distinguish arguments from nonarguments is the presence of premise and conclusion indicator words. These words, which we'll discuss in more detail in the next section, include "because," "so," "thus," "therefore," and "since" and suggest that the author is intending some of her statements to support another. But we should be a little careful. Although these words *usually* indicate the presence of an argument, they occasionally have other purposes. The word "thus," for example, is sometimes used to introduce an illustration, like this:

5. Whole numbers can be represented as fractions. Thus, 2 can be represented as 8/4, and 5 can be represented as 15/3.

In statement (5), the examples seem merely illustrative. Sometimes, however, examples are given not merely to explain or clarify but to support (provide evidence for) a thesis, in which case the passage in question is an argument rather than an illustration:

> **6.** You just said there are no twin primes greater than 1,000, but that is inaccurate; 1997 and 1999 are both prime.

And sometimes a passage can reasonably be interpreted either as an illustration or as an argument. It all depends on the answer to this question: Do the examples merely clarify (or explain) a statement, or are they used to *provide evidence* for it? If the examples are used to provide evidence, then the passage is an argument.

> An **illustration** is a statement together with an explanatory or clarifying example.

An **explanatory statement** provides a reason for the occurrence of some phenomenon. For example:

> **7.** Judy got sick because she ate too much.
> **8.** The dinosaurs are extinct because a "large comet or asteroid struck the earth some 65 million years ago, lofting a cloud of dust into the sky and blocking sunlight, thereby suppressing photosynthesis and . . . drastically lowering world temperatures. . . ."[2]

Such passages are easily confused with arguments since the word "because" is often used to indicate a premise—for example, "Not all mammals are land animals *because* whales are mammals." Here the word "because" indicates the premise "whales are mammals." (More on this use of "because" in the next section.) But consider cases (7) and (8) carefully. Statement (7) does not seem to be an argument for the conclusion that Judy got sick, with "she ate too much" as a premise. Rather, (7) is simply the *assertion* that Judy's sickness was caused by her overeating. And of course, there are other possible explanations for Judy's sickness, such as an encounter with viruses or food poisoning. But (7) provides no reason to think the "overeating explanation" is true; that is, (7) includes no premises. Hence, (7) is not an argument. Similarly, (8) doesn't seem to be an argument for the conclusion that dinosaurs are extinct. It is merely the assertion that one possible explanation of the extinction of the dinosaurs is correct.

To see the difference between arguments and explanations, contrast the following:

> **9.** War is wrong because it involves killing innocent people and that is always wrong.
> **10.** Wars happen because human beings are selfish.

In the first of these, the clause that precedes the word "because" is what the author is trying to convince us of. In the second, the clause that precedes "because" is what the author wants to explain. One indicator of the difference is that "war is wrong" is an interesting and controversial claim. It makes sense that someone would try to argue for it, whereas "wars happen" is an accepted fact that no one would need to argue for. Another indicator is that what follows the word "because" in (9) can be seen as providing a reason to believe that *war is wrong*, whereas *human beings are selfish* would not function well to convince someone who did not already know that wars happen.

Of course, sometimes an explanation can itself be the conclusion of an argument. If an explanatory hypothesis is supported by further statements, then we have an argument. For example, many arguments are arguments to the effect that a certain statement or hypothesis is the best explanation of some phenomenon (or that some statement is probably true because it is the best explanation of some phenomenon). These are arguments rather than mere assertions because premises are provided. For instance:

> **11.** Three explanations have been offered for the extinction of the dinosaurs. First, a global rise in temperature caused the testes of male dinosaurs to stop functioning. Second, certain flowering plants (namely, angiosperms) evolved *after* the dinosaurs evolved; these plants were toxic for the dinosaurs, which ate them and died. Third, a large comet struck the earth, causing a cloud of dust that blocked out the sunlight, which in turn created a frigid climate for which the dinosaurs were ill suited. Now, there is no way to get any evidence either for or against the first hypothesis. And the second hypothesis is unlikely because it is probable that angiosperms were in existence 10 million years before the dinosaurs became extinct. There is, however, some evidence in favor of the third hypothesis. If the earth was struck by a large comet at the time the dinosaurs became extinct (some 65 million years ago), then there should be unusually large amounts of iridium (a rare metal) in the sediments of that period, for most of the iridium on Earth comes from comets and other objects from outer space. And, as a matter of fact, unusually large amounts of iridium have been found in the sediments of that period. So, the third explanation seems best.[3]

Passage (11) is an argument because evidence is given to support the claim that one of the three explanations is best.

An **explanatory statement** provides a reason for the occurrence of some phenomenon.

A **conditional statement** is an if-then statement; taken by itself, a conditional statement is not an argument. For instance:

> **12.** If Lucy works hard, then she will get a promotion.

There is some temptation to think that the antecedent (if-clause) of a conditional is a premise and that the consequent (then-clause) is a conclusion. But this is typically not the case. Remember that a conditional statement is hypothetical in nature. Thus, statement (12) merely asserts that if Lucy works hard, then she will get a promotion. It does not assert that Lucy works hard. Nor does it assert that she will get a promotion. By contrast, consider the following argument:

> **13.** Lucy works hard. Therefore, Lucy will get a promotion.

Here, we clearly have a premise–conclusion structure. And the conclusion is asserted on the basis of the premise (which is also asserted).

A **conditional statement** is an if-then statement.

Although conditionals, taken by themselves, are not arguments, they may express an argument in context. For example, during a tournament, a chess coach might give this advice to one of his players: "If you want to beat Moy, you should use the French Defense." In this context, "you want to beat Moy" need not be explicitly stated; it can be assumed. So, by expressing a conditional, the coach is in effect offering a *modus ponens*–type argument: "If you want to beat Moy, you should use the French Defense. You want to beat Moy. So, you should use the French Defense." Here's a slightly more complicated example: A well-known bumper sticker says, "If you can't trust me with a choice, you can't trust me with a child." Clearly, the author of this bumper sticker intends a *modus tollens* argument that says (more or less): "If you can't trust me with a choice, you can't trust me with a child. It's not the case that you can't trust me with a child. So, it's not the case that you can't trust me with a choice." Note that adding unstated premises (and conclusions) to arguments can get tricky; we will return to this issue later in the chapter. The main point is that conditional statements are not by themselves arguments. If we are tempted to treat them as arguments, that's because context makes it obvious that authors intend them to be combined with other premises they have left implicit.

Summary of Definitions

A **report** is a set of statements intended to provide information about a situation, topic, or event.

An **illustration** is a statement together with an explanatory or clarifying example.

An **explanatory statement** provides a reason for the occurrence of some phenomenon.

A **conditional statement** is an if-then statement.

EXERCISE 2.1

PART A: Arguments and Nonarguments Which of the following passages are arguments? Which are not arguments? If a passage is an argument, identify its conclusion. If a passage is not an argument, classify it as a report, illustration, explanation, or conditional statement.

* **1.** Americans are materialistic because they are exposed to more advertising than any other people on Earth.

   2. A person is dead if his or her brain has stopped functioning.

   3. The world fish catch dropped from its 1989 high of 100 million tons to 97 million tons in 1990 and has remained at about that figure ever since. Harvests have increased in some oceans but have fallen in others. And rising catches of some species are offset by falling catches of others. Breaking with a historical trend of constantly growing catches, stagnation in the global catch now appears likely to continue . . . —Hal Kane, "Fish Catch No Longer Growing," in Lester Brown, Hal Kane, and Ed Ayres, eds., *Vital Signs 1993: The Trends That Are Shaping Our Future* (New York: Norton, 1993), p. 32

* **4.** Waging war is always wrong because it involves killing human beings. And killing humans is wrong.

   5. When we calculate what the surface temperature of the planet should be, based on the heat it radiates to space, we find the whole globe should be a frozen wasteland, colder than today by about 33 degrees Celsius (60 degrees Fahrenheit) on average. The force saving us from this frigid fate is the atmosphere. The layer of air surrounding our globe contains important gases such as water vapor and carbon dioxide, which absorb the heat radiated by Earth's surface and reemit their own heat at much lower temperatures. We say they "trap" Earth's radiation and call this planetary warming mechanism the "greenhouse effect." —National Oceanic and Atmospheric Administration, *The Climate System* (Winter 1991), p. 7

   6. Never has the nation been safer from foreign menaces, and never before has the nation been graduating students less well educated than those of the immediately preceding generation. These facts warrant this conclusion: Today the principal threat to America is America's public-education establishment. —George F. Will, *The Leveling Wind* (New York: Viking Press, 1994), p. 199

* **7.** It's certainly true that Pluto doesn't act much like the other planets. Not only is it small and obscure, it's so changeable in its motions that no one can tell you exactly where it will be in a century. Whereas the other planets orbit on more or less the same plane, Pluto's orbit shifts out of alignment at an angle of 17 degrees, like the brim of a hat tilted on someone's head. —Bill Bryson, *A Really Short History of Nearly Everything* (London: Random House, 2008), p. 17

   8. If corporations are people, then corporations have the right to marry.

9. U.S. food producers feed livestock 20 million tons of plant protein per year that could be consumed by humans, and the livestock yields only 2 million tons of protein.

*   **10.** Wars occur because humans desire to control other humans.

11. The earth is getting warmer. Why? There are many reasons, but here are two important ones. First, the burning of coal, oil, and natural gas has greatly increased the carbon dioxide in the atmosphere. And carbon dioxide retains heat. Second, chlorofluorocarbons, which are used in air conditioners and refrigerators, have attacked the ozone layer, thus leaving the earth exposed to ultraviolet rays from the sun.

12. In 1950, the population of the world was about 2.5 billion. In 1967, the population of the world was almost 3.5 billion. In 1980, the population of the world was almost 4.5 billion. And in 1992, the population of the world was almost 5.5 billion. In 2007, it was 6.6 billion. So, the population of the world has grown both steadily and rapidly since 1950.

*   **13.** Global oil demand still lies well below the peak level of 1979. Improved energy efficiency and the expanding role of natural gas in many countries is cutting into petroleum's market. But oil is still the world's leading source of energy, supplying 40 percent of the total . . . —Christopher Flavin and Hal Kane, "Oil Production Steady," in Lester Brown, Hal Kane, and Ed Ayres, eds., *Vital Signs 1993: The Trends That Are Shaping Our Future* (New York: Norton, 1993), p. 46

14. Either James died because he was shot or James died because he was hanged. It's false that James died because he was shot. Hence, James died because he was hanged.

15. Not all tyrants avoid prosecution because Hosni Mubarak was tried by his fellow Egyptians.

*   **16.** Prime numbers are divisible only by themselves and one. For example, 3, 5, 7, and 11 are prime numbers.

17. If U.S. special operations forces did not kill Osama Bin Laden, then someone else did.

18. Roman numerals as well as Arabic numerals can be used to stand for numbers. Thus, the Roman numeral IX stands for the number 9.

*   **19.** If one sets one's heart on humaneness, one will be without evil. —Confucius, *The Analects* (New York: Oxford University Press, 1993), p. 13

20. During the Cold War, the United States pursued a policy of nuclear deterrence. Missiles with nuclear warheads were aimed at many locations in the former Soviet Union. The threat of destruction was real. Had the missiles been launched, millions of innocent people would have been killed. But in my opinion, the U.S. policy of nuclear deterrence was immoral. Let me give you an analogy. Suppose two angry men face each other with machine guns. Behind each one stands many innocent bystanders. Each man holds the other in check by threatening to pull the trigger and thus kill many innocent people. I submit that it is obvious that such men would be acting immorally. Hence, the U.S. policy of nuclear deterrence was immoral also.

21. If it is permissible for humans to eat animals, then it is permissible for super-intelligent extraterrestrials to eat humans.

* **22.** The good don't always die young because Mother Teresa was a good person.

23. America is a powerful nation primarily because it has one of the strongest economies in the world.

24. Some metals are liquids at room temperature because mercury is a metal.

* **25.** If driving on the left side of the road is wrong simply because society disapproves of it, then stealing is wrong simply because society disapproves of it. And driving on the left side of the road is wrong simply because society disapproves of it. Therefore, stealing is wrong simply because society disapproves of it.

PART B: Constructing Arguments Each of the following statements can be made the conclusion of an argument. For each statement, write down at least one premise that provides some degree of support for it.

* **1.** It is morally permissible to experiment on nonhuman animals.

2. It is wrong to eat animals.

3. Marijuana should be legalized.

* **4.** Only violent criminals should be imprisoned.

5. Handguns should be outlawed.

6. Society has an obligation to provide housing for the homeless.

* **7.** Americans are too individualistic.

8. The world is overpopulated with humans.

9. It is foolish to live in a modern city.

* **10.** Beauty is in the eye of the beholder.

11. Large corporations have too much political power.

12. Nuclear deterrence is irrational.

* **13.** It is wrong to misrepresent one's income on a tax form.

14. It is not always wrong for a nation to wage war.

15. Torture is never morally permissible.

2.2   Well-Crafted Arguments

Arguments in ordinary English are often stated in ways that obscure their important logical features. For instance, excess verbiage may make it difficult to determine what the premises actually are. The conclusion may be "camouflaged" in a tangle of premises. Repetition may give the appearance of many premises where there are in fact few. An unhelpful variation in the vocabulary employed may obscure the linkage between the premises (and/or between the premises and the conclusion). And so on.

Obviously, arguments are easier to evaluate when stated in such a way that their important logical features are explicit. When an argument is so stated, we will refer to it as a **well-crafted argument.** Because well-crafted arguments are, from a logical point of view, easier to evaluate than their less-well-crafted cousins, one of the most important logical skills is the ability to take an argument in ordinary English and rewrite it as a well-crafted one.

> A **well-crafted** (version of an) **argument** is an argument that is stated in such a way that its important logical features are explicit.

It is worth noting that in converting a passage into a well-crafted argument, we are not suggesting that we can write the passage better than the author did or that we are in a better position to express his intentions than he was himself. No doubt he had excellent stylistic or rhetorical reasons for choosing the words he did. We are simply interested in separating the stylistic and rhetorical elements from the logical and evidential elements so that we can determine whether it is sound or cogent, whether it provides us with good reason for believing its conclusion.

How do we do this? The guiding idea is, on the one hand, to preserve the content of the original—what's being claimed, its truth value and whether it is valid—while, on the other hand, removing what is redundant or confusing or distracting. It's important to preserve the content of the original, so that we can be fair to the author and so that when we evaluate the well-crafted version and determine that if it is unsound, we can be sure that the original was unsound too. In this section, we will discuss six principles involved in producing well-crafted versions of arguments found in ordinary English.

Principle 1: Identify the premises and the conclusion.

Recall that the premises of an argument are the statements on the basis of which the conclusion is affirmed, and statements are sentences or parts of sentences that are either true or false. Each step of an argument, whether premise or conclusion, must be a statement. Consider the following simple example:

14. We should abolish the death penalty because it does not deter crime.

This is an argument. The word "because" indicates a premise, as it often does. A well-crafted version of argument (14) looks like this:

15. 1. The death penalty does not deter crime.
So, 2. We should abolish the death penalty.

From now on, when constructing well-crafted versions of arguments, let us adopt the convention of making the conclusion of the argument the final step. Let us also write "so" to mark a conclusion, as we have done here. Further, let us place a number before each step of the argument (whether premise or conclusion). A step of an argument without the word "so" in front of it will be understood to be a premise. In this case, statement (1) is the only premise. We can drop the word "because" since our convention tells us that (1) is a premise.

Argument (14) illustrates two things worth noting. First, the conclusion of an argument often comes first in English prose. Thus, one cannot assume that an author will first state his or her premises and then draw a conclusion later on. In ordinary prose, the order is often reversed.

Second, argument (14) illustrates a typical use of premise indicators—in this case, the word "because." Premise indicators are words or phrases that are typically followed by a premise. For example:

because	after all
since	the reason is that
for	in light of the fact that
as	based on the fact that

Now, one cannot assume that these words and phrases indicate premises on every occasion of their use. As we have already seen, the word "because" is often used in explanations. But the point here is that these words are frequently used as premise indicators, and knowing this is a great help when rewriting an argument as a well-crafted one.

Just as premise indicators typically signal premises, conclusion indicators typically signal conclusions. Common conclusion indicators include these:

so	thus
therefore	accordingly
hence	consequently
implies that	we may infer that
it follows that	which proves that

Consider the following argument:

16. I was bitten by several dogs when I was a child. Therefore, dogs are dangerous.

A well-crafted version of argument (16) looks like this:

17. 1. I was bitten by several dogs when I was a child.
So, 2. Dogs are dangerous.

Of course, this argument is weak, but a weak argument is still an argument.

The good news is that authors frequently use premise and conclusion indicators to clarify their intentions. The bad news is that authors often rely on more subtle methods (e.g., context, order, emphasis) to identify the structure of their reasoning. There is no substitute in such cases for logical and linguistic insight. But *a good rule of thumb is to identify the conclusion first.* Once you figure out what the author is trying to prove, the rest of the argument often falls into place.

Let's now consider a slightly more complicated argument:

> **18.** Since the average American consumes 30 times the amount of the earth's resources as does the average Asian, Americans (taken as a group) are selfish. After all, excessive consumption is a form of greed. And greed is selfish desire.

What is the conclusion of the argument? That Americans (taken as a group) are selfish. "Since" is a premise indicator, and so is "after all." Thus, a well-crafted version of the argument looks like this:

> **19.** 1. The average American consumes 30 times the amount of the earth's resources as does the average Asian.
> 2. Excessive consumption is a form of greed.
> 3. Greed is selfish desire.
> So, 4. Americans (taken as a group) are selfish.

You may be wondering whether the order of the premises matters. From the standpoint of logic, the order makes no difference, so we simply list the premises in the order in which they appear in the original. Note, however, that if an argument is well crafted, the premises must precede the conclusion because our conventions tell us that in a well-crafted version of an argument, the last statement *is* the conclusion.

As we saw in Chapter 1, conditional statements have a number of stylistic variants. The **standard form** of a conditional statement is "If A, then B." When writing a well-crafted version of an argument, you should put any conditional premises or conclusions into this form. There are two reasons for this. First, most people find it easier to grasp the logical meaning of conditionals when they are in standard form. Second, putting conditionals into standard form facilitates the recognition of argument forms. Consider the following example:

> **20.** It is not permissible to eat cows and pigs, for it is permissible to eat cows and pigs only if it is permissible to eat dogs and cats. But it is not permissible to eat dogs and cats.

Rewriting this argument as a well-crafted one, we get the following:

> **21.** 1. If it is permissible to eat cows and pigs, then it is permissible to eat dogs and cats.
> 2. It is not permissible to eat dogs and cats.
> So, 3. It is not permissible to eat cows and pigs.

The argument form is *modus tollens*. Recall that common stylistic variants of "If A, then B" include "B if A," "B assuming that A," "B given that A," "A only if B," "Given that A, B," and "Assuming that A, B."

> The **standard form** of a conditional statement is "If A, then B."

Before leaving the topic of identifying premises and conclusions, we need to address two slight complications involving rhetorical questions and commands. As noted in Chapter 1, not all sentences are statements. For example, questions are sentences, but questions are not statements. There is, however, one kind of question that serves as a disguised statement, namely, the so-called rhetorical question. A *rhetorical question* is used to emphasize a point. No answer is expected because the answer is considered apparent in the context. For example:

22. The common assumption that welfare recipients like being on welfare is false. Does anyone like to be poor and unemployed? Does anyone like to be regarded as a parasite?

In this context, the arguer clearly expects a "no" answer to both questions. So, these questions are in effect statements. And when producing a well-crafted version of the argument, we change them into statements, like this:

23. 1. No one likes to be poor and unemployed.

  2. No one likes to be regarded as a parasite.

So, 3. The common assumption that welfare recipients like being on welfare is false.

Commands (or imperatives) are also usually sentences but not statements. If someone issues the command "Shut the door!" it makes no sense to reply, "That's true" (or "That's false") because no truth claim has been made. However, imperatives sometimes turn up as premises or conclusions in arguments. Such imperatives are disguised "ought" statements. For example, consider the following argument:

24. Be a doctor! You've got the talent. You would enjoy the work. You could help many people. And you could make a lot of money!

In this case, the imperative "Be a doctor!" is naturally interpreted as "You ought to be a doctor," and this latter sentence expresses something either true or false.[4] When an imperative is a disguised "ought" statement, you should make this explicit when constructing a well-crafted version of the argument:

25. 1. You've got the talent.

  2. You would enjoy the work.

3. You could help many people.

4. You could make a lot of money.

So, 5. You ought to be a doctor.

It would be equally correct to write the conclusion this way: "You should be a doctor."

Principle 2: Eliminate excess verbiage.

Excess verbiage is a word or statement that adds nothing to the argument. This material should not be included in the well-crafted version of the argument.

> **Excess verbiage** is a word or statement that adds nothing to the argument.

Four types of excess verbiage are extremely common in arguments. One is discounts. A **discount** is an acknowledgment of a fact or possibility that might be thought to render the argument invalid, weak, unsound, or uncogent. For example:

26. Although certain events in the subatomic realm occur at random, I still say that the universe as a whole displays a marvelous order. Perhaps the best evidence for this is the fact that scientists continue to discover regularities that can be formulated as laws.

The conclusion of this argument is "the universe as a whole displays a marvelous order." The premise is "scientists continue to discover regularities that can be formulated as laws." But what are we to do with "Although certain events in the subatomic realm occur at random"? It does not seem to be a premise, for events that occur at random are not evidence of order. In fact, the statement "certain events in the subatomic realm occur at random" seems to be evidence *against* the conclusion of the argument. And that is why it is best regarded not as a premise but as a discount.

> A **discount** is an acknowledgment of a fact or possibility that might be thought to render the argument invalid, weak, unsound, or uncogent.

Discounts are very important rhetorically. Roughly speaking, **rhetorical elements** are elements in an argument that increase its psychological persuasiveness without affecting its validity, strength, soundness, or cogency. And discounts often increase the psychological persuasiveness of an argument by anticipating potential objections. An audience is often disarmed to some degree by the realization that the arguer has already considered a potential objection and rejected it. But discounts aren't premises because they don't support the conclusion.

Therefore, we shall omit them when producing a well-crafted version of an argument. To illustrate, here is a well-crafted version of argument (26):

27. 1. Scientists continue to discover regularities that can be formulated as laws.

So, 2. The universe as a whole displays a marvelous order.

Rhetorical elements are elements in an argument that increase its psychological persuasiveness without affecting its validity, strength, soundness, or cogency.

Discount indicators include these:

although	while it may be true that
even though	while I admit that
in spite of the fact that	I realize that . . . , but
despite the fact that	I know that . . . , but

A second type of excess verbiage is repetition. **Repetition** is a restatement of a premise or conclusion, perhaps with slightly altered wording. When this occurs, select the formulation that seems to put the argument in its best light and drop the others. Here's an example:

28. The study of logic will increase both your attention span and your patience with difficult concepts. In other words, if you apply yourself to the subject of logic, you'll find yourself able to concentrate for longer periods of time. You will also find yourself increasingly able to approach complex material without feeling restless or frustrated. Therefore, a course in logic is well worth the effort.

A well-crafted version of argument (28) might look like this:

29. 1. The study of logic will increase both your attention span and your patience with difficult concepts.

So, 2. A course in logic is well worth the effort.

Now, you may feel that something is lost in dropping the repetition in a case like this, and indeed, something of rhetorical importance *is* lost. Repetition itself aids memorization. And a slight alteration of terminology can correct possible misunderstandings and/or make an idea more vivid. But our well-crafted version has advantages of its own; in particular, it enables us to focus on the argument's essential logical features.

Repetition is a restatement of a premise or conclusion, perhaps with slightly altered wording.

A third type of excess verbiage is the assurance. An **assurance** is a statement, word, or phrase that indicates that the author is confident of a premise or inference. For example:

30. Ben will do well in the marathon, for he is obviously in excellent condition.

Here is a well-crafted version of the argument:

31. 1. Ben is in excellent condition.
So, 2. Ben will do well in the marathon.

The word "obviously" indicates the author's confidence in the premise, but it does not contribute to the validity, strength, soundness, or cogency of the argument. Common assurances include these:

obviously	everyone knows that
no doubt	it is well known that
certainly	no one will deny that
plainly	this is undeniable
clearly	this is a fact

Assurances are rhetorically important because confidence often helps win over an audience. But assurances seldom affect the validity, strength, soundness, or cogency of an argument, so they should seldom appear in the well-crafted version of an argument.

An **assurance** is a statement, word, or phrase that indicates that the author is confident of a premise or inference.

A fourth type of excess verbiage is the hedge, which is the opposite of an assurance. A **hedge** is a statement, word, or phrase that indicates that the arguer is tentative about a premise or inference. For instance:

32. In my opinion, we have lost the war on drugs. Accordingly, drugs should be legalized.

"In my opinion" is a hedge, so the well-crafted version of the argument would be as follows:

33. 1. We have lost the war on drugs.
So, 2. Drugs should be legalized.

Common hedges include these:

I think that	I believe that
it seems that	I guess that
perhaps	it is reasonable to suppose that
maybe	this seems reasonable
in my opinion	this is plausible

Hedges are rhetorically important because without them one sometimes sounds dogmatic and close-minded. But hedges usually do not contribute to the validity, strength, soundness, or cogency of an argument. So, hedges usually should not appear in the well-crafted version of an argument.

> A **hedge** is a statement, word, or phrase that indicates that the arguer is tentative about a premise or inference.

Assurances and hedges *usually* can be dropped when we are producing a well-crafted version of an argument. But they cannot always be dropped, for they sometimes contribute to the validity, strength, soundness, or cogency of the argument. For example:

> **34.** I am in pain if it seems to me that I am in pain. And it seems to me that I am in pain. Therefore, I am in pain.

Here's a well-crafted version of the argument:

> **35.** 1. If it seems to me that I am in pain, then I am in pain.
>
>   2. It seems to me that I am in pain.
>
> So, 3. I am in pain.

The main point of this argument is that in the case of pain, there is a special connection between what *seems* to be so and what *is* so. Hence, while we can usually drop "it seems to me that" as a hedge, in this case we cannot. This example underscores the fact that we must remain vigilant when rewriting an argument as a well-crafted one. The role of every word or phrase must be carefully evaluated in context.

Principle 3: Employ uniform language.

Compare the following two arguments:

> **36.** If it looks like a duck and quacks like a duck, then it probably is a duck. And it both resembles a duck and cackles like one. So, we have at least to consider the possibility that we have a small aquatic bird of the family *anatidae* on our hands.

37. If it looks like a duck and quacks like a duck then it probably is a duck. It looks like a duck and quacks like a duck. So, it probably is a duck.

Argument (36) appears to have been written by someone using a thesaurus, substituting "small aquatic bird of the family *anatidae*" for "duck," and so on. This nonuniform language obscures the link between the premises and the conclusion. By contrast, the premise–conclusion linkage is crystal clear in (37). And yet the underlying form of argument is the same in both cases, namely, *modus ponens*.

Here is one well-crafted version of argument (36):

38. 1. If it looks like a duck and quacks like a duck then it probably is a duck.

2. It looks like a duck and quacks like a duck.

So, 3. It probably is a duck.

Of course, you might just as well have used "resembles" in place of looks like. The important thing is to stick with one term throughout the argument so as to highlight the logical form or pattern of reasoning.

Before leaving the topic of uniform language, let's consider one more example:

39. If you study other cultures, then you realize what a variety of human customs there is. If you understand the diversity of social practices, then you question your own customs. If you acquire doubts about the way you do things, then you become more tolerant. Therefore, if you expand your knowledge of anthropology, then you become more likely to accept other people and practices without criticism.[5]

Once again, the lack of uniform language makes it difficult to see whether (and how) the premises logically connect with the conclusion. Here is one well-crafted version of the argument:

40. 1. If you study other cultures, then you realize what a variety of human customs there is.

2. If you realize what a variety of human customs there is, then you question your own customs.

3. If you question your own customs, then you become more tolerant.

So, 4. If you study other cultures, then you become more tolerant.

Now, we can see that the argument actually is a tightly linked chain of reasoning. The use of uniform language is enormously beneficial in exhibiting the logical structure of an argument. By clarifying the linkages between premises and conclusions, uniform language helps us to avoid fuzzy thinking, which frequently stems from the careless use of words. The guiding ideas for when to substitute a word are (a) the substitution makes the structure of the argument clearer and (b) the substitution, in this or any other context, does not change the intended content of the statement. Note that if a substitution loses some of the color or emotional force of the original, that is not a problem.

Note how these principles get applied in the transition from (39) to (40). We substituted "a variety of human customs" for "the diversity of social practices." This, and other changes, enabled us to see that (39) was really an example of hypothetical syllogism, and hence was valid. Moreover, "a variety of human customs" and "the diversity of social practices" have the same content. The result is less colorful, even more boring, but it suits our purposes in doing logic better.

Principle 4: Be fair and charitable in interpreting an argument.

Fairness involves being loyal to the original, not distorting the clear meaning. *Charity* is needed when the original is ambiguous in some respect; it involves selecting an interpretation that puts the argument in its best possible light. Both of these concepts need to be explained in some detail.

With regard to fairness, many people tend to read more into an argument than they should. Instead of letting the author speak for him- or herself, they re-create the argument in their own image. Key statements may be loosely reworded or couched in emotionally loaded phrasing. Important premises may be omitted. New premises not provided in the original may be added. And so on. Now, there is indeed a place for identifying assumed but unstated premises in evaluating an argument. (We'll get to this later in the chapter.) But before one can usefully identify unstated assumptions, one must first accurately represent the *stated* or *explicit* version of the argument without distorting the meaning.

Fairness demands that we not let our biases interfere with the process of providing a well-crafted version that is true to an author's original intent. For example, if an author argues in favor of euthanasia for permanently comatose patients, it almost certainly distorts his intent to describe himself as in favor of our "playing God." Similarly, a person who argues against promiscuity does not necessarily believe that all sex is evil, and she should not be so represented in the absence of solid evidence to the contrary. Or, again, someone who supports affirmative action isn't necessarily advocating the use of strict quotas to achieve greater equality. It is unfair to interpret this person as advocating strict quotas unless he or she has *clearly* stated or implied this.

At the same time, we must not conceive of fairness in too narrow or wooden a fashion. To interpret well, we must take into account various rhetorical devices, such as irony and deliberate exaggeration. Suppose an American newspaper reporter argues as follows:

41. Oh, yes, we are all deeply appreciative of the full and accurate information we received from our government during the Iraq War. So, how can anyone doubt that we received full and accurate information during the war in Libya?

It is widely believed that Americans were sometimes not told the truth by their own government during the Iraq War, so the reporter's real meaning is probably the exact opposite of the surface meaning of her words. A well-crafted version of the argument would therefore involve some changes, perhaps along these lines:

42. 1. Americans did not receive full and accurate information from their government during the Iraq War.

So, 2. Americans possibly (or probably) did not receive full and accurate information from their government during the war in Libya.

Incidentally, notice that in the well-crafted version, the rhetorical question is phrased as a statement.

Charity enters the picture when an argument has been presented unclearly. Perhaps a premise can be understood in either of two ways. Or perhaps the structure of the argument is unclear—which statement is supposed to support which? Where such ambiguities occur, charity demands that we put the argument in its best possible light. In other words, when we are confronted with an interpretive choice, we should try to select an interpretation that makes the argument valid, strong, sound, or cogent (as the case may be) rather than invalid, weak, unsound, or uncogent. For instance:

43. Flag burning should be outlawed. I realize that there are worse things than flag burning, such as murder or kidnapping, but it ought to be illegal. Many people are disturbed by it. And it is unpatriotic. How important is freedom of expression, anyway?

Consider the following attempt at a well-crafted version:

44. 1. Many people are disturbed by flag burning.
2. Flag burning is unpatriotic.
3. Freedom of expression is not important.

So, 4. Flag burning should be outlawed.

Premise (3) is stated in an uncharitable fashion. Admittedly, the meaning of the question "How important is freedom of expression, anyway?" is unclear. But as stated, premise (3) is an easy target. Charity demands that we rephrase premise (3), perhaps along these lines: "Freedom of expression is not the most important thing" or "Freedom of expression is not the highest value."

Sometimes there are several possible interpretations of an argument that is incomplete or ambiguous. For example, if you hear someone argue that "Every woman has a right to do what she wants with her body," and hence, that abortion is permissible, you may wonder whether she means, "Every woman has the right to do what she wants with her body—with no restrictions, no matter how it affects others—including, using her body to punch and kick etc.," or whether she means something more restricted, like "Every woman has the right to do what she wants with her body as long as it does not harm others." In such cases, if the person offering the argument is available, it is a good idea to ask her which interpretation she intended. If she is not available, it is a good idea to present and evaluate *both* versions of her argument.

> Principle 5: Do not confuse subconclusions with (final) conclusions.

In reconstructing arguments, you will often find that an author has argued by steps, first arguing for one claim, which we will call a "subconclusion," and then using that subconclusion to argue for a final conclusion. Consider this example:

45. It is not always moral to save five lives at the cost of one life. For if it is always moral to save five lives at the cost of one life, then it is moral to remove the organs of a healthy person *against his wishes* and transplant them in five people who need organ transplants. But it is not moral to perform such transplants because doing so violates the rights of the healthy person. Therefore, it is not always morally right to save five lives at the cost of one life.

Here is a well-crafted version of the argument:

46. 1. If it is always moral to save five lives at the cost of one life, then it is moral to remove the organs of a healthy person against his wishes and transplant them in five people who need organ transplants.

2. Removing the organs of a healthy person against his wishes and transplanting them in five people who need organ transplants violates the rights of the healthy person.

So, 3. It is not moral to remove the organs of a healthy person against his wishes and transplant them in five people who need organ transplants.

So, 4. It is not always moral to save five lives at the cost of one life.

Note that premise (2) supports subconclusion (3). This structure is required by the premise indicator "because" in argument (45). And final conclusion (4) follows from (3) and (1), which work together as a logical unit (the form is *modus tollens*). To make the structure of the argument clear, shorthand expressions in the original, such as "doing so," are here expanded and made explicit. (The extent to which this is helpful in a given case is a matter of judgment.)

Let us adopt the convention of always listing the (final) conclusion of the argument as the last step in the well-crafted version, marked by the word "So." Subconclusions are also marked by the word "So" and are distinguished from (final) conclusions because they have a dual role—that is, they are supposed to follow from earlier steps in the argument and to support later steps. Of course, a subconclusion in fact may not be adequately supported by earlier steps, and it may not adequately support any later steps. But the well-crafted version is supposed to represent the arguer's intentions, even if those intentions are logically flawed.

Another way to think about subconclusions is to think about why an author would use them. In the last section, there is an exercise that asks you to construct your own arguments for various conclusions. This exercise provides some useful insight, from a different point of view, into the structure of arguments. Suppose you believe and want to argue that capital punishment is wrong. To provide a good argument for this, you need premises that are true and provide good reasons to believe the conclusion. Well, why do you think capital punishment is wrong? Perhaps because you believe "Capital punishment kills human beings." You need to link that to the conclusion. So, let's add, "It is always wrong to kill human beings." But then perhaps you note that this isn't true (or at least isn't widely agreed to be true). Someone who disagrees with you will almost certainly bring up killing in self-defense or killing in the pursuit of a just war. So, to make your premise more plausible you modify it to read: "Killing a human being is always wrong unless doing so saves a larger number of lives." That still won't be universally accepted, but it is more plausible.

But now note that your argument reads:

47. Killing a human being is wrong unless doing so saves a larger number of lives. Capital punishment kills a human being. So, capital punishment is wrong.

Unfortunately, the changes have made the new argument invalid. To make it valid, change the second premise to read: "Capital punishment kills a human being without saving a larger number of lives." But now this premise is less obviously true. It is uncontroversial that capital punishment takes lives, but it is often argued that it saves a larger number of lives in the process. If you have reason to believe that this is false, it would be a good idea to include that reason as support for your claim "Capital punishment kills a human being without saving a larger number of lives." Perhaps you recall statistics you encountered in a sociology class that showed that, on average, the murder rate is higher in states that practice capital punishment than in states that do not practice capital punishment. Now, you can use that to support your contention that capital punishment is not a deterrent and, hence, does not save a larger number of lives.

Your resulting argument will look like this:

48. 1. Capital punishment kills a human being.
   2. The murder rate is higher in states that practice capital punishment than in states that do not practice capital punishment.
So, 3. Capital punishment is not a deterrent.
So, 4. Capital punishment does not save lives.
   5. Killing a human being is always wrong unless doing so saves a larger number of lives.
So, 6. Capital punishment is wrong.

Notice lines 3 and 4. They start with the word "So," which makes them conclusions, and yet they are used to support 6. In other words, they function as both premises and conclusions, that is, as subconclusions.

When evaluating an argument with subconclusions, you must evaluate the support for each subconclusion as well as the support for the final conclusion of the argument. For example, if the argument for a given subconclusion is weak or invalid, then the overall argument is logically flawed. However, even if a given subconclusion is poorly supported by a premise that is supposed to support it, the overall argument may still retain merit under two conditions: (a) The subconclusion is adequately supported by other premises in the argument or (b) the subconclusion is plausible taken all by itself.

Principle 6: Make explicit obviously implicit premises in a charitable way.

An **enthymeme** is an argument with an implicit premise or conclusion. For example:

49. Obviously, not all mammals are land animals. Think of whales, porpoises, dolphins, and so on.

In such a case, it would be inappropriate to object that this argument is invalid. It is clear that the author knows (and knows that we know) that whales and so on are mammals and that they are not land animals. To state this explicitly would be unnecessarily pedantic in everyday discourse. In the well-crafted version of the argument, however, where our goal is to make the logic of the argument as clear as possible, we need to make the implicit premise explicit. So, a well-crafted version of argument (49) would be as follows:

50. 1. Whales, porpoises, and dolphins are mammals.

    2. Whales, porpoises, and dolphins are not land animals.

So, 3. Not all mammals are land animals.

An **enthymeme** is an argument with an implicit premise or conclusion.

When we fill in missing steps in an argument, we must adhere to the principles of fairness and charity. This means that, to the extent possible, added steps should be intended by the speaker, should be true (or at least plausible), and should make the argument valid (if it is deductive) or strong (if it is inductive).

These latter goals sometimes conflict. There might be a way to complete the argument that makes all the premises true and a way to complete the argument that makes it strong or valid, but no way to do both. We might have to choose whether to treat the argument as inductive or as deductive. For example:

> **51.** Bob is a professional basketball player. So, Bob is tall.

What's the missing premise here: (a) "All professional basketball players are tall," or (b) "Most professional basketball players are tall," or (c) "98.7 percent of basketball players are tall"? We can rule out (c). Even if it is true, nothing in the context gives us reason to suppose that this is what the speaker intended. As a general point, note that we shouldn't put words in the speaker's or author's mouth unless her words or the context indicate that this is part of her intention. What about (a) and (b)? The addition of (a) makes the argument valid, but it is false. Rajon Rondo and Steve Nash aren't tall. The addition of (b), on the other hand, makes the argument cogent. Since it is more charitable to attribute a cogent argument to an arguer than a valid but unsound one, (b) seems the best choice.

Here's a more interesting example:

> **52.** Some of Shakespeare's plays were first published or performed after 1610. So, Shakespeare couldn't have (been the man who) died in 1604.

This argument is plainly an enthymeme. But what extra premise will best complete it? One suggestion is, (a) "Playwrights don't write plays after they are dead." Another is, (b) "Playwrights don't publish or perform their plays after they are dead." Another is, (c) "Plays are not first published or performed after the playwright is dead."

Premises (a) and (b) are true, but they leave the argument invalid. It just doesn't follow from the fact that a play was first published or performed at a certain date, and the fact that it couldn't have been written or performed by a dead man on that date, that it wasn't written earlier. On the other hand, although it makes the argument valid, premise (c) is not true.

This example illustrates an important aspect of principle 6. Use of this principle may seem to be a simple act of generosity to the arguer, helping her make her argument clearer. But it is also useful in rebutting an argument. If we do not make the implicit premise explicit, there is a danger that we will be swept along by it without examining it too carefully. If you hear argument (52), you might be tempted to think it obviously sound—perhaps because you don't carefully distinguish between the version with premise (a) and the version with (c). When you go to the trouble of making the implicit premise explicit, you see that there are two or more possible versions, each of which is flawed.

We should note that sometimes an arguer will leave his or her *conclusion* implicit. For example, the familiar bumper sticker that says, "Abortion stops a beating heart," plainly has both an implicit premise, "It is wrong to stop a beating heart," and an implicit conclusion, "So, abortion is wrong."

Summary of Principles for Constructing Well-Crafted Arguments

1. Identify the premises and the conclusion.
2. Eliminate excess verbiage (e.g., discounts, repetition, assurances, hedges).
3. Employ uniform language.
4. Be fair and charitable in interpreting an argument.
5. Do not confuse subconclusions with (final) conclusions.
6. Make explicit obviously implicit premises in a charitable way.

Summary of Definitions

The **standard form** of a conditional statement is "If A, then B."

Excess verbiage is a word or statement that adds nothing to the argument.

A **discount** is an acknowledgment of a fact or possibility that might be thought to render the argument invalid, weak, unsound, or uncogent.

Rhetorical elements are elements in an argument that increase its psychological persuasiveness without affecting its validity, strength, soundness, or cogency.

Repetition is a restatement of a premise or conclusion, perhaps with slightly altered wording.

An **assurance** is a statement, word, or phrase that indicates that the author is confident of a premise or inference.

A **hedge** is a statement, word, or phrase that indicates that the arguer is tentative about a premise or inference.

An **enthymeme** is an argument with an implicit premise or conclusion.

EXERCISE 2.2

PART A: Identifying Arguments If a given passage is an argument, write a well-crafted version of it. (Be sure to apply the first five principles developed in this section. Pay especially close attention to premise and conclusion indicators. Do NOT add unstated premises. Do NOT delete premises unless they are repetitious.) If a passage is not an argument, simply write "not an argument."

* **1.** The defendant is not guilty of murder since she is insane.

   2. One does not worry about the fact that other people do not appreciate one. One worries about not appreciating other people. —Confucius, *The Analects,* trans. Raymond Dawson (New York: Oxford University Press, 1993), p. 5

3. America is in many ways different from Britain, but the two countries today are alike in their extremes of inequality, and in the desire of many politicians to solve economic and social ills by reducing the power of the state. Britain's current crisis should cause us to reflect on the fact that a smaller government can actually increase communal fear and diminish our quality of life. Is that a fate America wishes upon itself? —Richard Sennett and Saskia Sassen, "Cameron's Broken Windows," *New York Times*, August 11, 2011

* **4.** All the world's farms currently produce enough food to make every person on the globe fat. Even though 800 million people are chronically underfed (6 will die of hunger-related causes while you read this article), it's because they lack money and opportunity, not because food is unavailable in their countries. The UN Food and Agriculture Organization (FAO) reports that current food production can sustain world food needs even for the 8 billion people who are projected to inhabit the planet in 2030. —Barbara Kingsolver, *Animal, Vegetable, Miracle* (New York: HarperCollins, 2007), p. 18

5. It can hardly be denied that people fear death more than they fear life imprisonment. Are we not then forced to conclude that the death penalty is a greater deterrent than life imprisonment?

6. "If you are in good health and averagely diligent about hygiene, you will have a herd of about one trillion bacteria grazing on your flesh—about 100,000 of them on every square centimeter of skin." —Bill Bryson, *A Really Short History of Nearly Everything* (London: Random House, 2008), p. 110

* **7.** Since affirmative action involves giving a less qualified person the job, affirmative action is unjust. After all, the most qualified person deserves the job.

8. Abraham Lincoln died because John Wilkes Booth shot him with a pistol.

9. If alcoholism is a disease, then it is treated medically. But alcoholism is not treated medically, for the primary mode of treatment is the 12-step program of Alcoholics Anonymous. And AA's 12-step program is religious in nature. Therefore, alcoholism is not a disease.

***10.** Since 9/11, America has been engaged in a war on terror in many parts of the world.

11. A galaxy is a complex system of many stars. The galaxy in which we live is called the Milky Way. It is shaped like a hamburger bun 10,000 light years thick and 100,000 light years in diameter. It contains most of the stars we are able to see at night. But there is one of these stars which we can never see at night; we call this star the Sun. It is about 93 million miles away. Orbiting the Sun at 66,600 miles per hour is our own personal space vehicle, the planet Earth. . . . The Milky Way is also spinning around. We are in orbit around the center of the Milky Way at the fantastic speed of 600,000 miles an hour. —A. R. Patton, *Science for the Non-Scientist* (Minneapolis: Burgess, 1962), p. 27

12. While it is true that people in general fear death more than they fear life in prison, most murders are crimes of passion. That is to say, most murderers, at the time when they commit the act, are so full of hate or anger that they are completely unconcerned with the long-term consequences of their actions. How, then, can anyone assert with confidence that the death penalty deters murder?

* **13.** As carbon dioxide warms the planet, it also seeps into the oceans and acidifies them. Sometime this century they may become acidified to the point that corals can no longer construct reefs, which would register in the geologic record as a "reef gap." Reef gaps have marked each of the past five major mass extinctions. The most recent one, which is believed to have been caused by the impact of an asteroid, took place 65 million years ago, at the end of the Cretaceous period; it eliminated not just the dinosaurs, but also the plesiosaurs, pterosaurs, and ammonites. The scale of what's happening now to the oceans is, by many accounts, unmatched since then. To future geologists, our impact may look as sudden and profound as that of an asteroid. —Elizabeth Kolbert, "Enter the Anthropocene: Age of Man," *National Geographic*, March 2011, p. 77

14. Pacifists are either deeply insightful or greatly mistaken. But if pacifists are deeply insightful, then it is immoral for a police officer to kill a sniper who is firing at schoolchildren. Frankly, I don't think it takes a moral genius to see that it isn't wrong for a police officer to kill a sniper who is firing at school-children. So, in my opinion, pacifists are not deeply insightful. And hence, in my estimation, they are greatly mistaken.

15. Robert Provine of the University of Maryland has found that people are thirty times more likely to laugh when they are with other people than when they are alone. When people are in bonding situations, laughter flows. Surprisingly, people who are speaking are 46% more likely to laugh during conversation than people who are listening. And they're not exactly laughing at hilarious punch lines. Only 15% of the sentences that trigger laughter are funny in any discernible way. —David Brooks, *The Social Animal* (New York: Random House, 2011), p. 42

* **16.** Obviously, empirical data are scientific. But only what can be falsified (i.e., what can in principle be shown false) is scientific. Therefore, although many people regard empirical data as fixed and unchangeable, empirical data can be falsified.

17. Joan and Carl had been living together for a year and had maintained their separate friendships with both sexes. They were in agreement that they were committed to monogamy, but did not want to sacrifice the opportunity to have close friends. This informal contract proved to be workable, until Carl began spending time with his young research assistant who was in the process of going through a divorce. In response, Joan found herself feeling jealous, threatened, and angry. —Harriet Goldhor Lerner, *The Dance of Anger* (New York: Harper & Row, 1985), p. 104

18. In spite of the fact that the vast majority of contemporary scientists and intellectuals accept the theory of evolution, it is highly questionable for at least two reasons. First, the probability of life evolving from nonlife is so low as to be in the category of the miraculous. Second, if evolution is true, then there are "missing links" (e.g., animals midway between reptiles and birds). But apparently there are no "missing links" since the fossil record contains none. Therefore, the theory of evolution is very much open to question.

*19. In Stanley Milgram's obedience experiments, first performed at Yale in 1963, subjects were ostensibly recruited to take part in a study of memory. They were then duped into believing they were to be "teachers" in an experiment in which they would administer painful electric shocks of increasing strength to "learners" whenever the latter made mistakes. The so-called learners were actually actors who grunted, screamed, begged to be released from the experiment. As the subject-teachers administered what they thought was ever stronger punishment, they were observed to see whether they continued or protested, and what their reactions were. A large fraction of them were induced to give the highest range of electric shock, even when the pseudo-learners cried out that they feared a heart attack. —Sissela Bok, *Lying: Moral Choice in Public and Private Life* (New York: Random House, 1978), p. 193

20. While many endorse the principle of *equal pay for equal work*, the principle is untrue, for it would have disastrous results if it were applied to college employees. Why? Because faculty salaries differ markedly by discipline (e.g., professors of engineering receive much higher salaries than professors of English literature). So, if colleges gave equal pay for equal work, they would either (a) go broke paying all faculty high salaries or (b) demoralize the more highly paid faculty with severe pay cuts. Obviously (a) would be disastrous, and so would (b).

PART B: Identifying Missing Premises Write well-crafted versions of these arguments, with implicit premises made explicit.

* **1.** Every woman has the right to do what she wants with her own body. So, we have a right to abortion.

  2. Abortion is wrong because it kills unborn human beings.

  3. Kurt is a cardiologist. So, he must be smart.

* **4.** Don't worry. Harry won't be killed at the beginning of book 2. He's the hero of the story.

  5. God created us. So, we ought to do whatever he tells us to do.

  6. It's your turn to wash the dishes. I did it yesterday.

* **7.** Capital punishment should be abolished. There have been documented cases of an innocent person being wrongly convicted and executed.

  8. The evidence regarding the deterrence effect of capital punishment is inconclusive. So, there's a chance that capital punishment saves lives. So, we should continue to practice capital punishment.

  9. William Shakspere of Stratford-on-Avon couldn't have been the author of *Hamlet*, *Macbeth*, and so forth. After all, William Shakspere was an uneducated man who had an illiterate daughter and owned no books.

*10. This class is too easy for me. I find it very boring.

11. I can't think of any reason that would justify God in allowing so many horrible instances of suffering. So, there is no reason that would justify God in allowing so many horrible instances of suffering.

12. The only people who did well in history 307 wrote essays that simply parroted the professor's opinions. I conclude that Janice simply parroted the professor's opinions.

* **13.** Don't tell me to behave myself! Well-behaved women rarely make history.

PART C: More Identifying Arguments If a given passage is an argument, write a well-crafted version of it. (Do NOT add unstated premises. Do NOT delete premises unless they are repetitious.) If a passage is not an argument, simply write "not an argument."

* **1.** The ozone layer has a hole in it primarily because of the large amounts of chlorofluorocarbons that have been released into the atmosphere. These chemicals are manufactured by human beings for use in refrigerators and air conditioners.

2. The most essential and fundamental aspect of culture is the study of literature, since this is an education in how to picture and understand human situations. —Iris Murdoch, *The Sovereignty of the Good* (London: Ark, 1970), p. 34

3. A significant motivation for anti-realism about morality is found in worries about the metaphysics of moral realism and especially worries about whether moral realism might be reconciled with (what has come to be called) naturalism. . . . According to naturalism, the only facts we should believe in are those countenanced by, or at least compatible with, the results of science. To find, of some putative fact, that its existence is neither established by, nor even compatible with science, is to discover, as naturalism would have it, that there is no such fact. If moral realism requires facts that are incompatible with science (as many think it does) that alone would constitute a formidable argument against it. —Sayre-McCord, Geoff, "Moral Realism," *The Stanford Encyclopedia of Philosophy* (Summer 2011 Edition), Edward N. Zalta (ed.)

* **4.** Americans put almost as much fossil fuel into our refrigerators as our cars. We're consuming about 400 gallons of oil a year per citizen—about 17% of our nation's energy use—for agriculture, a close second to our vehicular use. —Barbara Kingsolver, *Animal, Vegetable, Miracle* (New York: HarperCollins, 2007), p. 5

5. If someone believes something, we needn't always be able to answer the question "Why does he believe it?"; but if he knows something, then the question "How does he know?" must be capable of being answered. —Ludwig Wittgenstein, *On Certainty*, eds. G. E. M. Anscombe and G. H. von Wright (New York: Harper & Row, 1972), p. 72

6. We live in the best of all possible worlds. For there is a God. And if God exists, a perfect being exists. Moreover, if God exists, God created the world.

So, a perfect being created the world. But if a perfect being created the world, then we live in the best of all possible worlds.

* **7.** I emphatically deny that each culture should be judged only by its own moral standards, for if each culture should be judged only by its own moral code, then no culture's moral standards should be criticized. But the ethical standards of some cultures ought to be criticized because some cultures permit slavery, cannibalism, or the oppression of women. Hence, it is not the case that each culture should be judged only by its own ethical standards.

8. Failure to study literature in a technical way is generally blamed, I believe, on the immaturity of the student, rather than on the unpreparedness of the teacher. I couldn't pronounce on that, of course, but as a writer with certain grim memories of days and months of just "hanging out" in school, I can at least venture the opinion that the blame may be shared. At any rate, I don't think the nation's teachers of English have any right to be complacent about their service to literature as long as the appearance of a really fine work of fiction is so rare on the best-seller lists, for good fiction is written more often than it is read. —Flannery O'Connor, *Mystery and Manners* (New York: Noonday Press, 1957), p. 127

9. Americans of this generation read less than those of the previous generation. What explains this fact? In a word, television.

* **10.** We [Americans] had roughly 10,000 handgun deaths last year. The British had 40. In 1978, there were 18,714 Americans murdered. Sixty-four percent were killed with handguns. In that same year, *we had more killings with handguns by children 10 years old and younger than the British had by killers of all ages*. The Canadians had 579 homicides last year; we had more than 20,000. —Adam Smith, "Fifty Million Handguns," *Esquire*, April 1981, p. 24

11. Either murderers are rational enough to be deterred by the death penalty or they are not. If they are not rational enough to be deterred by the death penalty, then the death penalty is not necessary. On the other hand, if murderers are rational enough to be deterred by the death penalty, then they are rational enough to be deterred by life imprisonment. And if murderers are rational enough to be deterred by life imprisonment, then capital punishment isn't necessary. So, the death penalty is not necessary. Now, if the death penalty isn't necessary, it should be abolished. Therefore, we should get rid of capital punishment.

12. It may fairly be said that a just man becomes just by doing what is just, and a temperate man becomes temperate by doing what is temperate, and if a man did not so act, he would not have much chance of becoming good. But most people, instead of acting, take refuge in theorizing; they imagine that they are philosophers and that philosophy will make them virtuous; in fact, they behave like people who listen attentively to their doctors but never do anything that their doctors tell them. But a healthy state of the soul will no more be produced by this kind of philosophizing than a healthy state of the body by this kind of medical treatment. —*Aristotle's Nicomachean Ethics*, trans. James Weldon (New York: Macmillan, 1897), Bk. II, chap. 3

*13. It is now widely recognized that absolute proof is something which the human being does not and cannot have. This follows necessarily from the twin facts that deductive reasoning cannot have certainty about its premises and that inductive reasoning cannot have certainty about its conclusions. —Elton Trueblood, *A Place to Stand* (New York: Harper & Row, 1969), p. 22

14. Although advocates of the "pro-choice" view sometimes claim that a woman has an unlimited right over what happens in and to her own body, this claim is plainly false. For if a woman has an unlimited right over what happens in and to her own body, then she has the right to drink heavily during pregnancy. But if drinking lots of alcohol during pregnancy causes birth defects, then a woman does not have the right to drink heavily during pregnancy. And it is a well-known fact that heavy drinking during pregnancy does cause birth defects. So, a woman does not have the right to drink heavily during pregnancy. And therefore, a woman does not have an unlimited right over what happens in and to her own body.

15. Although rewards and punishments do indeed play a role in its formation, they do not by themselves *yield* the moral life. The tendency to avoid acting in a racist manner may first be developed in children by rewards and punishments, but they are not yet moral agents until they act in nonracist fashion even when discipline is not in view, and do so by acting *on the principle* of love and respect. —Nicholas P. Wolterstorff, *Educating for Responsible Action* (Grand Rapids, MI: Eerdmans, 1980), pp. 48–49

*16. The conscientious law breaking of Socrates, Gandhi, and Thoreau is to be distinguished from the conscientious law testing of Martin Luther King, Jr., who was not a civil disobedient. The civil disobedient withholds taxes or violates state laws knowing he is legally wrong but believing he is morally right. While he wrapped himself in the mantle of Gandhi and Thoreau, Dr. King led his followers in violation of state laws he believed were contrary to the federal Constitution. But since Supreme Court decisions in the end generally upheld his many actions, he should not be considered a true civil disobedient. —Lewis H. Van Dusen, Jr., "Civil Disobedience: Destroyer of Democracy," in Lynn Z. Bloom, ed., *The Essay Connection*, 4th ed. (Lexington, MA: Heath, 1995), pp. 564–565

17. In 1992, a small group of researchers in England went looking for talent. They couldn't find it. . . . By age twelve, the researchers found, the students in the most elite group were practicing an average of two hours a day versus about fifteen minutes a day for the students in the lowest group, an 800 percent difference. —Geoff Colvin, *Talent Is Overrated* (New York: Penguin, 2010), pp. 17–18

18. Terrorism is the threat or use of violence against noncombatants for political purposes. In ordinary war, the deaths of civilians are side effects of military operations directed against military targets. In terrorist operations, the civilian is the direct and intentional target of attack. Therefore, George Washington was not a terrorist; but neither were the truck-bombers who attacked the

Marine compound in Beirut in 1983, though they are commonly described as such; on the other hand, when states use murder and torture to crush political dissent (a common occurrence throughout the twentieth century), they engage in terrorism. —Douglas P. Lackey, *The Ethics of War and Peace* (Englewood Cliffs, NJ: Prentice-Hall, 1989), p. 85 (*Note:* Parts of the conclusion are paraphrased.)

* **19.** I find every [religious] sect, as far as reason will help them, make use of it gladly: And where it fails them, they cry out. It is a matter of faith, and above reason. —John Locke, *An Essay Concerning Human Understanding,* Bk. IV, chap. XVIII, p. 2

   20. All segregation statutes are unjust because segregation distorts the soul and damages the personality. It gives the segregator a false sense of superiority, and the segregated a false sense of inferiority. To use the words of Martin Buber, the great Jewish philosopher, segregation substitutes an "I-it" relationship for the "I-thou" relationship, and ends up relegating persons to the status of things. So segregation is not only politically, economically and sociologically unsound, but it is morally wrong and sinful. Paul Tillich has said that sin is separation. Isn't segregation an existential expression of man's tragic separation, an expression of his awful estrangement, his terrible sinfulness? So I can urge men to disobey segregation ordinances because they are morally wrong. —Martin Luther King, Jr., "Letter from the Birmingham City Jail," in James Rachels, ed., *The Right Thing to Do* (New York: Random House, 1989), pp. 242–243

PART D: Argument Forms and Well-Crafted Arguments Write a well-crafted version of each of the following arguments. Indicate which steps support each subconclusion. Also, identify the following forms wherever they appear: *modus ponens, modus tollens,* hypothetical syllogism, disjunctive syllogism, and constructive dilemma. To save laborious writing, use capital letters (as indicated) to stand for the statements composing the arguments. (See the Answer Key for an illustration.)

*   **1.** Large corporations have done much to weaken family ties given that the corporations require a high degree of mobility on the part of their employees, for a high degree of mobility ensures that families will be separated geographically. And the corporations do require a high degree of mobility on the part of their employees. Hence, large corporations have done much to weaken family ties. (L: Large corporations have done much to weaken family ties; M: The corporations require a high degree of mobility on the part of their employees; H: A high degree of mobility ensures that families will be separated geographically.)

   2. It is wrong to risk one's life unnecessarily. But given that it is wrong to risk one's life unnecessarily, it is wrong to race autos. Hence, it is wrong to race autos. And if it is wrong to race autos, then the Indy 500 should be banned, even though most Americans enjoy watching it. Therefore, the Indy 500 should be banned. (W: It is wrong to risk one's life unnecessarily; A: It is wrong to race autos; I: The Indy 500 should be banned.)

3. If the Democrats win, our taxes will go up. If the Republicans win, important government programs will be cut. Either the Democrats will win or the Republicans will win. So, either our taxes will go up or important government programs will be cut. (D: The Democrats win; R: The Republicans win; T: Our taxes will go up; P: Important government programs will be cut.)

* 4. God predestines human acts only if God fully causes human acts. God fully causes human acts only if humans lack free will. So, God predestines human acts only if humans lack free will. But humans do not lack free will. Hence, God does not predestine human acts. (P: God predestines human acts; C: God fully causes human acts; F: Humans lack free will.)

5. Nowadays many people are moral relativists; that is, they hold that one should act in the way one's society says one should act. But consider the following argument: "If moral relativism is true, then everyone who advocates reform (i.e., changing the societal code) is mistaken. Not everyone who advocates reform is mistaken. Therefore, moral relativism is not true." (M: Moral relativism is true; E: Everyone who advocates reform is mistaken.) —Fred Feldman, *Introductory Ethics* (Englewood Cliffs, NJ: Prentice-Hall, 1978), p. 166 (*Note:* The passage is slightly altered for use as an exercise.)

6. Either the order in the world is due merely to chance or the order in the world is due to intelligent design. The order in the world is not due merely to chance. So, the order in the world is due to intelligent design. Now, there is a God, assuming that the order in the world is brought about by intelligent design. Hence, God exists. (O: The order in the world is due merely to chance; D: The order in the world is due to intelligent design; G: God exists.)

* 7. Either ethical relativism is true or absolutism is true. It is not the case that absolutism is true since it is not always wrong to kill a human being. So, ethical relativism is true. (E: Ethical relativism is true; A: Absolutism is true. W: It is always wrong to kill a human being.)

8. Either the defendant should be put to death or he should be permanently hospitalized. For either the defendant is guilty or he is insane. And assuming that he is guilty, he should be put to death. But assuming that he is insane, he should be permanently hospitalized. Obviously, the defendant should not be put to death if the evidence is less than compelling. And the evidence is less than compelling. So, the defendant should not be put to death. And hence, the defendant should be permanently hospitalized. (D: The defendant should be put to death; H: The defendant should be permanently hospitalized; G: The defendant is guilty; I: The defendant is insane; E: The evidence is less than compelling.)

9. Humans have souls. For, assuming that humans are identical with their bodies, human acts are determined by prior states of the physical universe. And if human acts are determined by prior states of the physical universe, then humans lack free will. So, humans lack free will if humans are identical with their bodies. But obviously, humans do not lack free will. Therefore, humans are not identical with their bodies. And if humans are not identical with

their bodies, then they must have souls. (S: Humans have souls; B: Humans are identical with their bodies; D: Human acts are determined by prior states of the physical universe; F: Humans lack free will.)

* **10.** If Syria attacks Israel, Israel will counterattack. If Israel counterattacks, then the other Arab states will join in. So, if Syria attacks Israel, then the other Arab states will join in. If the other Arab states join in, then the United States will defend Israel. So, if Syria attacks Israel, the United States will defend Israel. And if the United States defends Israel, there will be a world war. Therefore, if Syria attacks Israel, there will be a world war. (S: Syria attacks Israel; C: Israel will counterattack; A: The other Arab states will join in; U: The United States will defend Israel; W: There will be a world war.)

2.3   **Argument Diagrams**

Arguments consist of premises and conclusions. Understanding the relationships between these makes an argument easier to evaluate. Does the argument consist of several premises that jointly support the conclusion? Does it consist of several premises that each, separately, support the conclusion? Does it consist of a series of steps, the first of which supports the second, the second of which supports the third? Which of these structures an argument has makes a difference to how one goes about evaluating it. For this reason, it is useful to be able to diagram the structure of an argument. Argument diagrams are of interest for at least two other reasons: (a) They provide a shorthand method of representing logical relationships and (b) they highlight certain important differences in the types of logical structure.

To diagram an argument, one first places brackets around each statement in the argument, taking note of any premise or conclusion indicators and numbering each statement. To illustrate:

> **53.** ¹[Campaign reform is needed] because ²[many contributions to political campaigns are morally equivalent to bribes.]

We will use an arrow to indicate the relationship of support between premise and conclusion. The arrow is drawn downward from the number that stands for the premise to the number that stands for the conclusion. Thus, the diagram for argument (53) looks like this:

The arrow means that (1), the conclusion, is affirmed on the basis of (2), the premise. In other words, (2) is given as a support for (1).

Subconclusions can readily be accommodated using this procedure. Here is an example:

54. ¹[Charles is unpleasant to work with] since ²[he interrupts people constantly.] Therefore, ³[I do not want to serve on a committee with Charles.]

This diagram says that premise (2) is given as a support for (1), the subconclusion, and that (1) is given as a support for (3), the conclusion.

Sometimes two or more premises provide *independent* support for a single conclusion. In such a case, if one of the premises were removed, the support provided by the other(s) would not decrease. For instance:

55. Although ¹[Americans like to think they have interfered with other countries only to defend the downtrodden and helpless], ²[there are undeniably aggressive episodes in American history.] For example, ³[the United States took Texas from Mexico by force.] ⁴[The United States seized Hawaii, Puerto Rico, and Guam.] And ⁵[in the first third of the twentieth century, the United States intervened militarily in all of the following countries without being invited to do so: Cuba, Nicaragua, Guatemala, the Dominican Republic, Haiti, and Honduras.]

The diagram is as follows:

Note that statement (1) is omitted from the diagram because it is a discount. The diagram says that the three premises support the conclusion *independently*.

Sometimes two or more premises are *interdependent*. In such a case, the premises work together as a logical unit, so that if one is removed, the support of the others is decreased. Here's an example:

56. ¹[No physical object can travel faster than light.] ²[A hydrogen atom is a physical object.] Hence, ³[no hydrogen atom can travel faster than light.]

If two or more premises provide *interdependent* support for a single conclusion (or subconclusion), write their numbers in a horizontal row, joined by plus signs, and underline the row. The plus signs serve as an abbreviation for "in conjunction with." To illustrate, the diagram for argument (56) looks like this:

$$\frac{1 + 2}{}$$
$$\downarrow$$
$$3$$

This diagram tells us that premises (1) and (2) provide *interdependent* support for conclusion (3).

Because English grammar is subtle and flexible, there are no hard-and-fast rules for bracket placement. But the main goal is to bracket the argument in a way that fully reveals the patterns of reasoning within it. The following rules of thumb will help you do this.

First, always take note of any premise and conclusion indicators. For instance, two statements joined by the premise indicator "because" need to be bracketed separately, since one is a premise and one is a conclusion (or subconclusion).

Second, recognize that statements joined by the words "and" or "but" often need to be separated into distinct units for the purpose of diagramming. For example, whenever the word "and" joins two premises, the diagram must indicate whether the premises operate independently or interdependently. Again, the overriding principle is to bracket the statements in such a way as to make an accurate picture of the logical structure of the argument. For instance:

> **57.** ¹[The defendant is guilty.] After all, ²[he confessed to stealing the jewels] and ³[he was undoubtedly present at the scene of the crime] since ⁴[his fingerprints are on the safe.]

The argument can be diagrammed as follows:

The diagram indicates that premises (2) and (3) support conclusion (1) *independently*. In addition, (4) supports (3) but not (2).

Third, note that conditionals (if-then statements) and disjunctions (either-or statements) should *never* be broken down into parts and joined with the plus sign. As noted previously, the plus sign is a special form of "and," linking statements that operate in a logically *interdependent* fashion. Of course, "and" is very different from "if-then" or "either-or." For example, take the statement "If I fall, then I will hurt myself." This conditional statement obviously does *not* have the same meaning as "I fall, *and* I will hurt myself." So, we must treat conditional statements as units for the purposes of diagramming. The same goes for disjunctions. The following words form compounds that should be treated as a single unit in diagramming arguments:

if . . . then	assuming that
only if	either . . . or
given that	neither . . . nor

Consider the following example:

> **58.** ¹[If China attacks Taiwan, Taiwan will fight,] for ²[the Taiwanese are ready to defend themselves.] ³[Their air force is formidable.] ⁴[And their navy is well trained and well equipped.]

Argument (58) can be diagrammed as follows:

Note that conclusion (1) stands for an entire conditional statement.

When bracketing and numbering an argument, simply take the statements in the order in which they appear in the original, marking the first statement (1), the second (2), and so on. This will help ensure that your numbering system is similar to that of your classmates. All statements should be numbered even though some statements, such as discounts and repeated statements, may not appear in your diagram. This convention helps in two ways: It makes the process of bracketing and numbering relatively mechanical, and it ensures that your numbering system is like that of your classmates. (This, in turn, is a great aid to communication.) Finally, where rhetorical questions and commands serve as premises or conclusions, they, too, should be bracketed and numbered.

The complexity of an argument diagram mirrors the complexity of the original. Accordingly, argument diagrams can become rather complex. Here's an example:

> **59.** Although ¹[some have argued that nuclear weapons introduce nothing genuinely new into the disputes about the morality of war,] I believe that ²[nuclear weapons raise novel moral issues.] First, ³[nuclear weapons have new and undreamed-of long-term effects] since ⁴[the radioactive fallout pollutes the environment and alters human genes.] Second, ⁵[a nuclear war could destroy human civilization in its entirety.] Third, ⁶[in case of nuclear war, the dust caused by the explosions would prevent the sun's rays from reaching the earth's surface.] So, ⁷[a nuclear war would result in a drastic lowering of the earth's temperature.] In other words, ⁸[a nuclear war would result in a "nuclear winter."] And ⁹[no human or human group has a right to gamble with the very climate upon which life itself is based.]

The argument can be diagrammed as follows:

A number of things are worthy of note in this diagram. First, statement (1) is omitted from the diagram because it is a discount. Second, statement (8) is omitted because it is a repetition of (7). Third, the conclusion is supported by three *independent* lines of reasoning:

- (4) supports (3), which, in turn, supports (2).
- (5) supports (2).
- (6) supports (7), and (7) operates in conjunction with (9) to support (2).

Each of these lines of reasoning is independent of the others because if we eliminate any one of them, the support of the others remains unaltered. Finally, statements (7) and (9) operate as an *interdependent* logical unit.

EXERCISE 2.3

PART A: Argument Diagrams Make a photocopy of the following arguments. Then, on your photocopy, bracket and number the statements in the arguments, using the techniques outlined in the previous section. Finally, construct a diagram for each argument, placing it beside the argument on the photocopy.

* **1.** Photography makes representational art obsolete because no one, not even the best artist, can be more accurate than a camera.

2. In spite of the fact that electrons are physical entities, they cannot be seen, for electrons are too small to deflect photons (i.e., light particles). Hence, electrons are invisible.

3. There is a healthy kind of individualism—the kind that is resistant to group tyranny. . . . But capitalist individualism is not concerned about promoting the growth of the person into emotional, intellectual, ethical and cultural fullness; rather, it fosters the development of individual traits only so far as these are useful for maximizing profits. Thus, ironically, capitalist individualism turns into a group despotism under which personal becoming is sacrificed to the external tyrannies of material gain. —Eugene C. Bianchi, "Capitalism and Christianity Are Contradictory," in David L. Bender, ed., *American Values: Opposing Viewpoints* (San Diego: Greenhaven Press, 1989), p. 147

* **4.** While there is much wickedness in the world, there is also much good. For if there is evil, then there must be good, since good and evil are relative, like big and small. And no one will deny that evil exists.

5. Since major historical events cannot be repeated, historians aren't scientists. After all, the scientific method necessarily involves events (called "experiments") that can be repeated.

6. The scientific method doesn't necessarily involve experimentation. For if anything is a science, astronomy is. But the great cosmic events observed by astronomers cannot be repeated. And, of course, an experiment is by definition a repeatable event.

7. Although people often say that beauty is in the eye of the beholder, there are various reasons for thinking that beauty is objective. First, there is wide agreement about natural beauty. After all, virtually everyone finds the Grand Canyon, Niagara Falls, and the Rocky Mountains beautiful. Second, even though art critics frequently disagree with one another, they do defend their views with principled reasoning. Third, art critics tend to agree among themselves about which historical works of art are truly great. And this agreement is no mere coincidence because the critics are not, in general, reluctant to disagree with one another.

8. In the new order, when voters are concerned about what benefits the elected officer will provide them, promises, hypocrisy, deceit, log-rolling and clout are fast becoming the characteristics of electability. As Harold Blake Walker noted, of 21 Congressmen linked in one way or another with political wrong-doing or personal scandal prior to the 1976 election, 19 were re-elected.
—John A. Howard, "Democratic Values Are Being Lost to Self-Interest," in David L. Bender, ed., *American Values: Opposing Viewpoints* (San Diego: Greenhaven Press, 1989), p. 57

* 9. Despite the fact that contraception is regarded as a blessing by most Americans, using contraceptives is immoral. For whatever is unnatural is immoral since God created and controls nature. And contraception is unnatural because it interferes with nature.

10. While some people seem to be under the impression that humans are making moral progress, I submit that the twentieth century is a movement backwards into violence and cruelty. For in spite of the fact that science and technology have developed rapidly, the greatest mass murders in history have all occurred in this century. Millions died on the battlefields of World Wars I and II. Six million Jews died in Nazi prison camps. And from 1917 until the end of Stalin's reign, 20 million people died in Soviet work camps. More recently, we have Pol Pot's slaughter of the Cambodians as well as the atrocities in the former Yugoslavia.

* 11. There is no life after death. For what's real is what you can see, hear, or touch. And you cannot see, hear, or touch life after death. Furthermore, life after death is possible only if humans have souls. But the notion of a soul belongs to a prescientific and outmoded view of the world. And hence, the belief in souls belongs to the realm of superstition.

12. Politicians are forever attributing crime rates to *policies*—if the crime rates are decreasing, to their own "wise" policies; if the crime rates are increasing, to the "failed" policies of their opponents. But the fact is that crime rates are best explained in terms of demographics. For crime is primarily a young man's game. Whenever there is a relatively large number of young men between the ages of 15 and 30, the crime rates are high. And whenever this part of the population is relatively small, the crime rates are relatively low.

13. A liberal arts education is vital to any great nation. Why? For one thing, a liberal arts education provides the best possible skills in communication. And without good communication at all levels, a nation cannot move forward. For another, work is not the whole of life. And it is well known that a liberal arts education increases one's capacity to enjoy life by substantially broadening the range of one's interests.

14. The human sciences have . . . made a major contribution to cynicism about human greatness, especially as they treat the subjects of motivation and freedom. We are told that human choice is not what it appears to be. If we accept the sophistications of some views of psychology, we know that what appears to be heroic—for example, a man or woman's act of courage in saving another's life—is, in fact, a desperate attempt to win the approval of a long-dead parent who had withheld love in the childhood years. What, then, has become of the hero? He or she is transformed in our minds into a neurotic, and with a slight turn of the mind, admiration is changed to pity and condescension. —Dick Keyes, "America Must Rediscover Heroism," in David L. Bender, ed., *American Values: Opposing Viewpoints* (San Diego: Greenhaven Press, 1989), p. 84

***15.** Violence as a way of achieving racial justice is both impractical and immoral. It is impractical because it is a descending spiral ending in destruction for all. The old law of an eye for an eye leaves everybody blind. It is immoral because it seeks to humiliate the opponent rather than win his understanding; it seeks to annihilate rather than to convert. Violence is immoral because it thrives on hatred rather than love. It destroys community and makes brotherhood impossible. —Martin Luther King, Jr., *The Words of Martin Luther King, Jr.*, selected and introduced by Coretta Scott King (New York: Newmarket Press, 1983), p. 73

PART B: More Argument Diagrams Make a photocopy of the following paragraphs. Then determine which of the paragraphs are arguments and which are not. If a paragraph is not an argument, write "not an argument" beside the paragraph. If a paragraph is an argument, bracket and number the statements involved on your photocopy; then, beside the argument, construct a diagram.

* **1.** John and Robert Kennedy and Martin Luther King were, like them or not, this country's last true national leaders. None of John Kennedy's successors in the White House has enjoyed the consensus he built, and every one of them ran into trouble, of his own making, while in office. In the same way, none of this country's national spokespeople since Robert Kennedy and Dr. King has had the attention and respect they enjoyed. —Warren Bennis, *Why Leaders Can't Lead* (San Francisco: Jossey-Bass, 1989), p. 61

2. If . . . our government is to function, it must have dissent. Only totalitarian governments insist upon conformity, and they—as we know—do so at their peril. Without criticism abuses will go unrebuked; without dissent our

dynamic system will become static. —Henry Steele Commager, "True Patrio-
tism Demands Dissent," in David L. Bender, ed., *American Values: Opposing
Viewpoints* (San Diego: Greenhaven Press, 1989), p. 248

3. It is because of the ideal of freedom that we have organized our particular
form of democracy, since the political structure of any society is . . . formed
to support the demands which the people make for the attainment of
certain values. Because of . . . the variety and richness of the social and
natural resources with which the country has abounded, in order to realize
the full potential which has always existed here, we have needed the idea
of freedom as a social instrument to be used for our full development.
—Harold Taylor, *Art and the Intellect* (New York: The Museum of Modern
Art, 1960), p. 53

* 4. For a variety of reasons, private colleges are in trouble. First, private colleges
have repeatedly increased tuition well beyond the rate of inflation. And any
business that increases prices in such a fashion is likely to run into trouble.
Second, many people are beginning to question the value of higher education since a college degree no longer guarantees an attractive salary. Third,
rightly or wrongly, the American public believes that colleges have not practiced good financial management, and hence the public thinks that tuition
dollars often subsidize inefficiency.

5. From 1979 through 1994, attacks by dogs resulted in 279 deaths of humans
in the United States. Such attacks have prompted widespread review of
existing local and state dangerous-dog laws, including proposals for adoption
of breed-specific restrictions to prevent such episodes. —*The Journal of the
American Medical Association*, 278(4) (1997): 278

6. The legalization of drugs is neither unwise nor immoral. It is not unwise because
by legalizing drugs we would eliminate the illegal drug trade. Hence, by legalizing drugs, we would rid our nation of all the violence that goes along with the
illegal drug trade. Furthermore, the legalization of drugs is not immoral because
it can be combined with a massive program of moral education.

7. During the 1930s, there were 1667 executions in the United States. During
the 1940s, there were 1284. During the 1950s, there were 717. And during the
rehabilitation-mad 1960s, the numbers plummeted to 191. Then came the
Furman v. Georgia decision in 1972, which resulted in a grand total of 3 executions during the 1970s. While the numbers began to creep back up in the
1980s, with a total of 117 executions in that decade, we are forced to conclude
that America has not had a serious practice of capital punishment since about
1960. Therefore, it is not true that America's currently high murder rate
proves the ineffectiveness of the death penalty.

8. It is difficult, and you may be sure that we know it, for us to oppose your
power and fortune, unless the terms be equal. Nevertheless we trust that the
gods will give us fortune as good as yours, because we are standing for what is
right against what is wrong; and as for what we lack in power, we trust that it
will be made up for by our alliance with the Spartans. . . . Our confidence,

therefore, is not so entirely irrational as you think. —The Melians to the Athenians, in Thucydides, *The Peloponnesian War*, trans. Rex Warner (New York: Penguin Books, 1954), p. 404 (The Athenians had demanded that the Melians surrender, but the Melians refused.)

9. Two distinct lines of reasoning support the thesis that the physical universe is temporally finite. First, the galaxies are speeding away from each other *and* from a central point. Moreover, there isn't enough matter in the universe to reverse this process. And if we trace this process back, it appears that the universe began with a "bang" roughly 15 billion years ago. Second, if the universe is temporally infinite, it must have gone through an infinite number of cycles (each Big Bang followed by a Big Crunch). But according to physicists, each Big Bang/Big Crunch cycle would cause a decrease in the overall amount of available energy. Thus, if the universe were temporally infinite, there would now be no energy available at all. But obviously, lots of energy is still available.

*10. While colleges and universities have come under heavy criticism in the last decade, they will undoubtedly remain a vital force in American social life for generations to come. For one thing, although both the public and the media seem to have a thirst for stories about people who've gotten rich or famous with only a high-school degree, the fact remains that a college or university degree is the surest way to increase one's social and occupational status. For another, college grads as a group indicate higher levels of satisfaction with their lives than do those with lesser educational attainments. Finally, you show me a nation with a weak system of higher education, and I'll show you a nation with little power. And Americans will never willingly accept a position of relative powerlessness among the nations of the world.

11. As I crisscross the United States lecturing on college campuses, I am dismayed to find that professors and administrators, when pressed for a candid opinion, estimate that no more than 25 percent of their students are turned on by classwork. For the rest, college is at best a social center or aging vat, and at worst a young folks' home or a prison that keeps them out of the mainstream of economic life for a few more years. —Caroline Bird, "College Is a Waste of Time and Money," in Stephen R. C. Hicks and David Kelley, eds., *The Art of Reasoning* (New York: Norton, 1994), p. 200

*12. There are no easy answers, no quick fixes, no formulas. It's time to face facts, lest we all follow Boesky, North, Hart, and the Bakkers into the abyss. We are not supermen. We cannot remake the world to suit us. It's not some mere trick of fate that the high and the mighty are tumbling off their pedestals in record numbers. It is rather the inevitable result of ambition outstripping competence and conscience. Whatever the question, competence and conscience are part of the answer. . . . —Warren Bennis, *Why Leaders Can't Lead* (San Francisco: Jossey-Bass, 1989), p. 154

13. Although the great majority of homicides in the United States involve assailants of the same race or ethnic group, current evidence suggests that socioeconomic status plays a much greater role in explaining racial and ethnic differences in the rate of homicide than any intrinsic tendency toward violence. For example, Centerwall has shown that when household crowding is taken into account, the rate of domestic homicide among blacks in Atlanta, Georgia, is no higher than that of whites living in similar conditions. Likewise, a recent study of childhood homicide in Ohio found that once cases were stratified by socioeconomic status, there was little difference in race-specific rates of homicide involving children 5 to 14 years of age. —John Henry Sloan et al., "Handgun Regulations, Crime, Assaults, and Homicide: A Tale of Two Cities," in Stephen R. C. Hicks and David Kelley, eds., *The Art of Reasoning* (New York: Norton, 1994), p. 305

*__14.__ The only proof capable of being given that an object is visible is that people actually see it. The only proof that a sound is audible is that people hear it; and so of the other sources of our experience. In like manner, I apprehend, the sole evidence it is possible to produce that anything is desirable is that people do actually desire it. [Thus,] no reason can be given why the general happiness is desirable, except that each person . . . desires his own happiness. —J. S. Mill, *Utilitarianism* (New York: Bobbs-Merrill, 1957), pp. 44–45

15. There is an undoubted psychological easing of standards of truthfulness toward those believed to be liars. It is simply a fact, for instance, that one behaves differently toward a trusted associate and toward a devious, aggressive salesman. But this easing of standards merely explains the difference in behavior; it does not by itself justify lies to those one takes to be less than honest. Some of the harm the liar may have done by lying may be repaid by the harm a lie can do to him in return. But the risks to others, to general trust, and to those who lie to liars in retaliation merely accumulate and spread thereby. Only if there are separate, and more compelling, excuses, can lying to liars be justified. —Sissela Bok, *Lying: Moral Choice in Public and Private Life* (New York: Random House, 1978), p. 134

NOTES

1. Alan Thein Durning, "World Spending on Ads Skyrockets," in Lester Brown, Hal Kane, and Ed Ayres, eds., *Vital Signs 1993: The Trends That Are Shaping Our Future* (New York: Norton, 1993), p. 80.
2. Stephen Jay Gould, "Sex, Drugs, Disasters, and the Dinosaurs," in Stephen R. C. Hicks and David Kelley, eds., *The Art of Reasoning: Readings for Logical Analysis* (New York: Norton, 1994), p. 145.
3. This argument is a summary of some of the main ideas in Gould, "Sex, Drugs, Disasters, and the Dinosaurs," pp. 144–152.

4. Some philosophers, such as the emotivists, have denied that "ought" judgments are either true or false. But we are here speaking from the standpoint of common sense. For a classic statement of the emotivist position, see Alfred Jules Ayer, *Language, Truth and Logic* (New York: Dover, 1952), pp. 102–120. This work was first published in 1935.
5. This example is borrowed from Anthony Weston, *A Rulebook for Arguments* (Indianapolis, IN: Hackett, 1987), p. 8. Our well-crafted version of this argument also is borrowed from Weston.

CHAPTER 3

Logic and Language

*T*o construct, analyze, and evaluate arguments *well*, one must pay close attention to language. Many errors of logic stem from a careless or imprecise use of language, and many misunderstandings about logic stem from misunderstandings about the nature of language. This chapter provides a series of clarifications about the relationships between logic and language.

 ## 3.1 Logic, Meaning, and Emotive Force

Let us begin by noting that the meaning of words can change over time. In Jane Austen's time, the term "mother-in-law" referred to stepmothers. So, at that time, someone might have said, "John sat in his mother-in-law's lap while she read him a story," without raising any eyebrows. We might also note that words can have different meanings in different parts of the world—even the English-speaking world. Peter plays soccer but is not permitted to play (American) football. His father might say, "Peter does not play football," while his British grandparents say, "Peter does play football," and both say something true. These phenomena have led some people to think that what is true varies from time to time and from place to place and is somehow a conventional matter. They believe this because they believe that truths are made up of words and the meaning of words, changes from time to time and from place to place and is a conventional matter that depends on our collective choices.

We need to be careful, however. In Chapter 1, we said that arguments are composed of statements and that statements are declarative sentences that have a truth value (i.e., are either true or false). Most philosophers and logicians would prefer to say that arguments are composed of propositions and that propositions, not sentences, are the real bearers of truth value. To grasp the concept of a proposition, consider the following sentences:

1. Grass is green.
2. Das Gras ist grun.

If someone said (2) and you didn't understand, it would be appropriate for a bilingual friend to say (1). In that case, she would have told you what the German speaker said. In some important sense, (1) and (2) *say the same thing*. This thing that (1) and (2) have in common is what philosophers and logicians call a **proposition**—a truth or falsehood that may or may not be expressed in a sentence.

> A **proposition** is a truth or falsehood that may or may not be expressed in a sentence.

Note that, just as a single proposition can be expressed in two different sentences, so a single sentence can express two different propositions. This happens when meaning changes over time or across cultures. The sentence "The boy is playing football" expresses different propositions in England and the United States. Similarly, if you say, "I am hungry," at 4 o' clock, it is, let us suppose, true. If you say, "I am hungry," after supper, it is false. The single sentence "I am hungry" has been used to express two different propositions, one true and one false.

If propositions are the bearers of truth value, the things that are really true or false, and if propositions get expressed by different sentences as meanings change, this gives us resources to respond to the suggestion, mentioned above, that truth changes as meaning changes and that, as a result, truth is merely conventional.

Consider the question "How many legs would a dog have if we called a tail a leg?" It is tempting to answer "five." But if that were right, then we could change how many legs a dog has by changing the meaning of our words. We might also imagine that we could make ourselves tall by redefining the word "tall" so that it means "over 4'7"" or make snow pink by switching the meaning of "white" and "pink." If this line of thought is right, then, you might think, anything is possible because it is always possible to change the meaning of a word, and any truth is expressed with words. This has led some people to deny the existence of necessary truths. If you changed the meaning of "square" to "curved figure," then there would be square circles, and if you changed the meaning of "4" to "5," then 2 + 2 would be 5. So, it is not necessarily true that there are no square circles, and not necessarily true that 2 + 2 = 4, and not necessarily true that if the premises of a *modus ponens* argument are true, then the conclusion is true also.

This would give us fantastic powers—we could make objects travel faster than light, make ourselves fantastically wealthy, raise the dead to life! It would be truly astonishing if we had these powers. Sadly, we don't.

To see this, think about what happens when you change the meaning of a word. For example, suppose you redefine "square" as "curved figure." Let's suppose you even manage to get all English speakers to accept this change. Before the change, you said, "There are square circles," and thereby expressed a false proposition—about figures with four corners and no corners. After the change, you say, "There are square circles." Now you have said something true, but you have expressed a *different proposition*—one that has nothing to do with figures with corners. There is no proposition that you have changed from being true to being false, and no geometric object that you have changed either. Similarly, if you change the meaning of "pink" so that it now refers to the color of vanilla ice-cream, you haven't changed the color of snow. You have made it the case that the sentence "Snow is pink" is true and that that sentence expresses a different proposition from the one it expressed before the change in meaning.

This means that what is true does not vary from time to time and from place to place as word meaning varies. "Peter plays football" expresses different propositions in two different places, one proposition that is true and one proposition that is false. The thing—the proposition—that is true in one place does not become false in another place. Moreover, although the meaning of a word is a conventional matter dependent on our collective choices, *truth* is not a conventional matter (except perhaps in unusual cases where the subject of the truth is itself a convention). So we don't have reason to deny that $2 + 2 = 4$ is a necessary truth or that it is necessarily true that if the premises of a *modus ponens* argument are true, then its conclusion is true also.

If this is right, then logic is about the relationship between truths and falsehoods. This means that logic is not simply a word game as some have supposed. It also means that in trying to clarify the nature of an argument, we can replace some words with others, as long as we don't alter the propositions thereby expressed. As we saw in Chapter 2, in reconstructing an argument, it is sometimes a good idea to replace a word with a synonym if that makes the underlying structure of the argument clearer. Notice that replacing words with synonyms doesn't alter the propositions expressed.

Statements often have emotive force as well as cognitive meaning. Failure to distinguish these two factors can easily lead to errors in logic. Consider the following statements:

3. There are approximately 20,000 homicides in the United States each year, with handguns being the most frequently used instrument of death.

4. The number of murders per year in America is now so high that you've got to have a death wish to walk the streets, day or night. Every lunatic and every thug carries a "heater," just waiting to blow you away.

Statement (3) is designed primarily to provide information, whereas statement (4) is designed, at least in part, to express feelings or elicit an emotional response.

The **cognitive meaning** of a sentence is the information conveyed by the sentence. Words such as "approximately," "20,000," and "homicides" help give (3) its cognitive meaning.

> The **cognitive meaning** of a sentence is the information conveyed by the sentence.

The **emotive force** of a sentence is the emotion the sentence expresses or tends to elicit. Words and phrases such as "death wish," "lunatic," "thug," and "blow away" contribute heavily to the emotive force of (4).

> The **emotive force** of a sentence is the emotion the sentence expresses or tends to elicit.

Of course, a single sentence can have both cognitive meaning and emotive force. Take (3), for instance. It conveys information, and so it has cognitive meaning, but the information conveyed is itself apt to provoke emotions such as fear or outrage; hence, (3) also has emotive force.

Logic has to do with cognitive meaning—that is, with the logical connections between the informational content of statements. So we often need to distinguish between the cognitive meaning and the emotive force of a sentence to understand its logical relationships, for emotionally loaded language is apt to interfere with logical insight. This can happen in at least two ways. First, loaded language can interfere with our attempt to understand the cognitive meaning of a sentence. We may be so carried away with or blinded by the feelings a sentence evokes that we fail to grasp its informational content precisely. Second, emotionally loaded language can blind us to the need for evidence. When our positive emotions are aroused, we may be inclined to accept a statement without argument even though an argument is definitely called for.

Let's consider some examples:

5. Should capital punishment be abolished? No way! The inmates on death row are nothing but human vermin.

6. You should ignore the company's arguments against the strike. Those arguments are nothing but capitalist propaganda aimed at workers.

The phrase "human vermin" in argument (5) is apt to have considerable emotive force. Vermin are small, troublesome animals (such as mice or rats) that we routinely kill without qualms. So, if we accept the label "vermin" for the inmates on death row, we may readily accept the claim that they should be killed. But what exactly is the *cognitive meaning* of the premise "The inmates on death row are nothing but human vermin"? Perhaps this: "The inmates on death row are very bad people, morally speaking." Putting the premise into emotionally neutral terms helps us not to be swayed too easily by the emotive force of the original wording. It also helps us to think of relevant critical questions to ask about the argument. For example, do we really believe that *all* "very bad people" should be put to death? Can't a person be very bad, morally speaking, without committing murder? If so, does argument (5) in effect extend the death penalty to many persons who have never killed anyone? It would seem so.

Argument (6) illustrates the way in which the emotive force of language may blind us to the need for evidence. Once we've labeled someone's reasoning as propaganda, we are apt to dismiss it out of hand. After all, propaganda is a systematic form of indoctrination, often involving deliberate deception or distortion of the facts. But if arguments have been offered, then we need to explain *why* they are rightly labeled as propaganda. For example, wherein lies the deception or distortion of facts? Perhaps some of the company's arguments against the strike are sound, even if it *is* in the company's interest to avoid a strike.

To underscore the distinction between cognitive meaning and emotive force, let's consider two further arguments:

> **7.** If we harvest the organs (hearts, liver, kidneys, etc.) of certain animals, such as baboons, and transplant the organs into humans who need them, many human lives will be saved. Therefore, we ought to harvest the organs of baboons and use the organs to save human lives.

> **8.** Most of the people at the party were bureaucrats. Therefore, not surprisingly, the party was quite boring.

Argument (7) illustrates how a word with positive emotive force can be used to downplay certain negative facts or aspects of an issue. Literally speaking, "to harvest" means "to gather in a crop," an agricultural activity that has everyone's approval. But, of course, "harvesting" the vital organs of animals involves killing the animals, and this unsavory or questionable aspect of obtaining the organs is to some degree obscured by the emotive force of the word "harvest." Again, there is less likelihood of downplaying negative aspects of the case if we express the argument in more neutral language—for instance, "If we remove the vital organs of certain kinds of animals, such as baboons, and transplant their organs into humans who need them, the animals will die, but many human lives will be saved. So, we ought to remove the vital organs of baboons and use the organs to save human lives."

As for argument (8), the word "bureaucrat" has a strong negative connotation. And the emotive force of the word may lead us to suppose that the premise of (8) supports its conclusion. But in less emotionally loaded language, the argument would look like this: "Most of the people at the party were government officials. So, the party was quite boring." Again, the more neutral language immediately suggests relevant critical questions: Are government officials on average less interesting than other people? If so, how is this known? What is the evidence? If not, then the premise seems to provide little support for the conclusion.

Emotionally loaded language appears in advertisements, as these examples illustrate:

> **9.** If you are facing criminal prosecution, hiring an aggressive and experienced defense attorney who has a proven record of ability and skill should be your first priority. An inadequate defense could cost you everything. That's why you need John Jacobsen!

> **10.** Give your child the gift of education. Seeing a child work toward a college degree is a parent's dream. But with rapidly escalating costs of higher education, this dream can become a financial nightmare.

Example (9) plays on the fear of someone facing criminal prosecution. Example (10) plays on the intensity of parental love and anxiety. We also find such emotionally loaded language in political contexts. For example:

> **11.** In the United States, an obscene alliance of corporate supremacists, desperate labor unions, certain ethnocentric Latino activist organizations and a majority of our elected officials in Washington works diligently to keep our borders open, wages suppressed and the American people all but helpless to resist the crushing financial and economic burden created by the millions of illegal aliens who crash our borders each year. (Lou Dobbs, CNN)

These examples are rather crass, suggesting that the use of emotionally loaded language is the province of political hacks and manipulative advertisers. Although that is often true, sometimes it is not.

For example, emotionally loaded language can be the stuff of great poetry. Consider these two examples, the first from a poem titled *Dulce et Decorum est* (which translated reads: "Sweet and right it is [to die for one's country]"):

> **12.** Bent double, like old beggars under sacks,
> Knock-kneed, coughing like hags, we cursed through sludge,
> Till on the haunting flares we turned our backs
> And towards our distant rest began to trudge.
> Men marched asleep. Many had lost their boots
> But limped on, blood-shod. All went lame; all blind;
> Drunk with fatigue; deaf even to the hoots
> Of tired, outstripped Five-Nines that dropped behind.[1]

The metaphors and choice of words and images that Owen uses in this passage evoke a horrific impression of war, expressing his own feelings about it, and moving readers to share those feelings.

Consider, by contrast, the following passage from Shakespeare's *Henry V*. In the play, which is loosely based on historical events, the English forces are poised for a decisive battle against the French, who vastly outnumber them. The

English are, understandably, pessimistic about their chances. Henry stands up and speaks to them in a passage known as the "St. Crispin's Day Speech" because the battle is fought on that day. Here's part of the speech:

> **13.** And Crispin Crispian shall ne'er go by,
> From this day to the ending of the world,
> But we in it shall be remembered—
> We few, we happy few, we band of brothers;
> For he today that sheds his blood with me
> Shall be my brother; be he ne'er so vile,
> This day shall gentle his condition;
> And gentlemen in England now-a-bed
> Shall think themselves accurs'd they were not here,
> And hold their manhoods cheap whiles any speaks
> That fought with us upon Saint Crispin's day.

This passage is filled with emotional language, designed to arouse (male) pride and confidence with thoughts of glory, fame, and comradeship. Note, however, in spite of their great beauty, that these passages encourage or discourage participation in a war without (at least in the passages quoted) giving any reasons for or against that particular war. Powerful and enriching as such passages are, if they are likely to move us to *action*, to fight and perhaps kill or die, or to refuse to fight for any cause at all, even to prevent the destruction of our country, we need to find and evaluate reasons for such action, and not simply be swept along by the passion and beauty of the words.

Although emotionally loaded language can interfere with logical insight, this does not mean that arguments should always be expressed in emotionally neutral language. In fact, it is neither possible nor desirable to rid argumentative speech and writing of emotive force. For example, the information conveyed in the premises of almost any argument about a controversial moral issue is apt to have emotive force. Furthermore, it is often appropriate to engage the emotions of your audience when defending an important belief or course of action. For example, it is entirely proper for a person to be stirred by a profound insight or by the revelation of serious injustice. "If you have a logical argument to back up a conclusion, there is nothing wrong with stating it in such a way that your audience will endorse it with their feelings as well as with their intellects."[2]

Summary of Definitions

A **proposition** is a truth or falsehood that may or may not be expressed in a sentence.

The **cognitive force** of a sentence is the information conveyed by the sentence.

The **emotive force** of a sentence is the emotion the sentence expresses or tends to elicit.

EXERCISE 3.1

Cognitive Meaning and Emotive Force Each of the following arguments involves the use of emotionally loaded language. Write well-crafted versions of the arguments, replacing the emotionally loaded wording with more neutral language. You may find it helpful to use a dictionary.

* **1.** Sir, terrorism in the Middle East is one of the greatest threats to world peace today. Therefore, I strongly recommend that we neutralize the leaders of each of the main terrorist groups.

   2. Since the Chinese have a lousy record on human rights, to give China "Most Favored Nation" status is simply to give in to injustice.

   3. What's wrong with playing the lottery? Nothing. Playing the lottery simply involves making a modest investment with the possibility of a substantial return.

* **4.** Ever since Franklin D. Roosevelt introduced welfare programs into American life, this country has become increasingly socialistic. But Americans reject socialism. So, the sooner we eliminate welfare, the better.

   5. Your reluctance to take this job is beyond comprehension. The pay is good and the hours are reasonable. Furthermore, the work of a sanitary removal engineer is of great importance.

   6. If you're against genetic engineering, you're against progress. So, why don't you just accept the fact that genetic engineering is here to stay?

* **7.** Plato lured us into a mystical realm of ideas separated from physical reality. Aristotle taught us how to be logic choppers. Descartes tried to frighten us with the possibility that we might be dreaming all the time. Kant did nothing but take ordinary moral rules and put them into his own pompous and obscure technical language. Haven't philosophers done a lot for the world?

   8. I utterly repudiate the notion that God will punish the immoral, for it is nothing but a deception used to frighten children and weak-minded adults.

   9. Gun control is utterly misguided! Do not be deceived: There is a war on. And politicians who promote gun control are collaborating with the enemy. But the enemy will remain fully armed—you can bet on that!

   10. The lyrics of many rock songs are obscene. We must cleanse our society of this moral filth. That's why I think rock music should be banned.

   11. While the right wing of the Republican party masquerades as the bastion of moral values, it has in fact done little but provide rationalizations for the selfishness of the yuppies. As for the Democrats, they are a loose-knit coalition of left-wing ideologues and social outcasts. So, cast your lot with the moderate Republicans.

* **12.** The world is full of horror, shocking cruelty, grinding poverty, starvation, and debilitating illness. In short, we humans inhabit one gigantic disaster area. And yet, some people believe that a loving God controls the universe. It just goes to show: People believe what they want to believe regardless of the facts.

13. If a gang of criminals were systematically executing 1.6 million citizens per year in our society, decent folks would take a stand, using force of arms if necessary. But this is precisely the situation America is in given the current rate of abortion. Hence, I think that those who have bombed abortion clinics are fully justified.

14. The insanity plea is a joke. Here's how the process works: (a) Vicious murderers go out and kill innocent people in cold blood; (b) the police haul the sadistic killers into court, where the killers claim to have been temporarily insane at the time they performed their cruel deeds; and (c) the psychotic killers spend a few months being treated in a mental hospital, are miraculously "cured," and then are released so they can go out and massacre more law-abiding citizens.

15. Son, you must not marry her! She's nothing but a selfish little Barbie Doll.

16. Once again, the hopeless cowardly Americans were back to repeat their cowardly act hiding behind a technological advance that God, most gracious, wanted it to be their curse and cause for shame.

   The aggressors came back launching their failed cowardly raids to commit a damned third attack which has very significant implications. The courageous resistance and great steadfastness of the noble Iraqi people gave the aggressors what they deserved. They will be taught a lesson and their wanton attack will be resisted.

   The missile attack on Iraq took place around 9 o'clock this morning, 3rd of September 1996, corresponding to 20th Rabi' Athani 1417 Hijri. This is going to be a glorious day. The Iraqi people will, in the name of God, add to their honorable record. It will be a day when the cowardly aggressors will be condemned by both history and the whole world, having been condemned by God Almighty.

   Oh, Iraqi people and members of the brave Iraqi armed forces, the apple of our eye, this is another day you can call your own. So, resist them as you have done. God Almighty wishes you to take your pride of place under the sun and on the heights of your good land—Saddam Hussein, speech to the Iraqi people, 1996

17. Obama has "pivoted" on unemployment so many times he's spun himself dizzy. And all of Obama's pirouettes are nothing but empty words—the man cares only about big bankers, and Obama disdainfully detests working people.

18. Would it be wrong to fight a nuclear war? Yes, of course. Just imagine it: Millions of people vaporized in a few moments. Millions more, including children and the aged, literally melting from the intense heat. Of those who aren't killed immediately, many freeze to death as great clouds of dust block out the sun's rays. The rest perish in agony from the nasty effects of radioactive fallout.

19. The public is being held hostage by avaricious employers who threaten us with economic collapse if we should become serious about border enforcement. A guest worker program, if properly implemented, might be an effective response.

20. The jobs issue is accurately described and if anything, understated. Democrats and Obama have been cowed by the undereducated blithering idiots who now lead the GOP, in the pay of the people who brought down the world economy through fraud and greed.

 ## Definitions

Ambiguous or vague language often interferes with clear thinking. A word is **ambiguous** if it has more than one meaning. For example, in the statement "He lies in this grave," the word "lies" might mean *tells a falsehood* or *is prostrate on a horizontal surface*.

> An **ambiguous** word has more than one meaning.

A word is **vague** if there are borderline cases in which there is no way to determine whether the word applies. For example, how much does a person have to have in the way of material possessions to count as rich? We would all agree that billionaires are rich. How about millionaires? How about multi-thousandaires? As we mention successively lesser sums, perhaps somewhere in the hundreds of thousands, there would come a point at which we would not be sure whether a person who has such-and-such a net worth is rich. Such a person would be a borderline case of "rich." "Tall," "bald," and "heap" are other vague terms.

> A **vague** word has borderline cases.

Definitions play an important role in argument because definitions can be used to clear up ambiguity and to make vague terminology more precise. In this section, we will examine various types of definitions, focusing on those types that are most helpful in clarifying and sharpening arguments.

Extensional and Intensional Definitions

We can attain greater clarity about linguistic meaning if we distinguish between the **extension** and the **intension** of a term. The extension of a term consists of the set of things to which the term applies. Thus, the extension of the term "mountain" consists of Mt. Rainier, Mt. Everest, Mt. Kilimanjaro, and so on. The intension of a term consists in the properties a thing must have to be included in the term's extension. In the case of "mountain," the intension includes *being a landmass that projects conspicuously above its surroundings* and *being higher than a hill*.

The **extension** of a term consists of the set of things to which the term applies.

The **intension** of a term consists of the properties a thing must have to be included in the term's extension.

As Wesley Salmon observes, we "may specify the meaning of a word through its extension, or we may specify its meaning through its intension. There is thus a basic distinction between extensional definitions and intensional definitions."[3] We will explore each of these kinds of definitions in what follows.

An **extensional definition** specifies the meaning of a term by indicating the set of things to which the term applies. Extensional definitions themselves come in two basic types: nonverbal (or ostensive) and verbal. To give an **ostensive definition,** one specifies the meaning of a term by pointing to objects in its extension. Usually, we can't point to them all, but only to a representative sample. Thus, if you are trying to teach a child the meaning of the word "rock," you might point to a rock, utter the word "rock," then point to another rock, utter the word "rock" again, and so on. Of course, this type of definition is not without its problems. For instance, if the rocks you point to are all small, the child may fail to realize that large rocks are rocks as well.

An **extensional definition** specifies the meaning of a term by indicating the set of things to which the term applies.

An **ostensive definition** specifies the meaning of a term by pointing to objects in its extension.

Many times, however, we use *verbal* extensional definitions to specify the meaning of a term. We can do this by naming the members of the extension *individually* or *in groups*. An **enumerative definition** names the members of the extension *individually*. For example:

> **14.** "Philosopher" means someone such as Socrates, Plato, Aristotle, Descartes, Kant, or Hegel.

Such a definition may be either partial or complete. Definition (14) is partial because we have not listed every philosopher. An enumerative definition is complete if all members of the extension are listed. For instance:

> **15.** "Scandinavia" means Denmark, Norway, Sweden, Finland, Iceland, and the Faroe Islands.

Generally speaking, however, it is either impossible or impractical to list all the members of a term's extension. For example, it is impossible to list all the whole numbers because there are infinitely many of them. And it would be impractical for most purposes to define "Ohioan" by listing all the inhabitants of that state.

> An **enumerative definition** specifies the meaning of a term by naming the members of its extension individually.

Another kind of verbal extensional definition names the members of the extension *in groups* (rather than individually). This is called a **definition by subclass.** For instance:

16. "Feline" means tigers, panthers, lions, leopards, cougars, cheetahs, bobcats, house cats, and the like.

Definitions by subclass can also be partial or complete. Definition (16) is partial because some classes (kinds or types) of felines have been omitted, such as jaguars and lynxes. Here is an example of a complete definition by subclass:

17. "North American marsupial" means an opossum.[4]

> A **definition by subclass** specifies the meaning of a term by naming the members of its extension in groups.

Although extensional definitions are sometimes very useful, they also have their drawbacks. One drawback is this: Some terms cannot be defined extensionally because their extensions are empty. To illustrate:

18. "Unicorn" means a horselike creature having one long, straight horn growing from the center of its forehead.

Because unicorns are mythical creatures, the extension of the term "unicorn" is empty. Nevertheless, "unicorn" has a meaning that can be specified via an intensional definition. A second drawback of extensional definitions is that they are often inadequate for the purposes of argument and rational dialogue. For example, suppose Smith and Jones are debating whether affirmative action is just. Jones requests a definition of "justice." Smith mentions a few examples of just social practices—for example, punishment only for the guilty, the progressive income tax, and the prohibition against poll taxes for voters. Even if Jones agrees that these practices are just, such an extensional definition is unlikely to facilitate an enlightening discussion of the justice of affirmative action. Careful and insightful thinking about controversial issues demands more precise terminology—hence the need for **intensional definitions,** which specify the meaning of a term by indicating the properties a thing must have to be included in the term's extension.

> An **intensional definition** specifies the meaning of a term by indicating the properties a thing must have to be included in the term's extension.

There are a number of different types of intensional definition with different criteria for success. It is important to understand the differences among these.

A **lexical definition** reports the conventional or established intension of a term. Dictionary definitions are standard examples of lexical definitions. For example:

19. "Immanent" means existing or remaining within, that is, inherent.

20. "Imminent" means about to occur.

Note that lexical definitions have truth values—that is, they are either true or false. They are true if they correctly report the established intension of the term and false if they fail to do this. For purposes of critical thinking, it is important to know when conventional meanings are at issue. To illustrate, if two people are debating the question of whether Bill Clinton was *impeached*, they might agree on all the nonlinguistic facts, but just attach slightly different meanings to the term "impeach." In that case, appeal to a dictionary would be appropriate and would settle the matter in favor of the claim that Clinton was indeed impeached because impeaching someone involves charging him with misconduct. As words change their meaning, there is often some disagreement about the correct lexical definition. Is it the established use, or is it the current, most widely heard use? The term "impeach" seems to be widely used to mean, "Remove from office on the grounds of misconduct." In response to such changes, dictionaries are regularly updated to reflect the way words are used.

> A **lexical definition** reports the conventional or established intension of a term.

A **stipulative definition** specifies the intension of a term independently of convention or established use. For various reasons, a writer or speaker may wish to introduce a new word into the language or give an old word a new meaning.

For example, the word "double-dodge" currently has no generally accepted meaning. But we could make a proposal:

> **21.** "Double-dodge" means the anticipatory movements people commonly make when they nearly collide (as when walking toward each other in a confined space) and are trying to avoid such collision.[5]

To illustrate: "Marsha and Fred nearly ran into each other in the hallway; but at the last moment they double-dodged and then came to a full stop, whereupon Fred burst into laughter." Thus, by introducing a stipulative definition, we can gain a shorthand means of expressing a complex idea.

A **stipulative definition** specifies the intension of a term independently of convention or established use.

Stipulative definitions are often useful in science. For example, in 1967, the physicist John Wheeler introduced the term "black hole" as shorthand for a star that has completely collapsed in on itself due to gravitational forces.[6] When first introduced, this definition was stipulative, for there was then no conventional use of "black hole" to refer to astronomical entities. (Of course, since 1967, "black hole" has come into common use so that it now has a conventional meaning that can be reported in a *lexical* definition.)

Note that a stipulative definition is a *recommendation* or *proposal* to use a term in a certain manner. In other words, a stipulative definition has the form "Let's use term X to mean . . ." And since a recommendation or proposal is neither true nor false, a stipulative definition is neither true nor false. However, if the recommendation to use a term in a certain manner takes hold and becomes part of established use, then the stipulative definition turns into a lexical one, as is the case with "black hole." And as we have seen, lexical definitions are true (or false) because they report conventional meanings.

A **precising definition** reduces the vagueness of a term by imposing limits on the conventional meaning. It differs from a stipulative definition because it is not independent of the conventional meaning, but it is like a stipulative definition in that it is a proposal to draw lines at a point not given by the conventional meaning.

A **precising definition** reduces the vagueness of a term by imposing limits on the conventional meaning.

For example, suppose we define a "very strong argument" as one such that there is at least a .95 probability that if the premises are true, then the conclusion is true. Obviously, this definition is more precise than the ordinary English phrase "very strong argument," but the definition is not stipulative because the conventional meaning is not ignored but is rendered more exact.

Precising definitions are common in both science and law. For example, the term "velocity" simply means "speed" in ordinary English, but physicists have given it a more precise meaning for their own purposes, namely:

22. "Velocity" means rate of motion in a particular direction.

Precising definitions are also essential in constructing workable laws. For instance, suppose Congress wishes to write legislation that provides a tax break for the poor. If left at that, the law will be excruciatingly difficult to apply because there will be disputes over who qualifies for the tax break. If someone receives the tax break, then someone in similar circumstances who earns a dollar more will insist that justice requires that he or she receive it too. And if so, then the next person will make the same claim, and pretty soon, everyone will have the tax break. We need to draw lines, even if they are somewhat arbitrary. So, for example, the law might contain a precising definition to the effect that a family of four counts as poor if it has an annual income of $15,000 or less. Or again, suppose a law is being written to determine when caregivers may remove a patient from life-support systems. A precising definition of "dead" will be helpful for this purpose because presumably there are no objections to removing life-support systems if the patient is dead. But is a person dead when her heart has ceased to function? When she stops breathing? When she is permanently unconscious? When her brain has stopped functioning? For legal purposes, we obviously want to be rather precise about this. In most states, a person is now considered legally dead if he or she is "brain-dead." That is, a precising definition along these lines is used:

23. A "dead" person is one whose brain functions have permanently ceased.

And an electroencephalograph can be used to determine whether this definition applies in a given case.

Keep in mind that precising definitions should draw lines within the range of borderline cases. Inappropriate uses of precision definitions draw lines in such a way that they classify clear cases incorrectly. For example, if legal purposes require that we precisify the concept of *a child*, it seems appropriate to offer the precising definition that anyone under 15 is a child, or that anyone under 16 is a child. It would not be appropriate to offer the precising definition that anyone under 25 is a child, since this would wrongly classify 24-year-olds, who are clear cases of adults.

A **theoretical definition** is an intensional definition that attempts to provide an adequate understanding of the thing(s) to which the term applies. For example, when philosophers or scientists disagree about the definition of important terms such as "knowledge," "virtue," "mass," "temperature," "space," or "time," they are not disagreeing about the lexical definitions. Nor are they simply trying to stipulate meanings or make conventional meanings more precise. They are trying to reach a deeper and more accurate understanding of the nature of things.

 A **theoretical definition** attempts to provide an adequate understanding of the things to which the term applies.

Philosophers have traditionally concerned themselves with questions like "What is knowledge?" "What is justice?" and "What is courage?" These questions were discussed by the ancient Greeks (in Greek) but may also come up in an introductory class you take next term. You may wonder why you cannot answer these questions simply by opening a dictionary. Well, let's consider one of them. *Merriam-Webster OnLine Dictionary* defines "knowledge" as "the fact or condition of knowing" and then defines "to know" as "(1) to perceive directly: have direct cognition of (2): to have understanding of . . . (3) to recognize the nature of: 2a: to be aware of the truth or factuality of: be convinced or certain of (b) to have a practical understanding of . . ." This definition doesn't answer the philosophical question, partly because it is somewhat circular—"knowledge" and "cognition" are synonyms; it is indeterminate, in shifting between different ideas; and some of the noncircular definitions seem open to counterexample. You can know something without having direct cognition of it, for example. You know that Sydney is in Australia even if you've never seen it with your own eyes. You can know something even if you are not absolutely certain of it. You can be certain of something even if you do not know it.

Philosophers for a long time favored the theoretical definition of knowledge as "justified true belief." This is different from the lexical, stipulative, or precising definitions. Rather, this definition attempts to provide a deeper insight into the nature of knowledge. Interestingly, however, philosophers have come to find fault with their own definition. In a groundbreaking article, Edmund Gettier described a series of cases of justified true beliefs that don't count as knowledge.[7]

The scientific definition of "temperature" as "the motion of molecules" also provides an example of a theoretical definition (the more rapid the motion of the molecules, the higher the temperature). Obviously, this definition of "temperature" could not be given prior to the development of molecular theory. Note that in offering this definition of "temperature," scientists are not reporting the conventional meaning. Nor are they offering a stipulative definition or making a conventional definition more precise. They are offering a theoretical definition intended to provide a deeper and more adequate understanding of the nature of temperature.

Lexical definitions are not always distinct from theoretical definitions. It sometimes happens that ordinary usage picks up on the best account of the nature of the thing(s). For example, the dictionary definition of "square" is equivalent to the mathematician's theoretical definition. One of the dictionary definitions for "true" comes close to capturing at least some philosophers' account of the nature of truth. Lexical definitions are correct insofar as they reflect standard usage. Theoretical definitions are correct insofar as they capture the true nature of the property or thing they purport to define.

Summary of Definitions

An **extensional definition** specifies the meaning of a term by indicating the set of things to which the term applies. For example:

> An **ostensive definition** specifies the meaning of a term by pointing to objects in its extension.

> An **enumerative definition** specifies the meaning of a term by naming the members of its extension individually.

> A **definition by subclass** specifies the meaning of a term by naming the members of its extension in groups.

An **intensional definition** specifies the meaning of a term by indicating the properties a thing must have to be included in the term's extension. For example:

> A **lexical definition** reports the conventional or established intension of a term.

> A **stipulative definition** specifies the intension of a term independently of convention or established use.

> A **precising definition** reduces the vagueness of a term by imposing limits on the conventional meaning.

> A **theoretical** definition attempts to provide an adequate understanding of the thing(s) to which the term applies.

Definition by Genus and Difference

One technique for constructing definitions is worth special attention because it can be applied in a wide variety of cases and because it is one of the best ways to eliminate ambiguity and vagueness. This is the method of definition by *genus* and *difference*. This method is often useful in constructing stipulative, precising, and theoretical definitions, but here we will focus primarily on lexical definitions.

To explain this method, we need some technical terms. First, as is customary among logicians, let us call *the word being defined* the **definiendum,** and let us call *the word or words that do the defining* the **definiens.** To illustrate:

24. "Puppy" means young dog.

Here, "puppy" is the *definiendum*, and "young dog" is the *definiens*.

> The **definiendum** is the word being defined.
> The **definiens** is the word or words that do the defining.

Second, we need to define *proper subclass*. A class X is a **subclass** of class Y given that every member of X is a member of Y. For example, the class of collies is a subclass of the class of dogs. Note, however, that the class of collies is also a subclass of itself. By contrast, class X is a **proper subclass** of class Y given that X is a subclass of Y but Y has members X lacks. Thus, the class of collies is a *proper* subclass of the class of dogs, but the class of collies is not a *proper* subclass of the class of collies.

> Class X is a **subclass** of class Y given that every member of X is a member of Y.
> Class X is a **proper subclass** of class Y given that X is a subclass of Y but Y has members X lacks.

Now we can say that a **genus** is a class of objects and a **species** is a proper subclass of a genus. This use of the terms differs from the use they are given in biology. For example, in logic (unlike biology), we may speak of the genus *dog* and the species *puppy*, of the genus *animal* and the species *dog*, or of the genus *animal* and the species *mammal*.

> A **genus** is a class of objects.
> A **species** is a proper subclass of a genus.

The **difference** (or specific difference) is the attribute that distinguishes the members of a given species from the members of other species in the same genus. For example, suppose *sibling* is the genus and *sister* is the species. Then the difference is the attribute of *being female*, which distinguishes sisters from brothers, which also belong to the genus *sibling*. Or suppose *dog* is the genus and *puppy* is the species. Then the difference is the attribute of *being young*, which distinguishes puppies from other species in the same genus—for example, adult dogs.

> The **difference** (or specific difference) is the attribute that distinguishes the members of a given species from the members of other species in the same genus.

The relationship among genus, species, and difference is shown in the following diagram, with the rectangles standing for classes.

```
┌─────────────────────────────────────────────────────────┐
│              GENUS (Example: horse)                      │
│                                                          │
│  ┌──────────────────────────┐  ┌──────────────────────┐  │
│  │  SPECIES: Filly          │  │  SPECIES: Colt       │  │
│  │                          │  │                      │  │
│  │  DIFFERENCE: Young female│  │  DIFFERENCE: Young male│ │
│  └──────────────────────────┘  └──────────────────────┘  │
└─────────────────────────────────────────────────────────┘
```

Now, one constructs a definition by genus and difference as follows. First, choose a term that is more general than the term to be defined. This term names the genus. Second, find a word or phrase that identifies the attribute that distinguishes the species in question from other species in the same genus. Here are some examples:

Species		Difference	Genus
"Stallion"	means	male	horse
"Kitten"	means	young	cat
"Banquet"	means	elaborate	meal
"Lake"	means	large	inland body of standing water

In many cases, of course, the difference is a rather complicated attribute that takes many words to describe. For example:

25. "Dinosaur" means any of a group of extinct reptiles of the Mesozoic Era, with four limbs and a long, tapering tail.[8]

The genus here is *reptile,* and the rest of the definition specifies the difference.

A definition by genus and difference is inadequate if it fails to meet certain criteria. Let us now examine the six standard criteria for evaluating definitions by genus and difference. The basic idea behind them is that, first, a definition should have the same extension as the term being defined, and, second, that it should be helpful and illuminating.

Criterion 1: A definition should not be too wide.

It is crucial that definitions be accurate, that is, that they pick out all and only the things that the definiendum applies to. A definition is too wide (or too broad) if the definiens applies to objects outside the extension of the definiendum. For instance:

26. "Bird" means an animal having wings.

Definition (26) is too wide because bats and flies have wings, and yet neither bats nor flies are birds. Bats and flies here constitute counterexamples to the definition, demonstrating that (26) has failed to capture a sufficient condition for being a bird.

Here's a more interesting example:

27. "Person" means something with human DNA.

This definition is too wide because we can think of counterexamples: things that have human DNA but are not persons—for example, a human fingernail clipping.

Criterion 2: A definition should not be too narrow.

A definition is too narrow if the definiens fails to apply to some objects in the extension of the definiendum. To illustrate:

28. "Bird" means a feathered animal that can fly.

Definition (28) is too narrow because some birds cannot fly—for example, penguins and ostriches. Penguins and ostriches here constitute counterexamples to the definition, demonstrating that (28) has failed to capture a necessary condition for being a bird.

A somewhat more interesting example is this:

29. "Person" means a being that can communicate on indefinitely many topics in sentences of indefinite length, can reason, and has a fully developed sense of self and a conscience.

Definition (29) is too narrow because we can think of counterexamples: things that lack the communication, reasoning, and so on skills but are nevertheless persons—a 2-year-old child or someone in a temporary coma, for example.

In general, a **counterexample** to a definition is something to which the term applies but which doesn't meet the conditions, or which meets the conditions but the term does not apply to it.

A **counterexample** to a definition is something to which the term applies but which doesn't meet the conditions, or which meets the conditions but the term does not apply to it.

Criterion 3: A definition should not be obscure, ambiguous, or figurative.

To illustrate:

> **30.** "Desire" is the actual essence of man, insofar as it is conceived, as determined to a particular activity by some given modification of itself.[9]

This definition employs obscure technical jargon. And since the point of defining a term is to clarify its meaning, one should use the simplest words possible in the definiens.

Sometimes, a definiens contains a word that, in the context, has two possible meanings. Then the definition is ambiguous:

> **31.** "Faith" means true belief.

Does "true belief" here mean "sincere or genuine belief," or does it mean "belief that is true as opposed to false"? Either meaning seems possible in the context of a definition of "faith," so the definition is ambiguous. Note, however, that many words have multiple meanings listed in the dictionary, and this mere fact does not render the words ambiguous in a given case. For instance, the word "store" may mean "a place where merchandise is sold," as in "I bought a shirt at the store"; or it may mean "to provide for a future need," as in "Squirrels store nuts for the winter." But the context usually indicates which of the meanings is relevant. It is only when the context does not make clear which meaning is relevant that ambiguity occurs.

Figurative (or metaphorical) definitions are generally either obscure or ambiguous. For example:

> **32.** "Art" is the stored honey of the human soul, gathered on wings of misery and travail.[10]

Definition (32) may be suggestive and interesting, but as is common with figurative language, it invites multiple interpretations and so is ambiguous.

> Criterion 4: A definition should not be circular.

A definition is **circular** if the definiendum (or some grammatical form thereof) appears in the definiens. To illustrate:

> **33.** "Metaphysics" means the systematic study of metaphysical issues.

Of course, if one doesn't know the meaning of the term "metaphysics," one isn't likely to find a definition employing the word "metaphysical" informative. Note, however, that depending on the context, some kinds of circularity in definitions are not problematic. For instance, suppose my audience knows what a triangle is but does not know what an acute triangle is. In such a context, I might define "acute triangle" as follows:

> **34.** "Acute triangle" means any triangle in which each of the three angles is less than 90 degrees.

This type of circularity is harmless because (in the context) the part of the definiendum that appears in the definiens (namely, "triangle") is not what needs to be defined.

> A definition is **circular** if the definiendum (or some grammatical form thereof) appears in the definiens.

> Criterion 5: A definition should not be negative if it can be affirmative.

For example:

> **35.** A "mineral" is a substance that is not an animal and not a vegetable.
>
> **36.** "Mammal" means an animal that is not a reptile, not an amphibian, and not a bird.

A relatively affirmative definition is more informative than a relatively negative one and is therefore to be preferred. However, it is impossible to give affirmative definitions in every case. For instance, a typical dictionary definition of "geometrical point" is "something that has position in space but no size or shape." And the word "spinster" is defined as "a woman who has never married." These definitions would be hard to improve on, though they are largely negative.

> Criterion 6: A definition should not pick out its extension via attributes that are unsuitable relative to the context or purpose.

For example, suppose we are trying to construct a lexical definition of the word "triangle." The following definition would violate criterion 6:

> **37.** "Triangle" means Steve's favorite geometrical figure.

Since triangles are Steve's favorite geometrical figure, the definiens applies to the correct extension, namely, the members of the class of triangles. But the attribute of *being Steve's favorite geometrical figure* is unsuitable to the context of forming a lexical definition. What would be suitable is the attribute English speakers implicitly agree to mean by the term "triangle," namely, *being a closed-plane figure with three angles (or three sides)*.

Because criterion 6 is not always easy to apply, let us consider some further examples. For instance:

38. "Seven" means the number of days in a week.

There are indeed seven days in a week, so the definiens picks out the right extension. But taken as a lexical definition, this definition is flawed because it does not make reference to the attribute associated with established usage, namely, *being one more than six*. (In principle, one could know the ordinary meaning of "seven" without knowing how many days there are in a week.) Furthermore, taken as a theoretical definition, (38) is flawed because it fails to pick out attributes relevant for mathematical purposes—for example, that of *being a whole number between six and eight*.

If we translate the proposal of certain ancient Greek philosophers into English, we get the following definition of "human":

39. "Human" means featherless biped.

Now, let's assume that this definition is neither too narrow nor too wide—that is, that all and only humans lack feathers *and* normally walk upright on two legs. Still, if (39) is taken as a lexical definition, it violates criterion 6. As evidence, we can cite the fact that the attribute of *being a featherless biped* is not alluded to in dictionary definitions of the term "human." We might add that the attribute seems unsuitable if the definition is taken to be theoretical in nature, for (39) surely fails to provide any noteworthy insight into the nature of human beings. In support of the thought that "featherless biped" is an inadequate theoretical definition of "human," philosophers often offer examples of *possible* objects that would satisfy the definiens without being examples of the definiendum. For example, a perfectly plucked chicken would be a featherless biped without being human. Similarly, we might object that a talking, thinking, feeling elephant would be a person and hence that "human being" is too narrow as a definition of "person."

To sum up, definitions can be used to eliminate ambiguity and vagueness. Both extensional and intensional definitions can be used for these purposes, but certain kinds of intensional definitions (e.g., stipulative, lexical, precising, and theoretical definitions) are especially useful in argumentation. The method of definition by genus and difference can often be used to construct stipulative, lexical, precising, and theoretical definitions; hence, this method is very useful for the purposes of constructing and evaluating arguments. Finally, definitions by genus and difference must conform to the six criteria set down in this section.

Summary of Criteria for Definitions by Genus and Difference

Criterion 1: A definition should not be too wide.

Criterion 2: A definition should not be too narrow.

Criterion 3: A definition should not be obscure, ambiguous, or figurative.

Criterion 4: A definition should not be circular.

Criterion 5: A definition should not be negative if it can be affirmative.

Criterion 6: A definition should not pick out its extension via attributes that are unsuitable relative to the context or purpose.

Summary of Definitions

An **ambiguous** word has more than one meaning.

A **vague** word has borderline cases.

The **extension** of a term consists of the set of things to which the term applies.

The **intension** of a term consists of the properties a thing must have to be included in the term's extension.

The **definiendum** is the word being defined.

The **definiens** is the word or words that do the defining.

Class X is a **subclass** of class Y given that every member of X is a member of Y.

Class X is a **proper subclass** of class Y given that X is a subclass of Y but Y has members X lacks.

A **genus** is a class of objects.

A **species** is a proper subclass of a genus.

The **difference** (or specific difference) is the attribute that distinguishes the members of a given species from the members of other species in the same genus.

A **counterexample** to a definition is something to which the term applies but which doesn't meet the conditions, or which meets the conditions but the term does not apply to it.

A definition is **circular** if the definiendum (or some grammatical form thereof) appears in the definiens.

EXERCISE 3.2

PART A: Types of Definitions Match the definition on the left to the letter of the item on the right that best characterizes it.

_____ * **1.** Let us use the word "grellow" to mean the color of things that are either green or yellow.

_____ **2.** "Vixen" means female fox.

_____ **3.** "Southern state" means Alabama, Arkansas, Georgia, Louisiana, Mississippi, North Carolina, South Carolina, Tennessee, Texas, and Virginia.

_____ * **4.** "Tall man" means male human over 6 feet in height.

_____ **5.** "Living things" means plants and animals.

_____ **6.** "Motorized vehicle" means cars, motorcycles, trucks, and the like.

_____ * **7.** "Tome" means large book.

_____ **8.** A "wrong act" is one that fails to promote the general happiness.

_____ **9.** "Aunt" means sister of one's father or mother.

_____ *__10.__ A "sound argument" is one that (a) has only true premises and (b) is valid (i.e., its conclusion cannot be false while its premises are true).

_____ **11.** "Religion" means Hinduism, Christianity, Judaism, Buddhism, Islam, Sikhism, and the like.

_____ **12.** Let us use the term "zangster" to mean a person who steals zirconium.

_____ *__13.__ "Human" means rational animal.

_____ **14.** "Subatomic particles" means electrons, protons, neutrons, quarks, and the like.

_____ **15.** "Miracle" means an event that (a) is an exception to a law of nature and (b) is brought about by the decision of a divine being.

A. Enumerative definition

B. Definition by subclass

C. Lexical definition

D. Stipulative definition

E. Precising definition

F. Theoretical definition

PART B: Lexical Definitions Identify one defect in each of the following definitions, using the six criteria for definition by genus and difference.

1. Too wide	**4.** Circular
2. Too narrow	**5.** Unnecessarily negative
3. Obscure, ambiguous, or figurative	**6.** Unsuitable attribute

Explain your answer briefly. For example, if you say a definition is too narrow, give an example that illustrates your point. Assume that the definitions are meant to be lexical definitions. You may find it helpful to use a dictionary.

  * **1.** "Penguin" means a bird that can't fly, but not an ostrich, cassowary, or emu.

    2. "Quadrilateral" means a closed-plane figure having four sides of equal length and four right (i.e., 90-degree) angles.

    3. "Marsupial" means an Australian mammal.

  * **4.** An "octagon" is a figure shaped like a stop sign.

    5. "Square" means a closed-plane figure having four right (i.e., 90-degree) angles.

    6. "Right" means not wrong.

  * **7.** A "triangle" is a closed-plane figure having three sides of equal length.

    8. "Jellyfish" means an animal without a spine.

    9. "Wine" means a beverage made from grapes.

 * **10.** An "ellipse" is a cross between a circle and a rectangle.

  11. "Coward" means a spineless person.

  12. "Wolf" is defined as a flesh-eating mammal having four legs.

* **13.** "Homosexual" means a man who is erotically attracted exclusively (or at least primarily) to other men.

  14. "Dog" means a flesh-eating domestic mammal similar to a wolf but having specifically doglike characteristics.

  15. A "murderer" is a human who has killed another human.

* **16.** A "wealthy person" is one who has as much money as Bill Gates or Donald Trump.

  17. "Camel" means ship of the desert.

  18. "Snake" means a widely feared animal that symbolizes evil or deception in many cultures.

* **19.** "Evil" is defined as the darkness that lies within the human soul.

  20. "Wife" means spouse who is not a husband.

PART C: More Lexical Definitions Evaluate the following definitions, using the six criteria for definition by genus and difference.

1. Too wide	**4.** Circular
2. Too narrow	**5.** Unnecessarily negative
3. Obscure, ambiguous, or figurative	**6.** Unsuitable attribute

Explain your answer briefly. For example, if you say a definition is too narrow, give an example that illustrates your point. Assume that the definitions are meant to be lexical definitions. If a definition meets all six criteria, simply write "OK."

* **1.** "Blue" means having a bluish color.
   2. "Fifty" means the number of states in the U.S.A.
   3. "Rectangle" means a plane figure having four equal sides and four right (i.e., 90-degree) angles.
* **4.** Time is the great container into which we pour our lives.
   5. "Wise person" means one who displays wisdom.
   6. A "trapezoid" is a closed-plane figure that is not a triangle or a rectangle or a circle or an ellipse.
* **7.** "Oligarchy" means a form of government in which the ruling power belongs to a few persons.
   8. A "circle" is a closed-plane figure bound by a single curved line, every point of which is equally distant from the point at the center of the figure.
   9. "Atheist" means person who believes that there is no God.
* **10.** "Spherical" means shaped like the earth.
   11. A "trumpet" is a brass wind instrument with three valves.
   12. A "painting" is a picture made with water colors.
* **13.** "Reptile" means snake.
   14. A "scrupulous person" is one who has scruples.
   15. "God" means a being Billy Graham often speaks about.

PART D: Precising Definitions Evaluate the following as precising definitions *in the context of making law.* Since these are precising definitions, they may, without fault, depart from ordinary usage in some degree, but if they inaccurately classify clear cases, they may appropriately be judged too wide or too narrow (or otherwise flawed).

* **1.** The elderly shall receive subsidized health care; "the elderly" means citizens over 92 years of age.
   2. Euthanasia is permissible when a patient is permanently comatose. A patient shall be deemed permanently comatose when he or she has been in a coma for at least one week.
   3. All serial killers shall receive the death penalty, a "serial killer" being anyone who has killed more than one person.
* **4.** Pacifists shall be exempt from the draft, a "pacifist" being anyone who is willing to swear under oath that he or she is opposed to the use of violence against human beings under any circumstances.
   5. Religion shall not be taught in public schools; "religion" means any belief system involving supernatural beings.

6. The penalty for terrorism shall be life imprisonment; "terrorism" means any use of violence against persons or property for political purposes.

* **7.** Evolution shall be taught in the public high schools; "evolution" means the view that all life, including human life, came into existence through entirely natural causes, there being no supernatural Creator.

8. Killing in self-defense is justifiable homicide; one kills in self-defense when one kills a person who is immediately threatening one's life. A person's life shall be deemed under immediate threat provided that he or she passes a lie detector test indicating that he or she believed (at the time of the event) that he or she was about to be attacked with a lethal weapon.

9. Torture, defined as *inflicting physical pain on another person*, is a grave offense and merits incarceration.

* **10.** The penalty for telling a lie shall be a fine of $1000; "one tells a lie" means one asserts a falsehood without being coerced.

11. It is illegal for adults to engage in sexual relations with minors. "A minor" is defined as someone under the age of 25.

12. Drive at 20 miles per hour when children are present. "Children" is defined as persons under the age of 10.

* **13.** Do Not Resuscitate forms signed by mentally competent patients shall be binding. "Mentally competent" patients are those who have been tested and found to have an IQ over 120.

PART E: Theoretical Definitions
Match the definiendum on the left with the *best* definiens available on the right. These definitions are theoretical in type.

_____ **1.** Courage

_____ **2.** Justice

_____ **3.** Faith

_____ * **4.** Evidence

_____ **5.** Wisdom

_____ **6.** Virtues

_____ * **7.** Belief

_____ **8.** Suspending judgment

_____ **9.** Vices

_____ ***10.** Disbelief

A. Confidence that a proposition is true

B. A tendency to perform acts the agent considers dangerous but worth the risk

C. Knowledge of which ends are worth achieving and of how to achieve them

D. Traits that hinder one from living well

E. Considerations relevant to the truth of the proposition in question

F. Confidence that a proposition is false

G. Believing in spite of factors that may tend to cause doubt

H. Giving each individual his or her due

I. Traits enabling one to live well

J. A lack of confidence in the truth of a proposition combined with a lack of confidence in its falsehood

3.3 Using Definitions to Evaluate Arguments

If we are not careful about language, two negative results are likely to occur: equiv‑ocation and merely verbal disputes. **Equivocation** occurs when a word (or phrase) is used with more than one meaning in an argument, but the validity of the argu‑ment depends on the word's being used with the same meaning throughout.

> **Equivocation** occurs when a word (or phrase) is used with more than one meaning in an argument, but the validity of the argument depends on the word's being used with the same meaning throughout.

For example:

40. John has a lot of pride in his work. He is already a superb craftsman, and he is constantly improving. But, unfortunately, pride is one of the seven deadly sins. So, John is guilty of one of the seven deadly sins.

Here, of course, the word "pride" is used with two different meanings. In the first occurrence, it means "appropriate self-respect." In the second occurrence, it means "arrogance" or "excessive self-regard." These two meanings differ, and it is invalid to argue that John has a serious moral flaw (namely, arrogance) simply because he has appropriate self-respect with regard to his work.

The use of the single word "pride" in argument (40) gives it a superficial appearance of validity. But if we rewrite the gist of the argument, plugging in words that capture the two different meanings of "pride," any appearance of validity vanishes completely:

41. John has appropriate self-respect with regard to his work. Arrogance is one of the seven deadly sins. So, John is guilty of one of the seven deadly sins.

Etymologically, "equivocate" comes from two Latin words, one meaning "equal" or "same" and one meaning "voice" or "word." When one equivocates, one makes it sound as if the same word (or phrase) is being used with the same meaning throughout the argument, when, in fact, more than one meaning is present. Let's consider another example of equivocation:

42. I cannot trust my son, Jack, to prepare and serve a five-course meal to 15 guests. I cannot trust my son! If one cannot trust someone, that means he is dishonest. So, that means my son is dishonest.

Here the phrase "cannot trust Jack" is used with two different meanings. In the first occurrence, it means "am not entitled to believe that Jack is willing and able to complete a certain task." In the second occurrence, it means "have reason to believe that Jack is dishonest." These two meanings differ, and it is invalid to argue that Jack is dishonest simply because he is incapable of completing a difficult task. The use of the phrase "cannot trust" in argument (42) gives it a superficial appearance of validity.

A **merely verbal dispute** occurs when two (or more) disputants appear to disagree (i.e., appear to make logically conflicting assertions), but an ambiguous word (or phrase) hides the fact that the disagreement is unreal.

> A **merely verbal dispute** occurs when disputants appear to disagree, but an ambiguous word (or phrase) hides the fact that the disagreement is unreal.

A really simple example of this occurs when two people use a single name with two different extensions. For example:

43. Mary: I'm travelling to Moscow this weekend.
Tom: Be careful! I've heard there are high rates of crime and corruption there.
Mary: Really, a small town in Idaho with high rates of crime and corruption! I'm surprised to hear that.

Tom and Mary are not disagreeing. They're simply talking about different cities.

Similarly, two people may be talking about the same person and may seem to be disagreeing about whether the person has a certain characteristic but, in fact, be talking about two different characteristics.

44. Mr. X: Bob is a good man. I can always count on him to do his job. And he doesn't make excuses. I wish I had more employees like him.
Ms. Y: I disagree. Bob is not a good man. He has been divorced four times, he drinks too much, and he is addicted to gambling.

For Mr. X, "good man" means "good man for the job"—that is, a man who does high-quality work efficiently. But for Ms. Y, "good man" means "a morally virtuous man." Accordingly, there is no real disagreement here between Mr. X and Ms. Y, for there is no logical conflict between the statement that Bob does high-quality work efficiently and the statement that Bob is not morally virtuous. Even if Bob does have some moral vices, it may still be true that he is a good employee.

A merely verbal dispute is similar to equivocation in that a double meaning is involved. But a merely verbal dispute necessarily involves *two or more people* who misunderstand each other because of the ambiguity of a key word or phrase, whereas equivocation occurs when an ambiguity destroys the validity of an argument (and no dialogue partner need be involved). The American philosopher and psychologist William James provides a striking and humorous example of a merely verbal dispute:

> Some years ago, being with a camping party in the mountains, I returned from a solitary ramble to find everyone engaged in a ferocious . . . dispute. The *corpus* of the dispute was a squirrel—a live squirrel supposed to be clinging to one side of a tree-trunk; while over against the tree's opposite side a human being was imagined to stand. This human witness tries to get sight of the squirrel by moving rapidly round the tree, but no matter how fast he goes, the squirrel moves as fast in the opposite direction, and always keeps the tree between himself and the man, so that never a glimpse of him is caught. The resultant . . . problem now is this: *Does the man go round the squirrel or not?* He goes round the tree, sure enough, and the squirrel is on the tree; but does he go round the squirrel? In the unlimited leisure of the wilderness, discussion had been worn threadbare. Everyone had taken sides, and was obstinate. . . .[11]

At this point, the dispute can be summed up as follows:

45. Side 1: The man goes around the squirrel.
Side 2: No. The man does not go around the squirrel.

James goes on to explain how he resolved the dispute:

> Mindful of the scholastic adage that whenever you meet a contradiction you must make a distinction, I immediately sought and found one, as follows: "Which party is right," I said, "depends on what you practically mean by 'going round' the squirrel. If you mean passing from the north of him to the east, then to the south, then to the west, and then to the north of him again, obviously the man does go round him, for he occupies these successive positions. But if on the contrary you mean being first in front of him, then on the right of him, then behind him, then on his left, and finally in front again, it is quite as obvious that the man fails to go round him, for by the compensating movements the squirrel makes, he keeps his belly turned toward the man all the time, and his back turned away."[12]

Here, the dispute is merely verbal because of the ambiguity in the phrase "going round." The disputants fail to communicate because they do not realize that their assertions are logically compatible. There is an appearance of contradiction, but no real logical conflict is present.

Consider one last example of a merely verbal dispute:

46. Mr. X: Modern physics has shown that medium-sized physical objects, such as bricks, walls, and desks, are not solid.
Ms. Y: How absurd! If you think this wall isn't solid, just try putting your fist through it, buster.[13]

Mr. X presumably has in mind the fact that according to modern physics, medium-sized physical objects are composed of tiny particles—atoms, protons, electrons, quarks, and the like. And, according to modern physics, these particles are not packed tightly together. Rather, the spaces between the particles are vast relative to the size of the particles (just as the spaces between the sun and the planets in the solar system are vast relative to the size of these bodies). In a nutshell, the two parties talk past each other because Mr. X uses "solid" to mean "dense or tightly packed," while Ms. Y uses "solid" to mean "hard to penetrate."

Sometimes, however, what looks like a mere verbal dispute is actually a genuine disagreement about definitions. So, in an earlier example, two people disagreeing about whether Clinton was impeached were engaged in a verbal dispute over the meaning of the word "impeach." It turned out, however, that one of them was wrong. This is particularly important in the case of theoretical definitions. Philosophers disagree about whether some claim is *true*—in part because they disagree about the nature of truth. For example, suppose some philosopher claimed that the statement "It is wrong to break a promise" was true, and another claimed that it was not true. When asked to defend her claim, the second of these philosophers may argue that moral claims cannot be true because they cannot be proven and add that, according to her, a statement is true if and only if it can be proven. The first philosopher may retort that this is not his notion of truth. It would not be appropriate to assert that the matter had now been resolved because these two philosophers will have shown themselves to have a deeper disagreement—a disagreement about the nature of truth.

At this point, we need to consider another error in reasoning that is sometimes confused with the merely verbal dispute. This is the improper use of persuasive definitions. A **persuasive definition** is one *slanted (or biased) in favor of a particular conclusion or point of view*. In practice, persuasive definitions often amount to an attempt to settle an argument by verbal fiat. Here's an example:

> **47.** "Affirmative action" means reverse discrimination. But discrimination is always wrong. So, affirmative action is wrong.

> A **persuasive definition** is a definition that is slanted (or biased) in favor of a particular conclusion or point of view.

By defining "affirmative action" as "reverse discrimination," one puts a particular slant on matters. But this definition hardly characterizes a useful concept for the purposes of rational discussion. Notice that a person who did not know the conventional meaning of "affirmative action" would not get a clear grasp of the concept from this definition. A better definition of "affirmative action" would be "preferential treatment of disadvantaged groups." This definition enables us to focus on the heart of the issue: Should disadvantaged groups receive special treatment?

Persuasive definitions sometimes have considerable rhetorical power, and this power is often exploited in politics. Here's a typical example:

> **48.** I will speak frankly and without the verbal fuzziness so typical of my opponent. "National health care" means socialized medicine. That's why I oppose it and why you should, too.

This argument may well succeed in associating national health care with something an audience fears or disapproves of, namely, socialism. But it is hardly a fair and neutral definition that will enable both sides to confront the issues squarely.

Persuasive definitions generally violate one or more of the six criteria for definition by genus and difference. Thus, they may be obscure, too wide, or too narrow, or they may involve attributes that are unsuitable relative to the context or purpose. The most common failing is this: When the context calls for a neutral (unbiased) definition of a key term for the purposes of rational discussion, then a persuasive definition makes reference to an attribute that is not suited to the purpose. A definition that slants things in favor of one side in the dispute is not a definition acceptable to all parties in the dispute.

The use of persuasive definitions is sometimes confused with the phenomenon of the merely verbal dispute. This is the case especially when disputants trade persuasive definitions slanted in favor of opposing points of view. For example, a political conservative may define "conservative" as "a liberal who has wised up." In retaliation, the liberal may define "conservative" as "a person bent on protecting his or her own privileges." But the use of persuasive definitions differs from the merely verbal dispute precisely because definitions are provided. By contrast, in a merely verbal dispute, different meanings are employed but no definitions are provided.

It is not necessarily an error in reasoning to employ persuasive definitions. The error comes only when persuasive definitions are substituted for substantive argument. This error can be exposed by restating the argument without using any persuasive definitions. If such a restatement is an argument whose premises do not support its conclusion, then an error in reasoning has occurred. But such a summary may reveal a valid or strong argument, with plausible premises, that does not depend on persuasive definitions. In that case, persuasive definitions may well have been used appropriately as a rhetorical device. Persuasive definitions can be both humorous and insightful, and thus legitimate rhetorical tools, provided they are not substituted for arguments where arguments are needed.

Summary of Definitions

Equivocation occurs when a word (or phrase) is used with more than one meaning in an argument, but the validity of the argument depends on the word's being used with the same meaning throughout.

A **merely verbal dispute** occurs when disputants appear to disagree, but an ambiguous word (or phrase) hides the fact that the disagreement is unreal.

A **persuasive definition** is a definition that is slanted (or biased) in favor of a particular conclusion or point of view.

EXERCISE 3.3

PART A: Equivocation Each of the following arguments is invalid because it uses a word or phrase that has a double meaning. Identify the ambiguous word or phrase in each argument, and succinctly describe the double meaning involved. (It is a common tendency to ramble on in an attempt to identify such double meanings. Avoid this. Instead, provide two brief definitions of the relevant word or phrase.) You may find it helpful to use a dictionary. (See the Answer Key for an illustration.)

* **1.** A boring job at the minimum wage is better than nothing. But nothing is better than going to heaven. So, a boring job at the minimum wage is better than going to heaven.

  2. If a tree falls in the forest and no one is there to hear it fall, does it make a sound? Modern science says, "Yes, for there are vibrations in the air even if no humans are nearby." But this is easily refuted. Sound is something heard. That's really quite obvious when you think about it. So, if no one was there to hear the sound, there was no sound.

  3. John's appendix is undoubtedly human. It is wrong to destroy a human. So, it is wrong to destroy John's appendix.

* **4.** You are standing in this grave and telling a lie when you say that it is your grave. If you lie in a grave, it is your grave. So, this is your grave. —Paraphrased from *Hamlet*, Act V, scene 1

  5. I phoned the museum, and the curator said that picture taking is permitted. So, when I visit the museum today, I should be allowed to take some of Rembrandt's pictures home with me.

  6. When the recession hit us, I lowered your salary by 20 percent. You moved from $30,000 to $24,000. I know that was tough, and I'm sorry about it. But I have some good news. Things are looking up again. We're showing a profit. So, I'm going to raise your salary by 20 percent. I hope you appreciate this. I lowered your salary by 20 percent; now I'm raising it by 20 percent. So, you see, this policy will bring you back up to where you were before the recession hit.

* **7.** People nowadays say they can't believe in the Christian religion. They say they can't believe in miracles. Is it that they can't or that they won't? They believe in the miracles of modern science, don't they? You bet they do. They believe in vaccines, space-walks, and heart transplants. They believe in fiber optics, laser surgery, and genetic engineering. They can believe in miracles, all right. They just don't want to believe in the Christian miracles.

  8. One milliliter of Nuclear Bug-Bomb Aerosol Spray will kill any pest. And Dennis McKenna is a pest. Hence, one-milliliter of Nuclear Bug-Bomb Aerosol Spray will kill Dennis.

  9. You are a free creature. So, you are free to do good or evil. But if you are free to do evil, then you should not be punished for doing evil. Hence, you should not be punished for doing evil.

* **10.** See how foolish and inconsistent it is to say, "I would prefer not to be, than to be unhappy." The man who says, "I prefer this to that," chooses something; but "not to be" is not something, but nothing. Therefore, you cannot in any way choose rightly when you choose something that does not exist. You say that you wish to exist although you are unhappy, but that you ought not to wish this. What, then, ought you to have willed? You answer, "Not to exist." But if you ought to have willed not to exist, then "not to exist" is better. However, what does not exist cannot be better; therefore, you should not have willed this. —St. Augustine, *On Free Choice of the Will,* trans. Anna S. Benjamin and L. H. Hackstaff (Indianapolis, IN: Bobbs-Merrill, 1964), p. 104

11. I have a duty to do what is right. And I have a right to run for office. Hence, I have a duty to run for office.

12. We can all agree that sick people should not be punished for displaying the symptoms of their sickness. For instance, you shouldn't punish a flu victim for having a high fever. But, you know, a person has to be sick to commit murder. Murder is a symptom of a sick mind. Thus, contrary to popular belief, murderers should not be punished.

13. Alice is crazy. She'll do anything to get a laugh! Of course, if she is crazy, then she should be put in a mental hospital. So, Alice should be put in a mental hospital.

14. Something is better than material well-being. And a speck of dust is something. It follows that a speck of dust is better than material well-being.

15. It is good to act natural. And it is natural for boys to fight. Therefore, it is good for boys to fight.

PART B: Merely Verbal Disputes and Persuasive Definitions

The following brief dialogues provide examples of either merely verbal disputes or the improper use of persuasive definitions. If a persuasive definition is employed, explain its weakness in terms of the six criteria for definitions. Remember, a persuasive definition occurs *only when* an explicit definition of the relevant word or phrase appears. (And, of course, not every explicit definition is persuasive.) In the case of a merely verbal dispute, identify the word or phrase that has a double meaning, and provide a definition for both meanings. (*Note:* A merely verbal dispute is similar to equivocation in that a double meaning is involved, but a merely verbal dispute necessarily involves *two or more people* who misunderstand each other because of the ambiguity of a key word or phrase. Equivocation occurs when an ambiguity destroys the validity of an argument, and no dialogue partner need be involved.)

* **1. Ms. X:** You promised to pay for the damage you caused to my car.

    Mr. Y: But I am a different person now. I no longer drink; I have a job; I jog every day. I'm not the man who promised to pay you.

    Ms. X: You are the same man: you have the same Social Security number, the same fingerprints, the same DNA, the same parents. Give me my money!

2. Ms. Y: Pacifists are the only hope for the future of the human species.

   Mr. X: I disagree. "Pacifist" means a wimp who's afraid to stand up for his own rights. I see nothing hopeful about that.

3. Ms. Y: Secular humanism is a religion, for it is just as much a worldview or way of life as Judaism or Christianity. And yet, secular humanists claim to be free of religious bias.

   Mr. X: No. Secular humanism is not a religion. After all, secular humanists deny the supernatural altogether.

* 4. Mr. X: The Republican party will be the salvation of this country.

   Ms. Y: Give me a break! The "Republican party" is best defined as the party whose primary concern is to protect the wealth of its own members. The only "country" Republicans will ever save is the country club.

5. Mr. X: I don't care for Reverend Boggs myself. Judging from his sermons, I don't even think he is a Christian. He denies the doctrine of the Trinity and the deity of Christ. Once he even preached a sermon claiming that heaven and hell are entirely mythical.

   Ms. Y: How can you say that! Reverend Boggs is a fine Christian man. He is genuinely loving, tolerant of others, and helps people in every way he can.

6. Ms. Y: This canyon is really beautiful. Look at these sweeping lines of natural geometry! And the background is the brightest blue sky imaginable.

   Mr. X: On the contrary, this canyon is nothing but a big, ugly hole in the ground.

   Ms. Y: You are mistaken. The word "beautiful" simply means enjoyable for the speaker to see or hear, and therefore the canyon is beautiful since I *do* enjoy looking at it.

* 7. Mr. X: You are guilty of false advertising, Madam. This orange is labeled "local" but it was grown 1,200 miles from here.

   Ms. Y: It's not false advertising. I'm selling the orange in the same state where it was grown.

8. Mr. X: Our society is losing its reverence for life. For example, euthanasia is widely practiced in American hospitals.

   Ms. Y: You are misinformed. Euthanasia is illegal, and in our litigious society, doctors have a tremendous motivation to avoid illegal procedures.

   Mr. X: But many patients are taken off respirators when their hearts are still pumping. Then they stop breathing and die. *That* is euthanasia.

   Ms. Y: No, it's not euthanasia because the electroencephalograms of the patients indicate that they were dead before the respirators were removed.

9. Ms. Y: We are not free because our behavior is determined by our genes in conjunction with environmental influences.

   Mr. X: I disagree. This is a free country. Americans are a free people!

***10. Ms. Y:** Moral codes vary from society to society. For example, polygamy is "right" in some societies but "wrong" in others.

   Mr. X: No. Polygamy is never right. It is degrading to women.

11. Mr. X: I know that I am reincarnated.

   Ms. Y: Nobody can know that.

   Mr. X: I disagree. "To know" means to believe with all your heart. And I believe with all my heart that I am reincarnated. Therefore, I know that I am reincarnated.

12. Ms. Y: Although many people claim to be atheists, there really are no atheists.

   Mr. X: I beg to differ.

   Ms. Y: Beg all you want, but "God" means the greatest being. And everyone thinks that something or other is the greatest being. For example, if you don't believe in supernatural entities, you will probably think that the entire physical universe is the greatest being. So, while not everyone accepts the traditional view of God, everyone does believe that God exists, and hence there are no atheists.

***13. Mr. X:** Did you have a nice weekend?

   Ms. Y: Yes, we went to the Jackson Pollock exhibit at the art museum. He is truly one of the greatest artists of the century.

   Mr. X: On the contrary, Pollock's abstract paintings aren't even art. You can't even tell what the paintings are supposed to be *of*.

14. Ms. Y: I'll never be a political conservative. Never!

   Mr. X: Oh, but you are mistaken. After all, the word "conservative" means a liberal who has been mugged. So, given the rate of violent crime, I think you will likely one day find yourself a conservative.

15. Mr. X: Nietzsche was one of the most intelligent people in the history of the world. His books caused a revolution in philosophy.

   Ms. Y: Intelligent? I don't think so. If Nietzsche was so smart, then why was his personal life such a total disaster? He couldn't keep a job, he alienated all his friends, and the older he got, the weirder he got. Personally, I think Nietzsche was stupid.

PART C: Equivocation and Persuasive Definition Identify any equivocations or persuasive definitions that appear in the following arguments. In the case of equivocation, provide definitions to clarify the double meaning. Where persuasive definitions occur, explain why they are biased or slanted.

* **1.** Every free action is prompted by a motive that belongs to the agent (i.e., the person who performs the action). So, every free act is pursued in an attempt to satisfy one of the agent's own motives. But, by definition, a "self-serving act" is one pursued in an attempt to satisfy one's own motives. Hence, every free act is self-serving.

2. Many people say there is poverty in America today. They cite the number of homeless men and women living on the streets. But there is no real poverty in America today. The people living on the streets of Calcutta are poor. They are literally starving. Now that's poverty. Therefore, poverty doesn't really exist in America today.

3. Whenever 2 gallons of water are poured into a barrel and 2 gallons of alcohol are added, the barrel will contain slightly less than 4 gallons of liquid (because of the way water and alcohol combine chemically). Thus, when you add 2 and 2, you do not always get 4. Of course, this is entirely contrary to what any mathematician will tell you—namely, when 2 and 2 are added, you always get 4. Therefore, mathematics is sometimes contrary to empirical fact.

* **4.** There ought to be a law against psychiatry, for "psychiatrist" means person who makes a living by charging money for talking with deeply troubled people. And it is wrong to exploit deeply troubled people.

5. Many atheists complain about the harshness of nature "red in tooth and claw." They say that a loving Creator would not set up a system in which some animals must kill and eat other animals in order to live. Hogwash! "The law of the survival of the fittest" is best defined as God's way of achieving population control among the animals. Thus, although the struggle for survival *appears* harsh to us, the law of the survival of the fittest is in fact a very good thing. For without it the environment would be destroyed by an overabundance of animals.

6. Wherever there is a law, there is a person or group who established it. So, since the law of gravity is a law, there is a person or group who established the law of gravity. Now, no human or group of humans could establish the law of gravity. Therefore, some superhuman person or group of superhumans established the law of gravity.

* **7.** Any fetus of human parents is itself human. And if any fetus of human parents is itself human, then abortion is wrong if human life is sacred. Furthermore, since being human consists in having faculties higher than those of other animals (such as the capacity to choose between good and evil), human life is sacred. It follows that abortion is wrong.

8. Frankly, it amazes me that there are people who oppose capitalism. "Capitalism" means an economic system characterized by a free market, fair competition for the goods available, minimal interference from the state, and the sacred right to keep what you've earned. Accordingly, capitalism is a good thing, indeed, a marvelous thing. I can only conclude that those who oppose capitalism are either seriously confused or perverse.

9. If you become a socialist, you will be making a very big mistake. For "socialist" means someone who thinks the government should own everything and that the individual person has no moral value and no rights. So, the very foundations of socialism are evil.

10. It is reasonable to appeal to legitimate authority to settle disputes. If it is reasonable to appeal to legitimate authority to settle disputes and legitimate authority in a democracy resides in the people, then in America, it is reasonable to appeal to the people to determine whether nuclear weapons are needed. And you will undoubtedly agree that legitimate authority in a democracy resides in the people. So, in America, it is reasonable to appeal to the people to determine whether nuclear weapons are needed. Now, if in America it is reasonable to appeal to the people to determine whether nuclear weapons are needed, then if the majority of Americans regard them as needed, they are needed. The majority of Americans regard nuclear weapons as needed. Hence, nuclear weapons are needed.

NOTES

1. Alexander W. Allison et al., *The Norton Anthology of Poetry*, 3rd ed. (New York: Norton, 1983), p. 1037.
2. David Kelley, *The Art of Reasoning*, exp. ed. (New York: Norton, 1990), p. 114.
3. Wesley Salmon, *Logic*, 3rd ed. (Englewood Cliffs, NJ: Prentice-Hall, 1984), p. 145.
4. This example is borrowed from Frank R. Harrison, III, *Logic and Rational Thought* (New York: West, 1992), p. 463.
5. We owe the interesting observation that the English language has no conventional term for this phenomenon to Dr. Gary Gleb, in conversation.
6. This example is borrowed from Irving M. Copi and Carl Cohen, *Introduction to Logic*, 9th ed. (Englewood Cliffs, NJ: Prentice-Hall, 1994), p. 170.
7. Edmund Gettier, "Is Justified True Belief Knowledge?" *Analysis* 23(1963): 121–123.
8. *Webster's New World Dictionary of the American Language* (New York: World, 1966), p. 412.
9. Benedict de Spinoza, *The Ethics*, trans. R. H. M. Elwes (New York: Dover, 1955), p. 173. Quote marks added.
10. Definition (32) is borrowed from H. L. Mencken, ed., *A New Dictionary of Quotations on Historical Principles from Ancient and Modern Sources* (New York: Knopf, 1978), p. 62. Quote marks added. Mencken attributes (32) to Theodore Dreiser.
11. William James, *Pragmatism and Four Essays from* The Meaning of Truth (New York: New American Library, 1974), p. 41. This quotation is from chap. 2 of *Pragmatism*, "What Pragmatism Means." *Pragmatism* was originally published in 1907 by Longman, Green.
12. James, *Pragmatism*, pp. 41–42.
13. The gist of this example is borrowed from Salmon, *Logic*, p. 162.

CHAPTER 4

Informal Fallacies

Some errors in reasoning are so obvious that no one is apt to be taken in by them. Other errors in reasoning tend to be psychologically persuasive. You might fall into them unintentionally while thinking through some issue for yourself, or someone might use them to trick you into believing something they have given you no good reason to believe. These errors are called "fallacies." In Chapter 1, we encountered a number of formal fallacies. In this chapter, we'll focus on informal fallacies. What's the difference? A **formal fallacy** involves the explicit use of an invalid form.

 A **formal fallacy** is an error in reasoning that involves the explicit use of an invalid form.

For example, the fallacy of affirming the consequent is a formal fallacy:

1. If 2,523 is divisible by 9, then it's divisible by 3. 2,523 is divisible by 3. So, it's divisible by 9.

The form here is invalid: "If A, then B; B; so, A." The fallacy of denying the antecedent is another formal fallacy.

2. If good intentions make good sermons, then Reverend McGuire is a good preacher. Unfortunately, they don't; so, he's not.

The form here is invalid as well: "If A, then B; not A; so, not B."
    We have also seen how to use counterexamples to expose formal fallacies. For instance:

3. All cantaloupes are melons. All watermelons are melons. So, all watermelons are cantaloupes.

The form of (3) is "All A are B; all C are B; so all C are A." Here is a counter-example that shows that this form is invalid: "All dogs are animals. All cats are animals. So, all cats are dogs."

Not all fallacies are formal fallacies. An **informal fallacy** is an error in reasoning that does not involve the explicit use of an invalid form.

> An **informal fallacy** is an error in reasoning that does not involve the explicit use of an invalid form.

Exposing an informal fallacy requires an examination of the argument's *content*. We took note of one kind of informal fallacy in Chapter 3, namely, equivocation. Here is a blatant example:

> **4.** My grandfather Joe is a child (he is the son of my great grandparents). If my grandfather Joe is a child, then he should not have to work for a living. So, Joe should not have to work for a living.

If we ignore the content, this argument appears to be an instance of *modus ponens*. But if we examine the content, we note that the word "child" is used with two different meanings. In the first premise, "child" means "human off-spring." In the second premise, "child" means "very young human being." Once we spot the double meaning, we see that it destroys the logical linkage between the two premises. Although the form initially appears to be *modus ponens*, an analysis of the content indicates that the form would be more accurately identified as follows: "A; if B, then C; so, C." This form is obviously invalid, but it is not explicitly employed in (4). It remains hidden because of the double meaning of the word "child." Thus, equivocation is an informal fallacy.

There are many types of informal fallacies, and logicians do not agree on the best way to classify them. However, an attempt to classify them has benefits, for it enables us to see some commonalities among them. In this text, informal fallacies are divided into three groups: (a) fallacies of irrelevance, (b) fallacies involving ambiguity, and (c) fallacies involving unwarranted assumptions. The reason for studying informal fallacies is simply this: By describing and labeling the more tempting ones, we increase our ability to resist their allure. A couple of notes of caution, however. It is important to note that, although the patterns described here are *almost always* fallacious, these patterns (or very similar patterns) are sometimes not fallacious. So, one shouldn't apply this material in an automatic way. At the same time, there is disagreement about exactly which patterns count as fallacies and how many there are. Moreover, no textbook could classify absolutely all the different argumentative errors. So, the fact that an argument doesn't commit one of the listed fallacies doesn't mean it doesn't commit some different logical error. The list of fallacies that follows is supposed to help you recognize common errors of reasoning and give you a general sense of how arguments can go wrong. It's not supposed to substitute for hard, rigorous thought about each argument you confront.

4.1   Fallacies of Irrelevance

Some fallacies involve the use of premises that are logically irrelevant to their conclusions, but that for psychological reasons may *seem* to be relevant. These fallacies are classified as fallacies of irrelevance. Seven varieties of this general class of fallacy are discussed in this section.

*Argument Against the Person (*Ad Hominem *Fallacy)*

The **argument against the person** (or *ad hominem* fallacy) involves attacking the person who advances an argument (or asserts a statement) as opposed to providing a rational critique of the argument (or statement) itself. (*Ad hominem* is a Latin phrase meaning "against the man.")

> The **argument against the person** (or *ad hominem* fallacy) involves attacking the person who advances an argument (or asserts a statement) as opposed to providing a rational critique of the argument (or statement) itself.

In its most blatant form, the **abusive *ad hominem,*** this fallacy involves an attempt to discredit a view or argument by launching a direct personal attack, for example, an insult or allegation that the arguer has a moral flaw.

> The **abusive *ad hominem*** involves an attempt to discredit an argument or view by launching a direct personal attack.

For example:

> **5.** Jones argues for vegetarianism. He says it is wrong to kill animals unless you really need them for food, and that, as a matter of fact, nearly everyone can get enough food without eating meat. But Jones is just a nerdy intellectual. So, we can safely conclude that vegetarianism remains what it has always been—nonsense.

Here, Jones's argument is not given a rational critique; rather, Jones himself is criticized. And even if Jones is a "nerdy intellectual," this does not show that Jones's argument is flawed, nor does it show that vegetarianism is nonsense. The personal attack on Jones is simply irrelevant to the soundness of Jones's argument and irrelevant to the issue of vegetarianism.

Ad hominem arguments need not employ outright verbal abuse. In more subtle forms, they involve the attempt to discredit an opponent by suggesting that the opponent's judgment is distorted by some factor in his or her circumstances—*even though the soundness of the opponent's argument (or truth of the opponent's view) is independent of the factor cited*. This form of *ad hominem* argument is sometimes called the *circumstantial ad hominem* because it involves an attempt to discredit an argument or view by calling attention to the circumstances or situation of those who advance it. For example:

> **6.** Ms. Fitch argues in favor of equal pay for equal work. She says it doesn't make sense to pay a person more for doing the same job just because he is male or Caucasian. But since Ms. Fitch is a woman, it's to her personal advantage to favor equal pay for equal work. After all, she would get an immediate raise if her boss accepted her argument! Therefore, her argument is worthless.

Here, an attempt is made to discredit the argument by showing that the arguer has something to gain if her conclusion is accepted. But this fact, by itself, does not prove that the arguer's reasoning is flawed. What is needed is a rational critique of the premises or inferences in question.

> The **circumstantial *ad hominem*** involves an attempt to discredit an argument or view by calling attention to the circumstances or situation of those who advance it.

Another form of the argument against the person is the *tu quoque* (pronounced "too kwo-kway"), meaning "you too." The *tu quoque* involves an attempt to undermine an argument or view by suggesting that one's opponent is hypocritical—that is, that his views or arguments conflict with his own practice or with what he has said previously.

> The ***tu quoque*** involves an attempt to discredit an argument or view by suggesting that one's opponent is hypocritical.

For instance, suppose a 12-year-old argues as follows:

> **7.** Dad tells me I shouldn't lie. He says lying is wrong because it makes people stop trusting one another. But I've heard my Dad lie. Sometimes he calls in "sick" to work when he isn't really sick. So, lying isn't actually wrong—Dad just doesn't like it when I lie.

The *tu quoque* fallacy may succeed in embarrassing or discrediting the opponent, but the logical error should be clear upon reflection. For example, with regard to argument (7), that some people (including one's parents) lie in no way shows that lying is morally permissible. In general, the fact that some people violate a given moral rule does not show that the rule is incorrect. So, the premise of (7), that "Dad lies," is irrelevant to the conclusion.

Before we leave *ad hominem* arguments, a few words of caution are in order. First, it is fairly rare for arguers in real life to state their *ad hominem* arguments as explicitly as the ones discussed here. It is especially rare for them to restate the opponent's arguments. It is also rare to conclude explicitly that the opponent's position is false. What is far more common is for the person offering the *ad hominem* argument to launch into a personal attack in an attempt to *distract* the listener or reader from the original argument. If you can be worked up into viewing the arguer with contempt as inconsistent or self-serving, then you will be much less likely to pay attention to what she says. Here's an example:

8. The mayor said the biggest problem for the city administration has been fighting people who have protested such things as industrial development. "We've had people fight highways, the school corporation, and county zoning," he said. "I didn't notice any of these people coming up here on horses and donkeys. They all drove cars up here, spewing hydrocarbons all over the place."

Second, there are two kinds of cases where attacks on a person are perfectly legitimate. During the run-up to an election, we are bombarded with many attack ads that criticize the candidates for various failings. Some of these advertisements are no doubt inappropriate, but the mere fact that they criticize the candidates does not make them guilty of the *ad hominem* fallacy. That is because what is at issue is whether this person would make a good president (governor, senator, dogcatcher, etc.). If it is true that this person lied or stole or was wildly promiscuous, that is good reason to think that he or she is not the right person for the office. Defects in the person (as premises) are relevant to the conclusion (that the person should not be elected). With typical *ad hominem* arguments, however, defects in the person (e.g., "My critics also damage the environment") are not relevant to the conclusion (e.g., "My damaging the environment is not wrong").

A second kind of case where personal criticisms are appropriate is the argument by authority. As we shall see in Chapter 10, it is common to argue by way of an appeal to authority—for example, "The surgeon-general has said that babies should receive the MMR vaccine. So, babies should receive the MMR vaccine." Such arguments are often cogent. But notice that the authority's say-so is offered as a premise. If it can be shown that the authority is unreliable, corrupt, or out to feather his or her own nest (e.g., suppose that the surgeon-general owns a large number of shares in the company that manufactures the vaccine), then this appeal to authority can be undermined. To do so is not to commit the *ad hominem* fallacy. Notice, again, that in this case, the attack on the person is not irrelevant to the conclusion because the original argument made use of an implicit premise that the authority was reliable.

Straw Man Fallacy

The **straw man fallacy** occurs when the arguer attacks a misrepresentation of the opponent's view. The idea is to describe something that *sounds like* the opponent's view but is easier to knock down and then to refute.

 The **straw man fallacy** occurs when the arguer attacks a misrepresentation of the opponent's view.

This fallacy can be very effective from a rhetorical point of view if one's audience is not aware that the misrepresentation has taken place. However, when put bluntly, it is obvious that the premise is irrelevant to the conclusion:

Premise: A misrepresentation of the view is false.

Conclusion: The view is false.

Notice that the straw man fallacy results from a failure to honor principle 4 of Chapter 2: *Be fair and charitable in interpreting an argument.* Fairness demands that we represent the original accurately; charity demands that we put an argument in its best light when we are confronted with interpretive choices.

To demonstrate that a straw man fallacy has occurred, one must provide a more accurate statement of the view that has been misrepresented. One does not always have in hand the information needed to do this. But one can often "smoke out" a straw man fallacy by asking such appropriate questions as these: What were the exact words used in the original? Have any key words or phrases been changed or omitted? Does the context suggest that the author was deliberately exaggerating or leaving obvious exception clauses unstated?

Here's an example:

9. These evolutionists believe that a dog can give birth to a cat. How ridiculous!

Argument (9) attacks a straw man rather than evolutionary theory itself. It is a fairly easy matter to read some standard account of evolutionary theory and discover that the view is not committed to anything this radical.

The straw man fallacy is also committed when a view or argument is alleged to involve assumptions that it does not (or need not) involve. For example:

10. Susan advocates the legalization of cocaine. But I cannot agree with any position based on the assumption that cocaine is good for you and that a society of drug addicts can flourish. So, I disagree with Susan.

Of course, one can consistently advocate the legalization of cocaine and yet believe that cocaine is not good for people. For example, one may think that although drugs are harmful, legalizing them is the best way to eliminate the illegal drug traffic (and hence the violence associated with it). Moreover, one can advocate the legalization of drugs without assuming or presupposing that a society of drug addicts can flourish. One might believe that legalization will not lead to a significant increase in the number of drug-addicted persons, especially if legalization is accompanied by a strong educational campaign on the dangers of using hard drugs.

Sometimes a persuasive (i.e., biased) definition is used to set up a straw man:

> **11.** Empiricism is the view that nothing should be believed in unless it can be directly observed. Now, no one can see, hear, taste, smell, or touch protons, electrons, or quarks. So, while empiricists pretend to be advocates of science, their views in fact rule out the most advanced physical science of our times.

Professor Anthony Flew, author of A *Dictionary of Philosophy*, defines "empiricism" as "the thesis that all knowledge or at least all knowledge of matters of fact (as distinct from that of purely logical relations between concepts) is based on experience."[1] Now, since the phrase "is based on" is somewhat vague, the concept of empiricism has rather fuzzy borderlines. But Flew's definition does not have the empiricists insisting that we know only those things we have *directly* observed. We might know about the existence of some entities by extrapolation or because the best theories presuppose their existence. This knowledge would still be "based on" experience because it would be inferred using observation statements. Thus, Flew's definition is fair to the empiricist tradition in philosophy, while the definition contained in argument (11) is biased. By including the phrase "direct observation," the arguer makes empiricism a straw man. Incidentally, argument (11) illustrates how the straw man fallacy can become quite subtle when complex issues are involved. If a seemingly minor but actually important aspect of a view is distorted or omitted, the view itself may appear much easier to refute than it really is.

Appeal to Force (Ad Baculum *Fallacy*)

The **appeal to force** (or *ad baculum* fallacy) occurs when a conclusion is defended by a threat to the well-being of those who do not accept it. (*Baculum* is Latin for "staff," the staff being a symbol of power.) The threat may be either explicit or implicit.

> The **appeal to force** (or *ad baculum* fallacy) occurs when a conclusion is defended by a threat to the well-being of those who do not accept it.

Let's start with a case involving the threat of physical harm, reminiscent of scenes in films about organized crime:

> **12.** Mr. Jones, you helped us import the drugs. For this, the Boss is grateful. But now you say you're entitled to 50 percent of the profits. The Boss says you're entitled to 10 percent. Unless you see things the Boss's way, you're going to have a very nasty accident. So, you're entitled to 10 percent. Got it?

Of course, the threatened "nasty accident" has no logical bearing on the conclusion ("Jones is entitled to 10 percent"). The logical error can be generalized as follows: "You can avoid harm by accepting this statement. So, the statement is true."

An autocratic employer might argue as follows:

> **13.** Lately there has been a lot of negative criticism of our policy on dental benefits. Let me tell you something, people. If you want to keep working here, you need to know that our policy is fair and reasonable. I won't have anybody working here who doesn't know this.

Here, the threat of job loss is obviously irrelevant to the truth of the conclusion (that the dental policy is fair and reasonable). Nevertheless, it may be tempting to suppose that if one can avoid harm by believing X, then X is true.

The *ad baculum* fallacy may involve any sort of threat to one's well-being, including one's psychological well-being. For instance:

> **14.** Listen, Valerie, I know you disagree with my view about the building project. You've made your disagreement clear to everyone. Well, it's time for you to see that you are mistaken. Let me get right to the point. I know you've been lying to your husband about where you go on Wednesday afternoons. Unless you want him to know where you really go, it's time for you to realize that I've been right about the building project all along. You follow me?

Of course, the threat to expose the lie in no way constitutes evidence for anyone's view on a building project. But again, it may be tempting to suppose that a statement is true if one can avoid harm by accepting it.

Finally, a note of caution. The fact that an argument mentions a threat doesn't necessarily make it a fallacy. For example:

> **15.** If you smoke, you increase your risk of getting lung cancer. It's not in your interest to do something that increases your risk of getting lung cancer. So, it's not in your interest to smoke.

This argument is perfectly reasonable. The danger of getting lung cancer is relevant to the question of whether it is in your interest to smoke. So, this is not an example of a fallacy. Now, of course, in this case, the arguer is *describing* a threat from an independent source, not making the threat herself. Does that make a difference? Suppose we changed the example to one in which the arguer is making the threat.

> **16.** If you don't get off my property right now, I'll call the police and have you arrested. [It's not in your interest to be arrested. So, it's not in your interest to stay on my property.]

The bracketed material would, in real life, be left implicit. But the explicit version of the argument is still clearly reasonable. Supposing the first premise of the argument is true (the speaker isn't just bluffing), this looks like a sensible and somewhat informative argument. So, even though the arguer is making a threat, she is not guilty of an *ad baculum* fallacy. Contrast this with example (12) earlier. In that case, the conclusion was, "You're entitled to 10 percent." The issue is whether the premises of the argument are relevant to the conclusion. In (16) they are, whereas in (12), they are not.

Appeal to the People (Ad Populum *Fallacy*)

The **appeal to the people** (or *ad populum* fallacy) is an attempt to persuade a person or group by appealing to the desire to be accepted or valued by others. (*Populum* is Latin for "people" or "nation.")

> The **appeal to the people** (or *ad populum* fallacy) is an attempt to persuade a person or group by appealing to the desire to be accepted or valued by others.

For instance, a speaker at a political rally may elicit strong emotions from the crowd, making each individual want to believe his conclusion so as to feel a part of the group:

> **17.** I look out at you all, and I tell you, I am proud to be here. Proud to belong to a party that stands for what is good for America. Proud to cast my lot with the kind of people who make this nation great. Proud to stand with men and women who can get our nation back on its feet. Yes, there are those who criticize us, who label our view of trade agreements as "protectionist." But when I look at you hard-working people, I know we're right and the critics are wrong.

Of course, the strong feelings of the crowd do not lend logical support to anyone's view about trade agreements. Premises to the effect that "I am proud to be associated with you" and "you are hard-working people" are irrelevant to the conclusion (that "our view of trade agreements is right").

One doesn't have to be addressing a large group to commit the *ad populum* fallacy. Any attempt to convince by appealing to the need for acceptance (or approval) from others counts as an *ad populum* fallacy. For instance:

> **18.** Ms. Sanchez, are you saying that President Bush made a moral error when he decided to go to war with Iraq? I can't believe my ears. That's not how Americans feel. Not true Americans, anyway. You are an American, aren't you, Ms. Sanchez?

The mere fact that Ms. Sanchez is an American provides her with no logical support for the conclusion that America's war with Iraq was just or moral. But like most Americans, Ms. Sanchez may wish to avoid being regarded as unpatriotic, and so an appeal to the people may influence her thinking.

The appeal to the people is common in advertising:

19. The new Electrojet 3000 cabriolet isn't for everyone. But then, you've always stood apart from the crowd, haven't you? So, the Electrojet 3000 is the car for you.

Here, the *ad populum* fallacy takes the form of "snob appeal," that is, an appeal to the desire to be regarded as superior to others.

Appeal to Pity (Ad Misericordiam *Fallacy*)

The **appeal to pity** (or *ad misericordiam* fallacy) is the attempt to support a conclusion merely by evoking pity in one's audience. (*Misericordiam* is Latin for "pity" or "mercy.")

> The **appeal to pity** (or *ad misericordiam* fallacy) is the attempt to support a conclusion merely by evoking pity in one's audience.

For example, a professor instructs his students as follows immediately before handing out teaching evaluations at the end of the term:

20. I hope you will make a careful, accurate, and positive assessment of this class. The university takes teaching evaluations very seriously and uses them to determine such matters as promotion and tenure. This is especially important to me as I have seven young children and a sick dog, all of whom I have brought to class for you to see and play with.

The premises here are simply irrelevant to the conclusion (that the speaker did a good job of teaching the class). Even if the speaker's family is very needy and failing to secure tenure would be bad for them, that is no reason to suppose that the class was well taught.

The appeal to pity is not, generally speaking, very subtle. But if the arguer succeeds in evoking sufficiently strong feelings of pity, he or she may distract the audience from the logic of the situation and create a desire to accept the conclusion. For this reason, lawyers often use the appeal to pity in an effort to convince judges and juries that their clients are not guilty or not deserving of a harsh sentence. For example:

21. You have heard that my client was seen in the vicinity of the crime scene on the day of the murder. But look at his narrow shoulders and frightened eyes. This is a man—a boy really—more sinned against than sinning.

The *ad misericordiam* fallacy must be distinguished from arguments that support the need for a compassionate response to persons whose plights call for compassion. For example, the following sort of argument is *not* an example of the *ad misericordiam* fallacy:

> **22.** Please help! On July 20, 2011, the United Nations declared a famine in parts of Somalia. On August 3, 2011, the UN declared that the famine had spread to three more regions of Somalia, including the camps for displaced families in the capital Mogadishu. Malnutritional levels for children have soared. In many regions of Somalia, 30% to 50% of the children are malnourished. The UN estimates that 29,000 children under the age of five have already died, while 640,000 Somali children are acutely malnourished and at risk of dying, unless helped immediately! (From MercyUSA website)

Although the information in the premises of this sort of argument is apt to evoke pity, the information is also logically relevant to the conclusion (that we ought to help the Somalis). The argument does not *merely* appeal to pity, so it does not commit the *ad misericordiam* fallacy.

Appeal to Ignorance (Ad Ignorantiam *Fallacy*)

The **appeal to ignorance** (or *ad ignorantiam* fallacy) involves one of the following: either (a) the claim that a statement is true (or may be reasonably believed true) simply because it hasn't been proven false or (b) the claim that a statement is false (or may be reasonably believed false) simply because it hasn't been proven true.

> The **appeal to ignorance** (or *ad ignorantiam* fallacy) involves one of the following: either (a) the claim that a statement is true (or may be reasonably believed true) simply because it hasn't been proven false or (b) the claim that a statement is false (or may be reasonably believed false) simply because it hasn't been proven true.

Here are two corresponding examples:

> **23.** After centuries of trying, no one has been able to prove that reincarnation occurs. So, at this point, I think we can safely conclude that reincarnation does not occur.
>
> **24.** After centuries of trying, no one has been able to show that reincarnation does not occur. Therefore, reincarnation occurs.

Put starkly, the claim that a statement is false because it hasn't been proven is manifestly erroneous. By such logic, scientists would have to conclude that their unproven hypotheses are false. And surely it is wiser for scientists to take a "wait-and-see" attitude. After all, we do not have to believe or disbelieve every statement we consider, for we often have the option of suspending judgment—that is, of not believing the statement is true and (simultaneously) not believing it is false. We can remain neutral. Similarly, the claim that a statement is true (or may reasonably be believed true) simply because it hasn't been disproven is illogical. By this principle, every new scientific hypothesis is true (or at least it can reasonably be believed to be true) unless it has been disproven—*no matter how flimsy the evidence for it is*.

The *ad ignorantiam* fallacy is often committed in organizations during periods of change. Those opposing change may argue along the following lines:

> **25.** It has not been proven that the proposed changes will be beneficial. Therefore, they will not be beneficial.

And the counterargument may be this:

> **26.** There is no solid evidence showing that the proposed changes will not be beneficial. Therefore, they will be beneficial.

Both arguments are flawed. As for (25), there may be no way of obtaining the evidence apart from organizational experimentation—that is, trying the proposal. So, demanding the evidence may be unrealistic and unreasonable. As for (26), problems with the proposal may become evident once it is tried, so the current lack of evidence against it is no guarantee that it will work.

One note of caution: Sometimes the absence of evidence really is evidence of absence. To see this, consider a species of the *ad ignorantiam* fallacy, the *Noseeum* argument. (*Noseeum* is a non-Latin term meaning "I do not see them.") The form of the Noseeum argument is this:

> I see (perceive) no X's.
> So, there are no X's.

Many substitution instances of this form are fallacious: "I see no germs on my hands, Mommy. So, there are no germs on my hands." But some substitution instances of this form are inductively strong. For example, "I see no orange juice jug in the fridge. So, there is no orange juice jug in the fridge." Or, "The coroner found no evidence of alcohol in the victim's blood. So, there was no alcohol in the victim's blood." What distinguishes these last two cases from the first is that in the last two cases, it seems reasonable to suppose that if there were any X's, those X's would have been discovered by the relevant search. The fact that they were not discovered is good evidence that they do not exist. Perhaps the point can best be put like this: It is not the mere fact that the coroner found no evidence of alcohol in the victim's blood that makes it reasonable to suppose that there was no alcohol in the victim's blood. It is that fact in combination with the (implicit) fact that if there had been alcohol in her blood, he would almost certainly have found it.

Some confusion regarding the *ad ignorantiam* fallacy may stem from the assumption used in courts of law that a defendant is innocent until proven guilty. Does this legal principle ask us to commit the *ad ignorantiam* fallacy? No, the legal principle instructs us to *treat* people *as if* they were innocent until they are proven guilty. It is not telling us that they are in fact innocent (i.e., that they did not commit the crime) before it has been proven that they are. It is not even telling us to believe that they are innocent before it has been proven that they are guilty. (Why would we prosecute them in that case?) Suppose the evidence presented in court suggests a 75 percent likelihood that the defendant committed the crime, and suppose that's the best the prosecution can do. How should the jury treat the defendant? Since 75 percent leaves room for "reasonable doubt," presumably, they should judge him "not guilty" and recommend that he not be punished. But, if we are simply attempting to form a belief about the matter, the most reasonable belief is presumably that he is *probably guilty* but that we cannot know for sure. To conclude that he is certainly innocent (he certainly did not commit the crime) would indeed be to commit a fallacy. Why treat him as innocent in that case? Undoubtedly, many defendants have committed the crimes they are accused of even though the evidence is not sufficient to prove them guilty according to accepted legal standards. Our legal system is deliberately designed to prevent one kind of unwanted result (namely, the punishment of the innocent) at the risk of allowing another unwanted result (namely, letting persons who have committed crimes go free).

Red Herring (Ignoratio Elenchi *Fallacy)*[2]

The **red herring fallacy** (or *ignoratio elenchi* fallacy) occurs whenever the premises of an argument are logically unrelated to the conclusion. It is thus the most general fallacy of irrelevance.

> The **red herring fallacy** (or *ignoratio elenchi* fallacy) occurs whenever the premises of an argument are logically unrelated to the conclusion.

But unlike some of the other fallacies of irrelevance that we have discussed, the typical example of a red herring fallacy is one where the premises focus on the topic of discussion but the conclusion is irrelevant to that topic. Instead of continuing on to the natural or appropriate conclusion that follows from the premises, the red herring introduces a new idea. A red herring is a fallacy in which an irrelevant topic is presented to divert attention form the original issue. The basic idea is to "win" an argument by leading attention away from the argument and to another topic.

The name of this fallacy comes from the sport of fox hunting in which a dried, smoked herring, which is red in color, is dragged across the trail of the fox to throw the hounds off the scent. Thus, a "red herring" argument is one that distracts the audience from the issue in question through the introduction of some irrelevancy. Here are a couple of examples:

27. Your friend Margie says that Taster's Choice coffee tastes better than Folgers. Apparently she is ignoring the fact that Taster's Choice is made by Nestlé, and Nestlé is the company that manufactured that terrible baby formula for Third World countries. Thousands of babies died when the dry milk formula was mixed with contaminated water. Obviously your friend was mistaken.

28. There is a good deal of talk these days about the need to eliminate pesticides from our fruit and vegetables. But many of these foods are essential to our

health. Carrots are an excellent source of vitamin A, broccoli is rich is iron, and oranges and grapefruits are high in vitamin C.[3]

In each of these cases, the arguer has changed the subject, and done so in a way liable to distract his or her audience. The death of babies is hugely significant and likely to turn one against a company responsible for it (especially if that company had any idea this would happen, or was otherwise culpable), but it is irrelevant to the question of which coffee tastes better. Similarly, in (28) the fact that various fruits and vegetables are good for us is irrelevant to the question of whether we need to eliminate pesticides from these foods—unless, of course, the arguer can show that we cannot get fruits and vegetables without pesticides. But no effort is made to argue for that. So, there is a glaring hole in the argument.

Summary of Definitions

A **formal fallacy** is an error in reasoning that involves the explicit use of an invalid form.

An **informal fallacy** is an error in reasoning that does not involve the explicit use of an invalid form.

The **argument against the person** (or *ad hominem* fallacy) involves attacking the person who advances an argument (or asserts a statement) as opposed to providing a rational critique of the argument (or statement) itself.

The **abusive *ad hominem*** involves an attempt to discredit an argument or view by launching a direct personal attack.

The **circumstantial *ad hominem*** involves an attempt to discredit an argument or view by calling attention to the circumstances or situation of those who advance it.

The ***tu quoque*** involves an attempt to discredit an argument or view by suggesting that one's opponent is hypocritical.

The **straw man fallacy** occurs when the arguer attacks a misrepresentation of the opponent's view.

The **appeal to force** (or *ad baculum* fallacy) occurs when a conclusion is defended by a threat to the well-being of those who do not accept it.

The **appeal to the people** (or *ad populum* fallacy) is an attempt to persuade a person or group by appealing to the desire to be accepted or valued by others.

The **appeal to pity** (or *ad misericordiam* fallacy) is the attempt to support a conclusion merely by evoking pity in one's audience.

The **appeal to ignorance** (or *ad ignorantiam* fallacy) involves one of the following: either (a) the claim that a statement is true (or may be reasonably believed true) simply because it hasn't been proven false or (b) the claim that a statement is false (or may be reasonably believed false) simply because it hasn't been proven true.

The **red herring fallacy** (or *ignoratio elenchi* fallacy) occurs whenever the premises of an argument are logically unrelated to the conclusion.

EXERCISE 4.1

PART A: Formal and Informal Fallacies   Most of the following passages exemplify either a formal fallacy or an informal fallacy. If a formal fallacy is committed, identify the argument form, using capital letters to stand for terms or statements (e.g., "All A are B; all C are B; so, all A are C"). If an informal fallacy is committed, name the type of fallacy and explain why the passage is an example of that type. (In the case of *ad hominem* fallacies, indicate whether they are abusive, circumstantial, or *tu quoque* in type.) If no fallacy is committed, simply write "Not a fallacy."

*   **1.** To put it bluntly but fairly, anyone today who doubts that the variety of life on this planet was produced by a process of evolution is simply ignorant—inexcusably ignorant. —Daniel Dennett, *Darwin's Dangerous Idea* (New York: Simon and Schuster, 1995), p. 46

   2. Your Honor, it's true that I killed my parents. I fully admit that I murdered them in cold blood. But I should get a light sentence. After all, I *am* an orphan.

   3. As I travel around and talk to people, I find that many do not even know what genetic engineering is. Well, genetic engineering is best defined as the most recent in a long line of attempts on the part of human beings to play God. Of course, the proponents of genetic engineering overlook just one little fact: We humans are not God. And that's why genetic engineering is profoundly immoral.

*   **4.** All the really hot new thinkers are using principles from sociobiology. It's the new wave in ethics. So, you should accept the principles of sociobiology.

   5. Any politician who has lied to the nation is a person who has betrayed the public trust. Some U.S. presidents are politicians who have lied to the nation. Accordingly, some U.S. presidents are persons who have betrayed the public trust.

   6. Although they've certainly tried, scientists have not been able to demonstrate that ESP is a myth. So, ESP is probably real.

*   **7.** It is quite clear what the proponents of legalized euthanasia are seeking. Put simply, they are seeking the power to kill anyone who has a serious illness. And that is why I stand opposed to legalized euthanasia.

   8. All beautiful paintings are colorful objects. No charcoal drawings are beautiful paintings. Therefore, no charcoal drawings are colorful objects.

   9. So many people these days are against prayer in the public schools! Of course, the assumptions underlying this view include (a) that there is no God, (b) that only matter exists, and (c) that life is essentially meaningless. That is why we must fight against these people who seek to remove prayer from our public schools.

*   **10.** Professor Jackson, this paper merits at least a "B." I stayed up all night working on it. And if I don't get a "B," I'll be put on academic probation.

11. If consuming large quantities of alcohol damages one's liver, then consuming large quantities of alcohol is unhealthy. Consuming large quantities of alcohol damages one's liver. Hence, consuming large quantities of alcohol is unhealthy.

12. Of course it is reasonable to believe that we have been visited by extraterrestrial beings. After all, plenty of skeptics have tried, but none has been able to disprove that such visitations have occurred.

* **13.** Since you became a member of this club, you've raised quite a ruckus about women's rights. And I know you sincerely believe in feminism. But if you go on holding these extreme views, I will see to it that you are never voted in as an officer of this club. And you know I can make good on that threat. I hope you follow me: Your feminist views are too radical and need to be toned down.

14. The future free actions of humans can be known in advance only if time travel is possible. But you're a fool if you think time travel is possible. So, it is not true that the future free actions of humans can be known in advance.

15. If Norway is the world leader in per-capita electrical power generation, then the U.S.A. is not the world leader. And indeed the U.S.A. is not the world leader in per-capita electrical power generation. Therefore, Norway is the world leader in per-capita electrical power generation.

* **16.** Dr. Herzheimer has written essays criticizing self-help books from the standpoint of logic and science. I realize Dr. Herzheimer is a famous philosopher, but I think it's immature and cold-hearted to criticize people who are trying to help others get their lives together. Thus, I myself give no credence to Dr. Herzheimer's work whatsoever.

17. Republicans are people who believe that the rich should get richer and the poor poorer. They are against welfare and against taxes for people who can well afford to pay taxes. Republicans also hold that the only good immigrants are either wealthy or well educated. Thus, I strongly urge you not to be a Republican.

18. Excuse me, Mr. Smith, did I hear you correctly? Did you say that boxing should be banned? Sure, boxing is a little dangerous, but real men love boxing. Therefore, boxing should not be banned.

* **19.** Mr. Johnson argues that we should stop eating meat. But did you know that Mr. Johnson owns the Vegetables Forever Produce Company? Oh yes, he stands to gain a lot, financially speaking, if the rest of us become vegetarians. I think we can safely ignore his line of argument.

20. Nowadays, everybody who is anybody knows that zumba is the coolest way to keep fit.

21. Given that most commuters are willing to ride trains, light rail is a good solution to gridlock on the highways. But most commuters are not willing to ride trains. Hence, light rail is not a good solution to gridlock on the highways.

* **22.** I do not have very much information about Mr. Reed, but there is nothing in his file to disprove that he's an eco-terrorist. So, he probably is one.

23. I find it mildly amusing that Mr. and Mrs. Billings are advocating school reforms. But I certainly do not see any reason to take their proposal seriously. Both of them were poor students in high school.

24. Intelligent, refined people insist on the best wines. And our Old World Merlot is the best red wine available. Obviously, Old World Merlot is for you.

***25.** The school needs a football team. I hope you agree. One thing I can tell you for sure: If you want to fit in around here, you'll see this issue the way the rest of us do. And we all think the school needs a football team.

26. Robert, I've heard you're a climate change denier. So, let me tell you something. Around here, we know climate change is real and manmade. And we have ways of making climate change deniers see the error of their ways. The last denier who passed through this town suddenly saw the light after some of the boys had a little "talk" with him one night. I hope these facts will clarify things for you. You do understand that climate change is real, don't you?

27. Yes, Jill argues for deconstruction. But her mind is so open, her brains are falling out. You can safely ignore whatever she has to say.

***28.** In 1742, Christian Goldbach conjectured that every even number greater than 2 is the sum of two primes. Mathematicians have been trying to prove Goldbach's conjecture ever since, but no one has succeeded in doing so. After two and a half centuries, I think we can safely conclude that Goldbach was wrong.

29. It's interesting how the family of David Walker, the African American shot by Seattle police, complains that none of the jurors at the fact-finding hearing are black but has no problem that their attorney suing the city for $5 million is not black. [Assume that the implicit conclusion is this: The complaint is groundless.] —Letter to the *Seattle Times*, July 19, 2000, B7

30. After centuries of trying, no one has been able to prove that God exists. The attempt seems to be futile. So, at this point, I think we can safely conclude that there is no God.

PART B: More Formal and Informal Fallacies

Most of the following passages exemplify either a formal fallacy or an informal fallacy. If a formal fallacy is committed, identify the argument form, using capital letters to stand for terms or statements (e.g., "All A are B; all C are B; so, all A are C"). If an informal fallacy is committed, name the type of fallacy and explain why the passage is an example of that type. (In the case of ad hominem fallacies, indicate whether they are abusive, circumstantial, or *tu quoque* in type.) If no fallacy is committed, simply write "Not a fallacy." *Note:* In some cases, more than one fallacy is exemplified in a single passage; where this occurs, identify all the fallacies.

* **1.** What is the prochoice view? This: It is permissible to kill innocent human beings at will as long as they are small and helpless. By implication, then, the prochoice view would permit the slaughter of children on a wide scale. And that is why we should all oppose the prochoice view.

2. Your Honor, my client does not deserve a year in prison. He has small children that need a father and a wife that needs a husband.

3. You really think that drugs should be legalized? Think again. Dad will cut you out of the inheritance if you go on thinking like that. That should make it clear to you just how far off base your views really are.

* 4. Clairvoyance is the alleged ability to "see" with the mind's eye what cannot literally be seen. For example, some clairvoyants have claimed to "see" the death of a loved one from whom they were separated by many miles. Of course, you can imagine the kind of attention clairvoyants receive from the media, not to mention the money they can squeeze out of weak-minded people who are curious about the paranormal. Thus, I think the alleged reports of clairvoyance are just hype.

5. Joe, I know you think that the new electronics plant should be located in Seattle. Well, you're wrong. It should be located in Spokane. How do I know? Joe, I'm your boss, right? And you're up for a promotion next month, right? You want the promotion, right? Well, then, the conclusion is obvious: The new electronics plant should be located in Spokane.

6. Smoking cigarettes can harm one's health. So, it's best to avoid smoking, assuming one wants to be healthy.

* 7. No one has ever shown that miracles do not happen. Therefore, miracles do happen.

8. Yates is guilty of murder, assuming that he pleads guilty. But Yates does not plead guilty. Therefore, Yates is not guilty of murder.

9. You have argued that it is wrong for me to hunt deer. Well, you eat hamburger, and that involves the killing of cows. Moreover, it is obvious that there is no moral difference between killing cows and killing deer, so your argument is unsound.

* 10. The poor people in many Third World countries are malnourished and highly susceptible to disease. These people are in need of help, for their poverty is so great that many of them can do little to help themselves. But many Americans have discretionary income well beyond what they need personally, and these (relatively) wealthy Americans could help the poor in the Third World—at least to some extent. Moreover, from a moral point of view, it is good to help those who really need help. So, from a moral point of view, it would be a good thing for these (relatively) wealthy Americans to help the poor in the Third World.

11. No one has been able to demonstrate that astrology is nonsense. For this reason, I have concluded that astrology is not nonsense—rather, it is an insightful way of viewing our lives and the world around us.

12. No nuclear power plants are pollution-free forms of generating electrical power. Some waterwheels are pollution-free forms of generating electrical power. It follows that no nuclear power plants are waterwheels.

* 13. Suzanne won the race only if she beat Marilyn. And Suzanne won the race. Therefore, Suzanne beat Marilyn.

14. Ingres' *Odalisque* is not a sexist painting. Of course, I admit that *Odalisque* is sexist if it treats women as sex objects. But you'd have to be the worst sort of uptight prude to think that *Odalisque* treats women as sex objects. In addition, no one has ever proven that *Odalisque* treats women as sex objects. Therefore, *Odalisque* does not treat women as sex objects, and so it is not sexist.

*15. No contracts that contain a deliberate lie are legal contracts. All legal contracts are binding contracts. So, no contracts that contain a deliberate lie are binding contracts.

16. I don't deserve a speeding ticket, officer. Yes, I admit I was doing 60 in a school zone. But I've had a really rough day. I was angry about some stuff that happened at work. Everybody has to let off some steam once in a while, don't they? Give me a break.

17. Your Honor, the witness has just lied to the court three times. This has been verified by the tape recordings and by the reports of all of the other witnesses. Therefore, I submit that the witness's testimony is untrustworthy.

18. My dear sir, there are two reasons why you should agree that the money in your wallet is rightfully mine. First, I've had a lot of bad luck in my life, but you obviously enjoy health, wealth, and prosperity. So, if you are a man of compassion, you'll see that I deserve the wallet. Second, since I'm pointing a gun at your head, you owe your very life to my generosity and patience.

19. According to mind–body dualism, human beings have both a body and a nonphysical soul. But if mind–body dualism is true, then new energy is introduced from the soul into the brain. But dualists have never been able to show that new energy is introduced from the soul into the brain. Thus, we can safely conclude that new energy is not introduced from the soul into the brain. Furthermore, it's just crazy to suppose that a nonphysical thing (i.e., the soul) can have causal interactions with a physical thing (i.e., the brain). This, too, supports the claim that new energy is not introduced from the soul into the brain. I must conclude that mind–body dualism is not true.

*20. My opponent, the evolutionist, denies that we have our origin in God. Rather, according to the evolutionist, we humans have our origin in lower forms of life. Instead of having the dignity of being made in the image of God, we have the ignominy of being "made" in the image of apes, snakes, and bacteria.

21. You bet I'm in favor of stiff punishments for violent crimes. After all, punishment deters crime—no doubt about that. Yes, I'm aware that many bleeding-heart liberals have tried to prove that punishment doesn't really deter crime, but their feeble efforts have all failed miserably. It's just plain common sense that punishment deters crime.

22. If you want to die young, be one of those animal rights advocates. I mean, it's your business, but around here, folks don't have much patience with stupidity. Now, I know you really don't want to die young. So, don't be an animal rights advocate. And don't say I didn't warn you.

23. Wow! Just when you thought every state agency that possibly could have overdosed on dumb pills, here comes yet another. Kudos to Washington State Fish and Wildlife for opening the Lake Washington sockeye season on July 4th. They must have trundled to the very depths of their department to find a mind so brilliant as to make this kind of decision. Why would someone mix 3,000 boatloads of fishermen who are chomping at the bit to finally have a viable fishery in their front yard with several thousand people trying to launch their boats to attend the fireworks display on Lake Union? —Letter to the *Seattle Times*, July 5, 2000, B7

* **24.** Everyone is selfish; everyone is doing what he believes will make himself happier. The recognition of that can take most of the sting out of accusations that you're being "selfish." Why should you feel guilty for seeking your own happiness when that's what everyone else is doing, too?

25. When the candidate was asked whether he'd name a running mate who was opposed to school prayer, he answered: "It would be presumptive for someone who has yet to earn his party's nomination to be picking a vice president. However, the main criterion I would use in choosing a running mate would be whether the person was capable of being president."

 ## **4.2 Fallacies Involving Ambiguity**

Arguments are sometimes flawed because they contain ambiguous words (phrases or statements) or because they involve a subtle confusion between two closely related concepts. These we will call *fallacies involving ambiguity*, and we will discuss four kinds of them.

Equivocation

We first discussed this fallacy in section 3.3. The **fallacy of equivocation** occurs when multiple meanings of a word (or phrase) are used in a context where validity requires a single meaning of that word (or phrase).

> The **fallacy of equivocation** occurs when multiple meanings of a word (or phrase) are used in a context where validity requires a single meaning of that word (or phrase).

Here is an example:

29. Only man is rational. But no woman is a man. Hence, no woman is rational.

Here, of course, the word "man" is used with two different meanings. In the first premise, it means "humans," but in the second premise, it means "male humans."

If we rewrite the argument making the two meanings explicit, the invalidity is apparent:

> **30.** Only humans are rational. No woman is a male human. So, no woman is rational.

The use of the single word "man" in argument (29) gives it a superficial appearance of validity. But our paraphrase, argument (30), indicates that in reality, the two meanings of the word "man" destroy the logical linkage between premises and conclusion. Etymologically, "equivocate" comes from two Latin words, one meaning "equal" or "same" and one meaning "voice" or "word." When one equivocates, one makes it sound as if the same word (or phrase) is being used with the same meaning throughout the argument, when, in fact, more than one meaning is present.

Is the following an example of equivocation?

> **31.** If you want to help me steal the car, you have a reason to do so. If you have a reason to steal the car, then you are justified in stealing the car. So, if you want to help me steal the car, then you are justified in stealing the car.

Yes. The phrase "have a reason to" is used in two different senses. In its first occurrence, "have a reason to" means, "have a motivating reason to, that is, have a motivation or desire to." In its second occurrence, "have a reason to" means, "there is some factor that wholly or partially justifies some behavior."

Now, let's consider a somewhat more subtle example of equivocation:

> **32.** These twins, Peter and William, are identical. If A and B are identical, then for any characteristic A has, B has it too. Peter is married to Sally. So, William is married to Sally.

This argument certainly looks valid. But it trades on an ambiguity in the term "identical." Philosophers distinguish between "qualitative identity" and "numerical identity." Two things are qualitatively identical when they share all of their intrinsic qualities. Two widgets made on the same assembly line are likely to be qualitatively identical, that is, virtual replicas of each other. Identical twins share most of their intrinsic qualities such as height, freckles, and eye color (although probably not absolutely all—as one could dye his hair). A and B are numerically identical if A is B, that is, if there is only one thing that has the names "A" and "B." No *two* things can be numerically identical with each other. The principle expressed in the second premise says that:

> **33.** If A and B are numerically identical, then for any characteristic A has, B has it too. (This principle is called "Leibniz's Law.")

So, to make the premises plausible and to make the equivocation clear, it would be best to translate argument 32 like this:

> **34.** Peter and William are the sort of twins who are (almost) qualitatively identical. If A and B are numerically identical, then for any characteristic A has, B has it too. Peter is married to Sally. So, William is married to Sally.

This paraphrase of the argument shows it to be clearly invalid.

Amphiboly

The **fallacy of amphiboly** occurs when multiple meanings of a sentence are used in a context where (a) validity requires a single meaning and (b) the multiple meanings are due to sentence structure (rather than the meaning of some words or phrases).

> The **fallacy of amphiboly** occurs when multiple meanings of a sentence are used in a context where (a) validity requires a single meaning and (b) the multiple meanings are due to sentence structure.

The ambiguity is often due to such infelicities as a missing comma, a dangling modifier, or an ambiguous antecedent of a pronoun. Here are some examples of such ambiguity:

> **35.** One morning I shot an elephant in my pajamas. How he got into my pajamas I'll never know. (Spoken by Groucho Marx in the movie *Animal Crackers*)
>
> **36.** Elephants: Stay off the Road. (On a road sign)
>
> **37.** Tuna biting off the coast of Florida. (Newspaper headline)

Such ambiguity is often the source of humor, but it can also mislead in less amusing ways. Here is an example:

> **38.** Author Myron Mobbins warns about the negative effects of subtle lies in his book *Liars Tell Lies*. So, given that Mobbins's book contains subtle lies, perhaps it is best not to read it.

Presumably, Mobbins is not warning people about subtle lies *that occur in his own book*; rather, in his book, he is warning people about the negative effects of subtle lies that originate from other sources. But the conclusion drawn in argument (38) results from a different interpretation of the syntactically flawed premise. Amphiboly often occurs when someone interprets a syntactically deficient statement in a way that was not intended by the original author (or speaker).

Here is another example of amphiboly:

39. You said you don't like her because she is beautiful. In that case, since you don't like her, I think you should reconsider marrying her.

The argument represented here by the speaker has a premise "I don't like her because she is beautiful," which has two meanings that need to be carefully distinguished. It could mean, "I dislike her because she is beautiful." (Compare, "I don't like driving behind the bus because of the diesel fumes.") Or it could mean, "It's not the case that I like her because of her beauty" (i.e., "My liking for her is caused by other qualities such as her intelligence and compassion"). In the absence of additional information, the arguer's interpretation is not justified, so (39) is an example of the fallacy of amphiboly.

Now, consider the following two arguments. Are both examples of amphiboly? How do you know?

40. We were disturbed to read in the *Times* that during the past five years many of the middle school students searched illegally carried firearms. Obviously, they should fire the school administrators for conducting these illegal searches.

41. I'm sure we can agree that mentally abnormal people, such as psychotics, should be hospitalized. They shouldn't be living on the streets, and they shouldn't be put in prison. However, we must be willing to apply this principle consistently. And consider this fact: Geniuses, such as Bobby Fischer, are mentally abnormal, for fewer than one in a million people have IQs as high as Fischer's. The conclusion is inescapable: Geniuses should be hospitalized.

Argument (40) is an example of amphiboly. Was it the searches or the carrying of firearms that was illegal? The arguer unjustifiably takes it to be the searches. Argument (41), on the other hand, is not an example of amphiboly; rather, it's an example of equivocation. The key phrase is "mentally abnormal." In its first use, "mentally abnormal" means "mentally ill." In its second use, "mentally abnormal" means simply "departing from the norm (or statistically rare)." Argument (41) is not an amphiboly because the ambiguity involved is not due to a structural flaw but simply due to the double meaning of the phrase "mentally abnormal."

In thinking about both equivocation and amphiboly, one question that may occur to you is why we are entitled to conclude that the arguer is using a term in two different senses in different parts of the argument. Wouldn't it be more charitable to interpret the arguer as using a single term consistently throughout the argument? Well, sometimes the context suggests that he or she is not. For example, in some of the previous examples, the arguer is using as a premise a claim that was made by someone else. In that case, we need to see what the original speaker meant by it.

In some cases, to interpret a term consistently throughout the argument would mean that one of the claims in which it occurs is obviously false. For example, recall (4):

> **4.** My grandfather Joe is a child. No child should have to work for a living. So, Grandfather Joe should not have to work for a living.

The word "child" is ambiguous. To interpret the argument as consistent, we would have to read the first premise as saying, "My grandfather Joe is an immature human being (under the age of, say, 15) or to read the second premise as saying, "Anyone who is the offspring of human parents should not have to work for a living." Both of these claims are obviously false. So, it is slightly more charitable to interpret the argument as invalid with true premises.

Sometimes the choice is more difficult. In such cases, it may be fairer to note that the argument can be interpreted in three (or even four) different ways (two different interpretations for each of two ambiguous occurrences) and then to go through each option and see if any of them is valid with plausible premises. If we find that each of the arguments either is invalid or has a false premise, then we can reject the original argument. For example, consider (31) earlier. The phrase "have a reason to" was, we said, ambiguous. One consistent reading of the argument is this:

> **31a.** If you want to help me steal the car, you are motivated to do so. If you are motivated to steal the car, then you are justified in stealing the car. So, if you want to help me steal the car, then you are justified in stealing the car.

It seems clear that we are not justified in doing whatever we want to do.

A second consistent reading is:

> **31b.** If you want to help me steal the car, there is some consideration that justifies you in doing so. If there is some consideration that justifies you in stealing the car, then you are justified in stealing the car. So, if you want to help me steal the car, then you are justified in stealing the car.

In this case, the first premise seems clearly false. The third interpretation, which uses two different interpretations of "has a reason" in the first and second premises, is, as we saw earlier, invalid. (There is, of course, a fourth interpretation, which uses two different interpretations of "has a reason" but uses the second in the first premise and the first in second premise. This interpretation has two false premises and is also invalid.)

The presence of an ambiguous word or phrase in an argument does not guarantee that the argument equivocates. For example, consider the old argument:

> **42.** All men are mortal.
>   Socrates is a man.
> So, Socrates is mortal.

"Man" is ambiguous between "human being" and "male human being." But both interpretations of this argument that use "man" consistently throughout are sound. These are the more charitable interpretations of the argument, so it is best not to treat this as an instance of equivocation.

Composition

The **fallacy of composition** involves either (a) an invalid inference from the nature of the parts to the nature of the whole or (b) an invalid inference from attributes of members of a group to attributes of the group itself.

> The **fallacy of composition** involves either (a) an invalid inference from the nature of the parts to the nature of the whole or (b) an invalid inference from attributes of members of a group to attributes of the group itself.

Here is an example of (a):

43. Each of the parts of this airplane is very light. Therefore, the airplane itself is very light.

Of course, if enough light parts are conjoined, the airplane itself may be quite heavy, and so the argument is invalid. Here is another example of the parts-to-whole type of fallacy of composition:

44. Each player on the football team is outstanding. Hence, the team itself is outstanding.

Even if each of the players on a team is outstanding, the team itself may not be outstanding if there is a lack of teamwork or insufficient opportunity to practice together.

Not all inferences from part to whole are invalid. For example:

45. Each part of the machine weighs more than one pound, and the machine has five parts. Consequently, the machine itself weighs more than one pound.

Argument (45) is valid. But (43) and (44) make it clear that the following argument form is not in general valid: "Each part of X has attribute Y; therefore, X itself has attribute Y." What distinguishes (45) from (43) and (44)? Presumably, one important difference is that it is a necessary truth that an object does not weigh less than any of its parts. This means that it is impossible for the premise of (45) to be true while its conclusion is false. So, (45) is valid. This means that one cannot be sure an argument commits the fallacy of composition unless one examines the content of the argument, especially the attribute in question.

The second type of fallacy of composition is an invalid inference from attributes of members of a group to attributes of the group itself. Here is an example:

> **46.** Elephants eat more than humans. So, elephants taken as a group eat more than humans taken as a group.

This argument illustrates the traditional distinction between *distributive* and *collective* predication. In the premise "Elephants eat more than humans," the attribute of "eating more than" is predicated distributively; that is, each *individual* elephant is said to eat more than any *individual* human eats. In the conclusion, however, the attribute of "eating more than" is predicated collectively; that is, elephants *taken as a group* are said to eat more than humans *taken as a group*. Thus, although the premise of (46) is true, its conclusion is false simply because there are so many more humans than elephants.

The two forms of the fallacy of composition are related because the relationship of parts to a whole is analogous to the relationship of members to a group (or collective). However, these relationships are not identical. A whole must have its parts organized or arranged in a particular way. For instance, if we take an automobile apart and ship the parts to hundreds of different locations, the automobile no longer exists, but the collection of parts still exists.

The fallacy of composition is here classified as a fallacy of ambiguity because it often gains its persuasive force from a confusion of concepts. Consider again this example: "The team members are excellent; so the team is excellent." Although on reflection there is a clear distinction between the team members and the team, the two concepts are easily confused because the team is merely its members *organized in a certain way*. So, a less-than-clear grasp of the concepts involved may obscure the error in reasoning.

In some cases, it is a matter of controversy whether an argument exemplifies the fallacy of composition. For instance, some philosophers think the following argument is an example of the fallacy of composition but others do not:

> **47.** Each part of the universe is a dependent entity (i.e., depends for its existence on some other entity). So, the universe itself is a dependent entity.

The conclusion of argument (47) has been used by some philosophers to argue for the existence of God. But does the premise of (47) support the conclusion? Some philosophers doubt that the concept of dependence is understood well enough to legitimate a conclusion about the universe as a whole (even if each part of the universe *is* a dependent entity). This controversy has yet to be settled in a definitive way.

Division

The **fallacy of division** is the reverse of the fallacy of composition—it involves either (a) an invalid inference from the nature of the whole to the nature of the parts, or (b) an invalid inference from the nature of a group to the nature of its members.

> The **fallacy of division** involves either (a) an invalid inference from the nature of the whole to the nature of the parts or (b) an invalid inference from the nature of a group to the nature of its members.

Here is an example of the whole-to-part type of fallacy:

48. The airplane is heavy. So, each of its parts is heavy.

Of course, some of the parts of a heavy airplane may be very light. Thus, the argument is invalid. Here is another example of the whole-to-part variety of the fallacy of division:

49. The soccer team is excellent. Hence, each member of the team is excellent.

A team may be excellent because of teamwork and a few outstanding players and yet have members who are not themselves excellent players.

The fallacy of division does not always involve an inference from a whole to its parts. It may involve an inference from a group (or collective) to its members. For instance:

50. Grizzly bears are rapidly disappearing. So, Freddy, the grizzly bear at the zoo, must be rapidly disappearing.

This argument moves invalidly from a statement about grizzly bears (taken as a group) to a statement about a member of that group. The fallacy of division (like the fallacy of composition) is classified as a fallacy of ambiguity because it gains its persuasive force from a confusion of meanings or concepts. For instance, "grizzly bears" may mean "grizzly bears taken as group" or "individual grizzly bears." If one fails to distinguish these two meanings, one is readily taken in by the fallacy.

Note that, as in the case with composition, not all inferences from whole to part are invalid. For example:

51. This machine is small enough to fit in the trunk of the car. So, each of its parts is small enough to fit in the trunk of a car.

Example (51) is valid, and that is presumably because it is a necessary truth that no part of an object is bigger than the object itself. This again means that one cannot be sure that an argument commits the fallacy of division unless one examines the content of the argument.

Summary of Definitions

The **fallacy of equivocation** occurs when multiple meanings of a word (or phrase) are used in a context where validity requires a single meaning of that word (or phrase).

The **fallacy of amphiboly** occurs when multiple meanings of a sentence are used in a context where (a) validity requires a single meaning and (b) the multiple meanings are due to sentence structure.

The **fallacy of composition** involves either (a) an invalid inference from the nature of the parts to the nature of the whole or (b) an invalid inference from attributes of members of a group to attributes of the group itself.

The **fallacy of division** involves either (a) an invalid inference from the nature of the whole to the nature of the parts or (b) an invalid inference from the nature of a group to the nature of its members.

EXERCISE 4.2

PART A: Fallacies Involving Ambiguity Most of the following passages exemplify a fallacy introduced in this section, but some of the passages do not exemplify fallacies, and some exemplify a fallacy introduced in section 4.1. Identify all of the fallacies. In the case of equivocation and amphiboly, briefly explain the double meaning involved. Finally, if no fallacy is committed, simply write "not a fallacy."

* **1.** The leader of this new religious group preaches the following message: "We shall wear no clothes to distinguish ourselves from our Christian brethren." Therefore, this religious group should be opposed. For it advocates nudity.

 2. No member of the crew can lift over 100 pounds. Therefore, the entire crew cannot lift over 100 pounds.

 3. Monty is so much fun at a party! He's a real ham! But if he's a ham, then he is high in cholesterol. So, he is high in cholesterol.

* **4.** Every sentence in my book is well written. Accordingly, my book is well written.

 5. The Acme Corporation is very important. So, since Ms. Griggs works for the Acme Corporation, she must be very important.

 6. Your Honor, the witness said he saw a photograph of the defendant lying on the coffee table. Therefore, the defendant must have lain on the coffee table at some point.

* **7.** The average Brazilian has 1.9 children. Maria is an average Brazilian. So, Maria has 1.9 children.

 8. Each brick in the building is larger than my logic textbook, and the building is composed of many bricks. It follows that the building itself is larger than my logic textbook.

9. Nuclear weapons are more destructive than conventional weapons. Therefore, over the course of human history, more destruction has resulted from nuclear weapons (taken as a group) than from conventional weapons (taken as a group).

*10. If I have a strong desire to believe in free will, then I have a motive for believing in free will. And if I have a motive for believing in free will, then I have a reason for believing in free will. However, if I have a reason for believing in free will, then I have evidence for my belief in free will. Therefore, if I have a strong desire to believe in free will, then I have evidence for my belief in free will.

11. You have asked our organization to contribute to the Krazykids Preschool fundraiser. I am sorry to inform you that we are unable to honor your request. We realize that you are under the impression that our previous director promised you that we would make a contribution this year. But what the previous director actually said was, "We promise to give $1000 and our best wishes to St. Mary's Hospital and Krazykids Preschool." So, St. Mary's gets the $1000, and Krazykids gets our best wishes.

12. Each cell in the human body is invisible. Therefore, the human body itself is invisible.

*13. Each square inch of the car's surface is red. It follows that the whole car is red.

14. If Maffeo Barberini was Pope Urban VIII, then if Pope Urban VIII had Galileo placed under house arrest, Maffeo Barberini had Galileo placed under house arrest. Maffeo Barberini was Pope Urban VIII. It follows that if Pope Urban VIII had Galileo placed under house arrest, Maffeo Barberini had Galileo placed under house arrest.

15. America is still a free country, right? You bet it is. That being so, how can you doubt that we are free to choose between good and evil? Every real American is free and knows it. I'm starting to wonder what country you're from.

*16. Immigrants come from every country in the world. Ms. Bashir is an immigrant. Consequently, Ms. Bashir comes from every country in the world.

17. Dear Sir: It is the duty of the *Williamsburg Post* to print all the news that's in the public interest. And whether you like it or not, there is tremendous public interest in clairvoyance. Hence, the *Post* would be remiss were it not to print articles on clairvoyance. —The Editors

18. Sparrows are plentiful. Pete, my pet bird, is a sparrow. Therefore, Pete is plentiful.

*19. All men are not losers. Therefore, all losers are nonmen.

20. According to the Declaration of Independence, all men are created equal. Well, I disagree. It is obvious that human beings differ in important respects from birth, for example, in intelligence, athletic ability, and physical attractiveness. Therefore, contrary to the Declaration of Independence, it is not the case that human beings are created equal.

21. Gareth Peterson argues that the war in Afghanistan is unjust. He claims that American military personnel are largely unable to distinguish friend from foe, and so they engage in a lot of indiscriminate killing. But Peterson is an embittered veteran of the conflict in Afghanistan. So, his argument has little value.

* **22.** Piet Mondrian's famous painting, *Composition with Red, Blue, and Yellow,* is made up of a number of distinct rectangles, each of which is brightly colored and beautiful. Hence, the painting itself is beautiful.

23. People do what they want to do. You said you wanted to go to the party, but in fact you stayed home to study for your logic exam. So, you didn't really want to go to the party—what you really wanted to do was to study for the logic exam.

24. We Americans have got to get rid of the Electoral College! Why? Well, this is supposed to be a democracy, but it's not a democracy and never has been. As long as we have an electoral college, a presidential candidate can win the popular vote and lose the election. And that's not democracy. Furthermore, in a democracy, each person's vote counts equally. But again, as long as we have an electoral college, the votes of some people count more than the votes of others. Is that democracy? No way. Now, you do believe in democracy, don't you? Of course you do; all good people do.

* **25.** According to the *Seattle Times,* this year the state of Washington will not issue parking permits to fish. So, I guess the salmon won't be allowed to park anywhere this year.

26. If Edwin Hubble is an astronomer, then he must necessarily be a scientist. Edwin Hubble is an astronomer. So, Hubble must necessarily be a scientist. But if Hubble must necessarily be a scientist, then he has no choice but to be a scientist. Consequently, Hubble has no choice but to be a scientist.

27. Dear Editor: I am writing to voice my opposition to the proposed light rail system, which is supposed to solve the traffic problems in Seattle. First, do the math. The project will cost $3.5 billion. If you divide by ridership predictions, the cost per ride over the first 10 years of operation will be $12.13. Apparently, backers of light rail are a bunch of fat cats with no conception of how the other half lives! Second, no one has proved that the proposed light rail system will solve the traffic problem. So, we have a proposal that is (a) outrageously expensive and (b) won't even solve the problem it's supposed to solve. The sooner we get a better plan for dealing with the traffic issue, the better.

* **28.** That which can not-be at some time is not. Therefore, if everything can not-be, then at one time there was nothing in existence. —St. Thomas Aquinas, *Summa Theologica* (I, Q. 2. Art. 3), in Anton C. Pegis, ed., *Introduction to St. Thomas Aquinas* (New York: Random House, 1948), p. 26

29. God is love. Love is a character trait. Therefore, God is a character trait.

30. The students at Seattle Pacific University are mostly female. Pat is a student at Seattle Pacific. So, Pat is mostly female.

* **31.** I read in the *Seattle Times* that most traffic accidents occur within 5 miles of your home. Now, given this fact, I'm forced to conclude that it would be a

good idea for you to relocate to someplace *more than 5 miles* distant from your home.

32. For Communication 101, I'm required to give a speech on drugs. But I am personally opposed to using drugs for any reason, so I think the professor is being unfair. I mean, sure, like most people, I've wondered what it would be like to be on drugs, but I shouldn't have to violate my personal ethical standards in order to meet the class requirements.

33. I'm sorry to hear that many of the bars tested illegally sell alcohol to people under 21. I infer that the governor should put a stop to such illegal testing.

*34. According to the letter we received, your previous employer recommends you with no qualifications. But I'm afraid we here at the Grove Company hire only people that do have qualifications. So, there's really no point in our talking further.

35. In a recent sermon, Pastor Bob said that a good marriage takes more than just two people in love. I found the sermon quite disturbing. Apparently Pastor Bob no longer believes in monogamy.

PART B: Equivocation For more examples of equivocation, see Exercise 3.3, Part A.

4.3 Fallacies Involving Unwarranted Assumptions

Some errors in reasoning result when the arguer makes an *unwarranted* assumption. An unwarranted assumption is one that, in context, stands in need of support. And because the support has not been provided, the assumption is illegitimate or unjustified, thus undermining the force of the argument. However, the unwary audience may not notice that an unwarranted assumption has been made, in which case the argument may be persuasive, although it *should not* be persuasive, and would not be to an ideally alert and rational audience.

Begging the Question (Petitio Principii)

The fallacy of **begging the question** (or *petitio principii fallacy*) occurs when an argument assumes the point to be proved. Begging the question is also known as *arguing in a circle*. (The Latin expression *petitio principii* means roughly "begging the first principle." It is pronounced variously but may be pronounced as "peh-TIT-ee-o prin-KIP-ee-ee.")

The fallacy of **begging the question** (or *petitio principii* fallacy) occurs when an argument assumes the point to be proved.

Here is an example:

52. The defendant is not guilty of the crime, for she is innocent of having committed it.

The conclusion of this argument is merely a slightly rephrased version of the premise. So, the conclusion cannot be false given that the premise is true. And hence, argument (52) is valid. Therefore, if the premise is, as a matter of fact, true, then the argument is sound (by definition). Still, even if (52) is sound, one can see that it is defective in that it *assumes the point to be proved*.

The phenomenon of begging the question is interesting from the standpoint of logical theory, for it shows us that ultimately we want something more than valid arguments *with true premises*. But what is that something more? Here, we must keep in mind the two basic purposes for arguing: (a) convincing others and (b) discovering truth. From the standpoint of convincing others, we need premises that are somehow more acceptable to them than the conclusion. Of course, it's one of the facts of life that we cannot always convince others. As the old saying goes, "Convince a man against his will, he's of the same opinion still." But insofar as we wish to use an argument to persuade a person or group on a given issue, we need to employ premises that are more plausible to that person or group than the conclusion. And what's "more plausible" is, at least to some extent, relative to the person or group.

We use arguments not only to convince others but also to discover truth. And arguments that beg the question are flawed from this perspective as well because one cannot reasonably claim to discover a truth *by inference* when that truth is itself included in the premises of one's argument. For one to discover a given truth via argument, each premise must be a different statement from the conclusion. Moreover, we usually want premises that we (rightly) take to be more probable than the conclusion before considering the argument.*

In sum, both from the standpoint of convincing others and from the standpoint of discovering truth, an argument that begs the question is deeply flawed. This is not to deny, of course, that question-begging arguments *do* sometimes convince a person or group. But such arguments *should not* be convincing because they illegitimately assume the point to be proved.

Does the following argument beg the question?

53. Everyone must be allowed to speak his or her mind because otherwise freedom of speech would be violated.[4]

The premise, written out more explicitly, says that if someone were not allowed to speak his or her mind, then freedom of speech would be violated. The word

---

*We say "usually" because sometimes a conclusion is well known on grounds independent of the premises of the argument, and yet the argument may be helpful from the standpoint of discovering the truth because it shows that the conclusion is supported by *more than one* line of evidence.

"violated" presumably signals something that *should not* happen, and this being so, the premise of the argument is similar in content to the conclusion. Is the premise better known than the conclusion? It's hard to see any good reason for thinking so. Thus, the argument seems to beg the question.

It is not always immediately obvious whether an argument involves a fallacy of begging the question. Consider the following case:

> **54.** God exists because the Bible says so. But how do I know that what the Bible says is true? Because it is God's Word.

In well-crafted form, argument (54) would look like this:

> **55.** 1. The Bible is God's Word.
> So, 2. What the Bible says is true. [from 1]
>   3. The Bible says that God exists.
> So, 4. God exists. [from 2 and 3]

None of the premises here simply *restates* the conclusion that God exists. But the first premise (all by itself) *presupposes* that God exists. Therefore, the argument seems to beg the question.

Here's another example:

> **56.** God does not exist. Why? Because natural selection is true, and according to natural selection, all species came into being by purely blind, natural forces. How do I know natural selection is true? Well, it is the best scientific theory. "Scientific theories" of course, by definition, exclude any supernatural claims or assumptions.

In well-crafted form, argument (56) would look like this:

> 1. No supernatural or theological theory is true.
> So, 2. The best explanation for the order in the universe is natural selection.
> So, 3. Natural selection is true.
> So, 4. God does not exist.

The first premise and the conclusion do not say exactly the same thing. But the first premise presupposes that God does not exist. So, this argument seems to beg the question too.

Sometimes, there is reasonable disagreement about whether an argument assumes the point to be proved. For one thing, there can be borderline cases because the extent to which a premise contains the information in the conclusion is a matter of degree. Furthermore, this entire issue is complicated by the fact that the premises of a *valid* argument, taken together, *must contain* the information in the conclusion. Ultimately, to identify a fallacy of begging the question, we need to determine whether each premise, taken by itself, is better known or more reasonably believed than the conclusion of the argument. If a given premise is similar in content to the conclusion but is *not* better known (or more reasonably believed) than the conclusion, then the argument begs the question. But there will sometimes be reasonable disagreement about whether a given premise is better known (or more reasonably believed) than the conclusion of the argument.

False Dilemma

The **false dilemma** fallacy occurs when one uses a premise that unjustifiably reduces the number of alternatives to be considered.

> The fallacy of **false dilemma** occurs when one uses a premise that unjustifiably reduces the number of alternatives to be considered.

For example, the arguer may assume, without justification, that there are only two possible alternatives, when in fact there are three or more. Consider the following argument:

> **57.** I'm tired of all these young people criticizing their own country. What I say is this, "America—love it or leave it!" And since these people obviously don't want to leave the country, they should love it instead of criticizing it.[5]

The argument presupposes that there are only two options: We can love America (uncritically) or we can emigrate. But there seem to be other possibilities. For example, surely it is morally permissible for one to respect one's country (i.e., respect its laws and traditions) without loving it (assuming that loving one's country involves being especially fond of it).

Notice that the fallacy of false dilemma does not involve an invalid inference. Given that I have just two options ("love it" or "leave it"), and given that one of these ("leave it") is ruled out, I must take the other. That is simply an instance of the valid argument form, disjunctive syllogism. Thus, as in the case of begging the question, the fallacy of false dilemma consists in assuming something without appropriate warrant or justification. In the case of a false dilemma, the arguer assumes that a certain list of alternatives is complete when it isn't. Here is a second example:

> **58.** Either everyone should pay exactly the same amount of income tax—like all members pay the same fee to join a country club—or else we are entitled to view the rich as a mere means, a resource to feed the rest of the population as a whale might feed a whole fishing village. Now, obviously, the latter view is completely immoral. So, everyone should pay exactly the same amount of income tax.

This argument ignores or overlooks several alternatives. For example, one might advocate a flat tax rate according to which everyone pays the same percentage of his or her income. Or one might advocate a progressive system of taxation that taxes the wealthy at a higher rate than the poor, on the grounds that government, and hence the taxes that support government, make it possible for the rich to earn what they earn. This latter approach can be combined with an upper limit on levels of taxation, say at 50 percent. Such an approach would not simply involve regarding the rich as a mere means.

We can't identify a false dilemma unless we can specify at least one alternative that has been ignored. This is not always easy. Consider the following example:

> **59.** Either your reasoning in any given case is based on an assumption or you have no place to start in your reasoning. If your reasoning is based on an assumption, then your conclusions are no more certain than a mere assumption. And if your conclusions are no more certain than a mere assumption, you do not gain knowledge by reasoning. Of course, if you have no place to start in your reasoning, then you are unable to make any inferences, and hence (once again) you do not gain knowledge by reasoning. Therefore, you do not gain knowledge by reasoning.

A chain of inferences has to start somewhere. And it seems that one cannot always defend one's premises with further arguments. Apparently, then, some of one's premises will be unsupported by further statements. Let us call these "first premises." Do first premises have the status of mere assumptions? If so, it would appear that all our reasoning is based on mere assumptions, in which case our reasoning never yields knowledge.

Many philosophers think there is a class of statements that do not *need* to be supported by further statements to be known or well grounded. But how do such statements differ from mere assumptions? How can a statement be known, warranted, or well grounded without being based on further statements? Here, some philosophers have called attention to allegedly self-evident statements, such as "No circles are squares." These are not *mere assumptions*, they claim, because to understand the statements is to see that they are true. Other philosophers have called attention to observation statements, such as "I see a piece of paper now." These are not *mere assumptions*, it is claimed, because they are somehow grounded in our sensory experience. But other philosophers have expressed doubts about the attempt to identify a privileged class of first premises. These philosophers are skeptical about the categories of self-evident statements and observation statements. The point here is simply that it takes philosophical creativity to explain how a first premise can be more than a mere assumption. Thus, it sometimes takes both creativity and hard intellectual work to make the case that a false dilemma fallacy has been committed.

Appeal to Unreliable Authority (Ad Verecundiam Fallacy)

The **appeal to unreliable authority** (or *ad verecundiam* fallacy) is an appeal to an authority when the reliability of the authority may be reasonably doubted. (*Ad verecundiam* is Latin for "appeal to authority.")

> The **appeal to unreliable authority** (or *ad verecundiam* fallacy) is an appeal to an authority when the reliability of the authority may be reasonably doubted.

A reliable authority is one who can be counted on, for the most part, to provide correct information in a given area. When an appeal to unreliable authority is made, the arguer assumes—*without sufficient warrant*—that the authority in question is reliable.

It is important to keep in mind that an appeal to *reliable* authority is generally appropriate. For example, when we cite encyclopedias, dictionaries, textbooks, or maps, we make an appeal to the authority of experts. This makes perfectly good sense as long as we are appealing to authorities whose reliability is not in doubt. However, when there is legitimate doubt about whether an authority is reliable, then the appeal to authority is fallacious.

Ad verecundiam fallacies are common in advertising when celebrities who lack the relevant expertise endorse products. For example:

> **60.** Mike "Monster" Malone, left tackle for the Seattle Sea Lions, says that Chocolate Zonkers are a nutritional breakfast cereal. So, Chocolate Zonkers are a nutritional breakfast cereal.

Malone may be a fine athlete, but we need to know whether he is an expert in nutrition, and the argument leaves us in doubt on that point. Thus, an *ad verecundiam* fallacy has occurred.

A more subtle appeal to unreliable authority occurs when a well-known expert in one field is cited as an expert in another field even though he or she lacks expertise in it. This form of the fallacy is especially subtle if the two fields are related (at least in the minds of the audience). For example:

> **61.** Professor Barrett, the well-known astronomer, has done extensive research on distant galaxies. He points out that human bodies are composed of atoms that were once part of distant stars. According to Barrett, this gives human life a sense of drama and significance equal to that inherent in the world's great mythologies and theologies. Thus, Barrett corrects the common error of supposing that materialism reduces the drama or significance of human life.

Even if it *is* an error to suppose that materialism reduces the drama or significance of human life, the reasoning in argument (61) is flawed. An astronomer is an expert in the science of the stars and other heavenly bodies. So, as an astronomer, Professor Barrett is in a position to tell us that the atoms in our bodies once belonged to the stars. But his authority about these matters does not automatically transfer to such philosophical topics as the comparative merits of mythologies, theologies, or worldviews in general. Expertise in one area doesn't necessarily "rub off" on another.

Argument (61) also reminds us of another point to keep in mind when evaluating an appeal to authority—namely, that the appeal to authorities in matters of controversy is often problematic. After all, in such matters, the authorities themselves often disagree. And when this occurs, if we have no good reason to suppose that one authority is more likely to be correct than another, then the appeal to authority should be unconvincing.

It is important to keep in mind the relationship between *ad hominem* arguments and appeals to unreliable authorities. Just as we warned earlier that it is not a fallacy (not an *ad hominem* argument) to challenge an appeal to authority by pointing out that the authority is unreliable or untrustworthy, we should make the converse warning here. If someone who is not a reliable authority in some area offers an argument that is not itself an appeal to authority, it is not appropriate to point out the arguer's unreliability. To do so would be to commit the *ad hominem* fallacy. So, for example, if a lawyer writes a book that raises objections to evolutionary theory, it is inappropriate to reject his arguments on the grounds that he is not a biologist (unless, of course, he argues like this: "I'm an expert. Trust me on this matter!").

False Cause Fallacy

The **false cause fallacy** occurs when one possible cause of a phenomenon is assumed to be a (or the) cause although reasons are lacking for excluding other possible causes.

> The **false cause fallacy** occurs when one possible cause of a phenomenon is assumed to be a (or the) cause although reasons are lacking for excluding other possible causes.

This fallacy comes in various forms. Perhaps the most common form is called in Latin *post hoc, ergo propter hoc*, which means "after this, therefore because of this." This form of the false cause fallacy occurs whenever an arguer illegitimately assumes that because event X preceded event Y, X caused Y. Here is an example:

> **62.** Since I came into office two years ago, the rate of violent crime has decreased significantly. So, it is clear that the longer prison sentences we recommended are working.

The longer prison sentences may be a causal factor, of course, but the mere fact that the longer sentences preceded the decrease in violent crime does not prove this. Many other possible causal factors need to be considered. For example, have economic conditions improved? Are more jobs available? Have the demographics of the area changed so that the population of young men (statistically the group most likely to commit violent crimes) is smaller relative to the population as a whole? Has there been an increase in the number of police officers on patrol?

Consider another example of the false cause fallacy:

> **63.** Since sex education has become common, we've had a marked increase in promiscuity. So, sex education causes promiscuity.

Here, the arguer fails in two ways: (a) by ignoring other possible causal factors and (b) by failing to explain the alleged linkage between sex education and promiscuity. Regarding (a), it may be that promiscuity actually results from a third factor, such as the breakdown of the broadly Protestant sexual code that historically typified American attitudes. (This breakdown seems to have occurred gradually during the first half of the twentieth century and then to have accelerated rapidly during the 1960s and 1970s.) Regarding (b), the arguer ignores the possibility that the causation may go *from* the phenomenon of promiscuity *to* sex education rather than vice versa. Surely the reason many people advocate sex education is that they are concerned about the increase in sexual activity among young people and seek to mitigate its negative consequences. So, it may be that promiscuity gives rise to sex education rather than vice versa. Again, the main point is that we cannot rightly assume that sex education causes promiscuity merely on the grounds that it precedes an increase in promiscuity.

Not all false cause fallacies involve the unwarranted assumption that if X precedes Y, then X causes Y. For instance:

> **64.** The best professional athletes receive big salaries. Therefore, in order to guarantee that Smith will become one of the best professional athletes, we should give him a big salary.

Here the arguer assumes—without sufficient warrant—that if big salaries and outstanding athletic performance are correlated, the former causes the latter. But surely the causal relation goes in the reverse direction: Successful athletic performance (in conjunction with the popular demand for spectator sports) leads to big salaries for some athletes. One cannot turn a mediocre athlete into a star simply by paying him a big salary.

Another version of the false cause fallacy occurs when many causes are (or may well be) operative but one of them is illegitimately assumed to be the sole cause:

> **65.** The scores on standardized tests have been dropping for several decades. What accounts for this? Well, during these same decades, the average time a child spends watching TV (per day) has increased. So, the cause is obvious: Kids are watching too much TV when they need to be reading instead.

The increase in time spent watching TV is a likely contributor to a drop in scores on such standardized tests as the SAT. But insufficient evidence is provided for the conclusion that the time spent watching TV is the *sole* cause. Other factors may be at work, such as a decrease in parental involvement or deficiencies in the public school system.

One special variety of the false cause fallacy is the *slippery slope* fallacy. This fallacy occurs when the arguer assumes that a chain reaction will occur but there is insufficient evidence that one (or more) events in the chain will cause the others. The chain of causes is supposedly like a steep slope—if you take one step on the slope, you'll slide all the way down. And since you don't want to slide all the way down, don't take the first step. Here is an example:

> **66.** Never buy a lottery ticket. People who buy lottery tickets soon find that they want to gamble on horses. Next, they develop a strong urge to go to Las Vegas and bet their life savings in the casinos. The addiction to gambling gradually ruins their family life. Eventually, they die, homeless and lonely.

The links in this alleged chain are weak. This is not to say that gambling is a risk-free practice. It is only to say that, logically speaking, when causal connections are claimed, there needs to be sufficient evidence that the connections are genuine. And to claim that buying a lottery ticket will cause one to die homeless and lonely is plainly to make a claim that is insufficiently supported by the evidence.

Therapists sometimes call the slippery slope fallacy "catastrophizing." For example, a person's fears may lead him to think that a relatively minor incident will lead to utter catastrophe:

> **67.** I told a joke at the party. It flopped. So, everyone there thought I was a loser. So, I'll never be invited again. In fact, if word gets out, I won't be invited anywhere. And I'm sure they're all talking about my stupid joke. So, I've completely ruined my chances for a decent social life. There's nothing left for me now but years of loneliness and misery. How I wish I'd never told that joke!

Although this example is extreme, it is a common human tendency to make rash assumptions about causal chains. The slippery slope fallacy is alive and well in the human heart.

In closing our discussion of the false cause fallacy, it may be helpful to note that in the English language there are many different ways to indicate a causal connection. For example, *depending on the context,* the following words and phrases may express a causal claim:

A produces B	A makes B	A leads to B
A creates B	A accounts for B	A brings about B
A generates B	A determines B	A is the source of B
A results in B	A is the origin of B	A gives birth to B
A gives rise to B	A brings B to pass	B occurs by A's influence

This list is by no means exhaustive. The key point to bear in mind is this: Since causal claims can be expressed in many different ways in English, causal fallacies can occur when the word "cause" does not appear.

Complex Question

The **complex question fallacy** involves asking a question that illegitimately presupposes some conclusion alluded to in the question.

The **complex question fallacy** involves asking a question that illegitimately presupposes some conclusion alluded to in the question.

Here's a classic example:

> **68.** Have you stopped beating your wife?

If the respondent answers "Yes," he admits that he has beaten his wife in the past. If he answers "No," he seems to be admitting that he has beaten his wife in the past and that he continues to do so. To expose a fallacy of complex question, one must call into question what it presupposes. For instance, in this case, the response might be along these lines: "To put it mildly, your question is misleading; I have never beaten my wife."

It is important to notice that virtually any question has one or more presuppositions. Consider the following example:

> **69.** Who is the governor of Ohio?

Question (69) presupposes that Ohio has a governor, but there is nothing illegitimate about this presupposition. Presuppositions are illegitimate when they are unwarranted by the evidence (and hence open to reasonable doubt).

In many cases, a fallacy of complex question involves two questions, the presupposition being that a single answer will satisfy both:

70. Will you please be kind and loan me $100?

Of course, the assumption here is that being kind involves lending the money. Again, an effective response will involve isolating the unwarranted presupposition and challenging it—for instance, "Being kind is one thing, lending the money is another. Let's not confuse the two."

Note that a complex question is not the same thing as a *leading* question. A leading question strongly suggests an answer the questioner wants to elicit, but a leading question need not involve an unwarranted assumption. For example, consider the following courtroom exchange:

> *Attorney:* Is it true that on the afternoon of February 4 you saw the defendant enter the Starbucks Coffee Shop at the corner of Boston and Queen Anne Streets?
>
> *Witness:* Yes.
>
> *Attorney:* And is it true that you saw the defendant reach into his coat pocket and pull out a knife?
>
> *Witness:* Yes.
>
> *Attorney:* Did the knife have serrated edge?
>
> *Witness:* Yes.
>
> *Attorney:* Did the defendant point the knife at a man standing behind the cash register and say, "Open the cash register or die"?
>
> *Witness:* Yes.

In asking such questions, the attorney may not be making any unwarranted assumptions. But a more open-ended question, such as "Would you please describe what you saw on the afternoon of February 4?" would give the witness a chance to describe the events in his or her own words and would thus lessen the likelihood that the witness will simply provide coached answers.

Which of the following are complex questions?

71. Who is the king of France?

72. What time is it now?

73. Why is math so boring?

Question (71) is complex because it illegitimately presupposes that France has a king. Question (73) is complex because it involves the unwarranted assumption that mathematics is very boring—an assumption that would certainly be rejected by anyone with a genuine interest in mathematics. Question (72) is not complex; it presupposes that there is some way to tell time and that "now" is a time, but these presuppositions are surely warranted.

In conclusion, fallacies are errors in reasoning that tend to be psychologically persuasive. In this chapter, we have distinguished formal from informal fallacies, and focused on some of the more common types of informal fallacies. Knowing about and having names for these fallacies can protect you from being misled, but be careful in classifying arguments as fallacies. Some arguments that appear to share the pattern of named fallacies are not fallacious. Many arguments are fallacious even though they do not commit any of the fallacies named here.

As a final note of caution, there is some debate about just which patterns of reasoning count as fallacies. The kinds identified so far in this chapter are universally recognized as fallacious. Be warned, however, that occasionally, an author will invent a fallacy simply to demonize some view that he or she disagrees with. By labeling a claim or argument form fallacious, the author is trying to make you think it's an error in reasoning that can be dismissed without much reflection, when in fact the argument may be sound and plausible, or, at the very least, the issue may be controversial, and may require substantive argument to show that the claim is false. Two historically important philosophical examples of this are "the intentional fallacy" and the "is-ought fallacy." The (so-called) intentional fallacy is an argument from the claim that the author or poet intended a certain interpretation of her work to the conclusion that this is the correct interpretation of the work. The theory that the author's intention constitutes the meaning of the work is a substantive theory that requires significant argument to refute and cannot simply be dismissed as fallacious. The (so-called) is-ought fallacy is an argument that proceeds from nonmoral premises to moral conclusions. If there are necessary truths connecting nonmoral facts to moral conclusions, then such arguments are not invalid. To demonstrate that such necessary truths do not exist, one needs to do more than simply label such arguments as fallacies. So, as always, be vigilant!

Summary of Definitions

The fallacy of **begging the question** (or *petitio principii* fallacy) occurs when an argument assumes the point to be proved.

The fallacy of **false dilemma** occurs when one uses a premise that unjustifiably reduces the number of alternatives to be considered.

The **appeal to unreliable authority** (or *ad verecundiam* fallacy) is an appeal to an authority when the reliability of the authority may be reasonably doubted.

The **false cause fallacy** occurs when one possible cause of a phenomenon is assumed to be a (or the) cause although reasons are lacking for excluding other possible causes.

The **complex question fallacy** involves asking a question that illegitimately presupposes some conclusion alluded to in the question.

EXERCISE 4.3

PART A: Identifying Fallacies Most of the following passages (but not all) exemplify fallacies. Many of the fallacies are fallacies involving unwarranted assumptions, but some are fallacies introduced in previous sections of this chapter. In some cases, a single passage exemplifies two or more fallacies. Identify all the fallacies that appear. In the case of fallacies involving an unwarranted assumption, identify the unwarranted assumption. If a passage does not contain a fallacy, simply write "not a fallacy."

* **1.** In a recent speech, the president of General Motors asserted that our country has drifted dangerously away from its religious and ethical moorings. In light of this pronouncement, the cheery optimism of the liberals is no longer reasonable.

  2. Every American is either a Republican or a Democrat. Dr. Porter is an American, but she is not a Republican. So, she must be a Democrat.

  3. On Monday, Bill drank scotch and soda and noticed that he got drunk. On Tuesday, Bill drank whiskey and soda and noticed that he got drunk. On Wednesday, Bill drank bourbon and soda and noticed that he got drunk. Bill concluded that soda causes drunkenness. —Adapted from Wesley Salmon, *Logic,* 3rd ed. (Englewood Cliffs, NJ: Prentice-Hall, 1984), p. 112

* **4.** If smoking is not harmful, then it is not wrong. And the tobacco companies say that smoking is not harmful. Therefore, smoking is not wrong.

  5. Sleeping pills work because they cause people to go to sleep.

  6. Left-turn signals frequently occur just before an automobile turns left. Right-turn signals frequently occur just before an automobile turns right. Consequently, turn signals cause automobiles to turn.

* **7.** Either men are superior to women or women are superior to men. Men are not superior to women. Hence, women are superior to men.

  8. Leonardo da Vinci's paintings are immoral if they incite rape. And the Reverend Posner states that da Vinci's paintings incite rape. Hence, da Vinci's paintings are immoral.

  9. Who's the fairest of them all, Scarlett Johansson or Beyonce?

* **10.** Obviously, humans have free will, since they have the power to make choices.

  11. Keegan is a reliable authority on military history. Keegan says that it was morally wrong for the Americans to fight in World War I. Hence, it was morally wrong for the Americans to fight in World War I.

  12. Day always follows night. The two are perfectly correlated. Therefore, night causes day.

* **13.** Last night we went to see *Hamlet.* The play was excellent since each scene was excellent. Plus, everybody who is anybody is raving about the play. I mean, the play was just excellent because it was really superb!

14. Either God created everything (including human beings) in six days or human life evolved gradually out of lower life forms over a very long period of time apart from any divine activity. But you are not a religious fanatic, so you know about fossils. And hence, you know that human life evolved gradually out of lower life forms over a very long period of time. Thus, God did not create everything in six days. I mean, I hate to break the news, but you are just about the last person on Earth who believes that humans were created by God.

15. Suicide is wrong for many reasons. First, because it involves killing. And killing is wrong because it is wrong to take a life. Second, suicide is wrong because it deeply wounds one's family and friends. And that is not cool—not cool at all. Third, suicide is the coward's way out. It's for weaklings who collapse the first time they run into a little adversity.

* **16.** Why was George W. Bush the worst U.S. president ever?

17. We could get control of the crime problem in the United States if we would just punish criminals harshly. In Saudi Arabia, for example, thieves get their hands chopped off. Murderers are immediately put to death. And the rate of crime in Saudi Arabia is much lower than the rate of crime in the United States. Therefore, harsh punishments would greatly reduce the rate of crime in the United States.

18. Time is composed of moments. Moments have no duration. Therefore, time has no duration. This rather surprising thesis is further supported by the following considerations: Time is illusory because time seems real but isn't real. Furthermore, down through the ages, the best and brightest people have always thought time was illusory.

* **19.** Without the discoveries of the great physicist Albert Einstein, the atomic bomb could not have been invented. And Einstein said that it was immoral for America to drop the atomic bomb on Hiroshima. Therefore, it was immoral for America to drop the atomic bomb on Hiroshima.

20. The largest slave revolt in U.S. history was one that occurred near New Orleans in 1811. Four or five hundred slaves were involved, lightly armed with cane knives, axes, and clubs. They wounded a plantation owner and killed his son. The revolt was put down by the U.S. Army, which attacked the slaves, killing 66 of them. This is all true, for I read about it in Howard Zinn's *A People's History of the United States* (New York: HarperCollins, 1995). And Dr. Zinn is a well-known historian.

21. What is the capital of Oregon?

* **22.** Gay rights activists claim that these marriages should be allowed because it doesn't hurt anyone, but it could start a chain reaction that destroys the whole idea of marriage. If someone wants to marry his dog, why shouldn't he be able to? What if someone wants to marry their brother or parent? What if someone wants to marry their blow-up doll or have 10 wives? What if someone wants to marry a tree, a corpse, herself? Let's put a stop to this madness before it starts.

23. Scientists have shown that a person loses a very small but measurable amount of weight at the time of death. This weight loss is probably due to the soul's leaving the body at that time. What else could account for this phenomenon? Here we have unexpected scientific evidence for the existence of an immaterial soul.

24. Violent crime rates have decreased in the last two decades. Abortion became more widespread roughly 20 years before that. We can only conclude that abortion has lowered the violent crime rate.

***25.** I have worn these socks to the last five baseball games. Each time, I've gotten a base hit. So, these are my lucky socks. I play better when I wear them.

26. Why is California the best place to live? Well, of course, it's very beautiful. And there are many job opportunities. But most important of all, California is a very progressive state in every way—so many important new trends begin there!

27. I warned those boys not to stand on Prince Valdinsky's grave. He was murdered, you know. And when he was being buried, his mother put a curse on anyone who showed disrespect for his grave. I was there—it was a very eerie thing to watch. Anyway, those boys wouldn't listen, and now look at them, all broken up from that automobile crash. I tell you, that curse worked!

***28.** Why is murder wrong? Because it takes away everything the victim has and everything he or she will ever have, including all the interesting experiences, fulfilling activities, and rewarding personal relationships.

29. The will states that the painting of a beautiful woman in the storage bin shall be given to the brother of the deceased. But this is not a painting of a beautiful woman in a storage bin. It is a painting of a beautiful woman walking across a field. Therefore, this painting does not belong to the brother of the deceased. Yes, I realize that the brother *thinks* the painting is his by right, but his mind is clouded by greed, and so his arguments are without force.

30. Either you approve of legalizing drugs or you disapprove. You can't have it both ways. Those who want to legalize drugs claim that we are losing the war on drugs. Indeed, they claim that we cannot win that war—the demand for drugs is high, and when demand is high, supply is inevitable. But we must not be taken in by this pseudo-reasoning. If we legalize drugs, they will be cheaper and easier to obtain. If drugs are cheaper and easier to obtain, more and more people will use drugs. As more people use drugs, the rate of absenteeism and work-related injuries will increase, productivity in the workplace will decline, and schools will be less effective in preparing students for the workforce. Thus, the economy will lose momentum and eventually collapse. Goodbye, America!

PART B: More Identifying Fallacies Most of the following passages (but not all) exemplify fallacies. Many of the fallacies are fallacies involving unwarranted assumptions, but some are fallacies introduced in previous sections of this chapter. In some cases, a single passage exemplifies two or more fallacies. Identify all the fallacies that appear. In the case of fallacies involving an unwarranted assumption, identify the unwarranted assumption. If a passage does not contain a fallacy, simply write "not a fallacy."

* **1.** Would you please be a good boy and eat your spinach?

   2. Please don't tell me you think that human vegetables should be kept on respirators! After all, brain-dead humans are already dead. We know this because they are not alive.

   3. Here's how to win the lottery: Consult an astrologer. How do I know this? Well, I was watching a TV program recently, and there was an interview with this very intelligent man who said that astrology is based on scientific principles. So, astrology is based on science. Furthermore, last week I took the advice of an astrologer who gave me a number based on my astrological sign. Using the number, I won the lottery. So, obviously, astrology works on things like the lottery.

* **4.** When it comes to criminal punishment, one must favor either rehabilitation or deterrence. The rehabilitationists think criminals are sick and need treatment. The deterrence crowd wants harsh punishments that will put a stop to crime. Since it is just silly to suppose that every shoplifter or car thief is mentally ill, the rehabilitationists are mistaken. Hence, the deterrence view is correct. And by the way, here's another way to see the same point: Rehabilitationists hold that even the most hardened criminals can be cured in a few sessions with a psychotherapist. But hardened criminals cannot be cured so easily! Once again, then, we see that rehabilitationists are mistaken.

   5. How do we know that there is life in other galaxies? Actually, that's not a difficult question. It's simply a matter of probabilities. With so many millions of planets out there, it's overwhelmingly likely that life has evolved on some of them, just as it has here on Earth.

   6. I've heard that St. Andrew's Episcopal Church is very wealthy. You are a member of St. Andrew's, so you must be wealthy. Anyway, I can tell you're wealthy because you have a lot of money.

* **7.** My psychology professor says that religious experience is generated out of the deep human need for a father figure, not by an encounter with an actual deity. So, religious experience is not really an experience of God.

   8. Surely Anthony loves me. For he told me he loves me, and he wouldn't lie to someone he loves.

   9. That young man was just fine until he read Kierkegaard's *Fear and Trembling*. It wasn't but a week or so later that he began to walk in his sleep and to emit those awful moans. Therefore, *Fear and Trembling* is a dangerous book.

10. How can anyone go on living in a world that contains 10 times as much misery as happiness?

   11. You either hate parties or you love them. So, since you say you don't hate parties, you must love them.

12. According to best-selling novelist, Dan Brown, Jesus and Mary Magdalene had a secret affair and a child whose descendants are around today. So, I'm pretty sure that's what happened, in spite of the fact that the Catholic Church has worked hard to suppress these facts.

* **13.** My sociology professor says that monogamy is an unjust form of social organization. Therefore, monogamy is an unjust form of social organization.

14. According to Lillian Roxon's *Rock Encyclopedia,* it was an English band called the Zombies that came out with the hit record "She's Not There" in 1965. So, while you say "She's Not There" was by the Beatles, it was really by the Zombies.

15. Before television came along, we didn't have much of a problem with illegal drugs. But people learn about drugs on TV, and then they want the drugs. So, TV is ruining this country.

* **16.** I was there, I tell you. I stood within 10 feet of the man. Either I was hallucinating or he levitated. And I wasn't hallucinating. Therefore, he levitated.

17. According to the *Encyclopedia Britannica,* Mary Cassatt, who is often considered America's greatest woman painter, was born in 1844 and died in 1926. So, Cassatt lived from 1844 until 1926.

18. When it comes to morality, a person is either a cultural relativist or a dogmatist. Since you won't allow that stoning a woman for adultery is right for Nigerians even if they approve of it, you obviously aren't a cultural relativist. So, you must be a dogmatist.

* **19.** We cannot intervene militarily in all countries with wicked dictators: Syria, Yemen, Zimbabwe, etc. To be consistent, we have to intervene everywhere or nowhere. So, we should intervene nowhere.

20. Either nonhuman animals are robots or they have thoughts and feelings just like humans have. Nonhuman animals are not robots. Hence, they have thoughts and feelings just like humans have.

21. Religion is the opiate of the people. Therefore, religion is like a drug that can be used to make people forget or ignore the miserable conditions they live in.

* **22.** Logic varies as languages vary. For logic is based on grammar. My chemistry professor said so. And any intelligent person will agree that different languages have different grammars. But if logic varies as languages vary, then logic is relative to cultures. Consequently, logic is relative to cultures.

23. People are either good or evil. And Doris is not good. Therefore, she is evil.

24. Would you please be a gentleman and refrain from talking politics?

* **25.** Either you believe that abortion is wrong or you believe it is right. Either way, you believe something about abortion. If you believe something, you think that's how things are. So, either way, you must think there are facts about right and wrong.

26. Why do all philosophical problems turn out, in the final analysis, just to be a question of how to define terms?

27. You should stop reading your horoscope. Why? First, because reading your horoscope is a waste of time. After all, you could be reading great literature instead. Second, people will think you are superstitious if you read your horoscope. Third, you should quit reading your horoscope because horoscopes are for idiots. Fourth, you don't want to turn out like that weird guy at work, Bob Crombie. And Bob reads horoscopes! So, obviously, horoscopes produce weirdness. Hence, you've got to stop reading them.

*28. When you get down to it, philosophers are just logic choppers who sit around trying to put reality into little boxes made of words. So, the philosophical arguments against time travel prove nothing. Hence, time travel is possible. Anyway, I know it's possible because it can happen. And besides, just about everyone *but* philosophers thinks that time travel is possible, so once again, time travel probably is possible.

29. Most Americans insist that terrorism is always wrong, but they are mistaken. Terrorism, after all, is simply the use of violence to further political ends. And no country on the face of the earth employs more violence to further its political ends than America does. So, Americans are in no position to condemn terrorism. Besides, one person's terrorist is another's freedom fighter. Why can't Americans see that their own revolutionary war heroes were all terrorists?

30. How do I know that mantras work? Consider this: Last week I said a mantra on Tuesday and on Friday. And guess what? Those days really went well for me. Furthermore, mantras work because they are effective. Finally, mantras are recommended by many great movie stars.

*31. Every nation in every region now has a decision to make. Either you are with us or you are with the terrorists. —George W. Bush, September 20, 2001

32. There are very few general laws of social science, but we can offer one that has a deserved claim: the restriction of the concept of humanity in any sphere never enhances a respect for human life. It did not enhance the rights of slaves, prisoners of wars, criminals, traitors, women, children, Jews, blacks, heretics, workers, capitalists, Slavs or Gypsies. The restriction of the concept of personhood in regard to the fetus will not do so either.[6]

33. Every woman has the right to do what she wants with her own body (as long as she harms no one else). Having an abortion is doing something with one's own body (and not harming anyone else). So, every woman has a right to have an abortion.

*34. Why should merely cracking down on terrorism help to stop it, when that method hasn't worked in any other country? Why are we so hated in the Muslim world? What did our government do there to bring this horror home to all those innocent Americans? And why don't we learn anything, from our free press, about the gross ineptitude of our state agencies, about what's really happening in Afghanistan, about the pertinence of Central Asia's huge reserves of oil and natural gas, about the links between the Bush and the bin Laden families?

NOTES

1. Anthony Flew, *A Dictionary of Philosophy*, rev. 2nd ed. (New York: St. Martin's Press, 1979), p. 104. We have slightly altered the punctuation.
2. There is some disagreement among writers on fallacies about whether the red herring fallacy should be classified with the *ignorantia elenchi* fallacy.
3. These two examples were taken from Doug Walton, "Classification of Fallacies of Relevance." http://io.uwinnipeg.ca/~walton/papers%20in%20pdf/04fall_rel.pdf.
4. This example is borrowed from Robert Baum, *Logic*, 3rd ed. (New York: Holt, Rinehart & Winston, 1989), p. 485.
5. We owe this example to Anthony Weston, *A Rulebook for Arguments* (Indianapolis, IN: Hackett, 1987), p. 88. We have elaborated the example somewhat.
6. Phillip Abbott, quoted by Helen M. Alvaré in "Abortion Is Immoral," from *The Abortion Controversy* (Greenhaven, CT 1995), p. 25.

CHAPTER 5

Categorical Logic: Statements

In this chapter and the next, we will explore an approach to logic that was first developed by Aristotle (384–322 BC). It focuses on categorical arguments, arguments whose validity depends on the relationships among classes, sets, or categories. It was the dominant approach to logic in the medieval and early modern periods and is still quite useful today.

 ## 5.1 Standard Forms of Categorical Statements

To understand categorical arguments, we must first understand categorical statements. As we saw in Chapter 1, a **categorical statement** is a statement that relates two classes or categories. For example:

1. All ducks are animals.
2. No humans are horses.
3. Some soldiers are cowards.
4. Some subatomic particles are not electrons.

Statement (1) says that every member of the class of ducks is a member of the class of animals. Statement (2) says that the class of humans and the class of horses have no members in common. Statement (3) says that some (i.e., at least one) member of the class of soldiers is a member of the class of cowards. And statement (4) says that some (i.e., at least one) member of the class of subatomic particles is not a member of the class of electrons.

There are four different **standard forms** of categorical statements, labeled **A**, **E**, **I**, and **O**. (This labeling stems from the medieval period when logic was studied in Latin. The letters are vowels from the Latin words *affirmo* and *nego,* meaning, respectively, "I affirm" and "I deny.") To be in standard form, the elements of a categorical statement must appear in the following order:

1. quantifier (i.e., the word "all," "no," or "some")
2. subject term (i.e., a word or phrase that names a class or category)
3. copula ("are" or "are not")
4. predicate term (i.e., a word or phrase that names a class or category)

The four standard forms are as follows:

Name	Form	Example
A	All S are P.	All trees are plants.
E	No S are P.	No plants are animals.
I	Some S are P.	Some trees are oaks.
O	Some S are not P.	Some trees are not oaks.

The letter S stands for the subject term; the letter P stands for the predicate term. For example, the word "trees" is the subject term in "All trees are plants," and the word "plant" is the predicate term. In the statement "Some trees are not oaks," the word "trees" is the subject term; the word "oaks" is the predicate term.

A term denotes a class or category; as such, a term is a noun or nounlike expression. Three brief comments will clarify what a term is. First, a term need not be a single word; it may be a long expression. For example, "All people who write best-selling novels are famous authors" is an **A** statement in standard form—the subject term is "people who write best-selling novels," and the predicate term is "famous authors." Second, a proper name is not a term because a proper name denotes a specific individual rather than a class. Hence, "Some philosopher is Socrates" is not a standard-form categorical statement because "Socrates" denotes a specific individual and not a class. Third, adjectives are not terms. Thus, "All paintings are beautiful" is not in standard form because "beautiful," being an adjective, does not denote a class; however, "All paintings are beautiful things" is in standard form because "beautiful things" is a nounlike expression that denotes the class containing all beautiful things.

To be in standard form, a statement must *strictly* possess one of the listed forms. For example, "Every tree is a plant" is not an **A** statement in standard form. To put it into standard form, we must replace "Every" with "All," "is" with "are," and "tree" with "trees" to arrive at "All trees are plants." We will discuss how to put statements into standard form shortly; for now, the four forms are to be interpreted quite strictly.

Quality and Quantity

Every categorical statement has a **quality**, affirmative or negative. If a statement affirms that one class is wholly or partially included in another class, then the statement's quality is *affirmative*. If a statement denies that one class is wholly or partially included in another, its quality is *negative*. Every categorical statement also has a **quantity**, universal or particular. *Universal* statements refer to all members of the class denoted by the subject term. *Particular* statements refer to only some members of the class denoted by the subject term.

An **A** statement ("All S are P") is a **universal affirmative** statement, which says that all members of class S are members of class P. "All wives are women" says that all members of the class of wives are members of the class of women.

An **E** statement ("No S are P") is a **universal negative** statement, which says that no members of class S are members of class P. In other words, a universal negative says that classes S and P have no members in common. "No men are women" says that no members of the class of men are members of the class of women.

An **I** statement ("Some S are P") is a **particular affirmative** statement, which says that some members of class S are members of class P. "Some animals are carnivores" says that some members of the class of animals are members of the class of carnivores. Note that for present purposes, the word "some" means "at least one." So, "Some S are P" does *not* imply that "Some S are not P"—for example, "Some dogs are animals" does not imply that "Some dogs are not animals."

An **O** statement ("Some S are not P") is a **particular negative** statement, which says that some members of class S are not members of class P. "Some mammals are not land animals" says that at least one member of the class of mammals is not a member of the class of land animals.

Summary of Standard Forms

Name	Form	Quantity	Quality
A	All S are P.	universal	affirmative
E	No S are P.	universal	negative
I	Some S are P.	particular	affirmative
O	Some S are not P.	particular	negative

Putting Categorical Statements into Standard Form

In ordinary English, categorical statements are often not in standard form. Our logical tools, however, only apply to statements in standard form. So, let us now consider some techniques for putting categorical statements into standard form.

First, when a statement is not in standard form because its predicate is an adjective, add an appropriate noun. Thus, we can write, "All humans are rational" as "All humans are rational animals" or "All humans are rational things."

Second, when the elements of a standard-form statement are all present but not in the right order, we merely rearrange the elements. Thus, to put "Rubies are all gems" into standard form, we simply write, "All rubies are gems."

Third, when a statement contains a verb other than "are," we can add "are" and shift the original verb into the predicate. For example, to put "All fish swim" into standard form, we can write, "All fish are swimmers." And to put "All criminals should be punished" into standard form, we may write, "All criminals are people who should be punished." Similarly, if the verb "to be" is in the past tense or future tense, we can add "are" and relocate the tensed verb in the predicate. Thus, to put "All workers were tired" into standard form, we may write, "All workers are people who were tired." And "No persons who confess will be prosecuted" may be rewritten as "No persons who confess are persons who will be prosecuted."

Fourth, each basic type of categorical statement has common stylistic variants. A **stylistic variant** is just another way of saying the same thing. Consider stylistic variants of **A** statements ("All S are P")—for example, each of these is a stylistic variant of "All cats are mammals":

> Every cat is a mammal.
> Each cat is a mammal.
> Any cat is a mammal.
> If anything is a cat, then it is a mammal.
> Things are cats only if they are mammals.
> Only mammals are cats.

We can put these into standard form as "All cats are mammals."

Take special note of the word "only." "Only P are S" means "All S are P"; it does *not* mean "All P are S." For example, "Only mammals are cats" means "All cats are mammals"; it does not mean "All mammals are cats." By contrast, "Only cats are mammals" means "All mammals are cats"; it does *not* mean "All cats are mammals."

Summary of Stylistic Variants

Universal Affirmative:
All S are P.

Every S is a P.
Each S is a P.
Any S is a P.
If anything is an S, then it is a P.
Things are S only if they are P.
Only P are S.

Universal Negative:
No S are P.

Nothing that is an S is a P.
A thing is an S only if it is not a P.
If anything is an S, then it is not a P.
Nothing is an S unless it is not a P.

Particular Affirmative:
Some S are P.

There are S that are P.
At least one S is a P.
There exists an S that is a P.
Something is both an S and a P.

Particular Negative:
Some S are not P.

At least one S is not a P.
Not all S are P.
Not every S is a P.
Something is an S but not a P.
There is an S that is not a P.

Next, consider stylistic variants of **E** statements ("No S are P"). For example, each of the following is a stylistic variant of "No whales are humans":

> Nothing that is a whale is a human.
> A thing is a whale only if it is not human.
> If anything is a whale, then it is not a human.
> Nothing is a whale unless it is not a human.

To put any of these into standard form, write "No whales are humans."

Now, consider stylistic variants of **I** statements ("Some S are P"). For example, each of the following is a stylistic variant of "Some fish are sharks":

> There are fish that are sharks.
> At least one fish is a shark.
> There exists a fish that is a shark.
> Something is both a fish and a shark.

To put any of these into standard form, we write "Some fish are sharks."

Finally, consider stylistic variants of **O** statements ("Some S are not P"). For example, each of the following is a stylistic variant of "Some fish are not sharks":

At least one fish is not a shark.

Not all fish are sharks.

Not every fish is a shark.

Something is a fish but not a shark.

There is a fish that is not a shark.

To put any of these into standard form, we write "Some fish are not sharks."

Prior to the late nineteenth century, many logicians thought that all valid arguments could be analyzed in terms of classes or categories. From this perspective, the four standard forms of categorical statements are the basic elements of deductive logic. Although logicians no longer hold this view, many insights still can be derived from the study of the logic of categorical statements.

EXERCISE 5.1

PART A: Categorical Statements Name the form of each of the following categorical statements (**A, E, I,** or **O**). Identify the subject and predicate terms in each case. Then state the quantity (universal or particular) and quality (affirmative or negative).

* **1.** All hungry cannibals are dangerous people.

  2. No Ohioans are Texans.

  3. Some diamonds are not valuable objects.

* **4.** No green vegetables are minerals.

  5. Some outlaws are heroes.

  6. All equilateral triangles are geometrical figures.

* **7.** Some poems are not sonnets.

  8. No junk-food addicts are people with healthy diets.

  9. Some scoundrels are people who have been mistreated.

***10.** Some numbers are not odd numbers.

  11. No pacifists are warmongers.

  12. All mammals are cats.

***13.** Some celebrities are highly moral people.

  14. Some criminals are evil people.

  15. All people who intentionally direct violence at noncombatants for political purposes are terrorists.

*16. No odd numbers are even numbers.

17. Some bank robbers are well-trained professionals.

18. All unreported crimes are lamentable events.

*19. Some art critics who like Picasso are snobs.

20. Some wealthy people are not nice people.

21. No sedimentary rocks are volcanic rocks.

*22. All individuals who lie frequently are deeply unhappy people.

23. No losers are winners.

24. Some people who voted for Gore are intelligent people.

*25. No photons are objects visible to the naked eye.

26. Some ancient gods are not morally perfect deities.

27. All people who worship money are lunatics.

*28. Some literature professors who love Tolstoy are not good lecturers.

29. No created entities are things that have always existed.

30. No humans who are truly happy are people who never work.

PART B: Standard Forms Which of the following are categorical statements in standard form? Which are not? (Remember, there are just four standard forms: "All S are P," "No S are P," "Some S are P," and "Some S are not P.") If a statement is already in standard form, simply name the form (**A, E, I,** or **O**) and indicate what the quantity and quality are. If a statement is not already in standard form, rewrite it so that it is; then name the form and indicate the quantity and quality.

* 1. No human being can swim across the Atlantic Ocean.

2. Every kangaroo is a marsupial.

3. At least one car is not a Ford.

* 4. At least one person is a nerd.

5. Nothing that is a spider is an insect.

6. All ancient Greeks worshiped Zeus.

* 7. There exists a poem that is not a sonnet.

8. There are saints who are reformed criminals.

9. Not all politicians are liars.

*10. Some morally virtuous human beings are atheists.

11. Each patriotic American loves justice.

12. No Vikings were wimps.

*13. Not every animal that can fly is a bird.

14. All people who have committed murder deserve death.

15. Some good-looking people are snobs.

* **16.** Shawnees were all skillful trackers.

 17. Nothing is a fool unless it is not a sage.

 18. Masai warriors are all superb athletes.

* **19.** No people who are unlucky are happy.

 20. All college students who listened to Jimi Hendrix opposed the war in Vietnam.

 21. Nothing is a snake unless it is not a mammal.

* **22.** Only reptiles are lizards.

 23. If anything is a chimpanzee, then it is not a fish.

 24. Not every bright green stone is an emerald.

* **25.** Things are birds only if they have feathers.

 26. Only diamonds are gems.

 27. World-class athletes all train vigorously.

* **28.** Something is a painting but not a masterpiece.

 29. Only physical objects are quarks.

 30. The voters will all be disappointed.

* **31.** There exists a mountain that is beautiful.

 32. If anything is a slug, then it is not intelligent.

 33. Soldiers who served under General George Patton all saw combat.

* **34.** At least one tree is ugly.

 35. Nothing that is an odd number is divisible by 2.

 36. Things are beautiful only if they are pleasant to behold.

* **37.** At least one animal is vicious.

 38. If anything is a bad-tempered person, then it is a curmudgeon.

 39. Only red things are scarlet.

* **40.** If anything is a sibling that is female, then it is a sister.

 41. Dogs over 15 years of age are all old.

 42. A thing is a tragedy only if it is not a fortunate event.

* **43.** Of the living survivors of the Nazi prison camps, some were tortured.

 44. Hindus all believe in reincarnation.

 45. No prisoners will be mistreated.

* **46.** At least one soldier will be wounded.

 47. Whole numbers between 1 and 5 are in some cases even numbers.

 48. Of the living veterans of World War I, none were generals.

* **49.** Not every person who chooses not to fight is a coward.

 50. There exists an animal that is a dog.

5.2   The Traditional Square of Opposition

We now turn to the logical relations between categorical statements. In this section and the next, we will focus on immediate inferences. An inference is **immediate** when a conclusion is drawn from only one premise.

> An inference is **immediate** when a conclusion is drawn from only one premise.

What are the logical relationships between standard-form categorical statements *having the same subject and predicate terms*? For example:

A All dogs are collies.
E No dogs are collies.
I Some dogs are collies.
O Some dogs are not collies.

Let us refer to categorical statements having the same subject term and the same predicate term as **corresponding statements.**

> **Corresponding statements** are categorical statements having the same subject term and the same predicate term.

Aristotelian logicians think that the following relationships hold between corresponding statements.

First, corresponding **A** and **O** statements are **contradictories**—that is they cannot both be true and they cannot both be false. (If one is true, the other must be false; and if one is false, the other must be true.)

> Two statements are **contradictories** if they cannot both be true and they cannot both be false.

For example, "All dogs are collies" contradicts "Some dogs are not collies." So, given that all dogs are collies, it is false that some dogs are not collies. And given that some dogs are not collies, not all dogs are collies.

Similarly, corresponding **E** and **I** statements are contradictories. For example, "No dogs are collies" contradicts "Some dogs are collies." Therefore, given that no dogs are collies, it is false that some dogs are collies. And given that some dogs are collies, it is false that no dogs are collies.

Second, corresponding **A** and **E** statements are contraries. Two statements are **contraries** if they cannot both be true but they can both be false.

Two statements are **contraries** if they cannot both be true but they can both be false.

For example, corresponding **A** and **E** statements such as "All dogs are collies" and "No dogs are collies" are contraries. These statements can both be false if some (but not all) dogs are collies. But if one of these statements is true, the other must be false.

One exception to the Aristotelian view of contraries should be noted, namely, the case in which **A** or **E** statements are necessary truths. A statement is a **necessary truth** if it is true and it cannot be false under any possible circumstances—for example, "All triangles are three-sided figures" or "No triangles are circles."

A statement is a **necessary truth** if it is true and it cannot be false under any possible circumstances.

If a statement is necessarily true, then it cannot be false, but two statements are contraries only if they can *both* be false. So, **A** or **E** statements that are necessary truths are not contraries.

Third, corresponding **I** and **O** statements are **subcontraries**—that is they cannot both be false but they can both be true.

Two statements are **subcontraries** if they cannot both be false but they can both be true.

For example, "Some dogs are collies" and "Some dogs are not collies" are subcontraries.

One exception to the Aristotelian view of subcontraries should be noted at this point, namely, the case in which **I** or **O** statements are necessarily false.

A statement is a **necessary falsehood** if it is false and it cannot be true in any possible circumstances—for example, "Some circles are triangles" or "Some triangles are not three-sided figures."

> A statement is a **necessary falsehood** if it is false and it cannot be true in any possible circumstances.

If a statement is necessarily false, then it cannot be true, but two statements are subcontraries only if they both can be true. So **I** or **O** statements that are necessarily false are not subcontraries.

Fourth, **A** statements logically imply their corresponding **I** statements. For example, the following argument is valid according to Aristotelians:

> 1. All ants are insects.
>
> So, 2. Some ants are insects.

Similarly, **E** statements logically imply their corresponding **O** statements. For example, the following argument is valid according to Aristotelians:

> 1. No ants are antelopes.
>
> So, 2. Some ants are not antelopes.

The logical relationship between a universal statement and its corresponding particular statement is **subalternation.** The universal statement is the **superaltern,** and the particular statement is the **subaltern.**

> **Subalternation** is the logical relationship between a universal statement and its corresponding particular statement. The universal statement is the **superaltern**, and the particular statement is the **subaltern**.

Thus, "All ants are insects" is a *superaltern* with "Some ants are insects" as its *subaltern*; and "No ants are antelopes" is a *superaltern* with "Some ants are not antelopes" as its *subaltern*. A *superaltern* implies its corresponding *subaltern*. This means that if the *superaltern* is true, the *subaltern* is true. But it also means that if the *subaltern* is false, then the *superaltern* is false (because any statement that implies a false statement is itself false). However, a *subaltern* does not imply its corresponding *superaltern* (e.g., "Some dogs are collies" does not imply "All dogs are collies").

All of these logical relationships can be pictured in a single diagram called the **Traditional Square of Opposition,** as shown here.

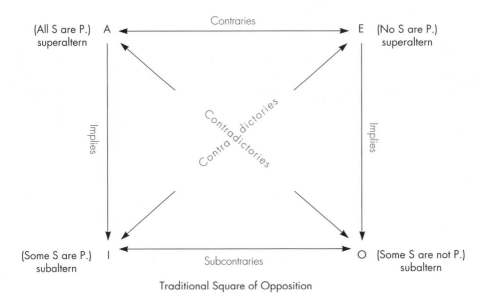

Traditional Square of Opposition

The Traditional Square of Opposition forms a helpful picture of a number of important logical relationships between corresponding statements.

1. Suppose an **A** statement (All S are P) is true; then
   a. its corresponding **E** statement or contrary (No S are P) is false.
   b. its corresponding **I** statement or subaltern (Some S are P) is true.
   c. its corresponding **O** statement or contradictory (Some S are not P) is false.

2. Suppose an **E** statement (No S are P) is true; then
   a. its corresponding **A** statement or contrary (All S are P) is false.
   b. its corresponding **O** statement or subaltern (Some S are not P) is true.
   c. its corresponding **I** statement or contradictory (Some S are P) is false.

Note: When the truth or falsehood of one statement, X, logically implies *neither* the truth *nor* the falsehood of another statement, Y, let us say that the truth value of Y is *not guaranteed* by the truth value of X.

3. Suppose an **I** statement (Some S are P) is true; then
   a. its corresponding **E** statement or contradictory (No S are P) is false.
   b. the truth value of the corresponding **A** statement (All S are P) is not guaranteed.
   c. the truth value of the corresponding **O** statement (Some S are not P) is not guaranteed.

4. Suppose an **O** statement (Some S are not P) is true; then
   a. its corresponding **A** statement or contradictory (All S are P) is false.
   b. the truth value of the corresponding **E** statement (No S are P) is not guaranteed.
   c. the truth value of the corresponding **I** statement (Some S are P) is not guaranteed.

Summary of Definitions

An inference is **immediate** when a conclusion is drawn from only one premise.

Corresponding statements are categorical statements having the same subject term and the same predicate term.

Two statements are **contradictories** if they cannot both be true and they cannot both be false.

Two statements are **contraries** if they cannot both be true but they can both be false.

A statement is a **necessary truth** if it is true and it cannot be false under any possible circumstances.

Two statements are **subcontraries** if they cannot both be false but they can both be true.

A statement is a **necessary falsehood** if it is false and it cannot be true in any possible circumstances.

Subalternation is the logical relationship between a universal statement and its corresponding particular statement. The universal statement is the **superaltern,** and the particular statement is the **subaltern.**

EXERCISE 5.2

PART A: Logical Relationships Give the names of the logical relations that hold between the following pairs of corresponding categorical statements. (In the case of subalternation, indicate which statement is the superaltern and which is the subaltern, in the order in which they appear.) If the pair of statements does not exemplify any of the logical relations discussed in this section, simply write "None."

* **1.** All roses are red flowers./No roses are red flowers.

  2. All souls are immortal substances./Some souls are immortal substances.

  3. Some people are jerks./Some people are not jerks.

* **4.** No Apaches are Shawnees./Some Apaches are Shawnees.

  5. No emeralds are plants./Some emeralds are not plants.

  6. Some people who believe in ghosts are smart people./Some people who believe in ghosts are not smart people.

* **7.** Some radical skeptics are profoundly miserable people./All radical skeptics are profoundly miserable people.

8. No truths are statements worth dying for./All truths are statements worth dying for.

9. All atoms are physical objects./Some atoms are not physical objects.

* **10.** Some odd numbers are numbers that can be divided by 2 (without remainder)./Some odd numbers are not numbers that can be divided by 2 (without remainder).

11. Some gems are not amethysts./Some gems are amethysts.

12. All liars are harmful people./No liars are harmful people.

* **13.** Some leaders are followers./Some leaders are not followers.

14. All positive whole numbers between 4 and 6 are odd numbers./No positive whole numbers between 4 and 6 are odd numbers.

15. Some dinosaurs are not rational animals./No dinosaurs are rational animals.

PART B: Immediate Inferences Which of the following immediate inferences are valid according to Aristotelian logicians? Which are not valid?

* **1.** All cougars are carnivores. So, it is false that some cougars are not carnivores.

2. All legal treaties are promises. Hence, it is not the case that no legal treaties are promises.

3. Some mosquitoes are evil beings. Therefore, it is not true that no mosquitoes are evil beings.

* **4.** All self-absorbed people are boring people. It follows that some self-absorbed people are boring people.

5. Some lawyers are shysters. So, all lawyers are shysters.

6. No five-star generals are humble people. Consequently, it is false that some five-star generals are humble people.

* **7.** Some heavenly bodies are not planets. Thus, it is false that all heavenly bodies are planets.

8. Some grapes are seedless fruit. So, some grapes are not seedless fruit.

9. It is false that all geometrical figures are trapezoids. Accordingly, some geometrical figures are not trapezoids.

* **10.** No fossils are traces of the missing link. Therefore, it is not true that all fossils are traces of the missing link.

11. No humans are morally perfect beings. It follows that some humans are not morally perfect beings.

12. All boxers who admire Hurricane Carter are winners. So, some boxers who admire Hurricane Carter are winners.

* **13.** Some persons who have landed on the moon are not women. Hence, no persons who have landed on the moon are women.

14. It is false that some grizzly bears are herbivores. It follows that some grizzly bears are not herbivores.

15. It is false that some wealthy Americans are political radicals. Thus, no wealthy Americans are political radicals.

* **16.** It is false that all dinosaurs are animals that existed prior to the Cambrian explosion. Accordingly, some dinosaurs are not animals that existed prior to the Cambrian explosion.

17. It is false that some Christians are not theists. Therefore, some Christians are theists.

18. All bureaucrats are spies. So, some bureaucrats are spies.

* **19.** Some senators are lovers of justice. It follows that some senators are not lovers of justice.

20. It is false that no astrologers are scientists. Consequently, some astrologers are scientists.

PART C: Generalizing Recall that when the truth value of one statement X logically implies neither the truth nor the falsehood of another statement Y, we say the truth value of Y is *not guaranteed* by X.

* **1.** Suppose an **A** statement is false. What can be logically inferred regarding the truth or falsehood of its corresponding **E**, **I**, and **O** statements?

2. Suppose an **E** statement is false. What can be logically inferred regarding the truth or falsehood of its corresponding **A**, **I**, and **O** statements?

3. Suppose an **I** statement is false. What can be logically inferred regarding the truth or falsehood of its corresponding **A**, **E**, and **O** statements?

* **4.** Suppose an **O** statement is false. What can be logically inferred regarding the truth or falsehood of its corresponding **A**, **E**, and **I** statements?

PART D: Standard Form Put the premise and conclusion of each of the following arguments into standard form. Then indicate whether each argument is valid.

* **1.** If anything is a capitalist, then it is not a hero. So, at least one thing is a capitalist but not a hero.

2. Only gods are immortal beings. Hence, there exist immortal beings that are gods.

3. Every misguided moralist is a menace to society. Consequently, a thing is a menace to society only if it is a misguided moralist.

* **4.** Things are positrons only if they are smaller than atoms. Therefore, not all positrons are smaller than an atom.

5. If anything is a falsehood, then it is not beneficial. So, only beneficial things are falsehoods.

6. There exists an athlete who can run the mile in under 4 minutes. Hence, not all athletes can run the mile in under 4 minutes.

* **7.** Nothing is an acid unless it is not a base. Therefore, each acid is a base.

 8. Only acts that conform to the Ten Commandments are right acts. So, an act is right only if it does not conform to the Ten Commandments.

 9. Nothing that is a categorical argument is valid. Hence, not every categorical argument is valid.

***10.** Any person who is kept awake for over a week will go crazy. Thus, only persons who are kept awake for over a week will go crazy.

 11. A thing is a wicked act only if it is an act committed with malice aforethought. Therefore, at least one wicked act is an act committed with malice aforethought.

 12. Some people who defended slavery were plantation owners. Thus, not all persons who defended slavery were plantation owners.

***13.** No person who invented the airplane died flying an airplane. It follows that only persons who died flying an airplane invented the airplane.

 14. Colonels are all authoritarian people. So, nothing that is a colonel is an authoritarian person.

 15. Only chemicals that turn blue litmus paper red are acids. Thus, there exists an acid that is a chemical that turns blue litmus paper red.

5.3 Further Immediate Inferences

Here we discuss some important types of immediate inferences *beyond* those associated with the Traditional Square of Opposition, namely conversion, obversion, and contraposition.

Conversion

The **converse** of a standard-form categorical statement is formed by interchanging its subject and predicate terms.

> The **converse** of a standard-form categorical statement is formed by interchanging its subject and predicate terms.

Here are four examples:

	Statement	Converse
A	All dogs are animals.	All animals are dogs.
E	No plants are animals.	No animals are plants.
I	Some plants are trees.	Some trees are plants.
O	Some plants are not trees.	Some trees are not plants.

Conversion is the inference from a categorical statement to its converse.

Conversion is the inference from a categorical statement to its converse.

Conversion is valid for **E** and **I** statements. For example, both of the following arguments are valid:

> **5.** No plants are animals. So, no animals are plants.
>
> **6.** Some plants are trees. So, some trees are plants.

In fact, every **E** statement is logically equivalent to its converse. Two statements are **logically equivalent** if each validly implies the other. For example, "No plants are animals" implies (and is implied by) "No animals are plants." Similarly, every **I** statement is logically equivalent to its converse. For example, "Some plants are trees" implies (and is implied by) "Some trees are plants."

But, as regards **A** and **O** statements, conversion is not a valid form of argument. The following clearly invalid arguments indicate why:

> **7.** All dogs are animals. So, all animals are dogs.
>
> **8.** Some plants are not trees. So, some trees are not plants.

However, Aristotelian logicians endorse an inference called **conversion by limitation,** in which we switch the subject and predicate terms of an **A** statement and change the quantity from universal to particular.

Conversion by limitation is the inference in which we switch the subject and predicate terms of an **A** statement and change the quantity from universal to particular.

Here is an example:

> 1. All seaweeds are plants.
> So, 2. Some plants are seaweeds.

The general pattern of the inference is this:

> 1. All S are P.
> So, 2. Some P are S.

To understand conversion by limitation, it may be helpful to note that, according to Aristotelian logicians, "All S are P" implies its subaltern "Some S are P," and then (because conversion is always valid for **I** statements) we can switch the subject and predicate terms to get "Some P are S." Thus, although *conversion* itself is not a valid argument form as applied to **A** statements, Aristotelian logicians endorse conversion by limitation.

We can picture what has been said about conversion as follows:

Standard Form		Converse
A	All S are P.	*All P are S.
		Converse by limitation: Some P are S.
E	No S are P.	No P are S.
I	Some S are P.	Some P are S.
O	Some S are not P.	*Some P are not S.

The asterisk (*) indicates those cases in which the inference from the standard form statement to its converse is not a valid form of argument.

Obversion

The concept of an obverse requires a bit of explanation. First, each class has a complement. The **complement** of a class X is the class containing all things that are *not* a member of X.

> The **complement** of a class X is the class containing all things that are *not* a member of X.

For instance, the complement of the class of trees is the class containing all nontrees, that is, everything that is not a tree (horses, hawks, humans, hamburgers, and so on).

Second, each term has a term-complement. The **term-complement** is the word or phrase that denotes the complement of a class.

> The **term-complement** is the word or phrase that denotes the class complement.

For instance, the term-complement of "dogs" is "nondogs," which denotes the class containing everything that is not a dog. And the term-complement of "nondogs" is simply "dogs," which denotes the class containing everything that is not a nondog. (*Note:* Do not confuse term-complements with contrary terms. For instance, the term-complement of "winner" is not "loser" but "nonwinner," and the class of nonwinners includes players who tie, nonplayers, *and* losers.)

When a term consists of more than one word, care must be taken in forming the term-complement. For example, what is the term-complement of "wild dogs"? Is it "nonwild dogs"? No. The term-complement must denote a class that includes *everything* outside the class denoted by the term. So, in this case the term-complement is "things that are not wild dogs," which denotes a class that includes both tame dogs and nondogs in general. Similarly, the term-complement of "good gymnast" would not be "nongood gymnast" but "things that are not good gymnasts." And the class of *things that are not good gymnasts* includes not only all the mediocre and poor gymnasts but also all the nongymnasts (atoms, apples, airplanes, etc.).

The **obverse** of a statement is formed by (a) changing its quality (from affirmative to negative, or vice versa) and (b) replacing the predicate term with its term-complement.

> The **obverse** of a standard-form categorical statement is formed by (a) changing its quality and (b) replacing the predicate term with its term-complement.

Here are four examples:

	Statement	Obverse
A	All trees are plants.	No trees are nonplants.
E	No cats are trees.	All cats are nontrees.
I	Some trees are oaks.	Some trees are not nonoaks.
O	Some trees are not oaks.	Some trees are nonoaks.

Obversion is the inference from a categorical statement to its obverse, which is always valid.

> **Obversion** is the inference from a categorical statement to its obverse.

In fact, every standard-form categorical statement is logically equivalent to its obverse. For example, "No boxers are wimps" implies (and is implied by) "All boxers are nonwimps."

We can picture what has been said about obversion like this:

	Standard Form	Obverse
A	All S are P.	No S are non-P.
E	No S are P.	All S are non-P.
I	Some S are P.	Some S are not non-P.
O	Some S are not P.	Some S are non-P.

The inference from a standard-form categorical statement to its obverse is always valid, and vice versa.

Contraposition

The **contrapositive** of a statement is formed by (a) replacing its subject term with the term-complement of its predicate term and (b) replacing the predicate term with the term-complement of its subject term.

> The **contrapositive** of a standard-form categorical statement is formed by (a) replacing its subject term with the term-complement of its predicate term and (b) replacing the predicate term with the term-complement of its subject term.

Here are four examples:

	Statement	Contrapositive
A	All cats are mammals.	All nonmammals are noncats.
E	No bats are elephants.	No nonelephants are nonbats.
I	Some plants are weeds.	Some nonweeds are nonplants.
O	Some plants are not weeds.	Some nonweeds are not nonplants.

Note: In every case, we switch the subject and predicate terms, then replace each with its term-complement.

   Contraposition is the inference from a statement to its contrapositive.

> **Contraposition** is the inference from a categorical statement to its contrapositive.

Contraposition is valid for **A** and **O** statements. So these arguments are valid:

   9. All rubies are stones. So, all nonstones are nonrubies.

   10. Some trees are not elms. So, some nonelms are not nontrees.

Interestingly, these same results can be achieved by a sequence of obversions and conversions. For instance, consider the inference from an **A** statement to its contrapositive:

   Step 1: All S are P.
   Step 2: No S are non-P. [obverse of Step 1]
   Step 3: No non-P are S. [converse of Step 2]
   Step 4: All non-P are non-S. [obverse of Step 3]

Note: An **A** statement and its contrapositive are logically equivalent. So "All collies are dogs" implies (and is implied by) "All nondogs are noncollies." Similarly, an **O** statement and its contrapositive are logically equivalent. So

"Some dogs are not collies" implies (and is implied by) "Some noncollies are not nondogs."

Contraposition is not a valid form of argument for **E** and **I** statements. For example, this inference from an **E** statement to its contrapositive is invalid:

11. No dogs are trees. So, no nontrees are nondogs.

Its premise is true, but its conclusion is false (some nontrees are nondogs, e.g. platypuses). And this inference from an **I** statement to its contrapositive is obviously invalid:

12. Some animals are nondogs. So, some dogs are nonanimals.

Although contraposition is not a valid form of argument as applied to **E** statements, Aristotelian logicians endorse an inference called **contraposition by limitation,** in which we (a) replace the subject term of an **E** statement with the term-complement of the predicate term, (b) replace the predicate term with the term-complement of the subject term, and (c) change the quantity from universal to particular.

Memory Device

1. **O**BVERSION is the **o**dd rule: It works on all four standard forms.

2. **CONVE**RSION works on **E** and **I** statements.

3. **CONTRAPO**SITION works on **A** and **O** statements.

Contraposition by limitation is the inference in which we (a) replace the subject term of an **E** statement with the term-complement of the predicate term, (b) replace the predicate term with the term-complement of the subject term, and (c) change the quantity from universal to particular.

Here's an example:

1. No flags are rags.

So, 2. Some nonrags are not nonflags.

We can move from (1) to (2) by way of inferences previously discussed:

Step 1. No flags are rags.
Step 2. Some flags are not rags. [subaltern of Step 1]
Step 3. Some flags are nonrags. [obverse of Step 2]
Step 4. Some nonrags are flags. [converse of Step 3]
Step 5. Some nonrags are not nonflags. [obverse of Step 4]

The general pattern of inference in contraposition by limitation is as follows:

> 1. No S are P.
>
> So,   2. Some non-P are not non-S.

We can sum up what has been said about contraposition as follows:

Standard Form		Contraposition
A	All S are P.	All non-P are non-S.
E	No S are P.	*No non-P are non-S.
		Contrapositive by limitation: Some non-P are not non-S.
I	Some S are P.	*Some non-P are non-S.
O	Some S are not P.	Some non-P are not non-S.

The asterisk (*) indicates those cases in which the inference from the standard-form statement to its contrapositive is not a valid form of argument.

Summary of Definitions

The **converse** of a standard-form categorical statement is formed by interchanging its subject and predicate terms.

Conversion is the inference from a categorical statement to its converse.

Conversion by limitation is the inference in which we switch the subject and predicate terms of an **A** statement and change the quantity from universal to particular.

The **complement** of a class X is the class containing all things that are *not* a member of X.

The **term-complement** is the word or phrase that denotes the class complement.

The **obverse** of a standard-form categorical statement is formed by (a) changing its quality and (b) replacing the predicate term with its term-complement.

Obversion is the inference from a categorical statement to its obverse.

The **contrapositive** of a standard-form categorical statement is formed by (a) replacing its subject term with the term-complement of its predicate term and (b) replacing the predicate term with the term-complement of its subject term.

Contraposition is the inference from a categorical statement to its contrapositive.

Contraposition by limitation is the inference in which we (a) replace the subject term of an **E** statement with the term-complement of the predicate term, (b) replace the predicate term with the term-complement of the subject term, and (c) change the quantity from universal to particular.

Summary Table: Conversion, Obversion, and Contraposition

Standard Form	Converse
A All S are P.	*All P are S.
	Converse by limitation: Some P are S.
E No S are P.	No P are S.
I Some S are P.	Some P are S.
O Some S are not P.	*Some P are not S.

Note: An asterisk indicates that the form of argument is not valid.

Standard Form	Obverse
A All S are P.	No S are non-P.
E No S are P.	All S are non-P.
I Some S are P.	Some S are not non-P.
O Some S are not P.	Some S are non-P.

Standard Form	Contrapositive
A All S are P.	All non-P are non-S.
E No S are P.	*No non-P are non-S.
	Contrapositive by limitation:
	Some non-P are not non-S.
I Some S are P.	*Some non-P are non-S.
O Some S are not P.	Some non-P are not non-S.

Note: An asterisk indicates that the form of argument is not valid.

EXERCISE 5.3

PART A: Term-Complements Rewrite the following categorical statements, replacing each term with its term-complement.

* **1.** No brown bears are herbivores.

 2. All corporals are nongenerals.

 3. Some large birds are eagles.

* **4.** Some unhappy entities are not people.

 5. No things that are not humans are rational animals.

 6. All drinkers are nondrivers.

* **7.** No great women are men.

8. Some athletes are poor losers.

9. Some nonsmokers are not healthy people.

*10. Some nonmetals are chemicals.

PART B: Conversion

Form the converse of each of the following statements. Then indicate whether conversion, as applied to the type of categorical statement in question, is a valid form of argument.

* 1. No magnates are maggots.

2. All miracles are acts of God.

3. Some rectangles are nonsquares.

* 4. Some explosives are not bombs.

5. All demons are angels.

6. No lovers are loners.

* 7. All forgeries are copies.

8. No roaches are coaches.

9. Some Africans are not Kenyans.

*10. Some leopards are nontigers.

PART C: Obversion

Form the obverse of each of the following statements. (Recall that obversion always results in a valid inference.)

* 1. All shar-peis are dogs.

2. No platypi are vegetarians.

3. Some prime ministers are women.

* 4. Some heroes are not martyrs.

5. All shamans are priests.

6. No tulips are weeds.

* 7. All colonels are objects weighing at least 100 pounds.

8. Some logicians are septuagenarians.

9. No giants are things less than 10 feet tall.

*10. No serigraphs are sculptures.

PART D: Contraposition

Form the contrapositive of each of the following statements. Then indicate whether contraposition, as applied to the type of categorical statement in question, is a valid form of argument.

* 1. All cynics are pessimists.

2. Some plants are nonroses.

3. Some dramas are not comedies.

* 4. Some noncollies are not nondogs.

  5. All photons are things that travel at the speed of light.

  6. No red oaks are elms.

* **7.** All things that can run at more than 50 miles an hour are cats.

  8. Some non-Fords are not nonautomobiles.

  9. All college students are entities having IQs of at least 100.

***10.** All great white sharks are nonguppies.

PART E: Inferences from A Statements

Assuming that "All ideologues are fools" is true, what is implied regarding the truth or falsehood of the following statements? (If neither the truth nor the falsehood of the statement is implied, simply write "Not guaranteed.") *Note:* To get the correct answer, you may need to make a series of inferences from the assumed statement.

* **1.** All fools are ideologues.

  2. No ideologues are nonfools.

  3. Some ideologues are fools.

* **4.** All nonfools are nonideologues.

  5. No nonfools are ideologues.

  6. Some fools are ideologues.

* **7.** No fools are nonideologues.

  8. Some ideologues are not fools.

  9. No ideologues are fools.

***10.** Some ideologues are not nonfools.

  11. Some fools are not nonideologues.

  12. All nonideologues are nonfools.

***13.** Some nonfools are nonideologues.

  14. No fools are ideologues.

  15. No nonideologues are nonfools.

PART F: Inferences from E Statements

Assuming that "No psychiatrists are optimists" is true, what is implied regarding the truth or falsehood of the following statements? (If neither the truth nor the falsehood of the statement is implied, simply write "Not guaranteed.") *Note:* To get the correct answer, you may need to make a series of inferences from the assumed statement.

* **1.** All psychiatrists are nonoptimists.

  2. No optimists are psychiatrists.

  3. Some psychiatrists are not optimists.

* **4.** No nonoptimists are nonpsychiatrists.

  5. All optimists are nonpsychiatrists.

  6. Some optimists are not psychiatrists.

* **7.** All psychiatrists are optimists.

   8. All nonpsychiatrists are optimists.

   9. Some psychiatrists are optimists.

* **10.** Some nonoptimists are not nonpsychiatrists.

   11. No nonpsychiatrists are optimists.

   12. Some optimists are nonpsychiatrists.

* **13.** No nonoptimists are psychiatrists.

   14. Some optimists are psychiatrists.

   15. Some psychiatrists are nonoptimists.

PART G: Inferences from I Statements Assuming that "Some chemicals are poisons" is true, what is implied regarding the truth or falsehood of the following statements? (If neither the truth nor the falsehood of the statement is implied, simply write "Not guaranteed.") *Note:* To get the correct answer, you may need to make a series of inferences from the assumed statement.

* **1.** Some poisons are chemicals.

   2. No chemicals are poisons.

   3. Some chemicals are not nonpoisons.

* **4.** Some nonchemicals are nonpoisons.

   5. No poisons are chemicals.

   6. All chemicals are poisons.

* **7.** Some nonpoisons are nonchemicals.

   8. No nonpoisons are nonchemicals.

   9. Some chemicals are not poisons.

* **10.** Some nonchemicals are not nonpoisons.

   11. All poisons are chemicals.

   12. Some chemicals are nonpoisons.

* **13.** Some nonchemicals are poisons.

   14. Some nonpoisons are chemicals.

   15. All chemicals are nonpoisons.

PART H: Inferences from O Statements Assuming that "Some celebrities are not saints" is true, what is implied regarding the truth or falsehood of the following statements? (If neither the truth nor the falsehood of the statement is implied, simply write "Not guaranteed.") *Note:* To get the correct answer, you may need to make a series of inferences from the assumed statement.

* **1.** No celebrities are saints.

   2. All celebrities are saints.

   3. Some celebrities are nonsaints.

* **4.** Some saints are not celebrities.

5. Some nonsaints are not noncelebrities.

6. Some celebrities are saints.

* **7.** Some nonsaints are celebrities.

8. All nonsaints are noncelebrities.

9. No celebrities are nonsaints.

***10.** Some noncelebrities are not nonsaints.

11. All celebrities are nonsaints.

12. No saints are celebrities.

***13.** Some celebrities are not nonsaints.

14. Some noncelebrities are saints.

15. No nonsaints are celebrities.

CHAPTER 6

Categorical Logic: Syllogisms

Categorical syllogisms are arguments composed entirely of categorical statements. Every categorical syllogism has two premises and one conclusion, and every categorical syllogism contains exactly three terms. For example:

1.   1. All human acts are behaviors caused by genes.
   2. All altruistic acts are human acts.
So, 3. All altruistic acts are behaviors caused by genes.

"Human acts," "altruistic acts," and "behaviors caused by genes" are the terms in this syllogism. Syllogisms are important and useful forms of argument. Many a long argument can be interpreted as a series of syllogisms, and it is often revealing to express the main steps as a syllogism.

 6.1   ## Standard Form, Mood, and Figure

Before we develop the tools to evaluate categorical syllogisms, let's develop a terminology for talking about them. Consider the following syllogism:

2.   1. All astronomers are scientists.
   2. Some astrologers are not scientists.
So, 3. Some astrologers are not astronomers.

Note that one of the terms, namely, "scientists," occurs once in each premise. The **middle term** of a categorical syllogism is the term that occurs once in each premise. The **major term** of a categorical syllogism is the predicate term of the conclusion. Thus, "astronomers" is the major term of syllogism (2). The **minor**

term of a categorical syllogism is the subject term of the conclusion. So, "astrologers" is the minor term of syllogism (2).

> The **middle term** of a categorical syllogism is the term that occurs once in each premise.
> The **major term** of a categorical syllogism is the predicate term of the conclusion.
> The **minor term** of a categorical syllogism is the subject term of the conclusion.

Just as there are standard forms for categorical statements, there is a standard form for categorical syllogisms. Our logical tools are designed to apply to syllogisms in standard form, so it is important to be able to put a syllogism into standard form. A categorical syllogism is in **standard form** when these conditions are met:

a. The premises and the conclusion are categorical statements in standard form ("All S are P," "No S are P," "Some S are P," or "Some S are not P").

b. The first premise contains the major term.

c. The second premise contains the minor term.

d. The conclusion is stated last.

The **major premise** of a syllogism contains the major term, and the **minor premise** contains the minor term. So, when a syllogism is in standard form, the first premise is the major premise and the second premise is the minor premise.

> The **major premise** contains the major term; in standard form, it's the first premise.
> The **minor premise** contains the minor term; in standard form, it's the second premise.

Which of the following categorical syllogisms are in standard form?

3. 1. All oaks are trees.
    2. All trees are plants.
So, 3. All oaks are plants.

4. 1. All trees are plants.
    2. All oaks are trees.
So, 3. All oaks are plants.

5. 1. All trees are plants.

2. Only trees are oaks.

So, 3. All oaks are plants.

Only (4) is in standard form. (3) is not because the minor premise comes first, and (5) is not because its second premise is not a categorical statement in standard form. We can put (5) into standard form by rewriting "Only trees are oaks" as "All oaks are trees."

The **logical form of a categorical syllogism** is determined by its mood and figure. The **mood** of a syllogism *in standard form* is determined by the kinds of categorical statements involved and the order in which they appear.

> The **mood** of a categorical syllogism *in standard form* is determined by the kinds of categorical statements involved and the order in which they appear.

For example:

6. 1. All psychiatrists are physicians.

2. Some psychologists are not physicians.

So, 3. Some psychologists are not psychiatrists.

The mood of this syllogism is **AOO.** That is, the first premise is an **A** statement, the second premise is an **O** statement, and the conclusion is an **O** statement. What is the mood of the following syllogism?

7. 1. No birds are mammals.

2. All bats are mammals.

So, 3. No bats are birds.

The mood is **EAE.** That is, the first premise is an **E** statement, the second premise is an **A** statement, and the conclusion is an **E** statement. Since the mood involves the *sequence* of the statements as well as their types, be sure that a syllogism is in standard form when trying to identify its mood.

Two syllogisms can have the same mood and yet differ in logical form. The following syllogism has the same mood as (7), but it differs in logical form:

8. 1. No mammals are birds.

2. All mammals are bats.

So, 3. No bats are birds.

We can bring out the difference in form by using letters to stand for terms. Let "S" stand for the minor term (the subject term of the conclusion), "P" for the major term (the predicate term of the conclusion), and "M" for the middle term. (Recall that the middle term occurs once in each premise but does not occur in the conclusion.) Then arguments (7) and (8) have the following forms, respectively:

No P are M.	No M are P.
All S are M.	All M are S.
So, no S are P.	So, no S are P.

In the Aristotelian scheme, (7) and (8) differ in figure. The **figure** of a categorical syllogism is specified by the position of the middle term.

> The **figure** of a categorical syllogism is specified by the position of the middle term.

There are four possible figures, which can be diagrammed as follows:

First Figure	Second Figure	Third Figure	Fourth Figure
M–P	P–M	M–P	P–M
S–M	S–M	M–S	M–S
So, S–P	So, S–P	So, S–P	So, S–P

In the first figure, the middle term is the subject term of the major premise and the predicate term of the minor premise. In the second figure, the middle term is the predicate term of both premises. In the third figure, the middle term is the subject term of both premises. In the fourth figure, the middle term is the predicate term of the major premise and the subject term of the minor premise.

The logical form of a syllogism is completely specified by its mood and figure. The Aristotelian approach works out which combinations of mood and figure result in valid forms and which result in invalid forms. For example, argument (7) is a syllogism in the *second figure* having the mood **EAE;** this form is valid. Argument (8) is a syllogism in the *third figure* having the mood **EAE;** this form is invalid. Thus, according to Aristotelian logic, formal validity is determined by mood and figure.

How many different forms of categorical syllogisms are there? Two hundred and fifty-six. As we have seen, there are four kinds of categorical statements and three categorical statements per categorical syllogism. Thus, there are $4^3 = 4 \times 4 \times 4 = 64$ possible moods (**AAA, AAE, AAI, AAO, AEA,** etc.). Moreover, there are four different figures, and $64 \times 4 = 256$. Out of all these possibilities, ancient and modern logicians agree that the following 15 forms are formally valid:

First figure: **AAA, EAE, AII, EIO**
Second figure: **EAE, AEE, EIO, AOO**
Third figure: **IAI, AII, OAO, EIO**
Fourth figure: **AEE, IAI, EIO**

It is not necessary to memorize this list of valid forms. It is much more important to learn how to test categorical syllogisms for formal validity, and we shall begin to do that in the next section. By the way, according to logicians in the Aristotelian tradition, an additional nine forms are valid:

> First figure: **AAI, EAO**
> Second figure: **AEO, EAO**
> Third figure: **AAI, EAO**
> Fourth figure: **AEO, EAO, AAI**

We will discuss why logicians in the Aristotelian tradition accept these additional nine forms as valid—and why many modern logicians do not—in section 6.4. For the moment, note that all the additional forms involve an inference from two universal premises to a particular conclusion. These forms do *not* test validity using the method we shall discuss in the next two sections.

Summary of Definitions

The **middle term** of a categorical syllogism is the term that occurs once in each premise.

The **major term** of a categorical syllogism is the predicate term of the conclusion.

The **minor term** of a categorical syllogism is the subject term of the conclusion.

The **major premise** contains the major term; in standard form, it's the first premise.

The **minor premise** contains the minor term; in standard form, it's the second premise.

The **mood** of a categorical syllogism *in standard form* is determined by the kinds of categorical statements involved and the order in which they appear.

The **figure** of a categorical syllogism is specified by the position of the middle term.

EXERCISE 6.1

PART A: Standard Form Which of the following categorical syllogisms are *in standard form*? If a syllogism is not in standard form, rewrite it so that it is.

* **1.** 1. Some works of art are books.
       2. All novels are books.
    So, 3. Some works of art are novels.

2.   1. Some poems are not masterpieces.
2. No limericks are masterpieces.
So, 3. Some limericks are not poems.

3.   1. All movies are films.
2. Some documentaries are not movies.
So, 3. Some documentaries are not films.

* **4.**   1. All sculptures are beautiful.
2. Some beautiful things are paintings.
So, 3. Some sculptures are not paintings.

5.   1. Some short stories are not interesting.
2. Every famous short story is interesting.
So, 3. Some short stories are not famous short stories.

6.   1. Some artists are millionaires.
2. No millionaires are poor.
So, 3. At least one artist is not poor.

* **7.**   1. All sadists are mean.
2. All art critics are mean.
So, 3. All art critics are sadists.

8.   1. All metaphors are figures of speech.
2. All metaphors are words.
So, 3. All figures of speech are words.

9.   1. All opera singers are cool people.
2. No rock singers are opera singers.
So, 3. No rock singers are cool people.

* **10.**   1. Some ballerinas are clumsy dancers.
2. All people who hate music are clumsy dancers.
So, 3. Some people who hate music are ballerinas.

11.   1. Some comedians are poets.
2. Some comedians are prophets.
So, 3. Some poets are prophets.

12.   1. Every author is insightful.
2. All novelists are authors.
So, 3. All insightful people are novelists.

* **13.**   1. No aspiring actor is a saint.
2. At least one aspiring actor is not an egoist.
So, 3. Some egoists are saints.

14.   1. Some musicians are not classically trained musicians.
2. All jazz musicians are musicians.
So, 3. Some jazz musicians are not classically trained musicians.

15.   1. Only artists are alive.
2. No ancient Greek poets are alive.
So, 3. No artists are ancient Greek poets.

PART B: Mood and Figure Specify the mood and figure of the following forms. Then use the list of valid forms provided in this section to determine whether the forms are valid.

* **1.** 1. Some P are M.
       2. All S are M.
   So, 3. Some S are P.

2. 1. Some M are P.
      2. Some M are S.
  So, 3. Some S are P.

3. 1. All P are M.
      2. No M are S.
  So, 3. No S are P.

* **4.** 1. No M are P.
        2. Some M are not S.
    So, 3. Some S are P.

5. 1. No M are P.
      2. All S are M.
  So, 3. No S are P.

6. 1. No P are M.
      2. All M are S.
  So, 3. No S are P.

* **7.** 1. All P are M.
        2. Some S are M.
    So, 3. Some S are P.

8. 1. Some P are not M.
      2. Some S are not M.
  So, 3. Some S are not P.

9. 1. Some M are not P.
      2. All M are S.
  So, 3. Some S are not P.

* **10.** 1. Some M are P.
         2. All S are M.
     So, 3. Some S are not P.

11. 1. All P are M.
       2. Some S are not M.
   So, 3. Some S are not P.

12. 1. No M are P.
       2. Some S are M.
   So, 3. Some S are not P.

* **13.** 1. All P are M.
         2. All S are M.
     So, 3. All S are P.

14. 1. All M are P.
       2. All M are S.
   So, 3. All S are P.

15. 1. All M are P.
       2. Some S are M.
   So, 3. Some S are P.

PART C: Putting Syllogisms into Standard Form Put the following syllogisms into standard form. Then specify the mood and figure. Finally, use the list of valid forms to determine whether the syllogisms are valid.

* **1.** Every cowboy loves horses. Not all farmers love horses. It follows that at least one farmer is not a cowboy.

2. Nothing is a rodeo unless it is not an opera. Each opera includes singers. So, nothing that is a rodeo includes singers.

3. Not everyone who loves country music is a rodeo star. For at least one rock star loves country music, and no rock stars are rodeo stars.

* **4.** No cowards ride bulls; therefore, some fools are not cowards because at least one bull rider is a fool.

5. No cowgirls are city slickers; hence, no city slicker is a talented rider because only talented riders are cowgirls.

6. There exists a drifter who is a sheriff; for at least one sheriff is a gunslinger, and a thing is a gunslinger only if it is a drifter.

* **7.** Only good guys are cowboys in white outfits. A thing is a cattle rustler only if it is not a good guy. It follows that no cowboys in white outfits are cattle rustlers.

8. Every barkeep who serves rotgut is a bad guy. Therefore, at least one person who won't live long is a bad guy because at least one barkeep who serves rotgut won't live long.

9. Only westerns are worth seeing because only good movies are worth seeing, and only westerns are good movies.

*10. At least one bronco is not hard to ride, for all bulls are hard to ride, and some broncos are not bulls.

11. Nothing is a wealthy landowner unless it is not a buckaroo. A thing is a cattle baron only if it is a wealthy landowner. Hence, nothing that is a buckaroo is also a cattle baron.

12. If anything is a bounty hunter, then it is not a sodbuster. At least one outlaw is a sodbuster; therefore, not every outlaw is a bounty hunter.

*13. A thing is a trail boss only if it is not a hired hand. There exists a rancher who is a hired hand. Consequently, at least one rancher is a trail boss.

14. Not all bandits will be hanged. After all, at least one bandit is not a horse thief, and every horse thief will be hanged.

15. Not all sheep ranchers are fast guns; hence, not all honest citizens are fast guns since only honest citizens are sheep ranchers.

PART D: Constructing Syllogisms Write your own syllogisms with forms as specified below. Then use the list of valid forms provided in this section to determine whether the syllogisms are valid.

1. First figure: **EIO**		**6.** Second figure: **EIO**	
2. Second figure: **AEE**		**7.** Third figure: **OAO**	
3. Third figure: **IAI**		**8.** Fourth figure: **IAI**	
4. Fourth figure: **EAE**		**9.** First figure: **EEA**	
5. First figure: **AAE**		**10.** Second figure: **AOO**	

6.2 Venn Diagrams and Categorical Statements

In this section and the next, we will examine a method for establishing the validity and invalidity of categorical arguments. This method was discovered around 1880 by the English logician John Venn. Venn's method involves the use of a special type of picture or diagram.

A Venn diagram consists of overlapping circles. Each circle stands for a class. Each categorical statement has two terms, with each term denoting a class, so the Venn diagram for a single categorical statement involves just two overlapping circles. For example, in the following diagram, the circle on the left denotes the class of dogs and the circle on the right denotes the class of animals. The numerals (1 through 4) are not normally part of the diagram but are added here temporarily to enable us to refer to the separate areas of the diagram.

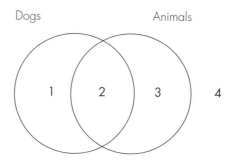

Area 1 stands for things that are dogs but not animals. Of course, in reality this area is empty because there are no dogs that are not animals. Area 2 (the area of overlap between the circles) stands for things that are both dogs and animals, that is, all the dogs. Area 3 stands for things that are animals but not dogs, such as cats, crickets, and kangaroos. Area 4 stands for things that are neither dogs nor animals, such as neutrons, nickels, and numbers.

To construct Venn diagrams, we indicate that the various areas of the diagram either contain objects or are empty. To show that an area contains at least one object, we use an "x." To show that an area is empty, we shade it in. If an area does not contain an "x" and is not shaded in, we simply have no information about it. Thus, to diagram a universal negative statement, such as "No dogs are cats," we indicate that the area of overlap between the two circles is empty by shading it in, as follows:

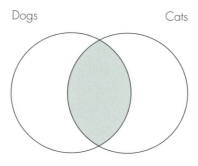

This sort of diagram, with shading in the area of overlap, is the sort you will always use for a universal negative statement. However, as previously noted, the English language provides various ways of saying that "No S are P," such as "If anything is an S, then it is not a P" and "Nothing that is an S is a P." When you encounter such stylistic variants in a syllogism, simply rewrite the statement in "No S are P" form and use a diagram similar to the one just shown. One last thing: Notice that the preceding diagram does not say that there are any dogs, nor does it say that there are any cats. It simply says that nothing belongs to the class (or set) of things that are both dogs and cats.

Universal affirmatives have the form "All S are P," and they say that all the members of set S are members of set P. Thus, the diagram for "All dogs are animals" looks like this:

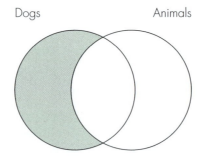

Dogs   Animals

Notice that this diagram does not say that there are any dogs, nor does it say that there are any animals. It simply says, "If there are any dogs, then they are animals" (or "Anything you put in the dog-circle has to go in the animal-circle"). This is the sort of shading you will always use when diagramming a universal affirmative statement. However, as previously noted, the English language contains numerous stylistic variants for "All S are P," such as "Every S is a P," "If anything is an S, then it is a P," and "Only P are S." When you encounter these stylistic variants, rewrite the statement into "All S are P" form and use a diagram similar to the one just shown.

Particular affirmatives have the form "Some S are P," and these say that sets S and P have at least one member in common. The diagram for "Some dogs are collies" looks like this:

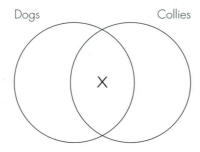

Dogs   Collies

This diagram asserts that there exists at least one dog that is a collie. ("Something is in the dog-circle *and* in the collie-circle.") This is the type of diagram you will always use for particular affirmative statements. However, as previously noted, the English language contains a number of stylistic variants for "Some S are P," including "At least one S is a P" and "There are S that are P." When you encounter these variants, simply rewrite the statement into "Some S are P" form and use a diagram similar to the one just shown.

Particular negatives have the form "Some S are not P." These statements say that set S has at least one member that does not belong to set P. The diagram for "Some dogs are not collies" looks like this:

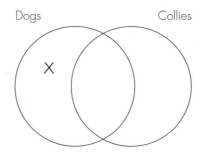

The diagram asserts that there exists at least one dog that is not a collie. ("Something is in the dog-circle but *not* in the collie-circle.") This is the type of diagram you will always use for particular negative statements. But as previously noted, the English language contains a number of stylistic variants for "Some S are not P," such as "Not all S are P" and "At least one S is not a P." When you encounter these variants, simply rewrite the statement in "Some S are not P" form and use a diagram similar to the one just shown.

Now that we know how to diagram the four relevant types of categorical statements, we can use Venn diagrams to evaluate arguments for validity. We begin with short arguments involving just one premise. To determine whether an argument is valid, we proceed as follows. First, we diagram the premise. Second, we look to see whether our diagram of the premise tells us that the conclusion is true. If it does, the argument is valid; if it does not, it is invalid.

Let's start with some examples of conversion:

   9. 1. No Namibians are Libyans.

   So, 2. No Libyans are Namibians.

To apply the Venn method, we draw two overlapping circles and label them. We use capital-letter abbreviations to label our circles. In our current example, let's use "N" for "Namibians" and "L" for "Libyans." For *single-premise* arguments, let us follow the convention of labeling the circle on the left with the *subject term* of the premise and the circle on the right with the *predicate term* of the premise, like this:

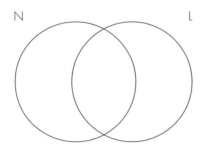

Now we diagram the premise:

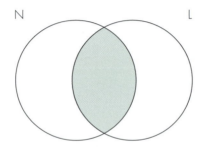

Next, we look to see whether the diagram of the premise tells us that the conclusion is true. In this case it does, for the shading indicates that no Libyan is a Namibian. So, the diagram tells us that the argument is valid, which is as it should be because conversion is valid for **E** statements.

Let's consider a second short argument:

10. 1. All Liberians are Africans.

So, 2. All Africans are Liberians.

As before, we draw two overlapping circles, label them, and diagram the premise:

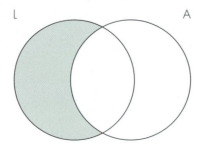

Now we look to see whether the diagram of the premise tells us that the conclusion is true. In this case, it does not. A diagram of the conclusion would have to shade in area 3, the part of the circle that stands for Africans who are not Liberians, like this:

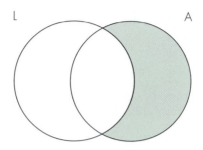

Thus, our diagram of the premise tells us that the argument is not valid.
   Consider another example of conversion:

11. 1. Some Moroccans are Spanish speakers.
So, 2. Some Spanish speakers are Moroccans.

Again, we diagram the premise:

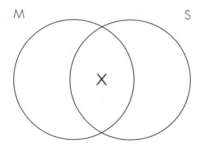

And now we look to see whether our diagram of the premise tells us that the conclusion of the argument is true. In this case, the answer is yes, the "x" tells us that some members of the class of Spanish speakers are also members of the class of Moroccans. So, our Venn diagram indicates that the argument is valid.
   Consider one last example of conversion:

12. 1. Some Africans are not Nigerians.
So, 2. Some Nigerians are not Africans.

As before, we diagram the premise:

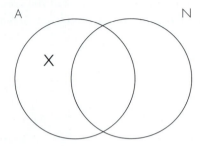

Does the diagram tell us that the conclusion is true? No, for this to be so, an "x" would have to appear in area 3, like this:

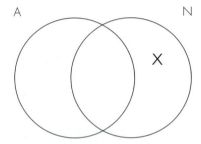

Consequently, the Venn method tells us that argument (12) is invalid.
    Now let's consider an example of obversion:

13. 1. No Cameroonians are Zimbabweans.
So, 2. All Cameroonians are non-Zimbabweans.

The diagram of the premise is as follows:

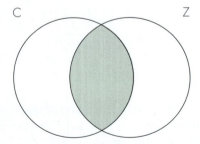

Does the diagram tell us that the conclusion is true? Yes, for it indicates that if there are any Cameroonians, they are not Zimbabweans (i.e., they must be in the part of the Cameroonian-circle that lies outside the Zimbabwean-circle). In the case of obversion, the conclusion of the argument is always logically equivalent to the premise, so a diagram of the premise is bound to tell us the conclusion is true.

This diagram raises the issue of dealing with negative terms, such as "non-Zimbabweans." To avoid certain complications, we will *not* label the circles in our diagrams with negative terms. But we will be forced at times (as in this case) to understand what sort of diagram is or would be needed where a negative term is involved. The essential question is, "For the statement to be true, where would the diagram need to be shaded or marked with an 'x'?" Sometimes it helps to experiment with a separate diagram on a sheet of scratch paper—do some shading or "x-ing" and ask, "Does that tell me that the statement is true?" A good working knowledge of obversion and contraposition is also helpful because it will help you identify statements that are (and are not) logically equivalent to the one containing a negative term. Let's consider some cases.

Here is an example of contraposition:

14. 1. All Ugandans are Africans.

So, 2. All non-Africans are non-Ugandans.

The diagram of the premise looks like this:

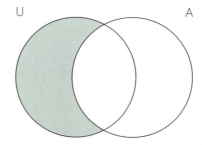

An **A** statement and its contrapositive are logically equivalent; so, the diagram of the premise is bound to contain the essential content of the conclusion, but the term-complements ("non-Africans" and "non-Ugandans") may make this less than obvious. To understand the diagram, note that "All non-Africans are non-Ugandans" says that if anything is outside of the circle labeled "Africans," then it is outside the circle labeled "Ugandans." And the diagram does indeed contain this information.

Here's another example of contraposition:

15. 1. Some Africans are non-Kenyans.

So, 2. Some Kenyans are non-Africans.

The diagram of the premise is as follows:

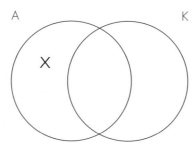

Does the diagram tell us that the conclusion is true? No, for there is no "x" in area 3, the area that stands for Kenyans who are non-Africans.

Now consider an especially difficult case involving negative terms, "No non-animals are nondogs." (If you recall the table on contraposition, you know that this is *not* logically equivalent to "No dogs are animals.") To diagram "No nonanimals are nondogs," we have to shade in the area of overlap between "nonanimals" and "nondogs." In a diagram in which the circles are labeled "animals" and "dogs," the area of overlap is the area *outside* of the circles, so the diagram looks like this:

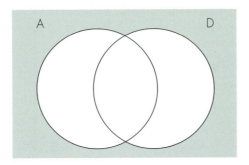

In closing this section, let's examine contradictories from the standpoint of the Venn method. Recall that if two statements are contradictories, then if one is true, the other must be false (and vice versa). Consider the following argument:

16. 1. Some Egyptians are not Muslims.

So, 2. It's false that all Egyptians are Muslims.

The premise may be diagrammed as follows:

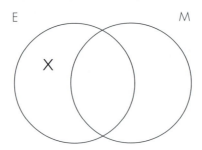

Does the diagram tell us that the conclusion of the argument is true? Yes. A diagram of "All Egyptians are Muslims" would declare area 1 of the diagram empty, but the "x" in area 1 tells us it isn't empty. Thus, given the truth of the premise, it's false that all Egyptians are Muslims. Accordingly, the Venn method nicely confirms the Aristotelian view of contradictories.

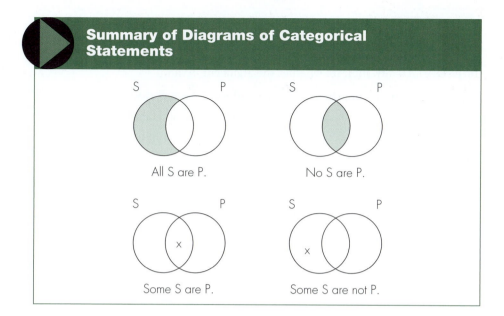

Summary of Diagrams of Categorical Statements

All S are P.

No S are P.

Some S are P.

Some S are not P.

EXERCISE 6.2

PART A: Venn Diagrams and Standard Form Put the following categorical statements into standard form, then construct a Venn diagram for each of them. Label the left circle of the diagram with an abbreviation of the subject term and the right circle with an abbreviation of the predicate term.

* **1.** At least one ancient philosopher believed in the unreality of change.
  2. Not every act of killing is an act of murder.
  3. If anything is a divine being, then it is not limited.
* **4.** Only tax-dodgers deserve harsh treatment from the IRS.
  5. At least one current musical hit will not be a hit next year.
  6. Only people who believe in life after death are people who believe in reincarnation.
* **7.** A thing is a chlorofluorocarbon only if it is not good for the ozone layer.
  8. At least one corporation is cheating the government.
  9. Only violent offenders should be incarcerated.
* **10.** Nothing is a physical entity unless it is not spiritual.

PART B: Venn Diagrams and Arguments Draw two Venn diagrams for each of the following arguments, one for the premise and one for the conclusion. First, draw a Venn diagram of the premise, labeling the left circle with an abbreviation of the subject term and the right circle with an abbreviation of the predicate term. Second, draw a Venn diagram for the conclusion, but label the circles as before (with the left circle labeled by an abbreviation of the subject term of the *premise* and the right circle labeled with an abbreviation of the predicate term of the *premise*). Finally, indicate whether the argument is valid.

* **1.** Some chairs are not thrones. So, some thrones are not chairs.

   2. All scallops are mollusks. Hence, no scallops are nonmollusks.

   3. All minds are brains. Therefore, all nonbrains are nonminds.

* **4.** Some married persons are persons who have attachment disorders. Thus, some persons who have attachment disorders are married persons.

   5. No laypersons are priests. It follows that all laypersons are nonpriests.

   6. Some political philosophers are egalitarians. Accordingly, some nonegalitarians are things that are not political philosophers.

* **7.** No elephants are beetles. Consequently, no nonbeetles are nonelephants.

   8. No Pickwickian interpretations are obvious interpretations. So, no obvious interpretations are Pickwickian interpretations.

   9. Some rays are devilfish. Hence, some devilfish are not nonrays.

* **10.** Some wines are not merlots. Therefore, some nonmerlots are not nonwines.

   11. All acts of torture are immoral acts. It follows that all immoral acts are acts of torture.

   12. Some vipers are not copperheads. Consequently, some vipers are noncopperheads.

* **13.** Some mammals are edentulous animals. Thus, all mammals are edentulous animals.

   14. Some boring events are colloquia. Accordingly, some boring events are not colloquia.

   15. Some theists are not predestinarians. Therefore, no theists are predestinarians.

6.3 Venn Diagrams and Categorical Syllogisms

The Venn method can be applied to categorical syllogisms. In fact, because the Venn method gives us a visual representation of the logic, many find it an especially insightful and intuitive way of testing syllogisms for validity.

To apply the Venn method to a categorical syllogism, we first check to see if the syllogism is in standard form. If it is, we can proceed immediately to construct a diagram. If the syllogism is not in standard form, we rewrite it so that it is. Next, because there are three terms in every categorical syllogism, with each term denoting a class, we need a diagram with three overlapping circles to represent the various possible relationships among the classes, as shown here:

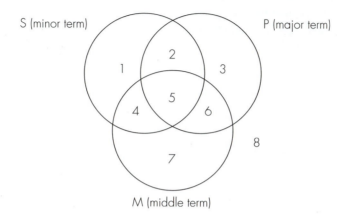

To ensure uniformity in our diagrams, we always let the circle in the middle stand for the class of things denoted by the *middle term* of the syllogism (the term that appears in both premises). We ordinarily label this circle with an abbreviation of the middle term. The circle in the upper left stands for the class of things denoted by the *minor term* (the subject term of the conclusion). We ordinarily label this circle with an abbreviation of the minor term. And the circle in the upper right stands for the set of things denoted by the *major term* (the predicate term of the conclusion). We ordinarily label this circle with an abbreviation of the major term. The numerals (1 through 8) are not normally part of a Venn diagram, but they are added here temporarily to enable us to refer to the separate areas of the diagram. Notice that there are eight areas (counting the region outside the circles). Each area represents a possible relationship among the three sets or classes. For example, if we placed an "x" in area 5, we would be saying that at least one thing belongs to all three of the sets or classes. If we shaded in area 5, we would be saying that no object belongs to all three sets. If we placed an "x" in area 8, we would be saying that at least one thing is not a member of any of the three classes in question. If we shaded in areas 4 and 5, we would be saying that nothing that belongs to the set denoted by the middle term also belongs to the set denoted by the minor term.

To determine whether a syllogism is valid, we proceed as follows. First, we diagram the premises. Second, we look to see whether our diagram of the premises tells us that the conclusion is true. If it does, the argument is valid; if it doesn't, it's invalid. Consider the following example:

17. 1. No rocks are sentient things.

2. All animals are sentient things.

So, 3. No animals are rocks.

We set up our diagram and label the circles as just prescribed: An abbreviation of the middle term ("S" for "sentient things") labels the middle circle; an abbreviation of the minor term ("A" for "animals") labels the circle in the upper left; and an abbreviation of the major term ("R" for "rocks") labels the circle in the upper right. Next, we diagram the first premise:

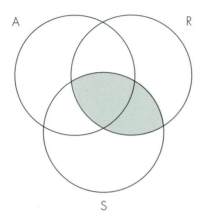

In diagramming the first premise, we focus on the two circles representing rocks and sentient things because only those classes are mentioned in the first premise. Next, we diagram the second premise:

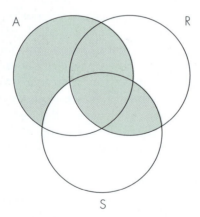

In diagramming the second premise, we need pay attention only to the circles representing animals and sentient things.

We now check whether the diagram tells us that no animal is a rock. It does, for the areas of overlap between the circles representing these two classes are shaded in. Therefore, the argument is valid.

Our first example involved only universal statements. Let us now consider a syllogism involving a particular negative statement:

18. 1. All humans are rational beings.
    2. Some animals are not rational beings.
So, 3. Some animals are not humans.

First, we draw and label the circles, and then we diagram the first premise:

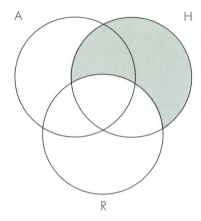

Next, we diagram the second premise:

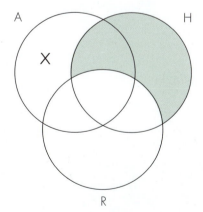

The "x" lies within the A-circle (which represents the class of animals) but outside the R-circle (which represents the class of rational beings). Why did we put our "x" in area 1 and not in area 2 of the diagram? We couldn't put it in area 2 because area 2 is shaded in. That is, the first premise tells us that area 2 is empty.

Now, we examine the diagram to see whether it tells us that some animals are not humans. It does. The "x" lies within the animal-circle but outside the human-circle.

In diagramming argument (18), we diagrammed the universal premise before we diagrammed the particular premise. *When a syllogism contains both universal and particular premises, always diagram the universal premise first.* Otherwise, you may run into obstacles in constructing your diagram. To illustrate, try to diagram the particular premise of argument (18) prior to diagramming the universal premise. (You won't know whether to put the "x" in area 1 or area 2.)

Now consider an invalid syllogism:

19. 1. All immoral persons are psychologically disturbed persons.
     2. No saints are immoral persons.
So, 3. No saints are psychologically disturbed persons.

We draw and label the circles and then diagram the first premise:

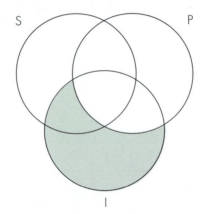

Next, we diagram the second premise:

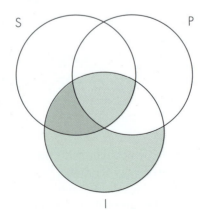

Notice that area 4 has been shaded in twice because the diagram for each prem-ise declares area 4 empty. This is not a problem; it merely means that our dia-gram is redundant regarding the emptiness of area 4.

Does our diagram tell us that the conclusion of the argument is true? No. Area 2 has not been declared empty. Thus, the diagram leaves open the possibil-ity that some saints are psychologically disturbed persons, and so the argument is invalid.

Let us now consider an example that brings out a slight complication:

20. 1. All famous actors are highly successful people.

2. Some highly successful people are people of average intelligence.

So, 3. Some people of average intelligence are famous actors.

We diagram the universal premise first:

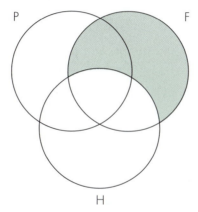

Now, when we try to diagram the second (or particular affirmative) premise, we see that the "x" could go in either area 4 or area 5. The premises do not contain more specific information than that. We indicate this by putting an "x" *precisely* on the line separating the two areas, like this:

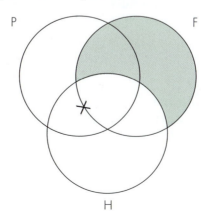

Now, for the argument to be valid, the premises must tell us that either area 2 or area 5 contains an object. But our diagram for the first premise declares that area 2 is empty. And our diagram for the second premise does not *assure* us that area 5 contains an object—it may or it may not. The "x" straddles areas 4 and 5, so the premises do not definitely say that the "x" belongs in area 4, nor do they say that the "x" belongs in area 5. Hence, the argument is invalid.

The Venn method can be used to test argument forms as well as arguments. Can you construct a Venn diagram for the following form?

> **21.** 1. All M are P.
> 2. Some S are not M.
> So, 3. Some S are not P.

The diagram looks like this:

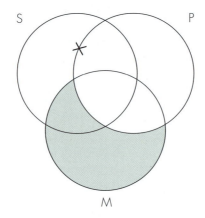

Note that the "x" straddles areas 1 and 2. The premises tell us that there is an "S" in at least one of these areas, but the premises do not tell us to place an "x" in area 1. And the argument form is valid *only if* the premises tell us to place an "x" within the S-circle but outside the P-circle. So, the argument form is not valid.

EXERCISE 6.3

PART A: Argument Forms Construct Venn diagrams to determine whether the following argument forms are valid. In labeling the circles of your diagrams, remember that "M" labels the circle in the middle, "S" labels the circle in the upper left, and "P" labels the circle in the upper right.

* **1.** 1. All M are P.
      2. Some M are not S.
   So, 3. Some S are not P.

2. 1. No P are M.
      2. Some M are not S.
   So, 3. Some S are P.

3. 1. No M are P.
     2. Some M are S.
So, 3. Some S are not P.

* **4.** 1. Some P are M.
       2. Some S are M.
So, 3. Some S are P.

5. 1. All P are M.
     2. Some M are not S.
So, 3. Some S are not P.

6. 1. All P are M.
     2. Some S are not M.
So, 3. Some S are not P.

* **7.** 1. No P are M.
       2. Some M are S.
So, 3. Some S are P.

8. 1. All P are M.
     2. No S are M.
So, 3. No S are P.

9. 1. No P are M.
     2. No S are M.
So, 3. No S are P.

* **10.** 1. All M are P.
        2. No S are M.
So, 3. No S are P.

PART B: Categorical Syllogisms
Use Venn diagrams to determine the validity of the following categorical syllogisms. If a given syllogism is not in standard form, be sure to put it into standard form before constructing your diagram. In labeling the circles of your diagrams, use an abbreviation of the *middle term* to label the circle in the middle, use an abbreviation of the *minor term* to label the circle in the upper left, and use an abbreviation for the *major term* to label the circle in the upper right.

* **1.** Only Greeks are Athenians. At least one human is not an Athenian. Therefore, not all humans are Greeks.

2. Every animal is sentient. And each sentient thing is a rights-holder. Hence, if anything is an animal, then it is a rights-holder.

3. No serial killer is good because every serial killer is evil, and no evil thing is good.

* **4.** Every wicked person is self-deceived, for all liars are wicked, and every liar is self-deceived.

5. Every person without a conscience is happy; hence, at least one criminal is happy because not every criminal has a conscience.

6. All those who have faith are virtuous. But there are highly moral people who do not have faith. Therefore, not all highly moral people are virtuous.

* **7.** No human is omniscient. Something is both divine and human. So, at least one divine being is not omniscient.

8. Only wars are great evils. Some wars are ordained by God. Hence, at least one great evil is ordained by God.

9. Not every hobby is worth doing well. But anything worth doing is worth doing well. Therefore, at least one hobby is not worth doing.

* **10.** If anything is a mental event, then it is not a brain event. For only physical events are brain events, and no mental events are physical.

11. Some philosophical views are not worth considering. Every philosophical view has been held by a genius. Thus, some views that have been held by geniuses are not worth considering.

12. No wicked person is utterly without a conscience. But all wicked persons are deeply confused individuals. Hence, no deeply confused individual is utterly without a conscience.

***13.** Only metaphorical statements are similarity statements. And every statement is a similarity statement. Accordingly, a thing is a statement only if it is metaphorical.

14. Contrary to what traditional Western morality says, some acts of suicide are morally permissible. For all morally permissible acts are ones that conform to the categorical imperative, and some acts of suicide conform to the categorical imperative.

15. Only acts that maximize utility are obligatory. Not all acts that maximize utility are prescribed by the Ten Commandments. Therefore, at least one act prescribed by the Ten Commandments is not obligatory.

***16.** Not every act is free, since every act foreknown by God is nonfree and some acts are foreknown by God.

17. Only acts approved of by God are moral. Some acts of killing are approved of by God. Hence, some acts of killing are moral.

18. No human is omnipotent. All divine beings are omnipotent. Therefore, no human is divine.

***19.** Only persons who have inner conflicts are unhappy. At least one successful comedian is unhappy. We may conclude that some successful comedians are persons who have inner conflicts.

20. At least one tycoon is a person who has walked over others to get to the top. Every person who has walked over others to get to the top is evil. It follows that at least one tycoon is evil.

21. Some trees are maples. Some trees are oaks. So, some oaks are maples.

***22.** No balalaika is a banjo. Some balalaikas are beautiful. Hence, some beautiful things are not banjos.

23. Each tyrant is mendacious. If anything is a tyrant, then it is a liar. Consequently, all liars are mendacious.

24. Every aphorism is an apothegm. Each epigram is an aphorism. Accordingly, only apothegms are epigrams.

***25.** Every Saint Bernard is a large dog. Not all large dogs are brown. So, not all brown dogs are Saint Bernards.

6.4   The Modern Square of Opposition

We now come to some points of disagreement between Aristotelian logicians and modern logicians such as George Boole (1815–1864), John Venn (1834–1923), Charles Sanders Peirce (1839–1914), Gottlob Frege (1848–1925), and Bertrand Russell (1872–1970).

Consider the following argument:

22. 1. All Egyptians are Africans.

So, 2. Some Egyptians are Africans.

The diagram of the premise looks like this:

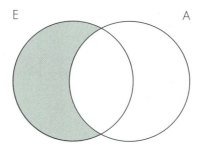

Does the diagram tell us the conclusion is true? No. An "x" would need to appear in the area of overlap between the two circles for the conclusion to be true. Note that argument (22) is an example of subalternation. Thus, our diagram in effect tells us that the Venn method we have presented does not confirm the Aristotelian view of the validity of subalternation. What's going on?

Aristotelian and modern logicians agree that particular statements have existential import. Categorical statements have **existential import** if (and only if) they imply that their subject terms denote nonempty classes.

> Categorical statements have **existential import** if (and only if) they imply that their subject terms denote nonempty classes.

For example, "Some Egyptians are Africans" implies that there *exists* at least one Egyptian (i.e., the class of Egyptians has at least one member and so is not empty). Similarly, "Some Rwandans are not marathoners" implies that there *exists* at least one Rwandan. Since the Venn diagrams for particular statements require an "x" within the circle labeled by the subject term, the Venn method presupposes that particular statements have existential import.

But modern logicians understand universal statements to have a conditional (if-then) aspect. From this perspective, "All Egyptians are Africans" is equivalent to "If anything is an Egyptian, then it is an African." So understood, "All Egyptians are Africans" does not imply that there are any Egyptians. After all, "If anything is a unicorn, then it is an animal" is true, but it does not imply that there actually are any unicorns. Similarly, "No Namibians are Libyans" is equivalent to "If anything is a Namibian, then it is not a Libyan," and so understood, it does not imply that there are any Namibians. This modern understanding of universal statements is built into the Venn method we presented. And this seemingly small point about universal statements has a series of ramifications for the Traditional Square of Opposition.

For example, consider the Aristotelian thesis that corresponding **A** and **E** statements are contraries (i.e., they cannot both be true but can both be false). If the Aristotelians are right, the following argument is valid:

> **23.** 1. No Malawians are Tanzanians.
>
> So, 2. It is false that all Malawians are Tanzanians.

A Venn diagram of the premise is as follows:

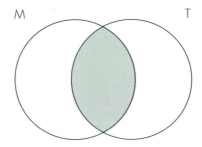

The diagram does not tell us that the conclusion is true since there is no "x" in area 1. Hence, according to the Venn method, argument (23) is not valid. The Venn method, therefore, disagrees with the Aristotelian view that corresponding **A** and **E** statements are contraries.

What about subcontraries? Aristotelian logicians claim that corresponding **I** and **O** statements are subcontraries (i.e., they can both be true but cannot both be false), in which case, this argument is valid:

> **24.** 1. It is false that some Chadians are Zambians.
>
> So, 2. Some Chadians are not Zambians.

Now the premise here is equivalent to "It's false that something is both a Chadian and a Zambian," which requires us to shade in the area of overlap.

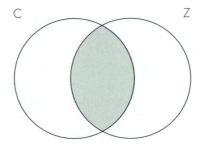

The diagram does not tell us that the conclusion is true since there is no "x" in area 1. So, according to the Venn method, argument (24) is not valid, and therefore disagrees with the Aristotelian view that corresponding **I** and **O** statements are subcontraries.

At this point, what's left of the Traditional Square of Opposition? Just the theses regarding contradictories, namely, *corresponding* **A** *and* **O** *statements are contradictories, and corresponding* **E** *and* **I** *statements are contradictories.* This is sometimes called the **Modern Square of Opposition** and may be represented pictorially as follows:

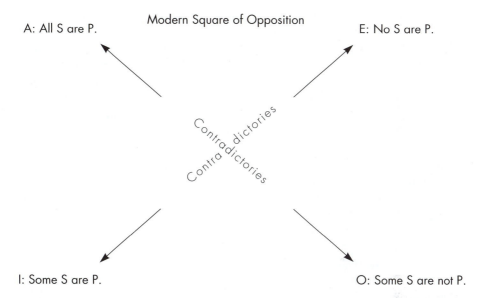

You may wish to stop a moment and compare this to the Traditional Square of Opposition discussed in section 5.2. The relationships along the sides of the Traditional Square have vanished (subalternation, contraries, subcontraries); only the diagonal relationships are retained (the contradictories).

The modern approach has at least one advantage over the Aristotelian approach that deserves special mention. Consider these pairs of statements:

> **25.** All unicorns are animals. Some unicorns are not animals.
>
> **26.** All ideal societies are perfectly just. Some ideal societies are not perfectly just.
>
> **27.** No perfect vacuums are spaces through which sound can be transmitted. Some perfect vacuums are spaces through which sound can be transmitted.

Are these pairs contradictories? Oddly enough, they are not *if we take an Aristotelian approach.* For in each case, the subject term refers to an empty class. (There exist no unicorns, ideal societies, or perfect vacuums.) It follows that these pairs are not contradictories given the Aristotelian approach. For according to Aristotelians, all of these statements have existential import. Thus, "All unicorns are animals" implies that at least one unicorn exists. And "Some unicorns are not animals" also implies that at least one unicorn exists. But any statement that implies a falsehood is itself false. Therefore, both "All unicorns are animals" and "Some unicorns are not animals" must be declared false by Aristotelians. But if two statements are contradictories, then if one is false, the other must be true. So, Aristotelians cannot preserve the thesis that corresponding **A** and **O** statements are always contradictories. And the same goes for corresponding **E** and **I** statements.

How does the modern approach differ? From this perspective, "All unicorns are animals" is equivalent to saying, "If anything is a unicorn, then it is an animal." This if-then statement seems to be true, and it doesn't imply that unicorns exist. But "Some unicorns are not animals" does imply that at least one unicorn exists, and so it is false. In this way, the modern approach preserves the thesis that corresponding **A** and **O** statements are contradictories *even when their subject terms refer to empty classes.* Similarly, if there are no unicorns, then "No unicorns are animals" is true, but "Some unicorns are animals" is false. So the modern approach also preserves the thesis that corresponding **E** and **I** statements are contradictories, *even when their subject terms refer to empty classes.*

Note that the differing understanding of universal statements affects the evaluation of conversion by limitation and contraposition by limitation. Consider conversion by limitation, which has this form:

28. 1. All S are P.
So, 2. Some P are S.

A diagram of the premise looks like this:

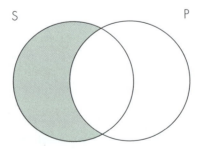

Does the diagram tell us that the conclusion is true? No, for there is no "x" in the area of overlap between the two circles. So, the Venn method tells us that conversion by limitation is not valid.

The differing understanding of universal statements also affects the assessment of certain syllogistic forms. In fact, nine syllogistic forms judged valid by Aristotelians are judged invalid via the modern approach. In every case, these syllogistic forms move from two universal premises to a particular conclusion. As an example, consider syllogisms in the first figure with the mood **AAI:**

29. 1. All M are P (e.g., all perfect spouses are spouses).

2. All S are M (e.g., all perfect husbands are perfect spouses).

So, 3. Some S are P (e.g., some perfect husbands are spouses).

A Venn diagram for (29) looks like this:

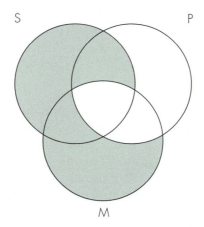

The diagram does not tell us the conclusion is true, for there is no "x" in the area of overlap between the S-circle and the P-circle. Indeed, given the modern understanding of universal statements as having a conditional (if-then) aspect, no categorical syllogism with two universal premises and a particular conclusion is valid.

These disagreements between Aristotelian and modern logicians may seem a bit troubling. But note that the disagreement has its source in the very specific issue of whether universal categorical statements have existential import. Let us suppose that the modern logicians are right that they do not. Still, in many actual cases, if an arguer appears to move from a universal categorical statement to a particular one, we can reasonably assume that the arguer has not stated all of his or her premises explicitly. (For practical purposes, it is often unnecessary to state every premise of an argument.) For example, the move from "All politicians are liars" to "Some politicians are liars" is valid if we add the premise "At least one politician exists." And in many cases, when someone asserts a premise of the form "All S are P," he or she is reasonably assuming that *there are some Ss*. Consider the following argument form:

30. 1. All S are P.

2. At least one S exists.

So, 3. Some S are P.

The second premise makes explicit the assumption that the class denoted by the subject term of the first premise is not empty. A diagram of the premises looks like this:

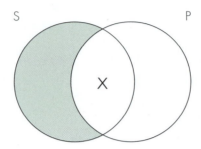

The second premise tells us we need an "x" within the S-circle, but the "x" can go only in the area of overlap between the two circles given our diagram of the first premise. (Here as elsewhere it is important tu diagram universal premises before diagramming particular ones.) Thus, the diagram of the premises tells us that the conclusion is true and the argument is valid. By making unstated premises explicit, we can thus accept the modern view of universal statements while recognizing an insight in the traditional Aristotelian view. In this case, an inference akin to superalternation ("All S are P, so some S are P") is valid if we add that there are Ss (i.e., if we add that the subject term of "All S are P" denotes a nonempty class).

A similar point can be made about the syllogistic forms that Aristotelians regard as valid but modern logicians reject as invalid. For example, consider syllogisms in the second figure with **EAO** as their mood:

31. 1. No P are M.
   2. All S are M.
So, 3. Some S are not P.

Here we need only add a premise to the effect that the subject term of the second premise denotes a nonempty class:

32. 1. No P are M.
   2. All S are M.
   3. At least one S exists.
So, 4. Some S are not P.

Of course, (32) does not have the form of a categorical syllogism because it has three premises instead of two, but we can easily diagram it, as long as we remember to diagram the universal premises first:

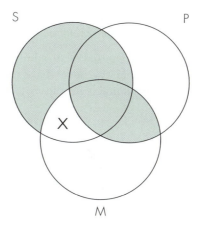

Premise 3 tells us to place an "x" within the S-circle, and the "x" can go only in area 4 given our diagrams for the universal premises. The diagram of the premises tells us that the conclusion is true, so argument form (32) is valid. Again, the point is that by adding unstated premises when it is reasonable to do so, we can in effect honor insights from both the Aristotelian and the modern traditions. Incidentally, arguments with unstated premises or conclusions are called *enthymemes*, and we shall take a closer look at them in the next section.

EXERCISE 6.4

PART A: Argument Forms Use Venn diagrams to test the following argument forms for validity. (Do not supply unstated premises.)

* **1.**   1. No M are P.
      2. All S are M.
  So, 3. Some S are not P.

2.   1. All P are M.
      2. No S are M.
  So, 3. Some S are not P.

3.   1. All M are P.
      2. All M are S.
  So, 3. Some S are P.

* **4.**   1. All M are P.
      2. All M are S.
      3. At least one M exists.
  So, 4. Some S are P.

5.   1. No M are P.
      2. All M are S.
  So, 3. Some S are not P.

6.   1. No M are P.
      2. All M are S.
      3. At least one M exists.
  So, 4. Some S are not P.

* **7.**   1. No S are P.
  So, 2. Some non-P are not non-S.

8.   1. All P are M.
      2. No M are S.
  So, 3. Some S are not P.

9.   1. All P are M.
      2. All M are S.
  So, 3. Some S are P.

* **10.**   1. No S are P.
       2. At least one S exists.
  So, 3. Some non-P are not non-S.

PART B: Testing Arguments Use Venn diagrams to test the following arguments for validity. (Do not supply unstated premises.)

* **1.** 1. All people who never make mistakes are admirable people.
  2. All ideal humans are people who never make mistakes.
  So, 3. Some ideal humans are admirable people.

2. 1. No plants are animals.
  2. All weeds are plants.
  So, 3. Some weeds are not animals.

3. 1. No perfect circles are perfect squares.
  2. Some perfect circles are objects of beauty.
  So, 3. Some objects of beauty are not perfect squares.

* **4.** 1. All persons who advocate the use of overwhelming nuclear force are persons who lack moral sensibility.
  2. All persons who advocate the use of overwhelming nuclear force are persons who should not serve as world leaders.
  3. At least one person who advocates the use of overwhelming nuclear force exists.
  So, 4. Some persons who should not serve as world leaders are persons who lack moral sensibility.

5. 1. All lions are cats.
  2. All cats are mammals.
  So, 3. Some mammals are lions.

6. 1. No terrorists who use nuclear weapons are good people.
  2. All terrorists who use nuclear weapons are people who mean well.
  3. At least one terrorist who uses nuclear weapons exists.
  So, 4. Some people who mean well are not good people.

* **7.** 1. All sycophants are flatterers.
  2. All flatterers are disgusting persons.
  3. At least one flatterer exists.
  So, 4. Some digusting persons are sycophants.

8. 1. Some highly educated people are sybarites.
  2. All sybarites are poor role models.
  So, 3. Some poor role models are highly educated people.

9. 1. No oaks are elms.
  2. All oaks are trees.
  3. At least one elm exists.
  So, 4. Some trees are not elms.

***10.** 1. No members of the IRA are members of the IRS.
  So, 2. It is false that all members of the IRA are members of the IRS.

11. 1. All great inventors are slightly odd people.
  2. At least one great inventor exists.
  So, 3. Some slightly odd people are great inventors.

12. 1. No anarchists are Republicans.
     2. At least one anarchist exists.
So, 3. Some non-Republicans are not nonanarchists.

* **13.** 1. All scarlet things are red things.
So, 2. It is false that no scarlet things are red things.

14. 1. No cities are nations.
     2. At least one city exists.
So, 3. Some cities are not nations.

15. 1. All people with perfect memories are people who remember everything.
So, 2. Some people with perfect memories are people who remember everything.

16. 1. It is false that some Germans are Zoroastrians.
So, 2. Some Germans are not Zoroastrians.

17. 1. It is false that some vampires are living things.
     2. At least one vampire exists.
So, 3. Some vampires are not living things.

18. 1. All people who do not care about social justice are heartless people.
So, 2. It is false that no people who do not care about social injustice are heartless people.

* **19.** 1. No kangaroos are karate experts.
So, 2. Some kangaroos are not karate experts.

20. 1. It is false that some tyrants are not humans.
     2. At least one tyrant exists.
So, 3. Some tyrants are humans.

6.5   Enthymemes

An **enthymeme** is an argument with one or more premises or its conclusion left implicit. If we use the more general term "step" to refer to premises or conclusions, an enthymeme is an argument with one or more steps left implicit.

Enthymemes are common both in ordinary discourse and in academic writing since many statements are presumed to be known to one's audience, and so it may be unnecessary to make them explicit. Here's an example:

> **33.** All Mozambicans are Africans. Hence, no Mozambicans are Asians.

A Venn diagram will show that (33), taken as it stands, is invalid. But obviously there is an unstated premise here, "No Africans are Asians" (or its converse, "No Asians are Africans"). And if we add this statement (or its converse) to the argument, we get a valid categorical syllogism:

> **34.** 1. No Africans are Asians.
>   2. All Mozambicans are Africans.
> So, 3. No Mozambicans are Asians.

Any kind of argument can have an implicit or unstated step, but we will here focus on categorical syllogisms. When we fill in missing steps in an argument, we must adhere to the principles of fairness and charity; that is, added steps should be true (or plausible) and make the argument valid.

To evaluate an enthymematic categorical syllogism for validity, we proceed in three stages. First, identify the missing step. The missing step may be a major premise, a minor premise, or the conclusion. Second, put the syllogism into standard form. Third, apply the Venn method.

How do we identify the missing step? The missing step will contain two terms that have been used only once each in the enthymeme. If the missing step is a premise, the form (**A, E, I,** or **O**) and order of the terms should be chosen with an eye toward the information needed to arrive at the conclusion. If the missing step is a conclusion, the form and order of terms should be chosen with an eye toward what the information in the premises would show to be true. For example, consider the following argument:

> **35.** If anything is a moral judgment, then it is a subjective opinion. It follows that judgments about the wrongness of theft are subjective opinions.

The missing step here is a minor premise: "All judgments about the wrongness of theft are moral judgments." Putting the syllogism into standard form, we get the following:

> **36.** 1. All moral judgments are subjective opinions.
>   2. All judgments about the wrongness of theft are moral judgments.
> So, 3. All judgments about the wrongness of theft are subjective opinions.

And now we can readily apply the Venn method:

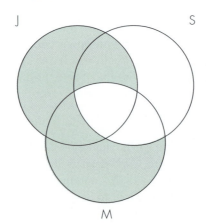

The diagram indicates that the argument is valid. The premise we have added seems to be true, but of course the first premise of the argument is highly controversial.

When adding steps to an enthymeme, it is not always possible to add a statement that is true (or plausible) and that makes the argument valid. Consider the following example:

37. All Ohioans are Americans. Hence, no Ohioans are socialists.

The missing step here is presumably "No Americans are socialists" (or its converse). Putting the syllogism into standard form, we get the following:

38. 1. No Americans are socialists.

    2. All Ohioans are Americans.

So, 3. No Ohioans are socialists.

Premise (1) is needed to make the argument valid, but (1) is false because some Americans are socialists. When a false or doubtful premise is needed to make an argument valid, we bring out an important weakness in the argument by making the premise explicit, for in doing so we have identified an important reason for doubting the soundness of the argument.

In some cases, the context forces us to make a hard choice between adding a blatantly false premise and adding a premise that makes the argument invalid. For example, what is the missing step in the following argument?

39. All Lutherans are Christians. Therefore, all Protestants are Christians.

The missing step seems to be either "All Protestants are Lutherans" or "All Lutherans are Protestants." If we add "All Protestants are Lutherans" to the argument, then it is valid but has a blatantly false premise. If we add "All Lutherans are Protestants" to the argument, then we add a true premise but one that makes the argument invalid. Thus, the argument is deeply flawed. It is up to us to choose whether to present that flaw as a flaw in the logical structure or as a false premise. When faced with this sort of choice, let us adopt the practice of adding a step that makes the argument valid, leaving the truth value of the added step as a matter for discussion. So, in standard form, argument (39) looks like this:

40. 1. All Lutherans are Christians.

    2. All Protestants are Lutherans.

So, 3. All Protestants are Christians.

Sometimes the conclusion of an argument is left unstated.

41. Every politician who wants to win slings mud, and every politician wants to win!

When we put the argument into standard form, we make the conclusion explicit:

42. 1. All politicians who want to win are mudslingers.

    2. All politicians are politicians who want to win.

So, 3. All politicians are mudslingers.

We add "All politicians are mudslingers" instead of "All mudslingers are politicians" because the former (unlike the latter) is guaranteed true by a diagram of the premises.

EXERCISE 6.5

PART A: Enthymemes Identify the missing step in each of the following arguments. Then put the argument into standard form. Finally, use a Venn diagram to check the argument for validity.

* **1.** No certainty should be rejected. So, no self-evident propositions should be rejected.
  2. Every virtue is beneficial. Therefore, no vice is a virtue.
  3. Only rational animals are humans. It follows that no ducks are humans.
* **4.** Atoms are indestructible because every simple substance is indestructible.
  5. Every envious person wants others to fail. Consequently, no good person is envious.
  6. Nothing is a liar unless it is not praiseworthy. At least one liar is a human being. Draw your own conclusion!
* **7.** Only scientific statements are rational. It follows that aesthetic judgments are never rational.
  8. All verdicts rendered in courts of law are relative because all value judgments are relative.
  9. Perfect beings have every virtue. Therefore, at least one god is not a perfect being.
* **10.** Some beliefs about aliens are not rational, for all rational beliefs are proportioned to the available evidence.
  11. No matter of faith is provable. At least one belief about life after death is a matter of faith. Draw your own conclusion!
  12. No bears are wolves, so some grizzlies are not wolves.
* **13.** Every vice is harmful. Accordingly, every vice is a form of laziness.
  14. Every composite substance is a substance that has parts. Hence, no soul is a composite substance.
  15. Every evil thing is to be avoided. But at least one evil thing is pleasurable. Need I say what follows?

PART B: More Enthymemes The following enthymemes are paraphrased or slightly altered versions of arguments found in the writings of the philosopher Gottfried Wilhelm Leibniz. (These are arguments Leibniz *discusses;* some he endorses and some he does not.) Identify the missing step in each of the arguments.

Then put the argument into standard form. Finally, use a Venn diagram to check the argument for validity.

* **1.** Every event that is foreseen by God is predetermined. Consequently, every event is predetermined.

  2. Every event that is predetermined is necessary. Every event is predetermined. Draw your own conclusion!

  3. Every event is necessary. Hence, every sin is necessary.

* **4.** No necessary event can be avoided. Only events that can be avoided are justly punished. Therefore, …

  5. Every being that is omnipotent and perfectly good creates the best of all possible worlds. Hence, some deity creates the best of all possible worlds.

  6. All composites are aggregates of simple substances. At least one composite exists. Draw your own conclusion.

* **7.** Nothing that has no parts can come apart. So, nothing that has no parts can be annihilated.

  8. If anything has the power to help everyone but helps only some, then it is not fair. Thus, some deity is not fair.

  9. Any being who punishes people who do their best is an unjust being. No perfectly good being is an unjust being. Need I say what follows?

* **10.** Every event is caused by a deity. It follows that every sin is caused by a deity.

6.6 Sorites and Removing Term-Complements

We have seen that ordinary language throws the logician many "curveballs" (i.e., complications). This section concerns two additional complications. First, we will discuss categorical syllogisms that are linked in a chain. Second, we will discuss categorical arguments that can be put into standard form through the elimination of term-complements.

Sorites

The term "sorites" (so-rī́-teez) comes from the Greek word *soros*, meaning "heap" or "pile." Roughly put, in the present context, a sorites is a "heap" of syllogisms. More precisely, a **sorites** is a chain of syllogisms in which the final conclusion is stated but the subconclusions are unstated.

A **sorites** is a chain of syllogisms in which the final conclusion is stated but the subconclusions are unstated.

Here is an example:

43. 1. All statements about beauty are statements known through the senses.

2. All statements known through the senses are empirical statements.

3. No mathematical statements are empirical statements.

4. All geometrical statements are mathematical statements.

So, 5. No geometrical statements are statements about beauty.

Premises (1) and (2) validly imply the following subconclusion:

Subconclusion 1: All statements about beauty are empirical statements.

When combined with premise (3), subconclusion 1 validly implies:

Subconclusion 2: No mathematical statements are statements about beauty.

Premise (4) and subconclusion 2 validly imply (5), the conclusion of the argument. Thus, the sorites is a chain of three valid categorical syllogisms.

In general, sorites are easier to evaluate when they are in standard form. A sorites in **standard form** has these features:

a. Each statement in the argument is in standard form ("All S are P," "No S are P," "Some S are P," or "Some S are not P").

b. The predicate term of the conclusion occurs in the first premise.

c. Each term appears twice, in two different statements.

d. Each premise (except the first) has a term in common with the immediately preceding premise.

Is argument (43) in standard form? Yes. This is perhaps easier to see by looking at the form of the argument. Using obvious abbreviations, the form of the argument is this:

44. 1. All B are K.

2. All K are E.

3. No M are E.

4. All G are M.

So, 5. No G are B.

When evaluating a sorites, we follow a three-step process. First, check to see if the sorites is in standard form. If it is, proceed to the next step. If it isn't, put it into standard form. We will freely use abbreviations for the terms as we put a sorites into standard form. Second, identify the subconclusions. Third, test each syllogism in the chain for validity, using a Venn diagram. If each syllogism in the chain is valid, the sorites is valid. If any of the syllogisms in the chain are invalid, the entire sorites is invalid.

To illustrate this three-step process, let us evaluate the following sorites:

45. No cruel and unusual punishments are proportioned to the offense. Every just punishment is deserved. Moreover, all deserved punishments are proportioned to the offense. Therefore, no cruel and unusual punishment is a just punishment.

First, we put the sorites into standard form, using obvious abbreviations for the various terms (J: just punishments; D: deserved punishments; P: punishments that are proportioned to the offense; C: cruel and unusual punishments). Incidentally, it often helps to begin with the conclusion and then work backward, making sure that the first premise contains the predicate term of the conclusion:

46. 1. All J are D.
  2. All D are P.
  3. No C are P.
So, 4. No C are J.

Premises (1) and (2) imply that all just punishments are punishments that are proportioned to the offense. Using our abbreviations:

Subconclusion 1: All J are P.

Let us adopt the practice of writing a subconclusion beside the last premise from which it is derived, like this:

47. 1. All J are D.
  2. All D are P.   Sub 1: All J are P.
  3. No C are P.
So, 4. No C are J.

Subconclusion 1 and premise (3) combine to yield (4), the conclusion of the argument. So, this sorites is a chain of two categorical syllogisms. And we now apply the Venn method to each of the two categorical syllogisms:

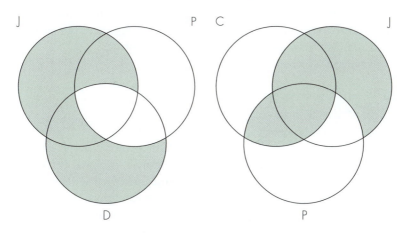

The diagram on the left evaluates the inference from premises (1) and (2) to subconclusion 1. The diagram on the right evaluates the inference from subconclusion 1 and premise (3) to the final conclusion of the argument, (4). Both of these syllogisms are valid, so the sorites itself is valid.

Removing Term-Complements

Consider the following argument:

> **48.** 1. All cats are nondogs.
>
> 2. Some mammals are dogs.
>
> So, 3. Some mammals are not cats.

This argument has four terms: "cats," "nondogs," "mammals," and "dogs." Hence, it is not a categorical syllogism in standard form. And if you try to evaluate this argument with a Venn diagram, questions arise regarding the label for the middle circle. You must label it either "dogs" or "nondogs." If you label the middle circle "dogs," then your diagram for the first premise cannot be the usual diagram for an **A** statement. If you label the middle circle "nondogs," then your diagram for the second premise cannot be the usual diagram for an **I** statement. (Try it!)

Note, however, that "dogs" and "nondogs" are term-complements. In arguments involving term-complements, we can often reduce the number of terms by applying conversion, obversion, or contraposition. For example, the obverse of "All cats are nondogs" is "No cats are dogs." Thus, we can rewrite argument (48) as:

> **49.** 1. No cats are dogs.
>
> 2. Some mammals are dogs.
>
> So, 3. Some mammals are not cats.

We have reduced the number of terms in the argument from four to three by removing a term-complement. Argument (49) is a categorical syllogism in standard form, and the Venn diagram for it is entirely routine.

Consider yet another argument:

> **50.** 1. No nonanimals are mammals.
>
> 2. All nonmammals are nondogs.
>
> So, 3. All dogs are animals.

Is this argument a categorical syllogism in standard form? No, it has six terms instead of three. But we can put it into standard form by a series of immediate inferences. First, we can convert the first premise to obtain "No mammals are nonanimals." Then, applying obversion, we get "All mammals are animals."

Second, we can apply contraposition to premise (2) to get "All dogs are mammals." With these changes, the argument looks like this:

51. 1. All mammals are animals.

2. All dogs are mammals.

So, 3. All dogs are animals.

Argument (51) is a syllogism in standard form, and it's easier to understand.

We can often put an argument into standard form by removing term-complements via conversion, obversion, or contraposition. And we are free to remove term-complements as long as the changes we make to each statement produce a *logically equivalent* statement. However, if the changes we make produce any statement that is *not* logically equivalent to the original, then we have significantly changed the meaning of the statement—in which case we are working with a different argument. When removing term-complements, the permissible changes are as follows:

Conversion

No S are P.   No P are S.

Some S are P.   Some P are S.

Contraposition

All S are P.   All non-P are non-S.

Some S are not P.   Some non-P are not non-S.

Obversion

All S are P.   No S are non-P.

No S are P.   All S are non-P.

Some S are P.   Some S are not non-P.

Some S are not P.   Some S are non-P.

In each case, the statement on the left is logically equivalent to the statement on the right, and vice versa.

In attempting to remove term-complements, the most common error involves misapplications of conversion and contraposition. When you apply conversion to **A** and **O** statements, you do not generally wind up with logically equivalent statements. So, *never* use conversion on **A** and **O** statements when removing term-complements. Similarly, when you apply contraposition to **E** and **I** statements, you do not generally wind up with logically equivalent statements. So, *never* apply contraposition to **E** and **I** statements when removing term-complements. On the other hand, because a statement and its obverse are *always* logically equivalent, we are always free to apply obversion when we are removing term-complements.

It is often convenient to remove term-complements to put a sorites into standard form. Here's an example:

52. 1. No F are G.
  2. All H are G.
  3. All non-H are non-K.
So, 4. All K are non-F.

This sorites is not in standard form because the terms F, H, and K do not appear twice (the term-complements appear instead). But we can easily put this sorites into standard form by applying contraposition to premise (3) and obversion to the conclusion:

53. 1. No F are G.
  2. All H are G.
  3. All K are H.
So, 4. No K are F.

Again, by removing term-complements, we have only put the argument into standard form and made it easier to grasp and to evaluate.

EXERCISE 6.6

PART A: Removing Term-Complements The following categorical arguments (and argument forms) all have more than three terms. Reduce the terms to three in each case by removing term-complements via applications of conversion, obversion, or contraposition. Use capital letters to abbreviate English terms.

* **1.** 1. All M are non-P.
    2. No S are non-M.
  So, 3. No S are P.

  2. 1. All logicians are nonpoets.
    2. Some logicians are not nondreamers.
  So, 3. Some dreamers are not poets.

  3. 1. All non-P are non-M.
    2. Some S are M.
  So, 3. Some S are not non-P.

* **4.** 1. All nonphysicians are nonsurgeons.
    2. All physicians are nonchiropractors.
  So, 3. No chiropractors are surgeons.

  5. 1. Some non-P are not non-M.
    2. No M are non-S.
  So, 3. Some S are not P.

6. 1. All mesomorphs are nonectomorphs.
   2. All nonectomorphs are things that are not slight persons.
So, 3. No slight persons are mesomorphs.

* **7.** 1. No M are non-P.
   2. All non-M are non-S.
So, 3. All S are P.

8. 1. No nonairplanes are jets.
   2. All nonjets are non-737s.
So, 3. All 737s are airplanes.

9. 1. All M are non-P.
   2. Some S are M.
So, 3. Some non-P are not non-S.

* **10.** 1. Some subatomic particles are mesons.
   2. No mesons are entities not subject to the strong nuclear force.
So, 3. Some entities subject to the strong nuclear force are subatomic particles.

PART B: Standard Form Put the following sorites into standard form, removing term-complements whenever possible. Then identify the unstated sub-conclusions and use Venn diagrams to test the sorites for validity.

* **1.** 1. Some A are B.
   2. All non-D are non-C.
   3. No B are non-C.
So, 4. Some D are A.

2. 1. Some F are G.
   2. All non-H are non-G.
   3. All H are non-E.
So, 4. Some non-E are not non-F.

3. 1. Some K are non-L.
   2. No M are non-N.
   3. All N are L.
So, 4. Some K are not M.

* **4.** 1. Some A are B.
   2. All non-E are non-D.
   3. All B are D.
   4. All E are non-C.
So, 5. Some A are not C.

5. 1. All F are non-M.
   2. All non-D are non-B.
   3. All D are M.
So, 4. All F are non-B.

6. 1. All U are non-T.
   2. All S are T.
   3. All non-S are non-R.

    4. All non-R are non-P.
So, 5. All P are non-U.

* **7.** 1. All non-B are non-A.
    2. No C are B.
    3. Some D are non-C.
So, 4. Some D are not A.

8. 1. No R are non-S.
    2. All T are V.
    3. All non-R are non-Q.
    4. All P are Q.
    5. No T are S.
So, 6. All V are non-P.

9. 1. All F are G.
    2. No G are non-H.
    3. No J are H.
    4. Some K are J.
So, 5. Some non-F are not non-K.

***10.** 1. Some B are A.
    2. All non-D are non-C.
    3. All B are C.
So, 4. Some D are A.

PART C: Sorites Put the following sorites into standard form. Use capital letters as abbreviations for the various terms. Then identify the unstated subconclusions and use Venn diagrams to test the sorites for validity.

* **1.** No theorists who hold that life evolved from nonlife are people who have solid evidence for their views. Every advocate of chemical evolution is a theorist who holds that life evolved from nonlife. At least one Darwinian is a person who has solid evidence for his or her views. Consequently, not all Darwinians are advocates of chemical evolution.

2. No voters who reject trickle-down economics are Republicans, for every voter who rejects trickle-down economics is a person who opposes tax cuts for the wealthy; all Democrats are non-Republicans; and only Democrats are persons who oppose tax cuts for the wealthy.

3. All folks who know that the oil reserves are running low are people who favor the development of alternative sources of energy. Every person who favors the development of alternative sources of energy is a voter who favors a tax increase. All well-informed citizens are folks who know that the oil reserves are running low. Not every highly educated person is a voter who favors a tax increase. Therefore, not all highly educated people are well-informed citizens.

* **4.** Each and every dualist is a moral realist. Nothing is an emotivist unless it is not a moral realist. Only dualists are Zoroastrians. At least one positivist is an emotivist. It follows that some non-Zoroastrians are not nonpositivists.

5. Every victim of sleep apnea is a sleep-deprived person. No sleep-deprived persons are nonunfortunates. At least one unfortunate is a college student. Therefore, some college students are victims of sleep apnea.

6. No humans with a sense of justice are consumers who are willing to buy clothing made in sweatshops. But only shoppers are persons looking for good deals. Hence, not all shoppers are humans with a sense of justice because some persons looking for good deals are consumers who are willing to buy clothing made in sweatshops.

* 7. Not all freethinkers are rational people. Every agnostic is a person who proportions his or her religious beliefs to the evidence. All people who proportion their religious beliefs to the evidence are rational people. Thus, not every freethinker is an agnostic.

8. Only reasons that override mere prudence are ethical reasons. Some motives for laying down one's life are ethical reasons. No motives for laying down one's life are intentions that make sense if there's no life after death. It follows that not all reasons that override mere prudence are intentions that make sense if there's no life after death.

9. There exist rapscallions that are human vermin. Only scalawags are moral freeloaders. All human vermin are moral freeloaders. Every scalawag is a nongangster. Hence, not every rapscallion is a gangster.

*10. No badly informed voters are responsible voters. Some folks who vote in every election are citizens who do not proportion their political beliefs to the evidence. Every citizen who does not proportion his or her political beliefs to the evidence is a badly informed voter. Only responsible voters are people who ought to vote. Accordingly, not all folks who vote in every election are people who ought to vote.

6.7 Rules for Evaluating Syllogisms

Before the invention of Venn diagrams, categorical syllogisms were evaluated by means of a set of rules. Although the rules lack the visual intuitiveness of Venn diagrams, they are equally effective in testing syllogisms for validity. In this section, we will explore a set of rules for evaluating categorical syllogisms.

Our first rule is:

> **Rule 1:** A valid standard-form categorical syllogism must contain exactly three terms, and each term must be used with the same meaning throughout the argument.

A *fallacy of equivocation* occurs if a term is used with more than one meaning in a categorical syllogism. For example:

54. Only man is rational. But no woman is a man. Hence, no woman is rational.

Argument (54) violates Rule 1 because in the first premise, "man" means "human beings," but in the second premise, "man" means "male human."

The next two rules depend crucially on the concept of a term's being *distributed*. So, the rather technical concept of distribution must be explained in some detail before we proceed any further. A term is **distributed** in a statement if the statement says something about every member of the class that the term denotes. A term is **undistributed** in a statement if the statement does not say something about every member of the class the term denotes.

> A term is **distributed** in a statement if the statement says something about every member of the class that the term denotes.
> A term is **undistributed** in a statement if the statement does not say something about every member of the class the term denotes.

For example:

    55. All ants are insects.

Statement (55) says something about all members of the class of ants—namely, that every member of the class of ants belongs to the class of insects. Hence, the term "ants" is distributed in (55). But the term "insects" is undistributed, for the statement does not say anything about every member of the class of insects. In general, the subject term of a universal affirmative (or **A**) statement is distributed, but the predicate term is not.

Both terms are distributed in a universal negative (or **E**) statement. For instance:

    56. No trumpets are flutes.

This says that every trumpet is excluded from the class of flutes and that every flute is excluded from the class of trumpets. Hence, both the subject term "trumpets" and the predicate term "flutes" are distributed.

Neither term is distributed in a particular affirmative (or **I**) statement. For example:

    57. Some precious stones are diamonds.

This statement makes no assertion about all precious stones. Furthermore, it makes no assertion about all diamonds. Both the subject term and the predicate term of a particular affirmative statement are undistributed.

The predicate term of a particular negative (or **O**) statement is distributed, but its subject term is undistributed. For example:

    58. Some precious stones are not diamonds.

Statement (58) does not say anything about *all* precious stones. But it does refer to all members of the class of diamonds, and it says that *all* diamonds are excluded from a portion of the class of precious stones.

To recap: Universal (**A** and **E**) statements distribute their subject terms, but negative (**E** and **O**) statements distribute their predicate terms. The following list summarizes our discussion of distribution:

Letter Name	Form	Terms Distributed
A	All S are P.	S
E	No S are P.	S and P
I	Some S are P.	None
O	Some S are not P.	P

We are now in position to state Rule 2.

> Rule 2: In a valid standard-form categorical syllogism, the middle term must be distributed in at least one premise.

Here is an example of a syllogism that violates Rule 2:

> **59.** All eagles are birds. All penguins are birds. So, all penguins are eagles.

The middle term, "birds," is not distributed in either premise because the predicate terms of **A** statements are not distributed. Within the Aristotelian scheme, a violation of Rule 2 is called a *fallacy of the undistributed middle*.

Why does the distribution of the middle term matter? Because the middle term has to serve as a link between the other terms. And if the middle term is undistributed, then neither premise makes an assertion about *all* the members of the class denoted by the middle term. Hence, it is possible that the minor term relates to one part of the class denoted by the middle term, while the major term relates to a different part of that class, with the result that there is no guaranteed link between the minor and major term.

Rule 3 also involves the concept of distribution.

> Rule 3: In a valid standard-form categorical syllogism, a term must be distributed in the premises if it is distributed in the conclusion.

This rule can be broken in two basic ways, depending on whether the major or minor term is distributed in the conclusion but not in the premises. Consider the following examples:

> **60.** All birds are animals. No bats are birds. So, no bats are animals.
>
> **61.** All squares are rectangles. All squares are figures. So, all figures are rectangles.

In argument (60), the major term, "animals," is distributed in the conclusion but not in the premises. This sort of violation of Rule 3 is called a *fallacy of the illicit major*. In argument (61), the minor term, "figures," is distributed in the conclusion but not in the second premise. This type of violation of Rule 3 is called a *fallacy of the illicit minor*.

Why is it important for a term to be distributed in the premises if it is distributed in the conclusion? Well, suppose a term is distributed in the conclusion but not in the premises. Then the conclusion contains more information than the premises warrant because the conclusion says something about *all* members of the class denoted by the term, while the premises do *not* say something about all the members of that class. Therefore, if a term is distributed in the conclusion but not in the premises, the conclusion "goes beyond" the information contained in the premises, and hence, the argument is invalid.

The next rule concerns the *quality* of the statements composing a categorical syllogism.

> Rule 4: In a valid standard-form categorical syllogism, the number of negative premises must be equal to the number of negative conclusions.[1]

A syllogism has only one conclusion, so this rule tells us that any categorical syllogism with two negative premises is invalid. For instance:

> **62.** No dogs are cats. Some cats are not cocker spaniels. So, some cocker spaniels are not dogs.

The premises of argument (62) are true, but the conclusion is false, so (62) is invalid.

Rule 4 also tells us that the conclusion of a categorical syllogism must be negative if one of the premises is negative. Thus, the following syllogism also violates Rule 4:

> **63.** No tigers are wolves. Some felines are tigers. So, some felines are wolves.

Summary of Rules for Determining the Validity of Categorical Syllogisms

Rule 1: A valid standard-form categorical syllogism must contain exactly three terms, and each term must be used with the same meaning throughout the argument.

Rule 2: In a valid standard-form categorical syllogism, the middle term must be distributed in at least one premise.

Rule 3: In a valid standard-form categorical syllogism, a term must be distributed in the premises if it is distributed in the conclusion.

Rule 4: In a valid standard-form categorical syllogism, the number of negative premises must be equal to the number of negative conclusions.

Rule 5: No valid standard-form categorical syllogism with a particular conclusion can have two universal premises.

Here again, the premises are true, while the conclusion is false, so the argument is invalid.

Finally, Rule 4 tells us that a categorical syllogism is invalid if it has a negative conclusion but no negative premises:

> **64.** All collies are dogs. Some animals are collies. So, some dogs are not animals.

Argument (64) has obviously true premises and an obviously false conclusion; therefore, it is plainly invalid. In fact, violations of Rule 4 are not common because the invalidity tends to be quite obvious.

At this point, our list of rules is complete from the traditional Aristotelian perspective. If we add the following rule, however, we can bring the Aristotelian system into agreement with modern systems of logic.

> Rule 5: No valid standard-form categorical syllogism with a particular conclusion can have two universal premises.[2]

Here is an example of a syllogism that violates Rule 5 but counts as valid in the traditional Aristotelian scheme:

> **65.** All Americans are humans. All morally perfect Americans are Americans. So, some morally perfect Americans are humans.

The conclusion asserts the existence of at least one morally perfect American. But from the standpoint of modern logic, we can assert that "all morally perfect Americans are Americans" without asserting that there actually *are* any morally perfect Americans. We can analyze the statement "All morally perfect Americans are Americans" as involving a conditional, along the following lines: "If anything is a morally perfect American, then it is an American." And such a statement can be true even if the term "employed" in the if-clause denotes an empty class.

EXERCISE 6.7

PART A: Forms   Apply the five rules set forth in this section to determine whether the following forms are valid. It may be useful first to determine the mood and figure of each argument form.

* **1.** No P are M. No M are S. So, no S are P.
  2. All M are P. No S are M. So, no S are P.
  3. All M are P. All M are S. So, all S are P.
* **4.** All P are M. All S are M. So, all S are P.
  5. No M are P. Some S are M. So, some S are not P.

   6. No M are P. All M are S. So, some S are not P.

* **7.** All P are M. Some S are not M. So, some S are not P.

   8. Some M are P. All S are M. So, some S are not P.

   9. All M are P. Some S are not M. So, some S are not P.

***10.** Some P are not M. Some S are not M. So, some S are not P.

 11. All P are M. Some S are M. So, some S are P.

 12. No P are M. All M are S. So, no S are P.

***13.** Some M are not P. All S are M. So, some S are not P.

 14. No M are P. Some M are not S. So, some S are not P.

 15. All P are M. No M are S. So, some S are not P.

***16.** All M are P. All S are M. So, some S are P.

 17. All P are M. All M are S. So, all S are P.

 18. No P are M. All S are M. So, some S are not P.

***19.** Some M are P. Some M are S. So, some S are P.

 20. Some P are M. All S are M. So, some S are P.

PART B: Valid or Invalid? For each of the following categorical syllogisms, specify the form using "S" to stand for the minor term, "P" for the major term, and "M" for the middle term. (If the English argument itself is not in standard form, be sure your form puts the major premise first, the minor premise second, and the conclusion last.) Then apply the five rules set forth in this section to determine whether the syllogism has a valid form.

* **1.** Some great scientists are famous. No TV stars are great scientists. So, some TV stars are not famous.

  2. No deathly ill people are hypochondriacs. All hypochondriacs are dysfunctional people. Accordingly, some deathly ill people are dysfunctional people.

  3. Some books written by Kant are not great books. For no great books are books that put their readers to sleep. But some books written by Kant are books that put their readers to sleep.

* **4.** No humans are animals. All members of *homo sapiens* are animals. Therefore, no humans are members of *homo sapiens*.

  5. All values that can be quantified are important values. No human emotions are values that can be quantified. Consequently, no human emotions are important values.

  6. No great altruists are great thinkers. Some great thinkers are people who make life better for humanity in general. It follows that some people who make life better for humanity in general are not great altruists.

* **7.** All cars are vehicles. All Ford automobiles are cars. Hence, some Ford automobiles are vehicles.

8. All banks are edges of rivers. Some banks are financial institutions. Thus, some financial institutions are edges of rivers.

9. All acts that promote the general welfare are commanded by God. For all acts commanded by God are obligatory acts. And all acts that promote the general welfare are obligatory acts.

* **10.** All of the greatest human achievements are accomplishments that have come at a great price. Some accomplishments that have come at a great price are not brilliant discoveries. We may conclude that some of the greatest human achievements are not brilliant discoveries.

11. All kleptomaniacs are troubled persons. No Bodhisattvas are troubled persons. So, some kleptomaniacs are not Bodhisattvas.

12. All biologists are vivisectionists. Some vivisectionists are well-intentioned people. Therefore, some biologists are well-intentioned people.

13. Every schipperke is a small dog. Some small dogs are not black. Hence, not all black dogs are schipperkes.

14. No bagatelle is important. Some important things are pleasurable. It follows that at least one bagatelle is not pleasurable.

15. All Mennonites are Protestants. No Mennonites are Roman Catholics. Accordingly, no Protestants are Roman Catholics.

NOTES

1. Our formulation of Rule 4 is borrowed from Wesley C. Salmon, *Logic*, 3rd ed. (Englewood Cliffs, NJ: Prentice-Hall, 1984), p. 57.
2. Our formulation of Rule 5 is borrowed from Irving Copi and Carl Cohen, *Introduction to Logic*, 9th ed. (Englewood Cliffs, NJ: Prentice-Hall, 1994), p. 266.

CHAPTER 7

Statement Logic: Truth Tables

*I*n Chapter 1, we saw that formally valid arguments are arguments that are valid by virtue of having a valid form. We exploited that fact in our effort to develop some methods for discerning the validity and invalidity of arguments. The famous forms method, in section 1.2, helped us discern the validity of many arguments. Unfortunately, it could not help us discern the validity of any argument that was not an instance of one of our famous forms. Moreover, it did nothing to help us discern invalidity. The counterexample method, in section 1.3, helped us discern the invalidity of many arguments, but it only gave us provisional results since we might not be able to identify the most logically sensitive form of an argument and, even when we do, we might lack the creativity to think of a good counterexample. In short, we had good reason to search for alternative methods.

In Chapters 5 and 6, we focused on methods that are useful for arguments involving categorical statements alone. But not all arguments are composed of categorical statements alone. For example:

1. 1. If you want to do well in logic, then you should read this chapter very carefully.
2. You want to do well in logic.
So, 3. You should read this chapter very carefully.

The methods developed in Chapters 5 and 6 do not recognize the validity of this argument even though it is an instance of *modus ponens*. In the next two chapters, Chapters 7 and 8, we will expand our focus to include two methods that are useful for arguments that involve statements other than categorical statements. In the present chapter, we will focus on the truth-table method developed by Charles Sanders Peirce (1839–1914).[1] But first we must learn how to translate English arguments into symbols.

7.1   Symbolizing English Arguments

Modern logicians have developed very useful ways of symbolizing an argument's form. Symbolizing an argument enables us to apply certain powerful techniques to determine its validity.

To symbolize statements properly, we must distinguish atomic from compound statements. An **atomic statement** is one that does not have any other statement as a component. For example:

2. Shakespeare wrote *Hamlet*.
3. China has a large population.
4. Roses are red.

A **compound statement** is one that has at least one atomic statement as a component. For instance:

5. It is not the case that Ben Jonson wrote *Hamlet*.
6. China has a large population, and Luxembourg has a small population.
7. Either Palermo is the capital of Sicily, or Messina is the capital of Sicily.
8. If Sheboygan is in Wisconsin, then Sheboygan is in the U.S.A.
9. The Democrats win if and only if the Republicans quarrel.

An **atomic statement** is one that does not have any other statement as a component.
A **compound statement** is one that has at least one atomic statement as a component.

We can symbolize the *atomic* statements in these compounds with capital letters, as follows:

B: Ben Jonson wrote *Hamlet*.
C: China has a large population.
L: Luxembourg has a small population.
P: Palermo is the capital of Sicily.
M: Messina is the capital of Sicily.
S: Sheboygan is in Wisconsin.
U: Sheboygan is in the U.S.A.
D: The Democrats win.
R: The Republicans quarrel.

When we assign each atomic statement a distinct capital letter, we provide what we will call a **scheme of abbreviation.** With this scheme of abbreviation in hand, statements (5)–(9) can be written as follows, in order:

10. It is not the case that B.

11. C and L.

12. Either P or M.

13. If S, then U.

14. D if and only if R.

Note that statement (10) is a compound even though it has only one statement as a component. It is a compound consisting of an atomic statement and the phrase "it is not the case that."

Throughout this chapter and the next, we will use capital letters to stand for atomic statements. We will also use symbols to stand for the key logical words in our example compounds, namely, "it is not the case that," "and," "or," "if ... then ... ," and "if and only if." We will symbolize these English expressions by means of **logical operators.** We can sum up the symbol system as follows*:

Operator	Name	Translates	Type of Compound
~	tilde	not	negation
•	dot	and	conjunction
∨	vee	or	disjunction
→	arrow	if-then	conditional
↔	double-arrow	if and only if	biconditional

Let us now turn to a discussion of each type of compound statement so that we can gain a better understanding of how to translate English statements into our symbol system.

Negations

The "~" symbol, called the **tilde,** is used to translate the English word "not" and its stylistic variants. Take the following example:

15. Roses are not blue. (R: Roses are blue)

---

*From a historical point of view, symbolic logic is relatively new and its notation is not yet standardized. Thus, although the symbols provided in this text are in common use, they are not the only ones in common use. Many texts employ one or more of the following alternatives: " ¬" to symbolize negations; "&" to symbolize conjunctions; " ⊃ " to symbolize conditionals; and " ≡ " to symbolize biconditionals. The lack of standard notation in logic is inconvenient, but it is not difficult to move from one notation to another once the basic principles have been mastered.

The scheme of abbreviation for (15) is in the parentheses to the right of the statement "Roses are not blue." We will often provide a scheme of abbreviation in this fashion. Using the tilde, we can then symbolize statement (15) as follows:

16. ~R

Of course, the English language provides a number of ways of negating a statement. For example:

a. It is not the case that roses are blue.
b. It is false that roses are blue.
c. It is not true that roses are blue.
d. Roses fail to be blue.

Statement (16) translates each of these English expressions into symbols.

Statement (15) is a negation of an atomic statement. Many negations are negations of compound statements, however. For example:

17. It is false that Christopher is a Buddhist or a Hindu. (B: Christopher is a Buddhist; H: Christopher is a Hindu)
18. It is not true that if Joshua finishes his dissertation this year, he is guaranteed a tenure-track job. (F: Joshua finishes his dissertation this year; T: Joshua is guaranteed a tenure-track job)
19. It is not the case that both the Orioles will win and the Mariners will win. (O: The Orioles will win; and M: the Mariners will win)

(17) is the negation of a disjunction, (18) is the negation of a conditional, and (19) is the negation of a conjunction. Using our logical operators and the scheme of abbreviation provided, we can symbolize these compounds as follows:

20. ~(B ∨ H)
21. ~(F → T)
22. ~(O • M)

These examples illustrate two important points. First, notice that we use *parentheses* as a form of punctuation. To understand why, consider what would happen if we removed them:

23. ~B ∨ H
24. ~F → T
25. ~O • M

(23) says "Christopher is not a Buddhist or Christopher is a Hindu," which is not the meaning of (17) at all. (24) says "If Joshua does not finish his dissertation, then he is guaranteed a tenure-track job," which hardly means (18). (25) says "The Orioles will not win and the Mariners will win," which (19) does not mean. So the placement of parentheses is important when translating English into symbols. Placing parentheses around B ∨ H and putting the tilde on the outside left makes it clear that it is B ∨ H (the disjunction) and not B (the atomic statement) that is negated. The same point applies to the other two examples.

Second, these examples also illustrate the difference between main logical operators and secondary logical operators. The **main logical operator** in a compound statement is the one that governs the largest component or components of a compound statement. A **minor logical operator** governs smaller components.

> The **main logical operator** in a compound statement is the one that governs the largest component or components of a compound statement. A **minor logical operator** governs smaller components.

In each of the previous examples the tilde is the main operator. In (20), the tilde governs (B ∨ H); in (21), the tilde governs (F → T); and in (22), the tilde governs (O • M). In (20), the minor operator is the vee, which governs B and H; in (21), the minor operator is the arrow, which governs F and T; in (22), the minor operator is the dot, which governs O and M.

Of course, negations can be more complex than the compounds just discussed. In that case, we may alternate parentheses and *brackets* because multiple sets of parentheses can appear confusing. For example:

26. It is false that, if God is omnipotent and perfectly good, then either horrific suffering is necessary in itself or necessary for some greater good. (P: God is omnipotent; G: God is perfectly good; I: Horrific suffering is necessary in itself; R: Horrific suffering is necessary for some greater good)

Using the scheme of abbreviation provided, we can symbolize (26) like this:

27. ~ [(P • G) → (I ∨ R)]

Each of the following statements is a negation. The main operator is the *tilde*.

~C

~(A ∨ B)

~(F → G)

Conjunctions

The "•" sign (called the **dot**) is used to translate the English word "and" as well as its stylistic variants. Take the following example:

> **28.** Hobbes was born in 1588, and Descartes was born in 1596. (H: Hobbes was born in 1588; D: Descartes was born in 1596)

Using the scheme of abbreviation indicated, statement (28) translates into symbols as follows:

> **29.** H • D

The statements composing a conjunction (H and D in this case) are called **conjuncts.** A partial list of stylistic variants for "and" is provided by the following set of sentences:

a. Hobbes was born in 1588, *but* Descartes was born in 1596.

b. Hobbes was born in 1588; *however,* Descartes was born in 1596.

c. *While* Hobbes was born in 1588, Descartes was born in 1596.

d. *Although* Hobbes was born in 1588, Descartes was born in 1596.

e. Hobbes was born in 1588, *yet* Descartes was born in 1596.

f. Hobbes was born in 1588; *nevertheless,* Descartes was born in 1596.

g. Hobbes was born in 1588 *even though* Descartes was born in 1596.

h. Hobbes was born in 1588 *though* Descartes was born in 1596.

(29) correctly symbolizes each of these variants. You may be thinking that such words as "but," "while," and "although" do not have quite the same connotation as "and" in ordinary English. Indeed, these words convey a sense of contrast that is lacking in "and." But bear in mind that some distortion often results when one language is translated into another. Moreover, *for the purpose of evaluating arguments for validity,* the expressions in the previous list can usually be translated adequately by means of the dot.

It should be noted, however, that the dot does not correctly translate *every* use of the English word "and." Consider the following statements:

> **30.** Stuart climbed Mount Baker and looked inside the sulfur cone.
> **31.** Stuart looked inside the sulfur cone and climbed Mount Baker.

In ordinary conversation, these two statements do not convey the same thing. Here, the word "and" conveys "and then," which indicates *temporal order.* The dot does not convey temporal order, so it cannot be used to translate what statements (30) and (31) convey. Here's another kind of case to be aware of:

32. Mike and Kirsten are married.

33. William and Peter are twins.

Typically, these statements are used to convey a *relationship*. Statement (32) normally conveys that Mike and Kirsten are married to each other, and (33) normally conveys that William and Peter are each other's twin. The dot does not convey such relationships, so it cannot be used to translate what these statements convey.

Each of the following statements is a conjunction. The main operator is the *dot*.

E • ~F

(G ∨ H) • K

(L → M) • (N ∨ O)

Disjunctions

The "∨" sign (called the **vee**) is used to symbolize disjunctions. (This symbol is borrowed from the first letter of the Latin word *vel*, meaning "or.") Consider this example:

34. Either Carol attends college or she gets a job. (C: Carol attends college; J: Carol gets a job)

Statement (34) can be translated into symbols this way:

35. C ∨ J

(35) also translates the stylistic variants of (34), such as the following:

a. Carol attends college *and/or* she gets a job.

b. Carol attends college *or* she gets a job.

c. *Either* Carol attends college *or* she gets a job (*or both*).

d. Carol attends college *unless* she gets a job.

In Chapter 1, section 1.2, we made several remarks about disjunctions, some of which bear repeating here. First, sometimes when people make statements of the form *Either A or B*, they mean *Either A or B (or both)*, which is called the *inclusive* sense of "or." For example, if Carol's parents say, "If you're going to live at home, then either you will go to college or you will get a job," they will not be unhappy if she lives at home as an employed college student. They had inclusive disjunction in mind. Second, sometimes people say something of the form *Either A or B* when they mean *Either A or B (but not both)*, which is called the *exclusive* sense of "or." For example, when a father tells his daughter, "Either you will apologize for hurting your brother or you will have a timeout," he does not intend for her to do both. He had exclusive disjunction in mind. Third, along with most logicians, we will assume that statements of the form *Either A or B* are inclusive disjunctions. That is, in our symbol system, the vee means inclusive "or," not exclusive "or." Fourth, when we want to communicate something of the form *Either A or B (but not both)*, we can represent it in our symbol system as the conjunction of two statements: *Either A or B, and not both A and B*. Consider this statement:

> **36.** Either the universe depends for its existence on something else or it depends for its existence on nothing, but not both. (S: The universe depends for its existence on something else; N: The universe depends for its existence on nothing)

It is correctly symbolized like this:

> **37.** (S ∨ N) • ~(S • N)

As a general rule, when symbolizing arguments containing disjunctions, assume that the word "or" is used in the inclusive sense unless this assumption renders the argument invalid. For example, consider the following argument, which has the form of a *disjunctive syllogism:*

> **38.** Lassie is either a cat or a dog. Lassie is not a cat. So, Lassie is a dog. (C: Lassie is a cat; D: Lassie is dog)

This argument is correctly symbolized as follows:

> **39.** C ∨ D, ~C ∴ D

Several things should be noted here. First, a comma is used to punctuate (or separate) the premises. Second, the vee is used in the first premise even though C and D cannot in fact both be true. The argument form is valid even if the "or" is inclusive: "Either C or D (or both) are true. It is not true that C. So, D is true." Third, it is customary among logicians to use the "∴" symbol (called the **triple-dot**) to mark the conclusion.

What if we need the exclusive "or" to represent an argument fairly? For example:

> **40.** Either the Sixers won or the Bulls won. The Sixers won. So, the Bulls did not win. (S: The Sixers won; B: The Bulls won)

Intuitively, the argument is valid, but the following symbolized version is invalid:

> **41.** S ∨ B, S ∴ ~B

Here's a counterexample: "Either trees are plants or flowers are plants (or both are plants). Trees are plants. So, flowers are not plants." To present the argument fairly, we need to interpret the first premise as follows:

42. Either the Sixers won or the Bulls won, but it is not true that both the Sixers won and the Bulls won.

The comma indicates that the main logical connective in (42) is the word "but," which is symbolized by the dot. The left conjunct is a disjunction ("Either the Sixers won or the Bulls won"), and the right conjunct is the negation of a conjunction ("It is not true that both the Sixers won and the Bulls won"). So, in symbols, (42) looks like this:

43. (S ∨ B) • ~(S • B)

With (43) as its first premise, argument (40) as a whole is symbolized as follows:

44. (S ∨ B) • ~(S • B), S ∴ ~B

This argument is intuitively valid, and we will prove that it is valid later in this chapter.

Before leaving disjunctions, let us note that statements of the form "Neither A nor B" can be symbolized in two ways. For instance:

45. Neither Sue nor Fred is happy. (S: Sue is happy; F: Fred is happy)

We can symbolize statement (45) by means of the vee, as follows:

46. ~(S ∨ F)

But we can also symbolize it by means of the dot, like this:

47. ~S • ~F

Each of the following statements is a disjunction. The main operator is the *vee.*

~P ∨ Q
(R • S) ∨ ~T
(U → W) ∨ ~(X • Y)

Conditionals

The "→" sign (called the **arrow**) is used to symbolize conditionals. For example:

48. If Fido is a dog, then he is an animal. (D: Fido is a dog; A: Fido is an animal)

(48) can be symbolized as follows:

    49. D → A

As we observed in Chapter 1, there are many stylistic variants for if-then statements. We will use the arrow to symbolize all of them. For example, expression (49) symbolizes (48) as well as each of the following:

  a. *Given that* Fido is a dog, Fido is an animal.
  b. Fido is an animal *given that* he is a dog.
  c. *Assuming that* Fido is a dog, he is an animal.
  d. Fido is an animal *assuming that* he is a dog.
  e. *Provided that* Fido is a dog, he is an animal.
  f. Fido is an animal *provided that* he is a dog.
  g. *On the condition that* Fido is a dog, he is an animal.
  h. Fido is an animal *on the condition that* he is a dog.
  i. Fido is an animal *if* he is a dog.
  j. Fido is a dog *only if* he is an animal.
  k. Fido's being a dog *is a sufficient condition for* Fido's being an animal.
  l. Fido's being an animal *is a necessary condition for* Fido's being a dog.

Items (k) and (l) merit comment. A *sufficient condition* is a condition that guarantees that a statement is true (or that a phenomenon will occur). For instance, *Fido's being a dog* guarantees that he is an animal. By contrast, *Fido's being an animal* does not guarantee that he is a dog, for he might be some other kind of animal. The *antecedent* (if-clause) of a true conditional statement provides a sufficient condition for the truth of the *consequent* (then-clause).

    A *necessary condition* is a condition that, if lacking, guarantees that a statement is false (or that a phenomenon will not occur). Thus, *Fido's being an animal* is a necessary condition for *Fido's being a dog,* for if Fido is not an animal, then he is not a dog. The consequent (then-clause) of a true conditional statement provides a necessary condition for the truth of the antecedent (if-clause).

    Each of the following statements is a conditional. The main operator is the *arrow.*

    ~X → Y
    Z → (A ∨ B)
    (C • ~D) → (E ∨ ~F)

Let us now symbolize an argument involving a conditional statement:

50. If humans have souls, then immaterial things can evolve from matter. Immaterial things cannot evolve from matter. So, humans do not have souls. (H: Humans have souls; M: Immaterial things can evolve from matter)

Using the scheme of abbreviation provided, argument (50) can be symbolized like this:

51. H → M, ~M ∴ ~H

Before leaving our discussion of conditionals, let us note that the word "unless" can be translated by means of the arrow as well as the vee. For example:

52. We will lose unless we do our best. (L: We will lose; B: We will do our best)

(52) can be symbolized as follows:

53. L ∨ B

But it can also be symbolized by a combination of the arrow and the tilde, like this:

54. ~L → B

In other words, (52) has the same meaning as "Our doing our best is a necessary condition for our not losing."

Biconditionals

The "↔" sign (called the **double-arrow**) is used to symbolize biconditionals. For example:

55. Mary is a teenager *if and only if* she is from 13 to 19 years of age. (M: Mary is a teenager; Y: Mary is from 13 to 19 years of age)

This statement may be symbolized as follows:

56. M ↔ Y

And (56) symbolizes not only (55) but also its stylistic variants, such as these:

a. Mary is a teenager *just in case* she is from 13 to 19 years of age.
b. Mary's being a teenager is a necessary and sufficient condition for Mary's being from 13 to 19 years of age.

Each of the following statements is a biconditional. The main operator is the *double-arrow*.

~H ↔ J

~K ↔ (P ∨ Q)

(L • M) ↔ (N → T)

Putting It All Together

We have been discussing how to translate English statements into the symbols of statement logic. Let us now consider several examples that will help us practice our translation skills and illustrate some of the finer points of translating arguments into symbols.

Let's begin with a simple argument:

> **57.** There is little doubt in the scientific community that carbon emissions contribute to global warming. If carbon emissions contribute to global warming, then we should reduce our carbon footprint. Therefore, we should reduce our carbon footprint. (C: Carbon emissions contribute to global warming; R: We should reduce our carbon footprint)

What is the conclusion of this argument? It is indicated by the word "Therefore" in the last sentence: What follows it is the conclusion and what precedes it are the premises. What follows it is the statement "we should reduce our carbon footprint," which the scheme of abbreviation assigns the letter R. Thus, the conclusion of the argument is symbolized as

> **58.** R

Now look at the first sentence. It begins with "There is little doubt in the scientific community." This phrase functions as an *assurance*. It should not be in our symbolic translation. (For more on the role of assurances, see Chapter 2.) So the first sentence offers us this statement as a premise: "carbon emissions contribute to global warming," which the scheme of abbreviation assigns the letter C. Thus, the first premise of the argument is symbolized as

> **59.** C

The second sentence of the argument is a conditional. Its antecedent is C and its consequent is R. Thus, it should be symbolized as

> **60.** C → R

Now let's put all the pieces together. Here is the argument in English and our symbolization of it:

> There is little doubt in the scientific community that carbon emissions contribute to global warming. If carbon emissions contribute to global warming, then we should reduce our carbon footprint. Therefore, we should reduce our carbon footprint. (C: Carbon emissions contribute to global warming; R: We should reduce our carbon footprint)
>
> *In symbols:* C, C → R ∴ R

Notice that when we put the argument into symbols, we can more easily see that it is formally valid because we can more easily see that it is an instance of *modus ponens*.

Let's consider another argument, one that is a bit more complex than the first one.

> **61.** It seems to me that we should stop buying factory-farmed meat and we should boycott fast-food restaurants. Why do I think that? Well, because that is what we should do if it is not morally permissible to eat factory-farmed animals. But it is morally permissible to eat factory-farmed animals only if factory farming does not cause them pain. And it is as obvious as your dog's shriek when you step on her toe that factory farming causes pain to animals. (S: We should stop buying factory-farmed meat; B: We should boycott fast-food restaurants; P: It is morally permissible to eat factory-farmed animals; F: Factory farming causes pain to animals)

Notice that the first sentence begins with the phrase "It seems to me that," which functions here as a hedge. It should not be included in our symbolic translation. (For more on the role of hedges, see Chapter 2.) Notice also that the second sentence is a rhetorical question that indicates that what follows it is a reason for what came before it. Thus, the conclusion is "We should stop buying factory-farmed meat *and* we should boycott fast-food restaurants." Note that this is a conjunction of two statements that, given the scheme of abbreviation, should be symbolized as

> **62.** S • B

The sentences that remain are the premises. The third sentence in the argument says "that is what we should do *if* it is not morally permissible to eat factory-farmed animals." Notice the word "if," which indicates a conditional. The antecedent of the conditional follows "if": "It is *not* morally permissible to eat factory-farmed animals." Notice the word "not" here, which indicates a negation; thus, given the scheme of abbreviation, the antecedent should be symbolized as ~P. The consequent is the phrase "that is what we should do." This is a way of referring back to the conclusion. Thus, the consequent of the conditional should be symbolized as S • B. Therefore, we should symbolize this premise as

63. ~P → (S • B)

The next sentence—"It is morally permissible to eat factory-farmed animals *only if* factory farming does not cause them pain"—is also a conditional. The antecedent precedes the "only if" and the consequent follows it. Given our scheme of abbreviation, the antecedent has been assigned the letter P. Notice that the consequent contains the word "not," which is a negation. Thus, given the scheme of abbreviation, it should be symbolized as ~F. Therefore, the premise should be symbolized like this:

64. P → ~F

Finally, the last sentence begins with a rhetorical flourish that we can safely leave out of our translation. The premise here is the straightforward claim that "factory farming causes pain to animals," which, given the scheme of abbreviation, should be symbolized as

65. F

With our symbolizations in hand, let's pull the pieces together. First the original argument and then the symbolization:

> It seems to me that we should stop buying factory-farmed meat and we should boycott fast-food restaurants. Why do I think that? Well, because that is what we should do if it is not morally permissible to eat factory-farmed animals. But it is morally permissible to eat factory-farmed animals only if factory farming does not cause them pain. And it is as obvious as your dog's shriek when you step on her toe that factory farming causes pain to animals. (S: We should stop buying factory-farmed meat; B: We should boycott fast-food restaurants; P: It is morally permissible to eat factory-farmed animals; F: Factory farming causes pain to animals.)
>
> *In symbols:* ~P → (S • B), P → ~F, F ∴ S • B

Let's try our symbolizing skills on another argument. It is common practice for doctors and therapists to breach the confidentiality of their relationship with their patients on the chance that doing so might serve the good of others. Against this practice, some people have argued along the following lines:

> **66.** Is it morally permissible for a doctor to breach the confidentiality of her patient for the sake of the public good? No. For it is morally permissible if and only if it is not wrong for a doctor to harm her patient, to contribute to the erosion of the institution of medical confidentiality, and to damage the honesty of her clinical relationships. But clearly, each of these things is wrong. (B: It is morally

permissible for a doctor to breach the confidentiality of her patient for the sake of the public good; H: It is wrong for a doctor to harm her patient; C: It is wrong for a doctor to contribute to the erosion of the institution of medical confidentiality; D: It is wrong for a doctor to damage the honesty of her clinical relationships)

Note several things about this argument. First, the conclusion of the argument—which is ~B—comes at the beginning of the passage because the word "for" indicates that what follows it is a reason for what comes before it. Nevertheless, when we represent the argument in symbols, the conclusion will come last. Second, the first premise of the argument is a biconditional because the main operator is "if and only if." The left side of the biconditional is B, while the right side is a conjunction of three statements: ~H, ~C, and ~D. Third, notice that it is not clear whether this conjunction should be symbolized as ((~H • ~C) • ~D) or (~H • (~C • ~D)). As it turns out, *in this case*, the two symbolic expressions mean the same thing; thus, we can arbitrarily choose one of them. But not every case is like this one. You must use your sense of the English language and the principle of charity to determine whether it is better to use one symbolic expression or another, or whether it is alright to make an arbitrary choice. We can represent the first premise as follows:

67. B ↔ [(~H • ~C) • ~D]

Finally, notice that the last statement in the argument is a shorthand way of saying three things: H, C, and D. Again, we face a choice that the text does not determine. We can treat this as three distinct premises H, C, D, or we can treat it as a conjunction, say

68. (H • C) • D

As it turns out, in this case, the two options are equivalent. But, again, you must exercise care and charity in making such a determination.

Putting the pieces together, here is the original argument and our symbolization of it:

Is it morally permissible for a doctor to breach the confidentiality of her patient for the sake of the public good? No. For it is morally permissible if and only if it is not wrong for a doctor to harm her patient, to contribute to the erosion of the institution of medical confidentiality, and to damage the honesty of her clinical relationships. But clearly, each of these things is wrong. (B: It is morally permissible for a doctor to breach the confidentiality of her patient for the sake of the public good; H: It is wrong for a doctor to harm her patient; C: It is wrong for a doctor to contribute to the erosion of the institution of medical confidentiality; D: It is wrong for a doctor to damage the honesty of her clinical relationships)

In symbols: B ↔ [(~H • ~C) • ~D], (H • C) • D ∴ ~B

If we'd like, we could format the argument a little bit differently like this, where the premises are numbered for handy reference:

1. B ↔ [(~H • ~C) • ~D]
2. (H • C) • D ∴ ~B

Let's symbolize one last argument. Doctors sometimes face the difficult choice of whether and when to tell dying patients the truth. Some people argue that doctors should never withhold the truth; others argue that sometimes it is permissible, and that doctors must use discretion on these occasions. Here's an argument for the second conclusion.

> **69.** Should a physician *never* withhold the truth from dying patients? I don't
> think so. For, although patients have a right to know the seriousness of
> their condition, it is permissible for a doctor to withhold the truth from
> dying patients sometimes, if either the patient is not ready to hear the
> bad news or the doctor is not ready to dispense it. Sometimes a doctor
> is not able to deliver bad news without communicating hopelessness
> about the patient's condition. If that is the case, then she is not ready to
> dispense the bad news. Sometimes a patient is repressing the gravity of
> his illness, or prone to severe emotional trauma, or even suicide. If that is
> the case, then the patient is not ready to hear the bad news. Therefore, it
> is permissible for a doctor to withhold the truth from her dying patient
> sometimes. (P: It is permissible for a doctor to withhold the truth from
> dying patients sometimes; H: The patient is ready to hear the bad news;
> D: The doctor is ready to dispense the bad news; A: Sometimes a doctor
> is able to deliver bad news without communicating hopelessness about
> the patient's condition; R: The patient is repressing the gravity of his
> illness; E: The patient is prone to severe emotional trauma; S: The patient
> is prone to suicide)

The conclusion of this argument—which is P, "It is permissible for a physician to withhold the truth from dying patients sometimes"—is indicated both at the outset of the text and, most clearly, at the end. Note that the third sentence of the text includes an acknowledgment that patients have a right to know the seriousness of their illness. This is an example of what we called in Chapter 2 a *discount*, an acknowledgment of a fact that might be thought to detract from the cogency or soundness of an argument. It is not a premise of the argument.

Now, setting aside the discount, the third sentence states, "It is permissible for a doctor to withhold the truth from dying patients sometimes *if* either the patient is *not* ready to hear the bad news or the doctor is *not* ready to dispense it." The main connective here is the "if," which indicates that the statement is a conditional. What comes after the "if," which is its antecedent, is a disjunction: "Either the patient is *not* ready to hear the bad news or the doctor is *not* ready to dispense it." Notice the negations. Given the scheme of abbreviation, we represent this disjunction as follows: ~H ∨ ~D. What comes before the "if," which is the consequent of the conditional, is the conclusion of the argument, which we have already identified as P. Thus, remembering that we must put the antecedent first in the expression of a conditional, we have as our first premise

70. (~H ∨ ~D) → P

We use parentheses around ~H ∨ ~D to represent the fact that the antecedent is a disjunction and that the main connective is the arrow.

The claim being made by the first premise is clear enough: *if* either ~H or ~D, *then* P. A natural question arises: Well, *is it the case* that either ~H *or* ~D? We would expect someone who asserted (~H ∨ ~D) → P and who wants to conclude that P to have an answer to that question. And, indeed, this is what we find. For the argument continues with reasons to think that both ~H and ~D are true.

First, we get a reason to think ~D is true: "Sometimes a doctor is *not* able to deliver bad news without communicating hopelessness about the patient's condition. *If* that is the case, *then* she is *not* ready to dispense the bad news." Notice the second sentence here is a conditional and that its antecedent is a quick way to refer back to the first sentence: "If *that* [i.e., the statement just before] is the case . . ." Also notice that the word "not" occurs twice. With these things in mind, and given the scheme of abbreviation, we can represent these two statements as follows:

71. ~A
72. ~A → ~D

Next, we get a reason to think ~H is true: "Sometimes a patient is repressing the gravity of his illness, *or* prone to severe emotional trauma, *or* even suicide. *If* that is the case, *then* the patient is not ready to hear the bad news." Again, notice that the second sentence here is a conditional: Its antecedent is a quick way to refer back to the first sentence and its consequent is ~H. Also notice that the first sentence contains the word "or" twice. This presents us with a choice: Using the scheme of abbreviation, do we represent that sentence as R ∨ (E ∨ S) or as (R ∨ E) ∨ S? As it turns out, *in this case,* the two expressions have the same meaing; thus, we can choose either one of them. But remember: not every case is like this one. You must rely on your grasp of the English language and use the principle of charity to determine whether, on the one hand, it is better to use one expression rather than another, or whether, on the other hand, it is alright to make an arbitrary choice. With these things in mind, and given the scheme of abbreviation, we can represent the disjunction and the conditional as follows:

73. (R ∨ E) ∨ S
74. [(R ∨ E) ∨ S] → ~H

The last statement in the text is a restatement of the conclusion: P.

Putting it all together, here is the original argument and our symbolization of it:

> Should a physician never withhold the truth from dying patients? I don't think so. For, although patients have a right to know the seriousness of their condition, it is permissible for a doctor to withhold the truth from dying patients sometimes, if either the patient is not ready to hear the bad news or the doctor is not ready to dispense it. Sometimes a doctor is not able to deliver bad news without communicating hopelessness about the patient's condition. If that is the case, then she is not ready to dispense the bad news. Sometimes a patient is repressing the gravity of his illness, or prone to severe emotional trauma, or even suicide. If that is the case, then the patient is not ready to hear the bad news. Therefore, it is permissible for a doctor to withhold the truth from her dying patient sometimes.
>
> *In symbols:* (~H ∨ ~D) → P, ~A, ~A → ~D, (R ∨ E) ∨ S, [(R ∨ E) ∨ S] → ~H ∴ P

At this point, we have introduced and illustrated the fundamentals of symbolization in statement logic. In effect, you have learned these fundamentals in the way people learn their first language, by immersion. In closing this section, it might be helpful to describe the grammar of our symbol system for statement logic more explicitly and precisely.

Symbol System for Statement Logic: A More Precise Formulation

The vocabulary of our symbol system for statement logic consists of parentheses, the logical operators (namely, ~, ∨, •, →, and ↔), and statement letters (i.e., capital letters A through Z). An *expression* of statement logic is *any* sequence of symbols in this vocabulary, such as (→ S ∨ ↔ (N~)). A grammatically correct symbolic expression is called a **well-formed formula** (WFF for short). To sum up what counts as a WFF, let us use the italicized, lowercase letters *p* and *q* as **statement variables,** which can stand for any statement. For instance, in the following summary, the statement variable *p* could stand for A, for ~B, for (C ∨ ~D), for (E • F), for (G → H), and so on.

> A **well-formed formula** (WFF) is a grammatically correct symbolic expression.
>
> A **statement variable** is a lowercase letter that serves as a placeholder for any statement—for example, *p, q, r, s.*

A symbolic expression is a WFF under the following conditions:

1. Capital letters (which stand for atomic statements) are WFFs.
2. If *p* is a WFF, then so is *~p.*

3. If p and q are WFFs, then so is $(p \bullet q)$.

4. If p and q are WFFs, then so is $(p \lor q)$.

5. If p and q are WFFs, then so is $(p \to q)$.

6. If p and q are WFFs, then so is $(p \leftrightarrow q)$.

Nothing counts as a WFF unless it can be demonstrated to be one by applications of the previous conditions.

Let us now apply our grammar to some expressions, making it explicit how our symbolic language works.

Consider the following expressions:

a. Platypuses purr.

b. p

c. M

d. (M)

e. ~M

f. (~M)

Expression (a) is not a WFF in statement logic because our vocabulary does not include the words or statements of any natural language. Expression (b) is not a WFF because no lowercase letter is in the vocabulary of our language. Lowercase letters are used only as statement variables to express the conditions under which an expression in our language is a WFF. Expression (c) is a WFF. Proof: Condition 1 says that capital letters are WFFs and M is a capital letter; therefore, M is a WFF. Expression (d) is not a WFF because none of our conditions says that we can place parentheses around a capital letter when it is by itself. Expression (e) is a WFF. Proof: According to Condition 2, ~M is a WFF if M is a WFF, and, according to Condition 1, M is a WFF. Expression (f) is not a WFF because Condition 2 does not say that we can place parentheses around negations, so we should not do so.

Now consider these expressions:

g. (M $\bullet$ N)   k. M $\bullet$ N

h. (M $\lor$ N)   l. M $\lor$ N

i. (M $\to$ N)   m. M $\to$ N

j. (M $\leftrightarrow$ N)   n. M $\leftrightarrow$ N

All of the expressions in the left column are WFFs. Expression (g) is a WFF because, according to Condition 3, (M $\bullet$ N) is a WFF if M and N are WFFs, and, according to Condition 1, they are. Expression (h) is a WFF because, according to Condition 4, (M $\lor$ N) is a WFF if M and N are WFFs, and, according to Condition 1, they are. Expression (i) is a WFF because, according to Condition 5,

(M → N) is a WFF if M and N are WFFs, and, according to Condition 1, they are. Expression (j) is a WFF because, according to Condition 6, (M ↔ N) is a WFF if M and N are WFFs, and, according to Condition 1, they are. None of the expressions in the right column are WFFs since no condition says that we can introduce a dot, vee, arrow, or double-arrow without parentheses around the resulting expression.

So far, the application of our conditions to symbolic expressions has been straightforward. Let us now look at some more complicated examples, highlighting how to use our rules of grammar to demonstrate that an expression is a WFF. Consider

   o. (A ∨ (B → C))

Expression (o) is a WFF. Note that the vee is the main operator, and, according to Condition 4, (A ∨ (B → C)) is a WFF if A and (B → C) are. Of course, A is a WFF, according to Condition 1, and, according to Condition 5, (B → C) is a WFF if B and C are and, according to Condition 1, they are. Here is a more complicated expression:

   p. ((A ∨ (B → C)) ↔ (D • E))

Expression (p) is also a WFF. Note that the double-arrow is the main operator, and, according to Condition 6, ((A ∨ (B → C)) ↔ (D • E)) is a WFF if (A ∨ (B → C)) and (D • E) are. Of course, as we proved earlier, (A ∨ (B → C)) is a WFF, and, according to Condition 3, (D • E) is a WFF if D and E are, which, of course, they are, according to Condition 1.

Thus far, we have applied the rules of our symbol system strictly. For the sake of convenience, we will relax these rules on two occasions. First, we are allowed to drop parentheses to avoid clutter provided that we do not create ambiguity. To illustrate: Since no ambiguity is created if we drop the outermost parentheses in expression (o), the following is a permissible departure from the rules:

   q. A ∨ (B → C)

But suppose we drop the innermost parentheses in expression (o), like this:

   r. (A ∨ B → C)

Expression (r) is not a permissible departure from the rules because an ambiguity is created: It could mean one of two very different things, on the one hand

   s. A ∨ (B → C)

or, on the other hand

   t. (A ∨ B) → C

Only drop parentheses when no ambiguity is created.

Second, even though our vocabulary makes no mention of brackets, we are allowed to alternate parentheses with brackets in long expressions, as this sometimes makes statements a bit easier to read. Thus, the expression

   u. $(A \lor (B \to C)) \leftrightarrow ((D \bullet E) \lor F)$

might be easier to read as follows:

   v. $[A \lor (B \to C)] \leftrightarrow [(D \bullet E) \lor F]$

The symbolic language we have developed in this section is extremely useful as a means of representing the forms of arguments.

Summary of Definitions

An **atomic statement** is one that does not have any other statement as a component.

A **compound statement** is one that has at least one atomic statement as a component.

The **main logical operator** in a compound statement is the one that governs the largest component or components of a compound statement.

A **minor logical** operator governs smaller components.

A **well-formed formula** (WFF) is a grammatically correct symbolic expression.

A **statement variable** is a lowercase letter that serves as a placeholder for any statement—for example, *p, q, r, s.*

EXERCISE 7.1

PART A: Well-Formed Formulas? Which of the following symbolic expressions are well-formed formulas (WFFs)? Which are not? (In answering these questions, use the six conditions for WFFs strictly, making no allowances for routine abbreviations.)

* **1.** $(A \to B \to C)$
  2. $(\sim B)$
  3. $(\sim(C) \to F)$
* **4.** $(E \to (\sim F \to G)$
  5. $\sim((H \to J) \to (K \to L)$
  6. $(M \to \sim\sim N)$
* **7.** $(O \to \sim(P \to R))$

  8. $((Q \to S) \to T)$
  9. $(\sim U \to (W))$
* **10.** $\sim Z$
  11. $\sim(B \bullet C)$
  12. $\sim(\sim W \lor \sim Z)$
* **13.** $\sim(m \leftrightarrow \sim h)$
  14. $(\sim E \bullet \sim F \bullet \sim\sim G)$

15. ~(~A → ~R)

*16. (~S ∨ ~R ∨ ~(T • U))

17. (~P ∨ Q ∨ ~R)

18. ((L ∨ M) → ~S)

*19. (~(D • E) ↔ (F ∨ ~G))

20. ((~H • ~~F) → ~(~K ↔ ~N))

PART B: Permissible Departures from Strict Grammar   What counts as a WFF is defined strictly in terms of six conditions, but in some cases, parentheses can be dropped without changing the meaning and without causing ambiguity. Also, in some cases, alternating brackets with parentheses makes a formula easier to read. Which of the following are examples of formulas that permissibly depart from a strict application of the six conditions by dropping a set of parentheses or by an appropriate use of brackets?

* 1. E ∨ ~F

2. ~G • ~H

3. ~J ↔ ~K

* 4. ~L ∨ [(M → N) → ~O]

5. (~Q ∨ ~R ∨ ~~S)

6. (A ∨ B) ↔ (C ↔ D)

* 7. ~U → ~X

8. [~Z • ~W ∨ ~~Y]

9. ~A → (~C → F)

*10. (B • E) • [(G ∨ H) • (J • K)]

PART C: Symbolizing   Translate the following statements into symbols, using the schemes of abbreviation provided.

* 1. The crops will fail unless it rains. (C: The crops will fail; R: It rains)

2. Humans are animals if they are mammals. (A: Humans are animals; M: Humans are mammals)

3. The statement "If humans are rational, then they are not animals" is false. (R: Humans are rational; A: Humans are animals)

* 4. Bats are mammals only if they nourish their young with milk. (M: Bats are mammals; N: Bats nourish their young with milk)

5. Coffee isn't good if it isn't fresh-brewed. (G: Coffee is good; F: Coffee is fresh-brewed)

6. Assuming that your test scores are high and you get your paper in on time, you will do well. (T: Your test scores are high; P: You get your paper in on time; W: You will do well)

* 7. Roberto lacks wisdom. (R: Roberto has wisdom)

8. The statement "Humans lack rationality" is false. (H: Humans have rationality)

9. Polly fails to be a parrot provided that she cannot talk and does not want a cracker. (P: Polly is a parrot; T: Polly can talk; C: Polly wants a cracker)

*10. Neither birds nor snakes are mammals. (B: Birds are mammals; S: Snakes are mammals)

11. Given that Linda is both smart and diligent, she will do well, but Linda is not diligent. (S: Linda is smart; D: Linda is diligent; W: Linda will do well)

12. Al wins only if Ed does not win, and Ed wins only if Al does not win. (A: Al wins; E: Ed wins)

* **13.** If Smith fails to win, then either Jones wins or Smith and Jones are tied. (S: Smith wins; J: Jones wins; T: Smith and Jones are tied)

14. Assuming that Julio is a bachelor, he is a man who is unmarried. (B: Julio is a bachelor; M: Julio is a man; J: Julio is married)

15. Erin's being penniless is a sufficient condition for her being miserable. (P: Erin is penniless; M: Erin is miserable)

* **16.** Dirk Nowitski's being tall is a necessary condition for his being on the team. (D: Dirk Nowitski is tall; T: Dirk Nowitski is on the team)

17. The statement "Santa does not exist" is false. (S: Santa exists)

18. We will be evicted unless we pay the rent. (E: We will be evicted; P: We pay the rent)

* **19.** Although reindeer exist, Santa does not exist, but adults are not honest if Santa does not exist. (R: Reindeer exist; S: Santa exists; H: Adults are honest)

20. Paula will pass the test just in case she studies diligently. (P: Paula will pass the test; S: Paula studies diligently)

PART D: More Symbolizing Translate the following statements into symbols, using the schemes of abbreviation provided.

* **1.** The picture frame is square only if it is rectangular. (S: The picture frame is square; R: The picture frame is rectangular)

2. You will not succeed if you lack common sense. (S: You will succeed; C: You have common sense)

3. If Sammy is a penguin, then Sammy is a bird that cannot fly. (P: Sammy is a penguin; B: Sammy is a bird; F: Sammy can fly)

* **4.** Either you work hard or you have fun, but not both. (W: You work hard; F: You have fun)

5. Given that Bozo has a bill, Bozo is either a duck or a platypus. (B: Bozo has a bill; D: Bozo is a duck; P: Bozo is a platypus)

6. Neither penguins nor ostriches can fly. (P: Penguins can fly; O: Ostriches can fly)

* **7.** If Alvin has a bill, then he is not a platypus if he has feathers. (B: Alvin has a bill, P: Alvin is a platypus; F: Alvin has feathers)

8. Neither Smith nor Jones wins if there is a tie, but Jones does not win given that Smith wins. (S: Smith wins; J: Jones wins; T: There is a tie)

9. While Miriam is both competent and hard-working, she is not interested in the job. (C: Miriam is competent; H: Miriam is hard-working; J: Miriam is interested in the job)

* **10.** Given that Murphy is a bat only if he can fly, Murphy is not a bat. (B: Murphy is a bat; F: Murphy can fly)

11. Sally will pass unless her mind goes blank. (P: Sally will pass; M: Sally's mind goes blank)

12. Either Floyd Mayweather Jr. wins or Manny Pacquiao wins, but not both. (F: Floyd Mayweather Jr. wins; M: Manny Pacquiao wins)

13. Stella's being in Arkansas is a sufficient condition for her being in the U.S.A. (A: Stella is in Arkansas; U: Stella is in the U.S.A.)

14. Humberto's being competent is a necessary and sufficient condition for his being hired. (C: Humberto is competent; H: Humberto is hired)

15. Solomon's growing older is a necessary condition for his becoming wiser, but it is not a sufficient condition for his becoming wiser. (S: Solomon grows older; W: Solomon becomes wiser)

16. Dan's being in Pennsylvania is a necessary condition for his being in Philadelphia. (D: Dan is in Pennsylvania; P: Dan is in Philadelphia)

17. It is always wrong to kill the innocent only if it is wrong to kill an insane person in self-defense. (K: It is always wrong to kill the innocent; S: It is wrong to kill an insane person in self-defense)

18. It is not the case that if the Seahawks win, the Cowboys win. (S: The Seahawks win; C: The Cowboys win)

19. It is not always wrong to kill the innocent just in case it is not wrong to kill an insane person in self-defense. (K: It is always wrong to kill the innocent; S: It is wrong to kill an insane person in self-defense)

20. Plato's being a rational animal is a necessary and sufficient condition for his being human. (R: Plato is rational; A: Plato is an animal; H: Plato is human)

PART E: More Symbolizing Symbolize the following statements, using the schemes of abbreviation provided.

* 1. Fido is a dog only if Fido is an animal. (D: Fido is a dog; A: Fido is an animal)

2. Josey is a mammal if Josey is a cat. (M: Josie is a mammal; C: Josey is a cat)

3. Physical laws cannot be changed given that they are either necessary or eternal. (C: Physical laws can be changed; N: Physical laws are necessary; E: Physical laws are eternal)

* 4. Snakes are mammals only if snakes nourish their young with milk, but snakes do not nourish their young with milk. (M: Snakes are mammals; N: Snakes nourish their young with milk)

5. The statement "If evil exists, then God does not exist" is false. (E: Evil exists; G: God exists)

6. If Smith is guilty only if Smith's blood is on the murder weapon, then Smith is not guilty if Smith's blood is not on the murder weapon. (G: Smith is guilty; B: Smith's blood is on the murder weapon)

* **7.** It is not true that if the Eiffel Tower is in Ohio, then it is in Europe. (O: The Eiffel Tower is in Ohio; E: The Eiffel Tower is in Europe)

  8. The defendant's having a motive is not a sufficient condition for his being guilty. (M: The defendant has a motive; G: The defendant is guilty)

  9. Jane will fail unless she studies. (F: Jane will fail; S: Jane studies)

* **10.** Assuming Fred is both rational and an animal, Fred is human, but Fred is not rational. (R: Fred is rational; A: Fred is an animal; H: Fred is human)

  11. Senator Crockett's approval of the war is not a necessary condition for her reelection. (W: Senator Crockett approves of the war; R: Senator Crockett will be reelected)

  12. Unless we stop using fossil fuels, the earth will continue to get warmer. (S: We stop using fossil fuels; E: The earth will continue to get warmer)

* **13.** Marie Curie's being a scientist is a necessary condition, but not a sufficient condition, for her being a physicist. (S: Marie Curie is a scientist; P: Marie Curie is a physicist)

  14. If God exists, then evil does not exist unless God has a good reason for allowing evil. (G: God exists; E: Evil exists; R: God has a good reason for allowing evil)

  15. Natalie Portman's being a movie star is a sufficient condition, but not a necessary condition, for her being famous. (M: Natalie Portman is a movie star; F: Natalie Portman is famous)

7.2 Truth Tables

In this section, we will examine the truth tables for the five basic types of compounds formed via the operators introduced in the previous section.

The main idea behind truth tables is that the truth value of certain compound statements is a function of the truth value of the atomic statements that make them up. A compound statement is said to be **truth-functional** if its truth value is completely determined by the truth value of the atomic statements that compose it. Let us now examine a series of truth-functional compounds.

A compound statement is **truth-functional** if its truth value is completely determined by the truth value of the atomic statements that compose it.

We will again use the italicized, lowercase letters *p* and *q* as statement variables that can stand for any statement. For instance, the statement variable *q* can stand for A, for ~B, for ~C ∨ D, for E ↔ F, and so on.

Negations

A negation (represented by the tilde) has the opposite truth value of the statement negated. For example, the statement "Bertrand Russell was born in 1872" is true; so its negation, "Bertrand Russell was not born in 1872," is false. And "John F. Kennedy was born in 1872" is false; so its negation, "John F. Kennedy was not born in 1872," is true. Thus, negations are truth-functional compounds. We can present this in a kind of diagram, called a **truth table,** as follows:

p	$\sim p$
T	F
F	T

This truth table has two vertical columns, one on the left and one on the right. The column on the left gives the possible truth values for any statement p, namely, T (true) and F (false). The column on the right gives the corresponding truth values for the negation, $\sim p$. The table also has two horizontal rows. In the first (or top) row, p is true, so its negation is false. In the second (or bottom) row, p is false, so its negation is true.

Conjunctions

A conjunction (represented by the dot) is true if both its conjuncts are true; otherwise, it is false. Thus, one false conjunct renders an entire conjunction false. For example, "St. Augustine and Abraham Lincoln were both born in 354" is false, for although St. Augustine was born in 354, Lincoln was not. We can sum up the relationship between the truth value of a conjunction and the truth value of its conjuncts as follows:

p	q	$p \bullet q$
T	T	T
T	F	F
F	T	F
F	F	F

Here, the two columns on the left list all the possible truth-value assignments for any two statements. Row 1 represents the situation in which both statements are true. Rows 2 and 3 represent the *two* situations in which the statements *differ* in truth value (p true, q false; and p false, q true). Finally, row 4 represents the situation in which both statements are false. The column under the dot indicates that the conjunction as a whole is true *only if* both conjuncts are true (namely, in row 1); otherwise, the conjunction as a whole is false.

Disjunctions

A *disjunction (represented by the vee) is false if both its disjuncts are false; otherwise, it is true.* Consider the following examples:

75. Either George Washington or John F. Kennedy was born in 2003 (or both were).

76. Either Abraham Lincoln or Andrew Jackson was born in 1809 (or both were).

77. Either Franklin D. Roosevelt or Jimmy Carter was a Democrat (or both were).

Statement (75) is false because both its disjuncts are false. (76) is true because Lincoln was born in 1809. (The statement as a whole is true even though Jackson was born not in 1809 but in 1767.) And (77) is true because both Roosevelt and Carter were Democrats.

The truth table for the vee is as follows:

p	q	$p \vee q$
T	T	T
T	F	T
F	T	T
F	F	F

Again, the columns on the left represent the four possible combinations of truth values for any two statements. The column under the vee indicates that the disjunction is false only when both disjuncts are false (namely, in row 4); otherwise, the disjunction as a whole is true.

Conditionals

English conditionals are rather complicated, and so we need to discuss the relationship between the arrow and the English if-then briefly. Consider the following examples:

78. If some dogs are collies, then no dogs are collies.

79. If George Washington was born before Jimmy Carter, then Jimmy Carter was born before George Washington.

80. If physical objects exert a gravitational attraction on each other, then a fist-sized chunk of lead released 3 feet from the surface of the earth will always float in midair.

Each of these conditionals has a true antecedent and a false consequent, and each conditional *is itself* false. Indeed, an English conditional is always false when its antecedent is true and its consequent is false. This fact is so important that logicians have defined a special type of conditional, called the

material conditional, that is *false only when its antecedent is true and its consequent is false*.

> A **material conditional** is a conditional that is false *only* when its antecedent is true and its consequent is false; otherwise, it is true.

The truth table for the material conditional, which is represented by the arrow, is as follows:

p	*q*	*p → q*
T	T	T
T	F	F
F	T	T
F	F	T

Now consider the following four English sentences, which correspond to the four rows in the truth table for the material conditional:

a. If the Eiffel Tower is in France, then the Eiffel Tower is in Europe.

b. If the Eiffel Tower is in France, then the Eiffel Tower is in the U.S.A.

c. If the Eiffel Tower is in Germany, then the Eiffel Tower is in Europe.

d. If the Eiffel Tower is in Ohio, then the Eiffel Tower is in the U.S.A.

With the exception of (b), each of these conditionals is true. In (a), both antecedent and consequent are true. In (c), the antecedent is false, while the consequent is true; however, the conditional itself is true because if the Eiffel Tower *is* in Germany, it is in Europe. It may seem odd that a conditional could be true when both antecedent and consequent are false, but (d) illustrates that this can be so: If the Eiffel Tower *is* in Ohio, then it is in the U.S.A.

Now it may seem that the English if-then is truth-functional and that the truth table for the material conditional is also a truth table for the English if-then. Unfortunately, things are not that simple. Consider the following:

a. If $1 + 1 = 2$, then the Eiffel Tower is in France.

b. If the Eiffel Tower is in Ohio, then it is in Europe.

c. If the Eiffel Tower is in Germany, then it is in the U.S.A.

In (a), both antecedent and consequent are true, yet we might well hesitate to pronounce it true because there is no relevance between the antecedent and the consequent. In (b), the antecedent is false and the consequent is true. If we went by the truth table for the material conditional, we would say that (b) is true, but it seems false. If the Eiffel Tower *is* in Ohio, then it is not in Europe. Similarly, (c) seems false. If the Eiffel Tower *is* in Germany, then it is not in the U.S.A. Yet, according to the truth table for material conditionals, (c) is true because both antecedent and consequent are false.

What good does it do to have a truth table for conditionals if it gives a questionable picture of the relationship between the truth value of English conditionals (in general) and the truth value of their constituent parts? Logicians disagree about the answer to this question, but they tend to agree that when the truth table method is applied to arguments, it nicely corroborates our belief in the validity of such intuitive inference rules as those introduced in Chapter 1—*modus ponens*, *modus tollens*, hypothetical syllogism, disjunctive syllogism, and constructive dilemma. Moreover, it confirms our belief in the *invalidity* of such common, formal fallacies as denying the antecedent and affirming the consequent. In short, the material conditional captures that part of the meaning of the English conditional that is essential for the validity of the basic argument forms of statement logic.

Biconditionals

As we've seen, biconditionals are, in effect, conjunctions of conditionals. Since we are treating conditionals as material conditionals, we will treat biconditionals as conjunctions of material conditionals. The result is what logicians call the **material biconditional,** which is *true when its constituent statements have the same truth value and false when they differ in truth value*.

> A **material biconditional** is a conjunction of two material conditionals; it is true when its constituent statements have the same truth value and false when they differ in truth value.

Thus, the truth table for the material biconditional, which is represented by the double-arrow, is as follows:

p	q	$p \leftrightarrow q$
T	T	T
T	F	F
F	T	F
F	F	T

The truth table for the biconditional is readily understandable if one keeps in mind that a biconditional is in effect a conjunction of two conditionals. Consider an example:

81. Lincoln won the election *if and only if* Douglas lost the election.

Statement (81) can be broken down into two conditional statements, as follows:

82. Lincoln won the election *if* Douglas lost the election.
83. Lincoln won the election *only if* Douglas lost the election.

In standard form, (82) and (83) look like this (respectively):

84. If Douglas lost the election, then Lincoln won the election.
85. If Lincoln won the election, then Douglas lost the election.

So, (81) can be rewritten as a conjunction of two conditionals:

86. If Lincoln won the election, then Douglas lost the election; and if Douglas lost the election, then Lincoln won the election. (L: Lincoln won the election; D: Douglas lost the election)

Similar remarks could be made about any biconditional. Let us symbolize (81) and (86) and then check to see if the truth tables for these statements are alike. In symbols, (81) and (86) look like this (respectively):

87. $L \leftrightarrow D$
88. $(L \rightarrow D) \bullet (D \rightarrow L)$

Let us work out the truth table for (88). The first row looks like this:

L D	$(L \rightarrow D) \bullet (D \rightarrow L)$
T T	T T T

When L and D are both true, then $L \rightarrow D$ is true, and so is $D \rightarrow L$. Hence, we place a T under the main operator, the dot, because both conjuncts are true. Now let us add the second row to the truth table:

L D	$(L \rightarrow D) \bullet (D \rightarrow L)$
T T	T T T
T F	F F T

With L true and D false, $(L \rightarrow D)$ is false, while $(D \rightarrow L)$ is true. (Remember, the material conditional is false *only when* its antecedent is true and its consequent is false.) So, we have a conjunction with one false conjunct and one true conjunct. We place an F under the dot because one false conjunct makes the entire conjunction false.

Next, we fill in truth values for the third row:

L	D	(L	→	D)	•	(D	→	L)
T	T		T		T		T	
T	F		F		F		T	
F	T		T		F		F	

With L false and D true, L → D is true; however, D → L is false. So, we again place an F under the dot because we have one false conjunct. We can now add the fourth and final row to the truth table:

L	D	(L	→	D)	•	(D	→	L)
T	T		T		T		T	
T	F		F		F		T	
F	T		T		F		F	
F	F		T		T		T	

With L and D both false, L → D is true, and so is D → L. We place a T under the dot because both conjuncts are true.

The column under the dot gives us the truth value of the entire statement, row by row. And the column under the dot is exactly like the column under the double-arrow in the truth table for the biconditional:

L	D	L ↔ D
T	T	T
T	F	F
F	T	F
F	F	T

Summary of Truth Tables for the Five Compounds

Negation		**Conjunction**			**Disjunction**			**Conditional**			**Biconditional**		
p	*~p*	*p*	*q*	*p • q*	*p*	*q*	*p ∨ q*	*p*	*q*	*p → q*	*p*	*q*	*p ↔ q*
T	F	T	T	T	T	T	T	T	T	T	T	T	T
F	T	T	F	F	T	F	T	T	F	F	T	F	F
		F	T	F	F	T	T	F	T	T	F	T	F
		F	F	F	F	F	F	F	F	T	F	F	T

Summary of Definitions

A compound statement is **truth-functional** if its truth value is completely determined by the truth value of the atomic statements that compose it.

A **material conditional** is a conditional that is false *only* when its antecedent is true and its consequent is false; otherwise, it is true.

A **material biconditional** is a conjunction of two material conditionals; it is true when its constituent statements have the same truth value and false when they differ in truth value.

EXERCISE 7.2

PART A: True or False? Determine the truth value of the following compound statements. Make the following assumptions: A is true, B is true, C is false, and D is false.

* **1.** A • C
  2. A ∨ C
  3. ~A
* **4.** B → D
  5. D → B
  6. A ↔ B
* **7.** C ↔ D
  8. ~(A • B)
  9. C ∨ D
* **10.** ~(C ∨ D)
  11. ~C → D
  12. ~(D → A)
* **13.** (A • C) → B

  14. C → (A → D)
  15. (C → A) → D
* **16.** ~(A ↔ D)
  17. ~C • ~D
  18. ~(~A ↔ ~B)
* **19.** (A • C) ∨ (B • D)
  20. (C ∨ A) • (D ∨ B)
  21. ~[A → (C ∨ B)]
* **22.** (D ↔ A) ∨ (C → B)
  23. (~C → A) ↔ (~A ∨ D)
  24. ~B ↔ (A • C)
* **25.** ~(D ∨ C) → B

PART B: More True or False Determine the truth value of the following compound statements.

* **1.** It is not the case that Abraham Lincoln was born in 1997.
  2. If water is H_2O, then water is not wet.
  3. Either New York City is the capital of Montana, or Seattle is the capital of Montana.
* **4.** Lady Gaga is a married man if and only if Lady Gaga is a husband.
  5. If Reno is in Nevada, then Reno is in the U.S.A.

6. Either Alabama is a southern state (of the U.S.A.) or Maine is a southern state.

* **7.** It is not the case that both Charlie Chaplin and George Washington are past presidents of the U.S.A.

8. If either Mozart or Beethoven was born in Korea, then it is false that both Mozart and Beethoven were born in Australia.

9. If the Taj Mahal is green, then the Taj Mahal is not invisible.

* **10.** If Paris is the capital of France, then neither Seattle nor Spokane is the capital of France.

11. Samuel Clemens wrote *Huckleberry Finn* if and only if Samuel Clemens is Mark Twain.

12. If Reno is in Nevada, then Reno is in Canada.

* **13.** If the Statue of Liberty is in Kentucky, then the Statue of Liberty is in the U.S.A.

14. Either Justin Bieber or Katy Perry is president of the U.S.A.

15. If Reno is in Nevada, then either Reno is in Canada or Reno is in the U.S.A.

PART C: Assigning Truth Values   What truth values must be assigned to the atomic statements to make the following compounds *false*?

* **1.** ~P ∨ Q

2. ~R → S

3. ~(E • G)

* **4.** ~(A → B) → C

5. (T ↔ ~W) ∨ T

6. ~(~G ∨ H) → ~K

* **7.** (Y → ~Z) ∨ ~Y

8. (L ↔ M) → ~M

9. ~A → ~(~B • C)

* **10.** ~(N ↔ P) ∨ ~P

11. ~(~A ∨ ~B) ∨ ~A

12. (~C ∨ E) → ~(E • C)

* **13.** ~(H • J) ∨ (K → L)

14. (M • N) → ~P

15. (R • ~S) → (R ↔ Q)

7.3   # Using Truth Tables to Evaluate Arguments

We are now in a position to use truth tables to establish the validity and invalidity of arguments. Let's begin by examining an argument having the form *modus tollens:*

89. If Lincoln is 8 feet tall, then Lincoln is over 7 feet tall. But it is not the case that Lincoln is over 7 feet tall. It follows that Lincoln is not 8 feet tall.
(L: Lincoln is 8 feet tall; S: Lincoln is over 7 feet tall)

The argument may be symbolized as follows:

90. L → S, ~S ∴ ~L

First, we generate all the possible truth-value assignments for L and S. There are two truth values (truth and falsehood), so our truth table must have 2^n rows, where n is the number of statement letters in the symbolic argument. In this case, we have just two statement letters, L and S, so our truth table will have 2^2 rows ($2^2 = 2 \times 2 = 4$). The truth-value assignments can be generated in a completely mechanical way; indeed, it is important to generate them mechanically both to avoid error and to facilitate communication. In the column nearest to the vertical line (in this case, the column under S), simply alternate Ts and Fs. In the next column to the left (in this case, the column under L), alternate couples (two Ts, followed by two Fs). Like this:

L	S	
T	T	
T	F	
F	T	
F	F	

We then write the steps of the argument out on the line at the top of the table and fill in the columns under each step of the argument, row by row. Row 1 looks like this:

L	S	L → S,	~S	∴ ~L
T	T	T	F	F

As we have seen, L → S is true when L and S are both true. Of course, ~S is false when S is true, and ~L is false when L is true.

Next, we fill in truth values in row 2:

L	S	L → S,	~S	∴ ~L
T	T	T	F	F
T	F	F	T	F

With its antecedent true and consequent false, L → S is false in this row of the table. S is false, so ~S must be true. And because L is true, ~L must be false.

Now we add row 3:

L	S	L → S,	~S	∴ ~L
T	T	T	F	F
T	F	F	T	F
F	T	T	F	T

The conditional premise is true when its antecedent is false and its consequent is true. ~S is false when S is true, and ~L is true when L is false.

To complete the table, we add the fourth and final row.

L	S	L → S,	~S	∴ ~L
T	T	T	F	F
T	F	F	T	F
F	T	T	F	T
F	F	T	T	T

The conditional premise is true in row 4. L and S are both false in this row, so ~S and ~L are true.

Now, what does the truth table tell us about the argument? Each row in the table describes a possible situation in very abstract terms. *What we are looking for is a row, and hence a possible situation, in which the premises are all true but the conclusion is false.* If we can find such a row (or situation), then the argument form is invalid. Recall that validity preserves truth—if you start with truth and reason validly, you'll get a true conclusion. So, if a form of argument *can* lead from true premises to a false conclusion, that form of argument is invalid. As we look at the table for the symbolic argument (90), which has the form *modus tollens*, we see that there is no row in which all of the premises are true and the conclusion is false. This means that the argument has a valid form; hence, the argument itself is valid. And because the English argument (89) has the same form, it too is valid.

Now let's see what happens when we apply the truth table method to one of the formal fallacies. Here is an argument having the form of the fallacy of denying the antecedent:

91. If society approves of genetic engineering, then genetic engineering is morally permissible. But society does not approve of genetic engineering. Therefore, genetic engineering is not morally permissible. (S: Society approves of genetic engineering; G: Genetic engineering is morally permissible)

We translate the argument into symbols as follows:

92. S → G, ~S ∴ ~G

The truth table looks like this:

S	G	S → G,	~S	∴ ~G
T	T	T	F	F
T	F	F	F	T
F	T	T	T	F *
F	F	T	T	T

Is there a row in which the premises are all true and the conclusion is false? Yes, row 3. This shows that the argument form is invalid, for it does not preserve truth. We will indicate which rows show invalidity with a star: *. The table gives us the additional bit of information that the invalidity of the form is revealed in situations in which the antecedent of the conditional premise (i.e., S) is false and its consequent (i.e., G) is true.

The pattern of reasoning is *always* invalid because it allows for all true premises and a false conclusion.

Of course, not all truth tables are as short as those we've examined thus far. Let us see what happens when we apply the truth table method to arguments having three statement letters.

> **93.** If the equatorial rain forests produce oxygen used by Americans, then either Americans ought to pay for the oxygen or they ought to stop complaining about the destruction of the rain forests. But either it is false that Americans ought to pay for the oxygen, or it is false that Americans ought to stop complaining about the destruction of the rain forests. Therefore, it is false that the equatorial rain forests produce oxygen used by Americans. (E: The equatorial rain forests produce oxygen used by Americans; P: Americans ought to pay for the oxygen; S: Americans ought to stop complaining about the destruction of the rain forests)

Using the scheme of abbreviation provided, the argument translates into symbols as follows:

> **94.** $E \rightarrow (P \lor S)$, $\sim P \lor \sim S$ $\therefore$ $\sim E$

Now we are ready to construct a truth table. We list the statement letters *in the order in which they appear* in our symbolization: E, P, S. Since a truth table must have 2^n rows, where n is the number of statement letters appearing in our symbolic notation, in this case we need a table with eight rows ($2^3 = 2 \times 2 \times 2 = 8$). To generate every possible combination of truth values for the three statement letters *mechanically*, we alternate Ts and Fs in the column nearest the vertical line, under S. Then we alternate couples (two Ts, followed by two Fs, etc.) in the next column to the left, under P. Next, we alternate quadruples (four Ts followed by four Fs) in the column on the far left, under E. Finally, we add the argument itself above the horizontal line. The result looks like this:

E	P	S	$E \rightarrow (P \lor S)$, $\sim P \lor \sim S$ $\therefore$ $\sim E$
T	T	T	
T	T	F	
T	F	T	
T	F	F	
F	T	T	
F	T	F	
F	F	T	
F	F	F	

It's important to generate the possible truth-value combinations *in the manner indicated*, for two reasons. First, doing so will enable you to construct truth tables quickly and accurately. Second, for purposes of comparing or checking for accuracy, a *standard method* of generating truth-value combinations is needed.

Next, we fill in the truth values for the premises and conclusion row by row. What follows are elaborate instructions for doing the first row. The point of these instructions is for you to see the reasoning behind the assignment of Ts and Fs. They should be enough for you to do the remaining seven rows of the truth table. At the end of our instructions, we will display the complete truth table.

Let's do the first premise first: E → (P ∨ S). The main operator is the arrow. We want to know what truth value to assign to it. To do that, we need to know the truth values of the antecedent, E, and the consequent, P ∨ S. We can see that on this row the atomic statement E is assigned a T. We now need to figure out what truth value to assign to P ∨ S, which is a disjunction. To do that we need to know the truth values of the disjuncts of P ∨ S. We see that on the first row the atomic statement P is assigned a T and the atomic statement S is assigned a T. Therefore, because a disjunction is true if at least one of its disjuncts is true, the disjunction P ∨ S is assigned a T. So we write a T on the first row of the truth table right beneath the vee in P ∨ S, like this:

E	P	S	E → (P ∨ S), ~P ∨ ~S ∴ ~E
T	T	T	T
T	T	F	
T	F	T	
T	F	F	
F	T	T	
F	T	F	
F	F	T	
F	F	F	

Now, because on the first row E is assigned a T, and we just learned that P ∨ S is assigned a T, the material conditional E → (P ∨ S) has a true antecedent and a true consequent. Therefore, because a material conditional is true when its antecedent is true and its consequent is true, E → (P ∨ S) is assigned a T. Write a T on the first row of the truth table just beneath the arrow, like this:

E	P	S	E → (P ∨ S), ~P ∨ ~S ∴ ~E
T	T	T	T T
T	T	F	
T	F	T	
T	F	F	
F	T	T	
F	T	F	
F	F	T	
F	F	F	

Now let's turn to the second premise: ~P ∨ ~S. The main operator is the vee. We want to know what truth value to assign to it. To do that, we need to know the truth values of both disjuncts, ~P and ~S. Let's begin with ~P. Because ~P is a negation, and the truth value of a negation is the opposite of the truth value of the statement that it negates, we need to know the truth value of P. We can see that on this row the atomic statement P is assigned a T. Therefore, we assign an F to ~P. Similar reasoning leads us to assign an F to ~S. So we write an F on the first row of the truth table right beneath the tilde in ~P and right beneath the tilde in ~S, like this:

E	P	S	E → (P ∨ S), ~P ∨ ~S ∴ ~E
T	T	T	T T F F
T	T	F	
T	F	T	
T	F	F	
F	T	T	
F	T	F	
F	F	T	
F	F	F	

Now, because a disjunction is false if both of its disjuncts are false, and because ~P is F and ~S is F, we assign F to ~P ∨ ~S. So we write an F on the first row of the truth table right beneath the vee in ~P ∨ ~S, like this:

E	P	S	E → (P ∨ S), ~P ∨ ~S ∴ ~E
T	T	T	T T F F F
T	T	F	
T	F	T	
T	F	F	
F	T	T	
F	T	F	
F	F	T	
F	F	F	

Now all we have left for the first row is the conclusion. Because it is a negation, and the truth value of a negation is the opposite of the truth value of the statement that it negates, we need to know the truth value of E. We can see that on this row the atomic statement E is assigned a T. Therefore, we assign an F to ~E. So we write an F on the first row of the truth table right beneath the tilde in ~E, like this:

E	P	S	E → (P ∨ S), ~P ∨ ~S ∴ ~E
T	T	T	T T F F F F
T	T	F	
T	F	T	
T	F	F	
F	T	T	
F	T	F	
F	F	T	
F	F	F	

Now we use similar reasoning to assign truth values for the remaining seven rows. You must *at least* provide a column of truth values under every logical operator and under every atomic statement that stands alone as a premise or the conclusion. (When you do truth tables on the website, you must provide this *and no more*. But on paper, it is sometimes helpful to provide more.) You will find this process moves *much* more quickly if, for each type of compound statement, you understand and memorize the conditions under which they are true and false. Here's a handy way to remember:

Remembering Truth Conditions

Compound	Tips to Remember Truth Conditions
Negation	Always the opposite
Conjunction	Always false except when both conjuncts are true
Disjunction	Always true except when both disjuncts are false
Material Conditional	Always true except when the antecedent is true and the consequent is false
Material Biconditional	Always true except when its two constituent statements have different truth values.

The completed truth table looks like this:

E	P	S	E → (P ∨ S),	~P ∨ ~S ∴	~E
T	T	T	T T F	F F	F
T	T	F	T T F	T T	F*
T	F	T	T T T	T F	F*
T	F	F	F F T	T T	F
F	T	T	T T F	F F	T
F	T	F	T T F	T T	T
F	F	T	T T T	T F	T
F	F	F	T F T	T T	T

Once the table is complete, we focus on the columns under the main operator of each premise and the conclusion. (If we are doing the truth table on paper, it might help to circle these columns, as indicated in the text.) Next, we examine the table to see whether there are any rows in which the premises are all true and the conclusion is false. (If we are doing the truth table on paper, it might help to note these rows with a star, as indicated in the text.) Rows 2 and 3 meet this condition, so the argument—argument (93), symbolized as argument (94)—is invalid. (An argument is invalid provided *at least* one row meets this condition.)

Using the hints provided by row 3 of the truth table, we can construct a counterexample to argument (94):

95. If George Washington was born before Harry Truman, then either Abraham Lincoln was born before George Washington or Abraham Lincoln was born before Harry Truman. Either it is false that Abraham Lincoln was born before George Washington or it is false that Abraham Lincoln was born before Harry Truman. So, it is false that George Washington was born before Harry Truman. (E: George Washington was born before Harry Truman; P: Abraham Lincoln was born before George Washington; S: Abraham Lincoln was born before Harry Truman)

Note that the counterexample matches the scenario described in row 3 of the truth table perfectly: E (i.e., Washington was born before Truman) is true, P (i.e., Lincoln was born before Washington) is false, and S (i.e., Lincoln was born before Truman) is true.

Truth tables can be used to evaluate for validity even when our English intuitions fail us. For example, is the following argument valid? Most people find it difficult to answer simply on the basis of logical intuition.

96. If Socrates works hard, he gets rich. But if Socrates doesn't work hard, he enjoys life. Moreover, if Socrates does not get rich, then he does not enjoy life. Hence, Socrates gets rich. (H: Socrates works hard; R: Socrates gets rich; L: Socrates enjoys life)

Using the scheme of abbreviation provided, the argument can be symbolized as follows:

97. H → R, ~H → L, ~R → ~L ∴ R

The truth table looks like this:

H	R	L	H → R, ~H → L, ~R → ~L ∴ R
T	T	T	T F T F T F T
T	T	F	T F T F T T T
T	F	T	F F T T T F F
T	F	F	F F T T T T F
F	T	T	T T T F T F T
F	T	F	T T F F T T T
F	F	T	T T T T F F F
F	F	F	T T F T T T F

There is no row in which all of the premises are true and the conclusion is false; therefore, the argument form is valid. Since argument (96) is one that most people find difficult to assess through unaided logical intuition, the fact that a truth table enables us to achieve a definitive evaluation illustrates the power of this method.

The truth table method does have an important limitation: It becomes unwieldy as arguments become longer. For instance, suppose we wish to evaluate an argument having the form of a constructive dilemma. In symbols, we have the following:

98. $A \lor B, A \to C, B \to D \therefore C \lor D$

Here, we have four statement letters, so we need 2^4 rows in our truth table ($2^4 = 2 \times 2 \times 2 \times 2 = 16$). The truth table looks like this:

A	B	C	D	$A \lor B,$	$A \to C,$	$B \to D$	$\therefore C \lor D$
T	T	T	T	T	T	T	T
T	T	T	F	T	T	F	T
T	T	F	T	T	F	T	T
T	T	F	F	T	F	F	F
T	F	T	T	T	T	T	T
T	F	T	F	T	T	T	T
T	F	F	T	T	F	T	T
T	F	F	F	T	F	T	F
F	T	T	T	T	T	T	T
F	T	T	F	T	T	F	T
F	T	F	T	T	T	T	T
F	T	F	F	T	T	F	F
F	F	T	T	F	T	T	T
F	F	T	F	F	T	T	T
F	F	F	T	F	T	T	T
F	F	F	F	F	T	T	F

It is clear which columns represent the main connectives, so we do not need to circle them. The argument is valid, for there are no rows in which all the premises are true and the conclusion is false. Note that the initial truth-value assignments on the left are generated in the mechanical way previously described: alternate Ts and Fs under the letter closest to the vertical line (D in the table); alternate couples under the next letter to the left (C); alternate quadruples under the next letter (B); finally, alternate groups of eight. How many rows would be needed for a truth table involving five statement letters? Thirty-two ($2^5 = 2 \times 2 \times 2 \times 2 \times 2 = 32$). And if six statement letters were involved, we would need a truth table with 64 rows. So, the truth table method is cumbersome when applied to arguments involving many statement letters. Nevertheless, it is a powerful method that is useful in many cases.

Summary of Truth-Table Method

1. Assign truth values mechanically.

   a. Place the capital letters of atomic statements in sequence from left to right in the order that they appear in our symbolization.

   b. The number of rows for atomic statements that you need is 2^n, where n is the number of atomic statements.

   c. Start assigning truth values to atomic statements in columns by first assigning truth values to the far right statement: alternate Ts and Fs in the column beneath it. The next column to the left: alternate pairs of Ts and Fs. The next column to the left: alternate quadruples of Ts and Fs. The next column to the left: alternate groups of eight, and so on (doubling).

2. Identify the main logical operator of each premise and the conclusion.

3. In the case of complex compound statements, work out the truth values of simpler compounds first, then work your way "outward" to the main logical operator.

4. Look for a row where all the premises are true and the conclusion is false. Assuming you've done everything correctly up to this point, if there is one, the argument is invalid; if not, it's valid.

EXERCISE 7.3

PART A: Truth Tables Construct truth tables to determine whether the following arguments are valid.

* **1.** A ∨ B, ~A ∴ B

  2. F → G, F ∴ G

  3. ~A ∨ ~B, ~B ∴ ~~A

* **4.** ~P → ~R ∴ ~(P → R)

  5. ~(X → Y) ∴ ~X → ~Y

  6. E ∴ D ∨ E

* **7.** A • B ∴ B

  8. ~(N • L) ∴ ~N → ~L

  9. (A ∨ B) • ~(A • B), A ∴ ~B

***10.** ~F • ~G ∴ ~F ↔ ~G

  11. ~(S • ~R), ~R ∴ ~S

  12. A ↔ B ∴ A • B

***13.** D ↔ (E ∨ C), ~D ∴ ~C

  14. A → (B → C) ∴ A → (B • C)

  15. N ↔ (M • L), ~L ∴ ~N

***16.** A → B, B → C ∴ A → C

  17. (Q • U) → Z, ~Z ∴ ~Q

  18. (E ↔ G) → H, ~H ∴ ~E ∨ ~G

***19.** A ∨ B, A → C, B → C ∴ C

  20. A → C, B → D, ~C ∨ ~D ∴ ~A ∨ ~B

PART B: More Truth Tables Construct truth tables to determine whether the following arguments are valid.

* **1.** A • ~B ∴ ~(A → B)

  2. F → G ∴ ~F → ~G

   3. ~E → ~G ∴ G → E

* **4.** ~(H • K) ∴ ~H • ~K

   5. A → B, B ∴ A

   6. X ∨ Y, Y ∴ ~X

* **7.** A ∴ (A ∨ B) • ~(A • B)

   8. ~(T ↔ ~S) ∴ ~T ∨ S

   9. ~F ∨ ~G ∴ ~(F ∨ G)

***10.** ~(H ↔ J) ∴ ~H ↔ ~J

  11. ~(A → B) ∴ A • ~B

  12. ~(N ↔ P) ∴ N → ~P

  13. ~(A ↔ B) ∴ (A • ~B) ∨ (B • ~A)

  14. (H • B) → S ∴ B → S

  15. P → Q, S → Q, ~Q ∴ ~P • ~S

  16. Z → (S ∨ G), Z ∴ S

  17. ~(L ∨ M), ~M ↔ ~N ∴ ~N

  18. P → (~Q ∨ R), P • ~R ∴ ~Q

  19. A → (B → C) ∴ (A • B) → C

  20. ~[~(D • E) ∨ (F ∨ ~D)] ∴ D • (E • ~F)

PART C: English Arguments Symbolize the following arguments. Then use truth tables to determine whether they are valid.

* **1.** Not having exceeded our natural resources is a necessary condition for its being appropriate to expand our city. Unfortunately, we have exceeded our natural resources. Consequently, it is not appropriate to expand our city. (E: We have exceeded our natural resources; A: It is appropriate to expand our city)

  2. Humans evolved from lower life forms given that either human life evolved from inanimate matter apart from divine causes or God created human life via the long, slow process we call evolution. God created human life via the long, slow process we call evolution. It follows that humans evolved from lower life forms. (H: Humans evolved from lower life forms; M: Human life evolved from inanimate matter apart from divine causes; G: God created human life via the long, slow process we call evolution)

  3. American foreign policy is bankrupt unless it is based on clear moral principles. American foreign policy is not based on clear moral principles just in case it is based primarily on the national interest. Unfortunately, American foreign policy is based primarily on the national interest. We may infer that American foreign policy is bankrupt. (B: American foreign policy is bankrupt; M: American foreign policy is based on clear moral principles; N: American foreign policy is based primarily on the national interest)

* **4.** You won't get an A unless you do well on all the exams. Therefore, if you do well on all the exams, you will get an A. (A: You will get an A; W: You do well on all the exams)

5. There are necessary truths (i.e., truths that cannot be false under any possible circumstances). For assuming that there are no necessary truths, there are no necessary connections between premises and conclusions. But there are no valid arguments if there are no necessary connections between premises and conclusions, and there are valid arguments. (N: There are necessary truths; C: There are necessary connections between premises and conclusions; V: There are valid arguments)

6. On the condition that land mines are designed to inflict horrible suffering, they ought to be banned unless inflicting horrible suffering is sometimes justified. It is not true that inflicting horrible suffering is sometimes justified, but it is true that land mines are designed to inflict horrible suffering. Accordingly, land mines ought to be banned. (L: Land mines are designed to inflict horrible suffering; B: Land mines ought to be banned; S: Inflicting horrible suffering is sometimes justified)

* **7.** The reduction of violence is a necessary and sufficient condition for making drugs legal. But more people will use drugs if drugs are made legal. And violence is not reduced if more people will use drugs. Hence, drugs are not made legal. (V: Violence is reduced; L: Drugs are made legal; P: More people will use drugs)

8. Augustine achieves heaven if Augustine is virtuous. But Augustine is happy provided that he is not virtuous. Augustine does not achieve heaven only if he is not happy. Therefore, Augustine achieves heaven. (A: Augustine achieves heaven; V: Augustine is virtuous; H: Augustine is happy)

9. Not all living things are able to feel pain. For all living things are able to feel pain only if all living things have nervous systems. But not all living things have nervous systems given that plants do not have nervous systems. And plants do not have nervous systems. (L: All living things are able to feel pain; N: All living things have nervous systems; P: Plants have nervous systems)

10. It is morally permissible for mentally superior extraterrestrials to eat humans on the condition that it is morally permissible for humans to eat animals. But either it is not morally permissible for mentally superior extraterrestrials to eat humans or human life lacks intrinsic value. However, human life has intrinsic value. We are forced to conclude that it is not morally permissible for humans to eat animals. (E: It is morally permissible for mentally superior extraterrestrials to eat humans; H: It is morally permissible for humans to eat animals; V: Human life has intrinsic value)

7.4 Abbreviated Truth Tables

As we have seen, the truth table method is rather cumbersome when applied to arguments having more than three statement letters. But there are ways to make it less cumbersome, and we will explore one of them in this section, namely, the

abbreviated truth table method. The essential insight behind abbreviated truth tables is this: If there is an assignment of truth values to *one row* of a truth table, *making all the premises true while the conclusion is false*, then the argument form in question is *invalid*. The central strategy of the abbreviated truth table method is to hypothesize that there is such a row, and then to *confirm* the hypothesis, thereby showing that the argument is *invalid*, or *disconfirm* it, thereby showing that the argument is *valid*.

Let's look at an example:

> **99.** If I am thinking, then my neurons are firing. Hence, if my neurons are firing, then I am thinking. (A: I am thinking; N: My neurons are firing)

Using the scheme of abbreviation provided, we may symbolize the argument as follows:

> **100.** $A \rightarrow N \therefore N \rightarrow A$

We begin by hypothesizing that the argument is invalid. If this hypothesis is true, then there will be an assignment of truth values to at least one row of a truth table where all of the premises are true and the conclusion is false. Here is how we represent our hypothesis:

$$\begin{array}{cc|c} A & N & A \rightarrow N \therefore N \rightarrow A \\ \hline & & \quad T \qquad\quad F \end{array}$$

Notice that, at this time, we leave the area under A and N to the left of the vertical line blank. Now we work backward from the conclusion. The conclusion, $N \rightarrow A$, is a material conditional, and the only way a material conditional can be false is when its antecedent is true and its conclusion is false. Thus, we assign a T to N and an F to A under the conclusion, like this:

$$\begin{array}{cc|c} A & N & A \rightarrow N \therefore N \rightarrow A \\ \hline & & \quad T \qquad\quad T\ F\ F \end{array}$$

We then fill in the truth values for N and A uniformly throughout the argument, arriving at this:

$$\begin{array}{cc|c} A & N & A \rightarrow N \therefore N \rightarrow A \\ \hline & & F\ T\ T \quad T\ F\ F \end{array}$$

This truth value assignment does indeed make the conclusion false and the premise true. We have in effect constructed a row in the truth table that shows the argument to be invalid: It is the row in which A is false and N is true. We add this information at the left to complete our abbreviated truth table:

A N	A → N ∴ N → A
F T	F T T T F F

We have thus confirmed our hypothesis and we have thereby shown the argument to be invalid.

Let's try a much more complicated example. Consider the following symbolic argument:

101. E ∨ S, E → (B • U), ~S ∨ ~U ∴ B

Again, we begin by hypothesizing that the argument is invalid; that is, we hypothesize that there is an assignment of truth values to at least one row of a truth table where all of the premises are true and the conclusion is false. We represent our hypothesis as follows:

E S B U	E ∨ S, E → (B • U), ~S ∨ ~U ∴ B
	T T T F

Then we work backward to determine the truth value of each constituent statement letter. We have assigned F to B, so we must uniformly assign F to B throughout the argument. So write an F under the B in the second premise. A conjunction is false if at least one of its conjuncts is false, and B is false, so we know that B • U is false. So write an F under the dot in B • U. (Note: Do *not* write an F under the U because we do not know yet whether it is false or true.) Thus we have this:

E S B U	E ∨ S, E → (B • U), ~S ∨ ~U ∴ B
	T T F F T F

Now, because B • U is false and it is the consequent of a material conditional, we know that the only way in which E → (B • U) can be true is if E is false. (If E were true and B • U were false, then E → (B • U) would be false, contrary to our hypothesis. Remember: Our goal is to see whether we can assign truths values *in accordance with* our hypothesis, not in conflict with it.) So write an F under the E in E → (B • U). We have assigned F to E, so we must uniformly assign F to E throughout the argument. So write an F under the E in the first premise. Thus we have this:

E S B U	E ∨ S, E → (B • U), ~S ∨ ~U ∴ B
	F T F T F F T F

Now, if E is false and, given our hypothesis, E ∨ S is true, then we know what truth value to assign to S. For the only way in which a disjunction can be true when one of its disjuncts is false is for the other disjunct to be true. Thus, S is true. So write a T under S in E ∨ S. We have assigned T to S, so we must uniformly assign T to S throughout the argument. So write a T under the S in the third premise, ~S ∨ ~U. (Note: Do *not* write a T under the tilde in ~S; write it under the S.) Thus we have this:

E	S	B	U	E ∨ S, E → (B • U), ~S ∨ ~U ∴ B
				F T T F T F F T T F

Now, because the truth value of a negation is the opposite of what it negates and S is true, ~S is false. So write an F under the tilde in ~S. Given our hypothesis, ~S ∨ ~U is true and ~S is false. But the only way in which a disjunction can be true when one of its disjuncts is false is for the other disjunct to be true. Thus, ~U is true. So write a T under the tilde in ~U. Thus we have this:

E	S	B	U	E ∨ S, E → (B • U), ~S ∨ ~U ∴ B
				F T T F T F F FT T T F

Since the truth value of a negation is the opposite of what it negates and ~U is true, U is false. So write an F under U in ~U. We have assigned F to U, so we must uniformly assign F to U throughout the argument. So write an F under the U in the second premise, E → (B • U). Thus we have this:

E	S	B	U	E ∨ S, E → (B • U), ~S ∨ ~U ∴ B
				F T T F T F F F FT T TF F

Now that we have assigned a truth value to every constituent statement letter and logical operator in such a way that all the premises are true and the conclusion is false, we can conclude that it is possible for all the premises to be true and the conclusion false. That possibility is when E is false, S is true, B is false, and U is false. Write these assignments under the atomic letters to the left of the vertical line, as follows:

E	S	B	U	E ∨ S, E → (B • U), ~S ∨ ~U ∴ B
F	T	F	F	F T T F T F F F FT T TF F

Argument (101) is therefore invalid. Notice that an argument that would require a 16-row truth table can be dealt with quickly by means of an abbreviated truth table.

The reasoning used in the last paragraph is long and complicated. Perhaps it's even intimidating. But rest assured: Each step will come in a flash of insight *if* you understand and memorize the truth table for each of the five types of compound statement.

So far, we have seen how the abbreviated truth table method can be used to show that an argument is invalid. It can also be used to show that an argument is valid. Let's try it out on an instance of disjunctive syllogism:

102. A ∨ B, ~A ∴ B

Again, we hypothesize that all of the premises can be true while the conclusion is false:

A B	A ∨ B, ~A ∴ B
	T T F

We have assigned F to B, so we must uniformly assign F to B throughout the argument. So write an F under the B in the first premise, A ∨ B. Now, because ~A is true, and the truth value of a negation is the opposite of what it negates, we know that A is false. So write an F under A in ~A. Given this assignment, we must uniformly assign F to A throughout the argument. So write an F under the A in the first premise, A ∨ B. Now our abbreviated truth table looks like this:

A B	A ∨ B, ~A ∴ B
	F TF TF F

There is something dreadfully wrong with it. What? This: It *can't* be right. It *can't* be right that A ∨ B is true, as our hypothesis says it is, when A and B are both false. *Given the hypothesis* that it is possible for all of the premises to be true while the conclusion is false, we have been led to say that A ∨ B is true. Moreover, *given that same hypothesis*, we have been led to say that both A and B are false, in which case we must say that A ∨ B is false. So, given our hypothesis, we are forced to say that A ∨ B is *both true and false*. But that's not possible! Thus, our hypothesis has led us to something impossible, so the hypothesis is false. That is, it is *not* possible for all the premises to be true while the conclusion is false, which is just to say that argument (102) is *valid*. We indicate that we are forced to assign both a T and an F to A ∨ B by writing the symbol "/" (a backslash) under the vee, as follows:

A B	A ∨ B, ~A ∴ B
	F / F TF F Valid

Notice that we do *not* write any truth values under the A and B to the left of the vertical line. That's because *there is no* assignment of truth values to A and B such that all of the premises are true and the conclusion is false.

Let's try our hand at a more complicated symbolic argument:

103. A ∨ ~B, ~A, ~B → (C → D) ∴ C → D

Once again, we hypothesize that it is possible for all the premises to be true while the conclusion is false, which we represent like this:

A B C D	A ∨ ~B, ~A, ~B → (C → D) ∴ C → D
	T T T F

This time we will streamline our explanation. If C → D is false, then C is true and D is false. But then the consequent of the third premise, ~B → (C → D), is false, and so its antecedent, ~B, is false. But if ~B is false, then B is true. So the ~B in the first premise, A ∨ ~B, has the same assignment. In that case, the A in A ∨ ~B is true. But if A is true there, it's true in the second premise, ~A, in which case our hypothesis has led us to say that ~A is *both* true and false. But that's impossible. So, given our hypothesis, we are led to an impossibility. Therefore, our hypothesis is false. That is, it is not possible for all the premises to be true while the conclusion is false. We represent it like this:

A B C D	A ∨ ~B, ~A, ~B → (C → D) ∴ C → D	
	T T FT / T FT T T F F T F F	Valid

Argument (103) is valid.

Using an abbreviated truth table is a bit more complicated when the conclusion of the argument is false on *more than one* assignment of truth values—for example, when the conclusion is a conjunction or a biconditional. In such cases, remember two principles:

Principle 1: If there is any assignment of values in which the premises are all true and the conclusion is false, then the argument is invalid.

Principle 2: If more than one assignment of truth values will make the conclusion false, then consider each such assignment; if each assignment that makes the conclusion false makes *at least one* premise false, then the argument is valid.

To illustrate Principle 1, consider the following symbolic argument:

104. F → G, G → H ∴ ~F • H

There are three ways to make the conclusion false: (a) Make both conjuncts false, (b) make the left conjunct false and the right one true, or (c) make the left conjunct true and the right one false. If we neglect this complexity, we can easily fall into error, for not every assignment that makes the conclusion false makes the premises true. For instance:

F G H	F → G, G → H ∴ ~F • H
	T / F F T F FTFF

With this assignment, the first premise is false. (We could make the first premise true by assigning T to G, but then the second premise would be false.) If we overlook the fact that other truth-value assignments render the *conclusion* false, we might suppose that this abbreviated truth table shows that the argument is valid. But it does not because there is a way of assigning F to the conclusion that makes all the premises true, namely:

F G H	F → G, G → H ∴ ~F • H
F F F	F T F F T F T F F F

And this proves that the argument form is invalid.

To illustrate Principle 2, consider the following example:

105. P → Q, Q → P ∴ P ↔ Q

A biconditional is false whenever its two constituent statements *differ* in truth value. So in this case, we must consider the assignment in which P is true and Q is false, *and* the assignment in which P is false and Q is true.

P Q	P → Q, Q → P ∴ P ↔ Q	
	T / F F T T T F F	
	F T T T / F F F T	Valid

Here, each assignment that makes the conclusion false also makes one of the premises false (which contradicts our hypothesis that all the premises can be true while the conclusion is false). Thus, we have shown the argument to be valid.

It is best to construct your truth table so that all of the ways in which the conclusion can be false are represented. For example, consider this symbolic argument:

106. ~[A • (B → C)] → D, E ∨ ~D, ~E ∴ A • (B → C)

We hypothesize that it is possible for all of the premises to be true while the conclusion is false. But notice that there are five ways for the conclusion to be false:

(1) A is true, and B → C is false because B is true and C is false
(2) A is false, and B → C is false because B is true and C is false
(3) A is false, and B → C is true because B is true and C is true
(4) A is false, and B → C is true because B is false and C is true
(5) A is false, and B → C is true because B is false and C is false

Each of these ways should be represented in our truth table, like this:

A	B	C	D	E	$\sim[A \cdot (B \to C)] \to D, E \vee \sim D, \sim E \therefore A \cdot (B \to C)$
					T F T F F
					F F T F F
					F F T T T
					F F F T T
					F F F T F

We must check each of these rows before we conclude that the argument is valid. Can you complete the truth table to show that argument (106) is valid? (In some cases where there are multiple ways in which the conclusion can be false, it's quicker to do a complete truth table than an abbreviated one.)

Summary of Abbreviated Truth Table Method

1. After placing the argument in a truth table, determine whether there are multiple ways in which the conclusion can be false.

2. If there is just one way, place an F under the (main operator of the) conclusion and a T under (the main operator of) each premise.

    a. To show invalidity, uniformly assign Ts and Fs to all of the components of the conclusion and the premises; write Ts and Fs under the atomic statements on the left of the table.

    b. To show validity, uniformly assign Ts and Fs to all of the components of the conclusion and the premises; write a backslash under (the main operator of) the premise you were led to say was both true and false. Do *not* write Ts and Fs under the atomic statements on the left.

3. If there is more than one way for the conclusion to be false, place one F under the (main operator of the) conclusion for *each* way it can be false, thereby creating as many rows as there are ways for the conclusion to be false. On each row, place a T under (the main operator of) each premise.

    a. To show invalidity, follow instruction 1b for *at least one* row.

    b. To show validity, follow instruction 2b for *every* row.

EXERCISE 7.4

PART A: Abbreviated Truth Tables Use abbreviated truth tables to show that the following arguments are invalid.

* **1.** $A \to (B \to C) \therefore B \to C$

   2. $\sim(E \leftrightarrow F) \therefore \sim E \cdot \sim F$

  3. ~(G ↔ H) ∴ ~G → ~H

* **4.** J → ~K ∴ ~(J ↔ K)

  5. (P • Q) → R, ~R ∴ ~P

  6. ~(Z • H), ~Z → Y, W → H ∴ ~W → Y

  How many rows would be needed in a complete truth table for argument 6?

* **7.** ~(S • H), (~S • ~H) → ~U ∴ ~U

  8. (F • G) ↔ H, ~H ∴ ~G

  9. ~(B → C), (D • C) ∨ E ∴ ~B

* **10.** (P → ~Q) ↔ ~R, R ∴ ~P

  11. S → (T → V) ∴ (S → T) → V

  12. A → (B → C) ∴ A → (B • C)

* **13.** (Z • Y) → W ∴ Z → (Y • W)

  14. ~(C ∨ D), (~C • ~E) ↔ ~D, ~E → (C ∨ F), S ∨ F ∴ S

  How many rows would be needed in a complete truth table for argument 14?

  15. (F ↔ G) ↔ H, ~H ∴ ~F • ~G

* **16.** P → Q, P → R, Q ↔ R, S, S → R ∴ P • Q

  17. S → (A • O), ~P ∨ ~R, P → (S ∨ Z), Z → (O → R) ∴ Z ∨ ~P

  18. A ∨ (B • C), ~A ∴ (A • B) ∨ (A • C)

* **19.** ~(Q ∨ S), ~T ∨ S, (U • W) → Q ∴ (~T • ~U) • W

  20. ~J • ~K, L → J, M → K, (M → ~L) → ~(N • O) ∴ ~N

PART B: More Abbreviated Truth Tables   Use abbreviated truth tables to show that the following arguments are invalid.

* **1.** ~(A • B), ~A → C, ~B → D ∴ C • D

  2. L ↔ (M • N), M ∨ N, ~L ∴ ~M

  3. (O ↔ P) → R, ~R ∴ ~O ∨ P

* **4.** ~(V • X) → ~Y ∴ ~[(V • X) → Y]

  5. ~(Z • H), ~Z → Y, W → H ∴ ~W → Y

  6. ~X ∨ (C • A), ~Y ∨ ~B, ~Y ∨ (X ∨ T), T → (A → B) ∴ T ∨ ~Y

* **7.** ~(Z → A), Z → B, ~A → C ∴ C • ~B

  8. B → (C • D), ~E ∨ ~F, E → (B ∨ G), G → (D → F) ∴ G ∨ ~E

  How many rows would be needed in a complete truth table for argument 8?

  9. ~(D ↔ E), ~D → F, E → G ∴ F • G

* **10.** H ∨ ~S, H → Z, ~S → P ∴ P ↔ Z

  11. ~[(J • K) → (M ∨ N)] ∴ K • N

  12. A → B, C → ~D, ~B ∨ D ∴ ~A ↔ ~C

13. ~E → (G • A), ~(P ↔ ~L) ∨ E, ~(P • L) ∨ Q, ~N → ~G ∴ Q • A
14. (G → E) ↔ S, ~(S ∨ H), ~(P • ~H) ∴ G • E
15. ~(C ↔ ~D) ∨ E, ~E → (G • H), (C • D) → K, ~N → ~G ∴ K • H

How many rows would be needed in a complete truth table for argument 15?

Part C: Still More Abbreviated Truth Tables Use abbreviated truth tables to show that the following arguments are valid.

  1. H → ~B, D → B, H ∴ ~D
  2. F → (G → H), ~F → J, ~(G → H) ∴ J
  3. (F ∨ E) → ~D, S ∨ D, E ∴ S
* **4.** ~A → F, A → D, ~D, F → S ∴ S ∨ X
  5. (A • E) → F, E, F → (D • ~C), A ∴ ~C
  6. ~F ∨ ~G, ~F → Z, ~G → ~R, (Z ∨ ~R) → (U → P), ~P ∴ ~U
  7. C → (T → L), ~L, ~E → C, L ∨ ~E ∴ ~T
  8. ~~A, B → ~A ∴ ~B
  9. (B • A) → C, ~D → (B • A), ~C ∴ ~~D
***10.** ~(S ∨ R), B → (S ∨ R), B ∨ P, ~Q ∨ B ∴ P • ~Q
 11. (G ∨ H) → (J ∨ K) ∴ ~(J ∨ K) → ~(H ∨ G)
 12. (M ∨ N) → ~S, T → (M ∨ N), ~S → ~(M ∨ N) ∴ T → ~(M ∨ N)
 13. X ↔ Y, ~~(X ∨ Y) ∴ X • Y
***14.** (X • Q) → (Z • ~T), R • (T ∨ ~Z) ∴ (~X ∨ ~Q) • R
 15. ~F, ~(F • ~S) → ~P, (~S • F) ∨ ~T ∴ ~(P ∨ T)

PART D: Valid or Invalid? Some of the following arguments are valid, and some are invalid. Use abbreviated truth tables to determine which are valid and which are invalid.

* **1.** ~A ∨ B ∴ A → B
  2. F → (G ↔ H), ~F • ~H ∴ ~G
  3. ~M ∴ ~N ∨ ~M
* **4.** A ∨ (B • C) ∴ (A • B) ∨ (A • C)
  5. P → ~(Q • R), P • R ∴ ~Q
  6. X → Z, Y → Z, ~Z ∴ X ↔ Y
  7. ~(S → R), S → J, ~R ↔ W ∴ W → ~J
  8. ~M → O, ~N → O, ~O ↔ ~P, ~P ∴ M • N

How many rows would be needed in a complete truth table for argument 8?

  9. (A ∨ B) • (A ∨ C) ∴ A • (B ∨ C)
 10. R ↔ ~Q, R ∨ Q, R ∨ P ∴ (P • Q) → R

PART E: English Arguments Translate the following English arguments into symbols, using the schemes of abbreviation provided. Use abbreviated truth tables to determine whether the arguments are valid.

* **1.** If you want to mess up your life, you should drink a lot of beer. There-fore, if you don't want to mess up your life, you should not drink a lot of beer. (W: You want to mess up your life; B: You should drink a lot of beer)

 2. Being undetermined is a necessary but not a sufficient condition for human behavior's being free. The laws of subatomic physics are statistical only if human behavior is not determined. And the laws of subatomic physics are statistical. It follows that human behavior is free. (D: Human behavior is determined; F: Human behavior is free; L: The laws of subatomic physics are statistical)

 3. Given that nuclear energy is needed if and only if solar energy cannot be harnessed, nuclear energy is not needed. For solar energy can be harnessed provided that funds are available; and funds are available. (N: Nuclear energy is needed; S: Solar energy can be harnessed; F: Funds are available)

* **4.** If the Afghanistan War was about overcoming terrorism, and if human life is more valuable than overcoming terrorism, then the Afghanistan War was immoral. Human life is more valuable than overcoming terrorism, but the Afghanistan War was not about overcoming terrorism. Therefore, the Afghanistan War was not immoral. (W: The Afghanistan War was about overcoming terrorism; H: Human life is more valuable than overcoming ter-rorism; I: The Afghanistan War was immoral)

 5. The rate of teenage drunk driving will decrease just in case the taxes on beer increase. The taxes on beer increase only if either the federal government or the state government will resist the liquor lobby. The state government will resist the liquor lobby, but the federal government will not. Accordingly, the rate of teenage drunk driving will not decrease. (R: The rate of teenage drunk driving will decrease; B: The taxes on beer increase; F: The federal government will resist the liquor lobby; S: The state government will resist the liquor lobby)

 6. Erik attains Valhalla given that he is valiant. And Erik is depressed assuming that he is not valiant. Furthermore, Erik fails to attain Valhalla only if he is not depressed. Thus, Erik is depressed. (E: Erik attains Valhalla; V: Eric is valiant; D: Eric is depressed)

* **7.** If society is the ultimate source of moral authority, then if society approves of polygamy, polygamy is right. But it is not true either that society is the ultimate source of moral authority or that society approves of polygamy. Hence, polygamy is not right. (S: Society is the ultimate source of moral authority; P: Society approves of polygamy; R: Polygamy is right)

 8. Either the earth is millions of years old or it is only 6000 years old. If the earth is millions of years old, then the traditional story of creation is a myth, and ultimate reality is nothing but atoms in motion. Now, either it is false that the earth is only 6000 years old or it is false that ultimate reality is nothing but atoms in motion. Therefore, the traditional story of creation is a myth. (E: The earth is millions of years old; S: The earth is only 6000 years old; B: The traditional story of creation is a myth; U: Ultimate reality is nothing but atoms in motion)

9. Wittgensteinians are right if logic is embedded in language. But logic is embedded in language if and only if logic varies as language varies. And logic is language-relative if logic varies as language varies. Moreover, given that logic is language-relative, contradictions may be true in some languages. Therefore, Wittgensteinians are right only if contradictions may be true in some languages. (W: Wittgensteinians are right; E: Logic is embedded in language; V: Logic varies as language varies; R: Logic is language-relative; C: Contradictions may be true in some languages)

10. Although most Americans approve of gun control, gun control is neither wise nor moral. For gun control is wise if and only if it prevents criminals from obtaining weapons. And gun control is moral if and only if it preserves our liberty. But it is not the case that gun control both preserves our liberty and prevents criminals from obtaining weapons. (W: Gun control is wise; M: Gun control is moral; P: Gun control prevents criminals from obtaining weapons; L: Gun control preserves our liberty)

 ## 7.5 Logically Significant Categories and Relationships

Truth tables can be used to sort statements into logically significant categories: tautologies, contradictions, and contingent statements. Truth tables can also be used to sort statements into logically significant relationships: equivalence, contradictoriness, consistency, and inconsistency. This section explains how to use truth tables to identify tautologies, contradictions, and contingent statements, as well as equivalence, contradictoriness, consistency, and inconsistency between statements. Finally, the section describes some interesting facts about statements that belong to these categories and enter into these relationships.

Tautology, Contradiction, and Contingency

A statement is a **tautology** if and only if it is true on every assignment of truth values to its atomic components.

> A statement is a **tautology** if and only if it is true on every assignment of truth values to its atomic components.

In a truth table, a statement is a tautology if it is true on every row. The tautologies of statement logic belong to a class of statements that are true simply by virtue of their form.* Here are some examples:

> **104.** Either it is raining or it is not raining. (R: It is raining)
> **105.** If trees are plants, then trees are plants. (P: Trees are plants)
> **106.** If neither atoms nor molecules exist, then atoms do not exist. (A: Atoms exist; M: Molecules exist)

These statements can be translated into symbols as follows, in order:

> **107.** R ∨ ~R
> **108.** P → P
> **109.** ~(A ∨ M) → ~A

If we construct truth tables for these statements, then every row under the main logical operator will contain a T:

R	R ∨ ~R
T	T
F	T

P	P → P
T	T
F	T

A M	~(A ∨ M) → ~A
T T	T
T F	T
F T	T
F F	T

(When you do truth tables on the *Power of Logic* website for Exercise 7.5, you must place a truth value under each logical operator. Here, for the sake of simplicity, we place a truth value only under the main logical operator.)

A statement is a **contradiction** if and only if it is false on every assignment of truth values to its atomic components.

> A statement is a **contradiction** if and only if it is false on every assignment of truth values to its atomic components.

---

*Not all statements that are true by virtue of their form are tautologies in the sense here defined. For example, the following statement is not a tautology, but it is true by virtue of its form: "If everything is human, then something is human." We will examine statements of this type in Chapter 9, "Predicate Logic." According to many philosophers, statements that are true by virtue of their form (including tautologies) belong to a larger class of statements called *necessary truths*. Necessary truths are truths that cannot be false under any possible circumstances. Here is an example of a necessary truth that does not appear to be true simply by virtue of its form: "If Al is older than Bob, then Bob is younger than Al."

In a truth table, a statement is a contradiction if it is false on every row. The contradictions of statement logic belong to a class of statements that are false simply by virtue of their form. Here are two examples:

110. Ants exist, and yet they do not exist. (A: Ants exist)

111. If lemons are yellow, then they are not blue, but lemons are both blue and yellow. (Y: Lemons are yellow; B: Lemons are blue)

In symbols, we have this:

112. A • ~A

113. (Y → ~B) • (B • Y)

If we construct a truth table for a contradiction, then every row under the main logical operator will contain an F:

A	A • ~A
T	F
F	F

Y	B	(Y → ~B) • (B • Y)
T	T	F
T	F	F
F	T	F
F	F	F

A statement is **contingent** if and only if it is true on some assignments of truth values to its atomic components and false on others.

> A statement is **contingent** if and only if it is true on some assignments of truth values to its atomic components and false on others.

In a truth table, a statement is contingent if it is true on some rows and false on other rows. For example, consider the statement *Platypuses purr, and if platypuses purr, then they are at rest,* which can be symbolized like this:

114. P • (P → R)

The truth table looks like this:

P	R	P • (P → R)
T	T	T
T	F	F
F	T	F
F	F	F

Equivalence, Contradictoriness, Consistency, and Inconsistency

So far, we have focused on three logically significant categories to which a single statement might belong. Now let's turn to four logically significant relationships statements might stand in to each other, and show how truth tables can be used to display these relationships.

Two statements are **logically equivalent** if and only if they agree in truth value on every assignment of truth values to their atomic components.

> Two statements are **logically equivalent** if and only if they agree in truth value on every assignment of truth values to their atomic components.

In a truth table, two statements are logically equivalent if they have the same truth value on each row. For example, consider the statements *If aardvarks aarkle, then baboons babooble* and *Aardvarks don't aarkle or baboons babooble*, which we can symbolize as A → B and ~A ∨ B.

A	B	A → B	~A ∨ B
T	T	T	T
T	F	F	F
F	T	T	T
F	F	T	T

Note that the columns under the arrow and the vee are exactly the same, row by row. Thus, A → B and ~A ∨ B are logically equivalent.

Two statements are **logically contradictory** if and only if they *disagree* in truth value on every assignment of truth values to their atomic components.

> Two statements are **logically contradictory** if and only if they disagree in truth value on every assignment of truth values to their atomic components.

In a truth table, two statements are logically contradictory if they have a different truth value on every row. For example, consider ~B → ~A and A • ~B:

A	B	~B → ~A	A • ~B
T	T	T	F
T	F	F	T
F	T	T	F
F	F	T	F

Note that the columns under the arrow and the dot are different, row by row. Thus, ~B → ~A and A • ~B are logically contradictory.

Two (or more) statements are **logically consistent** if and only if they are both (all) true on some assignment of truth values to their atomic components.

> Two (or more) statements are **logically consistent** if and only if they are both (all) true on some assignment of truth values to their atomic components.

In a truth table, two (or more) statements are logically consistent if they have the same truth value on at least one row. For example, consider A ∨ B and ~B ∨ A:

A	B	A ∨ B	~B ∨ A
T	T	T	T
T	F	T	T
F	T	T	F
F	F	F	T

Note that the columns under the two vees are the same on rows 1 and 2, even though they are different on rows 3 and 4. Thus, A ∨ B and ~B ∨ A are logically consistent. Also note that the definition of logical consistency allows for more than two statements to be logically consistent.

Two (or more) statements are **logically inconsistent** if and only if they are never both (all) true on any assignment of truth values to their atomic components.

> Two (or more) statements are **logically inconsistent** if and only if they are never both (all) true on any assignment of truth values to their atomic components.

In a truth table, two statements are logically inconsistent if there is no row on which they are both (all) true. For example, consider A ↔ B and ~(~A ∨ B):

A	B	A ↔ B	~(~A ∨ B)
T	T	T	F
T	F	F	T
F	T	F	F
F	F	T	F

Note that the columns under the double arrow and the tilde are never both true. Thus, A ↔ B and ~(~A ∨ B) are logically inconsistent. The definition of logical inconsistency allows for two statements to both be false. In a truth table, this appears as a row on which they are both false—for example, row 3. Also, the definition of logical inconsistency allows for more than two statements to be logically inconsistent. For example, consider A • B, (A • B) → ~C, and ~~C.

A	B	C	A • B	(A • B) → ~C	~~C
T	T	T	T	F	T
T	T	F	T	T	F
T	F	T	F	T	T
T	F	F	F	T	F
F	T	T	F	T	T
F	T	F	F	T	F
F	F	T	F	T	T
F	F	F	F	T	F

Note that there is no row on which all of these statements are true. Thus, they form what is called an *inconsistent triad,* three statements that cannot all be true.

Concluding Observations

Tautologies have some interesting and surprising properties. For example, every argument whose conclusion is a tautology is valid—regardless of the content of the premises. Consider the following example:

> **115.** The moon is made of green cheese. So, either Santa is real or Santa is not real. (M: The moon is made of green cheese; S: Santa is real)

Here is a symbolization and truth table for argument (115):

M	S	M ∴ S ∨ ~S	
T	T	T	T
T	F	T	T
F	T	F	T
F	F	F	T

As you can see, there is no row in which the premise is true while the conclusion is false, and so the argument is valid. This may seem puzzling because intuitively the premise is irrelevant to the conclusion. But the argument does satisfy our definition of validity—because the conclusion is a tautology, it is impossible for the conclusion to be false while the premise is true.

Like tautologies, contradictions have some interesting logical properties. For example, any argument that has a contradiction among its premises is a valid argument. For instance:

> **116.** Atoms exist, and yet they do not exist. So, God exists. (A: Atoms exist; G: God exists)

Here is the truth table:

A	G	A • ~A	∴ G
T	T	F	T
T	F	F	F
F	T	F	T
F	F	F	F

Note that there is no row in which the premise is true and the conclusion is false; hence, the argument is valid. This may seem strange, but the argument does satisfy our definition of validity. It is impossible for the conclusion to be false while the premise is true (because it is impossible for the premise to be true). Notice, however, that all arguments having a contradiction among their premises are *unsound* because contradictions are always false.

We can go a step further here: Any argument with logically inconsistent premises will be valid yet unsound. If the premises of an argument are inconsistent, then if we form a conjunction of the premises, that conjunction will be a contradiction. Here is an example:

117. P → Q, ~P → Q, ~Q ∴ R

If we form a conjunction of the premises, the argument looks like this:

P	Q	R	(P → Q)	•	[(~P → Q) • ~Q]	∴ R
T	T	T	T	F	F	T
T	T	F	T	F	F	F
T	F	T	F	F	T	T
T	F	F	F	F	T	F
F	T	T	T	F	F	T
F	T	F	T	F	F	F
F	F	T	T	F	F	T
F	F	F	T	F	F	F

The second column reveals that the conjunction is a contradiction. Again, the point is that, surprisingly, every argument with inconsistent premises is valid. (Of course, all such arguments are *unsound* because they have one or more false premises.) How will you know if the premises of an argument are inconsistent? Here's how: There will be no row in the truth table in which all of the premises are true. For instance:

M	N	L	M ↔ N,	M • ~N	∴ L
T	T	T	T	F	T
T	T	F	T	F	F
T	F	T	F	T	T
T	F	F	F	T	F
F	T	T	F	F	T
F	T	F	F	F	F
F	F	T	T	F	T
F	F	F	T	F	F

Because there is no row in which all the premises are true, the premises are inconsistent and the argument is valid.

Contingent statements have important logical relations to both tautologies and contradictions. For example, any argument that has a tautology as its premise but a contingent statement as its conclusion is invalid. (The premise will be true in every row of the truth table, while the conclusion will be false in at least one row.) And suppose that the premises of an argument, when made into a conjunction, form a contingent statement. Then, if the conclusion of the argument is a contradiction, the argument is invalid. (The conclusion will be false in every row, while the premise will be true in at least one row.)

Notice that tautologies and contradictions place limitations on the method of abbreviated truth tables that was introduced in the previous section. For instance, if an argument has a tautology as its conclusion, then there is no way to assign truth values so that the conclusion is false. One way to deal with such a case is to use a complete truth table to prove that the conclusion is a tautology (which simultaneously proves that the argument is valid). Similarly, if at least one premise is a contradiction (or if the premises are inconsistent), then there is no way to assign values so that the premises are all true, and a complete truth table may be needed to establish this, as in the case of argument (116). However, a complete truth table is not always needed in such cases, for consider the following (admittedly odd) argument:

118. B • ~B ∴ B

We can deal with this argument by means of an abbreviated truth table:

	B • ~B ∴ B		
	F / TF	F	Valid

There is only one way to make B false, and it forces an assignment of F to the premise, so the abbreviated truth table works in this case.

The concept of logical equivalence has an important relationship to the concept of a tautology—namely, if a biconditional statement is a tautology, then its two constituent statements (joined by the double-arrow) are logically equivalent. For instance, consider the following tautology:

F G	(F → G) ↔ (~G → ~F)		
T T	T	T	T
T F	F	T	F
F T	T	T	T
F F	T	T	T

From the fact that $(F \to G) \leftrightarrow (\sim G \to \sim F)$ is a tautology, we may infer that the following two statements are logically equivalent:

119. $F \to G$

120. $\sim G \to \sim F$

Note also that in the truth table, the same truth value occurs beneath the main operators of the two statements (i.e., the arrows) in each row.

    To sum up, truth tables can be used to sort statements into logically significant categories and to show logically significant relationships between statements. And, as we have seen, these categories and relationships have interesting logical properties.

Summary of Definitions

A statement is a **tautology** if and only if it is true on every assignment of truth values to its atomic components.

A statement is a **contradiction** if and only if it is false on every assignment of truth values to its atomic components.

A statement is **contingent** if and only if it is true on some assignments of truth values to its atomic components and false on others.

Two statements are **logically equivalent** if and only if they agree in truth value on every assignment of truth values to their atomic components.

Two statements are **logically contradictory** if and only if they disagree in truth value on every assignment of truth values to their atomic components.

Two (or more) statements are **logically consistent** if and only if they are both (all) true on some assignment of truth values to their atomic components.

Two (or more) statements are **logically inconsistent** if and only if they are never both (all) true on any assignment of truth values to their atomic components.

EXERCISE 7.5

PART A: Tautologies, Contradictions, and Contingent Statements

Use truth tables to determine whether the following statements are tautologies, contradictions, or contingent statements.

* **1.** $\sim A \to (A \to B)$

   2. $\sim F \to G$

   3. $\sim S \leftrightarrow S$

* **4.** $B \to (A \to B)$

   5. $F \to [\sim(F \bullet G) \to \sim G]$

   6. $A \to [(A \to B) \to B]$

* **7.** P → (P → Q)
  8. (A ↔ B) → (~A • ~B)
  9. ~P • ~(~P ∨ ~Q)
* **10.** (R • ~R) → S
  11. B → [~(A • B) → A]
  12. ~(F → G) • G
  13. ~(N ↔ M) → (N • ~M)

  14. [A → (B ∨ C)] → [(A → B) ∨ (A → C)]
  15. (~P ↔ P) → Q
  16. ~(K → L) → (K • ~L)
  17. [A → (B → C)] → [(A → B) → (A → C)]
  18. (H → J) → ~(H • ~J)
  19. (~Z • ~W) → (Z ↔ W)
  20. [(A → B) → A] → A

PART B: Logical Equivalence

Use truth tables to prove that the following pairs of statements are logically equivalent. It will be useful to know these particular equivalences as we move on to the material in the next chapter.

* **1.** ~(A • B)   ~A ∨ ~B
  2. ~(F ∨ G)   ~F • ~G
  3. P • (Q ∨ R)   (P • Q) ∨ (P • R)
* **4.** S → U   ~S ∨ U
  5. Q   ~~Q
  6. P ∨ (Q • R)   (P ∨ Q) • (P ∨ R)
  7. F ↔ G   (F • G) ∨ (~F • ~G)
  8. A ∨ B   B ∨ A
  9. K • K   K
  10. U ↔ Z   (U → Z) • (Z → U)

PART C: Logical Contradictoriness, Consistency, and Inconsistency

None of the following pairs of statements are logically equivalent. Use truth tables to prove that they are either logically contradictory, consistent, or inconsistent. *Note:* Some statements that are logically inconsistent are also logically contradictory.

* **1.** A • B   ~(A ∨ B)
  2. F → ~G   ~F → G
  3. X • ~Y   Y ∨ ~X
* **4.** ~M ↔ N   (~N • M) ∨ (M → ~N)
  5. (C ∨ D) • (~E ∨ C)   D ↔ ~C
  6. G → (H → I)   (G → H) → I
* **7.** J • (K ∨ ~L)   ~K • (~L → ~J)
  8. O ↔ (P • Q)   O • (Q → ~P)
  9. R • (~S → T)   ~(R • S) • ~(R • P)
  10. (Z • U) ∨ (W • U)   U → ~(Z ∨ W)

PART D: English Arguments Symbolize the following arguments. Then use truth tables to determine whether they are valid. Most of these arguments illustrate important logical properties of tautologies, contradictions, or contingent statements.

* **1.** Grass is green. So, if Obama wins, then Obama wins. (G: Grass is green; W: Obama wins)

  2. Light is both a wave and a particle. But if light is a wave, then it is not a particle. So, physicists are profoundly mistaken. (W: Light is a wave; P: Light is a particle; M: Physicists are profoundly mistaken)

  3. Either unicorns exist or unicorns do not exist. Therefore, trees exist. (U: Unicorns exist; T: Trees exist)

* **4.** Pain is an illusion if and only if it is not an illusion. It follows that everything is an illusion. (P: Pain is an illusion; E: Everything is an illusion)

  5. If it is wet, then it is wet if it is raining. Consequently, either Sasquatch exists or Sasquatch fails to exist. (W: It is wet; R: It is raining; S: Sasquatch exists)

  6. Human behavior is determined only if human behavior is not free. Human behavior is determined; nevertheless, it is free. Therefore, life is but a dream. (D: Human behavior is determined; F: Human behavior is free; L: Life is but a dream)

  7. The sky's being colored is a necessary condition for its being blue. It follows that the sky's being blue is a sufficient condition for its being colored. (C: The sky is colored; B: The sky is blue)

  8. It is not the case both that electrons exist and that electrons do not exist. Hence, electrons exist. (E: Electrons exist)

  9. If ultimate reality is divine, then it can be described in human language if and only if it cannot be described in human language. So, ultimate reality is not divine. (U: Ultimate reality is divine; L: Ultimate reality can be described in human language)

  10. If you do not accept me as I am, then you do not love me. You accept me as I am if and only if you accept me as a violent criminal. You love me, but you do not accept me as a violent criminal. Consequently, you do not love me. (A: You accept me as I am; L: You love me; C: You accept me as a violent criminal)

NOTE

1. C. S. Peirce, "On the Algebra of Logic: A Contribution to the Philosophy of Notation," *American Journal of Mathematics* 7 (1885): 180–202. The credit for the invention and development of truth tables should probably be spread around a bit. The idea occurs informally in Gottlob Frege's *Begriffsschrift* (Halle, Germany: L. Nebert, 1879). And the Austrian philosopher Ludwig Wittgenstein developed truth tables independently in his famous *Tractatus Logico-philosophicus* (London: Routledge & Kegan Paul, 1922).

CHAPTER 8

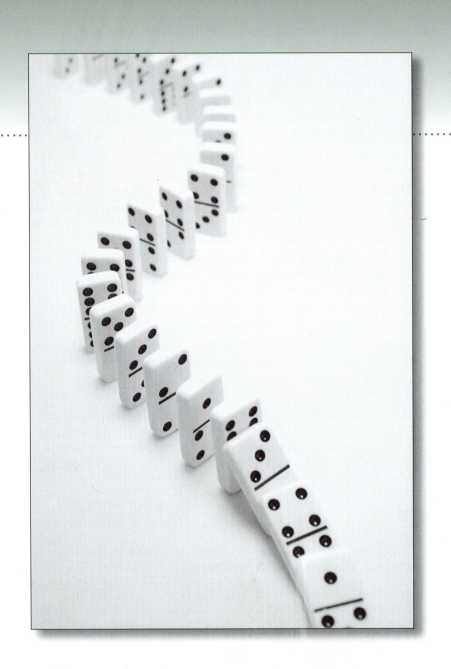

Statement Logic: Proofs

*I*n the previous chapter, we used truth tables to evaluate arguments in statement logic. We saw, however, that truth tables can be cumbersome. In this chapter, we will develop a system of natural deduction, a set of inference rules one can use to prove that the conclusion of an argument follows from its premises. A system of natural deduction has at least two advantages over the truth table method. First, it is less cumbersome. Second, it more clearly mirrors the ways we ordinarily argue. The German logician and mathematician Gerhard Gentzen (1909–1945) first developed a system of natural deduction.[1]

As we develop a system of natural deduction, we are pulled in two directions. On the one hand, we can develop a system with few inference rules, but then the proofs require much ingenuity and tend to be longer and to depart from ordinary reasoning. On the other hand, we can develop a system with many rules, but then we have to remember them all. The present system of natural deduction is a compromise that includes 20 rules altogether. We will introduce it in stages: 8 implicational rules (in 8.1), 10 equivalence rules (in 8.2 and 8.3), conditional proof (in 8.4), and *reductio ad absurdum* (in 8.5). Finally, in section 8.6, we discuss proving theorems.

8.1 Implicational Rules of Inference

Let us use the word **"proof"** in a technical sense to refer to a series of steps that leads from the premises of a symbolic argument to its conclusion.

A **proof** is a series of steps that leads from the premises of a symbolic argument to its conclusion.

The fundamental idea is to show that the premises lead, by way of valid rules of inference, to the conclusion. The underlying principle is this: *Whatever follows from a set of statements by means of valid inferences is true if all the statements in the set are true.*

Our first set of inference rules is mostly familiar. The first five were introduced as argument forms in Chapter 1. Once again, we use italicized, lowercase letters as variables that stand for any given statement: *p, q, r,* and *s*.

Rule 1: *Modus ponens* (MP): $p \to q$
p
$\therefore q$

Rule 2: *Modus tollens* (MT): $p \to q$
$\sim q$
$\therefore \sim p$

Rule 3: Hypothetical syllogism (HS): $p \to q$
$q \to r$
$\therefore p \to r$

Rule 4: Disjunctive syllogism (DS), in two forms:
$$p \lor q \qquad\qquad p \lor q$$
$$\sim p \qquad\qquad\quad \sim q$$
$$\therefore q \qquad\qquad\quad \therefore p$$

Rule 5: Constructive dilemma (CD): $p \lor q$
$p \to r$
$q \to s$
$\therefore r \lor s$

To these familiar forms we add three more.

Rule 6: Simplification (Simp), in two forms:
$$p \bullet q \qquad\qquad p \bullet q$$
$$\therefore p \qquad\qquad\quad \therefore q$$

Simplification says, in effect, that if you have a conjunction, then you may infer either conjunct. Here is an English example:

1. Both Pierre Curie and Marie Curie were physicists. Therefore, Marie Curie was a physicist.

This type of inference may seem so obvious as to be trivial, but it is nonetheless valid. And one aspect of the power of logic is its capacity to break complex reasoning down into easy steps.

The next rule tells us that if we have two statements as steps in an argument, we may conjoin them.

Rule 7: Conjunction (Conj): p
q
$\therefore p \bullet q$

Again, this rule is obviously valid. Here is an example:

> **2.** Thomas Aquinas died in 1274. William Ockham died in 1349. Consequently, Aquinas died in 1274, *and* Ockham died in 1349.

The rule of addition is perhaps a bit less obvious than the rules we have considered so far.

> **Rule 8:** Addition (Add) in two forms:
>
> $$p \qquad\qquad p$$
> $$\therefore p \vee q \qquad \therefore q \vee p$$

Addition tells us that from any given statement *p*, one may infer a disjunction that has *p* as one of its disjuncts—and the other disjunct may be anything you please. For instance:

> **3.** Thomas Paine wrote *Common Sense*. Hence, either Thomas Paine wrote *Common Sense* or Patrick Henry wrote *Common Sense*.

Although this type of inference may seem odd, recall that, in logic, disjunctions are treated as *inclusive* disjunctions, and only one disjunct must be true for an inclusive disjunction to be true. Thus, it is not possible for it to be true that Thomas Paine wrote *Common Sense* while it is false that either Thomas Paine wrote *Common Sense* or Patrick Henry wrote *Common Sense*. Indeed, it is not possible for it to be true that Thomas Paine wrote *Common Sense* while any of these are false:

> **4.** Either Thomas Paine wrote *Common Sense* or platypuses purr.
> **5.** Either Thomas Paine wrote *Common Sense* or 2 + 2 = 22.
> **6.** Either Thomas Paine wrote *Common Sense* or you're a monkey's uncle.

Is the following argument an example of addition?

> **7.** Adam stole the money. It follows that either Adam stole the money or Betty stole the money, but not both. (A: Adam stole the money; B: Betty stole the money)

No. Argument (7) has the following invalid form:

> **8.** A $\therefore$ (A $\vee$ B) $\bullet$ ~(A $\bullet$ B)

The following abbreviated truth table shows that it is invalid:

A B	A $\therefore$	(A $\vee$ B) $\bullet$ ~(A $\bullet$ B)
T T	T	T TT F F T T T

Do not confuse form (8) with the rule of addition.

The italicized, lowercase letters in the previous rules or argument schemas play a special role. They can be replaced by any symbolic statement *as long as the replacement is uniform throughout the schema.* For example, both of the following count as instances of *modus ponens:*

$$\begin{array}{ll} \sim\!F \rightarrow G & L \rightarrow (M \rightarrow N) \\ \sim\!F & L \\ \therefore G & \therefore M \rightarrow N \end{array}$$

In the inference on the left, ~F is substituted for the letter *p*, while G is substituted for the letter *q* in the original schema: *p* → *q*, *p* ∴ *q*. Note that we have replaced *p* with ~F throughout the argument schema; substitutions must be uniform in this sense. In the example on the right, L is substituted for *p*, while (M → N) is substituted for *q* in the original schema. In both cases, the pattern of reasoning is *modus ponens* because one premise is a conditional, the other is the antecedent of the conditional, and the conclusion is the consequent of the conditional.

In substituting symbolic formulas for lowercase letters, precision is required. Consider the following argument. Is it an instance of *modus tollens?*

$$\begin{array}{l} C \rightarrow \sim\!D \\ D \\ \therefore \sim\!C \end{array}$$

No, it is not. The schema for *modus tollens* is *p* → *q*, ~*q* ∴ ~*p*. If we replace the letter *q* with ~D in the first premise, we must replace *q* with ~D in the second premise as well, in which case we obtain the following argument:

$$\begin{array}{l} C \rightarrow \sim\!D \\ \sim\!\sim\!D \\ \therefore \sim\!C \end{array}$$

This *is* an instance of *modus tollens.* To apply *modus tollens,* we need a conditional *and* the negation of its consequent. If the consequent of the conditional is itself a negation, such as ~D, the other premise will be a double-negation, such as ~~D earlier.

To ensure an understanding of our new inference rules, let us consider a series of examples. Which rules of inference, if any, are instantiated by the following arguments?

$$\begin{array}{ll} \sim\!P \rightarrow (Q \bullet R) & X \vee (Y \leftrightarrow Z) \\ (Q \bullet R) \rightarrow S & \sim\!(Y \leftrightarrow Z) \\ \therefore \sim\!P \rightarrow S & \therefore X \end{array}$$

The argument on the left is an example of hypothetical syllogism. Note that ~P replaces *p*, (Q • R) replaces *q*, and S replaces *r* in the original schema: *p* → *q*, *q* → *r* ∴ *p* → *r*. The argument on the right is an example of disjunctive syllogism. Here, X replaces *p* and (Y ↔ Z) replaces *q* in the second form of disjunctive syllogism: *p* ∨ *q*, ~*q* ∴ *p*.

Which rules of inference, if any, are instantiated by the following arguments?

> ~M ∨ ~N
> ~M → ~O
> ~N → ~P   ~(B • ~C)
> ∴ ~O ∨ ~P   ∴ ~(B • ~C) ∨ ~D

The argument on the left is an instance of constructive dilemma. Here, ~M replaces *p*, ~N replaces *q*, ~O replaces *r*, and ~P replaces *s* in the schema for constructive dilemma: *p* ∨ *q*, *p* → *r*, *q* → *s* ∴ *r* ∨ *s*. The argument on the right is an instance of addition. Note that ~(B • ~C) replaces *p*, and ~D replaces *q* in the first form of addition: *p* ∴ *p* ∨ *q*.

Which rules of inference, if any, are instantiated by the following arguments?

>   A ∨ ~B
> (C → D) • (E ∨ F)   B
> ∴ E ∨ F   ∴ A

The argument on the left is an instance of simplification. Here, (C → D) replaces *p*, while (E ∨ F) replaces *q* in the second form of simplification: *p* • *q* ∴ *q*. The argument on the right, however, does *not* instantiate any of our inference rules. But if we changed the second premise to ~~B, then we would have an instance of the second form of disjunctive syllogism: *p* ∨ *q*, ~*q* ∴ *p*. (Substitute A for *p* and ~B for *q*.)

Let us now use our new inference rules to construct some proofs. We begin with an English argument:

> **9.** If some employees deserve 5 times the wages of others, then some employees are 5 times more valuable than others. It is not true that some employees are 5 times more valuable than others. So, it is not true that some employees deserve 5 times the wages of others. (D: Some employees deserve 5 times the wages of others; V: Some employees are 5 times more valuable than others)

Using the scheme of abbreviation provided, we can symbolize the argument like this:

> 1. D → V
> 2. ~V   ∴ ~D

The first lines of our proof, lines (1) and (2), contain the premises of the argument. To the right of the last premise we write the conclusion, marked by the triple-dot symbol. This reminds us what we are trying to derive from the premises. (Thus, the expression ∴ ~D is not really a part of the proof but merely a reminder of what we need to prove.) What we want to do is to arrive at the conclusion, ~D, by means of our inference rules. We have a conditional premise, and we also have the negation of its consequent. That is, we have here the makings of a *modus tollens*–type argument.

If you don't see this, try this procedure. Recall that the schema for *modus tollens* is this:

$$p \rightarrow q$$
$$\sim q$$
$$\therefore \sim p$$

Now, substitute D for *p* uniformly throughout the schema:

$$D \rightarrow q$$
$$\sim q$$
$$\therefore \sim D$$

Then, substitute V for *q* uniformly throughout the schema:

$$D \rightarrow V$$
$$\sim V$$
$$\therefore \sim D$$

So we can see that, given lines (1) and (2), D → V and ~V respectively, ~D follows by *modus tollens*.

Proper proof procedure requires that we list the lines to which we are applying the rule of inference, as well as the abbreviation of the inference rule. Accordingly, our completed proof looks like this:

1. D → V
2. ~V   ∴ ~D
3. ~D   1, 2, MT

Line (3) tells us that ~D follows from lines (1) and (2) by *modus tollens*. We have shown that the premises of the argument lead to the conclusion by way of a valid rule of inference. Notice that the only lines in the proof without annotation (without an explicit indication of how we arrived at them) are the premises. Let us adopt the convention that any step in an argument without annotation will be understood to be a premise.

Consider a slightly more complicated example:

10. If the workplace is a meritocracy, then the most qualified person always gets the job. But the most qualified person does not always get the job if networking plays a role in who gets most jobs. Furthermore, networking does play a role in who gets most jobs. Therefore, the workplace is not a meritocracy. (W: The workplace is a meritocracy; M: The most qualified person always gets the job; N: Networking plays a role in who gets most jobs)

Using the scheme of abbreviation provided, the argument should be symbolized as follows:

    1. W → M
    2. N → ~M
    3. N   ∴ ~W

The first lines of our proof contain the premises with the conclusion located to the right of the last premise. Here's the proof:

    1. W → M
    2. N → ~M
    3. N   ∴ ~W
    4. ~M   2, 3, MP
    5. ~W   1, 4, MT

Lines (2) and (3) imply ~M by the rule *modus ponens*. To see this, let's use our procedure again. Recall that the schema for *modus ponens* is this:

    p → q
    p
    ∴ *q*

Now, substitute N for *p* in the schema:

    N → *q*
    q
    ∴ N

And substitute ~M for *q*:

    N → ~M
    N
    ∴ ~M

Thus, given lines (2) and (3), N → ~M and N respectively, ~M follows by *modus ponens*. Lines (1) and (4) imply ~W by the rule *modus tollens*. To see this, recall the schema for *modus tollens*, earlier. Substitute W for **p** in the schema:

> W → **q**
>
> ~**q**
>
> ∴ ~W

Then substitute M for **q**:

> W → M
>
> ~M
>
> ∴ ~W

Thus, given lines (1) and (4), W → M and ~M respectively, ~W follows by *modus tollens*.

Here's a proof that employs our inference rules involving conjunctions:

11. Women earn only 75¢ for every dollar earned by men. If women earn only 75¢ for every dollar earned by men, and 90 percent of children who live with one parent live with their mothers, then men are better off than women, and women are victims of injustice. Ninety percent of children who live with one parent live with their mothers. Feminists are right if women are victims of injustice. So, feminists are right. (W: Women earn only 75¢ for every dollar earned by men; C: Ninety percent of children who live with one parent live with their mothers; M: Men are better off than women; V: Women are victims of injustice; F: Feminists are right)

Using the scheme of abbreviation provided, the translation looks like this:

> 1. W
> 2. (W • C) → (M • V)
> 3. C
> 4. V → F   ∴ F

The proof may be completed thus:

> 5. W • C   1, 3, Conj
> 6. M • V   2, 5, MP
> 7. V   6, Simp
> 8. F   4, 7, MP

Here's an explanation. Recall that rule of conjunction is this:

> **p**
>
> **q**
>
> ∴ **p** • **q**

If we substitute W for *p* and C for *q* in the schema, we get this:

> W
> C
> ∴ W • C

Thus, given lines (1) and (3), line (5) follows by conjunction. *Modus ponens* is this:

> *p → q*
> *p*
> ∴ *q*

Substitute W • C for *p* and M • V for *q* in the schema and the result is this:

> (W • C) → (M • V)
> W • C
> ∴ M • V

So, given lines (2) and (5), line (6) follows by *modus ponens*. Here's simplification:

> *p • q*
> ∴ *p*

If we substitute M for *p* and V for *q* in the schema, we have this:

> M • V
> ∴ M

Therefore, given line (6), line (7) follows by simplification. Finally, substitute V for *p* and F for *q* in the schema for *modus ponens* and the result is this:

> V → F
> V
> ∴ F

Hence, given lines (4) and (7), line (8) follows by *modus ponens*.

One last example will demonstrate some of the inference rules involving disjunctions.

12. If Pierre is an assassin, then either he should be put to death or he should be given a life sentence. He should be put to death only if murderers deserve death. He should be given a life sentence only if murderers forfeit their right to liberty. Pierre is an assassin, but murderers do not deserve death. Therefore, murderers forfeit their right to liberty. (A: Pierre is an assassin; D: Pierre should be put to death; L: Pierre should be given a life sentence; M: Murderers deserve death; F: Murderers forfeit their right to liberty)

Using the scheme of abbreviation provided, the argument may be symbolized like this:

    1. A → (D ∨ L)
    2. D → M
    3. L → F
    4. A • ~M   ∴ F

The proof may be completed as follows:

    5. A   4, Simp
    6. D ∨ L   1, 5, MP
    7. M ∨ F   6, 2, 3, CD
    8. ~M   4, Simp
    9. F   7, 8, DS

Note that line (7) derives from lines (6), (2), and (3) by substituting D for p, L for q, M for r, and F for s in the original schema for constructive dilemma: $p \lor q$, $p \to r, q \to s \therefore r \lor s$. And line (9) derives from lines (7) and (8) by substituting M for p and F for q in the first form of disjunctive syllogism: $p \lor q$, $\sim p \therefore q$.

Our first eight rules are called **implicational rules.** Note two things about them. First, since they are argument forms, they are *one-directional*. That is, although they allow us to move from a substitution instance of the premises to a substitution instance of the conclusion, they do *not* allow us to move from a substitution instance of the conclusion to a substitution instance of the premises. For example, although the rule of simplification—$p \bullet q \therefore p$—allows us to move from the conjunction *you and Santa exist* to the atomic statement *you exist*, it does *not* allow us to move from the atomic statement *you exist* to the conjunction *you and Santa exist*. Second, we can apply implicational rules *only* to entire lines of a proof; *we cannot apply them to parts of lines*. The need for this restriction is illustrated by this argument:

    13. If George W. Bush was president in 2010 and Barack Obama was president in 2010, then America had two presidents in 2010. So, George W. Bush was president in 2010. (B: George W. Bush was president in 2010; O: Barack Obama was president in 2010; A: America had two presidents in 2010)

If implicational rules could apply to parts of lines, we'd have the following proof:

    1. (B • O) → A ∴ B
    2. B   1, Simp

Plainly, this is an invalid inference. Simplification, like every other implicational rule, applies *only* to entire lines of a proof, *not* parts of lines.

Notice that we construct our proofs by means of *one* application of *one* rule of inference per line. We do this to ensure that each step in every proof is explicit and clearly justified by a rule in our system of logic. Which of the following proofs is properly constructed?

1. A → ~B		1. A → ~B	
2. A • C	∴ ~B	2. A • C	∴ ~B
3. ~B	1, 2, MP	3. A	2, Simp
		4. ~B	1, 3, MP

The proof on the right is correct; the proof on the left skips a required application of simplification and misapplies *modus ponens*.

The following tips will help you as you construct proofs. The first tip often goes unstated, but following it devotedly may well save you hours of useless head-scratching and painful consternation. When you do proofs, you will often copy the premises and the desired conclusion from one place, such as a textbook, to another place, such as a piece of paper.

Tip 1: Always, *always,* immediately check that you copied the proof correctly.

If you do not copy it correctly, you will waste your time trying to do a proof that can't be done. We recommend that you not fritter away your life in this way, nor any other way for that matter, but *especially* not in this way.

The second tip is this:

Tip 2: Scan the premises to see whether they fit any rule patterns.

As you become more skilled at using the rules, with little effort you will see patterns within the premises leap from the page. When that happens, go with the flow. Not infrequently, that flow becomes a stream and then a flood of rule recognition as a proof emerges right before your very eyes. At other times, the stream will subside into a trickle and then dry up. In either case, jot down the names of the rules as they come to mind, using their abbreviations. They might well prove useful later when you proceed to construct the proof, step by step.

The third tip is this:

Tip 3: Try to find the conclusion (or elements thereof) in the premises.

For example:

1. A → [B → (C ∨ D)]	
2. B • A	
3. ~D	∴ C

The conclusion here is C. Does it appear anywhere in the premises? Yes, it is embedded in the consequent of premise (1). And if we could obtain C ∨ D from premise (1), we could combine it with ~D—that is, premise (3)—to get C, by disjunctive syllogism. But how can we obtain C ∨ D? Consider another tip:

> **Tip 4:** Apply the inference rules to break down the premises.

We could get A from line (2) by simplification and use it together with line (1) to obtain B → (C ∨ D), by *modus ponens*. Then we could get B from line (2) (by simplification) and apply *modus ponens* again, to obtain C ∨ D. The whole proof would then look like this:

1. A → [B → (C ∨ D)]
2. B • A
3. ~D   ∴ C
4. A   2, Simp
5. B → (C ∨ D)   1, 4, MP
6. B   2, Simp
7. C ∨ D   5, 6, MP
8. C   3, 7, DS

Let's consider another example:

1. E ∨ F
2. E → G
3. F → H
4. (G ∨ H) → J   ∴ J ∨ K

Using Tip 3, we start by examining the conclusion. We look to see if the conclusion (or parts thereof) appears in the premises, noting that J is the consequent of premise (4). Now, is there any way to break premise (4) down, as Tip 4 suggests? Yes, we can use the rule of constructive dilemma to obtain G ∨ H from premises (1), (2), and (3), and then use *modus ponens* to get J. But where do we go from there? In particular, how can we obtain K when it appears nowhere in the premises? At this point, it will be helpful to bear in mind an additional tip.

> **Tip 5:** If the conclusion contains a statement letter that does not appear in the premises, use the rule of addition.

The whole proof looks like this:

1. E ∨ F
2. E → G

3. F → H
4. (G ∨ H) → J   ∴ J ∨ K
5. G ∨ H   1, 2, 3, CD
6. J   4, 5, MP
7. J ∨ K   6, Add

Thus far, we have mentioned five tips. We will mention more later. In closing this section, we want to commend a strategy for doing proofs that many students have found helpful. We call it **Ned's Wish List Strategy.**[2]

Suppose you are presented with a symbolic argument, say this one:

1. A → B
2. C → D
3. D → ~B
4. C   ∴ ~A

A simple question presents itself: What do you want? Naturally, world peace comes to mind, the abolition of AIDS, a cure for cancer, and so on. But setting aside such momentous matters, what do you want with respect to the argument before you? Well, you want to get ~A. Ned's Wish List Strategy begins with a piece of advice: Keep track of what you want to get. Indeed, write it down, like this:

1. A → B   Wish List
2. C → D   ~A
3. D → ~B
4. C   ∴ ~A

Next question: How are you going to get ~A? Well, using Tip 3, you see that A appears in line (1). *If* you can turn it into ~A, then you'll have what you want. But how can you do that? Well, *if* you had ~B, you could use *modus tollens* on A → B to get ~A. So you want ~B. Write it down:

1. A → B   Wish List
2. C → D   ~A
3. D → ~B   ~B   *(~B + line 1 + MT = ~A)*
4. C   ∴ ~A

What's between the parentheses reminds you of how you are going to use ~B to get ~A: You use ~B plus line (1) and *modus tollens* to get ~A.

Next question: How are you going to get ~B? Using an analogue of Tip 3—try to find what you want (or elements thereof) in the premises—you notice that ~B is the consequent of line (3). Well, *if* you had D, you could use *modus ponens* on D → ~B to get ~B. So you want D. Write it down:

			Wish List	
1. A → B				
2. C → D			~A	
3. D → ~B			~B	(~B + line 1 + MT = ~A)
4. C		∴ ~A	D	(D + line 3 + MP = ~B)

Next question: How are you going to get D? Using the analogue of Tip 3 again, you notice that D is the consequent of line (2). Well, if you had C, you could use *modus ponens* on C → D to get D. So, you want C. Write it down:

			Wish List	
1. A → B				
2. C → D			~A	
3. D → ~B			~B	(~B + line 1 + MT = ~A)
4. C		∴ ~A	D	(D + line 3 + MP = ~B)
			C	(C + line 2 + MP = D)

But wait a second! You already have C in line (4)! So now you have everything you need to do the proof.

First, because you have C on line (4), you get to have D, the item above C on the list. Write it down on line (5). Your parenthetical reminder indicates your justification of line (5). Don't forget to cross out C, and so forth:

			Wish List	
1. A → B				
2. C → D			~A	
3. D → ~B			~B	(~B + line 1 + MT = ~A)
4. C		∴ ~A	D	(D + line 3 + MP = ~B)
5. D		2, 4, MP	~~C~~	~~(C + line 2 + MP = D)~~

Next, since you have D on line (5), you get to have ~B, the next item up the list. Write it down on line (6) and use your parenthetical reminder for the justification; cross out D, and so forth:

			Wish List	
1. A → B				
2. C → D			~A	
3. D → ~B			~B	(~B + line 1 + MT = ~A)
4. C		∴ ~A	~~D~~	~~(D + line 3 + MP = ~B)~~
5. D		2, 4, MP	~~C~~	~~(C + line 2 + MP = D)~~
6. ~B		3, 5, MP		

Finally, you have ~B on line (6), so you get ~A, the next item up the list. Write it down on line (7), with the parenthetical reminder as a guide for the justification; cross out ~B, and so on. (And don't forget to cross out ~A too!) The whole proof, with completed Wish List, looks like this:

1. A → B   <u>Wish List</u>
2. C → D   ~~~A~~
3. D → ~B   ~~~B~~   ~~(~B + line 1 + MT = ~A)~~
4. C   ∴ ~A   ~~D~~   ~~(D + line 3 + MP = ~B)~~
5. D   2, 4, MP   ~~C~~   ~~(C + line 2 + MP = D)~~
6. ~B   3, 5, MP
7. ~A   1, 6, MT

Ned's Wish List Strategy is a systematic way to help you find what you need to do a proof and to keep track of the steps needed to do it properly.

A summary of all of the helpful tips for constructing proofs appears in section 8.5.

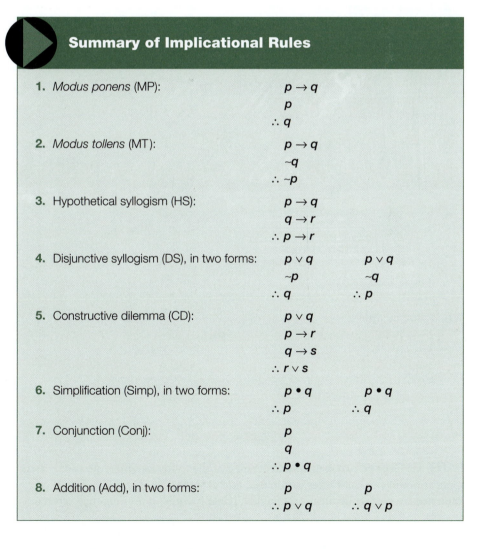

Summary of Implicational Rules

1. *Modus ponens* (MP): $p \rightarrow q$
                                          p
                                          ∴ q

2. *Modus tollens* (MT): $p \rightarrow q$
                                          ~q
                                          ∴ ~p

3. Hypothetical syllogism (HS): $p \rightarrow q$
                                          $q \rightarrow r$
                                          ∴ $p \rightarrow r$

4. Disjunctive syllogism (DS), in two forms: $p \lor q$ $p \lor q$
                                          ~p ~q
                                          ∴ q ∴ p

5. Constructive dilemma (CD): $p \lor q$
                                          $p \rightarrow r$
                                          $q \rightarrow s$
                                          ∴ $r \lor s$

6. Simplification (Simp), in two forms: $p \bullet q$ $p \bullet q$
                                          ∴ p ∴ q

7. Conjunction (Conj): p
                                          q
                                          ∴ $p \bullet q$

8. Addition (Add), in two forms: p p
                                          ∴ $p \lor q$ ∴ $q \lor p$

EXERCISE 8.1

PART A: Annotating For each of the following proofs, indicate from which steps each inference is drawn and by which rule the inference is made. (See the Answer Key for an illustration.)

* **1.** 1. F → G
  2. G → H ∴ F → H
  3. F → H

2. 1. ~S → ~P
  2. ~S ∴ K ∨ ~P
  3. ~P
  4. K ∨ ~P

3. 1. E → (T → S)
  2. ~(T → S)
  3. ~R ∨ E ∴ ~R
  4. ~E
  5. ~R

* **4.** 1. H ∨ ~C
  2. H → ~B
  3. ~C → D
  4. (~B ∨ D) → (K • J) ∴ J
  5. ~B ∨ D
  6. K • J
  7. J

5. 1. D
  2. ~H
  3. (D • ~H) → (E ∨ H) ∴ E
  4. D • ~H
  5. E ∨ H
  6. E

6. 1. ~A → ~B
  2. ~~B • C ∴ ~~A • C
  3. ~~B
  4. ~~A
  5. C
  6. ~~A • C

* **7.** 1. ~(P • Q) ∨ R
  2. (~E • ~R) → (A • B)
  3. E → (P • Q)
  4. ~R ∴ B ∨ (F • G)
  5. ~(P • Q)
  6. ~E
  7. ~E • ~R
  8. A • B
  9. B
  10. B ∨ (F • G)

8. 1. F ∨ S
  2. G
  3. [G • (F ∨ S)] → ~T
  4. ~B → T ∴ ~~B
  5. G • (F ∨ S)
  6. ~T
  7. ~~B

9. 1. F → B
  2. ~D
  3. (~D • G) → (B → S)
  4. G
  5. ~S ∴ G • ~F
  6. ~D • G
  7. B → S
  8. F → S
  9. ~F
  10. G • ~F

* **10.** 1. W → (X ∨ ~Y)
  2. ~~Y • W ∴ X ∨ ~Z
  3. W
  4. X ∨ ~Y
  5. ~~Y
  6. X
  7. X ∨ ~Z

PART B: Correct or Incorrect? Some of the following inferences are correct applications of the eight rules introduced in this section, and some are not. If an inference is a correct application of a rule, name the rule. If an inference is not a correct application of a rule, explain why it is not. (The question is whether the conclusion in each case can be reached *in a single step* from the premise(s) by an application of one of the rules.)

* **1.** $K \rightarrow L$
  $\sim L$
  $\therefore \sim K$

2. $G \rightarrow F$
  $E \rightarrow G$
  $\therefore E \rightarrow F$

3. $M \rightarrow N$
  $\sim M$
  $\therefore \sim N$

* **4.** $\sim B \vee \sim Y$
  $\sim B \rightarrow \sim X$
  $\sim Y \rightarrow Z$
  $\therefore \sim X \vee Z$

5. $(E \bullet F) \vee G$
  $\sim (E \bullet F)$
  $\therefore G$

6. $(N \bullet P) \rightarrow (O \vee S)$
  $O \vee S$
  $\therefore N \bullet P$

* **7.** $\sim E \vee \sim F$
  $\sim \sim F$
  $\therefore \sim E$

8. $A \rightarrow \sim \sim B$
  $\sim B$
  $\therefore \sim A$

9. $(P \rightarrow Q) \vee R$
  P
  $\therefore Q \vee R$

* **10.** $(R \bullet S) \rightarrow T$
  $\therefore S \rightarrow T$

11. $(K \vee L) \rightarrow M$
  $\sim M$
  $\therefore \sim (K \vee L)$

12. $(H \vee \sim S) \rightarrow \sim W$
  $H \vee \sim S$
  $\therefore \sim W$

* **13.** $T \rightarrow \sim U$
  U
  $\therefore \sim T$

14. $P \bullet Q$
  $\therefore (R \rightarrow S) \vee (P \bullet Q)$

15. $R \rightarrow \sim S$
  $\sim \sim S$
  $\therefore \sim R$

* **16.** $\sim C \vee \sim D$
  $X \rightarrow C$
  $Y \rightarrow D$
  $\therefore \sim X \vee \sim Y$

17. $\sim G \vee \sim P$
  G
  $\therefore \sim P$

18. $A \rightarrow (B \rightarrow C)$
  B
  $\therefore A \rightarrow C$

* **19.** $(\sim B \vee D) \rightarrow E$
  $\sim \sim B$
  $\therefore D \rightarrow E$

20. $\sim T \rightarrow \sim N$
  $\sim \sim N$
  $\therefore \sim \sim T$

PART C: Proofs Construct proofs to show that the following symbolic arguments are valid. Commas mark the breaks between premises. (See the Answer Key for an illustration.)

* **1.** $H \rightarrow \sim B, D \rightarrow B, H \therefore \sim D$

2. $F \rightarrow (G \rightarrow H), \sim F \rightarrow J, \sim (G \rightarrow H) \therefore J$

3. $(F \vee E) \rightarrow \sim D, S \vee D, E \therefore S$

* **4.** ~A → F, A → D, ~D, F → S ∴ S ∨ X
   5. (A • E) → F, E, F → (D • ~C), A ∴ ~C
   6. ~F ∨ ~G, ~F → Z, ~G → ~R, (Z ∨ ~R) → (U → P), ~P ∴ ~U
* **7.** ~(S ∨ R), B → (S ∨ R), B ∨ P, ~Q ∨ B ∴ P • ~Q
   8. C → (T → L), ~L, ~E → C, L ∨ ~E ∴ ~T
   9. ~~A, B → ~A ∴ ~B
* **10.** (B • A) → C, ~D → (B • A), ~C ∴ ~~D
   11. (~B • ~C) → (D → C), ~B, C → B ∴ ~D
   12. (D • H) → R, S → (D • H) ∴ S → R
* **13.** (T → C) → ~F, S → C, T → S, F ∨ ~P ∴ ~P
   14. (A ∨ ~B) → (F ∨ (R • G)), A, F → L, (R • G) → T, (L ∨ T) → S ∴ S
   15. P ∨ Q, (Q • ~R) → S, R → P, ~P ∴ S
* **16.** (E ∨ F) → ~G, ~H, H ∨ K, (K ∨ L) → E ∴ ~G
   17. (M ∨ N) → ~S, T → (M ∨ N), ~S → ~(M ∨ N) ∴ T → ~(M ∨ N)
   18. (E ∨ ~B) → (~S ∨ T), E, ~S → L, T → ~C, (L ∨ ~C) → A ∴ A
* **19.** ~~B, ~C → ~B, (~~C ∨ T) → P ∴ P
   20. B ∨ ~C, B → E, ~~C ∴ ~B ∨ E

PART D: More Proofs Construct proofs to show that the following arguments
are valid. Commas mark the breaks between premises.

* **1.** P → Q, R → ~S, P ∨ R, (Q ∨ ~S) → (~T ∨ ~W), ~~T ∴ ~W
   2. (A ∨ G) → K, K → (B → F), A • B ∴ F
   3. ~M, (~M • ~N) → (Q → P), ~N, P → R ∴ Q → R
* **4.** ~(R ∨ S), ~(T • V) → (R ∨ S), ~~(T • V) → W ∴ W ∨ ~R
   5. ~W • ~~Z, (~W • X) → Y, ~Z ∨ X ∴ Y
   6. F → A, ~J • ~K, H → (G → F), ~K → (~J → H) ∴ G → A
* **7.** ~F → J, ~F ∨ ~G, ~G → ~H, (J ∨ ~H) → ~K, ~L → K ∴ ~~L
   8. Y → W, (Z → W) → (V • ~T), Z → Y, Q → T ∴ ~Q
   9. (~N • M) → T, ~O → M, ~O • ~N ∴ T ∨ S
* **10.** ~A • ~C, ~C → D, (D • ~A) → (E → ~H), E • (~F → H) ∴ ~~F
   11. R → D, B → R, (B → D) → (E ∨ F), ~E ∴ F
   12. ~F → ~G, P → ~Q, ~F ∨ P, (~G ∨ ~Q) → (L • M) ∴ L
* **13.** (Z • A) ∨ ~Y, (Z • A) → U, W ∨ ~U, ~W ∴ ~Y
   14. (D • E) ∨ F, F → C, (D • E) → ~B, (~B ∨ C) → (A → P), ~P ∴ ~A
   15. O → N, ~M, S → R, P → O, R → P, (S → N) → (M ∨ L) ∴ ~P ∨ L
* **16.** (~M ∨ L) → (~A → B), ~S → T, R → ~S, ~M • J, R ∨ ~A ∴ T ∨ B
   17. F → ~G, ~~G • O, (~F • ~~G) → [(~H → E) • (C → F)], C ∨ ~H ∴ E

18. ~N • ~M, ~P → N, ~N → Z, (Z • ~~P) → K ∴ K • ~M

*19. A ∨ D, ~D, (C ∨ A) → ~E ∴ ~E

20. (C → Q) • (~L → ~R), (S → C) • (~N → ~L), ~Q • J,
~Q → (S ∨ ~N) ∴ ~R

21. ~(Z ∨ Y) → ~W, ~U → ~(Z ∨ Y), (~U → ~W) → (T → S), S → (R ∨ P),
[T → (R ∨ P)] → [(~R ∨ K) • ~K] ∴ ~R

*22. ~A, [~A ∨ (B • C)] → (D → ~E), ~E → ~F, (D → ~F) → G
∴ (G • ~A) ∨ ~H

23. (S ∨ U) • ~U, S → [T • (F ∨ G)], [T ∨ (J • P)] → (~B • E) ∴ S • ~B

24. ~X → (~Y → ~Z), X ∨ (W → U), ~Y ∨ W, ~X • T, (~Z ∨ U) → ~S
∴ (R ∨ ~S) • T

*25. (D ∨ C) → (F ∨ H), (H • G) → (F ∨ E), (D ∨ B) → (~F → G),
(F ∨ D) • (~F • A) ∴ E

PART E: English Arguments Symbolize the following arguments using the
schemes of abbreviation provided. Then construct proofs to show that the arguments are valid.

* 1. No one can know anything, for every piece of reasoning must start somewhere.
And if every piece of reasoning must start somewhere, then every piece of
reasoning begins with an unsupported premise. Now, if every piece of reasoning begins with an unsupported premise, then all human thinking is based on
mere assumption. And if all human thinking is based on mere assumption, no
one can know anything. (S: Every piece of reasoning must start somewhere;
U: Every piece of reasoning begins with an unsupported premise; A: All human
thinking is based on mere assumption; K: No one can know anything)

2. Theists say that God created the world. They say that the world must have a
cause. But why? The world must have a cause only if everything must have a
cause. But if everything must have a cause, then God has a cause. However,
God isn't God if God has a cause. And if God isn't God, God doesn't exist.
So, if the world must have a cause, there is no God. (W: The world must
have a cause; E: Everything must have a cause; H: God has a cause; G: God
is God; X: God exists)

3. Either we should stop going places, or we should develop hydrogen-powered
cars, or we should go on driving gasoline-powered cars. We should go on
driving gasoline-powered cars only if we should destroy the ozone layer. We
should not stop going places and we should not destroy the ozone layer.
Therefore, we should develop hydrogen-powered cars. (P: We should stop
going places; H: We should develop hydrogen-powered cars; G: We should
go on driving gasoline-powered cars; O: We should destroy the ozone layer)

* 4. Dinosaurs are extinct. And given that dinosaurs are extinct, they suffered
some catastrophe if they died suddenly. The dinosaurs died suddenly, assuming that they froze because of a sudden drop in temperature or were attacked
by a lethal virus. The dinosaurs froze because of a sudden drop in temperature

provided that the sun's rays were blocked. The earth's atmosphere was filled with dust because of the impact of a comet, and the sun's rays were blocked. Therefore, the dinosaurs suffered some catastrophe. (E: Dinosaurs are extinct; C: The dinosaurs suffered some catastrophe; D: The dinosaurs died suddenly; F: The dinosaurs froze because of a sudden drop in temperature; V: The dinosaurs were attacked by a lethal virus; S: The sun's rays were blocked; A: The earth's atmosphere was filled with dust because of the impact of a comet)

5. Even though advocates of suicide and euthanasia often claim that every right—including the right to life—can be waived, I think it's absurd to suggest that every right can be waived. (To waive a right is to agree, for good moral reasons, not to exercise it.) For if every right can be waived, then if I announce that I am waiving my right to liberty, you are morally permitted to enslave me. But obviously, it is not true that if I announce that I am waiving my right to liberty, then you are morally permitted to enslave me. (E: Every right can be waived; A: I announce that I am waiving my right to liberty; P: You are morally permitted to enslave me)

6. If morality is not subjective, then either morality is relative to cultures or God is the source of all moral values. If morality is subjective, then if I approve of racism, racism is right. Plainly, it's false that if I approve of racism, racism is right. Furthermore, if morality is relative to cultures, then the cannibalism in New Guinea is right, and the caste system in India is right. The statement "The cannibalism in New Guinea is right, and the caste system in India is right" is false. God exists if God is the source of all moral values. Accordingly, God exists. (S: Morality is subjective; M: Morality is relative to cultures; V: God is the source of all moral values; A: I approve of racism; R: Racism is right; C: The cannibalism in New Guinea is right; I: The caste system in India is right; G: God exists)

* 7. Al has precognition. And assuming that Al has precognition, Al experiences events before their occurrence. But if Al experiences events before their occurrence, then either events exist before their occurrence or Al predicts the future on the basis of what he knows about the past and present. It is simply nonsense to say that events exist before their occurrence. We may infer that Al predicts the future on the basis of what he knows about the past and present. (P: Al has precognition; A: Al experiences events before their occurrence; E: Events exist before their occurrence; F: Al predicts the future on the basis of what he knows about the past and present)

8. God's existence is either necessary or impossible, if it is not contingent. God's existence is a matter of metaphysical luck if it is contingent. God's existence is emphatically not a matter of metaphysical luck. God's existence is not impossible if the concept of an omnipotent and perfectly good being is coherent. The concept of an omnipotent and perfectly good being is coherent. Therefore, God's existence is necessary. (N: God's existence is necessary; I: God's existence is impossible; C: God's existence is contingent; M: God's existence is a matter of metaphysical luck; T: The concept of an omnipotent and perfectly good being is coherent)

9. Either the "eye for an eye" principle is interpreted literally or it is interpreted figuratively. If it is interpreted literally, then the state must do to criminals what they have done to their victims. If the state must do to criminals what they have done to their victims, then the state must torture torturers. On the other hand, if the "eye for an eye" principle is interpreted figuratively, the state need only mete out punishments that are proportional to the crime. If the state need only mete out punishments that are proportional to the crime, then the state is free to give murderers life imprisonment rather than the death penalty. Now, the state must not torture torturers if such acts are immoral. And it is indeed immoral to torture torturers. Hence, the state is free to give murderers life imprisonment rather than the death penalty.
(L: The "eye for an eye" principle is interpreted literally; F: The "eye for an eye" principle is interpreted figuratively; C: The state must do to criminals what they have done to their victims; T: The state must torture torturers; P: The state need only mete out punishments that are proportional to the crime; S: The state is free to give murderers life imprisonment rather than the death penalty; I: It is immoral to torture torturers)

10. Either Mary is in much pain or she isn't in much pain. And Mary lacks a capacity to make a rational decision about ending her life if she is in a lot of pain. On the other hand, given that Mary isn't in much pain, she is in no position to know what she will want when she is in much pain. Furthermore, Mary has no right to end her life if either she lacks a capacity to make a rational decision about ending her life or she is in no position to know what she will want when she is in much pain. But Mary has no right to "die with dignity" if she has no right to end her life. Therefore, Mary has no right to "die with dignity." (M: Mary is in much pain; R: Mary has the capacity to make a rational decision about ending her life; K: Mary is in a position to know what she will want when she is in much pain; E: Mary has a right to end her life; D: Mary has a right to "die with dignity")

8.2   **Five Equivalence Rules**

Recall that two statements are *logically equivalent* if and only if they agree in truth value on every assignment of truth values to their atomic components.[3] So, we can make a valid inference from one statement to another that is logically equivalent to it. For example, since $P \lor Q$ is logically equivalent to $Q \lor P$, the inference from $P \lor Q$ to $Q \lor P$ is valid and so is the inference from $Q \lor P$ to $P \lor Q$.

Now, an **equivalence rule,** as the name suggests, is based on a logical equivalence. Our use of the equivalence rules depends on this principle: *Within truth-functional logic, if we replace part of a compound statement with anything logically equivalent to that part, the resulting statement will have the same truth value as the original compound.* For example, if we start with $(P \lor Q) \rightarrow R$ and replace

$(P \lor Q)$ with $(Q \lor P)$, we get a statement that has the same truth value as the first, namely, $(Q \lor P) \rightarrow R$. The inference from $(P \lor Q) \rightarrow R$ to $(Q \lor P) \rightarrow R$ is clearly valid because the two statements must have the same truth value.

Five equivalence rules are introduced in this section and five more in the next section. Using the four-dot symbol $(: :)$ to indicate logical equivalence, we can state our first equivalence rule, the rule of **double-negation,** as follows:

> Rule 9: Double-negation (DN): $p : : \sim\sim p$

The rule of double-negation formalizes the intuition that any statement implies, and is implied by, the negation of its negation. Here are two English examples:

14. It is not true that Booth did not kill Lincoln. So, Booth killed Lincoln.

15. Booth killed Lincoln. So, it is not true that Booth did not kill Lincoln.

The usefulness of this rule is illustrated in constructing a proof for the following short argument:

16. If humans do not have free will, then they are not responsible for their actions. But obviously, humans are responsible for their actions. Thus, humans have free will. (F: Humans have free will; R: Humans are responsible for their actions)

Using the scheme of abbreviation provided, argument (16) translates into symbols as follows:

> 1. $\sim$F $\rightarrow$ $\sim$R
> 2. R $\therefore$ F

The proof must include two applications of the double-negation rule:

> 3. $\sim\sim$R   2, DN
> 4. $\sim\sim$F   1, 3, MT
> 5. F   4, DN

Note that we cannot obtain F from the premises in one step by applying MT. MT tells us that if we have a conditional in one line of a proof and *the negation of the conditional's consequent* in another line of the proof, then we can infer the negation of the antecedent. But line (2) of the proof does not give us the negation of the consequent of line (1). The negation of $\sim$R is $\sim\sim$R, and hence, we must use the double-negation rule before applying MT.

This is a good place to underscore the point that we must distinguish equivalence rules from implicational rules in two ways.

First, as we saw in section 8.1, implicational rules are one-directional; equivalence rules, however, are *two-directional*. For example, since P is logically equivalent to ~~P, not only is the inference from P to ~~P valid, so is the inference from ~~P to P.

Second, as we saw earlier, implicational rules can apply only to whole lines and not parts of lines; however, *equivalence rules can apply to both whole lines and parts of lines*. That's because we never change the truth value of a statement by replacing some part of it with a logically equivalent expression.

The proper use of both implicational and equivalence rules is illustrated in the following proof:

1. (A → B) → (A → ~~C)
2. A
3. A → D
4. D → B   ∴ C

At this point, if we tried to apply MP to lines (1) and (2) to derive B or ~~C, we would be misapplying MP. An implicational rule such as MP cannot be applied to a *part* of line (1); it must be applied to the whole line. So, we would need A → B to get A → ~~C from line (1) by MP. However, because double-negation is an equivalence rule, we can, if we wish, apply double-negation to a part of a line. Thus, we can complete our proof as follows:

5. (A → B) → (A → C)   1, DN
6. A → B   3, 4, HS
7. A → C   5, 6, MP
8. C   2, 7, MP

The fact that equivalence rules can be applied to parts of lines makes them very flexible tools to work with. But error will result if one fails to keep the distinction between implicational and equivalence rules firmly in mind.

Our second equivalence rule is **commutation,** which applies to both disjunctions and conjunctions:

Rule 10: Commutation (Com): (**p** ∨ **q**) :: (**q** ∨ **p**)
                            (**p** • **q**) :: (**q** • **p**)

Here are two English examples of commutation:

17. Either Sarah loves psychology or Harlan hates history. So, either Harlan hates history or Sarah loves psychology.

18. Frege is a logician, and Russell is a logician. So, Russell is a logician, and Frege is a logician.

The utility of the rule of commutation is revealed in constructing a proof for the following argument:

19. If pointless suffering occurs, then God is not both benevolent and omnipotent. But God is both omnipotent and benevolent. So, pointless suffering doesn't occur. (P: Pointless suffering occurs; B: God is benevolent; O: God is omnipotent)

1. P → ~(B • O)
2. O • B   ∴ ~P
3. B • O   2, Com
4. ~~(B • O)   3, DN
5. ~P   4, 1, MT

To underscore the difference between implicational and equivalence rules, it may be helpful to note that the following alternative proof is also correct:

3. P → ~(O • B)   1, Com
4. ~~(O • B)   2, DN
5. ~P   3, 4, MT

Here, the rule of commutation is applied to *part* of line (1) to obtain line (3).

The rule of **association** comes in two forms, one governing disjunctions and one governing conjunctions:

Rule 11: Association (As): $(p \lor (q \lor r)) :: ((p \lor q) \lor r)$
$(p \bullet (q \bullet r)) :: ((p \bullet q) \bullet r)$

In English, this sort of inference would normally be signaled by a shift in punctuation. Here is an example of the first form of association:

20. Either the alleged eyewitnesses of UFO landings are telling the truth, or they are lying, or they've been duped. So, either the alleged eyewitnesses of UFO landings are telling the truth, or they are lying, or they've been duped.

In our symbolic language, the parentheses play the role that the commas play in the English example.

The practical value of the rule of association is illustrated in constructing a proof for the following short argument:

21. Either cigarette manufacturers are greedy, or they are ignorant of cancer research, or they dislike young people. But it is not true that either cigarette manufacturers are ignorant of cancer research or they dislike young people. Therefore, cigarette manufacturers are greedy. (C: Cigarette manufacturers are greedy; R: Cigarette manufacturers are ignorant of cancer research; D: Cigarette manufacturers dislike young people)

1. (C ∨ R) ∨ D
2. ~(R ∨ D)   ∴ C
3. C ∨ (R ∨ D)   1, As
4. C   2, 3, DS

Our next rule—**De Morgan's laws**—was first made explicit by the English logician Augustus De Morgan (1806–1871). It comes in two forms.

Rule 12: De Morgan's laws (DeM): ~(***p*** • ***q***) : : (~***p*** ∨ ~***q***)

~(***p*** ∨ ***q***) : : (~***p*** • ~***q***)

Here is an English example of an inference endorsed by the first of De Morgan's laws:

22. Spot is not both a dog and a cat. So, either Spot is not a dog or Spot is not a cat.

Of course, since DeM is an equivalence rule, we can also validly infer the premise of (23) from the conclusion. Here is an English example of the second law:

23. It's not true that either hydrogen or oxygen is a metal. So, hydrogen is not a metal and oxygen is not a metal.

The second law also tells us that we may reverse this reasoning and infer the premise from the conclusion.

As the following example illustrates, De Morgan's laws are quite useful in constructing proofs.

24. Either people are equal and deserve equal pay for equal work, or else people are not equal and do not deserve equal pay for equal work. People are not equal. So, people do not deserve equal pay for equal work.
(E: People are equal; D: People deserve equal pay for equal work)

1. (E • D) ∨ (~E • ~D)
2. ~E   ∴ ~D
3. ~E ∨ ~D   2, Add
4. ~(E • D)   3, DeM
5. ~E • ~D   1, 4, DS
6. ~D   5, Simp

The strategy required in this proof is a bit indirect. The basic insight is that the second premise, ~E, is clearly incompatible with the left disjunct of the first premise, E • D. This means that an application of disjunctive syllogism is in the offing. But we have to use addition and one of De Morgan's laws before we can apply disjunctive syllogism.

Our next rule of inference relies on the logical equivalence between a conditional and its contrapositive. To form the contrapositive of a conditional, switch the antecedent and consequent and negate both. To illustrate, the contrapositive of "If Bob is an uncle, then Bob is male" is "If Bob is not male, then Bob is not an uncle." Let us call the inference rule itself **contraposition.**

> **Rule 13:** Contraposition (Cont): $(p \rightarrow q) :: (\sim q \rightarrow \sim p)$

The utility of this rule becomes apparent in evaluating the following argument:

25. If it is wrong to use drugs only if they impair the user's mental functions, then it is not wrong to use caffeine. And if drugs do not impair the user's mental functions, then it is not wrong to use drugs. Hence, it is not wrong to use caffeine. (W: It is wrong to use drugs; D: Drugs impair the user's mental functions; C: It is wrong to use caffeine)

1. $(W \rightarrow D) \rightarrow \sim C$	
2. $\sim D \rightarrow \sim W$	$\therefore \sim C$
3. $W \rightarrow D$	2, Cont
4. $\sim C$	1, 3, MP

To emphasize the point that equivalence rules can be applied to *part* of a line, let us note that the proof could also be completed as follows:

3. $(\sim D \rightarrow \sim W) \rightarrow \sim C$	1, Cont
4. $\sim C$	2, 3, MP

Here, contraposition is applied to *part* of line (1) to obtain line (3).

The five rules introduced in this section may seem obvious or even trivial, but some logicians have rejected one or more of them. This results from rejecting the **law of the excluded middle** (LEM), which says that for any given statement, either it is true or its denial is true. Using statement variables, we can state LEM as follows: $p \vee \sim p$.

> The **law of the excluded middle (LEM)** states that for any statement p, either p is true or $\sim p$ is true, that is, $p \vee \sim p$.

Intuitionists deny LEM. Their argument is this: The truth of a statement consists in its being provable. After centuries of trying, we have no proof for certain statements or their denials—for example, Goldbach's conjecture, which states that every even number greater than 2 is equal to the sum of two primes. Call this statement G. Because G is not provable, G is not true, and because ~G is not provable, ~G is not true. Thus, because neither of the disjuncts in G ∨ ~G is true, and a disjunction is true only if at least one of its disjuncts is true, it is *false* that for any statement **p**, either **p** is true or ~**p** is true—that is, LEM is false.[4]

However, given the rules introduced in this section, we cannot deny LEM unless we are prepared to deny the **law of noncontradiction** (LNC), which says that for any given statement, it is false that both it and its denial are true. Using statement variables, we can state LNC as follows: ~(**p** • ~**p**).

> The **law of noncontradiction (LNC)** states that for any statement **p**, it is false that both **p** and ~**p** are true, that is, ~(**p** • ~**p**).

And all logicians endorse LNC.[5] Now consider the following proof:

1. ~(G • ~G)   ∴ G ∨ ~G
2. ~G ∨ ~~G   1, DeM
3. ~G ∨ G   2, DN
4. G ∨ ~G   3, Com

Premise (1) states that it is false that both Goldbach's conjecture and its denial are true. And the conclusion states that either Goldbach's conjecture is true or its denial is true. It appears, then, that if we wish to deny LEM, we must deny at least one of the following: DeM, DN, Com, or LNC.

Intuitionists deny DN.[6] The system we develop here affirms DN and LEM. This is characteristic of a system of classical logic, and for the purposes of a beginning course in logic, it is best to learn classical logic. We would note, however, that we think that the intuitionist's argument for denying LEM (and so DN) is unsound. That's because we think that it is *false* that the truth of a statement consists in its provability. The truth of a statement consists in its describing things as they are. We would also note, however, that many philosophers agree with us about what the truth of a statement consists in, and still deny LEM (and so DN) for reasons having to do with vagueness, indeterminacy, and the nature of time. To assess those reasons would take us too far afield. We recommend, however, that you investigate these reasons after you learn the system of classical logic developed in this book, by taking higher-level university courses in logic, philosophy of language, and metaphysics.

As you complete the exercises that follow, keep in mind that the five helpful tips for constructing proofs provided in the previous section still apply. We now add two more. The first additional tip is

Tip 6. Consider logically equivalent forms of the conclusion and the premises.

Summary of the First Set of Equivalence Rules

9. Double-negation (DN): $p :: \sim\sim p$

10. Commutation (Com): $(p \lor q) :: (q \lor p)$

   $(p \bullet q) :: (q \bullet p)$

11. Association (As): $(p \lor (q \lor r)) :: ((p \lor q) \lor r)$

   $(p \bullet (q \bullet r)) :: ((p \bullet q) \bullet r)$

12. De Morgan's laws (DeM): $\sim(p \bullet q) :: (\sim p \lor \sim q)$

   $\sim(p \lor q) :: (\sim p \bullet \sim q)$

13. Contraposition (Cont): $(p \to q) :: (\sim q \to \sim p)$

For example, consider the following argument:

1. $\sim G \to \sim A$
2. $\sim H \to \sim B$
3. $\sim(G \bullet H)$ $\therefore \sim(A \bullet B)$

Notice that the conclusion, $\sim(A \bullet B)$, is equivalent to $\sim A \lor \sim B$ by one of De Morgan's laws. Also notice that $\sim A$ is the consequent of line (1) and $\sim B$ is the consequent of line (2), and recall that we can infer the disjunction of the consequents of two conditionals by constructive dilemma—*provided* we have the disjunction of their antecedents. But do we have $\sim G \lor \sim H$? Well, not exactly. But we do have something equivalent to it on line (3), namely $\sim(G \bullet H)$. We simply need to apply one of De Morgan's laws. Thus, by considering a logically equivalent form of the conclusion and one of the premises, we are led to a successful proof:

1. $\sim G \to \sim A$
2. $\sim H \to \sim B$
3. $\sim(G \bullet H)$ $\therefore \sim(A \bullet B)$
4. $\sim G \lor \sim H$ 3, DeM
5. $\sim A \lor \sim B$ 1, 2, 4, CD
6. $\sim(A \bullet B)$ 5, DeM

Here is another example. Consider this argument:

1. $\sim A \to \sim C$
2. $A \to D$ $\therefore \sim D \to \sim C$

Note, first, that the conclusion, $\sim D \to \sim C$, is equivalent to $C \to D$ by contraposition. Inspired by this observation, we might also note that line (1), $\sim A \to \sim C$, is equivalent to C → A. But C → A and A → D, which is line (2), gives us C → D, by hypothetical syllogism. Consequently, we have what we need, as we first noted, to draw the conclusion. The proof goes like this:

1. ~A → ~C
2. A → D   ∴ ~D → ~C
3. C → A   1, Cont
4. C → D   2, 3, HS
5. ~D → ~C   4, Cont

This is a good place to draw your attention to two questions about doing proofs that students often ask.

The first question is this: How can line (4) be justified by lines (2) and (3) and hypothetical syllogism? The schema for hypothetical syllogism is this:

p → *q*

q → *r*

∴ *p* → *r*

But lines (2) and (3) in the proof go like this:

2. A → D
3. C → A

They do not seem to be substitution instances of the premises of the schema at all!

Good question. Here's the answer. The *correct* application of an inference rule is not affected by the order of the premises or lines. Suppose we switch the order like this:

3. C → A
2. A → D

Now it is clear that we can move from lines (3) and (2) to line

4. C → D

by hypothetical syllogism. But notice: The logic remains the same even though the visual presentation is clearer. The order of the lines does not matter for logic even if it matters for clear visual presentation.

The second question is this: Is there more than one way to do a proof? Yes. The previous proof could have been done just as easily like this:

1. ~A → ~C
2. A → D   ∴ ~D → ~C
3. ~D → ~A   1 Cont
4. ~D → ~C   1, 3, HS

Indeed, insofar as simpler proofs are better than more complex ones, this proof is better than the original.

The second additional tip is this:

Tip 7: Both conjunction and addition can lead to useful applications of De Morgan's laws.

Consider the following examples:

1. ~E
2. ~F
3. ~E • ~F   1, 2, Conj
4. ~(E ∨ F)   3, DeM

1. ~G
2. ~G ∨ ~H   1, Add
3. ~(G • H)   2, DeM

As before, these helpful tips are to be taken as useful guides. They do not automatically provide a solution; only practice makes perfect.

EXERCISE 8.2

PART A: Annotating Annotate the following short proofs. (In each case, the argument has only one premise.)

* **1.**   1. ~~A → B ∴ A → B
    2. A → B

  2.   1. ~C → ~D ∴ D → C
    2. D → C

  3.   1. ~(E • ~D) ∴ D ∨ ~E
    2. ~E ∨ ~~D
    3. ~E ∨ D
    4. D ∨ ~E

* **4.**   1. ~(E ∨ D) ∴ ~D
    2. ~E • ~D
    3. ~D

  5.   1. ~A • [(A ∨ B) ∨ C] ∴ B ∨ C
    2. ~A
    3. (A ∨ B) ∨ C
    4. A ∨ (B ∨ C)
    5. B ∨ C

  6.   1. F • (G • R) ∴ G • F
    2. (F • G) • R
    3. F • G
    4. G • F

* **7.** 1. $[(P \rightarrow Q) \rightarrow R] \bullet (\sim Q \rightarrow \sim P)$ ∴ $\sim\sim R$
   2. $\sim Q \rightarrow \sim P$
   3. $P \rightarrow Q$
   4. $(P \rightarrow Q) \rightarrow R$
   5. R
   6. $\sim\sim R$

  8. 1. $[\sim(S \bullet T) \vee \sim\sim U] \bullet (T \bullet S)$ ∴ U
   2. $T \bullet S$
   3. $S \bullet T$
   4. $\sim(S \bullet T) \vee \sim\sim U$
   5. $\sim\sim(S \bullet T)$
   6. $\sim\sim U$
   7. U

  9. 1. $\sim W \vee (\sim X \vee \sim Y)$ ∴ $\sim Y \vee \sim(W \bullet X)$
   2. $(\sim W \vee \sim X) \vee \sim Y$
   3. $\sim(W \bullet X) \vee \sim Y$
   4. $\sim Y \vee \sim(W \bullet X)$

* **10.** 1. $[\sim O \rightarrow (\sim M \rightarrow \sim N)] \bullet \sim(N \rightarrow M)$ ∴ O
   2. $\sim O \rightarrow (\sim M \rightarrow \sim N)$
   3. $\sim(N \rightarrow M)$
   4. $\sim(\sim M \rightarrow \sim N)$
   5. $\sim\sim O$
   6. O

  11. 1. $\sim\sim P \bullet \sim P$ ∴ W
   2. $\sim\sim P$
   3. $\sim\sim P \vee W$
   4. $P \vee W$
   5. $\sim P$
   6. W

  12. 1. $\sim T$ ∴ $\sim(T \bullet \sim\sim S)$
   2. $\sim T \vee \sim S$
   3. $\sim(T \bullet S)$
   4. $\sim(T \bullet \sim\sim S)$

* **13.** 1. $\sim A$ ∴ $\sim[(B \bullet C) \bullet A]$
   2. $\sim(B \bullet C) \vee \sim A$
   3. $\sim[(B \bullet C) \bullet A]$

  14. 1. $(S \rightarrow G) \bullet (G \rightarrow T)$ ∴ $\sim T \rightarrow \sim S$
   2. $S \rightarrow G$
   3. $G \rightarrow T$
   4. $S \rightarrow T$
   5. $\sim T \rightarrow \sim S$

15. 1. ~R → ~S ∴ ~P ∨ (S → ~~R)
2. S → R
3. S → ~~R
4. ~P ∨ (S → ~~R)

PART B: Correct or Incorrect? Some of the following inferences are correct applications of our rules, and some are not. If an inference is a correct application of our rules, name the rule. If an inference is not a correct application of our rules, explain why it is not. (The question is whether the conclusion in each case can be reached in a single step from the premise(s) by an application of one of our rules.)

* **1.**   ~(~E ∨ B)
  ∴ ~~E • ~B

2.   ~B → ~C
  ∴ C → B

3.   ~(F ∨ G)
  ∴ ~F ∨ ~G

* **4.**   ~W ∨ ~Z
  ∴ ~(W • Z)

5.   A • ~B
  ∴ ~B • A

6.   ~D → ~E
  ∴ ~~E → ~~D

* **7.**   ~S ∨ T
  ∴ ~(S • ~T)

8.   ~J ∨ ~~K
  ∴ ~(J • ~K)

9.   P → ~Q
  ∴ Q → ~P

* **10.**   O → R
  ∴ ~R → ~O

11.   [B ∨ (C ∨ A)] ↔ D
  ∴ [(C ∨ B) ∨ A] ↔ D

12.   ~(D • C) → E
  ∴ (~D ∨ ~C) → E

* **13.**   ~(L • ~M)
  ∴ ~(~M • L)

14.   ~(U • ~Z)
  ∴ ~U ∨ ~~Z

15.   (~~N ∨ ~M) ↔ (L • K)
  ∴ ~(~N • M) ↔ (L • K)

* **16.**   ~[(O • ~P) • W]
  ∴ ~[O • (~P • W)]

17.   ~(R ∨ ~Q)
  ∴ ~R • ~~Q

18.   ~~S ↔ T
  ∴ S ↔ T

* **19.**   ~~(U ∨ W)
  ∴ ~(~U • ~W)

20.   ~(X → Y)
  ∴ ~X → ~Y

PART C: Proofs Construct proofs for each of the following symbolic arguments. Commas are used to mark the breaks between premises. (Each proof can be completed in fewer than 10 steps, including premises.)

* **1.** ~(C • D), ~C → S, ~D → T ∴ S ∨ T

  2. (W → U) • ~X ∴ ~U → ~W

  3. F → ~G, G ∴ ~F

* **4.** ~(~A ∨ B) ∴ A

  5. (~P → Q) • ~Q ∴ P

  6. ~(N ∨ M), ~L → (M ∨ N) ∴ L
* **7.** (A ∨ B) ∨ C, ~A ∴ C ∨ B
  8. (W • ~X) ∨ (Y • Z), (~X • W) → U, (Y • Z) → T ∴ U ∨ T
  9. ~(S ∨ R), P → R ∴ ~P
***10.** F → (G • H), (H • G) → J ∴ F → J
 11. K ∨ (L ∨ S), ~(K ∨ L) ∴ S
 12. ~P, ~(P ∨ Q) → ~R, ~Q ∴ ~R
***13.** ~S → (T • U), (~S → X) → ~Z, (U • T) → X ∴ ~Z
 14. ~(~B → A), C → (~A → B) ∴ ~C
 15. ~E, F → (D ∨ E), ~D ∴ ~F
***16.** (K ∨ P) ∨ X, K → ~O, (P ∨ X) → ~L ∴ ~(O • L)
 17. (G ∨ H) → (J ∨ K) ∴ ~(J ∨ K) → ~(H ∨ G)
 18. ~A → ~~R, G → ~U, ~A ∨ G ∴ ~(~R • U)
***19.** ~(L • M) → ~(N ∨ O) ∴ (O ∨ N) → (M • L)
 20. B → E, (B ∨ C) ∨ D, (D ∨ C) → F ∴ E ∨ F
 21. W → ~U, W ∨ X, ~T → (Z • U), X → ~Z ∴ T
***22.** ~(~P • Q), ~Q → R, P → ~S ∴ R ∨ ~S
 23. ~B, A → (B • C) ∴ ~A
 24. [S → (J • Q)] • ~Q ∴ ~S
***25.** ~B, ~(C • B) → C, ~F → ~C ∴ F

PART D: Longer Proofs Construct proofs to show that the following arguments are valid. Commas are used to mark the breaks between premises.

* **1.** ~~T ∨ ~R, ~(S ∨ ~R), (T • ~S) → ~Q, W → Q ∴ ~W
  2. ~(J • L), (~J ∨ ~L) → ~M, ~E ∨ (M ∨ ~S) ∴ ~(S • E)
  3. E → [~(H ∨ K) → R], ~~E • (~H • ~K) ∴ ~~R
* **4.** B → E, ~F ∨ G, (B • C) • D, (D • C) → F ∴ E • G
  5. P ∨ (Q ∨ R), (Q ∨ P) → ~S, R → ~T, U → (S • T) ∴ ~U ∨ Z
  6. ~~W • [(X ∨ W) → Y], H → ~Y ∴ ~H
* **7.** ~(B • ~C), ~B → D, C → ~E ∴ ~E ∨ D
  8. (F • G) → (H • J), (J • H) → (K ∨ L), (L ∨ K) → M ∴ (G • F) → M
  9. ~Y ∨ N, (Y • ~N) ∨ (Y • Z), (Z • Y) → ~~U ∴ U ∨ ~V
***10.** ~A → ~B, D → E, (B → A) → (C ∨ D), C → F ∴ E ∨ F
 11. ~(H ↔ G) ∨ ~J, K → (H ↔ G), ~L → J ∴ ~(K • ~L)
 12. (X • Q) → (Z • ~T), R • (T ∨ ~Z) ∴ (~X ∨ ~Q) • R
***13.** ~[(M ∨ N) ∨ O], (P • R) → N, ~P → T, ~R → S ∴ T ∨ S
 14. Z → (U • X), ~[(U • W) • X], W ∴ ~Z

15. ~(~A • B) ↔ ~(C ∨ ~D) ∴ (~B ∨ A) ↔ (D • ~C)

* **16.** ~[(E • F) ∨ G], (H ∨ ~E) → G ∴ ~(F ∨ H)

17. ~(R → S) → ~(~T → ~U), ~W → T, U → ~W, ~S ∴ ~R

18. ~[(L ∨ M) • N], (P → ~Q) → N, Q → ~P ∴ ~M

* **19.** [(A • B) ∨ ~C] → (~X • ~Y), ~(Y ∨ X) → Z, ~C ∨ (A • B) ∴ ~~Z

20. H ∨ G, ~(~D → E), (F ∨ G) → (~E → D) ∴ ~J ∨ H

21. ~(~P • ~Q), Q → (X ∨ R), P → Y ∴ X ∨ (Y ∨ R)

* **22.** A ∨ (B ∨ C), ~A • ~C ∴ [(B ∨ C) • ~(A ∨ C)] • (A ∨ B)

23. ~F, ~(F • ~S) → ~P, (~S • F) ∨ ~T ∴ ~(P ∨ T)

24. O → (H • M), (O → G) → (H → ~M), ~G → (~H ∨ ~M) ∴ H → ~M

* **25.** Z • Y, T → X, ~Y → ~S, ~(X ∨ Y) ∨ ~Z ∴ ~(T ∨ S) • Y

8.3 Five More Equivalence Rules

To this point, our system of natural deduction includes 8 implicational rules and 5 equivalence rules. In this section, we add 5 more equivalence rules.

The rule of **distribution** tells us how certain combinations of the dot and the vee interrelate. It comes in two forms.

> Rule 14: Distribution (Dist): $(p • (q ∨ r)) :: ((p • q) ∨ (p • r))$
> $(p ∨ (q • r)) :: ((p ∨ q) • (p ∨ r))$

Notice that when distribution is applied correctly, the main logical operator changes (either from the dot to the vee or from the vee to the dot). Here are some English examples of distribution:

> **26.** "Bats are animals, and they are either mammals or birds" implies (and is implied by) "Either bats are animals and mammals, or bats are animals and birds."

> **27.** "Either Bill lost the lottery, or Bill won and he is rich" implies (and is implied by) "Either Bill lost the lottery or he won, and either Bill lost the lottery or he is rich."

The utility of the rule of distribution is brought out when we construct a proof of the following argument:

> **28.** Either Fiona is insane or she is guilty and a liar. But if Fiona is either insane or a liar, then she is dangerous. It follows that Fiona is dangerous. (F: Fiona is insane; G: Fiona is guilty; L: Fiona is a liar; D: Fiona is dangerous)
>
> 1. F ∨ (G • L)
> 2. (F ∨ L) → D   ∴ D
> 3. (F ∨ G) • (F ∨ L)   1, Dist
> 4. F ∨ L   3, Simp
> 5. D   2, 4, MP

Perhaps because distribution appears a bit complex, there is some tendency to overlook occasions for its use when constructing proofs, but it is often quite useful.

The rule of **exportation** tells us that statements of the form "If *p* and *q*, then *r*" are logically equivalent to statements of the form "If *p*, then if *q*, then *r*." In symbols, we have the following:

Rule 15: Exportation (Ex): ((***p*** • ***q***) → ***r***) : : (***p*** → (***q*** → ***r***))

Here is an English example:

29. "If Sue is intelligent and she studies hard, then she gets good grades" implies (and is implied by) "If Sue is intelligent, then if she studies hard, she gets good grades."

A proof of the following argument illustrates a typical usage of exportation.

30. If World War I was not a war in defense of the U.S.A., and only wars of defense are just, then the American participation in World War I was not just. World War I was not a war in defense of the U.S.A. It follows that if only wars of defense are just, then the American participation in World War I was not just. (W: World War I was a war in defense of the U.S.A.; D: Only wars of defense are just; J: American participation in World War I was just)

1. (~W • D) → ~J
2. ~W   ∴ D → ~J
3. ~W → (D → ~J)   1, Ex
4. D → ~J   2, 3, MP

The **redundancy** rule is obviously valid, and as the name suggests, it allows us to eliminate certain types of redundancy.

Rule 16: Redundancy (Re): ***p*** : : (***p*** • ***p***)
                                       p : : (***p*** ∨ ***p***)

A proof of the following argument reveals a typical use of this rule.

31. Either pain is real or it is an illusion. If pain is real, then pain is bad. And if pain is an illusion, then pain is bad. Accordingly, pain is bad. (R: Pain is real; I: Pain is an illusion; B: Pain is bad)

1. R ∨ I
2. R → B
3. I → B   ∴ B
4. B ∨ B   1, 2, 3, CD
5. B   4, Re

Note that the rule allows us to introduce redundancy as well as to eliminate it. For example, the redundancy rule allows us to move from ~A to ~A • ~A and from R to R ∨ R.

The rule of **material equivalence** gives us a way of handling biconditionals. It comes in two forms. The first form tells us that a biconditional is logically equivalent to a *conjunction* of two conditionals. The second form makes sense if you remember the truth table for the biconditional: $(p \leftrightarrow q)$ is true if either p and q are both true or p and q are both false; otherwise, $(p \leftrightarrow q)$ is false.

> Rule 17: Material equivalence (ME): $(p \leftrightarrow q) : : ((p \rightarrow q) \bullet (q \rightarrow p))$
> $(p \leftrightarrow q) : : ((p \bullet q) \vee (\sim p \bullet \sim q))$

A proof of the following argument will illustrate a typical usage of the first version of material equivalence.

32. Withholding medical treatment is wrong if and only if either the patient has a valuable future life or the family insists on medical treatment. But the patient is brain dead. And if the patient is brain dead, then he has not got a valuable future life. Furthermore, it is not the case that the family insists on medical treatment. It follows that withholding medical treatment is not wrong. (W: Withholding medical treatment is wrong; L: The patient has a valuable future life; F: The family insists on medical treatment; B: The patient is brain dead)

1. W $\leftrightarrow$ (L $\vee$ F)		
2. B		
3. B $\rightarrow$ ~L		
4. ~F	$\therefore$ ~W	
5. ~L	2, 3, MP	
6. [W $\rightarrow$ (L $\vee$ F)] $\bullet$ [(L $\vee$ F) $\rightarrow$ W]	1, ME	
7. W $\rightarrow$ (L $\vee$ F)	6, Simp	
8. ~L $\bullet$ ~F	5, 4, Conj	
9. ~(L $\vee$ F)	8, DeM	
10. ~W	7, 9, MT	

The last of our equivalence rules is called **material implication.**

> Rule 18: Material implication (MI): $(p \rightarrow q) : : (\sim p \vee q)$

Without material implication, our proof system would lack the capacity to prove valid every argument that is valid according to the truth table method. But it is important to remember that $\sim p \vee q$ and $p \rightarrow q$ are equivalent because of the truth-functional definition we gave the arrow.

Our proof of the following argument makes a strategic use of both material implication and the rule of distribution.

33. If either humans do not need meat or eating meat is unhealthy, then humans should not eat meat. Hence, if humans do not need meat, then humans should not eat meat. (N: Humans need meat; E: Eating meat is unhealthy; S: Humans should eat meat)

1. (~N ∨ E) → ~S   ∴ ~N → ~S
2. ~(~N ∨ E) ∨ ~S   1, MI
3. ~S ∨ ~(~N ∨ E)   2, Com
4. ~S ∨ (~~N • ~E)   3, DeM
5. (~S ∨ ~~N) • (~S ∨ ~E)   4, Dist
6. ~S ∨ ~~N   5, Simp
7. ~~N ∨ ~S   6, Com
8. ~N → ~S   7, MI

This proof is rather complex, and it suggests the following helpful tips (to be added to the seven tips introduced previously):

Tip 8: Material implication can lead to useful applications of distribution.

This is illustrated by lines (2) through (5) in the previous proof. But here is a simpler case:

1. A → (B • C)
2. ~A ∨ (B • C)   1, MI
3. (~A ∨ B) • (~A ∨ C)   2, Dist

Tip 9: Distribution can lead to useful applications of simplification.

This tip is illustrated in lines (4) through (6) in the proof in (33), but here is another example:

1. (D • E) ∨ (D • F)
2. D • (E ∨ F)   1, Dist
3. D   2, Simp

At least one more tip may be helpful as you complete the exercises at the end of this section:

Tip 10: Addition can lead to useful applications of material implication.

Here are two examples:

1. B   1. ~F
2. ~A ∨ B   1, Add   2. ~F ∨ G   1, Add
3. A → B   2, MI   3. F → G   2, MI

Summary of the Second Set of Equivalence Rules

14.	Distribution (Dist):	$(p \bullet (q \lor r)) :: ((p \bullet q) \lor (p \bullet r))$
		$(p \lor (q \bullet r)) :: ((p \lor q) \bullet (p \lor r))$
15.	Exportation (Ex):	$((p \bullet q) \to r) :: (p \to (q \to r))$
16.	Redundancy (Re):	$p :: (p \bullet p)$
		$p :: (p \lor p)$
17.	Material equivalence (ME):	$(p \leftrightarrow q) :: ((p \to q) \bullet (q \to p))$
		$(p \leftrightarrow q) :: ((p \bullet q) \lor (\sim p \bullet \sim q))$
18.	Material implication (MI):	$(p \to q) :: (\sim p \lor q)$

EXERCISE 8.3

PART A: Annotating   Annotate the following short proofs. (In each case, the argument has only one premise.)

* **1.**   1. $B \leftrightarrow E \; \therefore \; E \to B$
      2. $(B \to E) \bullet (E \to B)$
      3. $E \to B$

   2.   1. $(B \bullet C) \lor (\sim B \bullet \sim C) \; \therefore \; B \leftrightarrow C$
      2. $B \leftrightarrow C$

   3.   1. $\sim(A \bullet A) \lor (B \lor B) \; \therefore \; A \to B$
      2. $\sim(A \bullet A) \lor B$
      3. $(A \bullet A) \to B$
      4. $A \to B$

* **4.**   1. $H \to (J \to \sim H) \; \therefore \; H \to \sim J$
      2. $H \to (\sim\sim H \to \sim J)$
      3. $(H \bullet \sim\sim H) \to \sim J$
      4. $(H \bullet H) \to \sim J$
      5. $H \to \sim J$

   5.   1. $P \bullet \sim Q \; \therefore \; P \bullet (\sim Q \lor R)$
      2. $(P \bullet \sim Q) \lor (P \bullet R)$
      3. $P \bullet (\sim Q \lor R)$

   6.   1. $F \lor (\sim G \bullet H) \; \therefore \; G \to F$
      2. $(F \lor \sim G) \bullet (F \lor H)$
      3. $F \lor \sim G$
      4. $\sim G \lor F$
      5. $G \to F$

* **7.** 1. M → ~N ∴ N → ~M
        2. ~M ∨ ~N
        3. ~N ∨ ~M
        4. N → ~M

  8. 1. ~S ↔ T ∴ (~S • T) ∨ (S • ~T)
        2. (~S • T) ∨ (~~S • ~T)
        3. (~S • T) ∨ (S • ~T)

  9. 1. (B • B) ∨ (C • D) ∴ B ∨ D
        2. B ∨ (C • D)
        3. (B ∨ C) • (B ∨ D)
        4. B ∨ D

* **10.** 1. (U → U) ∨ (~U → U) ∴ ~U ∨ U
        2. (~U ∨ U) ∨ (~U → U)
        3. (~U ∨ U) ∨ (~~U ∨ U)
        4. (~U ∨ U) ∨ (U ∨ U)
        5. (~U ∨ U) ∨ U
        6. ~U ∨ (U ∨ U)
        7. ~U ∨ U

  11. 1. ~(T ∨ T) ∴ T → ~T
        2. ~T • ~T
        3. ~T
        4. ~T ∨ ~T
        5. T → ~T

  12. 1. X • (Y ∨ Z) ∴ (X • Y) ∨ Z
        2. (X • Y) ∨ (X • Z)
        3. [(X • Y) ∨ X] • [(X • Y) ∨ Z]
        4. (X • Y) ∨ Z

* **13.** 1. ~P → P ∴ ~P → Q
        2. ~~P ∨ P
        3. ~~P ∨ ~~P
        4. ~~P
        5. ~~P ∨ Q
        6. ~P → Q

  14. 1. [(~R ∨ ~S) • ~S] ∨ [R • (~R ∨ ~S)] ∴ ~R → ~S
        2. [(~R ∨ ~S) • ~S] ∨ [(~R ∨ ~S) • R]
        3. (~R ∨ ~S) • (~S ∨ R)
        4. ~S ∨ R
        5. S → R
        6. ~R → ~S

  15. 1. Q ∨ (~P • T) ∴ (~Q → ~P) • (~Q → T)
        2. (Q ∨ ~P) • (Q ∨ T)
        3. Q ∨ ~P

4. ~P ∨ Q
5. P → Q
6. ~Q → ~P
7. Q ∨ T
8. ~~Q ∨ T
9. ~Q → T
10. (~Q → ~P) • (~Q → T)

PART B: Correct or Incorrect? Some of the following inferences are correct applications of our rules, and some are not. If an inference is a correct application of our rules, name the rule. If an inference is not a correct application of our rules, explain why it is not. (The question is whether the conclusion in each case can be reached in a single step from the premise by an application of one of our rules.)

* 1. (~B ∨ ~B) ↔ A
   ∴ ~B ↔ A

2. N ∨ M
   ∴ ~N → M

3. ~~P ∨ Q
   ∴ ~P → Q

* 4. (C • ~L) ∨ (C • S)
   ∴ C • (~L ∨ S)

5. (~M • N) → ~L
   ∴ ~M → (N → ~L)

6. S → (R • R)
   ∴ S → R

* 7. K ∨ (X • R)
   ∴ (K • X) ∨ (K • R)

8. ~H → P
   ∴ H ∨ P

9. X → (Y → Z)
   ∴ (X • Y) → Z

*10. (~U ∨ S) → Q
   ~~U
   ∴ S → Q

11. (~W ∨ ~U) → (~F ∨ ~F)
   ∴ (~W ∨ ~U) → ~F

12. ~A → ~B
   ∴ ~~A ∨ ~B

*13. ~A ∨ (N • Z)
   ∴ (~A ∨ N) • (~A ∨ Z)

14. F → (G • H)
   ∴ F → (G → H)

15. (~J • ~K) ∨ (~J • ~L)
   ∴ ~J • (~K ∨ ~L)

*16. M • (O ∨ U)
   ∴ (M • O) ∨ (M • U)

17. (S ∨ T) • (S ∨ ~W)
   ∴ S ∨ (T • ~W)

18. A • (~B ∨ C)
   ∴ (A ∨ ~B) • (A ∨ C)

*19. (E • H) → V
   ∴ E

20. (B → C) ∨ K
   B
   ∴ C ∨ K

PART C: Short Proofs Construct proofs for each of the following symbolic arguments.

* 1. ~M ∨ N ∴ ~N → ~M
2. ~B ↔ C, ~B ∴ C
3. ~S ∨ (R • T), ~R ∴ ~S

* **4.** ~A ∨ ~A, A ∨ P ∴ P
  5. (D → C) • (C → D), E → ~(D ↔ C) ∴ ~E
  6. F • (G ∨ H), ~F ∨ ~H ∴ F • G
* **7.** (~J • K) → L, ~J ∴ ~L → ~K
  8. (~N ∨ M) • (~N ∨ O) ∴ ~(M • O) → ~N
  9. P • P, Q → ~P ∴ ~Q
* **10.** ~R, (R → S) → T ∴ T
  11. U → (X → W), Z → ~[(U • X) → W] ∴ ~Z
  12. ~D ∴ C → ~D
* **13.** E → H, [(E ∨ F) • (E ∨ G)], [(F • G) → H] ∴ H
  14. (~J • K) ∨ (~J • L), M → J ∴ ~M
  15. ~N ↔ ~O, (~O → ~N) → P ∴ P
* **16.** ~~(R • S), T → (R → ~S) ∴ ~T
  17. ~C, (~A • B) ∨ (~A • C) ∴ B
  18. (~D ∨ E) • (~D ∨ ~F), (E • ~F) → ~G, ~D → ~G ∴ ~G
* **19.** H ∨ H, H ↔ ~J ∴ ~J
  20. X ↔ Y, ~~(X ∨ Y) ∴ X • Y
  21. [(L • M) ∨ ~L] • [(L • M) ∨ ~M] ∴ L ↔ M
* **22.** P • Q ∴ [(R ∨ P) • R] ∨ [(R ∨ P) • Q]
  23. R • ~R ∴ S • ~S
  24. ~O ∴ ~Q → ~(O • P)
* **25.** (A → B) ↔ C, ~(A → B) ∨ ~C ∴ ~C

PART D: Longer Proofs Construct a proof for each of the following symbolic arguments.

* **1.** (Z ∨ ~Y) • (Z ∨ W), Z → ~~U, ~Y → (W → U) ∴ U
  2. ~U → ~B, S → ~B, ~(U • ~S), T ∨ B ∴ T
  3. (Q • R) ∨ (~Q • ~R), N → ~(Q ↔ R), E ∨ N ∴ E
* **4.** ~H ∨ (G ∨ F), ~F, S → ~(H → G) ∴ ~S
  5. ~(J • L), (J → ~L) → (~M • ~X), E ∨ (M ∨ X) ∴ E
  6. (L ∨ M) • (L ∨ ~S), A → ~L, A → (~M ∨ S) ∴ ~A
* **7.** B ∨ (C • ~D), (D → B) ↔ P ∴ P
  8. (G • S) ∨ (G • ~T), ~R → ~G, (T → S) → Q ∴ R • Q
  9. ~X ↔ ~Y, ~X ∨ ~Y, Z ↔ Y ∴ ~Z
* **10.** (B • C) → D, B, Q → ~(~C ∨ D), ~Q ↔ T ∴ T
  11. (F • G) ∨ (F • ~H), (H → G) → L, L → (P → ~F) ∴ ~P
  12. ~X ∨ (M • O), (X → O) → ~M ∴ ~X

13. $(\sim Z \bullet W) \to Q, \sim Z, R \leftrightarrow (W \bullet \sim Q) \therefore \sim R$

14. $A \leftrightarrow B, \sim\sim(A \vee B) \therefore B$

15. $(A \vee B) \bullet (A \vee G), M \to \sim A, \sim Q \to (\sim B \vee \sim G) \therefore M \to Q$

16. $Y \bullet (\sim N \vee A), \sim Y \vee N, (A \bullet Y) \to \sim\sim K \therefore K$

17. $\sim G \to \sim F, (\sim F \vee G) \to (H \vee J), H \to Z, J \to \sim P \therefore P \to Z$

18. $(D \bullet E) \vee (\sim D \bullet \sim E), (H \bullet J) \to \sim(D \leftrightarrow E), \sim\sim H \vee J \therefore J \leftrightarrow \sim H$

19. $(\sim E \vee Z) \bullet (\sim E \vee W), \sim K \to E, \sim K \to (\sim Z \vee \sim W), K \leftrightarrow U \therefore R \to U$

20. $(R \bullet S) \vee (R \bullet \sim E), (Y \bullet O) \to (E \bullet \sim S), (O \to \sim Y) \to L \therefore L$

21. $\sim E, \sim(E \bullet D) \to F, (\sim F \vee B) \bullet (\sim F \vee C) \therefore A \vee (B \bullet C)$

22. $T \to R, R \to S, \sim R \leftrightarrow S \therefore \sim T \bullet S$

23. $(\sim K \to K) \to \sim L, \sim(\sim L \to \sim M) \to L, M \therefore K \leftrightarrow \sim L$

24. $W, \sim Y \to (\sim W \bullet \sim X) \therefore Y \bullet [(\sim W \bullet \sim X) \to Z]$

25. $F \vee \sim I, I \vee H, \sim(G \leftrightarrow J) \to \sim H \therefore [(\sim G \vee \sim J) \bullet (G \vee J)] \to F$

PART E: English Arguments Symbolize the following arguments, and then construct proofs to show that they are valid.

* **1.** If workers should be paid, then either they should be paid according to their needs (as Marx asserted) or they should be paid for services rendered. If workers should be paid according to their needs, then single mothers should be paid more (other things being equal) than their co-workers, and so should workers who have large families. If workers should be paid for services rendered, then workers should receive equal pay for equal work. Workers should be paid, but it is not the case that workers having large families should be paid more (other things being equal) than their co-workers. Hence, workers should receive equal pay for equal work. (P: Workers should be paid; N: Workers should be paid according to their needs; S: Workers should be paid for services rendered; M: Single mothers should be paid more (other things being equal) than their co-workers; F: Workers who have large families should be paid more (other things being equal) than their co-workers; E: Workers should receive equal pay for equal work)

2. If either the defendant refuses to take the stand or he confesses, then he is guilty. We may infer that the defendant is guilty if he refuses to take the stand. (R: The defendant refuses to take the stand; C: The defendant confesses; G: The defendant is guilty)

3. If beauty is in the eye of the beholder, then beauty is not objective. But beauty is objective if it is observable. And beauty can be seen, can't it? Furthermore, beauty can be seen if and only if beauty is observable. Therefore, popular opinion to the contrary, beauty is not in the eye of the beholder. (E: Beauty is in the eye of the beholder; B: Beauty is objective; O: Beauty is observable; S: Beauty can be seen)

* **4.** Either sex is for procreation or it is for interpersonal union and pleasure. If sex is for either procreation or interpersonal union, then societal rules are

needed to regulate sex. It follows that societal rules are needed to regulate sex. (S: Sex is for procreation; U: Sex is for interpersonal union; P: Sex is for pleasure; R: Societal rules are needed to regulate sex)

5. Young smokers either identify with their future selves or fail to identify with their future selves. If young smokers identify with their future selves, then they are irrational if they know smoking causes cancer. If young smokers fail to identify with their future selves, then they act without due regard for another person (namely, their future self), assuming that they know smoking causes cancer. And given that young smokers act without due regard for another person, they are immoral. But while young smokers do know that smoking causes cancer, they are not immoral. Therefore, young smokers are irrational, and they identify with their future selves. (I: Young smokers identify with their future selves; R: Young smokers are irrational; K: Young smokers know that smoking causes cancer; A: Young smokers act without due regard for another person; M: Young smokers are immoral) —This argument makes use of material in Derek Parfit, *Reasons and Persons* (New York: Oxford University Press, 1986), pp. 319–320

6. It is a biological fact that animals in most species will make greater sacrifices for near relatives than for others. (For instance, a calf's mother will defend it to the death but will not defend the calf of another cow.) Given this fact, there is a general law that animals act so as to preserve genes similar to their own. But if there is a general law that animals act so as to preserve genes similar to their own, then sociobiologists are right and it is biologically impossible to treat all people equally. Now, if it is biologically impossible to treat all people equally, then it is futile to preach the ideal of equality and futile to preach the ideal of universal love. Hence, it is futile to preach universal love if sociobiologists are right. [*Hint:* In symbolizing the argument, ignore the parenthetical remark.] (B: It is a biological fact that animals in most species will make greater sacrifices for near relatives than for others; G: There is a general law that animals act so as to preserve genes similar to their own; S: Sociobiologists are right; E: It is biologically impossible to treat all people equally; P: It is futile to preach the ideal of equality; U: It is futile to preach the ideal of universal love)

7. You can walk to the door only if you can walk to the halfway point between yourself and the door. But unfortunately, you can walk to the halfway point between yourself and the door only if you can walk to a point *halfway* to the halfway point! Now, if you cannot walk halfway to the halfway point only if you cannot walk to the door, then you can walk to the door only if you can perform an infinite number of acts in a finite period of time. Obviously, you cannot perform an infinite number of acts in a finite period of time. So, as Zeno of Elea concluded, in spite of what your senses may tell you, you cannot walk to the door. (D: You can walk to the door; H: You can walk to the halfway point between yourself and the door; P: You can walk halfway to the halfway point; F: You can perform an infinite number of acts in a finite period of time)

8. This is the best of all possible worlds. For God exists, and if God is not both morally perfect and omnipotent, then God does not exist. Now, if God is omnipotent, God can create just any possible world. And if God is morally

perfect, God will create the best possible world if God can create it. And God can create the best of all possible worlds if and only if God can create just any possible world. Moreover, this is the best of all possible worlds given that God will create the best of all possible worlds. (G: God exists; M: God is morally perfect; O: God is omnipotent; A: God can create just any possible world; W: God will create the best possible world; C: God can create the best possible world; B: This is the best of all possible worlds)

9. God cannot know the future free acts of his creatures if God is in time. For if God is in time, God's knowledge of the future is a prediction based on the past and present. However, if humans have free will, then their future acts are not infallibly predictable based on the past and the present. If the future acts of humans are not infallibly predictable based on the past and the present, then God cannot know the future free acts of God's creatures if God is in time. Finally, if humans do not have free will, then God's knowledge of the future is not a prediction based on the past and the present. (T: God is in time; P: God's knowledge of the future is a prediction based on the past and present; F: Humans have free will; I: The future acts of humans are infallibly predictable based on the past and present; K: God can know the future free acts of God's creatures)

10. All inductive arguments presuppose that the unobserved resembles the observed. (For example, "All observed emeralds have been green; therefore, the next emerald to be found will be green.") Given that all inductive arguments presuppose that the unobserved resembles the observed, induction is unjustified unless we have good reason to believe that the unobserved resembles the observed. If we have good reason to believe that the unobserved resembles the observed, then we have either a good deductive argument or a good inductive argument. We have a good inductive argument only if not all inductive arguments presuppose that the unobserved resembles the observed. We have a good deductive argument only if valid reasoning can begin with the observed and end with the unobserved. Sad to say, valid reasoning cannot begin with the observed and end with the unobserved. It thus appears that David Hume's skeptical conclusion is inescapable: Induction is unjustified. [*Hint:* In symbolizing the argument, ignore the parenthetical remark.] (P: All inductive arguments presuppose that the unobserved resembles the observed; J: Induction is justified; R: We have good reason to believe that the unobserved resembles the observed; D: We have a good deductive argument; I: We have a good inductive argument; V: Valid reasoning can begin with the observed and end with the unobserved)

8.4 **Conditional Proof**

Consider the following argument.

34. If Hank is a horse, then Hank is not a bird. So, if Hank is a horse, then Hank is a horse and not a bird. (H: Hank is a horse; B: Hank is a bird)

This argument may seem a bit odd, but it is plainly valid. Its form is as follows:

35. H → ~B ∴ H → (H • ~B)

Unfortunately, we cannot prove that the argument is valid using only the 18 rules we have in hand so far.[7] We need to add a rule called "conditional proof" (CP for short). Without this rule (or some equivalent addition to our system), we would be unable to construct proofs for many valid arguments. CP also greatly simplifies many proofs.

The basic idea behind CP is that *we can prove a conditional true by assuming that its antecedent is true and showing that its consequent can be derived from this assumption* (together with whatever premises are available). We need a way to formalize this basic idea. This means we need a way to include assumptions in our proofs, bearing in mind that an assumption is not a premise. Actually, because conditionals are hypothetical, the antecedent of a conditional may be false (and may be admitted to be false by the arguer) even though the conditional itself is true. So, we need a way of using assumptions temporarily—a way that keeps it clear that we are not treating them as premises. As an example, the formal proof of argument (36) would look like this:

1. H → ~B		∴ H → (H • ~B)
2. H		Assume (for CP)
3. ~B		1, 2, MP
4. H • ~B		2, 3, Conj
5. H → (H • ~B)		2–4, CP

The phrase "Assume (for CP)" indicates the special status of H as an assumption for conditional proof. The box indicates the *scope* of the assumption (i.e., the part of the proof in which the assumption is made). The steps from line (2) to line (4) do not prove that H • ~B follows from the argument's premise. (They *would* prove this if H were a premise and not a mere assumption.) Rather, lines (2) through (4) show only that H • ~B is true *on the assumption that* H is true. We box in the steps and enter line (5) to make it clear that only a conditional conclusion has been established. The annotation of line (5) mentions the steps falling within the scope of the assumption, as well as the type of proof used (CP). Note that line (5) follows logically from the premise of the argument, namely, H → ~B. We haven't added a premise to the argument in line (2). We have merely introduced a temporary assumption for the purpose of proving that the *conditional* conclusion follows from the premise.

Using lowercase letters as statement variables, we can make a diagram of conditional proof as follows:

Premises

p   Assume (for CP)

.

.

.

q

$p \rightarrow q$ CP

The vertical dots here stand for inferences from the premises and the assumption. In the typical case, $p \rightarrow q$ is the conclusion of the argument, though as we will see, this is not necessarily the case.

A **direct proof** is a proof that makes no use of assumptions. An **indirect proof** is a proof that does make use of assumptions.

A **direct proof** is a proof that makes no use of assumptions.
An **indirect proof** is a proof that makes use of assumptions.

In the system of statement logic we develop here, a direct proof is a proof that is done by using only the 18 inference rules that we have introduced, whereas an indirect proof is a proof that is done by using conditional proof (or *reductio ad absurdum* or some combination of them—see section 8.5), in addition to the 18 inference rules.

Let's consider another example:

36. If most Americans favor gun control, then if lobbies block gun control proposals, democracy is hindered. If most Americans favor gun control, then lobbies do block gun control proposals. Therefore, if most Americans favor gun control, democracy is hindered. (M: Most Americans favor gun control; L: Lobbies block gun control proposals; D: Democracy is hindered)

1. $M \rightarrow (L \rightarrow D)$
2. $M \rightarrow L$ $\therefore M \rightarrow D$
3. M   Assume (for CP)
4. $L \rightarrow D$ 1, 3, MP
5. L   2, 3, MP
6. D   4, 5, MP
7. $M \rightarrow D$ 3–6, CP

Notice that it would be a mistake to suppose that the statements within the box have been shown to follow from the premises alone. We box in the statements precisely to remind ourselves of their tentative status, dependent as they are on the assumption in line (3). We stop making our assumption at line (7). And our proof shows that line (7) follows logically from the premises—that is, lines (1) and (2).

When you are making an assumption for the purpose of conditional proof, always select the *antecedent* of the conditional statement that you are trying to obtain. CP is often useful when the conclusion of an argument is a conditional statement. So, we can state the following helpful tip:

Tip 11: If the conclusion of an argument is a conditional statement, use CP.

For instance, consider the following symbolic argument:

37. ~S → W, ~R → U, (U ∨ W) → T ∴ ~(S • R) → (T ∨ Z)

Because the conclusion of this argument is a conditional statement, CP is a good method to try. And we should assume the *antecedent* of the conclusion, ~(S • R). Accordingly, the proof looks like this:

1. ~S → W	
2. ~R → U	
3. (U ∨ W) → T	∴ ~(S • R) → (T ∨ Z)
4. ~(S • R)	Assume (for CP)
5. ~S ∨ ~R	4, DeM
6. W ∨ U	5, 1, 2, CD
7. U ∨ W	6, Com
8. T	3, 7, MP
9. T ∨ Z	8, Add
10. ~(S • R) → (T ∨ Z)	4–9, CP

Again, we box in the lines of the proof that fall within the *scope* of the assumption (the part of the proof in which the assumption is made). These lines tell us that if we have ~(S • R), then we can obtain T ∨ Z. The boxed-in steps are *hypothetical* in nature, for they depend on the assumption in line (4). We stop making our assumption at line (10). And our proof shows that line (10) follows validly from the premises—that is, lines (1), (2), and (3).

So far, we have considered cases in which only one assumption is introduced. But sometimes it is helpful to introduce more than one assumption—for example, when you are trying to prove a conditional whose *consequent* is a conditional. Here is an example:

38. If space travelers from another galaxy visit Earth, then aliens will rule us if our technology is inferior. But if our technology is inferior and aliens will rule us, then our liberty will decrease. So, if space travelers from another galaxy visit Earth, then our liberty will decrease if our technology is inferior. (S: Space travelers from another galaxy visit Earth; A: Aliens will rule us; T: Our technology is inferior; L: Our liberty will decrease)

We symbolize the argument and begin a conditional proof in line (3).

1. S → (T → A)
2. (T • A) → L   ∴ S → (T → L)
> 3. S   Assume (for CP)
> 4. T → A   1, 3, MP

Having derived line (4), we could turn our attention to premise (2), applying commutation, exportation, and so on, but with CP another strategy is possible. Note that the conclusion, S → (T → L), is a conditional with another conditional (namely, T → L) as its consequent. Thus, we can usefully introduce a second assumption (again, the antecedent of a conditional), as follows:

1. S → (T → A)
2. (T • A) → L   ∴ S → (T → L)
> 3. S   Assume (for CP)
> 4. T → A   1, 3, MP
> > 5. T   Assume (for CP)
> > 6. A   4, 5, MP
> > 7. T • A   5, 6, Conj
> > 8. L   2, 7, MP
> 9. T → L   5–8, CP

Now, at this point, we have shown that if T, then L, for by assuming T, we were able to obtain L. But all of this occurs within the scope of our first assumption (i.e., S), and *a proof is always incomplete as long as we are still making an assumption.* Furthermore, we have not yet reached the conclusion of the argument, so we need one additional step:

1. S → (T → A)
2. (T • A) → L   ∴ S → (T → L)
> 3. S   Assume (for CP)
> 4. T → A   1, 3, MP
> > 5. T   Assume (for CP)
> > 6. A   4, 5, MP
> > 7. T • A   5, 6, Conj
> > 8. L   2, 7, MP
> 9. T → L   5–8, CP
10. S → (T → L)   3–9, CP

Lines (3) through (9) indicate that if we have S, we can obtain T → L. In other words, the proof shows that line (10) follows logically from the premises—that is, lines (1) and (2). So, the argument is valid.

Here is the place to issue two important warnings. First, because the statements within the boxes are dependent on assumptions, we cannot make use of boxed-in statements in later parts of a proof. For example, in the previous proof, it may appear that we could write L on line (9) by applying *modus ponens* to lines (7) and (2), but line (7) is available only because of the assumption in line (5). And the box indicates that we *discharged* (i.e., ceased to make) that assumption when we got to line (9). So, we cannot make use of line (7) in subsequent parts of the proof. In general, boxed-in lines cannot be used to justify later steps in a proof, for the boxes indicate that we have ceased to make the assumption in question. Second, no proof involving CP is complete until all assumptions are discharged.

It should be noted that CP is sometimes useful even when the conclusion of the argument is not a conditional. Here is an example:

39. If God stops people from performing acts that cause unnecessary suffering, then *either* God denies creatures a choice between good and evil *or* God can cause the free acts of his creatures. If God can cause the free acts of his creatures, then the concept of free will is empty. The concept of free will is not empty. So, either God does not stop people from performing acts that cause unnecessary suffering or else God denies creatures a real choice between good and evil. (S: God stops people from performing acts that cause unnecessary suffering; G: God denies creatures a choice between good and evil; F: God can cause the free acts of his creatures; W: The concept of free will is empty)

We symbolize the argument and begin a conditional proof in line (4). This makes sense if one realizes that the conclusion, $\sim$S $\lor$ G, is logically equivalent to S $\rightarrow$ G.

1.	S $\rightarrow$ (G $\lor$ F)	
2.	F $\rightarrow$ W	
3.	$\sim$W	$\therefore$ $\sim$S $\lor$ G
4.	S	Assume (for CP)
5.	G $\lor$ F	1, 4, MP
6.	$\sim$F	2, 3, MT
7.	G	5, 6, DS
8.	S $\rightarrow$ G	4–7, CP
9.	$\sim$S $\lor$ G	8, MI

Note that *by CP we always obtain a conditional*, and this case is no exception. Lines (4) through (7) establish S $\rightarrow$ G. We then apply MI to obtain the conclusion of the argument.

CP can be used when the conclusion of an argument is a biconditional. For example:

40. (B $\lor$ A) $\rightarrow$ C, A $\rightarrow$ $\sim$C, $\sim$A $\rightarrow$ B $\therefore$ B $\leftrightarrow$ C

The basic strategy is to prove two conditionals, conjoin them, and then use ME:

1. (B ∨ A) → C
2. A → ~C
3. ~A → B   ∴ B ↔ C
   4. B   Assume (for CP)
   5. B ∨ A   4, Add
   6. C   1, 5, MP
   7. B → C   4–6, CP
   8. C   Assume (for CP)
   9. ~~C   8, DN
  10. ~A   2, 9, MT
  11. B   3, 10, MP
  12. C → B   8–11, CP
  13. (B → C) • (C → B)   7, 12, Conj
  14. B ↔ C   13, ME

Note that although two assumptions are made in this proof, neither falls within the scope of the other. So, at line (13), we are free to conjoin lines (7) and (12).

Conditional proof renders our system of statement logic complete. Whatever can be proved valid through the truth tables can be proved valid using our 8 implicational rules, 10 equivalence rules, and CP.

EXERCISE 8.4

PART A: Conditional Proofs Use CP to show that each of the following symbolic arguments is valid.

* **1.** Z → (~Y → X), Z → ~Y ∴ Z → X
  2. P → Q ∴ P → (Q ∨ R)
  3. (F ∨ ~G) → ~L ∴ L → G
* **4.** A → B, A → C ∴ A → (B • C)
  5. (H ∨ E) → K ∴ E → K
  6. (B → ~C) → D ∴ B → (~C → D)
* **7.** P ∴ (P → Q) → Q
  8. S ∴ ~(S • R) → ~R
  9. (G → H) → J ∴ H → J
***10.** C → (~D → E), (D → ~D) → (E → G) ∴ C → (~D → G)
 11. H → (J • K), ~L → (J • M) ∴ (~L ∨ H) → J
 12. ~X ∨ (O • W), (X → O) → (W → X) ∴ W → X

*13. $(A \lor N) \to \sim S, M \to [N \to (S \bullet T)] \therefore \sim(\sim M \lor \sim N) \to (S \bullet \sim A)$

14. $\sim P \lor (Q \bullet \sim R) \therefore (R \lor R) \to \sim P$

15. $(S \lor T) \leftrightarrow \sim E, S \to (F \bullet \sim G), A \to W, T \to \sim W \therefore (\sim E \bullet A) \to \sim G$

*16. $A \to (B \to C) \therefore (A \to B) \to (A \to C)$

17. $(G \bullet P) \to K, E \to Z, \sim P \to \sim Z, G \to (E \lor L) \therefore (G \bullet \sim L) \to K$

18. $S \to (\sim T \to U), \sim T \to (U \to O) \therefore \sim S \lor [(T \to \sim T) \to O]$

*19. $A \to (B \bullet C), B \to D, C \to \sim D \therefore A \to X$

20. $B \to [(E \bullet \sim G) \to M], \sim(\sim E \lor G) \to (M \to R) \therefore B \to [\sim(\sim G \to \sim E) \to R]$

21. $P \to (Q \to R) \therefore Q \to (P \to R)$

22. $Q \to R \therefore (P \lor Q) \to (P \lor R)$

23. $A \leftrightarrow B \therefore \sim B \leftrightarrow \sim A$

24. $C \leftrightarrow D, D \leftrightarrow \sim E \therefore C \leftrightarrow \sim E$

25. $\sim A \therefore [(A \bullet B) \lor (C \bullet D)] \leftrightarrow [(A \lor C) \bullet (A \lor D)]$

PART B: English Arguments Symbolize the following arguments, using the schemes of abbreviation provided. Then use CP to show that the arguments are valid.

* **1.** If Jones doesn't vote, then he shouldn't vote. For after all, if Jones doesn't vote, then either he lacks intelligence or he lacks a proper value system. And Jones shouldn't vote if he lacks intelligence. Furthermore, Jones shouldn't vote if he lacks a proper value system. (V: Jones does vote; I: Jones has intelligence; P: Jones has a proper value system; S: Jones should vote)

2. Euthanasia is wrong if either the patient prefers to go on living or she still maintains her higher faculties. Therefore, if the patient still maintains her higher faculties, then euthanasia is wrong. (P: The patient prefers to go on living; F: The patient maintains her higher faculties; E: Euthanasia is wrong)

3. If we should forgive our enemies, then it is wrong to punish criminals. For if we should forgive our enemies, then we should forget the offense and behave as if the offense never occurred. And we should punish criminals if and only if we should not behave as if the offense never occurred. Furthermore, it is wrong to punish criminals if and only if we should not punish criminals. (F: We should forgive our enemies; W: It is wrong to punish criminals; O: We should forget the offense; B: We should behave as if the offense never occurred; S: We should punish criminals)

4. If God believes on Monday that I'll tell a lie on Tuesday, then either I have the power to make one of God's past beliefs false or I cannot refrain from lying on Tuesday. I do not have the power to make one of God's past beliefs false if either God is infallible or the past is unalterable. The past is unalterable. It follows that if God believes on Monday that I'll tell a lie on Tuesday, then I cannot refrain from lying on Tuesday. (B: God believes on Monday that I'll tell a lie on Tuesday; F: I have the power to make one of God's past beliefs false; R: I can refrain from lying on Tuesday; I: God is infallible; P: The past is unalterable)

5. If humans lack free will, then there is no moral responsibility. Materialism is true if and only if only matter exists. Assuming that only matter exists, every event is the result of past states of the world plus the operation of natural laws. Now, if every event is the result of past states of the world plus the operation of natural laws, then human acts are under human control only if either humans have control over the past or humans have control over the natural laws. Humans do not have control over the past, and they do not have control over the natural laws. Finally, if human acts are not under human control, then humans do not have free will. We may conclude that if materialism is true, then there is no moral responsibility. (F: Humans have free will; R: There is moral responsibility; M: Materialism is true; O: Only matter exists; E: Every event is the result of past states of the world plus the operation of natural laws; C: Human acts are under human control; P: Humans have control over the past; N: Humans have control over the natural laws)

PART C: Valid or Invalid? Symbolize the following arguments. If an argument is invalid, prove this by means of an abbreviated truth table. If an argument is valid, construct a proof to demonstrate its validity.

1. If either moral judgments are products of biological causes or moral judgments are not based on empirical evidence, then morality is not objective. But if moral judgments are not products of biological causes, then moral judgments are not based on empirical evidence. Hence, morality is not objective. (M: Moral judgments are products of biological causes; E: Moral judgments are based on empirical evidence; O: Morality is objective)

2. It is false that if we continue to use gasoline, then the air will not be polluted. Either we do not continue to use gasoline or we use solar power. If we continue to use gasoline and air-pollution control devices are perfected, then the air will not be polluted. Therefore, we use solar power if and only if air-pollution control devices are perfected. (G: We continue to use gasoline; A: The air will be polluted; S: We use solar power; P: Air-pollution control devices are perfected)

3. Given that Henri Rousseau's *The Dream* is pornographic if and only if Rousseau painted it with the intention of inciting lust in the viewers, Rousseau's *The Dream* is not pornographic. For Rousseau painted it with the intention of inciting lust in the viewers only if every nude painting is painted with the intention of inciting lust in the viewers. And the latter suggestion is wildly false! (P: Henri Rousseau's *The Dream* is pornographic; L: Rousseau painted *The Dream* with the intention of inciting lust in the viewers; N: Every nude painting is painted with the intention of inciting lust in the viewers)

4. If Boethius is morally virtuous, then he achieves heaven. But if he isn't morally virtuous, then his longings are satisfied. On the other hand, if Boethius doesn't achieve heaven, then his longings are not satisfied. So, Boethius's longings are satisfied. (M: Boethius is morally virtuous; H: Boethius achieves heaven; L: Boethius's longings are satisfied)

5. Either God has a reason for his commands or morality is ultimately arbitrary. If God has a reason for his commands, then reasons that are independent of God's will make actions right. Consequently, reasons that are independent of God's will make actions right provided that morality is not ultimately arbitrary. (R: God has a reason for his commands; M: Morality is ultimately arbitrary; I: Reasons that are independent of God's will make actions right)

8.5 *Reductio ad Absurdum*

Although our system of statement logic is already complete, we will add one more rule that simplifies proofs in many cases, namely, *reductio ad absurdum* (RAA for short). The basic principle behind RAA is this: *Whatever implies a contradiction is false.*

Using the italicized, lowercase letters *p* and *q* as statement variables (which can stand for any statement), we can see that RAA is closely related to *modus tollens*. Suppose we know that a given statement ~*p* implies a contradiction:

41. ~*p* → (*q* • ~*q*)

Now, we know that contradictions are false. So, we also know this:

42. ~(*q* • ~*q*)

But, then if we apply *modus tollens* to (41) and (42), we get ~~*p* and, hence, *p* by DN. This is the essential logic underlying **reductio ad absurdum**. Because ~*p* leads to (or "reduces" to) a logical absurdity (i.e., a contradiction), ~*p* is false. Hence, by DN, *p* is true.[8]

Now, in practice, the contradiction does not usually follow from a single statement all by itself. Rather, the contradiction usually follows from the premises of the argument (which are taken as true for the purpose of establishing validity) *together with* the temporary assumption, ~*p*, where *p* is the conclusion of the argument.

Look at it this way. Suppose we have three statements that together imply a contradiction. For instance:

~A → (B • ~C)
B → C
~A

Using MP, Simp, and Conj, we can derive C • ~C from these statements in only a few steps. Because these statements imply a contradiction, we know that at least one of them is false. Now, given that the first two statements are true, we can conclude that ~A is false and, hence, that A is true. This reasoning shows the following argument to be valid:

43. ~A → (B • ~C), B → C ∴ A

The formal proof runs as follows:

```
1. ~A → (B • ~C)
2. B → C                ∴ A
3. ~A                   Assume (for RAA)
4. B • ~C               1, 3, MP
5. B                    4, Simp
6. C                    2, 5, MP
7. ~C                   4, Simp
8. C • ~C               6, 7, Conj
9. A                    3–8, RAA
```

The phrase "Assume (for RAA)" indicates the special status of ~A as an assumption for *reductio ad absurdum*. For the purpose of establishing the *validity* of an argument, the truth of the premises is a given. So, since the premises, together with ~A, imply a contradiction, we may conclude that ~A is false and, hence, that A is true. As with CP, we box in the lines that fall within the scope of the assumption and add line (9) to indicate that A follows not from our assumption but from the premises of the argument. The annotation for line (9) mentions the lines falling within the scope of the assumption and adds "RAA" for *reductio ad absurdum*.

　　When the conclusion of an argument is the *negation* of a statement, (e.g., ~B), your assumption line should usually be the statement itself (in this case, B) rather than a double-negation. This procedure will usually save some steps. For example, consider the following proof:

```
1. B ↔ ~A
2. ~A → ~C
3. C v D
4. ~C → ~D                          ∴ ~B
5. B                    Assume (for RAA)
6. (B → ~A) • (~A → B)  1, ME
7. B → ~A               6, Simp
8. ~A                   5, 7, MP
9. ~C                   8, 2, MP
10. D                   3, 9, DS
11. ~D                  4, 9, MP
12. D • ~D              10, 11, Conj
13. ~B                  5–12, RAA
```

Note that in line (5), we assume B rather than ~~B. It wouldn't be a logical error to assume ~~B, but it would add an unnecessary step. (We'd have to apply DN to drop the double-negation before performing a *modus ponens* step.)

Thus, a proof involving RAA may proceed in two ways. Using lowercase letters as statement variables, we can diagram these two ways as follows:

To Prove a Negation: *~p*		**To Prove a Statement That Is Not a Negation: *p***	
Premises		Premises	
p	Assume (for RAA)	*~p*	Assume (for RAA)
.		.	
.		.	
.		.	
(q • ~q)		*(q • ~q)*	
~p	RAA	*p*	RAA

The procedure is essentially the same in both cases: We show that a statement (together with the premises) implies a contradiction and conclude that the statement is false. *Note:* As with CP, no proof involving RAA is complete until all assumptions have been discharged.

When should one use RAA? There is usually no way to know for sure, apart from experiment, whether RAA will prove useful, but here are some points to keep in mind. First, RAA will always work (assuming, of course, that the argument is valid), but RAA may unnecessarily complicate a proof. Second, when direct proof seems difficult or impossible and the conclusion of the argument is not a conditional, try RAA. (If the conclusion is a conditional, CP is usually preferable to RAA.) Consider an example:

44. $(F \vee {\sim}F) \rightarrow G \therefore G$

Applying MI to the premise, we get $\sim(F \vee {\sim}F) \vee G$. By DeM, we can then obtain $(\sim F \bullet {\sim}{\sim}F) \vee G$. Com will give us $G \vee (\sim F \bullet {\sim}{\sim}F)$. And Dist will yield $(G \vee {\sim}F) \bullet (G \vee {\sim}{\sim}F)$. Now we can simplify to obtain $G \vee {\sim}F$ as well as $G \vee {\sim}{\sim}F$. But where do we go from here? Maybe it would help to have an assumption to work with. And because the conclusion is not a conditional, let's try RAA:

1. $(F \vee {\sim}F) \rightarrow G$	$\therefore G$
2. $\sim G$	Assume (for RAA)
3. $\sim(F \vee {\sim}F)$	1, 2, MT
4. $\sim F \bullet {\sim}{\sim}F$	3, DeM
5. G	2–4, RAA

Summary of Tips for Constructing Proofs

1. Always, *always*, immediately check that you copied the proof correctly.
2. Scan the premises to see whether they fit any rule patterns.
3. Try to find the conclusion, or elements thereof, in the premises.
4. Apply the inference rules to break down the premises.
5. If the conclusion contains a statement letter that does not appear in the premises, use the rule of addition.
6. Consider logically equivalent forms of the conclusion and the premises.
7. Both conjunction and addition can lead to useful applications of De Morgan's laws.
8. Material implication can lead to useful applications of distribution.
9. Distribution can lead to useful applications of simplification.
10. Addition can lead to useful applications of material implication.
11. If the conclusion of an argument is a conditional statement, use CP.
12. If direct proof is difficult and the conclusion of the argument is not a conditional, try RAA.

In this case, RAA makes the proof short and easy. Let us now add a twelfth helpful tip:

> **Tip 12:** If direct proof is difficult and the conclusion of the argument is not a conditional, try RAA.

It is possible to combine RAA and CP. Here is an example:

1. ~(S • ~R) ∨ (S → T)	∴ S → (R ∨ T)	
2. S	Assume (for CP)	
3. ~(R ∨ T)	Assume (for RAA)	
4. ~R • ~T	3, DeM	
5. ~R	4, Simp	
6. S • ~R	2, 5, Conj	
7. ~~(S • ~R)	6, DN	
8. S → T	1, 7, DS	
9. T	2, 8, MP	
10. ~T	4 Simp	
11. T • ~T	9, 10, Conj	
12. R ∨ T	3–11, RAA	
13. S → (R ∨ T)	2–12, CP	

In line (2), we begin a conditional proof. Having begun a CP proof, we need to obtain the consequent of the conditional in question, namely, R ∨ T. If we assume ~(R ∨ T) and derive a contradiction, we will have shown that R ∨ T must be true given that S is true. The preceding proof spells out the details. Note that in this case, an RAA proof falls within the scope of a CP proof.

As we have seen, when using RAA, one typically derives a contradiction from the assumption that the *conclusion* of the argument is false. But other assumptions can be useful. Here's an example:

1. L → H		
2. L → ~H		
3. ~L → (S ∨ R)		
4. ~R	∴ S	
5. L	Assume (for RAA)	
6. H	1, 5, MP	
7. ~H	2, 5, MP	
8. H • ~H	6, 7, Conj	
9. ~L	5–8, RAA	
10. S ∨ R	9, 3, MP	
11. S	10, 4, DS	

Why assume L at line (5)? This assumption makes sense for two reasons. First, if we can obtain ~L, then we can derive S from premises (3) and (4). Second, given premises (1) and (2), if we assume L, we can easily derive a contradiction.

Note: As with CP, because the statements within the boxes of an RAA proof depend on one or more assumptions, we cannot make use of boxed-in statements in *later* parts of a proof. For example, could we enter ~L • H at line (10) in the previous proof, using "6, 9, Conj" as our annotation? No. For at that point in the proof, line (6) is off limits—we obtained H by making an assumption, and (as the box indicates) we stopped making that assumption when we got to line (9).

In closing this section, let us reflect briefly on the value of proofs. What good are they? First, many valid arguments are sufficiently complex to dazzle one's logical intuitions. In such cases, our proof system comes into its own by enabling us to show how we can get from the premises to the conclusion *using only the rules we have explicitly adopted.* So, unless we have doubts about our system of rules, a proof should settle all doubts about the validity of even very complicated arguments. Second, suppose you claim that an argument is valid and someone else claims that it isn't. What can you do? Well, if the argument can be shown to be valid by means of a proof, then this should settle the matter (unless the other person rejects one or more of the rules in our system). Logic is powerful because in so many cases, it can settle the question of an argument's validity. And once we determine that an argument is valid, the question of its soundness turns entirely on whether its premises are true. Of course, if an argument is valid and has all true premises, then the truth of the premises will be preserved in the conclusion. That's why the soundness of an argument is so valuable. Thus, to the extent that it is reasonable to believe the premises, it will be reasonable to believe the conclusion.

EXERCISE 8.5

PART A: Proofs Construct proofs to show that the following symbolic arguments are valid. Use RAA but not CP.

* **1.** A → B ∴ ~(A • ~B)
  2. P → Q, ~P → J, ~Q → ~J ∴ Q
  3. F → G, F ∨ G ∴ G
* **4.** (H ∨ R) • (H ∨ ~R) ∴ H
  5. (M → L) → M ∴ M
  6. ~P ↔ Q, ~(Q ∨ R), (P • ~R) → S ∴ S
* **7.** Z → (X ∨ Y), X → ~W, Y → ~W, ~W → ~Z ∴ ~Z
  8. E ∨ T, T → (B • H), (B ∨ E) → K ∴ K
  9. (O ∨ N) → (O • N) ∴ N ↔ O
* **10.** ~A • ~B ∴ A ↔ B
  11. ~W ∨ (Z → Y), ~X → (W ∨ Y), W → Z ∴ Y ∨ X
  12. ~P → (R • S), ~Q → (R • T), ~(S ∨ T) ∴ P • Q
* **13.** D → ~(A ∨ B), ~C → D ∴ A → C
  14. E ∴ (E • H) ∨ (E • ~H)
  15. ~Q → (L → F), Q → ~A, F → B, L ∴ ~A ∨ B
* **16.** W → (X ∨ G), G → M, ~M ∴ ~W ∨ X
  17. (~H ∨ K) • (~H ∨ L), ~N → H, ~N → (~L ∨ ~K), P ↔ N ∴ S → P
  18. C → (D → H), D • ~H, H ∨ T ∴ ~C • T
* **19.** ~S → (T • U), ~R → ~(T ∨ U), (T ↔ U) → (~~S • R) ∴ R • S
  20. (A → B) → (C → A) ∴ C → A
  21. (S ∨ T) ∨ (V ∨ W) ∴ (V ∨ T) ∨ (S ∨ W)
  22. S → T ∴ (U ∨ S) → (U ∨ T)
  23. X → Y ∴ (Y ∨ X) → Y
  24. R • P, R → (S ∨ Q), ~(Q • P) ∴ S
  25. K, D → E, D → F, D → G, J → ~K, E → H, H → [I → (~J → ~G)],
     F → (K → I) ∴ ~D

PART B: Valid or Invalid? For each of the following pairs of arguments, one is valid and one is invalid. Use an abbreviated truth table to determine which argument is invalid. Then construct a proof to show that the other member of the pair is valid, using either RAA or CP.

* **1.** $(F \rightarrow G) \rightarrow H \therefore F \rightarrow (G \rightarrow H)$
* **2.** $F \rightarrow (G \rightarrow H) \therefore (F \rightarrow G) \rightarrow H$
  3. $\sim L \rightarrow L, \sim L \leftrightarrow N \therefore \sim N$
  4. $(E \bullet F) \rightarrow G \therefore F \rightarrow G$
  5. $(\sim D \vee H) \bullet (\sim D \vee \sim P), \sim D \rightarrow S, (H \bullet P) \rightarrow \sim U \therefore S \vee \sim U$
  6. $\sim(S \rightarrow R) \therefore S \bullet \sim R$
  7. $(Z \vee Y) \bullet (Z \vee W) \therefore Z \bullet (Y \vee W)$
  8. $P \rightarrow \sim Q \therefore Q \rightarrow \sim P$
  9. $\sim S \rightarrow (F \rightarrow L), F \rightarrow (L \rightarrow P) \therefore \sim S \rightarrow (F \rightarrow P)$
  10. $A \rightarrow (B \vee C) \therefore (A \rightarrow B) \bullet (\sim A \vee C)$

PART C: English Arguments Symbolize the following arguments using the schemes of abbreviation provided. Then construct proofs to show that the arguments are valid. Use only RAA.

* **1.** If the rate of literacy has declined, then either TV or parental neglect is the cause. If TV is the cause, then we can't increase literacy unless we can get rid of TV. If parental neglect is the cause, then we can't increase literacy unless we are willing to support early childhood education with our tax dollars. The rate of literacy has declined, but we can't get rid of TV and we certainly aren't willing to support early childhood education with our tax dollars. So, we can't increase literacy. (R: The rate of literacy has declined; T: TV is the cause of the decline in the rate of literacy; P: Parental neglect is the cause of the decline in the rate of literacy; L: We can increase literacy; C: We can get rid of TV; W: We are willing to support early childhood education with our tax dollars)

  2. Either vegetarians are misguided or factory farming is cruel and the grain fed to animals could save thousands of starving people. Vegetarians are misguided only if feeding grain to animals is an efficient way to make protein. And if the grain fed to animals could save thousands of starving people, then American consumers are insensitive if they insist on eating meat at the current rate. American consumers insist on eating meat at the current rate. Therefore, either American consumers are insensitive or feeding grain to animals is an efficient way to make protein. (V: Vegetarians are misguided; F: Factory farming is cruel; G: The grain fed to animals could save thousands of starving people; E: Feeding grain to animals is an efficient way to make protein; A: American consumers are insensitive; M: American consumers insist on eating meat at the current rate)

  3. We should maximize the general welfare if and only if utilitarianism is true. If we should maximize the general welfare, we should promote the greatest sum of pleasure. If we should promote the greatest sum of pleasure, then we are morally obligated to increase the size of the population provided that we can increase the size of the population without reducing the standard of living. We can increase the size of the population without reducing the standard of living, but we are not morally obligated to increase the size of the population if either increasing the size of the population will destroy the environment or no individual experiences the sum of pleasure. Obviously, no individual experiences the sum of pleasure. It follows that utilitarianism is not true. (W: We should maximize the general welfare; U: Utilitarianism is true; P: We should promote the greatest sum of pleasure; M: We are morally obligated to increase the size of the population; R: We can increase the size of the population without reducing the standard of living; E: Increasing the size of the population will destroy the environment; N: No individual experiences the sum of pleasure)

4. According to some Hindu traditions, reincarnation is true, but reality is undifferentiated being. However, it is not the case that *both* reincarnation is true *and* reality is undifferentiated being. For reincarnation is true if and only if a person's soul transfers to another body at death. But if a person's soul transfers to another body at death, then each individual soul is real and each individual soul differs from all other souls. But if reality is undifferentiated being, then all apparent differences are illusory. And if each individual soul is real, then souls are not illusory. However, if each individual soul differs from all other souls and souls are not illusory, then not all apparent differences are illusory. (R: Reincarnation is true; U: Reality is undifferentiated being; T: A person's soul transfers to another body at death; E: Each individual soul is real; D: Each individual soul differs from all other souls; S: Souls are illusory; A: All apparent differences are illusory)

5. Some hold the view that although contradictions *could* be true, we happen to know that they are always false. This view is mistaken. For if contradictions could be true, then if the evidence for some statements is counterbalanced by equally strong evidence for their negations, some contradictions are true for all we know. Now, if there are areas of controversy among scholars, then the evidence for some statements is counterbalanced by equally strong evidence for their negations. And it almost goes without saying that there are areas of controversy among scholars. Finally, some contradictions are true for all we know if and only if we do not know that contradictions are always false. (C: Contradictions could be true; K: We know that contradictions are always false; E: The evidence for some statements is counterbalanced by equally strong evidence for their negations; S: Some contradictions are true for all we know; A: There are areas of controversy among scholars)

PART D: Valid or Invalid? Symbolize the following arguments using the schemes of abbreviation provided. If an argument is invalid, demonstrate this by means of an abbreviated truth table. (Only one of the arguments is invalid.) If an argument is valid, demonstrate this by constructing a proof. You can use CP, RAA, or direct proof.

1. If Smith works hard, then he gets elected. But if he doesn't work hard, then he is happy. Moreover, if he doesn't get elected, then he isn't happy. We may infer that Smith gets elected. (W: Smith works hard; E: Smith gets elected; H: Smith is happy)

2. If either mathematical laws are due to arbitrary linguistic conventions or mathematical laws are not based on empirical evidence, then math is merely a game played with symbols. If mathematical laws are not based on empirical evidence, then they are not due to arbitrary linguistic conventions. So, math is merely a game played with symbols. (M: Mathematical laws are due to arbitrary linguistic conventions; E: Mathematical laws are based on empirical evidence; G: Math is merely a game played with symbols)

3. God is not outside of time if time is real. For, as St. Thomas Aquinas pointed out, if God is outside of time, then God sees all of time (past, present, and future) at a glance. But if God sees all of time at a glance, then all of time (past, present, and future) already exists. Now, if all of time already exists, then the future already exists. However, if the future already exists, then I have already committed sins that I will commit in the future. But if time is real, I have emphatically *not* already committed sins that I will commit in the future. (O: God is outside of time; S: God sees all of time at a glance; A: All of time already exists; F: The future already exists; I: I have already committed sins that I will commit in the future; T: Time is real)

4. Television has destroyed the moral fiber of our country if it has both stifled creativity and substantially interfered with communication between children and parents. Of course, television has not destroyed the moral fiber of our country, assuming that our country still has moral fiber. However, one must admit that television has substantially interfered with communication between children and parents. Furthermore, the statement "Television has stifled creativity if and only if television is a good thing" is false. It follows that television is a good thing given that our country still has moral fiber. (T: Television has destroyed the moral fiber of our country; S: Television has stifled creativity; C: Television has substantially interfered with communication between children and parents; M: Our country still has moral fiber; G: Television is a good thing)

5. There is life after death if and only if there is a God. For either God exists or only matter exists. And if only matter exists, then when we die our bodies simply decay and we cease to exist permanently. Of course, if we cease to exist permanently, then there is no life after death. But God exists if and only if God is both perfectly good and omnipotent. If God is omnipotent, God is able to raise humans from the dead. If God is perfectly good, then God wants to raise humans from the dead if resurrection is necessary for their fulfillment. Resurrection is necessary for human fulfillment if most people die with their deepest longings unsatisfied, and as a matter of fact

most people do die in that condition. If God is able *and* wants to raise humans from the dead, then there is life after death. (L: There is life after death; G: God exists; M: Only matter exists; D: When we die our bodies simply decay; E: We cease to exist permanently; P: God is perfectly good; O: God is omnipotent; A: God is able to raise humans from the dead; W: God wants to raise humans from the dead; R: Resurrection is necessary for human fulfillment; U: Most people die with their deepest longings unsatisfied)

8.6   Proving Theorems

A **theorem** is a statement that can be proved independently of any premises.

> A **theorem** is a statement that can be proved independently of any premises.

The theorems of statement logic are identical with the tautologies of statement logic. (Recall that a *tautology* is a statement that is true on every assignment of truth values to its atomic statements.) Theorems belong to a class of statements that are true by virtue of their logical form. Many philosophers regard theorems as one type of necessary truth. A **necessary truth** is a truth that cannot be false under any possible circumstances.

Theorems have some rather surprising logical properties. For instance, any argument that has a theorem as its conclusion is valid, regardless of the information in the premises. This is so because it is impossible for a theorem to be false, and hence, it is impossible for the conclusion of such an argument to be false while the premises are true. Note that this implies that each theorem is validly implied by any other theorem.

To prove a theorem, use either CP or RAA. If the theorem is itself a conditional statement, it is usually best to use CP. Here is an example:

$$\therefore \sim A \rightarrow [(A \lor B) \rightarrow B]$$

1.	~A	Assume (for CP)
2.	A ∨ B	Assume (for CP)
3.	B	1, 2, DS
4.	(A ∨ B) → B	2–3, CP
5.	~A → [(A ∨ B) → B]	1–4, CP

The theorem itself is indicated by the triple-dot symbol. This proof shows that if we have ~A, then if we have A ∨ B, we can derive B. In other words, the proof shows that the statement beside the triple-dot symbol is indeed a theorem: It can be proved without appealing to any premises.

In some cases, RAA is the best approach. Here is a simple example:

$$\therefore P \lor {\sim}P$$

1. ${\sim}(P \lor {\sim}P)$	Assume (for RAA)
2. ${\sim}P \bullet {\sim}{\sim}P$	1, DeM
3. $P \lor {\sim}P$	1–2, RAA

In other cases, a combination of CP and RAA works best. For instance:

$$\therefore [(F \to G) \to F] \to F$$

1. $(F \to G) \to F$	Assume (for CP)
2. ${\sim}F$	Assume (for RAA)
3. ${\sim}(F \to G)$	1, 2, MT
4. ${\sim}({\sim}F \lor G)$	3, MI
5. ${\sim}{\sim}F \bullet {\sim}G$	4, DeM
6. ${\sim}{\sim}F$	5, Simp
7. ${\sim}F \bullet {\sim}{\sim}F$	2, 6, Conj
8. F	2–7, RAA
9. $[(F \to G) \to F] \to F$	1–8, CP

Sometimes it is necessary to introduce multiple assumptions to prove a theorem. Here is an example:

$$\therefore [A \to (B \to C)] \to [(A \to B) \to (A \to C)]$$

1. $A \to (B \to C)$	Assume (for CP)
2. $A \to B$	Assume (for CP)
3. A	Assume (for CP)
4. B	2, 3, MP
5. $B \to C$	1, 3, MP
6. C	4, 5, MP
7. $A \to C$	3–6, CP
8. $(A \to B) \to (A \to C)$	2–7, CP
9. $[A \to (B \to C)] \to [(A \to B) \to (A \to C)]$	1–8, CP

There is an important connection between valid arguments and theorems. To understand this connection, we first need the concept of a corresponding conditional. In the case of an argument with a single premise, one forms the corresponding conditional simply by connecting the premise and conclusion with an arrow. Here is an example:

> *Argument: ~(A ∨ ~B) ∴ B*
> *Corresponding conditional: ~(A ∨ ~B) → B*

In the case of an argument with multiple premises, forming the corresponding conditional is a two-step process. First, one conjoins the premises—that is, one forms a conjunction of the premises. Second, one connects this conjunction with the conclusion of the argument by means of an arrow. To illustrate:

> *Argument: P → Q, ~Q ∴ ~P*
> *Conjunction of premises: (P → Q) • ~Q*
> *Corresponding conditional: [(P → Q) • ~Q] → ~P*

Note that in this case, the form of the argument is *modus tollens*. Of course, the argument is valid, and the corresponding conditional is a theorem. So, in general, *p → q* is the **corresponding conditional** of the argument *p ∴ q*, where *p* is a single premise of the argument or the conjunction of the premises.

> *p → q* is the **corresponding conditional** of the argument *p ∴ q*, where *p* is a single premise of the argument or the conjunction of the premises.

This is a relationship that can be counted on for every symbolic argument of statement logic: A symbolic argument is valid if and only if its corresponding conditional is a theorem.

Consider a second example. The argument form is traditionally known as *destructive dilemma*:

> *Argument: ~A ∨ ~B, C → A, D → B ∴ ~C ∨ ~D*

To form the corresponding conditional, we first make a conjunction out of the premises, like this:

> (~A ∨ ~B) • [(C → A) • (D → B)]

Next, we connect this conjunction to the conclusion of the argument with an arrow, to obtain the corresponding conditional:

> ((~A ∨ ~B) • [(C → A) • (D → B)]) → (~C ∨ ~D)

Now, we can prove that the argument is valid by proving that its corresponding conditional is a theorem:

$$\therefore\ ((\sim A \lor \sim B) \bullet [(C \to A) \bullet (D \to B)]) \to (\sim C \lor \sim D)$$

1.	$(\sim A \lor \sim B) \bullet [(C \to A) \bullet (D \to B)]$	Assume (for CP)
2.	$\sim A \lor \sim B$	1, Simp
3.	$(C \to A) \bullet (D \to B)$	1, Simp
4.	$C \to A$	3, Simp
5.	$D \to B$	3, Simp
6.	$\sim(\sim C \lor \sim D)$	Assume (for RAA)
7.	$\sim\sim C \bullet \sim\sim D$	6, DeM
8.	$\sim\sim C$	7, Simp
9.	C	8, DN
10.	A	4, 9, MP
11.	$\sim\sim A$	10, DN
12.	$\sim B$	2, 11, DS
13.	$\sim\sim D$	7, Simp
14.	D	13, DN
15.	B	5, 14, MP
16.	$B \bullet \sim B$	15, 12, Conj
17.	$\sim C \lor \sim D$	6–16, RAA
18.	$((\sim A \lor \sim B) \bullet [(C \to A) \bullet (D \to B)]) \to (\sim C \lor \sim D)$	1–17, CP

EXERCISE 8.6

PART A: Theorems Prove the following theorems using either CP or RAA.

* **1.** $\sim(P \to Q) \to (P \bullet \sim Q)$
  2. $\sim(A \bullet \sim A)$
  3. $[(S \lor R) \bullet \sim R] \to S$
* **4.** $(X \to Y) \to \sim(X \bullet \sim Y)$
  5. $(\sim F \bullet \sim G) \to (F \leftrightarrow G)$
  6. $\sim(H \bullet [(H \to J) \bullet (H \to \sim J)])$
* **7.** $K \to [(K \to L) \to L]$
  8. $\sim(M \leftrightarrow \sim M)$
  9. $(\sim N \to O) \lor (N \to O)$
* **10.** $(P \bullet \sim Q) \to \sim(P \leftrightarrow Q)$
  11. $[(\sim B \to \sim A) \to A] \to A$

12. ~[(X ↔ Y) • ~(X ∨ ~Y)]
13. ~F → (F → G)
14. [~H ∨ (~J ∨ K)] → [(~H ∨ J) → (~H ∨ K)]
15. [(~M ∨ M) → M] → M
16. [(P → Q) • (R → ~Q)] → ~(P • R)
17. D → (C → D)
18. ~[(E ∨ F) • ((E → G) • [(F → G) • ~G])]
19. (~X → Y) ∨ (X → Z)
20. [(A → B) ∨ (A → C)] → [A → (B ∨ C)]

PART B: Challenging Theorems Prove the following theorems using either CP or RAA.

* **1.** (T → U) ∨ (U → T)
  2. (D → E) → [(F → E) → ((D ∨ F) → E)]
  3. [(H → I) → H] → H
* **4.** [P ∨ (~P • Q)] ↔ (P ∨ Q)
  5. (R ↔ S) → [((T → R) ↔ (T → S)) • ((R → T) ↔ (S → T))]
  6. [(S ∨ T) • (Q ∨ R)] → [((S • Q) ∨ (S • R)) ∨ ((T • Q) ∨ (T • R))]
* **7.** [((L • M) ∨ (L • N)) ∨ ((P • M) ∨ (P • N))] → [(L ∨ P) • (M ∨ N)]
  8. [(K → J) • (Q → R)] → [((~K • ~Q) ∨ (~K • R)) ∨ ((J • ~Q) ∨ (J • R))]
  9. [((~E • ~G) ∨ (~E • H)) ∨ ((F • ~G) ∨ (F • H))] → [(E → F) • (G → H)]
***10.** [(A • B) ∨ (C • D)] → [((A ∨ C) • (A ∨ D)) • ((B ∨ C) • (B ∨ D))]

PART C: Corresponding Conditionals Form the corresponding conditional for each of the following symbolic arguments. Then construct a proof to show that each of the conditionals is a theorem.

* **1.** ~A ∨ ~B, B ∴ ~A
  2. C ↔ D, C ∴ D
  3. ~E ∴ E → F
  4. G → J, ~K → ~H, G ∨ H ∴ J ∨ K
  5. ~M ∨ ~S, ~L ∴ (~L • ~M) ∨ (~L • ~S)
  6. N • O ∴ P → N
  7. ~R, Q ∴ ~(Q → R)
  8. ~S ∨ T, ~T ∨ U ∴ U ∨ ~S
  9. ~(W → X), Z → X ∴ ~Z
  10. A ↔ ~A ∴ B

NOTES

1. The relevant work is Gerhard Gentzen, "Untersuchungen über das logische Schliessen," *Mathematische Zeitschrift* 39 (1934): 176–210, 405–431.
2. We learned this from our colleague, Ned Markosian.
3. For more on logical equivalence, see section 7.5.
4. The most famous intuitionist is the Dutch mathematician Luitzen Egbertus Jan Brouwer (1881–1966). See Anthony Flew, *A Dictionary of Philosophy* (New York: St. Martin's Press, 1979), p. 178.
5. Alas, the old adage that, for any statement you please, at least one extraordinarily intelligent philosopher has denied it, holds true here as well. See Graham Priest, *In Contradiction: A Study of the Transconsistent* (Oxford: Oxford University Press, 2006), expanded edition.
6. That's because, in intuitionistic logic, it is provable that $\sim\sim(p \lor \sim p)$, by *reductio ad absurdum* (see section 8.5) and DeM, and given $\sim\sim(p \lor \sim p)$, as a premise, LEM follows by two applications of DeM and DN, as follows.

1. $\sim\sim(p \lor \sim p)$	$\therefore p \lor \sim p$
2. $\sim(\sim p \bullet \sim\sim p)$	1, DeM
3. $\sim\sim p \lor \sim\sim\sim p$	2, DeM
4. $\sim\sim p \lor \sim p$	3, DN
5. $p \lor \sim p$	4, DN

7. The form of the argument and the observation that it cannot be proved directly from the rules of inference adopted thus far are borrowed from Howard Kahane, *Logic and Philosophy: A Modern Introduction*, 6th ed. (Belmont, CA: Wadsworth, 1990), p. 88.
8. As we pointed out earlier, intuitionists, and others besides, deny DN because they deny LEM. Thus, although they will agree that the essential logic underlying *reductio ad absurdum* is that because $\sim p$ leads to a contradiction, $\sim p$ is false, they will disagree that we can infer that p is true by DN. This textbook develops a system of classical logic, which affirms both LEM and DN. In classical logic, the appeal to DN is legitimate.

CHAPTER 9

Predicate Logic

*T*he system of natural deduction developed in Chapter 8 is powerful, but incomplete. Consider the following example:

> **1.** All skeptics are depressed. Some logicians are skeptics. So, some logicians are depressed.

This argument is obviously valid, but suppose we try to symbolize it, using the techniques of statement logic. Our scheme of abbreviation would look something like this:

> S: All skeptics are depressed; L: Some logicians are skeptics; D: Some logicians are depressed.

Using this scheme of abbreviation, (1) translates into symbols as follows:

> **2.** S, L ∴ D

But argument (2) is invalid. We can easily show this with an abbreviated truth table. (Simply assign falsehood to D and truth to S and L.) So, the validity of (1) is not revealed through the techniques of statement logic.

In Chapter 6, we explored the classical approach to categorical syllogisms like argument (1). In this chapter, we will see how categorical logic can be developed by adding certain elements to our system of statement logic. This modern treatment of categorical logic is due to the great German mathematician, Gottlob Frege (1848–1925)[1] and the current chapter draws heavily on his pioneering work.

The Language of Predicate Logic

In order to extend our system of natural deduction to cover categorical logic, we must first develop a method of symbolizing categorical statements. And in order to do that, we must first say a few words about predicates, constants, variables, and quantifiers.

Predicates, Constants, and Variables

Let us begin with a simple subject-predicate sentence:

3. Kripke is a logician.

This sentence says that a particular person or thing, Kripke, has a certain property or attribute, namely, *the property of being a logician.* If we let the lowercase letter k abbreviate the name "Kripke," and let the capital letter L abbreviate the predicate "is a logician," we can symbolize (3) as follows:

4. Lk

Similarly, if we let the lowercase letter b name the philosopher George Boolos and let the capital letter P express the property of *being a philosopher,* we can symbolize the statement "Boolos is a philosopher" as follows:

5. Pb

In this chapter, we will use capital letters A through Z to express properties (such as being human, being mortal, being rational, etc.). When so used, we will call these symbols **predicate letters.**

Predicate letters are capital letters—A through Z—used to express properties.

(Note that capital letters can still be used to stand for statements as needed, but we are here expanding their use.) Lowercase letters a through u will be used to name people, places, and things (such as Boethius, Rome, etc.). We will call these symbols **individual constants.**

Individual constants are lowercase letters—a through u—used to name individuals.

The remaining lowercase letters—v, w, x, y, and z—will serve as **individual variables.** Variables do not name individuals; they are used primarily as placeholders.

Individual variables are lowercase letters—v through z—used primarily as placeholders.

To grasp the idea of a placeholder, consider the following expression:

6. _____ is Greek.

The blank space here can be filled with the name of any individual. If we place a name for Socrates or Plato in the blank, a true statement results. If we place a name for George Washington or Abraham Lincoln in the blank, a false statement results. We can therefore symbolize (6) by letting the capital letter G abbreviate "is Greek" and by replacing the blank with a variable:

7. Gx

The expression "x is Greek" is neither true nor false, just as "_____ is Greek" is neither true nor false. So, Gx is not a statement (i.e., a sentence that is either true or false). We will instead call it a *statement function*, for if we replace the variable with a constant, we arrive at a statement. For example:

8. Gs

(A more careful definition of a statement function is given below.) It is very important to keep the distinction between individual constants and individual variables in mind. Remember: Individual constants (a through u) are always used as names, whereas individual variables (v through z) are primarily used as placeholders.

It is also very important to keep in mind the distinction between predicate letters and statement letters. When a capital letter is coupled with an individual constant or variable, it is a predicate letter that is being used to express a property—for example, Fa, Gd, and Px. When a capital letter is not coupled with an individual constant or variable, it is being used to stand for a statement—for instance, F, G, and P.

The Universal Quantifier

Suppose that we want to symbolize the statement "Everything is human." How do we go about this? First, we need a scheme of abbreviation to tell us what capital letter stands for the predicate "is human." We indicate the scheme of abbreviation in parentheses following the statement to be symbolized, like this:

9. Everything is human. (Hx: x is human)

Now, to symbolize this statement, we must employ a **quantifier.** A quantifier is an expression that is used to indicate how many things have a given property. For example, the words "all" and "some" are quantifiers in English.

 A **quantifier** is an expression used to indicate how many things have a given property.

To illustrate the concept of a quantifier, let us note that statement (9) bears a close relationship to the following expression:

10. _____ is human.

To say that everything is human is to say that (10) is true no matter how we fill in the blank. We can therefore express (9) this way:

11. For all x, x is human. (Hx: x is human)

For the sake of brevity, we will use a variable enclosed in parentheses to stand for the phrase "for all x." Thus, we can symbolize statement (11) as follows:

12. (x)Hx

(12) correctly symbolizes both (11) and (9). The symbol (x) is called a *universal quantifier*. It may be read variously as "for any x," "for every x," "for each x," and "for any individual x." Note that we could use a variable other than x to translate statement (9), since the variables in the scheme of abbreviation are merely placeholders. So, the following is also a correct symbolization of (9):

13. (y)Hy

The universal quantifier can also be used to symbolize a *universal affirmative* statement, such as the following:

14. All humans are mortal. (Hx: x is human; Mx: x is mortal)

Let us begin by rephrasing this universal affirmative. Statement (14) says, in effect, that *if anything is human, then it is mortal.* In other words, it says that the following expression is true no matter how we fill in the blank "If _____ is human, then _____ is mortal." We can therefore rewrite "All humans are mortal" as follows:

15. For all x, if x is human, then x is mortal.

The advantage of this technical language, which we will call "logicese," is that it is easily translated into symbols. Using the scheme of abbreviation provided, we can translate statement (15), and hence (14), into symbols as follows:

16. (x)(Hx → Mx)

Note that *universal affirmative statements involve the arrow.* This analysis of universal statements partially in terms of conditionals provides one of the crucial links between statement logic and categorical logic. Shortly, we will provide a similar analysis of universal negatives, particular affirmatives, and particular negatives. Each of these analyses essentially involves elements of statement logic. These Frege-style translations of Aristotelian categorical statements enable us to develop a system of proof for predicate logic that builds on the system of proof for statement logic.

Note that it would be wrong to symbolize (14) as:

17. (x)(Hx • Mx)

This says that everything in the entire universe is both human and mortal, which is clearly false. So, (17) is not equivalent to (16).

Universal affirmatives can be expressed in a variety of ways in English. For example, each of the following is a stylistic variant of "All humans are mortal":

a. Every human is mortal.

b. Each human is mortal.

c. Any human is mortal.

d. If anything is a human, then it is mortal.

e. A thing is human only if it is mortal.

f. Only mortals are humans.

Each of (a) through (f) is correctly symbolized by (16): (x)(Hx → Mx). Note that in (f), the order of the terms is reversed. The word "only" often causes con-fusion. For example, "All trees are plants" is *not* equivalent to "Only trees are plants"; the first statement is true, while the second is false. "All trees are plants" is equivalent to "Only plants are trees" because "Only plants are trees" is equiv-alent to "If a thing is not a plant, then it is not a tree," which, in turn, is equivalent to "If a thing is a tree, then it is a plant."

Let us now turn from the universal affirmative to the *universal negative:*

18. No trees are animals. (Tx: x is tree; Ax: x is an animal)

This says, in effect, that if anything is a tree, then it is not an animal. In logicese, statement (18) looks like this:

19. For any x, if x is a tree, then x is not an animal.

So, we can symbolize (18) by means of a universal quantifier, the arrow, and the tilde:

20. (x)(Tx → ~Ax)

There are various ways of expressing universal negatives in English. For example, (18) has the following stylistic variants:

a. Nothing that is a tree is an animal.

b. All trees are nonanimals.

c. If anything is a tree, then it is not an animal.

d. A thing is a tree only if it is not an animal.

e. Nothing is a tree unless it is not an animal.

f. Only nonanimals are trees.

(20) symbolizes each of (a) through (f).

Note that the placement of tildes is very important when translating universal negative statements. Consider the following examples:

21. Nothing is human. (Hx: x is human)

22. Not everything is human. (Hx: x is human)

23. Not every human is a hero. (Hx: x is a human; Ox: x is a hero)

In logicese, (21) becomes "For all x, x is not human." In symbols, we have (x)~Hx. We can rephrase (22) as "It is not the case that, for all x, x is human." In symbols, we have ~(x)Hx. And (23) translates into "It is not true that for all x, if x is a human, then x is a hero." In symbols, we have ~(x)(Hx → Ox). These examples underscore the fact that the placement of tildes requires careful attention.

The Existential Quantifier

We now introduce a second quantifier, called the *existential quantifier*. Our symbol for the existential quantifier looks like this: (∃x). (The "E" is backwards so it won't be confused with a predicate letter.) This symbol is read, "There exists some x such that" or "There is some x such that" or simply "For some x." Consider, for example, the following statement:

24. Something is mortal. (Mx: x is mortal)

To say that something is mortal is to say that there is some way of filling in the following blank that results in a true statement: "_____ is mortal." In logicese, "For some x, x is mortal." In symbols, we have this:

25. (∃x)Mx

The existential quantifier allows us to symbolize *particular affirmatives*, such as the following:

26. Some dogs are collies. (Dx: x is a dog; Cx: x is a collie)

(26) translates into logicese as "For some x, x is a dog and a collie." This translates into symbols as:

27. (∃x)(Dx • Cx)

Note that (27) is *not* equivalent to either of the following:

28. For some x, if x is a dog, then x is a collie.
29. (∃x)(Dx → Cx).

Both (28) and (29) tell us that something is such that *if* it is a dog, *then* it is a collie. Applying the rule MI, we see that (29) is logically equivalent to (∃x)(~Dx ∨ Cx). But this statement is true given that something is *either* not a dog or a collie. So, the mere existence of one thing that is not a dog—say, a desk or a duck—is sufficient to ensure the truth of (29). Hence, (29) is a far cry from "Some dogs are collies." *Therefore, when symbolizing particular affirmatives, we need to combine the existential quantifier with the dot rather than the arrow.*

Stylistic variants of "Some dogs are collies" include the following:

a. At least one dog is a collie.
b. There are dogs that are collies.
c. Something is both a dog and a collie.
d. There exists a dog that is a collie.
e. There is some dog that is a collie.

Each of these is correctly symbolized as follows: (∃x)(Dx • Cx).

The symbolization for *particular negative* statements is now apparent. Consider:

30. Some dogs are not collies. (Dx: x is a dog; Cx: x is collie)

Statement (30) translates into logicese as follows: "For some x, x is a dog and x is not a collie." In symbols, we have this:

31. (∃x)(Dx • ~Cx)

There are numerous ways of expressing particular negatives in English. For example, stylistic variants of "Some dogs are not collies" include the following:

a. At least one dog is not a collie.
b. There are dogs that are not collies.
c. Something is a dog but not a collie.
d. Not all dogs are collies.
e. Not every dog is a collie.

Note that (d) and (e) can be translated using either the existential quantifier or the universal quantifier:

32. (∃x)(Dx • ~Cx)
33. ~(x)(Dx → Cx)

Later in the chapter, we will be able to prove that these two statements are logically equivalent.

One final note of caution: The existential quantifier can sometimes be used to translate the word "any," since "any" can sometimes means "even one." This is clearest in the case of "if any" conditionals like:

34. If anyone complains, Dad is going to turn this car around.

What (34) says is that Dad will turn the car around if *even one* person complains—that is, if *there is* some person who complains. We must therefore use the existential quantifier when translating this into logicese:

35. If, for some x (x is a person and x complains), then Dad turns the car around. (Px: x is a person; Cx: x complains; d: Dad; Tx: x turns the car around)

In symbols, (35) becomes:

36. (∃x)(Px • Cx) → Td

The Language of Predicate Logic: A More Precise Formulation

To this point, our introduction to the language of predicate logic has been informal. But for clarity, we must provide a formal description of that language. This description may seem needlessly technical, but it is required if we are to avoid serious misunderstandings. In particular, we must have a clear grasp of what counts as a well-formed formula of predicate logic.

The vocabulary of predicate logic consists of statement letters (capital letters A through Z), individual constants (lowercase letters a through u), individual variables (v, w, x, y, and z), predicate letters (capital letters A through Z when coupled with individual constants or variables, e.g., Fa, Gx, and Hxy), the logical operators (~, ∨, •, →, and ↔), the quantifier symbols, and parentheses. An *expression* of predicate logic is any sequence of symbols in this vocabulary, such as (B → Fy ∨ (∃z)~. An *atomic formula* of predicate logic is either a statement letter, such as P or S, or a predicate letter coupled with individual constants or variables, such as Fa or Gxy.

In what follows, we will use the capital, cursive letters *P* and *Q* to stand for any expressions in the language of predicate logic. And we will use the bold

letter **x** to stand for any individual variable (v, w, x, y, and z). Using this notation, we can say that a symbolic expression is a **well-formed formula** (WFF) of
predicate logic under the following conditions:

1. Every atomic formula is a WFF.
2. If $\mathcal{P}$ is a WFF, then so is $(\mathbf{x})\mathcal{P}$.
3. If $\mathcal{P}$ is a WFF, then so $(\exists\mathbf{x})\mathcal{P}$.
4. If $\mathcal{P}$ is a WFF, then so is ~$\mathcal{P}$.
5. If $\mathcal{P}$ and $\mathcal{Q}$ are WFFs, then so is $(\mathcal{P} \bullet \mathcal{Q})$.
6. If $\mathcal{P}$ and $\mathcal{Q}$ are WFFs, then so is $(\mathcal{P} \vee \mathcal{Q})$.
7. If $\mathcal{P}$ and $\mathcal{Q}$ are WFFs, then so is $(\mathcal{P} \rightarrow \mathcal{Q})$.
8. If $\mathcal{P}$ and $\mathcal{Q}$ are WFFs, then so is $(\mathcal{P} \leftrightarrow \mathcal{Q})$.

Nothing counts as a WFF of predicate logic unless it can be demonstrated to be
one by application of the above conditions.*

Although nothing counts as a WFF unless it can be demonstrated to be
one via the previous conditions, we continue to allow some informal uses for the
sake of convenience; for example, we permit the omission of parentheses when
no ambiguity results. Thus, we may write Fa ∨ (y)Gy instead of (Fa ∨ (y)Gy).
Similarly, brackets may be employed to increase readability; accordingly, we may
write (x)[(Ax • Bx) → Cx] instead of (x)((Ax • Bx) → Cx).

Which of the following are WFFs? Which are not WFFs?

((x)Fx ∨ (∃y)Gy)
(x)(Hx → (∃x)(Hx))
(∃x)Kb
(j)Lj
(∃H)Hb

The first expression is a WFF. Fx and Gy are both atomic formulas, so both
are WFFs. Also, any WFF prefixed by a quantifier is a WFF, so (x)Fx and (∃y)Gy
are both WFFs. Finally, the disjunction of any two WFFs is a WFF, so ((x)Fx ∨
(∃y)Gy) is a WFF.

The second expression differs from the first in that it contains two x-
quantifiers and two appearances of the same predicate. Despite these differences,
it is also a WFF. Hx is an atomic formula, so it is a WFF. Any WFF prefixed by a

---

quantifier is a WFF, so (∃x)(Hx) is a WFF. And any conditional linking two WFFs is a WFF, so (Hx → (∃x)(Hx)) is a WFF. Finally, adding another quantifier to the front gives us yet another WFF.

The third expression differs from the previous two in that it contains an x-quantifier, but no occurrence of x. Despite this difference, it is also a WFF (essentially, it says that something is such that b is K). Kb is atomic, so it is a WFF. And affixing a quantifier to a WFF always results in a WFF.

The fourth expression is *not* a WFF because j is an individual constant, not a variable, and a quantifier must contain a variable: v, w, x, y, or z. The expression (j)Lj is therefore nonsense, like saying, "For all Abraham Lincoln, Abraham Lincoln is tall."

The fifth expression is *not* a WFF because H is a predicate letter and quantifiers in predicate logic must contain individual variables.[2] The expression (∃H) Hb is therefore nonsense, like saying, "There is some hairy, such that Bill Clinton is hairy."

Given an understanding of what counts as a WFF of predicate logic, we can easily grasp the important concepts of the *scope* of a quantifier, and of *free* and *bound* variables. The **scope** of a quantifier within a formula is the shortest WFF immediately to the right of the quantifier.

> The **scope** of a quantifier within a formula is the shortest WFF immediately to the right of the quantifier.

Here is an example:

37. (x)Hx → Mx

In (37), the scope of the quantifier (x) is Hx. And (37) must not be confused with the following:

38. (x)(Hx → Mx)

In (38), the scope of the quantifier is the conditional, (Hx → Mx). Here it may help to note that (Hx is not a WFF. Applying the conditions for being a WFF strictly—as we must—a parenthesis may appear only with the dot, the vee, the arrow, the double-arrow, or as part of a quantifier.

An occurrence of a variable **x** is **bound** if it lies within the scope of an **x**-quantifier.

> An occurrence of a variable **x** is **bound** if it lies within the scope of an **x**-quantifier.

To clarify, by this definition, (z) or (∃z) can bind only occurrences of z-variables; z-quantifiers cannot bind occurrences of, for example, y-variables. An occurrence of a variable is **free** if it is not bound.

> An occurrence of a variable is **free** if it is not bound.

Now, ignoring the variable contained in the quantifier, which variables in (37) are bound? Which are free? The x in "Hx" is bound, for it lies within the scope of the (x) quantifier; the x in "Mx" is free because it does not lie within the scope of any quantifier. By contrast, in (38), the quantifier binds both the x in "Hx" and the x in "Mx," for both fall within the scope of the quantifier.

Why does it matter whether a variable is bound or free? Let Hx mean "x is human" and Mx mean "x is mortal." Given this scheme of abbreviation, (38) means:

39. If anything is human, then *it* is mortal.

As we have seen, this is a stylistic variant of "All humans are mortal." The case of (37) is quite different. Here, the second occurrence of x is free, which means that it is functioning as a placeholder. In effect, (37) says something like the following:

40. If everything is human, then ___ is mortal.

In other words, (37) expresses a statement *function*, rather than a statement. In fact, the concept of a free occurrence of a variable allows us to state a precise definition of a statement function: A **statement function** is a WFF of predicate logic that includes a free occurrence of a variable.

> A **statement function** is a WFF of predicate logic that includes a free occurrence of a variable.

To ensure clarity regarding scope, consider one last example:

41. (∃y)(Ny → (x)Rx) • Sw

What is the scope of (∃y)? The shortest WFF immediately to the right of (∃y) is the conditional, (Ny → (x)Rx). And the y in "Ny" is bound by the (∃y) quantifier. What is the scope of (x)? Answer: Rx. And the x in "Rx" is bound by the quantifier (x). Note that (∃y) does not bind the x in "Rx." Quantifiers can bind only occurrences of the variables they contain, so (∃y) can bind only occurrences of y. Finally, because the occurrence of the variable w in (41) does not fall within the scope of any quantifier, the w in "Sw" is free.

We now have a precise understanding of the language of predicate logic. We also have the concept of the scope of a quantifier and of the concept of free and bound variables. The following table helps to summarize our method for symbolizing categorical statements.

Summary of Symbolizations

English	Logicese	Symbols
1. All ruffians are dangerous. (Rx: x is a ruffian; Dx: x is dangerous)	For all x (if x is a ruffian, then x is dangerous).	(x)(Rx → Dx)
2. No plants are minerals. (Px: x is a plant; Mx: x is a mineral)	For all x (if x is a plant, then x is not a mineral).	(x)(Px → ~Mx)
3. Some people are stingy. (Px: x is a person; Sx: x is stingy)	For some x (x is a person and x is stingy).	(∃x)(Px • Sx)
4. Some students are not bored. (Sx: x is a student; Bx: x is bored)	For some x (x is a student and x is not bored).	(∃x)(Sx • ~Bx)
5. Electrons exist. (Ex: x is an electron)	For some x, x is an electron.	(∃x)Ex
6. Everything is an electron. (Ex: x is an electron)	For all x, x is an electron.	(x)Ex
7. Vampires do not exist. (Vx: x is a vampire)	For all x, it is not the case that x is a vampire.	(x)~Vx
8. Something is a logician. (Lx: x is a logician)	For some x, x is a logician.	(∃x)Lx
9. Someone is a logician. (Px: x is a person; Lx: x is a logician)	For some x (x is a person and x is a logician).	(∃x)(Px • Lx)
10. If Aristotle is a logician, then there is at least one logician; (Lx: x is a logician, a: Aristotle)	If Aristotle is a logician, then for some x, x is a logician.	La → (∃x)Lx
11. Either Abelard is a logician or no one is a logician. (Lx: x is a logician; a: Abelard; Px: x is a person)	Either Abelard is a logician, or for all x (if x is a person, then x is not a logician).	La ∨ (x)(Px → ~Lx)

Summary of Symbolizations (*Continued*)

English	Logicese	Symbols
12. If everything is beautiful, then nothing is ugly. (Bx: x is beautiful; Ux: x is ugly)	If for all x, x is beautiful, then for all x, x is not ugly.	(x)Bx → (x)~Ux
13. Only women are mothers. (Wx: x is a woman; Mx: x is a mother)	For all x (if x is a mother, then x is a woman).	(x)(Mx → Wx)
14. If anything is red or blue, then it has a color. (Rx: x is red; Bx: x is blue; Cx: x has a color)	For all x [if (x is red or x is blue), then x has a color].	(x)[(Rx ∨ Bx) → Cx]
15. Some but not all humans are rational. (Hx: x is human; Rx: x is rational)	For some x (x is human and x is rational) and it is not the case that for all x (if x is human, then x is rational).	(∃x)(Hx • Rx) • ~(x)(Hx → Rx)

Summary of Definitions

Predicate letters are capital letters—A through Z—used to express properties.

Individual constants are lowercase letters—a through u—used to name individuals.

Individual variables are lowercase letters—v through z—used primarily as placeholders.

Quantifiers are expressions used to indicate how many things have a given property.

The **scope** of a quantifier within a formula is the shortest WFF immediately to the right of the quantifier.

An occurrence of a variable **x** is **bound** if it lies within the scope of an **x**-quantifier.

An occurrence of a variable is **free** if it is not bound.

A **statement function** is a WFF of predicate logic that includes a free occurrence of a variable.

EXERCISE 9.1

PART A: Well-Formed Formulas? Which of the following are well-formed formulas (WFFs)? Which are not?

* **1.** (x)Ax
 2. (x)(Ax)
 3. ~(∃y)By
* **4.** (a)Ca
 5. (z)~Tz
 6. (~x)Hx
* **7.** ~(x)~Jx
 8. Cx
 9. (z)P~z

* **10.** (∃z)(Sx • Rz)
 11. (∃u)Gu
 12. (w)(~Dw)
* **13.** (P • (x)Fx)
 14. ((x)Gx → (x)Nx)
 15. (y)(My → ~Oy)
* **16.** ~b
 17. (y)(Hy ∨ (∃y)Fy)
 18. ((y)Ry ∨ (∃z)~Sz)

* **19.** (x)((Fx ∨ Gx) → Hx)
 20. (Q • (Rg ∨ (x)Ex))
 21. (∃x)Ba
* **22.** (z)M
 23. (∃y)Gx
 24. (∃x)(∃x)Fx
* **25.** (y)(∃x)Sxy

PART B: Free and Bound Variables Ignoring the variables contained in the quantifiers, determine which occurrences of variables are free and which are bound in the following formulas.

* **1.** (x)(Hx ∨ Gy)
 2. (x)(y)(Ax ↔ By) ∨ ~Bz
 3. (∃y)(Cy ∨ Db) • Ed
* **4.** (z)[(Fz ∨ Gz) → Jx]
 5. (∃x)Kx • (x)Lx
 6. (x)(Mx ∨ (y)~Ny)
* **7.** (x)(y)Pxy • Qx
 8. (∃y)(R • Sy)
 9. (x)[(Tx ∨ Ux) → ~Ax]
* **10.** (x)[(Bx • (y)Dy) ↔ (z)Ez]
 11. (x)(∃y)[(∃z)Fxz ∨ (z)Fyz]
 12. (z)[~Ge → (Hz ∨ Ky)]
* **13.** (∃x)Lx • (∃x)Nx
 14. (y)[(Ox ∨ (x)Px) ↔ Wy]
 15. (x)[(y)(Abz ∨ By) → Cyx]

PART C: Symbolizing Symbolize the following statements using the schemes of abbreviation provided.

* **1.** No Zoroastrians are Muslims. (Zx: x is a Zoroastrian; Mx: x is a Muslim)
 2. All kangaroos are marsupials. (Kx: x is a kangaroo; Mx: x is a marsupial)

3. Peter Abelard is a logician, but Jacob Boehme is not. (Lx: x is a logician; a: Peter Abelard; b: Jacob Boehme)

* **4.** Not every marsupial is a kangaroo. (Mx: x is a marsupial; Kx: x is a kangaroo)

5. Nothing is right. (Rx: x is right)

6. Not everything is right. (Rx: x is right)

* **7.** Something is right. (Rx: x is right)

8. Something is not right. (Rx: x is right)

9. Only dogs are animals. (Dx: x is a dog; Ax: x is an animal)

* **10.** At least one mortal is human. (Mx: x is mortal; Hx: x is human)

11. A thing is a logician only if it is rational. (Lx: x is a logician; Rx: x is rational)

12. All trees are nonanimals. (Tx: x is a tree; Ax: x is an animal)

* **13.** Some people are good and some people are not good. (Px: x is a person; Gx: x is good)

14. Something is both good and evil. (Gx: x is good; Ex: x is evil)

15. There exists a person who is good. (Px: x is a person; Gx: x is good)

* **16.** Only blue things are sky-blue. (Bx: x is blue; Sx: x is sky-blue)

17. If Socrates is not a philosopher, then Aristotle is not a philosopher. (s: Socrates; Px: x is a philosopher; a: Aristotle)

18. Not all animals are rational. (Ax: x is an animal; Rx: x is rational)

* **19.** There exists an animal that has a soul. (Ax: x is an animal; Sx: x has a soul)

20. If all bats are mammals, then some mammals have wings. (Bx: x is a bat; Mx: x is a mammal; Wx: x has wings)

21. All birds except penguins can fly. (Bx: x is a bird; Px: x is a penguin; Fx: x can fly)

* **22.** All and only circles are perfect. (Cx: x is a circle; Px: x is perfect)

23. One fails the course when blowing off the final exam. (Px: x is a person; Fx: x fails the course; Bx: x blows off the final exam)

24. If any explorer discovers gold, then he or she will become famous. (Ex: x is an explorer; Dx: x discovers gold; Fx: x will become famous)

* **25.** Humans are featherless bipeds. (Hx: x is human; Fx: x is featherless; Bx: x is a biped)

PART D: More Symbolizing Symbolize the following statements using the schemes of abbreviation provided.

* **1.** A thing is a cat only if it is an animal. (Cx: x is a cat; Ax: x is an animal)

2. Some people are wicked. (Px: x is a person; Wx: x is wicked)

3. Some diseases are not fatal. (Dx: x is a disease; Fx: x is fatal)

* **4.** Every logic student is wise. (Lx: x is a logic student; Wx: x is wise)

5. No soldier is a sailor. (Sx: x is a soldier; Ax: x is a sailor)

   6. Only animals are wolves. (Ax: x is an animal; Wx: x is a wolf)

* **7.** Everything is an illusion. (Ix: x is an illusion)

   8. Not everything is an illusion. (Ix: x is an illusion)

   9. Either something is an illusion or nothing is an illusion. (Ix: x is an illusion)

***10.** Nothing is right unless it is not wrong. (Rx: x is right; Wx: x is wrong)

  11. If neither Aristotle nor Boole is a logician, there are no logicians. (Lx: x is a logician; a: Aristotle; b: Boole)

  12. Some but not all paintings are forgeries. (Px: x is a painting; Fx: x is a forgery)

***13.** If everything is mental, then nothing is physical. (Mx: x is mental; Px: x is physical)

  14. If nothing is mortal, then nothing is human. (Mx: x is mortal; Hx: x is human)

  15. If everyone is sad, then no one is happy. (Sx: x is sad; Px: x is a person; Hx: x is happy)

***16.** If anyone is sad, then he or she is not happy. (Sx: x is sad; Px: x is a person; Hx: x is happy)

  17. If Cudworth is a logician and all logicians are bores, then he is a bore. (Lx: x is a logician; Bx: x is a bore; c: Cudworth)

  18. Something is red all over and something is green all over, but it is not true that something is both red all over and green all over. (Rx: x is red all over; Gx: x is green all over)

***19.** If ghosts do not exist, then no houses are haunted. (Gx: x is ghost; Hx: x is a house; Nx: x is haunted)

  20. If any number is odd, then not every number is even. (Nx: x is a number; Ox: x is odd; Ex: x is even)

  21. No bears, with the exception of teddy bears, are safe. (Bx: x is a bear; Tx: x is a teddy bear; Sx: x is safe)

***22.** Only large rodents are capybaras. (Lx: x is large; Rx: x is a rodent; Cx: x is a capybara)

  23. Among sports, only football is painful. (Sx: x is a sport; Fx: x is football; Px: x is painful)

  24. All and only hip cats play jazz. (Hx: x is hip; Cx: x is a cat; Jx: x plays jazz)

***25.** None but surfers are cool. (Sx: x is a surfer; Cx: x is cool)

PART E: Quiz on Symbolizing Symbolize the following statements using the schemes of abbreviation provided.

   1. Every wombat is a marsupial. (Wx: x is a wombat; Mx: x is a marsupial)

   2. No wombat is a duck. (Wx: x is a wombat; Dx: x is a duck)

   3. Some rectangles are squares. (Rx: x is a rectangle; Sx: x is a square)

   4. At least one rectangle is not a square. (Rx: x is a rectangle; Sx: x is a square)

   5. Not every person is a vegetarian. (Px: x is a person; Vx: x is a vegetarian)

6. Something is both green and not green. (Gx: x is green)

7. Only cats are mammals. (Cx: x is a cat; Mx: x is a mammal)

8. A thing is a sphere only if it is not a cube. (Sx: x is sphere; Cx: x is a cube)

9. There exists a tree that is an oak. (Tx: x is a tree; Ox: x is an oak)

10. If everything is blue, then nothing is red. (Bx: x is blue; Rx: x is red)

PART F: Challenging Translations

Translate the following statements into symbols using the schemes of abbreviation provided. (*Note:* Some of these are rather difficult.)

* **1.** No rectangle is a square unless it is equilateral. (Rx: x is a rectangle; Sx: x is a square; Ex: x is equilateral)

2. Not all murderers deserve capital punishment, but Smith is a murderer who deserves capital punishment. (Mx: x is a murderer; Dx: x deserves capital punishment; s: Smith)

3. If Darwin is not a biologist, then no one is a biologist. (d: Darwin; Bx: x is a biologist; Px: x is a person)

* **4.** None but citizens can vote. (Cx: x is a citizen; Vx: x can vote)

5. Only citizens can vote. (Cx: x is a citizen; Vx: x can vote)

6. If everything is a human, then Fido is a human. (Hx: x is a human; f: Fido)

* **7.** If all humans are mortal but Socrates is not mortal, then Socrates is not human. (Hx: x is human; Mx: x is mortal; s: Socrates)

8. If everyone is wise, then no one is a fool. (Px: x is a person; Wx: x is wise; Fx: x is a fool)

9. If anyone is wise, then he or she is not a fool. (Px: x is a person; Wx: x is wise; Fx: x is a fool)

* **10.** Fetuses lack a right to life if they are neither humans nor moral agents. (Fx: x is a fetus; Rx: x has a right to life; Hx: x is human; Mx: x is a moral agent)

11. None but men are fathers. (Mx: x is a man; Fx: x is a father)

12. If anyone is either courageous or just, then he is virtuous. (Px: x is a person; Cx: x is courageous; Jx: x is just; Vx: x is virtuous)

* **13.** If Bob is a dog and all dogs are animals, then Bob is an animal. (b: Bob; Dx: x is a dog; Ax: x is an animal)

14. Either no one is wise or Solomon is wise. (Px: x is a person; Wx: x is wise; s: Solomon)

15. All and only married men are husbands. (Mx: x is married; Nx: x is a man; Hx: x is a husband)

* **16.** If anyone is both happy and sad, then he is confused. (Px: x is a person; Hx: x is happy; Sx: x is sad; Cx: x is confused)

17. At least one nonphysical thing exists given that God exists. (Px: x is physical; G: God exists)

18. Only benevolent deities are worthy of worship. (Bx: x is benevolent; Dx: x is a deity; Wx: x is worthy of worship)

*19. Nothing is good unless something is evil. (Gx: x is good; Ex: x is evil)

20. No animal is a dog unless it is a mammal. (Ax: x is an animal; Dx: x is a dog; Mx: x is a mammal)

21. When it rains, it pours, and an old man snores. (R: It is raining; P: It is pouring; Mx: x is a man; Ox: x is old; Sx: x snores)

*22. The whale is neither a killer nor a fish. (Wx: x is a whale; Kx: x is a killer; Fx: x is a fish)

23. Some artists are not painters but dancers. (Ax: x is an artist; Px: x is a painter; Dx: x is a dancer)

24. No shark attacks unless provoked. (Sx: x is a shark; Ax: x attacks; Px: x is provoked)

*25. If anyone can play chess, Kasparov can. (Px: x is a person; Cx: x can play chess; k: Kasparov)

9.2   Demonstrating Invalidity

An **algorithm** is a precisely described and finite procedure for solving a problem. The truth tables we studied in Chapter 7 are an algorithm for statement logic. If we follow the correct procedures for constructing a truth table, we can determine the validity of any argument within statement logic. Unfortunately, there is no such algorithm for predicate logic. This was proved in 1936 by the American logician Alonzo Church.[3] Nevertheless, there are methods similar to truth tables that can be used to evaluate many arguments in predicate logic. We will examine one such method in this section, *the finite universe method.*

> An **algorithm** is a precisely described and finite procedure for solving a problem.

An argument is invalid if it is *possible* for its conclusion to be false while its premises are true. Thus, if we can describe a possible situation in which the conclusion of an argument is false while its premises are true, then we have shown the argument to be invalid. This is the essential principle underlying the finite universe method. And the finite universe method enables us to describe such situations simply and abstractly by imagining universes with a small number of objects.

To understand the finite universe method, we must first understand the meaning of quantified statements in universes containing a small number of objects. For instance, let us imagine a universe containing only two objects—a and b. We can picture it like this:

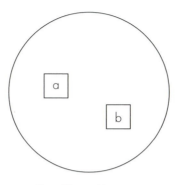

Two-Object Universe

Let us first consider the meaning of universally quantified statements in a two-object universe. A **universally quantified statement** is a WFF of the form $(\mathbf{x})\mathcal{P}$, where the bold **x** stands for any variable.

 A **universally quantified statement** is a WFF of the form $(\mathbf{x})\mathcal{P}$.

For example:

> **42.** Everything is red. (Rx: x is red)
> *In symbols:* (x)Rx

Because a and b are the only items in this universe, (x)Rx is equivalent *in this universe* to the following conjunction:

Ra • Rb

In general, in a finite universe, a universally quantified statement is equivalent to a certain conjunction.

We also need to consider the meaning of existentially quantified statements. An **existentially quantified statement** is a WFF of the form $(\exists\mathbf{x})\mathcal{P}$, where the bold **x** stands for any variable.

 An **existentially quantified statement** is a WFF of the form $(\exists\mathbf{x})\mathcal{P}$.

For example:

> **43.** Something is red. (Rx: x is red)
>   *In symbols:* (∃x)Rx

This statement is equivalent, in our two-object universe, to the following disjunction:

Ra ∨ Rb

In general, in a finite universe, an existentially quantified statement is equivalent to a certain disjunction.

To ensure understanding, let us consider a slightly larger universe containing three objects—a, b, and c:

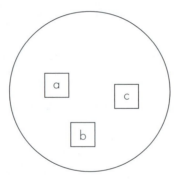

Three-Object Universe

In this universe, (x)Rx is equivalent to the following conjunction:

Ra • (Rb • Rc)

And in this universe, (∃x)Rx is equivalent to the following disjunction:

Ra ∨ (Rb ∨ Rc)

We could continue working out these equivalences for universes of larger (but finite) sizes. However, the general principle should be clear at this point: Universally quantified statements become conjunctions; existentially quantified statements become disjunctions.

A special case worth noting is that of a universe with only one object:

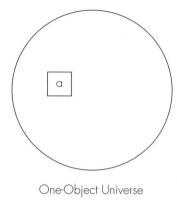

One-Object Universe

In this universe, "Everything is red" is equivalent to "a is red" (in symbols, Ra). But "Something is red" is also equivalent (in our one-object universe) to "a is red" (in symbols, Ra). Thus, in a one-object universe, (x)Rx is equivalent to (∃x)Rx.

Let us now consider the meaning of *universal affirmative* and *particular affirmative* statements in a two-object universe. Here is a universal affirmative statement in both English and symbols:

    44. All collies are dogs. (Cx: x is a collie; Dx: x is a dog)
        In symbols: (x)(Cx → Dx)

In a universe containing just two objects, a and b, this universal affirmative statement is equivalent to the following conjunction:

    (Ca → Da) • (Cb → Db)

As before, universally quantified statements become conjunctions, but note that an arrow appears in each conjunct.

Here is a particular affirmative statement in both English and symbols:

    45. Some dogs are collies. (Dx: x is a dog; Cx: x is a collie)
        In symbols: (∃x)(Dx • Cx)

In a universe containing only two objects, a and b, this particular affirmative statement is equivalent to the following disjunction:

    (Da • Ca) ∨ (Db • Cb)

Note that the dot appears in each disjunct.

The process of translating universally quantified statements into conjunctions, and existentially quantified statements into disjunctions, should now be clear. To apply the finite universe method, we first translate the premises and conclusion of an argument into atomic formulas (for a one-object universe) or conjunctions and disjunctions (for a multiple-object universe). We then apply the method of abbreviated truth tables to determine whether the conclusion can be false while the premises are true. The basic idea is that the validity of an argument does not depend on there being a large number of objects in the universe. For instance, if a pattern of reasoning allows for true premises and a false conclusion in a two-object universe, then that pattern of reasoning is invalid. No further proof is needed.

Let's try the method out on a short argument:

46. Nothing red is blue. Something is not blue. So, something is red. (Rx: x is red; Bx: x is blue)

In symbols: (x)(Rx → ~Bx), (∃x)~Bx ∴ (∃x)Rx

To keep things as simple as we can, we first translate the premises and conclusion for a one-object universe, like this:

Ra → ~Ba, ~Ba ∴ Ra

Now, we apply the method of abbreviated truth tables. If we can find a truth-value assignment in which the premises are true while the conclusion is false, we have shown the argument to be invalid:

Ra	Ba	Ra → ~Ba, ~Ba ∴ Ra
F	F	F T T F T F F

This assignment does the job. We have shown that it is possible for an argument of the preceding pattern to have true premises and a false conclusion. Hence, the form is invalid. (We could obtain the same result by translating the premises and conclusion for a two-object universe, a three-object universe, and so on, but there is no need to do so.)

A one-object universe will not always be adequate for our purposes. Consider the following argument:

47. Nothing good is evil. Something is good. So, nothing is evil. (Gx: x is good; Ex: x is evil)

In symbols: (x)(Gx → ~Ex), (∃x)Gx ∴ (x)~Ex

For a one-object universe, the argument translates as follows:

Ga → ~Ea, Ga ∴ ~Ea

Now, we apply the abbreviated truth table method:

Ga Ea	Ga → ~Ea, Ga ∴ ~Ea
	T / F T T F T

Although we hypothesized that the premises could be true (while the conclusion is false), we were forced to contradict the hypothesis, as the symbol "/" indicates. So, let's try a two-object universe:

Ga Ea Gb Eb	(Ga → ~Ea) • (Gb → ~Eb), Ga ∨ Gb ∴ ~Ea • ~Eb
T F F T	T TTF T T F TFT TT F TF FF T

Here, the premises are true and the conclusion is false. This shows that the argument form is invalid, for there are circumstances in which it leads from true premises to a false conclusion.

To show that certain kinds of arguments are invalid, we need to consider a universe containing at least three objects. Here is an example:

48. (∃x)(Ax • ~Bx), (∃x)(Bx • ~Ax) ∴ (x)(Ax ∨ Bx)

Aa Ba Ab Bb Ac Bc	(Aa • ~Ba) ∨ [(Ab • ~Bb) ∨ (Ac • ~Bc)],
F F T F F T	F FTF T T TTF T F FFT

(Ba • ~Aa) ∨ [(Bb • ~Ab) ∨ (Bc • ~Ac)] ∴ (Aa ∨ Ba) • [(Ab ∨ Bb) • (Ac ∨ Bc)]

F FTF T F FFT TTTTF   F F F   TTF T FTT

This method becomes rather unwieldy as we consider universes with more than two members. The good news is that in many cases, a one- or two-object universe will be sufficient to reveal the invalidity of an argument.

The bad news here is multiple. First, there are invalid arguments within predicate logic whose invalidity *cannot* be shown via the finite universe method. These arguments belong to the logic of relations, the more advanced part of predicate logic (see section 9.5).[4] Second, there are cases in which a large (though finite) universe would be needed to apply the finite universe method, making it impractical without a computer. For instance, some invalid arguments can be shown to be invalid only in a universe with at least 2^n objects, where n is the number of predicate letters. So, if such an argument has only three predicate letters, then the finite universe method would require a universe with eight objects.

In spite of these limitations, the finite universe method can deepen our understanding of the meaning of quantified statements by revealing a great many invalid inferences. In practice, it is usually best to consider a one-object universe first and then try a two- or three-object universe as needed.

Using the finite universe method, we can now sort out some issues that arose in Chapter 5 as we discussed the Aristotelian Square of Opposition. Recall that *corresponding* categorical statements have the same subject and predicate terms. And from an Aristotelian perspective, a universal affirmative statement implies its corresponding particular affirmative—for example, "All unicorns are animals" implies "Some unicorns are animals." Similarly, a universal negative statement implies its corresponding particular negative—for example, "No unicorns are horses" implies "Some unicorns are not horses." Modern logicians, following George Boole, deny that these inferences are valid. Let's examine the inference from a universal affirmative to its corresponding particular affirmative, using the finite universe method.

49. All unicorns are animals. So, some unicorns are animals. (Ux: x is a unicorn; Ax: x is an animal)

In symbols: $(x)(Ux \rightarrow Ax)$ ∴ $(\exists x)(Ux \bullet Ax)$

The invalidity is demonstrable in a one-object universe:

Ua Aa	$Ua \rightarrow Aa$ ∴ $Ua \bullet Aa$
F T	F T T F F T

In general, the inference from a universal affirmative to its corresponding particular affirmative will move from truth to falsehood when the subject terms denote an empty class. The inference from universal negative statements to their corresponding particular negatives is invalid for the same reason.

Here is a related point. In the Aristotelian scheme, corresponding universal affirmative and universal negative statements are said to be **contraries.** Contraries cannot both be true, but they can both be false.

 Contraries are statements that cannot both be true, but can both be false.

To illustrate, "All unicorns are animals" and "No unicorns are animals," according to Aristotelians, are contraries. But according to modern logicians, these statements are not contraries because they can both be true. Now, if the Aristotelians are right, the following argument should be valid:

50. All unicorns are animals. So, it is false that no unicorns are animals. (Ux: x is a unicorn; Ax: x is an animal)

That is, if "All unicorns are animals" and "No unicorns are animals" are contraries, then if "All unicorns are animals" is true, "No unicorns are animals" must be false. Here's the argument in symbols:

$(x)(Ux \rightarrow Ax)$ ∴ $\sim(x)(Ux \rightarrow \sim Ax)$

We translate for a one-object universe and assign truth values as follows:

Ua Aa	Ua → Aa ∴ ~(Ua → ~Aa)
F T	F T T F F T F T

On this truth-value assignment, the premise is true and the conclusion is false, so the inference is invalid. The reason is this: The conditionals Ua → Aa and Ua → ~Aa are both true when Ua is false. And, of course, Ua is false assuming the class of unicorns is empty. We can generalize this point as follows: *Whenever the subject term of corresponding universal affirmative and universal negative statements denotes an empty class, both statements are true.* This is why modern logicians deny the Aristotelian thesis that corresponding universal affirmative and universal negative statements are contraries.

Before bringing our discussion of the finite universe method to a close, let us consider a special complication that arises when one quantifier falls within the scope of another. For example:

(∃x)(Sx → (y)Ry) ∴ (y)[(∃x)Sx → Ry]

Note that in the premise, the scope of (∃x), is (Sx → (y)Ry), so that the (y) quantifier falls within the scope of (∃x). The situation is reversed in the conclusion, where the scope of (y) is [(∃x)Sx → Ry], and the (∃x) quantifier lies within the scope of (y). How do we translate such formulas for a two-object universe? It may help to translate them in two stages, one quantifier at a time. Let's start with the premise:

Stage 1: (Sa → (y)Ry) ∨ (Sb → (y)Ry)
Stage 2: (Sa → [Ra • Rb]) ∨ (Sb → [Ra • Rb])

In stage 1, we translated the existential quantifier and in stage 2 the universal quantifier. (The order doesn't matter.) The translation of the conclusion is as follows:

Stage 1: [(∃x)Sx → Ra] • [(∃x)Sx → Rb]
Stage 2: [(Sa ∨ Sb) → Ra] • [(Sa ∨ Sb) → Rb]

In stage 1, we translated the universal quantifier and in stage 2 the existential quantifier. The following truth-value assignment reveals the invalidity of the argument:

Sa Ra Rb Sb	(Sa → [Ra • Rb]) ∨ (Sb → [Ra • Rb])
F F F T	F T F F F T T F F F F

∴ [(Sa ∨ Sb) → Ra] • [(Sa ∨ Sb) → Rb]

F T T   F   F   F   F T T   F   F

The fact that the argument is invalid underscores the importance of the scope of the quantifiers, from the standpoint of logic.

Summary of the Finite Universe Method

1. Translate the premises and conclusion of the argument into symbols.
2. In a one-object universe, translate all quantified statements into atomic formulas.
3. In a multiple-object universe, translate universally quantified statements into conjunctions.
4. In a multiple-object universe, translate existentially quantified statements into disjunctions.
5. Apply the method of abbreviated truth tables to determine whether it is possible for the conclusion to be false while the premises are true.

Summary of Definitions

An **algorithm** is a precisely described and finite procedure for solving a problem.

A **universally quantified statement** is a WFF of the form $(x)\mathcal{P}$.

An **existentially quantified statement** is a WFF of the form $(\exists x)\mathcal{P}$.

Contraries are statements that cannot both be true, but can both be false.

EXERCISE 9.2

PART A: Demonstrating Invalidity Use the finite universe method to show that the following symbolic arguments are invalid. All of these exercises can be completed using either one-object or two-object universes.

* **1.** $(x)(Ax \to Bx) \therefore (\exists x)(Ax \bullet Bx)$

  2. $(\exists x)Cx \therefore (x)Cx$

  3. $(z)(Fz \to {\sim}Gz), (\exists z)(Fz \bullet {\sim}Hz) \therefore (\exists z)(Gz \bullet Hz)$

* **4.** $(\exists y)Ky \to (\exists y)Ly \therefore (y)(Ky \to Ly)$

  5. $(\exists x)(Ax \to Bx) \therefore (x)(Ax \to Bx)$

  6. $(\exists x)(Rx \to Sx) \therefore (x)Rx \to (x)Sx$

* **7.** $(x)Hx \to (x){\sim}Jx \therefore (x)(Jx \to {\sim}Hx)$

  8. $(\exists z)Mz, (\exists z)Nz \therefore (\exists z)(Mz \bullet Nz)$

  9. $(x)(Ax \to Bx), (\exists x)Bx \therefore (\exists x)Ax$

 10. $(\exists y)(Ry \to Sy) \therefore (\exists y)Ry \to (\exists y)Sy$

 11. $(x)(Cx \to {\sim}Dx) \therefore {\sim}(x)(Cx \to Dx)$

 12. $(\exists z)(Nz \leftrightarrow Pz) \therefore (z)(Nz \leftrightarrow Pz)$

*13. (y)(Ay → By), Bd ∴ Ad

14. (x)Fx → (x)Gx ∴ (x)(Fx → Gx)

15. (∃x)Dx, (∃x)Cx ∴ (x)(Dx • Cx)

*16. (x)(Mx → Nx), (∃x)Mx ∴ (x)Nx

17. ~(∃y)(Sy • Py) ∴ (∃y)(Sy • ~Py)

18. (x)Tx ↔ (x)Ux ∴ (x)(Tx ↔ Ux)

*19. (∃z)(Az • Bz), (∃z)(Cz • Bz) ∴ (∃z)(Az • Cz)

20. (x)(Ox ∨ Px) ∴ (x)Ox ∨ (x)Px

21. ~[(∃x)Hx → (y)Ny] ∴ (∃x)(Hx → (y)Ny)

*22. ~(x)(Ax → (∃y)By) ∴ (x)Ax → (∃y)By

23. (∃x)(Lx → (z)Mz) ∴ (∃x)Lx → (z)Mz

24. (y)Fy → (∃x)Gx ∴ (x)[(y)Fy → Gx]

*25. (x)Sx → (∃y)Ry ∴ (x)(Sx → (∃y)Ry)

26. (x)(Lx → Nx) ∴ (∃x)Lx → (x)Nx

27. (x)Fx → (y)Gy ∴ (x)[Fx → (y)Gy]

*28. ~(x)(Ax → Bx) ∴ (x)Ax → (x)Bx

29. (x)[(∃y)Uy • Zx] ∴ (x)(Ux • Zx)

30. (∃x)[(y)Ry → Tx] ∴ (y)Ry → (x)Tx

PART B: English Arguments Translate the following English arguments into symbols. Then use the finite universe method to show that the arguments are invalid.

* 1. All students who take logic are courageous. Therefore, some students who take logic are courageous. (Sx: x is a student; Lx: x takes logic; Cx: x is courageous)

2. All human beings are moral agents. Hence, all moral agents are human beings. (Hx: x is a human being; Mx: x is a moral agent)

3. Every general is arrogant. There are lieutenants who are not generals. It follows that at least one lieutenant is not arrogant. (Gx: x is a general; Ax: x is arrogant; Lx: x is a lieutenant)

* 4. All saints are good people. Some bankers are good people. Consequently, some bankers are saints. (Sx: x is saint; Gx: x is a good person; Bx: x is a banker)

5. Nothing is a lover unless it is not a fighter. If anything is a fighter, then it is not a peacemaker. Accordingly, no lovers are peacemakers. (Lx: x is a lover; Fx: x is a fighter; Px: x is a peacemaker)

6. There is an x such that if x is a tycoon, then x is a rapscallion. Thus, some tycoons are rapscallions. (Tx: x is a tycoon; Rx: x is a rapscallion)

7. If everything is a circle, then everything is a square. Therefore, if anything is a circle, then it is square. (Cx: x is a circle; Sx: x is a square)

8. Something is guilty. We may infer that Bob Smith is guilty. (Gx: x is guilty; b: Bob Smith)

9. Nothing that is a ghost is also a vampire. So, there exists a ghost who is not a vampire. (Gx: x is a ghost; Vx: x is a vampire)

10. All anarchists are fanatics. All communists are fanatics. We may infer that all communists are anarchists. (Ax: x is an anarchist; Fx: x is a fanatic; Cx: x is a communist)

11. If anything is a human, then it is a sinner. Dracula is not a human. Hence, Dracula is not a sinner. (Hx: x is a human; Sx: x is a sinner; d: Dracula)

12. Everything that is fully caused by material antecedents is determined. Some determined events are not free. Consequently, some things that are fully caused by material antecedents are not free. (Cx: x is fully caused by material antecedents; Dx: x is a determined event; Fx: x is free)

13. Only acts that promote the general happiness are morally obligatory. Not all acts that promote the general happiness are socially acceptable. Therefore, at least one act that is socially acceptable is not morally obligatory. (Ax: x is an act; Px: x promotes the general happiness; Mx: x is morally obligatory; Sx: x is socially acceptable)

14. All scientists who are engaged in cancer research are vivisectionists. Some vivisectionists are well intentioned but misguided. Therefore, some scientists who are engaged in cancer research are well intentioned but misguided. (Sx: x is a scientist; Cx: x is engaged in cancer research; Vx: x is a vivisectionist; Wx: x is well intentioned; Mx: x is misguided)

15. Only things approved of by either God or society are morally permissible. Some acts of violence are approved of by either God or society. Hence, some acts of violence are morally permissible. (Gx: x is approved of by God; Sx: x is approved of by society; Mx: x is morally permissible; Vx: x is an act of violence)

9.3 Constructing Proofs

In this section and the next, we will extend our practice of employing proofs to establish validity. We begin by observing that all the rules of statement logic still apply within predicate logic. For example, consider the following argument:

51. If Christine is not intimidated by predicate logic, then she has not been paying attention. But Christine has been paying attention. So, she is intimidated by predicate logic. (c: Christine; Lx: x is intimidated by predicate logic; Px: x has been paying attention)

We can symbolize this argument and prove it valid as follows:

1. ~Lc → ~Pc
2. Pc   ∴ Lc
3. ~~Pc   2, DN
4. ~~Lc   1, 3, MT
5. Lc   4, DN

Because Lc and Pc are statements, they can be moved about in accordance with the rules of statement logic, just as statement letters can. Here's another example:

52. If something is a moral agent, then it is rational. So, everything is either rational or not a moral agent. (Mx: x is a moral agent; Rx: x is rational)

1. (x)(Mx → Rx)   ∴ (x)(Rx ∨ ~Mx)
2. (x)(~Mx ∨ Rx)   1, MI
3. (x)(Rx ∨ ~Mx)   2, Com

This inference is permitted because material implication and commutation are both equivalence rules, and equivalence rules, unlike implicational rules, can be applied to parts of lines in a proof (as well as to entire lines).

We will now move beyond statement logic to add four implicational rules of inference that are specific to predicate logic. To grasp these rules, however, one must first understand what it is to be an *instance* of a quantified formula. The idea is straightforward. Begin with a quantified formula:

A. (x)[Fx → (∃y)(Gy ∨ Hx)]

Removing the (x) quantifier from the front of this formula leaves us with two free occurrences of the x-variable:

B. Fx → (∃y)(Gy ∨ Hx)

(Note that the y in "Gy" remains bound by (∃y).) Because (B) contains free occurrences of a variable, it is not a statement, but a statement function—it says, in essence, "If ___ is F, then (something is G or ___ is F)." However, we can turn (B) into a statement by filling in the blanks:

C. Fa → (∃y)(Fy ∨ Ha)

We now have an *instance* of the universally quantified formula (A). The operation that takes us from (A) to (C) is called *instantiation*, while the constant introduced at the final step—in this case, a—is called the *instantial constant*.

More generally, let the cursive letter 𝒫 stand for any WFF of predicate logic, the bold letter **x** stand for any individual variable, and the bold letter **c** stand for any individual constant. We can then say that an instance of a quantified WFF (**x**)𝒫 or (∃**x**)𝒫 is any WFF obtained by the following steps:

Step 1: Remove the initial quantifier, (**x**) or (∃**x**) as the case may be.

Step 2: In the WFF resulting from Step 1, uniformly replace all free occurrences of the variable **x** in 𝒫 with occurrences of **c**. (We use 𝒫**c** to stand for the resulting instance.)

There are four important features of this definition, which can be brought out by considering four more examples:

D. (x)[Fx → (Ga ∨ Hx)]
E. Fb → (∃y)(Gy ∨ Hc)
F. Fa → (∃y)(Ga ∨ Ha)
G. Fz → (∃y)(Gy ∨ Hz)

(D) through (G) are *not* instances of (A). Each fails for a different reason. The problem with (D) is that it does not remove the *initial* quantifier in (A). The problem with (E) is that it does not *uniformly* replace all free occurrences of the x-variable. The problem with (F) is that it replaces a *bound* occurrence of the y-variable with a constant. And the problem with (G) is that it replaces the occurrences of one variable with those of another *variable*, rather than a constant. Remember: Instantiation always takes us from variables to constants.

With our definition in place, we can now proceed to the rules.

Universal Instantiation

Our first new implicational rule is *universal instantiation* (UI, for short). The following argument illustrates the need for this rule:

53. All humans are mortal. Socrates is human. Therefore, Socrates is mortal.
(Hx: x is human; Mx: x is mortal; s: Socrates)

1. (x)(Hx → Mx)
2. Hs   ∴Ms

One might be tempted to apply *modus ponens* to lines (1) and (2), but this would be a mistake. We require a conditional to apply *modus ponens*, and (1) is not a conditional, but a universally quantified statement. However, the first premise does tell us that, for every x, if x is human, then x is mortal. What goes for everything goes for Socrates, so from (1) we can infer:

3. Hs → Ms   1, UI

We call the rule of inference that permits this move "universal instantiation" because it allows us to instantiate a universally quantified formula. The remainder of the proof is now merely statement logic:

1. (x)(Hx → Mx)
2. Hs   ∴Ms
3. Hs → Ms   1, UI
4. Ms   3, 2, MP

There are no restrictions on universal instantiation—UI allows us to move from *any* universally quantified formula to *any* instance of that formula. We can therefore formulate UI as follows, where $\mathcal{P}$ stands for any WFF, **x** stands for any variable, and **c** stands for any constant:

Universal Instantiation (UI)

$(\mathbf{x})\mathcal{P}$

$\therefore \mathcal{P}\mathbf{c}$ (where $\mathcal{P}\mathbf{c}$ is an instance of $(\mathbf{x})\mathcal{P}$)

Which of the following are correct applications of UI? Which are incorrect?

A. 1. (y)(Ac • By)
    2. Ac • Bc   1, UI
B. 1. (y)(Ac • By)
    2. Ac • Bd   1, UI
C. 1. (x)(∃z)(Gx ↔ Hz)
    2. (∃z)(Ga ↔ Hz)   1, UI
D. 1. (x)Fx
    2. Fz   1, UI
E. 1. (y)(Ay → By)
    2. Ac → Bd   1, UI
F. 1. (z)Gz • (y)Hy
    2. Ga • (y)Hy   1, UI

(A) through (C) are all correct applications of UI; (D) through (F) are all incorrect. The problem with (D) is that a variable has been replaced with a variable, so the second line is not an instance of the first. Remember: Instantiation is always to a constant. The problem with (E) is that different constants have been used to replace occurrences of the same variable, so the second line is not an instance of the first. Remember: Instantiation must always be done uniformly. Finally, the problem with (F) is that the first line is not a universally quantified statement at all, but a *conjunction* of two such statements. As our formulation of UI makes clear, the rule applies only to formulas of the form $(\mathbf{x})\mathcal{P}$, not $\mathcal{P} \bullet \mathcal{Q}$. Remember: UI is an implicational rule (like addition), not an equivalence rule (like commutation). Hence, UI can be applied only to whole lines in a proof, not to parts thereof. In (F), UI is applied to part of a conjunction, and for that reason is incorrect.

Let's consider two final mistakes that are easy to make. First:

1. ~(y)Gy
2. ~Gs   1, *incorrect use of UI*

This is like arguing, "Not everything is Greek; therefore, Socrates is not Greek," which is plainly invalid. The problem with this inference is that the first line is not a universally quantified statement, but the *negation* of a universally quantified statement. Hence, UI has no application.

Second, UI does not permit the following sort of inference:

1. (x)Ex → (y)Dy
2. Es → (y)Dy   1, *incorrect use of UI*

This is like arguing, "If everything is an even number, then everything is divisible by 2 (without remainder). Hence, if 6 is an even number, then everything is divisible by 2 (without remainder)." The premise of this argument is true, but the conclusion is false (it has a true antecedent and a false consequent). Once again, the problem is that the first line is not a universally quantified statement, but a *conditional* linking two such statements. Once again, UI has no application.

What all of these examples bring out is that one must exercise *extreme* caution in classifying formulas because not every formula that includes a quantifier is a quantified formula. We cannot emphasize this enough. Before using UI, you must make sure that you are working with a universally quantified formula. To do this, you must follow two steps. First, make sure that a universal quantifier appears at the *beginning* of the line in question. In the first example, ~(y)Gy is *not* a universally quantified formula because (y) does *not* appear at the very start of the line. Second, make sure that the quantifier has scope over the *entire* line in question. In the second example, (x)Ex → (y)Dy is *not* a quantified formula because (x) does *not* have scope over the entire line (remember that the scope of a quantifier is the shortest WFF to the right of the quantifier—in this case, Ex). If a line passes both of these tests, it is a universally quantified formula, in which case you may apply UI.

(Before moving onto the next rule, you may wish to complete Exercise 9.3C, which gives you some practice using UI.)

Summary of Universal Instantiation (UI)

(x)$\mathcal{P}$

∴ $\mathcal{P}$c

Where $\mathcal{P}$c is an instance of (x)$\mathcal{P}$.

Correct Applications		Incorrect Applications	
1. (z)Fz		1. ~(y)Ay	
2. Fa	1, UI	2. ~Ac	1, *incorrect use of UI*
1. (x)(Dx • Ex)		1. (x)Fx → (y)Gy	
2. Db • Eb	1, UI	2. Fd → (y)Gy	1, *incorrect use of UI*

The incorrect applications on the right involve the same basic error: applying UI to part of a line.

Existential Generalization

Our second inferential rule is *existential generalization* (EG). The need for this rule is illustrated by the following argument and proof:

54. All humans are mortal. Socrates is human. Therefore, someone is mortal.
(Hx: x is human; Mx: x is mortal; s: Socrates)

1. (x)(Hx → Mx)
2. Hs   ∴(∃x) Mx
3. Hs → Ms   1, UI
4. Ms   3, 2, MP
5. (∃x)Mx   4, EG

Until the last line, this is just like the earlier proof for (53). Having shown that *Socrates* is mortal, we now conclude that *someone* is mortal because Socrates is obviously someone. We call the rule that permits this move "existential generalization" because it allows us to existentially *generalize* an instance of a quantified formula. The operation of generalization is essentially the opposite of instantiation—instead of moving from a quantified formula to an instance, we move from an instance to a quantified formula; instead of *removing* a quantifier and replacing variables with constants, we *introduce* a quantifier and replace constants with variables.

As with UI, there are no restrictions on the application of EG—the rule allows us to infer *any* existentially quantified formula from *any* instance of that formula. We can therefore formulate EG as follows, where $\mathcal{P}$ stands for any WFF, **x** stands for any variable, and **c** stands for any constant:

Existential Generalization (EG)

$\mathcal{P}$**c**

∴(∃**x**)$\mathcal{P}$ (where $\mathcal{P}$**c** is an instance of (∃**x**)$\mathcal{P}$)

Which of the following are correct applications of EG? Which are incorrect?

A. 1. Fa
    2. (∃x)Fx   1, EG
B. 1. Gx
    2. (∃y)Gy   1, EG
C. 1. Ac • Bc
    2. (∃z)(Az • Bz)   1, EG
D. 1. Sb ∨ Rc
    2. (∃y)(Sy ∨ Ry)   1, EG
E. 1. Ma • Sa
    2. (∃x)(Mx • Sa)   1, EG
F. 1. Ja • ~Kb
    2. (∃x)Jx • ~Kb   1, EG

(A), (C), and (E) are correct applications of EG; (B), (D), and (F) are incorrect. The problem with (B) is that the first line is not an instance of the second, which is a requirement for using EG. Remember: Instances are the result of removing the initial quantifier and replacing free occurrences of the variable with *constants*. The problem with (D) is similar: The first line is not an instance of the second because instances are the result of removing the initial quantifier and *uniformly* replacing free occurrences of the variable. The problem with (F) is that EG has been applied to part of a line, rather than to the whole. Remember: As an implicational rule, EG can be applied only to whole lines, so an application of EG should always result in an existentially quantified formula. We know that the application of EG is incorrect in (F) because the result—(∃x)Jx • ~Kb—is not an existentially quantified statement, but a *conjunction* (in which the first conjunct is an existentially quantified statement). One final note: The inference in (E) might appear questionable, but it is actually a correct application of EG because Ma • Sa is an instance of (∃x)(Mx • Sa). The inference is therefore valid, like arguing, "Al is mad and Al is sad; hence, there is an x such that (x is mad and Al is sad)."

Let's consider one more proof that makes use of both EG and UI. Are both rules applied correctly in this case?

1. (x)Rx	∴(∃x)Rx
2. Rb	1, UI
3. (∃x)Rx	2, EG

Yes. Given that *everything* has the property R, our rules allow us to infer that *something* is R. This brings out an interesting feature of our system that is shared by other classical systems of logic—it includes the assumption that at least one thing exists. Without this assumption, we could not instantiate to b in line (2) because that move assumes that there is at least one individual corresponding to the constant.[5]

(Before moving onto the next rule, you may wish to complete Exercise 9.3D, which gives you some practice using EG.)

Summary of Existential Generalization (EG)

$\mathcal{P}$**c**
∴(∃x)$\mathcal{P}$
Where $\mathcal{P}$**c** is an instance of (∃x)$\mathcal{P}$.

Correct Applications		**Incorrect Applications**	
1. Fa		1. ~Gc	
2. (∃x)Fx	1, EG	2. ~(∃z)Gz	1, *incorrect use of EG*
1. Db • Eb		1. Gd → Hd	
2. (∃y)(Dy • Ey)	1, EG	2. (∃y)Gy → Hd	1, *incorrect use of EG*

The incorrect applications on the right involve the same basic error: applying EG to part of a line.

Existential Instantiation

Our third inferential rule is *existential instantiation* (EI). The following argument illustrates the need for this rule.

55. All baseball players are athletes. Some baseball players take performance enhancing drugs. So, some athletes take performance enhancing drugs. (Bx: x is a baseball player; Ax: x is an athlete; Dx: x takes performance enhancing drugs.)

1. (x)(Bx → Ax)
2. (∃x)(Bx • Dx)   ∴(∃x)(Ax • Dx)

The second premise tells us that at least one baseball player takes drugs, but it does not tell us which one (or which ones). However, if we know that someone satisfies this description, we can give that someone a name to go on talking about him—let's call our mystery person "Balco Bob" (b: Balco Bob). From (2), we can then infer:

3. Bb • Db   2, EI

The remainder of the proof is straightforward:

4. Bb   3, Simp
5. Db   3, Simp
6. Bb → Ab   1, UI
7. Ab   6, 4, MP
8. Ab • Db   7, 5, Conj
9. (∃x)(Ax • Dx)   8, EG

The rule invoked at line (3) is called "existential instantiation" because it allows us to instantiate an existentially quantified formula, subject to certain restrictions. Which restrictions?

First: *One cannot instantiate to a constant that has already occurred in the proof.* To see the need for the restriction, simply think about the previous example. We introduced the name "Balco Bob" for a baseball player who uses performance enhancing drugs. Crucially, "Balco Bob" is a new name in this context—we have simply made up a name for some baseball player who uses the drugs, whoever that player might be. Given that the name was introduced in this way, all we know about Balco Bob is that he plays baseball and that he uses drugs. Suppose instead that we had reasoned as follows: "Some baseball players take performance enhancing drugs—let's just call one of those players 'Ichiro Suzuki.' Ichiro Suzuki plays for the Seattle Mariners. So, someone on the Seattle Mariners uses performance enhancing drugs." The problem with this line of reasoning is obvious: "Ichiro Suzuki" is not a made-up name that is new to the context—there is already a famous baseball player who goes by the name, so it would be a mistake to use this name in this way. In the same way, it would be a mistake to existentially instantiate to a constant that is already being used in a proof. Here is an illustration:

1. (∃x)(Ax • Bx)	
2. (∃x)(Ax • ~Bx)	∴ (∃x)(Bx • ~Bx)
3. Ac • Bc	1, EI
4. Ac • ~Bc	2, *incorrect use of EI*
5. Bc	3, Simp
6. ~Bc	4, Simp
7. Bc • ~Bc	5, 6, Conj
8. (∃x)(Bx • ~Bx)	7, EG

The argument in this case is clearly invalid, like arguing, "Some athletes are baseball players and some athletes are not baseball players, so someone is both a baseball player and not a baseball player." The mistake comes at line (4). When we instantiate to the same constant in (4) that we did in (3), we in effect assume that some *single* individual makes *both* (1) and (2) true. We are not in a position to make this assumption, so we must introduce a new instantial constant.

    The second restriction on EI is related to the first: *One cannot instantiate to a constant that occurs in the conclusion to be proved.* In other words, the instantial constant introduced by EI must not appear in the final line of the proof. To understand the need for this restriction, imagine talking to someone who admits that some baseball players use performance enhancing drugs, but denies that Barry Bonds has ever done anything of the sort. The following argument would do little to change that person's mind: "Some baseball players use performance enhancing drugs—let's just call one of those players 'Barry Bonds.' So, Barry Bonds uses performance enhancing drugs." The following proof is therefore mistaken:

1. (∃x)(Bx • Dx)	∴ Db
2. Bb • Db	1, *incorrect use of EI*
3. Db	2, Simp

    With the previous discussion in mind, we can now formulate EI as follows, where $\mathcal{P}$ stands for any WFF, **x** stands for any variable, and **c** stands for any constant:

Existential Instantiation (EI)

(∃**x**)$\mathcal{P}$

∴ $\mathcal{P}$**c** (where $\mathcal{P}$**c** is an instance of (∃**x**)$\mathcal{P}$ and **c** does not occur in an earlier line
    of the proof or in the last line of the proof)

Which of the following are correct applications of EI? Which are incorrect?

A. 1. (∃x)Fx
    2. Fa   1, EI
B. 1. (∃x)Fx
    2. Fy   1, EI
C. 1. (∃y)(Sy • (x)Rx)
    2. Sb • (x)Rx   1, EI
D. 1. (∃x)[Fx • (∃y)(Fy • Gb)]
    2. Fb • (∃y)(Fy • Gb)   1, EI
E. 1. (∃z)(Pz → Tz)
    2. Pc → Tc   1, EI
F. 1. (∃z)(Rz ∨ Sz) ∴Rc
    2. Rc ∨ Sc   1, EI
G. 1. (∃z)Rz ∨ (∃z)Sz
    2. Rd ∨ (∃z)Sz   1, EI

(A), (C), and (E) are correct applications of EI; (B), (D), (F), and (G) are incorrect. The problem with (B) is that the second line is not an instance of the first—the initial quantifier has been dropped, but the variable has not been replaced with a constant. The problem with (D) is that the instantial constant b occurs in a previous line of the proof, which is disallowed by EI. Similarly, (F) is incorrect because the instantial letter c appears in the conclusion to be proved. Finally, (G) is incorrect because the first line is not an existentially quantified statement, but a *disjunction* of existentially quantified statements—once again, implicational rules cannot be applied to parts of lines.

Before moving on, it will be instructive to consider one final proof that employs EI:

56. Every ESPN anchor is funny. Some ESPN anchors are philosophers. So, some philosophers are funny. (Ex: x is an ESPN anchor; Fx: x is funny; Px: x is a philosopher)

1. (x)(Ex → Fx)
2. (∃x)(Ex • Px)   ∴(∃x)(Px • Fx)
3. Ea • Pa   2, EI
4. Ea → Fa   1, UI
5. Ea   3, Simp
6. Pa   3, Simp
7. Fa   4, 5, MP
8. Pa • Fa   6, 7, Conj
9. (∃x)(Px • Fx)   8, EG

Note that the application of EI at line (3) comes before the application of UI at line (4). What if we had reversed the order of application and universally instantiated to a at line (3)? In that case, we could no longer existentially instantiate to a, because that constant would no longer be new to the argument. This observation leads to our first tip for predicate logic:

Tip 1: Apply EI before you apply UI.

(Before moving onto the next rule, you may wish to complete Exercise 9.3E, which gives you some practice using EI.)

Summary of Existential Instantiation (EI)

(∃x)$\mathcal{P}$
∴$\mathcal{P}$c

Where $\mathcal{P}$c is an instance of (∃x)$\mathcal{P}$ and **c** does not occur in an earlier line of the proof or in the last line of the proof.

Correct Applications

1. (∃z)Fz
2. Fa   1, EI

1. (∃x)(Dx • Ex)
2. Db • Eb   1, EI

Incorrect Applications

1. (∃x)(Gb → Hx)
2. Gb → Hb   1, *incorrect use of EI*

1. (∃x)Fx   ∴Fb
2. Fb   1, *incorrect use of EI*

The incorrect applications on the right involve two distinct errors: (a) existentially instantiating to a constant that occurs in an earlier line of the proof and (b) existentially instantiating to a constant that occurs in the last line of the proof.

Universal Generalization

Our fourth inferential rule is *universal generalization* (UG). Consider the following argument and the accompanying proof, which illustrates a typical use of UG.

57. All trees are plants. All plants are living things. So, all trees are living things. (Tx: x is a tree; Px: x is a plant; Lx: x is a living thing)

1. (x)(Tx → Px)
2. (x)(Px → Lx)   ∴ (x)(Tx → Lx)
3. Td → Pd   1, UI
4. Pd → Ld   2, UI
5. Td → Ld   3, 4, HS
6. (x)(Tx → Lx)   5, UG

The addition of the universal quantifier in line (6) is legitimate because the validity of the earlier steps in the proof did not require any specific constant. We instantiated to d, but we could just as easily have instantiated to b or c or any other constant. In fact, we could have gone one-by-one and composed a version of this argument for everything in the universe: "If Aristotle is a tree, then he is a plant. If Aristotle is a plant, then he is a living thing. So, if Aristotle is a tree, then he is a living thing . . . If the moon is a tree, then it is a plant. If the moon is a plant, then it is a living thing. So, if the moon is a tree, then it is a living thing . . . If Robert Plant is a plant, then . . ." The inference from line (5) to (6) is similar to certain types of inferences often made in mathematics. For example, a geometer may prove that all rectangles have such-and-such a property by arguing that a certain figure, f, about which we assume only that it is a rectangle, has that property. If one makes no other assumptions about f, then the conclusion that it has such-and-such a property may be generalized to all rectangles.

Of course, there are several restrictions on the application of UG, just as there were restrictions on the application of EI—UG allows us to move from an instance of a universally quantified formula to a universally quantified formula, *provided that certain conditions are met.* Which conditions?

First: *One cannot generalize from a constant that occurs in a premise of the argument.* The need for this restriction should be clear—just because some individual has a property, one cannot infer that everything has that property. Without this restriction in place, our rule would endorse the following:

1. Os   ∴(x)Ox

2. (x)Ox   1, *incorrect use of UG*

This proof is mistaken, like arguing, "Seven is an odd number. So, everything is an odd number."

Second: *One cannot universally generalize from a constant that appears in a line derived by an application of EI.* The need for this restriction should also be clear—without it, our rule would endorse the following:

1. (∃x)Ex   ∴(x)Ex

2. Et   1, EI

3. (x)Ex   2, *incorrect use of UG*

This proof is mistaken, like arguing, "Something is an even number—let's just call it 'Ted.' Ted is even. So, everything is even."

It may be helpful to note that these first two restrictions on UG can be derived from the following prescription: *One should only universally generalize from a constant that is introduced by UI.* To understand this point, simply ask yourself the following question: How does an individual constant get into a proof in the first place? If we limit our attention to direct proofs, there are only three possibilities. An individual constant can be introduced by (i) a premise of the argument, (ii) existential instantiation, or (iii) universal instantiation. The first two restrictions on UG prevent us from generalizing from constants that are introduced by (i) and (ii), which leaves only those constants that are introduced by (iii). Looking at things from this perspective helps us understand the justification for UG: We can generalize *to* a universal statement because the constant comes *from* a universal statement.

The third restriction on UG is this: *One cannot universally generalize from a constant that appears in the resulting formula.* Without this restriction, our rule would endorse the following:

1. (x)(Mx → Px)	∴ (x)(Mc → Px)
2. Mc → Pc	1, UI
3. (x)(Mc → Px)	2, *incorrect use of UG*

This proof is mistaken, like arguing, "For all x, if x is a monkey, then x is a primate. So, if Curious George is a monkey, then Curious George is a primate. So, for all x, if Curious George is a monkey, then x is a primate." The premise in this case is true, but the conclusion is false (Curious George is a monkey, but not everything is a primate). The lesson is this: When applying UG, be sure to uniformly replace *all* occurrences of the relevant constant with free occurrences of a variable before introducing the universal quantifier.

We will introduce one further restriction on UG in section 9.4 when we discuss indirect proofs, but for now, we can formulate UG as follows, where $\mathcal{P}$ is any WFF, **x** is any variable, and **c** is any constant:

Universal Generalization (UG)

$\mathcal{P}$**c**

∴ (**x**)$\mathcal{P}$ (where $\mathcal{P}$**c** is an instance of (**x**)$\mathcal{P}$ and **c** does not occur in a premise of
    the argument, a previous line derived by an application of EI, or (**x**)$\mathcal{P}$)

Which of the following are correct applications of UG? Which are incorrect?

A.	1. Fa	
	2. (y)Fy	1, UG
B.	1. Gb • (∃y)(Hy)	
	2. (x)(Gx • (∃y)Hy)	1, UG
C.	1. Sb ∨ Tc	
	2. (x)Sx ∨ Tc	1, UG
D.	1. Qa • (Rb → Sa)	
	2. (y)[Qy • (Ry → Sy)]	1, UG

(A) and (B) are correct applications of UG, assuming that the relevant constants do not come from argument premises or lines derived by EI. (C) is incorrect because it applies UG to part of a line, rather than the whole. And (D) is incorrect because (1) in this case is not an instance of (2)—note that there is no way of uniformly replacing the variables in [Qy • (Ry → Sy)] to arrive at [Qa • (Rb → Sa)].

(Exercise 9.3F will give you some practice using this rule.)

Summary of Universal Generalization (UG)

$\mathcal{P}$**c**

∴(**x**)$\mathcal{P}$

Where $\mathcal{P}$**c** is an instance of (**x**)$\mathcal{P}$ and **c** does not occur in a premise of the argument, a previous line derived by an application of EI, or (**x**)$\mathcal{P}$.

Correct Applications		Incorrect Applications	
1. Fa		1. Ab ∴(x)Ax	
2. (x)Fx	1, UG	2. (x)Ax	1, *incorrect use of UG*
1. Db • Eb		1. (∃y)Gy	
2. (y)(Dy • Ey)	1, UG	2. Gc	1, EI
		3. (y)Gy	2, *incorrect use of UG*
		1. Ra • Sa	
		2. (x)(Rx • Sa)	1, *incorrect use of UG*

The incorrect applications on the right involve three distinct errors: (a) universally generalizing from a constant that appears in a premise, (b) universally generalizing from a constant that occurs in a line derived by an application of EI, and (c) universally generalizing from a constant that occurs in (**x**)$\mathcal{P}$.

EXERCISE 9.3

PART A: Annotating Annotate the following proofs.

* **1.** 1. (x)(Rx → Tx)
    2. ~Tc ∴ ~Rc
    3. Rc → Tc
    4. ~Rc

  2. 1. Km
    2. (∃x)Kx → (x)Lx ∴ Lm
    3. (∃x)Kx
    4. (x)Lx
    5. Lm

3. 1. $(z)(Az \rightarrow Bz)$
   2. $(\exists y)Ay$ $\therefore$ $(\exists y)By$
   3. Ab
   4. $Ab \rightarrow Bb$
   5. Bb
   6. $(\exists y)By$

* **4.** 1. Hn $\therefore$ $(\exists x)Hx$
   2. $(\exists x)Hx$

5. 1. $(x)(Rx \rightarrow {\sim}Ox)$
   2. $(\exists y)(Sy \bullet Ry)$ $\therefore$ $(\exists z)(Sz \bullet {\sim}Oz)$
   3. $Sb \bullet Rb$
   4. $Rb \rightarrow {\sim}Ob$
   5. Rb
   6. ${\sim}Ob$
   7. Sb
   8. $Sb \bullet {\sim}Ob$
   9. $(\exists z)(Sz \bullet {\sim}Oz)$

6. 1. $(z)(Mz \bullet Lz)$
   2. $(z)Mz \rightarrow Kd$ $\therefore$ $(\exists y)Ky$
   3. $Mc \bullet Lc$
   4. Mc
   5. $(z)Mz$
   6. Kd
   7. $(\exists y)Ky$

* **7.** 1. $(y)(Ry \rightarrow Ny)$
   2. ${\sim}Ng$ $\therefore$ $(\exists y){\sim}Ry$
   3. $Rg \rightarrow Ng$
   4. ${\sim}Rg$
   5. $(\exists y){\sim}Ry$

8. 1. $Ab \lor (Bb \bullet Cb)$
   2. $(x){\sim}Cx$ $\therefore$ $(\exists x)Ax$
   3. $(Ab \lor Bb) \bullet (Ab \lor Cb)$
   4. $Ab \lor Cb$
   5. ${\sim}Cb$
   6. Ab
   7. $(\exists x)Ax$

9. 1. $(x)(Fx \rightarrow Gx)$
   2. $(x)(Gx \rightarrow Fx)$ $\therefore$ $(x)(Fx \leftrightarrow Gx)$
   3. $Fa \rightarrow Ga$
   4. $Ga \rightarrow Fa$
   5. $(Fa \rightarrow Ga) \bullet (Ga \rightarrow Fa)$
   6. $Fa \leftrightarrow Ga$
   7. $(x)(Fx \leftrightarrow Gx)$

* **10.** 1. $(\exists y)Py \rightarrow (z)(\sim Nz \vee Oz)$
   2. Pn
   3. $\sim Om$ $\therefore$ $(\exists x)\sim Nx$
   4. $(\exists y)Py$
   5. $(z)(\sim Nz \vee Oz)$
   6. $\sim Nm \vee Om$
   7. $\sim Nm$
   8. $(\exists x)\sim Nx$

11. 1. $(x)(Kx \rightarrow Lx)$
   2. $(x)(Lx \rightarrow Mx)$ $\therefore$ $(x)(Kx \rightarrow Mx)$
   3. $Ka \rightarrow La$
   4. $La \rightarrow Ma$
   5. $Ka \rightarrow Ma$
   6. $(x)(Kx \rightarrow Mx)$

12. 1. $(x)[(Ax \vee Bx) \rightarrow Cx]$
   2. $(x)\sim Cx$ $\therefore$ $(x)\sim Bx$
   3. $(Aa \vee Ba) \rightarrow Ca$
   4. $\sim Ca$
   5. $\sim(Aa \vee Ba)$
   6. $\sim Aa \bullet \sim Ba$
   7. $\sim Ba$
   8. $(x)\sim Bx$

* **13.** 1. $(y)(Dy \bullet Ey)$ $\therefore$ $(y)Dy \bullet (y)Ey$
   2. $Db \bullet Eb$
   3. Db
   4. $(y)Dy$
   5. Eb
   6. $(y)Ey$
   7. $(y)Dy \bullet (y)Ey$

14. 1. $(\exists x)(Jx \bullet Kx)$ $\therefore$ $(\exists x)Jx \bullet (\exists x)Kx$
   2. $Jb \bullet Kb$
   3. Jb
   4. $(\exists x)Jx$
   5. Kb
   6. $(\exists x)Kx$
   7. $(\exists x)Jx \bullet (\exists x)Kx$

15. 1. $(x)[Ma \vee (Lx \bullet Nx)]$
   2. $\sim Ma$ $\therefore$ $(x)Nx$
   3. $Ma \vee (Lb \bullet Nb)$
   4. $Lb \bullet Nb$
   5. Nb
   6. $(x)Nx$

PART B: Correct or Incorrect? Which of the following inferences are permitted by our inference rules? Which are not permitted? (In each case, assume that the last line shown is the final line of the proof.)

* **1.** 1. (x)Ax → (x)Bx
    2. Aa → (x)Bx   1, UI

  2. 1. (∃x)(Dx • Fx)
    2. (∃x)Gx
    3. Da • Fa   1, EI
    4. Da   3, Simp
    5. (x)Dx   4, UG
    6. Fa   3, Simp
    7. (∃x)Fx   6, EG
    8. Ga   2, EI

  3. 1. (∃y)Hy → (∃y)Jy
    2. Hb → (∃y)Jy   1, EI

* **4.** 1. (∃z)(Kz • Lz)
    2. (∃z)Kz   1, Simp

  5. 1. (∃y)(Ry • Sy)
    2. Rx • Sx   1, EI

  6. 1. (x)(Mx → Nx)
    2. (x)(Nx → Ox)
    3. Ma → Na   1, UI
    4. Na → Oa   2, UI
    5. Ma → Oa   3, 4, HS
    6. (x)(Mx → Ox)   5, UG
    7. Md → Od   6, UI
    8. (∃y)(My → Oy)   7, EG

* **7.** 1. (x)(y)(My ↔ Nx)
    2. (y)(My ↔ Ny)   1, UI

  8. 1. ~(x)(Tx ∨ Ax)
    2. ~(Ta ∨ Aa)   1, UI

  9. 1. (x)((y)Fy ∨ Hx)
    2. (y)Fy ∨ Ha   1, UI
    3. (y)Fy ∨ (∃z)Hz   2, EG

* **10.** 1. (x)(Bx → (z)Cz)
    2. (x)Bx
    3. (z)Cz   1, 2, MP

 11. 1. (x)(Px → Sx)
    2. Pa → Sc   1, UI
    3. (y)(Sy → Sy)   2, UG

 12. 1. (x)[(Fx • (∃y)Gy) → Hx]
    2. (Fa • (∃y)Gy) → Hx   1, UI

* **13.** 1. (x)(Ax ∨ Bx)
         2. Aa ∨ Ba   1, UI
         3. (y)(Aa ∨ By)   2, UG

  14. 1. (∃x)(Px • Sx)
         2. Pb • Sb   1, EI
         3. (∃z)(Pz • Sb)   2, EG
         4. Pc • Sb   3, EI
         5. (∃z)(Pz • Sz)   4, EG

  15. 1. (x)[Cx → (∃y)((Fy • My) • Kx)]
         2. (∃z)Cz
         3. Ca   2, EI
         4. Ca → (∃y)[(Fy • My) • Ka]   1, UI
         5. (∃y)[(Fy • My) • Ka]   3, 4, MP
         6. (Fb • Mb) • Ka   5, EI
         7. Fb • Mb   6, Simp
         8. (y)(Fy • My)   7, UG

PART C: Proofs Construct proofs to show that the following symbolic arguments are valid. Use only statement logic and UI. Use direct proof rather than CP or RAA.

  1. (z)(~Gz ∨ Fz), ~Fa ∴ ~Ga

  2. Hc ∨ Jd, (x)(Hx → (∃y)Ky), (x)(Jx → (∃y)Ly) ∴ (∃y)Ky ∨ (∃y)Ly

* **3.** (y)(~Py → ~Ly), Lc ∨ Ld ∴ Pd ∨ Pc

  4. (x)(~Tx → ~Hx), Ha ∴ Ta

  5. (x)(y)[Lx → (Mx • Ny)], ~Mb ∴ Lb → Ob

* **6.** (x)(Ax ↔ ~Ax) ∴ Bc

  7. (x)[Lx → (Mx ↔ Nx)], La • Lb, Na • ~Nb ∴ Ma • ~Mb

  8. (y)[(Fy • Gy) → Hy], Fb • ~Hb ∴ ~Gb

* **9.** (z)~[~(x)Jx ∨ ~Kz] ∴ Jc • Kc

  10. (z)(Jz→Kz), (y)(~Ky ∨ Jy) • Ld ∴ Jd ↔ Kd

PART D: More Proofs Construct proofs to show that the following symbolic arguments are valid. Use only statement logic, UI, and EG. Use direct proof rather than CP or RAA.

* **1.** (x)(Fx → ~Gx), Fa ∴ (∃x)~Gx

  2. Ra → Sa, (x)(Sx → Tx) ∴ (∃y)(Ry → Ty)

  3. (z)Hz, (x)(Gx → ~Hx) ∴ (∃y)(Gy → (x)Kx)

  4. (x)(Fx → Gx), (x)(Hx → Jx), Fa ∨ Ha ∴ (z)(Fz ∨ Hz) → (∃x)(Gx ∨ Jx)

* **5.** (x)(Mx → Ox), ~(Nc ∨ ~Md) ∴ (∃x)Ox

  6. ~~(v)Fv ∨ ~(w)Gw, ~ [(∃x)Hx ∨ ~(w)Gw], [(v)Fv • ~(∃x)Hx] → ~(y)Jy, Ka → (y)Jy ∴ (∃z)(Kz → Lz)

  7. Ja → Hb, (y)~Hy ∴ (∃x)~Jx

8. (x)(y)(z)[(Ox ∨ ~Ny) • (Ox ∨ Mz)], (x)(y)(Ox → ~ ~Ly),
   (x)(y)(z)[~Nx → (My → Lz)] ∴ (∃x)(Lx)

* 9. ~(z)Hz ∨ ((y)Gy ∨ ~(∃x)Fx), Fc, Sc → ~((z)Hz → (y)Gy) ∴ (∃z)~Sz

10. (y)(Fy → Gy), Fb ∴ (∃y)(Fy • Gy)

PART E: Still More Proofs   Construct proofs to show that the following symbolic arguments are valid. Use only statement logic, UI, EG, and EI. Use direct proof rather than CP or RAA.

1. (∃x)(Ax • Bx) ∴ (∃x)Ax • (∃x)Bx

* 2. (x)(Dx → Lx), (∃x)Dx ∴ (∃x)(Dx • Lx)

3. (z)(Hz → Jz), (∃z)(Hz • Kz) ∴ (∃z)(Jz • Kz)

4. (x)[(Ax ∨ Bx) → Cx], (∃x)Bx ∴ (∃x)Cx

5. (∃x)(Dx • ~Rx), (x)(Dx → Wx) ∴ (∃x)(Wx • ~Rx)

* 6. (z)[Uz → (Kz ∨ Sz)], (z)Uz, (∃z)~Sz ∴ (∃z)Kz

7. (x)[(Bx → (z)Az) → ~P], (∃x)~Bx ∴ ~P

8. (x)[(Sx • ~(z)Rz) → Nd], (x)~Nx, (∃x)Sx ∴ Rc

* 9. (x)[Px → (∃y)Oy], (∃z)Pz ∴ (∃y)Oy

10. (∃x)(Jx • Kx) ∴ (∃x)Jx • (∃x)Kx

11. (x)(Gx → Hx), (∃x)(~Fx • Gx) ∴(∃x)(~Fx • Hx)

12. (x)(Jx → ~Ex), (∃x)(Jx ∨ Jd) ∴ (∃y)(Ey → ~Ed)

*13. (x)(Sx → Tx), (∃y)(Ry • ~Ty) ∴ (∃z)(Rz • ~Sz)

14. (x)(Bx → Cx), (x)(Ax → Bx), (x)(Cx → Dx), (∃x)~Dx ∴ (∃x)~Ax

15. (x)(Dx → ~Kx), (∃x)(Ex • Hx), (x)(Hx → Dx), (x)(Jx → Kx)
    ∴ (∃x)(Ex • ~Jx)

16. (x)[Fx ↔ (Hx • ~(y)Gy)], (∃x)~Fx, (z)Hz ∴ Gc

*17. (x)[Bx → (Cx • Dx)], (∃x)Bx ∴(∃x)~(~Cx ∨ ~Dx)

18. (x)[Mx → (∃y)(Ny • Px)], (x)(Nx → ~G), (∃x)Mx ∴ ~G

19. (x)(Fx → Gx) • La, (∃y)[Hy • (~Gy • Lb)] ∴(∃z)(Hz • ~Fz)

20. (y)(Hy → ~Ky), (∃z)(Kz • Jz) ∴ (∃x) (Jx • ~Hx)

PART F: Still More Proofs   Construct proofs to show that the following symbolic arguments are valid. You may use statement logic, UI, EG, EI, and UG. Use direct proof rather than CP or RAA.

1. (y)~(Ly → My), (y)Ly → (∃x)Dx ∴ (y)~My • (∃x)Dx

* 2. (z)(Nz → ~Ez), (z)(Sz → Nz) ∴ (z)(Sz → ~Ez)

3. (x)[(Ax • Bx) → Cd], (x)(Ax → ~Bx) → (x)Ex, ~Cd ∴ Ed

4. (x)(Fx • Gx), ~(x)Gx ∨ Ha ∴ (∃x)Hx

* 5. (∃y)Fy → (y)My, Fg ∴ Mg

6. (x)(Lx → Mx) → (x)(Nx → Lx), (x)~Lx ∴ (x)~Nx

7. $(x)(Rx \leftrightarrow Sx) \therefore (x)(Rx \rightarrow Sx) \bullet (x)(Sx \rightarrow Rx)$

* 8. $(x)[(Bx \lor Ax) \leftrightarrow Cx], (x)\sim Cx \therefore (x)(Ax \leftrightarrow Bx)$

9. $(x)[Rx \rightarrow (Sx \lor (y)Ty)], (x)(Rx \rightarrow Sx) \rightarrow Pb, \sim(y)Ty \therefore Pb$

10. $(x)[Mx \rightarrow (\exists y)(Ny \bullet Px)], (x)(Nx \rightarrow \sim G), (\exists x)Mx \therefore \sim G$

PART G: English Arguments
Symbolize the following arguments using the schemes of abbreviation provided. Then construct proofs to show that the arguments are valid. Use direct proof rather than CP or RAA.

* 1. Only humans have inherent value. No chimps are humans. So, no chimps have inherent value. (Hx: x is a human; Ix: x has inherent value; Cx: x is a chimp)

2. Every fetus has an immortal soul. A thing has an immortal soul only if it has a right to life. Hence, each and every fetus has a right to life. (Fx: x is fetus; Sx: x has an immortal soul; Rx: x has a right to life)

3. There are rights that cannot be waived. But alienable rights can be waived. It follows that some rights are inalienable. (Rx: x is right; Wx: x can be waived; Ax: x is an alienable right)

* 4. God is a perfect being. Nothing perfect is unreal. Therefore, God is real. (g: God; Px: x is a perfect being; Rx: x is real)

5. At least one instance of intentional killing is not wrong. But every murder is wrong. Hence, some instances of intentional killing are not murder. (Kx: x is an instance of intentional killing; Mx: x is murder; Wx: x is wrong)

6. Some wars are just. No war of aggression is just. Accordingly, there are wars that are not wars of aggression. (Wx: x is a war; Jx: x is just; Ax: x is a war of aggression)

* 7. A person deserves the death penalty if and only if he is a serial killer. Bundy is a serial killer, but Oswald is not. Both Bundy and Oswald are persons. Hence, Bundy deserves the death penalty, but Oswald does not. (Px: x is a person; Dx: x deserves the death penalty; Sx: x is a serial killer; b: Bundy; o: Oswald)

8. All contingent beings are causally dependent. No necessary beings are causally dependent. Every physical entity is contingent. All atoms are physical entities. We may conclude that no atom is a necessary being. (Cx: x is a contingent being; Dx: x is causally dependent; Nx: x is a necessary being; Px: x is a physical entity; Ax: x is an atom)

9. At least one instance of killing an innocent human is not wrong. For some instances of killing an innocent human are either accidental or in self-defense. But accidental killing is not wrong. And killing in self-defense is not wrong. (Kx: x is an instance of killing an innocent human; Wx: x is wrong; Ax: x is an accidental killing; Sx: x is a case of killing in self-defense)

10. Only things having human bodies are human. No soul has a human body. Only souls survive the death of the body. Thus, no humans survive the death of the body. (Bx: x has a human body; Hx: x is human; Sx: x is a soul; Dx: x survives the death of the body)

9.4 Quantifier Negation, RAA, and CP

In this section, we add an equivalence rule to our system and explain how to use conditional proof and *reductio ad absurdum* within predicate logic.

To begin, consider the following four pairs of statements.

58. Something is human. It is not the case that everything is nonhuman.

59. Something is nonhuman. It is not the case that everything is human.

60. Everything is human. It is not the case that something is nonhuman.

61. Everything is nonhuman. It is not the case that something is human.

The statements in each pair are logically equivalent. These examples illustrate the **rule of quantifier negation** (QN), which comes in four forms:

Quantifier Negation (QN)

$(\exists \mathbf{x})\mathcal{P} :: \sim(\mathbf{x})\sim\mathcal{P}$

$(\exists \mathbf{x})\sim\mathcal{P} :: \sim(\mathbf{x})\mathcal{P}$

$(\mathbf{x})\mathcal{P} :: \sim(\exists \mathbf{x})\sim\mathcal{P}$

$(\mathbf{x})\sim\mathcal{P} :: \sim(\exists \mathbf{x})\mathcal{P}$

The four-dot symbol indicates that QN is an equivalence rule, which means that it can be applied to parts of lines in a proof, as well as to whole lines.

Here is a simple tip for mastering the rule of quantifier negation: Whenever you see a quantifier, think of it as having a "slot" on either side, where these slots are always filled by tildes or blank spaces. QN allows you to change any quantifier to its opposite (i.e., replace an existential quantifier with a universal quantifier or vice versa), provided that you also do the same for whatever is in the slot on either side (i.e., change tildes to blank spots and vice versa). In the first form of QN, for example, you can think of there being a blank space on either side of the existential quantifier. When we switch to the universal quantifier, we also have to switch each blank to a tilde, which gives us $\sim(\mathbf{x})\sim\mathcal{P}$. In the second form of QN, you can think of there being a blank space on the left of the existential quantifier and a tilde on the right. When we switch to the universal quantifier, we have to switch to a tilde on the left and a blank on the right, which gives us $\sim(\mathbf{x})\mathcal{P}$.

Here are some typical examples of inferences permitted by the QN rule:

A. 1. $(\exists x)(Ax \bullet Bx)$
    2. $\sim(x)\sim(Ax \bullet Bx)$ 1, QN
B. 1. $(\exists y)\sim(Cy)$
    2. $\sim(y)(Cy)$ 1, QN
C. 1. $(x)(Dx \rightarrow Ex)$
    2. $\sim(\exists x)\sim(Dx \rightarrow Ex)$ 1, QN
D. 1. $(z)\sim(Fz)$
    2. $\sim(\exists z)(Fz)$ 1, QN

Because QN is an *equivalence* rule, it can be applied to *parts* of a line. For example:

E. 1. (x)~Hx → (y)Ky

2. ~(∃x)Hx → (y)Ky   1, QN

F. 1. (y)By → ~(x)Ax

2. (y)By → (∃x)~Ax   1, QN

Note that in example (E), QN is applied to the antecedent of a conditional, and in example (F), it is applied to the consequent of a conditional.

The following argument and proof illustrate the utility of the quantifier negation rule:

62. Not all animals are moral agents. Only moral agents have rights. Hence, some animals do not have rights. (Ax: x is an animal; Mx: x is a moral agent; Rx: x has rights)

1. ~(x)(Ax → Mx)

2. (x)(Rx → Mx)   ∴ (∃x)(Ax • ~Rx)

3. (∃x)~(Ax → Mx)   1, QN

4. ~(Aa → Ma)   3, EI

5. ~(~Aa ∨ Ma)   4, MI

6. ~~Aa • ~Ma   5, DeM

7. ~Ma   6, Simp

8. Ra → Ma   2, UI

9. ~Ra   8, 7, MT

10. ~~Aa   6, Simp

11. Aa   10, DN

12. Aa • ~Ra   11, 9, Conj

13. (∃x)(Ax • ~Rx)   12, EG

When a tilde appears on the left side of a quantified statement, it is often useful to apply QN so that one can apply EI or UI. Lines (1), (3), and (4) illustrate this type of sequence, which suggests a second tip for predicate logic:

Tip 2: When a tilde appears on the left side of a quantifier, it is often useful to apply QN and instantiate.

Using QN, we can prove the equivalence of statements such as these:

63. Not all animals are cats. (Ax: x is an animal; Cx: x is a cat)
64. Some animals are not cats. (Ax: x is an animal; Cx: x is a cat)

The following proofs show that we can move logically from either one of these statements to the other; hence, they are logically equivalent.

1. ~(x)(Ax → Cx)	∴ (∃x)(Ax • ~Cx)
2. (∃x)~(Ax → Cx)	1, QN
3. (∃x)~(~Ax ∨ Cx)	2, MI
4. (∃x)(~~Ax • ~Cx)	3, DeM
5. (∃x)(Ax • ~Cx)	4, DN

1. (∃x)(Ax • ~Cx)	∴ ~(x)(Ax → Cx)
2. (∃x)(~~Ax • ~Cx)	1, DN
3. (∃x)~(~Ax ∨ Cx)	2, DeM
4. (∃x)~(Ax → Cx)	3, MI
5. ~(x)(Ax → Cx)	4, QN

Sometimes, the QN rule enables us to make use of statement logic rules without instantiating. Here is an example:

1. (x)~Ax → (z)Bz	
2. (∃z)~Bz	∴ (∃x)Ax
3. ~(z)Bz	2, QN
4. ~(x)~Ax	1, 3, MT
5. (∃x)~~Ax	4, QN
6. (∃x)Ax	5, DN

The QN rule is often useful when employing the *reductio ad absurdum* (RAA) method. For example:

1. (x)(Lx → Mx)	
2. (∃x)Lx	∴ (∃x)Mx
3. ~(∃x)Mx	Assume (for RAA)
4. (x)~Mx	3, QN
5. La	2, EI
6. La → Ma	1, UI
7. Ma	6, 5, MP
8. ~Ma	4, UI
9. Ma • ~Ma	7, 8, Conj
10. (∃x)Mx	3–9, RAA

But although RAA and CP can be used in predicate logic as well as in statement logic, the use of these methods demands an additional restriction on universal generalization: *One cannot universally generalize from a constant that occurs in an undischarged assumption.* Thus, our official formulation of UG is as follows, where $\mathscr{P}$ stands for any WFF, **x** stands for any variable, and **c** stands for any constant:

Universal Generalization (UG)

$\mathscr{P}\mathbf{c}$

$\therefore (\mathbf{x})\mathscr{P}$ (where $\mathscr{P}\mathbf{c}$ is an instance of $(\mathbf{x})\mathscr{P}$ and **c** does not occur in (a) $(\mathbf{x})\mathscr{P}$, (b) a premise of the argument, (c) a line derived by an application of EI, or (d) an undischarged assumption)

To appreciate the need for this further restriction, consider the following erroneous proof:

65. If everything is red, then everything is blue. So, all red things are blue. (Rx: x is red; Bx: x is blue)

In symbols: (x)Rx → (x)Bx ∴ (x)(Rx → Bx)

1. (x)Rx → (x)Bx	∴ (x)(Rx → Bx)
2. Ra	Assume (for CP)
3. (x)Rx	2, *incorrect use of UG* [violates the new restriction]
4. (x)Bx	1, 3, MP
5. Ba	4, UI
6. Ra → Ba	2–5, CP
7. (x)(Rx → Bx)	6, UG

The invalidity of this argument is quickly revealed by the finite universe method:

Ra Rb Ba Bb	(Ra • Rb) → (Ba • Bb) ∴ (Ra → Ba) • (Rb → Bb)
T F F T	T F F T F F T T F F F F T T

Our new restriction on UG prevents us from "proving" that such invalid arguments are valid.

Let us consider some further examples of CP and RAA in predicate logic. Here is a correct use of CP:

1. (x)(Rx → Bx)	∴ (x)Rx → (x)Bx
2. (x)Rx	Assume (for CP)
3. Ra → Ba	1, UI
4. Ra	2, UI
5. Ba	3, 4, MP
6. (x)Bx	5, UG
7. (x)Rx → (x)Bx	2–6, CP

Here, we have *not* violated the new restriction on UG because the constant does not occur in the assumption in line (2). The following is also permissible:

1. (x)(Fx → Gx)
2. (x)(Fx → Hx)   ∴ (x)[Fx → (Gx • Hx)]
   3. Fa   Assume (for CP)
   4. Fa → Ga   1, UI
   5. Fa → Ha   2, UI
   6. Ga   3, 4, MP
   7. Ha   3, 5, MP
   8. Ga • Ha   6, 7, Conj
9. Fa → (Ga • Ha)   3–8, CP
10. (x)[Fx → (Gx • Hx)] 9, UG

This proof does *not* violate our new restriction on UG since UG is applied after we have discharged the assumption. Hence, the relevant constant does not occur in an *undischarged* assumption. Here, we may add a third tip for predicate logic:

> **Tip 3:** If the conclusion is a universally quantified statement containing an arrow, use CP to prove an instance of the relevant conditional and then apply UG.

When the conclusion of an argument is an existentially quantified statement, RAA is often useful. For example:

1. (x)(Px → Sx)
2. Pa ∨ Pb   ∴ (∃x)Sx
   3. ~(∃x)Sx   Assume (for RAA)
   4. (x)~Sx   3, QN
   5. Pa → Sa   1, UI
   6. ~Sa   4, UI
   7. ~Pa   5, 6, MT
   8. Pb   2, 7, DS
   9. Pb → Sb   1, UI
   10. Sb   9, 8, MP
   11. ~Sb   4, UI
   12. Sb • ~Sb   10, 11, Conj
13. (∃x)Sx   3–12, RAA

This argument illustrates our fourth and final tip for predicate logic:

> **Tip 4:** When the conclusion of an argument is an existentially quantified statement, RAA is often useful.

As in statement logic, it is sometimes useful to employ more than one assumption in the same proof. In the following proof, CP and RAA are combined:

1. (x)Ax ∨ (x)Bx	∴ (x)(~Ax → Bx)
2. ~Aa	Assume (for CP)
3. (x)Ax	Assume (for RAA)
4. Aa	3, UI
5. Aa • ~ Aa	4, 2, Conj
6. ~(x)Ax	3–5, RAA
7. (x)Bx	1, 6, DS
8. Ba	7, UI
9. ~Aa → Ba	2–8, CP
10. (x)(~Ax → Bx)	9, UG

Once again, this proof does not violate our new restriction on UG because the relevant constant does not occur in an *undischarged* assumption. We could also construct a proof for this argument using RAA alone, but it would be longer.

Summary of Tips for Predicate Logic

1. Apply EI before you apply UI.
2. When a tilde appears on the left side of a quantifier, it is often useful to apply QN and instantiate.
3. If the conclusion is a universally quantified statement containing an arrow, use CP to prove an instance of the relevant conditional and then apply UG.
4. When the conclusion of an argument is an existentially quantified statement, RAA is often useful.

EXERCISE 9.4

PART A: Proofs Construct proofs to show that the following arguments are valid. You may use direct proof, CP, or RAA.

* **1.** (x)Ax → (x)Bx, ~(x)Bx ∴ (∃x)~Ax
  2. ~(∃y)Cy, (y)~Cy → (z)Dz ∴ Db
  3. ~(x)~Fx ∴ (∃x)Fx
* **4.** ~(∃x)~Gx ∴ (x)Gx
  5. (∃y)Hy → (∃y)Jy, (y)~Jy ∴ ~Ha
  6. (z)[(Kz ∨ Lz) → Mz] ∴ (z)(Lz → Mz)
* **7.** (x)(Nx → Ox) ∴ ~(x)Ox → ~(x)Nx

8. ~(∃x)~Px, ~(∃y)Sy ∨ ~(x)Px   ∴ ~Sd

9. (x)~Rx → (∃x)~~Tx   ∴ (x)~Tx → (∃x)Rx

*10. (x)(Ax → ~Bx), (y)Ay   ∴ (z)~Bz

11. ~(∃x)(Fx • ~Gx)   ∴ (x)(Fx → Gx)

12. (x)(Jx → Kx)   ∴ (x)[Jx → ((y)(Ky → Ly) → Lx)]

*13. (∃x)[Bx → (y)~Cy], ~(∃y)Cy → ~(∃z)Dz   ∴ (x)Bx → (z)~Dz

14. (∃x)[Fx • (y)(Gy → Hx)], (x)[Fx → (y)(By → ~Hx)]   ∴ (x)(Gx → ~Bx)

15. (x)[Dx → (∃y)(Fy • Gy)]   ∴ (x)~Fx → ~(∃y)Dy

*16. ~(x)Mx ∨ (∃x)~Mx, (∃x)Sx → (x)Mx, Sb ∨ (x)~Px   ∴ ~Pa

17. [(x)Hx → (∃x)Gx] → ~(∃y)(Fy ∨ (∃z)Tz), ~(x)Fx → (∃x)Gx,
    (x)Hx → (∃x)~Fx   ∴ (∃x)~Tx

18. (x)Hx ∨ [(x)Kx • (∃x)~Lx], (x)Hx → ~(x)Nx, ~(x)Lx → (∃x)~Nx,
    (x)Mx ∨ (x)Nx   ∴ Mc

*19. (x)(Lx ↔ (y)My)   ∴ (x)Lx ∨ (x)~Lx

20. (x)Ax ∨ (x)Bx   ∴ (x)(Ax ∨ Bx) [*Hint:* Use two assumptions.]

PART B: More Proofs Construct proofs to show that the following symbolic arguments are valid. You may use direct proof, CP, or RAA.

* 1. (∃x)Fx → (∃x)(Gx • Hx), (∃x)Hx → (x)Jx   ∴ (x)(Fx → Jx)

   2. (x)(Wx → Sx)   ∴ (∃x)Wx → (∃x)Sx

   3. (x)~Kx ∨ (∃x)Lx, (x)~Lx   ∴ ~Kb

* 4. ~(∃x)Mx → (∃x)(Nx • Px), (x)~Px   ∴ (∃x)Mx

   5. ~(∃x)(Rx ∨ Sx) ∨ (x)Tx, (∃x)~Tx   ∴ ~(∃x)Sx

   6. (x)(Ax → (y)By)   ∴ (x)Ax → (x)Bx

* 7. (x)(Cx → Dx), ~(∃x)Cx → (∃x)Dx   ∴ ~(x)~Dx

   8. (z)(Ez → (∃x)Fx), (z)Gz → (∃z)Ez   ∴ (z)Gz → (∃z)Fz

   9. ~(x)~Ax, (∃x)Ax → (x)Bx, (x)[(Bx ∨ Cx) → Dx]   ∴ (x)Dx

*10. (∃x)~Kx → ~(∃x)Dx, ~(x)Kx, Db ↔ Qa   ∴ ~Qa

11. ~[(x)Fx ∨ (∃x)Gx], (∃x)~Fx → (y)Hy, (x)~Gx → (z)Jz   ∴ (x)(Hx • Jx)

12. ~(x)Kx → (∃x)Lx, (∃x)~Kx → (x)(Lx → Mx)   ∴ ~(x)Kx → (∃x)Mx

*13. ~[(x)Ax → (∃x)Bx], (∃x)~Cx → (∃x)Bx, (x)[(Ax • Cx) → Da]   ∴ Da

14. ~[(y)Zy • (y)Wy], (∃y)~Zy → (y)Uy, (∃y)Ry → (y)Wy   ∴ (y)(Uy ∨ ~Ry)

15. Ba ↔ ~(∃x)Cx, (∃x)Ax ∨ (x)Bx, (x)~Ax   ∴ ~Ce

*16. (x)[(Ax → ~Bx) ∨ Cb], ~(∃x)Cx, (∃y)By   ∴ ~(y)Ay

17. (∃x)Sx → (y)(~Ty → Uy), (∃x)Rx → (∃x)~Tx   ∴ (∃x)(Sx • Rx) → (∃z)Uz

18. (x)(~Gx ∨ ~Hx), (x)[(Jx → Fx) → Hx]   ∴ ~(∃x)(Fx • Gx)

*19. [~(x)(R • Px) → (R → ~(x)Px)] → (∃x)[Ax • (y)(~Ay ∨ ~By)]   ∴ ~(x)Bx

20. (x)Px   ∴ (∃x)[Px • (Qx → (y)Qy)]

PART C: Logical Equivalents Construct proofs to show that the following are valid. By constructing these proofs, you will show that each pair of statements is logically equivalent. Take special note of the fourth and fifth pairs, as these indicate the somewhat surprising behavior of quantifiers that bind variables in the antecedent of a conditional.

* **1.** (x)(Ax • Bx) ∴ (x)Ax • (x)Bx
  2. (x)Ax • (x)Bx ∴ (x)(Ax • Bx)
  3. (∃x)(Ax ∨ Bx) ∴ (∃x)Ax ∨ (∃x)Bx
* **4.** (∃x)Ax ∨ (∃x)Bx ∴ (∃x)(Ax ∨ Bx)
  5. (x)(P → Ax) ∴ P → (x)Ax
  6. P → (x)Ax ∴ (x)(P → Ax)
* **7.** (x)(Ax → P) ∴ (∃x)Ax → P

  8. (∃x)Ax → P ∴ (x)(Ax → P)
  9. (∃x)(Ax → P) ∴ (x)Ax → P
  10. (x)Ax → P ∴ (∃x)(Ax → P)
  11. (∃x)(P → Ax) ∴ P → (∃x)Ax
  12. P → (∃x)Ax ∴ (∃x)(P → Ax)
  13. (x)Ax ∨ P ∴ (x)(Ax ∨ P)
  14. (x)(Ax ∨ P) ∴ (x)Ax ∨ P

PART D: English Arguments Symbolize the following arguments, using the schemes of abbreviation provided. Then construct proofs to show that the arguments are valid. You may use either direct proof, CP, or RAA.

* **1.** Every act of terrorism is deplorable. If there is an act of terrorism that either promotes the general welfare or corrects an injustice, then some acts of terrorism are not deplorable. So, no act of terrorism corrects an injustice. (Tx: x is an act of terrorism; Dx: x is deplorable; Wx: x promotes the general welfare; Cx: x corrects an injustice)

  2. All brain processes are physical processes. No mental processes are tangible. Therefore, every brain process that is a mental process is also an intangible physical process. (Bx: x is a brain process; Px: x is a physical process; Mx: x is a mental process; Tx: x is tangible)

  3. Either Smith is a criminally insane person or all kleptomaniacs are criminally insane persons. But it is not the case that there are persons who are criminally insane. We may infer that Smith is not a kleptomaniac. (Cx: x is criminally insane; Px: x is a person; Kx: x is a kleptomaniac; s: Smith)

* **4.** An act of killing is wrong if and only if it eliminates the prospect of future valuable life. To kill a potential person is to kill. To kill a fetus is to kill a potential person. To kill a potential person is to eliminate the prospect of future valuable life. It follows that killing a fetus is wrong. (Kx: x is an act of killing; Wx: x is wrong; Ex: x eliminates the prospect of future valuable life; Px: x is an act of killing a potential person; Fx: x is an act of killing a fetus)

  5. If there are any gods, then all free creatures are predestined. If there are any free creatures, then whatever is predestined is morally responsible. Accordingly, if there are any gods, then all free creatures are morally responsible. (Gx: x is a god; Fx: x is a free creature; Px: x is predestined; Mx: x is morally responsible)

  6. No absolute right can be denied. Every right can be denied if one person's right to life can conflict with another person's right to life. Unfortunately, one person's right to life can conflict with another person's right to life. Therefore, no rights are absolute rights. (Ax: x is an absolute right; Rx: x is a right; Dx: x can be denied; P: One person's right to life can conflict with another person's right to life)

* **7.** Some reprobates are boring. Some highly moral individuals are humorous. If there are any reprobates, then highly moral individuals are fascinating if they are humorous. We may conclude that there are highly moral individuals who are fascinating. (Rx: x is a reprobate; Bx: x is boring; Mx: x is highly moral; Hx: x is humorous; Fx: x is fascinating)

8. If some poltergeists are not ghosts, then some haunted houses are dangerous. But it is not the case that there are any ghosts or haunted houses. Therefore, it is not the case that there are any poltergeists. (Px: x is a poltergeist; Gx: x is a ghost; Hx: x is a haunted house; Dx: x is dangerous)

9. Contraception is not right if it violates the purpose of sex or obviates valuable life. Some acts of contraception obviate valuable life. If a thing is not right, then it is wrong. Hence, some acts of contraception are wrong. (Cx: x is an act of contraception; Rx: x is right; Vx: x violates the purpose of sex; Ox: x obviates valuable life; Wx: x is wrong)

10. If some acts of torturing the innocent are not wrong, then all acts of torturing the innocent are right. Some acts of torturing the innocent are approved by society. Consequently, if no acts of torturing the innocent are right, then some things approved by society are wrong. (Tx: x is an act of torturing the innocent; Wx: x is wrong; Rx: x is right; Sx: x is approved by society)

PART E: Ready for a Challenge? Try the following proof. It's a bit on the long side: (x)Px ∴ ~(∃x)Qx ↔ ~[(∃x)(Px • Qx) • (y)(Qy → Py)]

9.5   The Logic of Relations: Symbolizations

Thus far, we have considered only *monadic* (one-place) predicate letters, such as Ax, By, and Cz. Monadic predicate letters are adequate for ascribing an attribute (e.g., being human) to an individual. But individuals not only have attributes, they also bear relations to one another. For example, we can say that Smith *is older than* Jones or that Elizabeth *is a sister of* John. Modern predicate logic encompasses the logic of relations, but to symbolize relations, we need predicate letters with more than one place. These are called *polyadic* predicate letters. For instance, we can use Oxy to abbreviate "x is older than y" or Sxy to abbreviate "x is a sister of y."

Here is a simple example of an argument that involves a relational predicate:

66. Al is taller than Bob. Bob is taller than Chris. If one thing is taller than a second and the second is taller than a third, then the first is taller than the third. So, Al is taller than Chris.

We need a polyadic predicate letter to symbolize the relation of *being taller than*, so here is a scheme of abbreviation for argument (66):

Txy: x is taller than y; a: Al; b: Bob; c: Chris

Using this scheme of abbreviation, "Al is taller than Bob" becomes simply Tab, and "Bob is taller than Chris" becomes Tbc. To symbolize the third premise, we first translate it into logicese: "For all x, for all y, and for all z, if x is taller than y and y is taller than z, then x is taller than z." The complete symbolization looks like this:

67. Tab, Tbc, (x)(y)(z)[(Txy • Tyz) → Txz] ∴ Tac

And the proof runs as follows:

1. Tab
2. Tbc
3. (x)(y)(z)[(Txy • Tyz) → Txz]   ∴ Tac
4. (y)(z)[(Tay • Tyz) → Taz]   3, UI
5. (z)[(Tab • Tbz) → Taz]   4, UI
6. (Tab • Tbc) → Tac   5, UI
7. Tab • Tbc   1, 2, Conj
8. Tac   6, 7, MP

Although we already have the inference rules needed for constructing proofs that involve relations, we will delay a detailed discussion of such proofs until the next section. For now, let us turn our attention to symbolizing statements involving relations.

Statements involving relations can be rather difficult to symbolize, but much of the difficulty can be removed by working through a series of well-chosen examples. Perhaps the most important skill to develop here is that of translating English into logicese. How would you symbolize the following sentence?

68. Someone loves everyone. (Px: x is a person; Lxy: x loves y)

First, let's rewrite it in logicese: "There is some x such that x is a person, and for all y, if y is a person, then x loves y." Once we have the logicese, symbolizing is easy:

69. (∃x)[Px • (y)(Py → Lxy)]

Now, examine the following closely related sentences, along with their symbolic translations. (The scheme of abbreviation remains the same.)

70. Everyone loves someone.

In logicese, we have "For all x, if x is a person, then there is some y such that y is a person and x loves y." In symbols:

71. (x)[Px → (∃y)(Py • Lxy)]

How would you symbolize the following sentence?

72. No one loves everyone.

In logicese, we have "For all x, if x is a person, then it is not true that for all y, if y is a person, x loves y." In symbols:

73. (x)[Px → ~(y)(Py → Lxy)]

Statement (69) can also be translated into logicese as follows: "It is not the case that there is some x such that x is a person and for all y, if y is a person, then x loves y." So, we can also symbolize (69) this way:

74. ~(∃x)[Px • (y)(Py → Lxy)]

We can prove that statements (73) and (74) are logically equivalent. To do this, we must show that (73) implies (74), and vice versa. The following proof shows that (74) implies (73). That (73) implies (74) is left as an exercise.

1. ~(∃x)[Px • (y)(Py → Lxy)] ∴ (x)[Px → ~(y)(Py → Lxy)]	
2. Pa	Assume (for CP)
3. (x)~[Px • (y)(Py → Lxy)]	1, QN
4. (y)(Py → Lay)	Assume (for RAA)
5. ~[Pa • (y)(Py → Lay)]	3, UI
6. ~Pa ∨ ~(y)(Py → Lay)]	5, DeM
7. ~~(y)(Py → Lay)	4, DN
8. ~Pa	6, 7, DS
9. Pa • ~Pa	2, 8, Conj
10. ~(y)(Py → Lay)	4–9, RAA
11. Pa → ~(y)(Py → Lay)	2–10, CP
12. (x)[Px → ~(y)(Py → Lay)]	11, UG

Now, try to symbolize the following sentence:

75. No one loves anyone.

In logicese, we have "For all x, if x is a person, then for all y, if y is a person, x does not love y." In symbols:

76. (x)[Px → (y)(Py → ~Lxy)]

Statement (75) can also be translated into logicese as follows: "It is not the case that there is some x such that x is a person and there is some y such that y is a person, and x loves y." In symbols:

77. ~(∃x)[Px • (∃y)(Py • Lxy)]

Predicate letters can be of more than two places. For example, the following sentence involves the three-place predicate "x steals y from z":

78. Every thief steals something valuable from someone. (Tx: x is a thief, Sxyz: x steals y from z; Vx: x is valuable; Px: x is a person)

In logicese, we have "For all x, if x is a thief, then there is some y such that y is valuable, and there is some z such that z is a person, and x steals y from z." The symbolization looks like this:

79. (x)(Tx → (∃y)[Vy • (∃z)(Pz • Sxyz)])

Again, our symbolization brings out the logical complexity that can be present in rather ordinary English sentences.

As mentioned previously, the best way to ensure accuracy of translation into symbols within predicate logic is first to translate English into logicese and then to translate logicese into symbols. The following short list of examples should serve as a useful guide for this process.

Summary of Symbolizations

English	Logicese	Symbols
1. No woman is smarter than Eve. (Wx: x is a woman; Sxy: x is smarter than y; e: Eve)	For all x (if x is woman, then it is not the case that x is smarter than e).	(x)(Wx → ~Sxe)
2. If Adam is taller than Eve, then someone is taller than Eve. (a: Adam; e: Eve; Txy: x is taller than y; Px: x is a person)	If a is taller than e, then there is some x such that (x is a person and x is taller than e).	Tae → (∃x) (Px • Txe)
3. No one is shorter than himself. (Px: x is a person; Sxy: x is shorter than y)	For all x (if x is a person, then it is not the case that x is shorter than x).	(x)(Px → ~Sxx)
4. No one is shorter than everyone. (Px: x is a person; Sxy: x is shorter than y)	For all x [if x is a person, then it is not the case that for all y (if y is a person, then x is shorter than y)].	(x)[Px → ~(y)(Py → Sxy)]

Continued

Summary of Symbolizations (*Continued*)

English	Logicese	Symbols
5. Everyone is shorter than someone. (Px: x is a person; Sxy: x is shorter than y)	For all x [if x is a person, then there is some y such that (y is a person and x is shorter than y)].	(x)[Px → (∃y)(Py • Sxy)]
6. Every adult gives a present to some child. (Ax: is an adult; Gxyz: x gives y to z; Px: x is a present; Cx: x is a child)	For all x [if x is an adult, then there is some y such that (y is a present and there is some z such that (z is a child, and x gives y to z))].	(x)[Ax → (∃y)(Py • (∃z)(Cz • Gxyz))]

In closing this section, let us note certain general characteristics of relations. First, a relation R is **symmetrical** just in case: For all x and y (if x bears R to y, then y bears R to x). For example, the relation *being a sibling of* is symmetrical, for if Jeff is a sibling of Jane, then Jane must be a sibling of Jeff. On the other hand, the relation *being a mother of* is asymmetrical, for if Thelma is the mother of Sharlene, then Sharlene is not the mother of Thelma. More generally, a relation R is **asymmetrical** just in case: For all x and y (if x bears R to y, then it is not the case that y bears R to x). Note that some relations are **nonsymmetrical**— that is, they are neither symmetrical nor asymmetrical. The relation *being a sister of* is nonsymmetrical, for if Jane is a sister of Chris, Chris may or may not be a sister of Jane—it all depends on whether Chris is male or female.

A relation R is **reflexive** just in case: For all x (x bears R to x). For example, each thing is identical with itself. So, identity is a reflexive relation. On the other hand, a relation R is **irreflexive** just in case: For all x (it is not the case that x bears R to x). For example, nothing can be larger than itself, so *being larger than* is an irreflexive relation. And a **nonreflexive** relation is one that is neither reflexive nor irreflexive. *Being proud of* is nonreflexive because a person may or may not be proud of himself or herself.

Next, a relation R is **transitive** just in case: For all x, y and z (if x bears R to y and y bears R to z, then x bears R to z). For example: If Al is taller than Bob, and Bob is taller than Chris, then Al must be taller than Chris. Hence, *being taller than* is transitive. On the other hand, *being father of* is an intransitive relation, for if Earl is the father of John and John is the father of Drew, then Earl cannot be the father of Drew. In general, a relation R is **intransitive** just in case: For all x, y and z (if x bears R to y and y bears R to z, then it is not the case that x bears R to z). Finally, a relation is **nontransitive** if it is neither transitive nor intransitive. The relation *being an acquaintance of* is nontransitive. If Rick is an acquaintance of Dawn and Dawn is an acquaintance of Pete, then Rick may or may not be an acquaintance of Pete.

Summary of Definitions

A relation R is **symmetrical** just in case: For all x and y (if x bears R to y, then y bears R to x).

A relation R is **asymmetrical** just in case: For all x and y (if x bears R to y, then it is not the case that y bears R to x).

A relation is **nonsymmetrical** just in case it is neither symmetrical nor asymmetrical.

A relation R is **reflexive** just in case: For all x (x bears R to x).

A relation R is **irreflexive** just in case: For all x (it is not the case that x bears R to x).

A relation is **nonreflexive** just in case it is neither reflexive nor irreflexive.

A relation R is **transitive** just in case: For all x, y, and z (if x bears R to y and y bears R to z, then x bears R to z).

A relation R is **intransitive** just in case: For all x, y, and z (if x bears R to y and y bears R to z, then it is not the case that x bears R to z).

A relation is **nontransitive** just in case it is neither transitive nor intransitive.

EXERCISE 9.5

PART A: Matching Match the item on the left with the appropriate characteristic on the right.

_____ **1.** If x is older than y and y is older than z, then x is older than z.

_____ **2.** Nothing is bigger than itself.

_____ **3.** If x is shorter than y, then y is not shorter than x.

_____ **4.** Everything is the same size as itself.

_____ **5.** If x is married to y, then y is married to x.

_____ **6.** If x is greater than y, then y is not greater than x.

_____ **7.** If x is equal to y, then y is equal to x.

_____ **8.** If x is the mother of y and y is the mother of z, then x is not the mother of z.

_____ **9.** If x loves y and y loves z, then x may or may not love z.

_____ **10.** If x admires y, then y may or may not admire x.

_____ **11.** A person may or may not hate himself.

_____ **12.** If x is obligated to y and y is obligated to z, then x may or may not be obligated to z.

A. Symmetrical

B. Asymmetrical

C. Nonsymmetrical

D. Reflexive

E. Irreflexive

F. Nonreflexive

G. Transitive

H. Intransitive

I. Nontransitive

PART B: Symbolizing Symbolize the following statements using the schemes of abbreviation provided.

* **1.** Nothing stands to the left of itself. (Lxy: x stands to the left of y)

2. No human is taller than Goliath. (Hx: x is human; Txy: x is taller than y; g: Goliath)

3. No human is taller than himself. (Hx: x is human; Txy: x is taller than y)

* **4.** Some financier is richer than everyone. (Fx: x is a financier; Rxy: x is richer than y; Px: x is a person)

5. Someone gives everyone something. (Px: x is a person; Gxyz: x gives to y [object] z)

6. Someone gives someone everything. (Px: x is a person; Gxyz: x gives to y [object] z)

* **7.** No deity is weaker than some human. (Dx: x is a deity; Hx: x is human; Wxy: x is weaker than y)

8. No one gives anyone anything. (Px: x is a person; Gxyz: x gives to y [object] z)

9. Everyone gives someone something. (Px: x is a person; Gxyz: x gives to y [object] z)

* **10.** No one who is poor is richer than someone who is wealthy. (Ox: x is a person; Px: x is poor; Rxy: x is richer than y; Wx: x is wealthy)

11. No one is more fun than Chris. (Px: x is person; Fxy: x is more fun than y; c: Chris)

12. No cat is smarter than some horse. (Cx: x is cat; Sxy: x is smarter than y; Hx: x is a horse)

* **13.** No mouse is mightier than himself. (Mx: x is a mouse; Mxy: x is mightier than y)

14. Every woman is stronger than some man. (Wx: x is a woman; Sxy: x is stronger than y; Mx: x is a man)

15. If Apollo is better than Hera and Hera is better than Cronos, then Apollo is better than Cronos. (Bxy: x is better than y; a: Apollo; h: Hera; c: Cronos)

* **16.** Every moviegoer admires Bogart. (Mx: x is moviegoer; Axy: x admires y; b: Bogart)

17. Some moviegoers admire themselves as well as Bogart. (Mx: x is a moviegoer; Axy: x admires y; b: Bogart)

18. Some saints help someone everyday. (Sx: x is a saint; Hxyz: x helps y on z; Px: x is person; Dx: x is a day)

* **19.** No saint helps everyone everyday. (Sx: x is a saint; Hxyz: x helps y on z; Px: x is person; Dx: x is a day)

20. Everyone falls in love with someone at some enchanted moment. (Px: x is a person; Lxyz: x falls in love with y at z; Ex: x is enchanted; Mx: x is a moment)

21. The relation *being older than* is asymmetrical. (Oxy: x is older than y)

* **22.** The relation *being the father of* is intransitive. (Fxy: x is the father of y)

23. The relation *being larger than* is irreflexive. (Lxy: x is larger than y)

24. The relation *being south of* is transitive. (Sxy: x is south of y)

* **25.** The relation *being near to* is symmetrical. (Nxy: x is near to y)

PART C: More Matching Match the item on the left with the appropriate characteristic on the right.

_____ **1.** Nothing is smaller than itself.

_____ **2.** If x hates y, then y may or may not hate x.

_____ **3.** If x is the same size as y, then y is the same size as x.

_____ **4.** Everything is the same weight as itself.

_____ **5.** If x is near y, then y is near x.

_____ **6.** If x is less than y, then y is not less than x.

_____ **7.** If x likes y and y likes z, then x may or may not like z.

_____ **8.** If x is the father of y and y is the father of z, then x is not the father of z.

_____ **9.** If x is taller than y, then y is not taller than x.

_____ **10.** If x is younger than y and y is younger than z, then x is younger than z.

A. Symmetrical

B. Asymmetrical

C. Nonsymmetrical

D. Reflexive

E. Irreflexive

F. Nonreflexive

G. Transitive

H. Intransitive

I. Nontransitive

PART D: More Symbolizing Symbolize the following statements using the schemes of abbreviation provided.

* **1.** Someone gets angry at everyone. (Px: x is a person; Axy: x gets angry at y)

2. Everyone laughs at someone. (Px: x is a person; Lxy: x laughs at y)

3. Everything is either colorless or the same color as itself. (Cx: x has a color; Sxy: x has the same color as y)

* **4.** Some people like themselves, but some people do not like themselves. (Px: x is a person; Lxy: x likes y)

5. No one laughs at anyone. (Px: x is a person; Lxy: x laughs at y)

6. Some students find Kant boring, but Amy is a student who does not find Kant boring. (Sx: x is a student; Bxy: x finds y boring; k: Kant; a: Amy)

* **7.** Everything is caused by something (or other). (Cxy: x is caused by y)

8. Nothing causes everything. (Cxy: x causes y)

9. Something causes everything. (Cxy: x causes y)

* **10.** Nothing causes anything. (Cxy: x causes y)

11. Everyone gets angry at someone about something. (Px: x is a person; Axyz: x gets angry at y about z)

12. Everything has a cause; but for all x and y, if x precedes y, then y does not cause x. (Cxy: x causes y; Pxy: x precedes y)

13. Every entity is either necessary or dependent on a necessary entity. (Nx: x is necessary; Dxy: x is dependent on y)

14. No logician argues about every subject with everyone. (Lx: x is a logician; Sx: x is a subject; Px: x is a person; Axyz: x argues about y with z)

15. Either nothing is dependent on anything or everything is dependent on something. (Dxy: x is dependent on y)

16. No one is obligated to everyone. (Px: x is a person; Oxy: x is obligated to y)

17. Everyone is obligated to someone. (Px: x is a person; Oxy: x is obligated to y)

18. The relation *being to the north of* is transitive. (Nxy: x is north of y)

19. The relation *being next to* is symmetrical. (Nxy: x is next to y)

20. The relation *being the same shape as* is reflexive. (Sxy: x is the same shape as y)

21. Some number is greater than itself. (Nx: x is a number; Gxy: x is greater than y)

22. Voldemort hates all muggles. (v: Voldemort; Mx: x is a muggle; Hxy x hates y)

23. Some philosopher studies every book with some teacher. (Px: x is a philosopher; Sxyz: x studies y with z; Bx: x is a book; Tx: x is a teacher)

24. Every philosopher studies some book with every teacher. (Px: x is a philosopher; Sxyz: x studies y with z; Bx: x is a book; Tx: x is a teacher)

25. No philosopher studies any book with any teacher. (Px: x is a philosopher; Sxyz: x studies y with z; Bx: x is a book; Tx: x is a teacher)

PART E: Ready for a Challenge? Symbolize the following sentences. Some of these are rather difficult.

* **1.** Someone is having her cake and eating it too. (Hxy: x is having y; Px: x is a person; Cx: x is a cake; Exy: x is eating y)

  2. There is some particular thing that is between any two things. (Bxyz: x is between y and z)

  3. Between any two things there is something or other. (Bxyz: x is between y and z)

* **4.** All metaphysicians except idealists postulate the existence of at least one corporeal entity. (Mx: x is a metaphysician; Ix: x is an idealist; Pxy: x postulates the existence of y; Cx: x is a corporeal entity)

  5. Some guys have all the luck. (Gx: x is a guy; Hxy: x has y; Lx: x is a bit of luck)

  6. Everybody needs somebody sometime. (Px: x is a person; Tx: x is a time; Nxyz: x needs y at z)

* **7.** Everyone who hates someone hates herself. (Px: x is a person; Hxy: x hates y)

  8. There is someone who loves and is loved by Brit. (Px: x is a person; Lxy: x loves y; b: Brit)

9. No bank is without at least some money. (Bx: x is a bank; Pxy: x is in y; Mx: x is a unit of money)

*10. Some planets' moons are Jupiter's moons. (Px: x is a planet; Mxy: x is a moon of y; j: Jupiter)

11. Nobody weds anyone to anyone, unless she meets them both. (Px: x is a person; Wxyz: x weds y to z; Mxy: x meets y)

12. Once upon a time in a place far away, there lived a mighty warrior. (Tx: x is a time; Px: x is a place; Fx: x is far away; Wx: x is a mighty warrior; Lxyz: x lived at y during z)

*13. There was a time when nobody lived anywhere. (Tx: x is a time; Rx: x is a person; Px: x is a place; Lxyz: x lived at y during z)

14. A dog's bark is worse than his bite. (Dx: x is a dog; Bxy: x is a bark of y; Wxy: x is worse than y; Txy: x is a bite of y)

15. Every even number has a successor. (Ex: x is even; Nx: x is a number; Hxy: x has y; Sx: x is a successor)

*16. A rolling stone gathers no moss. (Rx: x rolls; Sx: x is a stone; Gxy: x gathers y; Mx: x is moss)

17. If anything can kill a fast-moving mammal, the cheetah can. (Kxy: x can kill y; Fx: x is fast-moving; Mx: x is a mammal; Cx: x is a cheetah)

18. An Italian's dinner is spicier than a Norwegian's. (Ix: x is an Italian; Dxy: x is a dinner of y; Sxy: x is spicier than y; Nx: x is a Norwegian)

*19. If anyone is married to anyone, then someone wed them both. (Px: x is a person; Mxy: x is married to y; Wxyz: x wed y to z)

20. You can fool some of the people all of the time and all of the people some of the time, but you can't fool all of the people all of the time. (Fxyz: x can fool y at z; Px: x is a person; Tx: x is a time)

9.6   The Logic of Relations: Proofs

The inference rules for predicate logic introduced in sections 9.3 and 9.4 are sufficient for the logic of relations. But it will be helpful to highlight some new types of situations that can arise and to issue some important reminders regarding restrictions on our inference rules.

First, if you have a premise with more than one quantifier, apply UI or EI to remove the quantifiers one at a time, from left to right. Here is an example:

1. $(\exists x)(y)Hxy$	$\therefore (\exists x)Hxx$
2. $(y)Hay$	1, EI
3. Haa	2, UI
4. $(\exists x)Hxx$	3, EG

In this connection, remember that UI and EI are implicational rules, and hence they cannot be applied to *parts* of statements. For this reason, the following use of UI is incorrect:

1. (∃x)(y)Hxy	∴ (∃x)Hxx
2. (∃x)Hxa	1, *incorrect use of UI*

We can apply UI only to *universally* quantified statements, and (∃x)(y)Hxy is not a universally quantified statement. Similarly, we can apply EI only to *existentially* quantified statements. Consider the following proof:

1. (∃x)(∃y)Fxy → Gb	
2. (x)(y)Fxy	∴ Gb
3. (y)Fay	2, UI
4. Fab	3, UI
5. (∃y)Fay	4, EG
6. (∃x)(∃y)Fxy	5, EG
7. Gb	1, 6, MP

May we infer (∃y)Fay → Gb from premise (1) by EI? No, for in doing so, we would be applying EI to *part* of a statement (specifically, to the antecedent of a conditional). In the first premise, (∃x) has scope over only (∃y)Fxy. Incidentally, notice that just as we removed the quantifiers on premise (2) one at a time, we put quantifiers back on one at a time also, at lines (5) and (6).

Second, remember that EG and UG are implicational rules. Is the following application of EG correct?

1. (x)Ax → Bac	∴ (x)Ax → (∃y)Byc
2. (x)Ax → (∃y)Byc	1, EG

No. Here EG has been applied to part of a statement, specifically to the consequent of a conditional. However, the following proof is correct:

1. (x)Ax → Bac	∴ (x)Ax → (∃y)Byc
2. (x)Ax	Assume (for CP)
3. Bac	1, 2, MP
4. (∃y)Byc	3, EG
5. (x)Ax → (∃y)Byc	2–4, CP

Is the following use of UG correct?

1. (x)[(y)Lxy → Ma]	∴ (x)(y)Lxy → Ma
2. (y)Lby → Ma	1, UI
3. (x)(y)Lxy → Ma	2, UG

No. We cannot apply UG to part of a statement, and here we have applied UG to the antecedent of a conditional. We can, however, show that the argument is valid using CP:

1. (x)[(y)Lxy → Ma]	∴ (x)(y)Lxy → Ma
2. (x)(y)Lxy	Assume (for CP)
3. (y)Lby → Ma	1, UI
4. (y)Lby	2, UI
5. Ma	3, 4, MP
6. (x)(y)Lxy → Ma	2–5, CP

Third, when using UI, remember that constants must be substituted *uniformly*. Here are some correct and incorrect applications of UI:

1. (x)[Mx • (Lx ∨ (y)Kxy)]	
2. Mb • (Lb ∨ (y)Kby)	1, UI (correct)
3. Ma • (Lb ∨ (y)Kby)	1, UI (incorrect)

Similarly, when using EI, constants must be substituted *uniformly*. Here are some correct and incorrect applications:

1. (∃x)(y)(Pxy ↔ ~Oxy)	
2. (y)(Pay ↔ ~Oay)	1, EI (correct)
3. (y)(Pay ↔ ~Oby)	1, EI (incorrect)

Fourth, remember that we may never existentially instantiate to a constant that occurs previously in the proof. For example:

1. (x)(∃y)Gyx	
2. (∃y)Gya	1, UI
3. Gaa	2, *incorrect use of EI*
4. (∃x)Gxx	3, EG

This is like arguing, "For every natural number x, there is some natural number y such that y is greater than x. So, there is some natural number that is greater than itself." Clearly, the argument is invalid.

Fifth, recall the special restrictions on UG. UG lets us move from $\mathcal{P}c$ to $(\mathbf{x})\mathcal{P}$ provided that **c** does not occur in (i) $(\mathbf{x})\mathcal{P}$, (ii) a premise of the argument, (iii) a line derived by an application of EI, or (iv) an undischarged assumption. Is the following application of UG correct?

1. (y)Eyy	
2. Eaa	1, UI
3. (x)Exa	2, UG???
4. (∃y)(x)Exy	3, EG

Moving from (1) to (4) is like arguing, "Every number is equal to itself. There-fore, there is some number such that all numbers are equal to it." Because the premise is true and the conclusion is false, the argument is invalid. The problem is with step 3. This is a misapplication of UG because the constant being gener-alized on still appears in line (3).

The logic of relations enables us to see the subtlety of many rather ordinary-looking English sentences. For example, consider the following argument:

80. Each thing causes at least one thing. So, something causes something. (Cxy: x causes y)

In symbols: (x)(∃y)Cxy ∴ (∃x)(∃y)Cxy

Note that it would be wrong to switch the order of the quantifiers in the premise as follows: (∃y)(x)Cxy. This formula says that *at least one thing is such that every-thing causes it,* which is quite different from the premise of argument (80). The proof for (80) is short and simple:

1. (x)(∃y)Cxy	∴ (∃x)(∃y)Cxy
2. (∃y)Cay	1, UI
3. (∃x)(∃y)Cxy	2, EG

Now, compare argument (80) to the following fallacious argument:

81. Each thing causes at least one thing. So, at least one thing is such that everything causes it. (Cxy: x causes y)

In symbols: (x)(∃y)Cxy ∴ (∃y)(x)Cxy

Even if each thing causes at least one thing, we cannot infer that something is caused by everything. So, we shouldn't be able to construct a (correct) proof for argument (81). Which of the following steps cannot be justified by our rules?

1. (x)(∃y)Cxy	∴ (∃y)(x)Cxy
2. (∃y)Cby	?
3. Cbc	?
4. (x)Cxc	?
5. (∃y)(x)Cxy	?

Line (2) follows from line (1) by UI, and line (3) follows from line (2) by EI. The problem comes at line (4). It may seem that line (4) derives from line (3) by UG, but this is not so. The third restriction on UG tells us that we cannot generalize from a constant that appears in a line derived by an application of EI. In this case, we are generalizing from *b*, which appears in line (3), which is derived by an application of EI. Hence, this is a misapplication of UG.

In closing, let us consider an argument that involves a grammatically complicated conclusion:

82. The *Mona Lisa* is beautiful. So, anyone who steals the *Mona Lisa* steals something beautiful. (a: The *Mona Lisa;* Bx: x is beautiful; Px: x is a person; Sxy: x steals y)

The symbolization is as follows:

83. Ba ∴ (x)[(Px • Sxa) → (∃y)(By • Sxy)]

Here is a proof for argument (83). Note the use of two assumptions.

1. Ba	∴ (x)[(Px • Sxa) → (∃y)(By • Sxy)]
2. Pb • Sba	Assume (for CP)
3. ~(∃y)(By • Sby)	Assume (for RAA)
4. (y)~(By • Sby)	3, QN
5. ~(Ba • Sba)	4, UI
6. ~Ba ∨ ~Sba	5, DeM
7. ~~Ba	1, DN
8. ~Sba	6, 7, DS
9. Sba	2, Simp
10. Sba • ~Sba	9, 8, Conj
11. (∃y)(By • Sby)	3–10, RAA
12. (Pb • Sba) → (∃y)(By • Sby)	2–11, CP
13. (x)[(Px • Sxa) → (∃y)(By • Sxy)]	12, UG

EXERCISE 9.6

PART A: Correct or Incorrect? Which of the following inferences are permitted by our inference rules? Which are not? (In each case, assume that the first line shown is a premise and the last line shown is the final line of the proof.)

* **1.** 1. (x)(y)(Mx • Nxy)
     2. (y)(My • Nyy)   1, UI

2. 1. (x)(y)Axy
     2. (y)Aay   1, UI
     3. Aaa   2, UI
     4. (y)Ayy   3, UG

3. 1. (x)Fx ↔ Gab
     2. (x)Fx ↔ (∃x)Gxb   1, EG

* **4.** 1. (x)[(∃y)Lxy → Kx]
       2. (∃y)Lby → Kb   1, UI

  5. 1. (∃x)Bax → (y)Cyb
       2. Bac → (y)Cyb   1, EI

  6. 1. (∃x)Dxb
       2. Dbb   1, EI

* **7.** 1. Eab → Fab
       2. (x)(Exb → Fxb)   1, UG

  8. 1. ~(x)Jxd
       2. ~Jad   1, UI

  9. 1. (x)(Gxb → Hxb)
       2. Gab → Hab   1, UI
       3. (x)Gxb → Hab   2, UG

* **10.** 1. (∃x)(y)(Kyx ∨ ~Lxa)
        2. (y)(Kya ∨ ~Laa)   1, EI

  11. 1. (x)[(∃y)Ayx ∨ ~Bx]
        2. (∃y)Ayc ∨ ~Bc   1, UI

  12. 1. (x)(y)Pxy
        2. (x)Pxb   1, UI

* **13.** 1. (x)[Sxb → (y)Rxy]
        2. Sbb → (y)Rby   1, UI

  14. 1. (∃x)(Hxb • ~Hab)
        2. Hab • ~Hab   1, EI
        3. (∃y)(Hyb • ~Hyb)   2, EG

  15. 1. Nad   Assume (for CP)
        2. (x)Nxd   1, UG
        3. Nad → (x)Nxd   1–2, CP

* **16.** 1. (x)(∃y)Jyx
        2. (∃y)Jya   1, UI
        3. Jba   2, EI
        4. (x)Jbx   3, UG

  17. 1. (x)Mxd
        2. Mad   1, UI
        3. (∃y)May   2, EG
        4. (z)(∃y)Mzy   3, UG

  18. 1. (z)(∃y)Pzy
        2. (∃y)Pay   1, UI
        3. Paa   2, EI

* **19.** 1. ~Lnn
        2. (∃x)~Lxx   1, EG
        3. (∃x)~Lxn   1, EG
        4. (∃x)~Lnx   1, EG

20. 1. (∃x)(y)Axy
    2. (y)Aay   1, EI
    3. Aab   2, UI
    4. (x)Axx   3, UG

21. 1. (x)[~~Jxb • (~Jxb ∨ Kxx)]
    2. ~~Jab • (~Jab ∨ Kaa)   1, UI
    3. ~~Jab   2, Simp
    4. ~Jab ∨ Kaa   2, Simp
    5. Kaa   3, 4, DS

***22.** 1. (∃x)Fxd
    2. Fad   1, EI
    3. (x)Fxd   2, UG

23. 1. (∃x)[Ax • (y)(Ay → Bxy)]
    2. Aa • (y)(Ay → Bay)   1, EI
    3. Aa   2, Simp
    4. (y)(Ay → Bay)   2, Simp
    5. Aa → Baa   4, UI
    6. Baa   5, 3, MP
    7. (x)Bxx   6, UG

24. 1. (x)(Cxb • Dxb)
    2. Cab • Dcb   1, UI

25. 1. (y)Fby
    2. (x)(y)Fxy   1, UG

PART B: Proofs Construct proofs to show that the following arguments are valid. You may use direct proof, CP, or RAA.

* **1.** (x)(y)(Rxy → Ryx), Rab ∴ Rba

  2. (∃x)~Rxx, ~(x)Rxx → (x)(y)~Txy ∴ ~Tba

  3. (x)(y)(z)[(Wxy • Wyz) → Wxz], Wab, Wbc ∴ Wac

* **4.** (y)(Bay ∨ Bya) ∴ Baa

  5. Meb → Nbb, (z)~Nzz ∴ ~Meb

  6. (x)(Tx → (y)[Vy → (∃z)(Pz • Sxyz)]), Tb • Ve ∴ (∃z)(Pz • Sbez)

* **7.** (∃x)[Hx • (y)(Hy → Lyx)] ∴ (∃x)(Hx • Lxx)

  8. (x)[Px → ~(y)(Py → Lxy)] ∴ ~(∃x)[Px • (y)(Py → Lxy)]

  9. (x)[Px → (y)(Py → ~Lxy)] ∴ ~(∃x)[Px • (∃y)(Py • Lxy)]

***10.** ~(∃x)[Px • (∃y)(Py • Lxy)] ∴ (x)[Px → (y)(Py → ~Lxy)]

 11. (∃y)(z)~Kzy ∴ (y)(∃z)~Kyz

 12. (x)(y)(Sxy → ~Syx) ∴ (x)~Sxx

 13. (x)[Px → ~(∃y)Mxy] ∴ ~(∃x)(Px • Mxb)

 14. (∃x)(y)(Jx • Ny), (∃x)(Jx • Nx) → ~(∃x)Ux ∴ ~Ud

15. $(x)(Kbx \rightarrow Gxc)$, $(\exists x)Gxc \rightarrow (\exists y)Gcy$ $\therefore$ $(\exists x)Kbx \rightarrow (\exists y)Gcy$

16. $(\exists x)(\exists y)(z)Pxyz$ $\therefore$ $(z)(\exists x)(\exists y)Pxyz$

17. $(x)(y)(Rxy \rightarrow \sim Ryx)$ $\therefore$ $(x)(y)[(\sim Sxy \bullet Rxy) \rightarrow \sim Ryx]$

18. $(\exists y)(x)(Lxy \rightarrow Mxy)$ $\therefore$ $(\exists x)(y)Lxy \rightarrow (\exists y)(\exists x)Mxy$

19. $(x)(Gx \rightarrow Fx)$, $(\exists x)Fx \rightarrow \sim(\exists y)(\exists z)Hyz$ $\therefore$ $(\exists x)Gx \rightarrow \sim Hbc$

20. $(x)[Fx \rightarrow (y)(Sy \rightarrow Rxy)]$, $(x)[Px \rightarrow (y)(Rxy \rightarrow Ty)]$,
    $\therefore$ $(\exists x)(Fx \bullet Px) \rightarrow (y)(Sy \rightarrow Ty)$

21. $(x)(\sim Rx \vee Nx)$, $\sim(\exists x)Nx \vee (\exists y)(z)Szy$ $\therefore$ $\sim(\exists x)Rx \vee (z)(\exists y)Szy$

22. $(\exists x)(Mx \bullet Nx)$, $(\exists x)[Mx \bullet (y)(Ny \rightarrow \sim Lxy)]$
    $\therefore$ $(\exists x)[Mx \bullet \sim(y)(My \rightarrow Lyx)]$

23. $(x)(y)(Hxy \rightarrow \sim Ia)$, $(\exists x)Hbx \bullet (x)(y)(z)Jxyz$ $\therefore$ $\sim(Jabc \rightarrow Ia)$

24. $(x)(y)[\sim Cxy \vee (Dx \rightarrow Dy)]$, $(x)(\sim Dx \rightarrow \sim Ax)$, $(x)[Ax \rightarrow (\exists y)(By \bullet Cxy)]$,
    $(\exists x)Ax$ $\therefore$ $(\exists x)(Bx \bullet Dx)$

25. $(x)(y)(Rxy \rightarrow (\exists z)Szxy)$, $(x)(y)(z)[Szxy \rightarrow (Tzx \bullet Tzy)]$, $(x)Rxa$
    $\therefore$ $(x)(\exists y)(Syxa \bullet Tya)$

PART C: English Arguments Symbolize and construct proofs to show that
the following arguments are valid.

* **1.** Ormazd is morally superior to Ahriman. For all x, for all y, if x is morally superior to y, then y is not morally superior to x. Hence, Ahriman is not morally superior to Ormazd. (o: Ormazd; a: Ahriman; Sxy: x is morally superior to y)

2. There is an entity that is more powerful than all entities. Therefore, at least one entity is more powerful than itself. (Mxy: x is more powerful than y)

3. There is at least one person. For all x, for all y, x loves y if and only if x loves x. Mad Eye loves no one. It follows that Mad Eye does not love himself. (Px: x is a person; Lxy: x loves y; m: Mad Eye)

* **4.** Any rational animal is of greater intrinsic value than any nonrational animal. Karen is a rational animal, but she is not of greater intrinsic value than George. So, if George is an animal, then he is rational. (Rx: x is rational; Ax: x is an animal; Gxy: x is of greater intrinsic value than y; k: Karen; g: George)

5. Something is such that everything was created by it. We may infer that everything was created by something. (Cxy: x was created by y)

6. Carl is not on the team. For Carl is a sprinter, and Carl is faster than any sprinter on the team. But no sprinter is faster than himself. (c: Carl; Sx: x is a sprinter; Fxy: x is faster than y; Tx: x is on the team)

7. All horses are animals. Therefore, every tail of a horse is a tail of an animal. (Hx: x is a horse; Ax: x is animal; Txy: x is a tail of y)

8. It is not the case that there exists a nation more just than Norway. Every utopia is more just than Norway. Hence, no utopia is a nation. (Nx: x is a nation; Jxy: x is more just than y; n: Norway; Ux: x is a utopia)

9. God does not cause any free act that he wants to occur. Moreover, if there are any free acts that God does not want to occur, God does not cause them. Hence, God does not cause any free acts. (g: God; Cxy: x causes y; Fx: x is a free act; Wxy: x wants y to occur)

*10. There are sets. Hence, it is not the case that there is a set that contains all and only those sets that do not contain themselves. (Sx: x is a set; Cxy: x contains y)

11. If Dumbledore is wiser than Harry and Harry is wiser than Dudley, then Dumbledore is wiser than Dudley. Harry is a wizard-in-training. Dumbledore is wiser than every wizard-in-training. Dudley is a muggle. Every wizard-in-training is wiser than every muggle. So, Dumbledore is wiser than Dudley. (Wxy: x is wiser than y; d: Dumbledore; Tx: x is a wizard-in-training; h: Harry; Mx: x is a muggle; u: Dudley)

12. Every physical event has a physical cause. Every brain event is a physical event. If any brain event has a physical cause, then it lacks a mental cause. It follows that no brain event has a mental cause. (Px: x is physical; Ex: x is an event; Cxy: x causes y; Bx: x occurs in the brain; Mx: x is mental)

13. Whatever is not observable by both Einstein and Feynman is outside the realm of science. If an electron is observable by Feynman, then it is observable by Einstein. Accordingly, if any electron is not observable by Einstein, then it is outside the realm of science. (Oxy: x is observable by y; e: Einstein; f: Feynman; Sx: x is outside the realm of science; Ex: x is an electron)

14. If Lindsay has greater intrinsic worth than Lassie and Lassie has greater intrinsic worth than every insentient creature, then Lindsay has greater intrinsic worth than every insentient creature. Lassie is a merely sentient creature. Lindsay has greater intrinsic worth than every merely sentient creature. Every plant is an insentient creature. Every merely sentient creature has greater intrinsic worth than every insentient creature. So, Lindsay has greater intrinsic worth than every plant. (l: Lindsay; Gxy: x has greater intrinsic worth than y; s: Lassie; Ix: x is an insentient creature; Sx: x is a merely sentient creature; Px: x is a plant)

15. Every act is caused by a desire. Every desire is caused by a brain process. For all x, y, and z, if x is caused by y and y is caused by z, then x is caused by z. Thus, every act is caused by a brain process. (Ax: x is an act; Dx: x is a desire; Cxy: x is caused by y; Bx: x is brain process)

PART D: A System Without UG and EG? The rules UG and EG are standard in systems of predicate logic because these rules mirror intuitive inferences. However, the special restrictions on the first rule make it relatively difficult to master. So, you may be interested to know that our system of predicate logic is complete without these rules. That is, any proof we can complete using our statement logic rules (including CP and RAA), UI, EI, UG, EG, and QN, *can also be completed without* using UG and EG. However, the price we would pay for doing without UG and EG is that most proofs must be completed by CP and RAA, which tends to make the proofs longer. Symbolize the following arguments, then construct two proofs for each argument—one that uses neither UG nor EG and one that uses at least one of these rules. Compare the length of the proofs.

1. Every number is divisible by itself. Some even number is a number. So, some even number is divisible by itself. (Nx: x is a number; Dxx: x is divisible by x; Ex: x is an even number)

2. All even numbers are divisible by 2. Nothing divisible by 2 is odd. So, no even number is odd. (Ex: x is an even number; Dxy: x is divisible by y; t: 2; Ox: x is odd)

9.7   Identity: Symbolizations

Among the many different types of relations, one is particularly important for logic, namely, *identity*. For instance, consider the following argument:

84. George Orwell wrote *1984*. George Orwell is identical with Eric Blair. Therefore, Eric Blair wrote *1984*. (o: George Orwell; Wxy: x wrote y; n: *1984*; Ixy: x is identical with y; b: Eric Blair)

This argument is valid, but we cannot prove it valid given the inference rules introduced thus far. Using the scheme of abbreviation provided, the symbolization looks like this:

1. Won

2. Iob ∴ Wbn

Now what do we do? We have no useful moves to make because as yet we have no inference rules concerning the identity relation.

To introduce identity into our system of logic, we will borrow a symbol from arithmetic—namely, the equality sign—but we will refer to it as the *identity sign*. Except for the addition of the identity sign, the language for predicate logic with identity is exactly like the language for predicate logic. So, we can symbolize the statement "George Orwell is identical with Eric Blair" as follows:

85. o = b

In our system, (85) is treated as an atomic formula, like Fa or Gab, so there is no need to use parentheses.

Here are some additional examples of identity claims, together with their symbolizations:

86. Thomas Edward Lawrence was Lawrence of Arabia. (t: T. E. Lawrence; a: Lawrence of Arabia)

In symbols: t = a

87. Kareem Abdul-Jabbar is Lew Alcindor. (k: Kareem Abdul-Jabbar; a: Lew Alcindor)

In symbols: k = a

88. Muhammed Ali is the same individual as Cassius Clay. (m: Muhammed Ali; c: Cassius Clay)

In symbols: m = c

And we can symbolize negations of identity statements by means of the negation sign, as follows:

89. Jon Stewart is not identical with Stephen Colbert. (s: Jon Stewart; c: Stephen Colbert)

In symbols: ~s = c

90. John Milton is distinct from William Shakespeare. (m: John Milton; s: William Shakespeare)

In symbols: ~m = s

Note that statements or statement functions are formed by placing a *constant* or a *variable* on each side of the identity sign—for example, a = b, x = y, and a = y. Also note that to negate an identity statement, we simply attach a tilde to it—no parentheses are employed. Thus, to negate a = b, we simply write ~a = b, which is read as "It is not the case that a is identical with b." To clarify how the new symbols work, consider the following English sentence together with its symbolization:

91. Everything identical with the number 7 is an odd number. (s: the number 7; Ox: x is an odd number)

In symbols: (x)(x = s → Ox)

Here the parentheses indicate that the scope of the quantifier is x = s → Ox. Without the parentheses, we would have (x)x = s → Ox, in which case the scope of the quantifier would be x = s.

By means of the identity sign we can symbolize many complicated types of statements. The following list provides you with a guide for moving from English to logicese to symbols.

Only

English: Only Edison invented the phonograph. (e: Edison; Px: x invented the phonograph)

Logicese: e invented the phonograph, and for all x, if x invented the phonograph, then x is identical with e.

Symbols: Pe • (x)(Px → x = e)

The Only

English: The only person who is guilty is David. (Px: x is person; Gx: x is guilty; d: David)

Logicese: d is a person and d is guilty, and for all x, if x is a person and x is guilty, then x is identical with d.

Symbols: (Pd • Gd) • (x)[(Px • Gx) → x = d]

No . . . Except

English: No one except Bell invented the telephone. (Px: x is a person; b: Bell; Tx: x invented the telephone)

Logicese: b is a person and b invented the telephone, and for all x, if x is a person and x invented the telephone, then x is identical with b.

Symbols: (Pb • Tb) • (x)[(Px • Tx) → x = b]

All . . . Except

English: All European countries except Switzerland declared war. (Ex: x is a European country; s: Switzerland; Dx: x declared war)

Logicese: s is a European country and s did not declare war, and for all x, if x is a European country and x is not identical with s, then x declared war.

Symbols: (Es • ~Ds) • (x)[(Ex • ~x = s) → Dx]

Superlatives

English: The tallest mountain is Mount Everest. (Mx: x is a mountain; Txy: x is taller than y; e: Mount Everest)

Logicese: e is a mountain, and for all x, if x is a mountain and x is not identical with e, then e is taller than x.

Symbols: Me • (x)[(Mx • ~x = e) → Tex]

Note: The strategy regarding superlatives is to say, first, that a certain individual *e* falls into a class and, second, that *e* has a certain property in greater degree than anything else that falls into that class.

At Most

English: There is at most one god. (Gx: x is a god)

Logicese: For all x, for all y, if x is a god and y is a god, then x is identical with y.

Symbols: (x)(y)[(Gx • Gy) → x = y]

English: There are at most two gods. (Gx: x is a god)

Logicese: For all x, for all y, for all z, if x is a god and y is a god and z is a god, then either x is identical with y or x is identical with z or y is identical with z.

Symbols: (x)(y)(z)([(Gx • Gy) • Gz] → [(x = y ∨ x = z) ∨ y = z])

Note: These "at most" statements do not assert that there are any gods. The first merely states that if there are any gods, then the maximum number is one.

And the second states that if there are any gods, then the maximum number is two.

At Least

English: There is at least one utilitarian. (Ux: x is a utilitarian)

Logicese: There exists an x such that x is a utilitarian.

Symbols: $(\exists x)Ux$

English: There are at least two utilitarians. (Ux: x is a utilitarian)

Logicese: There is some x and there is some y such that x is a utilitarian and y is a utilitarian and x is distinct from y.

Symbols: $(\exists x)(\exists y)[(Ux \bullet Uy) \bullet \sim x = y]$

Note: If we had omitted $\sim x = y$ from our symbolization of "There are at least two utilitarians," we would have left open the possibility that x and y are one and the same thing.

Exactly One

English: There is exactly one solipsist. (Sx: x is a solipsist)

Logicese: There is some x such that x is a solipsist, and for all x, for all y, if x is a solipsist and y is a solipsist, then x is identical with y.

Symbols: $(\exists x)Sx \bullet (x)(y)[(Sx \bullet Sy) \rightarrow x = y]$

Note: Here "exactly one" is viewed as a conjunction of "at least one" and "at most one." However, there is a more elegant way of symbolizing "exactly one." To illustrate, "There is exactly one solipsist" can be written in logicese as "There is some x such that x is a solipsist and for all y, if y is a solipsist, then y = x." In symbols:

$$(\exists x)[Sx \bullet (y)(Sy \rightarrow y = x)]$$

Similarly, "There are exactly two solipsists" can be symbolized as follows:

$$(\exists x)(\exists y)([(Sx \bullet Sy) \bullet \sim x = y] \bullet (z)[Sz \rightarrow (z = x \lor z = y)])$$

The identity sign has been used to provide an important analysis of *definite descriptions*. A definite description is an expression of the form "the so-and-so," such as "the smallest prime number," "the discoverer of polonium," or "the author of *War and Peace*." Such expressions seem intended to denote exactly one object or person. But consider the following example, which Bertrand Russell discussed in "On Denoting"[6]:

92. The present King of France is bald.

France presently has no king, so the expression "the present King of France" apparently fails to refer to anyone or anything. How then can (92) be a meaningful sentence (as it appears to be)? Russell suggested that statements involving definite descriptions, such as (92), make three claims:

   a. A thing of a certain type exists (in this case, a present King of France).

   b. It is unique.

   c. It has a certain property (in this case, it is bald).

From Russell's perspective, then, we can rewrite (92) in logicese as follows: There is some x such that x is a present King of France, and for all y, if y is a present King of France, then y is identical with x, and x is bald. Letting Kx abbreviate "x is a present King of France" and Bx stand for "x is bald," the symbolization looks like this:

   93. $(\exists x)[Kx \bullet (y)(Ky \rightarrow y = x) \bullet Bx]$

This analysis of (92) does not invite the question "To what object, if any, does 'the present King of France' refer?" Rather, this analysis simply invites us to ask whether there are any actual objects having the property of being a present King of France. Of course, the answer is no. Thus, the meaning of the sentence is clear; indeed, we can see that it is false. Because Russell's analysis of statements involving definite descriptions has been very influential, we will adopt it on a provisional basis. Let us consider one further example of a statement involving a definite description, together with its symbolization:

Definite Descriptions

English: The discoverer of polonium is Polish. (Dx: x discovered polonium; Px: x is Polish)

Logicese: There is some x such that x discovered polonium, and for all y, if y discovered polonium, y is identical with x, and x is Polish.

Symbols: $(\exists x)(Dx \bullet (y)[(Dy \rightarrow y = x) \bullet Px])$

EXERCISE 9.7

PART A: Symbolizing Symbolize the following sentences using the schemes of abbreviation provided.

* **1.** Timberlake is not identical to Timbaland. (j: Timberlake; t: Timbaland)

  2. Samuel Clemens is identical with Mark Twain. (s: Samuel Clemens; m: Mark Twain)

  3. Everything is identical with something.

* **4.** Nothing is distinct from itself.

   5. Everything differs from something.

   6. Nothing differs from everything.

* **7.** Each thing is identical with itself.

   8. If two things are identical to a third thing, then they are identical to each other.

   9. Only Faraday discovered electromagnetic induction. (f: Faraday; Dx: x discovered electromagnetic induction)

***10.** At least two people invented the airplane. (Px: x is a person; Ax: x invented the airplane)

   11. No one except Dostoyevsky wrote *Crime and Punishment*. (Px: x is a person; d: Dostoyevsky; Wxy: x wrote y; c: *Crime and Punishment*)

   12. Goliath is the tallest human. (g: Goliath; Hx: x is human; Txy: x is taller than y)

   13. At most two persons invented the airplane. (Px: x is a person; Ax: x invented the airplane)

   14. There is exactly one dollar in my wallet. (Dx: x is a dollar in my wallet)

   15. At least two physicists discovered polonium. (Px: x is a physicist; Dx: x discovered polonium)

   16. Dane Cook is the worst comedian. (d: Dane Cook; Cx: x is a comedian; Wxy: x is worse than y)

   17. Every star except the sun is outside our solar system. (Sx: x is a star; s: the sun; Ox: x is outside our solar system)

   18. The most brilliant physicist is Einstein. (Px: x is a physicist; Bxy: x is more brilliant than y; e: Einstein)

   19. There is at most one mountain in Ohio. (Mx: x is a mountain; Ox: x is in Ohio)

   20. There are at most two wizards. (Wx: x is a wizard)

PART B: More Symbolizing Symbolize the following sentences, using the schemes of abbreviation provided.

* **1.** If something is distinct from itself, then nothing makes sense. (Mx: x makes sense)

   2. If anything is distinct from itself, then it is strange. (Sx: x is strange)

   3. Everything is identical with itself if and only if nothing is distinct from itself.

* **4.** There are exactly two entities.

   5. There are at least two honest politicians. (Hx: x is honest; Px: x is a politician)

   6. Everything but the Big Bang has a cause. (b: Big Bang; Cx: x has a cause)

* **7.** Exactly one person shot Abraham Lincoln. (Px: x is a person; Sxy: x shot y; a: Abraham Lincoln)

8. The author of *The Brothers Karamazov* is Russian. (Wxy: x wrote y; Rx: x is Russian; b: *The Brothers Karamazov*)

9. The star of the movie *Patton* is George C. Scott. (Sxy: x is a star of y; p: *Patton*; g: George C. Scott)

* **10.** No Dane except Kierkegaard is gloomy. (Dx: x is a Dane; k: Kierkegaard; Gx: x is gloomy)

11. No movie star is identical with both Jennifer Lopez and Jennifer Aniston. (Mx: x is a movie star; j: Jennifer Lopez; a: Jennifer Aniston)

12. If Meriwether Lewis is an explorer and William Clark is an explorer, then there are at least two explorers. (m: Meriwether Lewis; c: William Clark; Ex: x is an explorer)

13. The whole number between 6 and 8 is an odd number. (Wxyz: x is a whole number between y and z; s: 6; e: 8; Ox: x is an odd number)

14. Everyone who loves someone else also loves herself. (Px: x is a person; Lxy: x loves y)

15. At least one person is angry at everyone except himself. (Px: x is a person; Axy: x is angry at y)

9.8   Identity: Proofs

To construct proofs involving the identity relation, we will add three new rules of inference.[7] The first of these is called **Leibniz' law** (LL), after the philosopher who first made it explicit, Gottfried Wilhelm Leibniz (1646–1716). Leibniz' law is the principle that if m and n are identical, then every property of m is a property of n, and vice versa. Here are some typical inferences permitted by Leibniz' law:

A. 1. $a = b$
    2. Fa
    3. Fb   1, 2 LL

B. 1. $c = d$
    2. Wbc
    3. Wbd   1, 2 LL

C. 1. $e = f$
    2. ~Ge
    3. ~Gf   1, 2 LL

In each case, we substitute one individual constant for another that denotes the same entity. To state our inference rules in a general fashion, we will use the bold letters **m** and **n** to stand for any individual constant. And we will use $\mathcal{P}$m and

$\mathcal{P}$n to stand for WFFs containing **m** and **n**, respectively. Leibniz' law comes in two forms, as follows:

Leibniz' Law (LL)

m = n	n = m
$\mathcal{P}$m	$\mathcal{P}$m
∴ $\mathcal{P}$n	∴ $\mathcal{P}$n

Here, we obtain $\mathcal{P}$n by replacing *one or more* occurrences of **m** in $\mathcal{P}$m with occurrences of **n**. Which of the following are correct applications of LL? Which are incorrect?

A. 1. b = c
    2. (x)(Ax → Bx)
    3. Ab → Bb   2, UI
    4. Ac → Bc   1, 3, LL

B. 1. Ca • Da
    2. b = a
    3. Cb • Db   1, 2, LL

C. 1. (y)(My ∨ Ny)
    2. a = d
    3. Ma ∨ Na   1, UI
    4. Md ∨ Na   2, 3, LL

(A) through (C) are all correct applications of LL. Armed with Leibniz' law, we can easily prove the validity of the argument that appears at the beginning of the previous section: "George Orwell wrote *1984*. George Orwell is identical with Eric Blair. Therefore, Eric Blair wrote *1984*." The symbolization and proof are as follows:

    1. Won
    2. o = b   ∴ Wbn
    3. Wbn   1, 2, LL

The following argument and proof illustrate another application of LL:

94. William Ockham died of the black plague. Billy the Kid did not die of the black plague. So, William Ockham is not Billy the Kid. (o: William Ockham; Dx: x died of the black plague; b: Billy the Kid)

    1. Do
    2. ~Db   ∴ ~o = b
    3. o = b   Assume (for RAA)
    4. Db   1, 3, LL
    5. Db • ~Db   4, 2, Conj
    6. ~o = b   3–5, RAA

This proof illustrates the general principle that if x has a certain property and y lacks that property, then x is not identical to y.

Our next inference rule is called **symmetry** (Sm). Where the bold **m** and **n** stand for any individual constants, the rule may be stated as follows. It comes in two forms:

Symmetry (Sm)

m = n	~m = n
∴ n = m	∴ ~n = m

Symmetry justifies such intuitive inferences as these:

95. Lewis Carroll was Charles Lutwidge Dodgson. Therefore, Charles Lutwidge Dodgson was Lewis Carroll. (c: Lewis Carroll; d: Charles Lutwidge Dodgson)

96. Woody Allen is not Gottfried Wilhelm Leibniz. So, Gottfried Wilhelm Leibniz is not Woody Allen. (a: Woody Allen; g: Gottfried Wilhelm Leibniz)

The proofs are short and simple:

1. c = d	∴ d = c	1. ~a = g	∴ ~g = a
2. d = c	1, Sm	2. ~g = a	1, Sm

Our third and final rule of inference governing the logic of identity is the principle that *each thing is identical with itself.* We will call this simply the **identity** (Id) rule. It differs from all our previous rules in that it does not involve a premise. We may represent it as follows:

Identity (Id)

∴ n = n

Here, the bold **n** stands for any individual constant. The Id rule allows us to enter statements of self-identity, such as b = b, as lines in a proof. This rule isn't used very often in constructing proofs, but our system of logic would not be complete without it. Here are an argument, symbolization, and proof that illustrate an application of Id:

97. Everything that is identical with Lewis Black is a comedian. So, Lewis Black is a comedian. (b: Lewis Black; Cx: x is a comedian)

In symbols: (x)(x = b → Cx) ∴ Cb

1. (x)(x = b → Cx)	∴ Cb
2. b = b → Cb	1, UI
3. b = b	Id
4. Cb	2, 3, MP

Note: The parentheses in premise (1) indicate that the scope of the quantifier is x = b → Cx. Without the parentheses, we would have (x)x = b → Cx, in which case the scope of the quantifier would be x = b and we could not apply UI at step 2.

EXERCISE 9.8

PART A: Proofs Construct proofs to show that the following arguments are valid.

* **1.** Na • ~Nb ∴ ~a = b
  2. ~a = b ∴ (∃x)(∃y)~x = y
  3. Rab • (∃x)~Rxb ∴ (∃x)~x = a
* **4.** c = d → e = g, d = c, Fg ∴ Fe
  5. (x)x = a → ~b = b ∴ (∃x)~x = a
  6. (x)(~Gx → ~x = d) ∴ Gd
* **7.** (y)(Ay → By), Ab, b = c ∴ Bc
  8. (z)(Cz → Dz), ~Dg • Ca ∴ ~g = a
  9. (x)(~Fx → ~Ex), (x)(Fx → Gx), ~Gb • Ea ∴ ~a = b
* **10.** (x)(Hx → Jx), (x)(Kx → Lx), Hd • Kc, c = d ∴ Jc • Ld
  11. (x)(Gx → x = d), (∃x)(Fx • Gx) ∴ Fd
  12. (x)(y)[Cyx → ~(z)Dz], (x)n = x, (∃x)[Ax • (y)(Ay → Cxy)] ∴ ~Dn
* **13.** (∃x)Hx, (x)(y)[(Hx • Hy) → x = y] ∴ (∃x)[Hx • (y)(Hy → x = y)]
  14. (x)(y)y = x, (x)Mxx ∴ Mab
  15. (x)[(∃y)Kxy → (∃z)Kzx], (x)(Kxg • x = b) ∴ (∃z)Kzb
* **16.** (∃x)([(Ax • Bxa) • (y)((Ay • Bya) → y = x)] • Dxb), Ac • Bca ∴ Dcb
  17. (x)x = a ∴ (x)(y)x = y
  18. (∃x)Wx • (x)(y)[(Wx • Wy) → x = y] ∴ (∃x)[Wx • (y)(Wy → x = y)]
  19. (x)[Mx → (x = a ∨ x = b)], (∃x)(Mx • Nx) ∴ Ma ∨ Mb
  20. (∃x)[Fx • (y)(Fy → x = y)] → ~(x)(∃y)x = y, Fb ∴ (∃y)(Fy • ~b = y)

PART B: English Arguments Symbolize the following arguments using the schemes of abbreviation provided. Then construct proofs to show that the arguments are valid.

* **1.** No one antedates himself. Augustine antedates Boethius. Augustine and Boethius are both persons. Therefore, Augustine is not identical with Boethius. (Px: x is a person; Axy: x antedates y; a: Augustine; b: Boethius)
  2. I am not my body. The clump of cells in the corner of the room is my body. It follows that I am not identical with the clump of cells in the corner of the room. (i: I; b: my body; c: the clump of cells in the corner of the room)

3. Every mental state is identical with some brain state or other. All mental states are introspectible. There is at least one mental state. Hence, some brain state is introspectible. (Mx: x is a mental state; Bx: x is a brain state; Nx: x is introspectible)

* **4.** There are exactly two omniscient beings. Apollo is omniscient. We may infer that there is an omniscient being distinct from Apollo. (Ox: x is omniscient; a: Apollo)

5. The only suspect who confessed is Benjamin Bondurant. The only suspect with a motive is Charles Ashworth. At least one suspect who confessed also has a motive. Consequently, Benjamin Bondurant is one and the same individual as Charles Ashworth. (Sx: x is suspect; Cx: x confessed; b: Benjamin Bondurant; c: Charles Ashworth; Mx: x has a motive)

6. The perfect triangle is not a material object. Hence, there is a perfect triangle. (Px: x is perfect; Tx: x is a triangle; Mx: x is a material object)

7. There are at least two physical objects. Jupiter is a physical object. Accordingly, there is at least one physical object other than Jupiter. (Px: x is a physical object; j: Jupiter)

8. The perfect being is divine. All divine beings are benevolent. We may conclude that the perfect being is benevolent. (Px: x is a perfect being; Dx: x is a divine being; Bx: x is benevolent)

9. The greatest painter is Rembrandt. Michelangelo is greater than Rembrandt. Michelangelo is not the same individual as Rembrandt. If one thing is greater than another, then the latter is not greater than the former. Therefore, Michelangelo is not a painter. (Px: x is a painter; Gxy: x is greater than y; r: Rembrandt; m: Michelangelo)

10. The most powerful god is Zeus. The most powerful god is not morally weak. If one thing is more powerful than another, then the latter is not more powerful than the former. If Zeus is not morally weak, then Zeus is morally good. It follows that Zeus is morally good. (Mxy: x is more powerful than y; Gx: x is a god; z: Zeus; Wx: x is morally weak; Ox: x is morally good)

NOTES

1. See A. N. Prior, "History of Logic," in Paul Edwards, ed., *The Encyclopedia of Philosophy*, Vol. 4 (New York: Macmillan Free Press, 1967), p. 520; and Anthony Flew, "Logic," *A Dictionary of Philosophy*, 2nd ed. (New York: St. Martin's Press, 1979), pp. 208–212. Flew remarks, "The advance in Frege's system . . . is the introduction of quantifiers. . . .This enabled him to unify the logic of propositions [i.e. statement logic] . . . with the study of those logical relationships which had previously been treated in the theory of the syllogism" (p. 211). Gottlob Frege's *Begriffsschrift* was first published in 1879; an English translation is available in J. van Heijnoort, ed., *From Frege to Gödel: A Source Book in Mathematical Logic, 1879–1931* (Cambridge, MA: Harvard University Press, 1967).

2. The focus throughout this book is on first-order logic, in which all variables are *individual* variables (e.g., x, y, and z) that range over the domain of particular people, places, and things (e.g., Michael Jordan, New York City, and the Eiffel Tower). However, there are also higher-order logics that include second-order variables (for example) that range over properties, relations, and sets of individuals (e.g., the property of *being a basketball player,* the *north of* relation or the set of Parisian landmarks). For a brief introduction to higher-order logic, see Stewart Shapiro, "Classical Logic II—Higher-Order Logic," in Lou Goble, ed., *The Blackwell Guide to Philosophical Logic* (Oxford: Blackwell, 2001), pp. 33–54.

3. See Flew, *A Dictionary of Philosophy,* p. 63. The relevant work is Alonzo Church, "A Note on the *Entscheidungsproblem,*" *Journal of Symbolic Logic* I (1936): pp. 40–41.

4. See Donald Kalish, Richard Montague, and Gary Mar, *Logic: Techniques of Formal Reasoning,* 2nd ed. (New York: Harcourt Brace Jovanovich, 1980), p. 238. These authors give the following example: $(x)(y)(z)[(Fxy \bullet Fyz) \rightarrow Fxz]$, $(x)(\exists y)Fxy \therefore (\exists x)Fxx$.

5. Not all systems of logic involve the assumption that at least one thing exists. Those that do not make this assumption are called "Free Logics." ("Free Logic" means "logic free of assumptions about existence.") For an excellent discussion of Free Logics, see Stephen Read, *Thinking About Logic: An Introduction to the Philosophy of Logic* (New York: Oxford University Press, 1995), pp. 131–144.

6. Bertrand Russell, "On Denoting," *Mind,* Vol. 14 (Oxford University Press, 1905), pp. 479–493.

7. The system of rules here employed for the logic of identity is based on a system developed by Kalish, Montague, and Mar, *Logic,* chap. 5.

CHAPTER 10

Inductive Logic

So far, we have focused primarily on deductive logic, and hence on tests for the validity and invalidity of arguments. In this chapter, we turn our attention to inductive logic. **Inductive logic** is the part of logic that is concerned with tests for the strength and weakness of arguments.

> **Inductive logic** is the part of logic that is concerned with the study of methods of evaluating arguments for strength and weakness.

Our approach will be to consider three different areas in which inductive logic is common: ordinary reasoning (10.2), scientific reasoning (10.3), and probabilistic reasoning (10.4). But first, a few words of introduction are in order.

10.1 Inductive and Deductive Logic

We begin by reviewing some terminology from Chapter 1 and by bringing out some important contrasts between inductive and deductive logic.

First, recall that a **strong argument** is one in which it is probable (but not necessary) that if the premises are true, then the conclusion is true. In other words, it is unlikely that the premises are true, given that the conclusion is false.

> A **strong argument** is one in which it is probable (but not necessary) that if the premises are true, then the conclusion is true.

For example:

> **1.** Ninety percent of 40-year-old American women live to be at least 50. Helen is a 40-year-old American woman. So, Helen will live to be at least 50.

Argument (1) is not valid, but its premises do provide some support for its conclusion. Just consider this: If you have to place a bet, and the premises of (1) sum up the relevant information you have in hand, then you should bet on the conclusion of (1) rather than on its negation.

A **weak argument** is one in which it is *not* probable that if the premises are true, then the conclusion is true.

> A **weak argument** is one in which it is *not* probable that if the premises are true, then the conclusion is true.

For example:

> **2.** Fifty percent of 30-year-old American women live to be 80. Alice is a 30-year-old American woman. So, Alice will live to be 80.

Is it probable that if the premises of this argument were true, then its conclusion would be true? Let us assume for the moment that the premises are true. If 50 percent of 30-year-old American women will live to be 80, then 50 percent of 30-year-old American women will *not* live to be 80. So, given only the information provided in the premises, we could just as well conclude that *Alice will not live to be 80.* In short, the premises give us no reason to prefer the conclusion of the argument to its negation. Thus, it is *not* probable that if the premises were true, then the conclusion would be true. Hence, the argument is weak.

A **cogent argument** is a strong argument in which all of the premises are true. An **uncogent argument** is either a weak argument or a strong argument with at least one false premise.

> A **cogent argument** is a strong argument in which all of the premises are true.

> An **uncogent argument** is either a weak argument or a strong argument with at least one false premise.

Note that "uncogent argument" is *not* defined as an argument that either is weak or has a false premise. This latter definition is too broad because it would classify *valid arguments with false premises* as uncogent. It is unhelpful to classify valid arguments as uncogent because they meet a higher logical standard than strength.

Let us now contrast deduction and induction. First, note that a sound argument cannot have a false conclusion, but a cogent argument can. A sound argument cannot have a false conclusion because if an argument is valid and has only true premises, then it must have a true conclusion. But if an argument is strong and has only true premises, it is still possible (though unlikely) that its conclusion is false. To illustrate, suppose the premises of the following argument are true:

> **3.** Ninety percent of the cars in the parking lot were vandalized last night. Michael's car was in the parking lot. So, Michael's car was vandalized last night.

Suppose Michael goes to the parking lot and discovers that his car was not vandalized. Does that mean the argument is weak? No, it simply means that his car was among the 10 percent not vandalized. Again, the main point is that the conclusion of a cogent argument can be false.

Here is a second important contrast between deduction and induction. Validity is an all-or-nothing affair; it does not come in degrees. For instance, if two arguments are valid, it makes no sense to say that one of them is *more valid* than the other. But strength does come in degrees. Suppose that we altered the first premise of argument (3) so that it read, "Ninety-nine percent of the cars in the parking lot were vandalized last night." The resulting argument would be *stronger* than (3) in the sense that the conclusion would be even more likely to be true, given the truth of the corresponding premises. Hence, strength—unlike validity—comes in degrees.

Finally, although every argument with a valid form is valid, the strength of an argument is not ensured by its form. To grasp this point, let us consider an example of a *statistical syllogism*.

> **4.** Ninety-five percent of women over 30 years of age cannot run the mile in under 5 minutes. Rebekah is a woman over 30 years of age. Hence, Rebekah cannot run the mile in under 5 minutes.

The form of a statistical syllogism can be represented as follows:

> 1. _____ percent of A are B.
> 2. c is an A.
> So, 3. c is a B.

In our example, A stands for the set of women over 30, and B stands for the set of things that cannot run the mile in under 5 minutes. The lowercase letter c stands for a particular person, Rebekah. (In another case, c might stand for a particular thing, event, or situation.) The blank space is to be filled with numbers greater than 50 and less than 100. If we place the number 50 in the blank, we get a weak argument. If we place the number 100 in the blank, we get a valid argument—it is as if we had said, "All A are B." So, we will stipulate that the numbers filling the blank in a statistical syllogism must lie between 50 and 100 *exclusive.* By the way, in ordinary English, a statistical syllogism may be formulated without the use of specific percentages. For instance, the following counts as a statistical syllogism: "The vast majority of violent criminals are unhappy. Jones is a violent criminal. So, Jones is unhappy."

Now, consider argument (4) in light of the following statistical syllogism:

> **5.** Eighty percent of women over 30 who are world-class marathoners can run the mile in under 5 minutes. Rebekah is a woman over 30 who is a world-class marathoner. Therefore, Rebekah can run the mile in under 5 minutes.

The premises of arguments (4) and (5) could all be true. But their conclusions contradict each other (assuming "Rebekah" names the same person in both arguments). This situation cannot arise in the case of valid arguments. If the premises of two *valid* arguments can be combined to form a consistent set of statements, then the conclusions of those arguments must be consistent as well.

What is going on? Assuming one is fully aware of the information contained in the premises of argument (5), one cannot rightly pronounce argument (4) strong. Yet, (4), like (5), has the form of a statistical syllogism. So, although arguments having the form of a statistical syllogism *can* be strong, having that form is not a guarantee of strength.

Logicians are not agreed on how to characterize what is wrong with argument (4) *given that* the premises of both arguments are true. Perhaps the best we can say is this: If someone were to advance (4) *while aware* of the information contained in the premises of (5), that person would be leaving out relevant evidence, evidence that has a bearing on the truth of the conclusion of (4). We might call such a culpable omission the **fallacy of incomplete evidence.**[1] And, in general, when one seeks to meet the standard of strength but *knowingly omits relevant evidence,* one is apt to fall short of the standard. The main point for the moment, however, is simply that form does not ensure strength. This fact greatly complicates the process of testing arguments for strength and weakness. Let us briefly expand on this point.

> The **fallacy of incomplete evidence** is the culpable omission of relevant evidence.

We have already seen that a knowledge of valid argument forms is a powerful tool in evaluating arguments for validity. But when evaluating arguments for strength, the identification of form only rules out certain types of errors. For example, consider the following argument:

> **6.** Five percent of adults can do 50 push-ups. Minoru is an adult. So, Minoru can do 50 push-ups.

This argument may appear to be a statistical syllogism, but it is not really of that form because the percentage is too low. The percentage must lie between 50 and 100 (exclusive) to meet the requirements for a statistical syllogism. And given only the information provided in the premises of (6), we have more reason to deny the conclusion than to affirm it. ("Ninety-five percent of adults cannot do 50 push-ups. Minoru is an adult. So, Minoru cannot do 50 push-ups.") Accordingly, the form of argument (6) is flawed.

As we have just seen, however, *given only the information provided in the premises*, arguments having a certain form will appear strong, and yet they may be weak, if relevant information has been omitted. This is so, for example, whenever the argument has the form of a statistical syllogism. And this leaves us with the question "When does the omission of relevant evidence count as a logical error?" It is clearly an error to omit evidence (or information) when one knows full well that it reduces the strength of one's argument. But consider the following cases:

- The relevant evidence is readily available, and most people are aware of it. The arguer is not aware of it, but his ignorance is excusable for some reason (e.g., due to illness or other circumstances beyond his control, he has been isolated from the ordinary sources of information).

- The relevant evidence is readily available, and most people are aware of it. The arguer is not aware of it, but her ignorance is culpable (i.e., she should be aware of it).

- The relevant evidence is available but only through some investigation (e.g., a trip to the library), and the arguer is not aware of the evidence.

Do we want to say that a fallacy of incomplete evidence has been committed in some or all of these kinds of cases? This issue is under dispute among logicians, and we cannot attempt to resolve it here. But the very nature of the issue underscores the fact that induction is far less tidy than deduction.

At this point, we have highlighted three key contrasts between inductive and deductive arguments. In closing, it may be helpful to discuss one common mistake about this distinction. One often hears it said that "deductive arguments proceed from the general to the specific, whereas inductive arguments proceed from the specific to the general." There are at least six problems with this thesis.[2]

First, some valid arguments move from general premises to a general conclusion:

> **7.** All Shiites are Muslims. All Muslims are monotheists. Hence, all Shiites are monotheists.

Second, some valid arguments go from particular premises to a particular conclusion:

> **8.** William of Ockham died in 1349. Bertrand Russell did not die in 1349. Therefore, William of Ockham is not identical with Bertrand Russell.

Third, some valid arguments even go from particular to general:

> **9.** Franklin Roosevelt was a Democrat. So, anyone who voted for Roosevelt voted for a Democrat.

Fourth, some strong arguments have a general premise but a particular conclusion:

> **10.** All lemons previously tasted have been sour. Therefore, the next lemon to be tasted will be sour.

Note that the premise here concerns only *previously* tasted lemons, but the conclusion concerns a lemon as yet untasted. So, the argument is not valid, but it is nevertheless strong.

Fifth, certain types of strong arguments move from particular premises to particular conclusions:

> **11.** The 2011 Packers did very well. The 2012 Packers are very similar to the 2011 Packers in terms of personnel, coaching, and schedule. So, the 2012 Packers will do well.

This argument appears strong, but it is certainly not valid. It is possible–though perhaps unlikely–for a promising team to do quite poorly. Finally, some strong arguments have general premises and a general conclusion:

> **12.** All five starters on the basketball team performed well throughout the season. All five starters have shown a willingness to sacrifice personal glory for the sake of the team throughout the season. All five starters are experienced competitors. All five starters are rested and in good health. All five starters are highly motivated to do their best. So, all five starters on the basketball team will perform well in the competition tomorrow.

Note that the conclusion of argument (12) could be false even if the premises are true. For instance, one of the players may perform poorly because she received some dismaying news just before the game. So, the argument is not valid, but it seems to be strong.

To sum up, it is a mistake to suppose that strong arguments always move from particular statements to general statements. And it is equally erroneous to suppose that valid arguments always move from general statements to particular ones. These characterizations are at best gross oversimplifications. The key point to keep in mind, then, is that a strong argument has this essential feature: It is probable (but not necessary) that if its premises are true, then its conclusion is true.

Summary of Definitions

Inductive logic is the part of logic that is concerned with the study of methods of evaluating arguments for strength and weakness.

A **strong argument** is one in which it is probable (but not necessary) that if the premises are true, then the conclusion is true.

A **weak argument** is one in which it is *not* probable that if the premises are true, then the conclusion is true.

A **cogent argument** is a strong argument in which all of the premises are true.

An **uncogent argument** is either a weak argument or a strong argument with at least one false premise.

The **fallacy of incomplete evidence** is the culpable omission of relevant evidence.

EXERCISE 10.1

PART A: True or False? Which of the following statements are true? Which are false?

* **1.** If an argument is cogent, then it has true premises.
  2. If an argument is cogent, then it is strong.
  3. If an argument is cogent, then it is invalid.
* **4.** If an argument is strong and has only true premises, then it is cogent.
  5. If an argument is weak, then it is probable that if its premises are true, its conclusion is false.
  6. If an argument is strong, then it is possible that its conclusion is false even if its premises are true.
* **7.** If an argument is weak, then it is uncogent.
  8. If an argument has a false premise, then it must be uncogent.
  9. If an argument has true premises and a false conclusion, then it is weak.
* **10.** If an argument is valid, then it is strong.
  11. If an argument is strong, then it is valid.
  12. If an argument is uncogent, then it is weak.
* **13.** If an argument is weak, then it must be invalid.

14. If the conclusion of an argument is *exactly as probable* as its negation, given the premises of the argument, then the argument is weak.

15. If an argument is uncogent, then it is strong but has at least one false premise.

* **16.** Strong arguments always proceed from the specific to the general.

17. Valid arguments always proceed from the general to the specific.

18. Some valid arguments proceed from the general to the general.

* **19.** If an argument is valid and has at least one false premise, then it is uncogent.

20. If an argument is weak, then it is not likely that if its premises are true, then its conclusion is true.

PART B: Identifying and Evaluating Statistical Syllogisms Which of the following arguments have the form of a statistical syllogism? Which do not? Some of the arguments contain information that suggests a possible fallacy of incomplete evidence. Explain why.

* **1.** Fifty percent of the marbles in container 3 are green. The next marble to be drawn is a marble from container 3. Hence, the next marble to be drawn is green.

2. Two-thirds of the students at Seattle Pacific University are women. Chris is a student at Seattle Pacific. Consequently, Chris is a woman.

3. The vast majority of Americans approved of the Gulf War. John Montgomery is an American. So, John Montgomery approved of the Gulf War even though he belongs to a religious group whose members are mostly pacifists.

* **4.** More than half of all voters in the state of Washington favor campaign reform. Gordon Johnark, a U.S. senator, is a voter in the state of Washington. Accordingly, Gordon Johnark favors campaign reform.

5. Philosophy 301 is similar to Philosophy 101 in that both are philosophy courses. Philosophy 101 is a course Diana dislikes. So, Philosophy 301 is a course Diana dislikes.

6. Most college students do not work full-time. Jane is a college student. Therefore, Jane does not work full-time.

* **7.** Seventy percent of the citizens of Salt Lake City do not drink coffee. Phil Goggans is a citizen of Salt Lake City. So, even though Phil owns and operates the Caffeine Club Coffee House, he probably does not drink coffee.

8. One hundred percent of Texans love Texas. Jeanine Diller is a Texan. Therefore, Jeanine loves Texas.

9. Eighty-two percent of those in a randomly chosen sample of 4000 Americans eat meat. Therefore, about 82 percent of Americans eat meat.

* **10.** Nearly all Mennonites are (were, and will be) pacifists. John Howard Yoder was a Mennonite. Accordingly, John Howard Yoder was a pacifist.

11. According to the *National Enquirer*, last week a woman gave birth to a baby whose father came from Mars. Therefore, last week a woman gave birth to a baby whose father came from Mars.

12. Fifty-one percent of Marines are under 19 years old. Captain Lawrence is a Marine. So, Captain Lawrence is under 19 years old.

* **13.** Jack is 65 years old. So, Jack is not currently making a living as a professional boxer.

14. Ninety percent of abortions in the 1980s were performed in the first 12 weeks of pregnancy. Ms. Brown's abortion occurred in the 1980s. Thus, Ms. Brown's abortion was performed in the first 12 weeks of her pregnancy.

15. Ninety-nine percent of lemons are sour. The fruit I am about to eat is a lemon. Therefore, the fruit I am about to eat is sour.

10.2 Ordinary Reasoning: Authority, Analogy, and Enumeration

In this section, we consider three of the most common kinds of inductive arguments: arguments from authority, arguments from analogy, and arguments by enumeration. All of these arguments are familiar from our everyday way of reasoning. In each case, we identify the form of the argument and offer some observations on what makes for a strong instance of that form. We also highlight some potential pitfalls and fallacies.

Arguments from Authority

Let us begin with **arguments from authority,** which have the following form:

> 1. R sincerely asserts that S.
>
> So, 2. S.

Here, R stands for any source of information (e.g., a person, a paper, or a reference work), and S stands for any statement. We use arguments from authority when we appeal to dictionaries, encyclopedias, maps, or experts in any field. For instance:

> **13.** In his *Dictionary of Philosophy,* Anthony Flew defines "logicism" as the view that "mathematics, in particular arithmetic, is part of logic." So, that is what logicism is.[3]

In this context, an **authority** is a reliable producer of true statements on some topic. (An authority in this sense is to be distinguished from an "organizational" authority, like an elected official or a company president.)

An **authority** is a reliable producer of true statements on some topic.

The strength of an argument from authority is largely determined by the reliability of the relevant source—the more reliable the source, the stronger the argument. Of course, even highly reliable sources can sometimes be mistaken, so arguments from authority are not typically valid. (Note that an appeal to an infallible source would no longer be a case of induction, since an assertion from an infallible authority would guarantee the truth of the conclusion.)

An appeal to a reliable source usually makes for a strong inductive argument. However, there are also many ways for an argument from authority to go wrong. We will mention three.

First and most obviously, an argument from authority is weak when it appeals to a nonreliable source. This is known as the **ad verecundiam fallacy.** In some cases, this fallacy is obvious—an Orson Welles endorsement of frozen peas provides no evidence for their quality, since Welles knew little of frozen produce. In other cases, this fallacy is less obvious. Suppose, for example, that one appealed to the famous physicist, Richard Feynman, in arguing for a particular view about the value of science. That might seem like a strong argument from authority—after all, Feynman is a leading authority in the scientific community. However, questions about the *value* of science are not themselves scientific questions (they are philosophical) and, as Feynman himself says, "A scientist looking at nonscientific problems is just as dumb as the next guy."[4] So this would be yet another instance of the *ad verecundiam* fallacy.

The **ad verecundiam fallacy** occurs when an argument from authority appeals to a non-reliable source.

A second problem occurs when someone makes an appeal to an authority while ignoring conflicting reports from equally reliable sources. For example, suppose that you pick up Steven Cahn's *Classics of Western Philosophy* and read that Thomas Aquinas was born in 1225. You know that Cahn is an authority on such matters, so you conclude that Aquinas was born in 1225. However, you go on to read James Ross's *Introduction to the Philosophy of Religion*, which says that Aquinas was born in 1224. Still later, you read in Bertrand Russell's *History of Western Philosophy* that Aquinas was born in *either* 1225 or 1226. These subsequent discoveries do not challenge the credentials of your original source—Cahn *is* an authority on the history of philosophy. Nor do they undermine the premise of your original argument—Cahn *does* assert that Aquinas was born in 1225. But these discoveries *do* weaken your original argument. In light of your *total* current evidence, Cahn's assertion does not make your conclusion more likely than not. To cling to the original argument in this context would be to commit what we earlier called *the fallacy of incomplete evidence*.

Arguments from authority can also go wrong through misquotation or misinterpretation. Suppose, for example, that one argues as follows: The eminent biologist Stephen J. Gould admits that evolution is "a theory" (i.e., an unsupported hunch). So, evolution is an unsupported hunch. Here, the nonparenthetical part of the premise is true—Gould *does* say that evolution is a theory. But the parenthetical part involves an obvious misinterpretation of his words—in science, the word "theory" does *not* mean "unsupported hunch." Since the premise involves a misinterpretation, the argument is uncogent.

To sum up, an argument from authority can be cogent, provided that we have correctly represented a reliable source and we have not ignored conflicting claims from other authorities in the field.

Summary of Arguments from Authority

Form

    1. R sincerely asserts that S.

So, 2. S.

Questions to Ask

1. Is the source reliable on this topic?
2. Are there authorities (other than R) that assert that S is false? If so, are these authorities more, less, or equally reliable on the subject at issue?
3. Is the authority being misquoted or misinterpreted?

Arguments from Analogy

Another common kind of inductive argument is the argument from analogy, which has the following form:

    1. A is similar to B.

    2. B has property P.

So, 3. A has property P.

Here, A and B can stand for many different things. For example, they may stand for particular people, places, or things (e.g., Socrates, Seattle, or last night's soccer game) or kinds of objects and events (e.g., cities or soccer matches in general). P stands for any sort of property (e.g., the property of being fast, the property of being intelligent, or the property of being dangerous). To illustrate, let's consider an example:

14. *The Tempest* and *A Midsummer Night's Dream* are both plays written by William Shakespeare. These two plays are very similar in length. Hud was able to read *A Midsummer Night's Dream* in the space of an evening. So, Hud is able to read *The Tempest* in the space of an evening.

Here, "*The Tempest*" replaces A and "*A Midsummer Night's Dream*" replaces B in the original schema. P is the property of being readable (by Hud) in the space of an evening.

In order to evaluate an argument from analogy, we must examine the relevant resemblance. In particular, we must determine the degree to which. A's similarity to B provides support for the statement that A has property P. Unfortunately, there is no simple formula or mechanical method for determining this degree of support. But the following questions are often a good place to start.

> **Question 1:** What are the respects in which A and B are similar, and are they relevant to the issue at hand? Ideally, the one who offers the argument supplies this information, but often the information is provided only in part. Similarities are relevant if they increase the likelihood of A's having property P. And, generally speaking, the more relevant respects A and B share, the stronger the argument.

> **Question 2:** Are A and B dissimilar in any relevant respects? That is, does the analogy between A and B break down at any relevant points? Dissimilarities are relevant if they decrease the likelihood of A's having property P. Relevant differences between A and B tend to weaken the argument.

> **Question 3:** Are there things (other than A) that are similar to B in the relevant respects? If so, do these things have property P? To the extent that there are things relevantly similar to B that lack P, the analogy breaks down. To the extent that there are things relevantly similar to B that have P, the analogy holds up.

Let us evaluate argument (14) in terms of these three questions.

Question 1: In what respects are A (*The Tempest*) and B (*A Midsummer Night's Dream*) similar? They are similar in length, and both are written in Elizabethan English. The style of writing is also similar. Are these similarities relevant to the issue at hand? That is, does the fact that these plays are similar in length, language, and style support the claim that they can be read in roughly the same amount of time? Yes.

Question 2: Are A (*The Tempest*) and B (*A Midsummer Night's Dream*) dissimilar in any relevant respects? *The Tempest* is a more serious play than *A Midsummer Night's Dream*, and in places *The Tempest*, unlike *A Midsummer Night's Dream*, is rather pessimistic in tone. So, it might take a little longer to read *The Tempest*.

Question 3: Are there things other than A (*The Tempest*) that are similar to B (*A Midsummer Night's Dream*) in the relevant respects and that have property P (i.e., can be read by Hud in an evening)? Yes, Hud once read another of

Shakespeare's plays, *As You Like It,* in an evening. And it is similar in length, type of English, and style to *A Midsummer Night's Dream.*

To sum up, the answer to Question 1 indicates that there are several relevant respects in which *The Tempest* and *A Midsummer Night's Dream* are similar. The answer to Question 2 notes a relevant dissimilarity, but the dissimilarity does not seem to weaken the analogy much. The answer to Question 3 indicates that as we consider related examples, the analogy holds up. Accordingly, the argument appears to be strong.

Let's consider a second argument from analogy:

> **15.** Parrots and humans can both talk. Humans can think rationally. Therefore, parrots can think rationally.

Here, "parrots" replaces A and "humans" replaces B in the original schema. P is the property of being able to think rationally.

Question 1: What are the similarities between parrots and humans? The most obvious similarity is the ability to talk. Is this similarity relevant to the question of whether parrots can think rationally? There is *some* sort of linkage between the ability to talk and the ability to think rationally because it is primarily in the linguistic behavior of humans that their capacity for rational thought is exhibited.

Question 2: Are parrots dissimilar to humans in any relevant respects? Yes, in at least two relevant respects. First, as far as we can tell, parrots merely *mimic* what they hear. They do not produce their own sentences in a spontaneous, creative fashion. And, of course, mimicking is not a reliable indication of rational thought. Second, the brain of a parrot is much smaller than that of a human. And this raises a legitimate doubt about whether parrots are capable of the kind of thinking of which humans are capable.

Note that not all dissimilarities are relevant ones. For example, parrots have feathers and humans do not. But this dissimilarity has no apparent bearing on the issue at hand (i.e., can parrots think rationally?), and so it is irrelevant for present purposes. Relevant dissimilarities are those that affect the likelihood of A's having property P.

Question 3: Are there any examples of things (other than parrots) that can talk but cannot think rationally? Apparently so, for some deranged persons are able to talk but only in a highly disconnected and illogical fashion. So, apparently, there are things that talk but do not think rationally. This observation again draws attention to a weakness in the analogy between parrots and humans (in general).

To sum up, our answer to Question 1 indicates that there are *some* relevant similarities between parrots and humans but not many. Our answers to Questions 2 and 3 indicate that these similarities are *not* sufficient to make it likely that if the premises of argument (15) are true, then its conclusion is true. Therefore, argument (15) is weak.

Arguments from analogy are often used in moral and legal reasoning. For example:

16. The prohibition of so-called hard drugs such as cocaine and heroin is similar to the prohibition of alcohol. The prohibition of alcohol was well intentioned and based on legitimate concerns about the dangers of alcohol consumption. The prohibition of alcohol also led to a highly profitable black market ruled by organized crime and marked by violence. Now, we can all agree that the prohibition of alcohol was, in the final analysis, a mistake. Therefore, the prohibition of hard drugs is also a mistake—hard drugs should be legalized.

Here, A is the prohibition of hard drugs and B is the prohibition of alcohol. Property P is that of being a mistake. Is this argument strong or weak? That is a difficult question, and we cannot hope to answer it here. But we can begin working toward an answer by asking some preliminary questions.

Question 1: In what ways are A and B similar? The premises spell out a number of ways in which the prohibition of hard drugs is similar to the prohibition of alcohol, and these similarities seem relevant to the issue of legalization.

Question 2: Are A and B dissimilar in any relevant respects? Critics of argument (16) might claim that prohibiting hard drugs is relevantly different from prohibiting alcohol in at least two ways. For instance:

a. Drugs such as cocaine and heroin are more addictive than alcohol and might therefore be more dangerous.

b. The current social context is different from that in which alcohol was legalized. When alcohol was legalized, drug abuse was not a serious social problem in America. But now it is. Therefore, legalizing hard drugs will probably add to current problems such as death and injury resulting from traffic accidents, babies born with health problems because their mothers abuse chemical substances, and workplaces that are less efficient because of the number of people who use drugs while working.

Surely, these alleged dissimilarities, if accurate, are relevant and weaken the analogy at least to some degree.

Question 3: Are there things other than A (the prohibition of hard drugs) that are similar to B (the prohibition of alcohol) in the relevant respects but that lack P (the property of being a mistake)? Critics of argument (16) may point out that there are many drugs that cannot be used legally without a doctor's prescription. Surely, then, it is not in general a mistake to prohibit the use of a drug (except under doctor's orders). Proponents of argument (16) might reply, however, that prescription drugs are not in general relevantly similar to cocaine and heroin, for prescription drugs are not being sold in large quantities through black markets, and they are not under the control of organized criminals.

The foregoing discussion illustrates the kinds of issues that arise when evaluating arguments by analogy. It also illustrates how this process of evaluation can teach valuable lessons, and raise important questions, even when we are unable to reach a final verdict on the argument under dispute.

Summary of Arguments from Analogy

Form

1. A is similar to B.
2. B has property P.

So, 3. A has property P.

Questions to Ask

1. What are the respects in which A and B are similar, and are they relevant to the issue at hand?
2. Are A and B dissimilar in any relevant respects?
3. Are there things (other than A) that are similar to B in the relevant respects? If so, do these things have property P?

Induction by Enumeration

We turn, finally, to a third kind of inductive argument. This type of argument is called **induction by enumeration,** and the form is as follows:

1. _____ percent of a sample of A are B.

So, 2. Approximately _____ percent of A are B.

A **sample** of a population, A, is a set of observed members from that group. The blanks may be filled by numbers from 0 to 100, inclusive. For instance:

17. Twenty-five percent of a sample of the students at St. Ambrose College are members of the Republican Party. So, approximately 25 percent of the students at St. Ambrose College are members of the Republican Party.

Here, "twenty-five" fills the blanks, the set of students at St. Ambrose College replaces A, and the set of persons belonging to the Republican Party replaces B.

A **sample** of a population is a set of observed members from that group.

Argument (17) is correct in form, but it may still be weak since the sample may not be a good one. For instance, if our sample consists of only 4 students, and St. Ambrose has 3000 students enrolled, then our sample is too small to warrant the inference. Or suppose our sample is large but biased—it was taken at a meeting of the Young Democrats Club. Then, again, the argument will be weak.

How large does a sample need to be? How can one avoid biased samples? These turn out to be very complicated questions. We will focus on three points: A good sample must be *random*, of *appropriate size*, and not distorted by *psychological factors*.[5]

RANDOM SAMPLES

A good sample is *random* rather than *biased*. "Random" here has a technical meaning. A **random sample** is one in which each member of the population has an equal chance of being selected for observation.

A **random sample** is one in which each member of the population has an equal chance of being selected for observation.

A famous case of sample bias illustrates the importance of randomness. In 1936, *Literary Digest* magazine conducted a poll to determine who would win the presidential election—Republican Alf Landon or Democrat Franklin D. Roosevelt. The *Digest* sent out 10 million questionnaires, of which roughly 2 million were returned. A sample of 2 million is a very large sample compared with those used in a Gallup poll, so there was no problem with the size of the sample. And based on the sample, the *Digest* predicted that Landon would win the election, but in fact Roosevelt won by a landslide. What went wrong? First, the names of those surveyed had been taken mainly from lists of telephone subscribers and lists of automobile registrations. Second, the election occurred during the Great Depression, when many people could not afford a telephone or an automobile. Thus, the poorest members of the population did not have a equal chance of being selected for the survey. This bias explains the poll results, since the poor voted overwhelmingly for Roosevelt.

How can a random sample be obtained? In some cases, this is easy—for example, when the members of a population are known to have a high degree of uniformity. To take an extreme case, suppose that our argument concerns hydrogen atoms. Hydrogen atoms are exceedingly similar to one another, each having one proton and one electron. So, although the total number of hydrogen atoms is very large (approximately 10^{80}!), a relatively small sample would support an inference about the total population. Similarly, police detectives can learn much from a few strands of hair or a few drops of blood at the scene of a crime since a person's hairs tend to be very similar to one another, and one drop of a victim's (or suspect's) blood will be very similar to another.

However, if we are concerned with human opinions about, say, which foods taste best, our population will have a very low degree of uniformity, for humans have widely varying views about which foods taste best. In cases like this we need to take elaborate precautions to ensure a random sample. Bias can creep into a sample in many ways, some of them rather subtle. To cite just one common problem, when a sample consists of questionnaires that must be voluntarily returned, people on one side of an issue may have much stronger feelings than those on the other side, and those with stronger feelings may be more likely to return the questionnaire.

Researchers today employ many different methods for avoiding biases of this sort. For example, election pollsters typically divide their target population into geographical regions and then randomly interview representatives from each area. This helps to avoid sample bias, since voting preferences tend to vary from region to region.[6]

APPROPRIATE SAMPLE SIZE

A good sample is of the appropriate size. It would be nice if a simple mathematical formula could be applied to determine the appropriate sample size in any given case. Unfortunately, this is not the case. As we have just seen, the appropriate size of the sample depends on such factors as the degree of uniformity within the population. It also depends on the size of the population and the acceptable degree of error. We will say a few words about each of these factors.

First, the appropriate sample size depends partly on the size of the population. This is especially true when the population is relatively small. For instance, if we are taking an opinion poll at a small elementary school, our sample can be smaller than it would need to be if we were polling students at a large state university. However, one common misconception about samples is that a larger population will always require a larger sample. But that is not the case when dealing with sufficiently large populations. For example, a typical election poll with a margin of error of (+/−) 3 percent requires approximately 1500 interviews—and that is the case whether the election is for the mayor of Dallas, the governor of Texas, or the president of the United States. To illustrate this point:

Suppose we are drawing a sample of 500 marbles from a barrel containing 10,000 marbles, half of them red and half blue. And let us stipulate that our sample is chosen randomly so that each marble in the barrel has an equal chance of being selected. Our sample likely will contain approximately 250 red marbles (give or take a few), and approximately 250 blue ones (give or take a few). Now, suppose the barrel contains 1 million marbles instead of 10,000. If we select 500 marbles at random, we should still get approximately 250 red and 250 blue. Thus, a larger population does not necessarily require a larger sample.[7]

The appropriate sample size will also depends upon the acceptable degree of error. The **sampling error** is the difference between the percentage of the sample that has the attribute in question and the percentage of the population that has it.

> The **sampling error** is the difference between the percentage of the sample that has the attribute in question and the percentage of the population that has it.

For instance, suppose we take a random sample of 10 marbles from a population of 100: 6 marbles in our sample are red, 4 are blue. We conclude that 60 percent of the marbles in the population are red. Let us suppose that exactly 50 percent of the marbles in the population are red. The sampling error in this case is 10 percent.

Based on experience with the Gallup polls, the relationship between sample size and sampling error can be stated with remarkable precision for studies of large populations.[8]

Number of Interviews	Margin of Error (in percentage points)
4000	± 2
1500	± 3
1000	± 4
750	± 4
600	± 5
400	± 6
200	± 8
100	±11

Let us suppose that we are conducting a poll, and our (randomly selected) sample contains 1000 registered voters, of whom 700 say they currently favor Smith for president. We conclude that 70 percent of the registered voters currently favor Smith for president, with a sampling error of ±4 percentage points. In other words, given our evidence, it is probable that between 66 and 74 percent of the registered voters currently favor Smith for president. And, as the data indicate, we can reduce the margin of error by increasing the size of our sample. Of course, it takes more time and effort to obtain larger samples (and hence more money), so we may rest content with a smaller sample if we do not have a strong need for greater accuracy.

PSYCHOLOGICAL FACTORS

One last potential problem with samples should be noted: distortion caused by psychological factors. In some case, the very *nature* of a question is liable to lead to inaccurate results, as when one asks "Are you planning any upcoming felonies?" In other cases, the *wording* of a question can significantly affect the answers one receives. For example, a 2011 CBS News/New York Times poll found that 34 percent of Americans strongly favored "homosexuals" serving in the military. The very same poll found that 51 percent of Americans strongly favored "gay men and lesbians" serving in the military.[9] In still other cases, it is the question*er*, rather than the question, that can produce unwanted psychological effects. For example, a certain facial expression or tone of voice from an interviewer can subtly affect the answers given by interviewees.

To sum up, arguments from enumeration can be cogent, provided that we use a random sample of appropriate size and avoid psychological factors that can cause inaccuracies.

Summary of Induction by Enumeration

Form

1. _____ percent of a sample of A are B.

So, 2. Approximately _____ percent of A are B.

Questions to Ask

1. Is the sample random?
2. Is the sample of an appropriate size?
3. Is the sample inaccurate due to psychological factors?

Summary of Definitions

An **authority** is a reliable producer of true statements on some topic.

The ***ad verecundiam* fallacy** occurs when an argument from authority appeals to a nonreliable source.

A **sample** of a population is a set of observed members from that group.

A **random sample** is one in which each member of the population has an equal chance of being selected for observation.

The **sampling error** is the difference between the percentage of the sample that has the attribute in question and the percentage of the population that has it.

EXERCISE 10.2

PART A: Identifying Inductive Arguments   Which of the following arguments are examples of the types of inductive argument introduced in this section? Which are not? (a) If an argument is not an example of any of the types of arguments introduced in this section, simply write "Incorrect form." (b) If an argument is an example of a type of argument introduced in this section, identify the type. (c) Specify the sampling error wherever possible. (d) Identify any fallacies of incomplete evidence, and briefly indicate why a fallacy has been committed.

*   **1.** One hundred percent of the dogs that have been dissected have had kidneys. Hence, 100 percent of the members of the class of dogs have kidneys.

    2. In a recent study, a randomly chosen sample of 1500 American husbands were asked how many times they had had extramarital affairs. Eighty-four percent of those in the sample stated that they had never had an extramarital affair. Hence, approximately 84 percent of American husbands have never had an extramarital affair.

    3. The word "obviate" means "to do away with or prevent" because that is what *Webster's Dictionary* says it means.

*   **4.** According to a recent poll, 50 percent of a random sample of 1500 voters in Ohio favor Quigley for governor. Thus, roughly 50 percent of voters in Ohio favor Quigley for governor.

    5. Bertrand Russell, a noted logician, states that the social mores concerning sex outside of marriage are harmful and oppressive. So, the social mores concerning sex outside of marriage are harmful and oppressive.

    6. Ron Paul and George W. Bush are both Republican. And Ron Paul advocates the decriminalization of marijuana. So, George W. Bush favors the decriminalization of marijuana.

*   **7.** The *Bantam Medical Dictionary* says that an *ectopic pregnancy* is "the development of a fetus at a site other than the womb" (e.g., the fallopian tube). So, an ectopic pregnancy is the development of a fetus at a site outside the womb.

    8. According to a recent poll, zero percent of a randomly chosen sample of five U.S. voters favor Mack Smith for president. So, zero percent of U.S. voters favor Mack Smith for president.

    9. Chimpanzees have intrinsic moral worth. After all, human beings have intrinsic moral worth, and over 98 percent of their DNA is present in chimpanzees.

* **10.** The noted astrologer Vashti Zinia states that the stars determine the course of human history. So, our fate is in the hands of the stars.

  11. The following information is gleaned from Howard Zinn, *A People's History of the United States* (New York: HarperCollins, 1995), p. 585: In February 1991, U.S. aircraft dropped bombs on an air raid shelter in Baghdad. Between 400 and 500 people were killed. The Pentagon claimed the shelter was a military target. But reporters who were allowed to inspect the site asserted that there was no evidence of any military presence. Now, given this information from Zinn, we may conclude that the Pentagon was right: The shelter was a military target.

12. In a recent study involving 600 male prison inmates in Georgia, 80 percent of those in the sample indicated disapproval of the death penalty. Hence, 80 percent of men in Georgia disapprove of the death penalty.

* **13.** Sixty-seven percent of those in a randomly chosen sample of 4000 Americans are overweight. Therefore, about 67 percent of Americans are overweight.

14. *The Tempest* is perfectly analogous to *The Tempest*, since everything perfectly resembles itself. And *The Tempest* is boring. So, by analogy, *The Tempest* is boring.

15. Eighty-two percent of a randomly chosen sample of 600 American college students are sleep-deprived. Therefore, approximately 82 percent of American college students are sleep-deprived.

* **16.** According to a recent poll, 80 percent of a randomly chosen sample of 10 Americans prefer football to soccer. Hence, about 80 percent of Americans prefer football to soccer.

* **17.** Of a randomly selected sample of 1000 Americans, only 140 had red hair. So, about 14 percent of Americans have red hair.

18. I'm awesome at Madden 12. So I'm sure I'll be awesome at Madden 13 too.

* **19.** According to Dee Brown, *Bury My Heart at Wounded Knee* (New York: Washington Square Press, 1981), 153 Native Americans are known to have been killed in the massacre at Wounded Knee, although the actual number may well be as high as 300. Only 25 U.S. soldiers were killed, most of them by "friendly fire" from other soldiers. According to Brown, the soldiers ordered the Native Americans to give up their rifles, but a young Minneconjou named Black Coyote did not give up his rifle. Some eyewitnesses say that Black Coyote opened fire on the soldiers; others say he was deaf and did not understand the soldiers. Therefore, based on this information, we may conclude that Black Coyote started the incident at Wounded Knee by firing on the soldiers.

20. According to a recent poll, 90 percent of a randomly chosen sample of 4000 men in Mississippi reported that they believe that racism is more widespread than sexism. Hence, approximately 90 percent of Americans believe that racism is more widespread than sexism.

PART B: Analyzing and Evaluating Analogies Analyze the following arguments in terms of the schema for arguments from analogy, identifying A and B (the things being compared) and property P. Below each argument is a suggested criticism or reply. Does the reply point to an important weakness in the analogy? Why or why not?

* **1.** Mars is similar to the earth in that both are planets that orbit the sun. The earth is inhabited by living things. Therefore, Mars is inhabited by living things.

   Reply: The moon also orbits the sun, but we know that the moon is not inhabited by living things.

2. Having an abortion is like using contraception. In both cases, the intent is the same: to avoid having a baby. And plainly, contraception is morally permissible. Thus, abortion is morally permissible also.

   Reply: Abortion involves taking life, whereas contraception prevents life from occurring.

3. Marijuana is as much a gift from the earth as is lettuce. Therefore, because it is not wrong to enjoy lettuce, it is not wrong to enjoy marijuana.

   Reply: Marijuana is usually smoked, but lettuce is eaten.

* **4.** Logic, like whiskey, loses its beneficial effects when taken in very large quantities. Therefore, very large quantities of logic should be avoided. —Lord Dunsany, *My Ireland,* as quoted in H. L. Mencken, ed., *A New Dictionary of Quotations* (New York: Knopf, 1978), p. 705 (*Note:* This quotation is slightly altered—we've made the conclusion explicit, and the original has "too" where we've used "very.")

   Reply: Whereas whiskey has alcohol in it, logic does not.

5. Surrogate motherhood is slave owning, for both slave owning and surrogate motherhood involve the buying and selling of human beings. (The only difference is that in the case of surrogate motherhood, the humans who are bought and sold are always babies.) And yet everyone will agree that slave owning is immoral. We may therefore conclude that surrogate motherhood is immoral also.

   Reply: Surrogate mothers do not sell their babies; rather, surrogate mothers "rent" the use of their own reproductive capacities.

6. Can nonhuman animals feel pain? Well, the higher mammals have nervous systems that are similar to human nervous systems. Furthermore, higher mammals behave in ways similar to humans when damage is inflicted. (For example, just as a human is apt to cry out and withdraw his finger if it is stabbed with a pin, so a dog is apt to yelp and withdraw its paw if it is stabbed with a pin.) Therefore, higher mammals can feel pain.

   Reply: Animals cannot talk to us and explain how they feel, but humans can.

7. Taxation of earnings from labor is on a par with forced labor . . . it is like forcing the person to work n hours for another's purpose. Therefore, because it is wrong to force one person to work for another's purpose, it is wrong for the government to tax our earnings. —Robert Nozick, *Anarchy, State, and Utopia* (New York: Basic Books, 1974), p. 169 (*Note:* We have made the conclusion explicit.)

   Reply: All governments tax their citizens, but only corrupt or tyrannical governments have programs of forced labor.

8. If at times force can be used to counter force, why should lies never be used to counter lies? . . . just as someone forfeits his rights to noninterference by others, when he threatens them forcibly, so a liar has forfeited the ordinary right to be dealt with honestly. —Sissela Bok, *Lying: Moral Choice in Public and Private Life* (New York: Random House, 1979), p. 133 (*Note:* Bok states the argument to discuss it, not to endorse it.)

Reply: Lying involves the use of language, whereas force need not involve the use of language.

9. For the first six to eight weeks of pregnancy, the fetus has no brain waves. So, during this period, the fetus is similar to a brain-dead adult. Therefore, if a brain-dead adult is not living, neither is a fetus during the first six to eight weeks of pregnancy. —Adapted from Baruch Brody, "Fetal Humanity and the Theory of Essentialism," in Robert Baker and Frederick Elliston, eds., *Philosophy and Sex* (Buffalo: Prometheus Books, 1975), pp. 348–352

Reply: A brain-dead adult is not growing and gaining new powers, but a fetus is growing and gaining new powers.

* **10.** A computer, like the human brain, is capable of responding to stimuli in astonishingly complex ways. Computers can play chess, enter into dialogues, and solve extremely difficult mathematical problems. Now, humans are aware of their own thoughts and feelings. Therefore, computers are aware of their own thoughts and feelings also.

Reply: Computers are made mostly of metal and plastic, but humans are not.

11. Suppose a wicked tyrant threatens to kill 10 innocent people unless you give him all your discretionary income. If you refuse to give the money, you will not be harmed, but the 10 innocent people will be put to death. If you give the money, both you and the 10 innocent people will go unharmed. (Assume that you have no other options such as overthrowing the tyrant or helping the 10 people escape.) Clearly, in such circumstances, you are morally obligated to give up your discretionary income to save the 10 people. Now, you are in fact in a situation quite like this. World hunger is the wicked tyrant. The 10 innocent people are the starving poor of the Third World. Therefore, you are morally obligated to give up your discretionary income to save the starving poor. —Adapted from Louis Pascal, "Judgement Day," in Peter Singer, ed., *Applied Ethics* (New York: Oxford University Press, 1986), pp. 105–111

Reply: In the wicked tyrant case, you can identify exactly who will die, but in the case of world hunger, you cannot identify the individuals who will die.

12. Suppose you have been kidnapped by the Society of Music Lovers and your kidneys have been connected to the circulatory system of a famous violinist who lies unconscious beside you. You know that if you detach yourself from his circulatory system, the violinist will die. You also know that if you stay attached to the violinist for nine months, he'll regain his health (and your health will not suffer). In such circumstances, would you be morally obligated to remain connected to the violinist? Surely not. It would be very nice of you to remain connected, but it is not your moral duty to do so. Therefore, it is not wrong for a woman to have an abortion in the case of pregnancy through rape. —Adapted from Judith Jarvis Thomson, "A Defense of Abortion," in Peter Singer, ed., *Applied Ethics* (New York: Oxford University Press, 1986), pp. 37–56

Reply: Detaching yourself from the famous violinist is not killing—it is not like shooting him in the head with a gun. In other words, detaching yourself from the violinist is merely letting him die. By contrast, abortion involves killing the fetus.

13. Rich nations are tiny lifeboats surrounded by masses of drowning people. Thus, it is impossible for rich nations to save many of those living in the poorest nations. —Adapted from Garrett Hardin, "Lifeboat Ethics: The Case Against Helping the Poor," in Stephen Satris, ed., *Taking Sides: Clashing Views on Controversial Moral Issues*, 4th ed. (Guilford, CT: Dushkin, 1994), pp. 350–357

Reply: Rich nations such as the United States own vast amounts of land. So, obviously, they can hold a lot more people than a lifeboat can.

14. When the technique of in vitro fertilization is employed, eggs are withdrawn from the woman by laparoscopy and fertilized in a Petri dish (usually by the husband's sperm but sometimes by a donor's sperm). A number of eggs are removed at one time and fertilized, for various reasons. For one thing, women who seek in vitro fertilization typically have a history of difficulties in achieving pregnancy. Thus, multiple attempts at inserting embryos (i.e., fertilized eggs) into the womb are often required. Also, the pain and expense of multiple surgeries are saved by removing more than one egg per laparoscopy. Now, after the eggs are fertilized, they must be frozen, and if the woman becomes pregnant, there may be unneeded or superfluous frozen embryos. These embryos are simply thawed and discarded if the pregnancy results in the birth of a baby. And obviously, there is nothing immoral about discarding such superfluous frozen embryos. But note that this has implications for the abortion debate. Since discarding a frozen embryo is not and cannot reasonably be equated with murder, early abortions cannot reasonably be equated with murder either.

Reply: Frozen embryos cannot grow; but under normal circumstances, a zygote can.

15. The experiences of a clairvoyant person are similar to the experiences of a sighted person. Both types of experience involve vivid images. And both types of experience seem to tell us about events in the real world. Now, admittedly, not everyone is clairvoyant, but not everyone is sighted either. Furthermore, while the experiences of clairvoyant persons sometimes prove illusory, the experiences of sighted persons sometimes prove to be illusory, too. After all, optical illusions are common enough. Nevertheless, it is reasonable to believe that the experience of seeing is a source of truth about the world. Hence, it is reasonable to believe that the experiences of clairvoyant persons are a source of truth about the world.

Reply: Most people are sighted, but at best only a small minority are clairvoyant.

10.3 Scientific Reasoning: Mill's Methods

Much of what we do is based on causal knowledge. We turn the keys in the ignition because we know this will start the car (i.e., it will *cause* the car to start). We step on the accelerator because that causes the car to go. And we honk at slow drivers because that causes them to get out of the way. But how do we come to know these causal truths? As the great Scottish philosopher David Hume (1711–1776) pointed out, we cannot directly observe causation. We see the match strike the flint and we see the match burst into flame, but we do not literally *see* the causal relationship between these events. Causal knowledge is therefore indirect knowledge, which we arrive at by means of induction.

In his book *A System of Logic*, the English philosopher John Stuart Mill (1806–1873) identified five methods for attaining causal knowledge. In this section, we explain Mill's ideas and then apply them to a classic case of scientific reasoning.

Mill's Methods

First, Mill proposed the **method of agreement.** To apply this method, one attempts to identify a common factor in a range of cases.

> The **method of agreement** involves identifying a common factor, that is, one that is present whenever the effect is present.

For example, suppose five students at Vernon Elementary School become nauseated shortly after lunch. The school nurse makes a list of what each student ate for lunch:

Student 1: Milk, tuna salad, candy bar

Student 2: Tuna salad, Coke, potato chips

Student 3: Milk, tuna salad, chocolate cake

Student 4: Apple, orange juice, tuna salad

Student 5: Tuna salad, milk, carrots, cupcake

The nurse observes that all of these students ate the tuna salad in the school cafeteria. Thus, eating the tuna salad is a factor common to all five cases. Of course, this is not enough, by itself, to prove that the tuna salad caused the nausea, but the search for a common factor gives us a good place to start in identifying the cause.

Second, Mill proposed the **method of difference.** To apply this method, we compare two cases, one in which the effect is present and one in which the effect is absent.

> The **method of difference** involves comparing two cases, one in which the effect is present and one in which it is absent. If when the effect is absent, the possible cause C is also absent, the test lends support to C as the cause.

To continue with our school lunch example, the "effect" is the nausea. To apply this method, the school nurse would find out what one or more students *who didn't become nauseated* ate for lunch. For example, suppose students (6) and (7) didn't become nauseated:

> Student 6: Pizza, Coke, tossed salad
> Student 7: Hot dog, milk, potato chips

The effect (nausea) is absent, so the cause is absent as well. And because students (6) and (7) did not eat the tuna salad, the nurse gains an additional line of evidence in favor of the tuna salad as the cause of the nausea. (Of course, it could be that those who became ill just happen to have an intolerance of tuna. Then the common factor is more subtle and complex—a combination of the material ingested and the conditions specific to the students who became ill, such as food allergies.)

Mill's third method, his so-called **joint method,** is simply a combination of the method of agreement and the method of difference. And, as we have just seen, it is entirely natural to combine the two.

> The **joint method** involves combining the method of agreement and the method of difference.

Mill's fourth method is called the **method of concomitant variation.** To employ this method, we show that as one factor varies, another varies in a corresponding way.

> The **method of concomitant variation** involves showing that as one factor varies, another varies in a corresponding way.

A simple example would be the speed of a car and the extent to which the accelerator is pressed down. The more you press down on the accelerator, the faster the car goes. In the case of the nauseated schoolchildren, the nurse may find that some students are sicker than others and that the more tuna salad a student ate, the sicker he or she is. This would give the nurse yet further evidence that eating the tuna salad caused the nausea.

Mill's fifth method is called the **method of residues.** The method of residues is applied when some of the causes of a phenomenon have already been verified; we then conclude that a remaining factor completes the causal account.

> The **method of residues** involves "subtracting out" those aspects of the effect whose causes are known and concluding that the rest of the effect ("the residue") is due to an additional cause.

For example, suppose a room in your house is very cold in the winter. You identify three possible causes: (a) a broken windowpane, (b) a hole in the ceiling, and (c) a clogged furnace duct. You replace the windowpane and unclog the furnace duct; the room is not as cold as it was, but it is still relatively cool. You conclude that the hole in the ceiling accounts for the *residual* coldness. To generalize, in applying the method of residues, we "subtract out" those aspects of the effect whose causes are known and conclude that the rest of the effect ("the residue") is due to an additional cause.

It should be obvious that arguments employing Mill's methods are not valid, for even if the premises are true, it is possible that the conclusion is false. The following example (which we first encountered in Chapter 4) illustrates this point:

18. On Monday, Bill drank scotch and soda and noticed that he got drunk. On Tuesday, Bill drank whiskey and soda and noticed that he got drunk. On Wednesday, Bill drank bourbon and soda and noticed that he got drunk. Bill concluded that soda causes drunkenness.[10]

Here, Bill applies the method of agreement. Soda is indeed a common factor in the three cases. And yet Bill has arrived at a false conclusion. The problem is that Bill failed to recognize another, very important common factor, namely, alcohol. In this case, Bill's oversight is outlandish. But in the history of science, there are many cases in which the most important common factor was something that most people did not even regard as a possible cause. For example, before Louis Pasteur's famous experiments in 1881, virtually no one thought that vaccination could produce immunity to rabies and anthrax. And until 1900, when Walter Reed proved that mosquitoes can transmit yellow fever, most people had never even regarded mosquito bites as a possible cause of the disease.

The soda and alcohol example illustrates something very important about Mill's methods: To make effective use of the methods, we have to make intelligent guesses about which conditions are causally relevant in a given case. For example, just before Bill's getting intoxicated, he may have been wearing a white shirt, breathing regularly, thinking about summer vacation, and eating a sandwich. Why do we ignore these prior conditions as we consider possible causes of Bill's inebriated state? Well, our background knowledge gives us some ideas about the kinds of conditions that might produce the effect in question. Accordingly, out of the myriad conditions present in any given case, we hypothesize that only some of them are causally relevant. Thus, our discussion of Mill's methods leads naturally to a discussion of the formation and testing of hypotheses. In other words, our discussion of Mill's methods leads naturally to a discussion of scientific reasoning.

Scientific Reasoning

The scientific method involves (a) observing a phenomenon, (b) formulating a hypothesis that would explain the phenomenon, and then (c) testing that hypothesis. To illustrate this process, let us consider the work of one scientist, Ignaz Semmelweis, a physician who worked in the Vienna General Hospital. In the 1840s, he made an important discovery concerning the cause of childbed (puerperal) fever. His discovery saved many lives, since childbed fever was a frequent cause of death among pregnant women in Europe at the time.[11]

Semmelweis began by observing a puzzling asymmetry. The Vienna General Hospital had two maternity divisions. In one of these divisions, the First Maternity Division, 8.2 percent of the mothers died of childbed fever in 1844, 6.8 percent died in 1845, and 11.4 percent died in 1846. In the Second Maternity Division, however, the death rate was much lower: 2.3, 2.0, and 2.7 during the same years. In order to explain this asymmetry, Semmelweis formulated a number of hypotheses. Some hospital workers had complained that the First Maternity Division was too crowded, so Semmelweis formulated the following hypothesis:

> H_1: Childbed fever is caused by the crowded conditions in the First Maternity Division.

Semmelweis tested this hypothesis by considering its implications. He observed that the Second Division was actually more crowded than the First. (Because of the notorious reputation of the First Division, women understandably went to great lengths to avoid being assigned to it.) Thus, he reasoned that if H_1 were true, then the rate of childbed fever should be at least as high in the Second Division as in the First. But, as noted previously, the rate was in fact lower in the Second Division. So, Semmelweis concluded that H_1 was false.

Note that Semmelweis's initial reasoning involved Mill's method in several different ways. Semmelweis began with H_1 because crowded conditions were thought to be a common factor. In doing so, he was tacitly using Mill's method of agreement. Semmelweis subsequently rejected this hypothesis because he noted that the effect—that is, the higher mortality rate—was lacking in the Second Division, even though the hypothesized cause was present. His rejection of the hypothesis was therefore based on Mill's method of difference.

Semmelweis next observed that the women in the two divisions delivered their babies in different positions—those in First Division delivered lying on their backs, and those in the Second Division delivered lying on their sides. In accordance with Mill's joint method, Semmelweis formulated the following hypothesis:

> H_2: Childbed fever is caused by the position of delivery (specifically, by the mother lying on her back rather than on her side).

To test this hypothesis, Semmelweis instructed the First Division to use the same method of delivery as that used in the Second Division. But this change did not affect the rates of mortality and, following the method of difference, Semmelweis concluded that H_2 was false.

Desperate for answers, Semmelweis tried a psychological hypothesis. He noted that the priest who administered the sacraments to the dying women was readily visible to the women in the First Division. Using the method of agreement, he formulated this hypothesis:

> H_3: The appearance of the priest terrifies the patients, making them more susceptible to childbed fever.

To test this hypothesis, Semmelweis instructed the priest to come by a different route so that he would not be seen or heard except by those who were already gravely ill. But this made no difference in the rate of childbed fever or the rate of death; following the method of difference, Semmelweis rejected H_3.

At length, a tragic accident led Semmelweis to an insightful hypothesis. A colleague of Semmelweis's named Kolletschka was accidentally cut by an assistant's scalpel while performing an autopsy. Shortly thereafter, Kolletschka died from an illness whose symptoms were the same as those of childbed fever. Semmelweis intuited that Kolletschka's death had been caused by the "cadaveric matter" introduced into his bloodstream during the autopsy. Furthermore, Semmelweis knew that the doctors and medical students often examined the women in the First Division immediately after performing dissections in the autopsy room, and although the medical personnel washed their hands, an unmistakable odor indicated that some of the cadaveric matter was still present. The method of agreement led Semmelweis to the following hypothesis:

> H_4: Childbed fever is caused by cadaveric matter on the hands of medical examiners.

Again, Semmelweis tested the hypothesis in accordance with the method of difference. If H_4 was correct, then childbed fever could be prevented by removing the infectious material from the hands of those examining the pregnant women. Accordingly, he required all those who participated in such examinations to wash their hands in a solution containing chlorinated lime. As a result of this measure, the rate of childbed fever dropped dramatically in the First Division; indeed, it became lower than the rate in the Second Division.

Semmelweis also noted that H_4 explained why the rates of disease and mortality had differed between the two divisions, for the patients in the Second Division had been cared for by midwives rather than by those whose training involved the dissection of cadavers. Semmelweis concluded that H_4 was true.

Let us now consider the general principles involved in testing hypotheses. Let us use H to stand for a hypothesis and I to stand for an implication of the hypothesis. You may have noticed that Semmelweis employed the following pattern of reasoning in rejecting hypotheses:

> 1. If H, then I.
> 2. It is not the case that I.
> So, 3. It is not the case that H.

This is the general pattern for rejecting an empirical hypothesis as a result of an unfavorable test outcome (i.e., one that conflicts with the predictions made on the basis of the hypothesis). Note that the form is *modus tollens*, which meets the standard of deductive logic, namely, validity. For this reason, and because valid forms may be employed in deriving test implications from a hypothesis, this picture of scientific hypothesis testing is often called the "hypothetico-deductive method."

It would, however, be a gross oversimplification to suggest that rejecting a scientific hypothesis is simply a matter of applying *modus tollens*. In a typical case, one must make many background assumptions to obtain the premises. For example, suppose an astronomical hypothesis implies that a planet will be in a certain location at a certain time. An astronomer uses her telescope to observe whether the planet is present at the location and time implied by the hypothesis, but she does not see the planet. Has the hypothesis been disproved? Not necessarily. The astronomer may have made an error in aiming the telescope. The telescope may have malfunctioned. And note that using the telescope presupposes that the various hypotheses concerning optics, which are employed in the design and construction of the telescope, are true. So, in testing one hypothesis, we may need to assume that another hypothesis or theory is true. The point is that although *modus tollens* may be employed in testing hypotheses, applying it in scientific situations involves making many background assumptions that may be open to question in a given case (e.g., the telescope did not malfunction, the astronomer used the telescope properly, and so on).

How is a hypothesis confirmed? It may seem that Semmelweis used the following pattern of reasoning (where H stands for the hypothesis and I stands for an implication of the hypothesis):

> 1. If H, then I.
> 2. I.
> So, 3. H.

("If cadaveric matter causes childbed fever, then the patients currently being treated in the First Division do not get childbed fever when the cadaveric matter is absent. The patients currently being treated in the First Division do not get childbed fever when the cadaveric matter is absent. So, cadaveric matter causes childbed fever.") But the form of argument here is the fallacy of affirming the consequent. Are we saying, then, that scientific reasoning rests on a fallacy? No. It would indeed be a fallacy to argue that if one specific implication of a hypothesis holds true, then the hypothesis holds true. But if we can identify many specific implications of a hypothesis, and observation (or experiment) indicates that all the implications are true, we can accumulate a significant amount of support for the hypothesis. Each case in which an implication of a hypothesis is observed to be true is called a **confirming instance.** And at some point, as the number (or kind) of confirming instances for a hypothesis increases, scientists find it unreasonable to attribute this to chance or mere coincidence. However, it is extremely difficult to specify clear and general logical principles for determining when a hypothesis is strongly supported by the evidence, and we cannot enter into a discussion of these complicated issues here.[12]

A **confirming instance** is a case in which an implication of a hypothesis is observed to be true.

What do scientists look for in a hypothesis?[13] At least four things. First, generally speaking, a hypothesis should be logically consistent with hypotheses or theories that are already well established. There are exceptions to this general rule, however. For example, Einstein's theories were not consistent with Newton's, and yet they came to be accepted because they explained things Newton's theories could not explain.

Second, a hypothesis should have explanatory power. A hypothesis has explanatory power to the extent that known facts can be inferred from it. And, of course, the "known facts" mentioned here must include those we are seeking to explain; otherwise, the hypothesis is irrelevant. To illustrate, Semmelweis's hypothesis that cadaveric material (when introduced into the bloodstream) causes childbed fever has explanatory power. From it, we can infer that persons who have had cadaveric material introduced into their bloodstreams are apt to contract childbed fever, which explains the high rate of childbed fever in the First Maternity Division.

Third, a good scientific hypothesis should be liable to empirical tests. Suppose Semmelweis had hypothesized that the higher rate of childbed fever in the First Division was caused by ghosts who haunt the First Division (but not the Second Division). Is there any way to test this hypothesis? There might be. Perhaps the ghosts can be seen or heard at certain times, or perhaps their influences can be thwarted by the work of an exorcist. But suppose no tests are allowed. The alleged ghosts, it is asserted, cannot be seen or heard. No traces of them can be found, not even in principle. Nor are they the type of ghosts who will respond to the work of exorcists. And so on. Such an untestable hypothesis is not acceptable within any scientific discipline.

But at least two cautionary remarks are warranted here. First, scientists routinely form hypotheses concerning entities that are not directly observable, such as electrons and protons. Nevertheless, many observable events can be explained in terms of these unobserved entities. For instance, if a hypothesis states that electrons behave in such-and-such a way, implications concerning observable events can be derived from the hypothesis. Scientists can then check to see if these events occur. Second, it is one thing to say that an untestable hypothesis is unscientific and another to say that it is untrue. There may well be things that cannot be explained scientifically—for example, the very existence of physical reality—and such things may have to be explained via untestable hypotheses or else not explained at all.

Finally, other things being equal, scientists generally prefer a simpler hypothesis to one that is more complicated. But consider an example outside of science for a moment. When investigating a murder, police do not typically begin with a complicated hypothesis to the effect that the victim was assassinated as part of an international conspiracy. Rather, it seems best to start with a relatively simple hypothesis and complicate it only as necessary to explain the phenomenon.

To take a scientific case, suppose we are testing a steel spring that hangs from the ceiling.[14] We place a 1-pound weight on the spring, and it extends 1 inch; we place a 2-pound weight on the spring, and it extends 2 inches; we place a 3-pound weight on the spring, and it extends 3 inches; and so on. We hypothesize that the behavior of the spring conforms to the formula $x = y$ (where x is the force in pounds and y is the extension in inches).

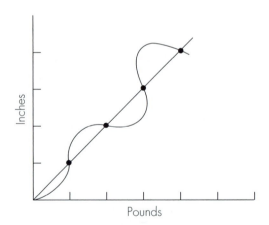

In the graphical representation, our hypothesis is represented by the straight diagonal line. The dots stand for specific observations we have made—for example, "A 2-pound weight extends the spring 2 inches." The curvy line represents an alternative hypothesis that is far more complicated but that still accounts for each of the observations. The point, once again, is that a good scientific hypothesis avoids unnecessary complications. If a relatively simple hypothesis works, one should not complicate it.

To sum up: Mill's methods provide us with some helpful strategies for reaching conclusions of the form "A causes B." But to use Mill's methods effectively, we have to make intelligent guesses about which conditions are apt to cause the phenomenon in question. That is, we have to formulate hypotheses. Scientific reasoning involves observing a phenomena, formulating hypotheses, and testing them. Hypotheses are tested by drawing out their implications and checking to see if the implications are true. A good scientific hypothesis is consistent with well-established hypotheses, has explanatory power, can be tested, and is relatively simple.

Summary of Definitions

The **method of agreement** involves identifying a "common factor," that is, one that is present whenever the effect is present.

The **method of difference** involves comparing two cases, one in which the effect is present and one in which it is absent. If when the effect is absent the possible cause C is also absent, the test lends support to C as the cause.

The **joint method** involves combining the first two methods.

The **method of concomitant variation** involves showing that as one factor varies, another varies in a corresponding way.

The **method of residues** involves "subtracting out" those aspects of the effect whose causes are known and concluding that the rest of the effect ("the residue") is due to an additional cause.

A **confirming instance** is a case in which an implication of a hypothesis is observed to be true.

EXERCISE 10.3

PART A: Mill's Methods   Which of Mill's methods is illustrated in each of the following examples? If, in your opinion, the conclusion reached indicates that an inadequate hypothesis was employed, formulate a better hypothesis.

* **1.** By his third shot of whiskey, Robert noticed that he was feeling intoxicated. He drank another shot of whiskey and found that the feeling increased. Curious, he drank yet another shot, and his head really began to spin. Robert concluded that the whiskey was making him drunk.

  2. Dick and Jane took a history exam. Both did poorly, although both studied for many hours. Both had pulled an "all-nighter." They concluded that the cause of their poor performance on the exam was a lack of sleep.

  3. Tom, Tanya, and Teri ate dinner at a Japanese restaurant. Tom had rice, squid, and salad. Tanya had rice, octopus, and salmon. Teri had rice, squid, and cucumber rolls. After the meal, Tom and Teri had upset stomachs, but Tanya did not. They concluded that the squid caused their upset stomachs.

* **4.** Alonzo has done well on his last three math exams. In each case, he studied very intensely for three hours the night before the exam. Also, in each case, he departed from his usual informal style of dress and wore a tie to the exam. Alonzo concluded that wearing a tie increases the quality of his performance on examinations.

5. Joe is weighing cargo on trucks, using a drive-on scale. A truck pulls onto the scale, and Joe records the total weight of 6000 pounds. He subtracts the weight of the truck, which is 4500 pounds, to determine the weight of the cargo, 1500 pounds.

6. An economist noted a correlation between the length of women's skirts and the price of stocks. As fashion trends moved in the direction of shorter skirts, stock prices increased. But as fashion trends moved in the direction of longer skirts, stock prices fell. The economist concluded that fashion trends regarding the length of women's skirts cause stock prices to rise and fall.

* **7.** A certain physics professor got into his car to drive home from work. As he backed out of the parking place, he noticed a large oil spot. The next day he parked in a different parking place, one that had no oil spot. But as he backed out of the parking place at the end of the day, he once again noticed a large oil spot. He concluded that an oil leak from his car had caused the oil spots.

8. Pasteur gave each of 25 farm animals a vaccination for anthrax. These animals, as well as 25 who had not been vaccinated, were subsequently given a large dose of anthrax germs. None of the vaccinated animals came down with the disease, but all of the others died of anthrax. Pasteur concluded that his vaccine produced immunity to anthrax.

9. A mechanic is trying to fix a car that leaks a small puddle of oil every day. Looking under the hood, he notices oily stains in two places: (a) near the back of the valve cover at the top of the engine and (b) near the bottom of the engine, where the oil pan is attached. The mechanic replaces the gasket in the valve cover, and the leaking decreases by about half, but a puddle of oil still appears whenever the car is parked for several hours. The mechanic concludes that the remaining leakage is coming from the bottom of the engine, where the oil pan is attached.

* **10.** A doctor had 10 patients suffering from a rare form of cancer. By investigating the life histories of his patients, he found that each of them had worked for several years at a nuclear power plant and each had been exposed to significantly high amounts of radiation on at least one occasion. The doctor concluded that the radiation was the cause of cancer in each of the 10 cases.

11. Bobby pulled the lever on the little black box. His electric train began to move forward. He pulled the lever a bit further. The train went faster. He pulled the lever further, and the train went so fast that it flew off the track. Bobby concluded that pulling the lever caused the train to go faster.

12. A psychiatrist treated five soldiers who wished to stop stuttering. He discovered that each of the soldiers had begun to stutter shortly after undergoing a frightening experience in combat. The psychiatrist concluded that the stuttering was caused by extreme fear.

* **13.** Galvani was dissecting a dead frog. By chance, he touched the nerves of the frog's leg with an instrument that conveyed an electrical impulse. The frog's leg muscles contracted suddenly. Galvani touched the frog's nerves many times with the instrument, and each time the frog's leg muscles contracted sharply. Galvani then touched the frog's nerves with a metal instrument that did not convey an electrical impulse. The frog's leg did not contract. Galvani concluded that an electrical impulse had caused the dead frog's muscles to contract.

14. A Martian visited a large city in North America. While walking the streets incognito, he observed the traffic closely. He noted that when lights blinked on the left side of a vehicle, it nearly always turned left, and when lights blinked on the right side of a vehicle, it nearly always turned right. The Martian concluded that the blinking lights caused the vehicles to turn.

15. Mary is trying to determine the source of water in her basement. Possible causes include a leaky pipe and water seeping through the basement walls. Mary fixes the leaky pipe, and the amount of water in the basement decreases substantially but still remains at a significant level. She concludes that the rest of the problem is due to water seeping through the basement walls.

* **16.** On Wednesday night, Fran had shrimp, fries, and a salad with blue cheese dressing. She broke out in hives. The following Sunday, she ate the same meal, and again she broke out in hives. She suspected that the blue cheese dressing was the problem. So, a few days later, she ate shrimp, fries, and a salad with Italian dressing. She did not break out in hives. Fran concluded that the blue cheese dressing had indeed caused the hives.

17. Sharon drank one cup of coffee with cream on an empty stomach. She began to feel more alert. So, she had a second cup of coffee, again with cream. She noticed that she felt a bit jittery, but the coffee was delicious, so she had a third cup, adding a generous portion of cream. Suddenly, Sharon began to feel very nervous and to talk excitedly. She concluded that the cream was making her feel nervous.

18. A psychiatrist treated six men who wanted to be married but always wound up in profoundly unsatisfying relationships with women. He found that all of the men had been neglected as children by their parents. He concluded that parental neglect had left the men without resources for maintaining satisfying relationships with women.

* **19.** At one point in his research on the causes of yellow fever, Walter Reed confined some volunteers to a carefully sealed room. The room contained a number of mosquitoes that were known to have bitten persons having yellow fever. All

the volunteers were bitten by the mosquitoes, and all contracted yellow fever. In another room, mosquitoes were carefully sealed out, and the people staying in that room did not contract yellow fever. Reed concluded that the mosquitoes were spreading yellow fever.

20. "On one occasion, . . . [Semmelweis] and his associates, having carefully disinfected their hands, examined first a woman in labor who was suffering from a festering cervical cancer; then they proceeded to examine twelve other women in the same room, after only routine washing without renewed disinfection. Eleven of the twelve patients died of puerperal fever. Semmelweis concluded that childbed fever can be caused not only by cadaveric material, but also by 'putrid matter derived from living organisms.'" —Carl G. Hempel, *Philosophy of Science* (Englewood Cliffs, NJ: Prentice-Hall, 1966), p. 6

21. Colette took one Benadryl capsule and felt a bit drowsy. She took a second Benadryl capsule and began to feel very sleepy. She took a third Benadryl capsule and could scarcely keep her eyes open. She concluded that Benadryl causes sleepiness.

*22. Betty, a department store manager, seeks an explanation for a register that often shows a shortage of cash at the end of the day. Betty suspects that one of the employees, Frank, is dipping from the till. But she also suspects that another employee, Jon, is making frequent mistakes in counting change. Betty confronts Frank about the matter; he admits to stealing and is fired. The frequency and amounts of the shortfall decrease sharply but are still nontrivial. Betty concludes that the persisting problem is likely caused by Jon's mistakes in counting change.

23. Marla ate some cookies that she obtained from a vending machine. Shortly after she ate the cookies, her lips began to tingle, and then they swelled up. Because the swelling didn't last very long, she quickly forgot about the incident. But a few weeks later, she again ate some cookies from a vending machine, and once again her lips swelled up immediately. She concluded that something in the cookies was causing her lips to swell up.

24. The chief of police is trying to account for a recent upsurge in violent crime in the subways. He suspects that two causes are operating: first, a reduction in allocation of funds to the police department, which leads to fewer police on duty in the subways, and second, the appearance of the subway cars—specifically, they are covered with graffiti and often full of trash. (The chief suspects that the appearance of the subway cars tends to make people feel that no one cares what goes on in the subways.) A discussion with the mayor solves the funding problem. The number of police on duty in the subways doubles, and the rate of violence drops significantly but does not return to the same level as before the recent upsurge. The chief concludes that the appearance of the subway cars accounts for what remains of the higher-than-usual rate of violence in the subways.

25. A sociologist closely observed correlations between demographics and the rate of violent crime. He noted that the rate of violent crime rose as the percentage of young men (15 to 25 years of age) *relative to the rest of the population* increased. For example, he noted that about 15 years after each baby boom, there is an increase in the rate of violent crime and the rate remains high for approximately 10 years. After about 10 years, the rate of violent crime falls off. The sociologist concluded that increases in the rate of violent crime are largely caused by an increase in the number of young men (as a percentage of the population).

PART B: Hypotheses In the following arguments, identify any hypotheses that fail to meet the four criteria for good scientific hypotheses. State which criterion is violated, and explain your answer.

* **1.** Frederick has been having trouble with his watch. It keeps losing time. He had the battery replaced, but that didn't help. So, Frederick hypothesized that an invisible demon had possessed his watch, slowing down the mechanism. He took the watch to a priest for an exorcism, but that didn't help either. Frederick concluded that the demon must be the type of demon that cannot be exorcised.

2. Robert was behind in his lab work in Chemistry 101. He heated some chemicals in a test tube. A gas was generated, and Robert filled a balloon with the gas. The balloon floated upward when released. Robert concluded that boiling the chemicals had somehow produced a situation in which the law of gravity was temporarily suspended. He excitedly wrote up his lab reports, expecting an A for his remarkable discovery.

3. Jennifer has been having trouble with her computer. For example, occasionally a few letters in a document get misplaced (without any action on her part). In an effort to account for these glitches, Jennifer hypothesizes that the computer has developed free will and is now occasionally making its own choices.

* **4.** A certain biology professor noted a correlation between increased activity among bees and the beginning of spring. He hypothesized that as bees flap their wings, their body heat increases, which warms the air around them, thus bringing about the changes in seasons from winter to spring.

5. A mechanic is trying to discover why your car won't start. He hypothesizes that the trouble is due to poltergeistic activity. When you state your intention of obtaining a second opinion, he indicates that this will do you no good because he is the only mechanic who can intuit the presence of poltergeists in cars and no observational checks are possible.

6. A certain professor got into his car to drive home from work. As he backed out of the parking place, he noticed a large oil spot. The next day he parked in a different parking place, one that had no oil spot. But as he backed out of the parking place at the end of the day, he once again noticed a large oil spot. He concluded that a group of pranksters had lifted his car up via blimp and poured oil under it on both days.

* **7.** A detective is trying to explain two murders that are remarkably similar in detail yet happened at the same time in very different locations—one in Florida and one in Alaska. The detective hypothesizes that the murderer has somehow learned to travel faster than the speed of light.

8. A biologist is trying to account for the extinction of the dinosaurs. He hypothesizes that the dinosaurs simply decided to stop having sex.

9. A detective is assigned to a murder case. The victim has been shot six times with a large-caliber handgun. Forensic tests indicate that the bullets all came from the same gun. With virtually no other facts to go on, the detective hypothesizes that there were six murderers who took turns shooting the victim, each of them firing one shot.

10. Martha has received her logic exam back from the instructor. She did well but lost a few points on one item. Specifically, on the exam, an inference of the form "If A, then B; not A; so not B" is identified as *modus tollens*. The answer is in Martha's handwriting. But Martha knows that the inference form is actually the fallacy of denying the antecedent, so she hypothesizes that the CIA stole her exam from the instructor, erased her original answer, and wrote an incorrect answer in her handwriting.

PART C: For Discussion Suppose you are a detective trying to solve a burglary. The specific evidence under consideration is this:

> *Evidence:* Ms. Vogel's TV is missing. It's a small TV set easily carried by one person. McGraw was seen lurking about Vogel's house while she was on vacation, and McGraw's fingerprints are on the table where Vogel kept her TV.

As a detective, you happen to have some relevant background information:

> *Background information:* McGraw and Kingston both have a record of petty theft, and both live within easy walking distance of Vogel's house.

Now, based on these givens, which of the following hypotheses is preferable, and why?

> *Hypothesis 1:* McGraw stole the TV.
>
> *Hypothesis 2:* Kingston stole the TV.
>
> *Hypothesis 3:* Spies from a foreign country stole the TV, and they framed McGraw (forcing him to walk around Vogel's house while she was on vacation and forcing him to touch her TV table).
>
> *Hypothesis 4:* McGraw and Kingston both stole the TV.

Which hypotheses have the most explanatory power? Which accord best with the background information? Which, if any, are preferable on grounds of simplicity?

10.4 Probabilistic Reasoning: The Rules of Probability

We have said that inductive logic is the part of logic that is concerned with strength, rather that validity. And we have characterized strength in terms of *probability*: A strong argument is one in which it is probable (but not necessary) that if the premises are true, then the conclusion is true. Probability thus figures into the definition of inductive logic. It also figures prominently into the *practice* of induction, both in our ordinary reasoning and in our scientific endeavors. For these reasons, it is important to explore the topic of probability.

We begin by introducing the basic rules of the probability calculus. We then discuss an important theorem of probability—Bayes' theorem—and show how that theorem can shed light on some traditional philosophical disputes.

The Rules of Probability

Many philosophers disagree about the exact nature of probability and the question of how we are to determine the likelihood of particular events. However, there is widespread agreement about how the probability of a compound statement is determined by the probabilities of its component parts. These rules are set forth in the *probability calculus*, which is analogous to the truth-table method in certain respects. As we saw in Chapter 7, a truth table does not tell us the truth value of noncompound statements such as F, G, and H, but it does tell us the value of $(F \vee G)$, for example, given truth-value assignments for F and for G. Similarly, the probability calculus does not tell us the probability of noncompound statements, but it does enable us to determine the probability of compound statements whenever we can assign probabilities to the noncompound statements involved.

Our discussion of probability presupposes the truth-functional logic introduced in Chapter 7. Accordingly, we will employ the symbols for statement logic first introduced in that chapter—specifically, "~" for negation, "∨" for disjunctions, "•" for conjunctions, "→" for material conditionals, and "↔" for material biconditionals. In addition, we will use the uppercase letter "P" for the probability operator; "P(A)" is to be read as "the probability that A."

Probability values are expressed as numbers from 0 to 1. Zero is the lowest degree of probability; 1 is the highest. It is customary to assign a probability of 1 to the tautologies of statement logic (which are true in every row of the truth table). So, for example, $P(A \vee {\sim}A) = 1$. We may state this first rule of probability as follows:

Rule 1: If a statement ***p*** is a tautology, then $P(\textbf{\textit{p}}) = 1$.

Here, the italicized, lowercase ***p*** stands for any statement whatever, including compound statements such as $[B \rightarrow (B \vee C)]$. Since a truth table reveals that $[B \rightarrow (B \vee C)]$ is a tautology, Rule 1 tells us that $P[B \rightarrow (B \vee C)] = 1$.

It is also customary to assign a probability of 0 to contradictions, which are false in every row of the truth table. This is our second rule of probability:

Rule 2: If a statement ***p*** is a contradiction, then $P(\textbf{\textit{p}}) = 0$.

For example, Rule 2 tells us that $P(H \bullet {\sim}H) = 0$ and that $P(B \leftrightarrow {\sim}B) = 0$.

Next, two statements are **mutually exclusive** if they cannot both be true. For example:

19. Tom Brady threw 36 touchdowns in 2010.
20. Tom Brady threw 46 touchdowns in 2010.

Two statements are **mutually exclusive** if they cannot both be true.

A set of statements is **exhaustive** if one of the statements must be true. For example:

21. Stefani Germanotta was born before 1986.
22. Stefani Germanotta was born after 1986.
23. Stefani Germanotta was not born before or after 1986.

Note that any statement and its negation are mutually exclusive as well as jointly exhaustive.

A set of statements is **exhaustive** if one of the statements must be true.

Now, suppose two statements, *p* and *q*, are mutually exclusive. For example, perhaps we are rolling a single six-sided die of the type used in ordinary board games. Let T stand for "The die will turn up three," and let S stand for "The die will turn up six." Now, assuming the die is not loaded, there is one chance in six that it will turn up on any given side. So, $P(T) = 1/6$ and $P(S) = 1/6$. And our chances of rolling *either three or six* on the next roll are two out of six. In other words, we add the probabilities: $P(T \vee S) = 1/6 + 1/6 = 2/6 = 1/3$. Examples such as this give us an intuitive grasp of the **restricted disjunction rule:**

> **Rule 3:** If *p* and *q* are mutually exclusive, then $P(p \vee q) = P(p) + P(q)$.

(This is called the "*restricted* disjunction rule" because it governs only the case in which two statements are mutually exclusive.) Two examples will illustrate the plausibility of this principle.

First, suppose that we are about to draw 1 card from an ordinary, well-shuffled deck of 52 playing cards. What is the probability that we will select either the ace of clubs or the ace of diamonds? Assuming each of the 52 cards has an equal chance of being drawn, $P(\text{draw ace of clubs}) = 1/52$, and P(draw ace of diamonds) = 1/52. So, intuitively, we have 2 chances out of 52 of selecting either the ace of clubs or the ace of diamonds (on the next draw), and this is just what the restricted disjunction rule tells us:

> P(draw ace of clubs ∨ ace of diamonds) = P(draw ace of clubs) +
> P(draw ace of diamonds) = 1/52 + 1/52 = 2/52 = 1/26

What is the probability of drawing a queen from a well-shuffled deck (on the next draw)? Since there is one queen per suit and four suits, the intuitively correct answer is 4 out of 52, and again this is just what the restricted disjunction rule tells us:

> P(draw queen of clubs ∨ draw queen of hearts ∨ draw queen of diamonds
> ∨ draw queen of spades) = P(draw queen of clubs) + P(draw queen of
> hearts) + P(draw queen of diamonds) + P(draw queen of spades) =
> 1/52 + 1/52 + 1/52 + 1/52 = 4/52 = 1/13

Next, the restricted disjunction rule allows us to calculate the probability of a negation from the probability of the statement negated. Take the statement S. Since S and ~S are mutually exclusive, the restricted disjunction rule allows us to conclude:

> P(S ∨ ~S) = P(S) + P(~S)

And since S ∨ ~S is a tautology, Rule 1 allows us to infer:

> P(S ∨ ~S) = 1

Now, it is a general principle of mathematics that two quantities equal to a third quantity are equal to each other. (If $x = z$ and $y = z$, then $x = y$.) So, from the two prior equations, we can deduce:

> P(S) + P(~S) = 1

Finally, we subtract the P(S) from both sides of the equation:

> P(~S) = 1 − P(S)

Generalizing, we have the **negation rule:**

> **Rule 4:** P(~*p*) = 1 − P(*p*)

The negation rule is very useful. For example, if we know that the probability of rolling a four on the next throw of the die is 1/6, then the negation rule allows us to immediately calculate the probability that a four will not turn up on the next throw:

P(not roll 4) = 1 − P(roll 4) = 1 − 1/6 = 5/6

Again, there are 13 cards in each suit, so the probability that we will select a spade on the next draw from a well-shuffled deck is 13/52. What is the probability that we will *not* select a spade on the next draw?

P(not select spade) = 1 − P(select spade) = 52/52 − 13/52 = 39/52 = 3/4

Of course, not every pair of statements is mutually exclusive. So, we need a more general disjunction rule to take care of cases in which the disjuncts can both be true. For example, suppose we want to know the probability of getting either a king or a club on the next draw. There is a king of clubs, so these two possibilities are not mutually exclusive. How shall we proceed? We have to subtract the probability of drawing a king that is also a club:

P(draw king ∨ club) = P(draw king) + P(draw club) − P(draw king • club)

If we do not subtract this quantity, we in effect count the king of clubs twice— once as a king and once as a club—which skews the result. Now, because there is one king per suit, the probability that we will draw a king (on the next draw) is 4/52. The probability that we will draw a club is 13/52 because there are 13 cards in each suit. But what is the probability that we will draw both a king *and* a club? Because there is only one king that is also a club, the probability that we will draw a king and a club is simply the probability that we will draw the king of clubs, that is, 1/52. Plugging these values into our formula, we get the following:

P(draw king ∨ club) = 4/52 + 13/52 − 1/52 = 16/52 = 4/13

This example illustrates the **general disjunction rule:**

Rule 5: P(p ∨ q) = P(p) + P(q) − P(p • q)

Note that we can apply the general disjunction rule even when p and q are mutually exclusive, for in such a case, P(p • q) will always be 0. For example, what is the probability that the next card to be drawn will be either a club or a diamond? Applying Rule 5 we get the following:

P(club ∨ diamond) = P(club) + P(diamond) − P(club • diamond)

And because a card cannot be both a club and a diamond, we may write this:

P(club ∨ diamond) = 13/52 + 13/52 − 0 = 26/52 = 1/2

To take another example: What is the probability of drawing either a red card or an eight (on the next draw)? Because half the cards (i.e., 26) are red, and there are 4 eights (1 in each suit), one might be tempted to answer 30/52. But this would be a mistake because 2 of the eights are red and they've been counted twice. The general disjunction rule gives the correct answer:

P(red ∨ eight) = 26/52 + 4/52 − 2/52 = 28/52 = 7/13

Before leaving our discussion of the general disjunction rule, let us note that it enables us to handle the material conditional, for $p \rightarrow q$ is logically equivalent to ~$p \vee q$, and hence P($p \rightarrow q$) is equal to P(~$p \vee q$). However, as we noted in Chapter 7, the material conditional does not adequately capture the meaning of the English "if-then" in every context. For this reason, logicians have developed a rule of probability that is designed to capture the meaning of English conditionals as they are used in contexts involving judgments about probability.

Suppose we want to know the probability that q is true *conditional on p's* being true. Following standard notation in probability theory, we will write "The probability of q conditional on p" as P(q/p). This notation is read variously as "The probability of q *on the condition that p*," "The probability of q on p," or "The probability of q *given p*." The **conditional rule** is as follows:

Rule 6: $P(q/p) = \dfrac{P(p \bullet q)}{P(p)}$

Stated in the abstract, this rule may not seem all that obvious. Why suppose that conditional probability equals the probability of the conjunction of its antecedent and consequent *divided by* the probability of its antecedent? Let us consider some specific examples. First, suppose that we are about to draw exactly one card from a well-shuffled deck. Consider the probability that we will draw a club *given that* we will draw the ace of clubs. Intuitively, the probability is 1 because if the card drawn is the ace of clubs, it must be a club. And this is exactly what Rule 6 tells us:

$$P(\text{club/ace of clubs}) = \frac{P(\text{ace of clubs} \bullet \text{club})}{P(\text{ace of clubs})}$$

The probability of drawing the ace of clubs is 1/52. The probability of drawing a club *that is also the ace of clubs* is simply the probability of drawing the ace of clubs. Thus:

$$P(\text{club/ace of clubs}) = \frac{1/52}{1/52} = 1$$

Consider a second example. What is the probability that we will draw a spade *given that* we will draw a heart? Intuitively, the probability is 0 because if we draw just one card and it is a heart, we certainly do not draw a spade. Let's see if the conditional rule bears this out:

$$P(\text{spade}/\text{heart}) = \frac{P(\text{heart} \bullet \text{spade})}{P(\text{heart})}$$

The probability of drawing a heart on a given draw is 13/52. Because a card cannot be both a heart and a spade, the probability of drawing a heart *and* a spade (on a given draw) is 0. Plugging in these values, we get:

$$P(\text{spade}/\text{heart}) = \frac{0}{13/52} = 0$$

Thus, the conditional rule once again gives us the intuitively correct answer.

A third example: What is the probability that we will draw the king of hearts from a well-shuffled deck *given that* we will draw a king? There are four kings altogether, but only one king of hearts, so this probability is intuitively 1/4. Applying the conditional rule, we get this:

$$P(\text{king of hearts}/\text{king}) = \frac{P(\text{king} \bullet \text{king of hearts})}{P(\text{king})}$$

The probability of drawing a king on a single draw from a well-shuffled deck is 4/52. The probability of drawing a king that is also the king of hearts is simply the probability of drawing the king of hearts, that is, 1/52. Therefore:

$$P(\text{king of hearts}/\text{king}) = \frac{1/52}{4/52} = 1/52 \times 52/4 = 52/208 = 1/4$$

Once again, the conditional rule accords with our intuitions.*

One last example: What is the probability that we will draw a club *given that* we will draw a black card? Half the black cards are clubs and half are spades, so the answer is intuitively 1/2. The conditional rule tells us:

$$P(\text{club}/\text{black}) = \frac{P(\text{black} \bullet \text{club})}{P(\text{black})}$$

Since half the cards in a deck are black, $P(\text{black}) = 1/2$. And the probability of drawing a card that is both black *and* a club is simply the probability of drawing

---

*Keep in mind that a/b divided by c/d = a/b times d/c. For example, 1/3 divided by 4/5 = 1/3 times 5/4 = 5/12. Thus, the division of a fraction may be interpreted as multiplication by the reciprocal of its *divisor*. (In the previous formula, the divisor is c/d.)

a club, namely, 13/52, or 1/4. Once again, the conditional rule gives us the intuitively correct answer:

$$P(\text{club}/\text{black}) = \frac{1/4}{1/2} = 1/4 \times 2/1 = 2/4 = 1/2$$

The conditional rule is important, not only for what it tells us about conditional probability but also because from it we can immediately deduce the **general conjunction rule:**

Rule 7: $P(p \bullet q) = P(p) \times P(q/p)$

To prove this, we begin with the conditional rule:

$$P(q/p) = \frac{P(p \bullet q)}{P(p)}$$

Next, we multiply both sides of the equation by $P(p)$:

$$P(p) \times P(q/p) = P(p) \times \frac{P(p \bullet q)}{P(p)}$$

Now, because $a \times \dfrac{b}{a} = \dfrac{a \times b}{a} = \dfrac{a}{a} \times b = 1 \times b = b$, we can transform the right-hand side of the equation as follows:

$$P(p) \times P(q/p) = P(p \bullet q)$$

And this is just what the general conjunction rule says. For example, consider the situation in which one draws a card from a well-shuffled deck and, *without* replacing it, draws a second card. What is the probability of drawing the ace of spades on the first draw *and* the ace of spades on the second draw? The answer is 0, because there is only one ace of spades and it was removed on the first draw. This is exactly the answer given by the general conjunction rule:

P(ace of spades on 1 • ace of spades on 2) = P(ace of spades on 1) ×
P(ace of spades on 2 *given* ace of spades on 1) = 1/52 × 0 = 0

What is the probability of drawing a red card on the first draw and a red card on the second draw? P(red on 1) = 1/2. But if we do select a red card on the first draw, only 51 cards will be left, 25 of them red. So, our chances of getting a red card the second time will be 25/51. How do we ascertain P(red on 1 • red on 2)? The general conjunction rule gives the answer:

P(red on 1 • red on 2) = P(red on 1) × P(red on 2 *given* red on 1) =
1/2 × 25/51 = 25/102

In other words, the probability is just a bit shy of 1/4. Of course, the numerically precise answer is something virtually no one can directly intuit. But because the general conjunction rule follows from the conditional rule, and we have seen that the conditional rule accords with our intuitions about probability, we can trust the answer given by the general conjunction rule.

What is the probability of drawing an ace on the first draw *and* (without replacing the first card drawn) another ace on the second draw?

P(ace on 1 • ace on 2) = P(ace on 1) × P(ace on 2 *given* ace on 1)

Now, the probability of getting an ace on the first draw is only 4/52. But if we do draw an ace and lay it aside, 51 cards remain in the deck, 3 of them aces. So, the probability of selecting an ace on the second draw, given that we drew an ace on the first draw, is 3/51. Therefore:

P(ace on 1 • ace on 2) = 4/52 × 3/51 = 12/2652 = 1/221

In other words, the probability of drawing two consecutive aces is quite low. Here again, although virtually no one can directly intuit the precise numerical probability, the answer is reliable assuming the conditional rule (from which we derived the general conjunction rule) is reliable.

Two statements, *p* and *q*, are **independent** if neither affects the probability of the other. In such a case, P(*q*/*p*) = P(*q*) and P(*p*/*q*) = P(*p*).

> Two statements are **independent** if neither affects the probability of the other.

For example, "The German philosopher Gottfried Wilhelm Leibniz died in 1716" and "The next card to be drawn will be a jack" are independent. Thus, the probability that "The next card to be drawn will be a jack *given that* Leibniz died in 1716" is simply the probability that the next card to be drawn will be a jack, namely, 4/52. In such cases, we can apply the **restricted conjunction rule:**

Rule 8: If *p* and *q* are independent, P(*p* • *q*) = P(*p*) × P(*q*).

For example, consider the probability of selecting an ace twice by drawing from a well-shuffled deck, replacing the card, reshuffling, and drawing a second time. Because, in this sort of case, what one gets on the first draw has no effect on what one gets on the second draw, it is convenient to apply the restricted conjunction rule:

P(ace on 1 • ace on 2) = P(ace on 1) × P(ace on 2)

Plugging in numerical values, we get:

P(ace on 1 • ace on 2) = 4/52 × 4/52 = 1/13 × 1/13 = 1/169

It is instructive to compare this with the probability calculated previously of drawing two aces consecutively *without* replacing the card selected on the first draw.

The restricted conjunction rule highlights an important fact about probability. Suppose we have a conjunction of independent statements, each of which has a probability of less than 1 but greater than 1/2. For example, suppose P(A) = 7/10, P(B) = 7/10, and P(C) = 7/10. What is the probability of the whole conjunction?

P[A • (B • C)] = 7/10 × 7/10 × 7/10 × 343/1000

Note that although each conjunct is more probable than not, the entire conjunction has a probability of less than 1/2. The upshot is that a conjunction of likely truths can itself be unlikely.

Bayes' Theorem

Having introduced the basic rules of the probability calculus, we will now focus on one important implication of our system: *Bayes' theorem*, which is named after the English theologian and mathematician Thomas Bayes (1702–1761). According to many philosophers, Bayes' theorem gives us an important insight into the relationship between the evidence for a hypothesis and the hypothesis itself. If this is correct, then Bayes' theorem promises a deeper understanding of the scientific method and other kinds of inductive reasoning.

We will use the italicized, lowercase letter *h* to stand for any hypothesis and *e* to stand for a statement that summarizes the observational evidence for that hypothesis. We begin with the conditional rule:[15]

$$P(h/e) = \frac{P(e \bullet h)}{P(e)}$$

This tells us that the probability of a hypothesis *given* the evidence is equal to the probability of the conjunction of the evidence and the hypothesis *divided by* the probability of the evidence.

A proof or truth table will reveal that *e* is logically equivalent to (*e* • *h*) ∨ (*e* • ~*h*). Therefore, we may replace *e* with (*e* • *h*) ∨ (*e* • ~*h*) wherever we wish, and it is useful to do so in the denominator:

$$P(h/e) = \frac{P(e \bullet h)}{P[(e \bullet h) \vee (e \bullet \sim h)]}$$

Now, by the restricted disjunction rule, $P[(e \bullet h) \vee (e \bullet \sim h)]$ is equal to $P(e \bullet h) +$ $P(e \bullet \sim h)$. Thus:

$$P(h/e) = \frac{P(e \bullet h)}{P(e \bullet h) + (e \bullet \sim h)}$$

Next, we apply the rule of commutation from Chapter 8 to the three conjunctions on the right side of the equation, as follows:

$$P(h/e) = \frac{P(h \bullet e)}{P(h \bullet e) + P(\sim h \bullet e)}$$

Finally, we apply the general conjunction rule three times, to arrive at **Bayes' theorem:**

$$P(h/e) = \frac{P(h) \times P(e/h)}{[P(h) \times P(e/h)] + [P(\sim h) \times P(e/\sim h)]}$$

Bayes' theorem tells us the degree to which a given hypothesis is supported by the evidence, provided that we have three pieces of information: $P(h)$, $P(e/h)$, and $P(e/\sim h)$. (Remember, if we have $P(h)$, we can calculate $P(\sim h)$ using the negation rule.) $P(h)$ stands for the **prior probability** of the hypothesis—that is, the likelihood of the hypothesis independent of the new evidence *e*. Normally, *e* is a statement summarizing the latest observational evidence so that we have some background evidence to appeal to in estimating $P(h)$.[16] $P(e/h)$ is the likelihood that the evidence (or phenomenon in question) would be present, assuming the hypothesis is true. $P(e/\sim h)$ is the likelihood that the evidence (or phenomenon in question) would be present, assuming the hypothesis is false. An example will help make these abstractions concrete.

> The **prior probability** of a hypothesis is the likelihood of the hypothesis independent of the new evidence.

Suppose a doctor has diagnosed a patient as having *either* some minor stomach troubles *or* stomach cancer. And let us assume that the doctor knows that the patient does not have *both* minor stomach troubles *and* stomach cancer. The doctor also knows that, given the symptoms, 30 percent of patients have stomach cancer; the rest have minor stomach troubles. Accordingly, the doctor initially suspects that the patient has only minor stomach troubles. But the doctor proceeds to conduct a test. Experience indicates that 90 percent of cases of stomach cancer yield a positive result when this test is applied, but only 10 percent of cases of minor stomach troubles yield a positive result. What is the probability that the patient has stomach cancer *given that the test turns out positive?*

Following our practice of using capital letters to stand for specific statements, here's a scheme of abbreviation that will help us apply Bayes' theorem:

H: The patient has stomach cancer.

E: The test is positive.

We want to find P(H/E), that is, the probability that the hypothesis is true given the evidence. To do this, we need three bits of information. First, we need P(H), that is, the prior or antecedent probability of the hypothesis. Second, we need P(E/H), that is, the probability of a positive test result *assuming that* the hypothesis is true. Finally, we need to know P(E/~H), that is, the probability of a positive test result *assuming that* the hypothesis is not true. It is built into the case that if the patient does not have cancer, then he or she has minor stomach troubles. So, given the parameters of the case, information about ~H is given by way of information about "minor stomach troubles."

The doctor's background knowledge provides the prior or antecedent probability that the patient has stomach cancer, for given the symptoms, 30 percent of patients have stomach cancer. In other words, P(H) = 30/100 = 3/10. We can obtain P(~H) by the negation rule: $1 - 3/10 = 7/10$. And because 90 percent of cases of stomach cancer yield a positive result when the test is applied, P(E/H) = 90/100 = 9/10. Furthermore, because we are assuming that the patient has minor stomach troubles if he or she does not have stomach cancer, and because 10 percent of cases of minor stomach troubles yield a positive result when the test is applied, then P(E/~H) = 10/100 = 1/10. Plugging these values into Bayes' theorem, we get:

$$P(H/E) = \frac{3/10 \times 9/10}{[3/10 \times 9/10] + [7/10 \times 1/10]} = \frac{27/100}{27/100 + 7/100} = \frac{27}{34}$$

So, the probability of the hypothesis given the evidence is 27/34, or approximately .79.

You may be wondering whether P(~*h*/*e*) = 1 − P(*h*/*e*). The answer is yes.[17] In our proof of Bayes' theorem, we saw that P(*e*) = P(*e* • *h*) + P(*e* • ~*h*). Now, if we divide both sides of the equation by P(*e*), we get this:

$$\frac{P(e)}{P(e)} = \frac{P(e \bullet h) + P(e \bullet \sim h)}{P(e)}$$

Therefore:

$$1 = \frac{P(e \bullet h)}{P(e)} + \frac{P(e \bullet \sim h)}{P(e)}$$

By the conditional rule, we can replace P(*e* • *h*)/P(*e*) with P(*h*/*e*). Similarly, we can replace P(*e* • ~*h*)/P(*e*) with P(~*h*/*e*). Making these replacements, we get the following:

$$1 = P(h/e) + P(\sim h/e)$$

Finally, subtracting P(*h*/*e*) from both sides, we obtain:

P(~*h*/*e*) = 1 − P(*h*/*e*)

Thus, if we know P(*h*/*e*) = 7/10, we may conclude that P(~*h*/*e*) = 1 − 7/10 = 3/10.

In many cases, we do not have adequate grounds for assigning precise numerical values to P(*h*), P(*e*/*h*), and/or P(*e*/~*h*). Does it follow that Bayes' theorem is inapplicable in such cases? Not necessarily. Even if we cannot assign precise numerical values, we may be able to assign relative values. For example, in a given case, we may have good reason to suppose that P(*h*) ≥ P(~*h*). And we may be able to settle, by argument, that P(*e*/*h*) > P(*e*/~*h*). In such a case, we can conclude that the evidence under consideration favors *h* over ~*h*. This is so because whenever P(*h*) ≥ P(~*h*), evidence *e* favors *h* provided that P(*e*/*h*) > P(*e*/~*h*). After all, as we saw previously P(*h*) + P(~*h*) = 1. Hence, if P(*h*) ≥ P(~*h*), then P(*h*) ≥ 1/2 and P(~*h*) ≤ 1/2. And in this situation, if P(*e*/*h*) > P(*e*/~*h*), then P(*h*/*e*) > P(~*h*/*e*). To illustrate this concretely, suppose P(*h*) = P(~*h*) = 1/2, P(*e*/*h*) = 3/5, and P(*e*/~*h*) = 2/5. Then, applying Bayes' theorem, we get:

$$P(h/e) = \frac{1/2 \times 3/5}{[1/2 \times 3/5] + [1/2 \times 2/5]} = \frac{3/10}{3/10 + 2/10} = 3/5$$

P(~*h*/*e*) = 2/5

To generalize, if P(*h*) ≥ P(~*h*) and P(*e*/*h*) > P(*e*/~*h*), then P(*h*/*e*) > P(~*h*/*e*). The important point is that we can sometimes apply Bayes' theorem even when we cannot set precise numerical values.

In many cases, there are more than two hypothesis competing for our credence. Can a Bayesian approach accommodate a situation in which multiple hypotheses are being compared? Yes. To illustrate, if h_1, h_2, and h_3 are three *mutually exclusive hypotheses that exhaust the possibilities*, then:

$$P(h_1/e) = \frac{P(h_1) \times P(e/h_1)}{[P(h_1) \times P(e/h_1)] + [P(h_2) \times P(e/h_2)] + [P(h_3) \times P(e/h_3)]}$$

In other words, we can accommodate as many hypotheses as we like (provided they are mutually exclusive and exhaust the possibilities), simply by adding relevant clauses to the denominator. To apply Bayes' theorem, we must assign values for $P(e/h_1)$, $P(e/h_2)$, and $P(e/h_3)$, as well as for the prior probabilities of at least two of the three hypotheses. We are assuming that the three hypotheses are mutually exclusive and exhaust the possibilities, so we can assume that the sum of their prior probabilities is one, just as P(*h*) + P(~*h*) = 1. And given that $P(h_1) + P(h_2) + P(h_3) = 1$, then $P(h_1) = 1 - P(h_2) - P(h_3)$. Similarly, $P(h_2) = 1 - P(h_1) - P(h_3)$, and $P(h_3) = 1 - P(h_1) - P(h_2)$.

Some philosophers have tried to apply Bayes' theorem to major philosophical issues such as the existence of God.[18] Although we cannot here enter into a detailed discussion of such matters, it is important to understand how Bayes' theorem can be used to organize a rational dialogue and develop strategies for argument. To this end, let us briefly consider a version of the cosmological argument for God's existence. Let H be "God exists" and E be "There is a physical universe." A theist may argue that $P(E/H) > P(E/\sim H)$ on the following grounds: first, that God would have a good reason to create the physical universe as an appropriate environment for intelligent creatures, and second, that if there is no God, then there is no explanation for the existence of physical reality—it can only be regarded as a coincidence. Using Bayes' theorem to structure the discussion, the nontheist might respond in three ways:

- Refute the theist's arguments for the thesis that $P(E/H) > P(E/\sim H)$.

- Argue that the prior probability of "God exists" is lower than the prior probability of "God does not exist." If a good case can be made that $P(H) < P(\sim H)$, then this could destroy the force of the cosmological argument, *even if* $P(E/H) > P(E/\sim H)$. (To illustrate, some have argued that $P(H) < P(\sim H)$ because the divine attributes lead to conceptual puzzles—for example, if God is all-powerful, can God create a stone too big for God to lift?)

- Argue that the probability that God exists is low given some evidence *other than* the existence of the physical universe, such as the suffering or evil in the world.

These strategies can be combined. The point here is not to recommend either the cosmological argument or any of these strategies for replying to it but merely to illustrate how the Bayesian perspective can help us structure a rational dialogue on a controversial topic.

Summary of the Rules of Probability

1. If a statement p is a tautology, then $P(p) = 1$.
2. If a statement p is a contradiction, then $P(p) = 0$.
3. **Restricted disjunction rule:** If p and q are mutually exclusive, then $P(p \vee q) = P(p) + P(q)$
4. **Negation rule:** $P(\sim p) = 1 - P(p)$
5. **General disjunction rule:** $P(p \vee q) = P(p) + P(q) - P(p \bullet q)$
6. **Conditional rule:** $P(q/p) = \dfrac{P(p \bullet q)}{P(p)}$
7. **General conjunction rule:** $P(p \bullet q) = P(p) \times P(q/p)$
8. **Restricted conjunction rule:** If p and q are independent, $P(p \bullet q) = P(p) \times P(q)$.

Summary of Definitions

Two statements are **mutually exclusive** if they cannot both be true.

A set of statements is **exhaustive** if one of the statements must be true.

Two statements are **independent** if neither affects the probability of the other.

The **prior probability** of a hypothesis is the likelihood of the hypothesis independent of the new evidence.

EXERCISE 10.4

PART A: Atomic Statements Suppose that you have an ordinary deck of playing cards. What is the probability of each of the following statements? (An ordinary deck consists of 52 playing cards in four suits: hearts, diamonds, clubs, and spades. Each suit contains 13 cards: an ace, a two, a three, a four, a five, a six, a seven, an eight, a nine, a ten, a jack, a queen, and a king. Hearts and diamonds are red; clubs and spades are black.)

* **1.** You select the jack of diamonds on the next draw.
  2. You select a queen on the next draw.
  3. You select a red card on the next draw.
* **4.** You select a heart on the next draw.
  5. You select a black card on the next draw.
  6. You select the ace of spades on the next draw.
* **7.** You select the three of diamonds on the next draw.
  8. You select an ace on the next draw.
  9. You select the five of hearts on the next draw.
  10. You select a club on the next draw.

PART B: Disjunctions Suppose you have an ordinary deck of playing cards. Assuming that you are as likely to draw one card as another, what is the probability that on your next draw you will select each of the following?

* **1.** A spade or a diamond?
  2. A jack or a queen?
  3. A king or a nonking?
* **4.** The queen of diamonds or a heart?
  5. A king or a spade?
  6. A club or a red card?
* **7.** A red card or an ace?

8. A black card or the 10 of hearts?

9. A black card or the 10 of spades?

10. A black card or a 10?

PART C: Conjunctions and Conditionals You have an ordinary deck of
cards. You draw one card, do *not* replace it, and then draw a second card. Assuming
you are as likely to draw one card as another, find the following probabilities.

* **1.** P(jack on first draw • queen on second draw)

2. P(ace on first • ace on second)

3. P(ace of hearts on first • red on second)

* **4.** P(club on first • club on second)

5. P(club on first • diamond on second)

6. P(black on first • black on second)

* **7.** P(queen of hearts on first • queen of hearts on second)

8. P(spade on first • black on second)
[*Note:* Because the conditional rule and the general conjunction rule are
interdependent, you must answer the last two items by thinking intuitively.
For example, regarding item 9, if you select an ace on the first draw and do
not put it back in the deck, what are your chances of selecting a king on the
second draw?]

9. P(king on second draw *given* ace on first draw)

10. P(red on second *given* jack of spades on first)

PART D: Various Compound Statements Let G be "Ben will get a game
for his birthday," M be "Ben will get a birthday present from Mary," T be "A → A,"
and D be "Zoe will get a doll for her birthday." Assume that P(G) = 3/5, P(M) =
3/10, P(D) = 9/10, and P(G/M) = 9/10. Also assume that D and M are independent. Determine the following probabilities.

* **1.** P(~G)

2. P(~M)

3. P(G • ~G)

* **4.** P(M ∨ ~M)

5. P(T)

6. P(~T)

* **7.** P(M • G)

8. P(M ∨ G)

9. P(D/M)

* **10.** P[D → (G → D)]

11. P(M/D)

12. P(~D)

13. P(D • M)

14. P(D ∨ M)

15. P[G → (M ∨ G)]

PART E: The Strength of Arguments Use the rules of probability to
determine the strength of the following arguments. In other words, given that the
premises are true, how likely is the conclusion? (*Note:* To say that *the odds of A are*

x-to-y is to say that $P(A) = x/(x + y)$. For example, to say that the odds of drawing a spade from a normal deck are 1-to-3 is to say that $P(\text{draw spade}) = 1/(1 + 3) = \frac{1}{4}$. Note also that this differs from common usage: When people say that the odds *of something* are a million-to-one, they usually mean that there is a million-to-one odds *against that thing*.)

* **1.** The odds are 5 to 1 that the Packers will beat the Bears in the division championship.The odds are 4 to 1 that the Steelers will beat the Jets in the division championship. Therefore, the Packers will play the Steelers in the Superbowl.

  2. The odds are 6 to 1 that Chris is lying. Therefore, it is not the case that Chris is lying.

  3. The odds are 1 to 3 that Frodo has the ring. The odds are 2 to 1 that Sam has the ring. There is a probability of 0 that Frodo and Sam both have the ring. Therefore, either Frodo or Sam has the ring.

* **4.** The die is fair (not loaded or off balance), and I will roll it twice. Therefore, I will roll a five twice.

  5. The odds are 1 to 4 that Tracy stole the TV. The odds are 1 to 3 that Jack stole the TV. The odds are 1 to 9 that Jack and Tracy both stole the TV. Therefore, either Tracy or Bill stole the TV.

  6. Jack and Jill are married, and they are both 30 years of age. The probability that a 30-year-old man will live to age 80 is .63, and the probability that a 30-year-old woman will live to age 80 is .71. Therefore, Jack and Jill will both live to age 80.

* **7.** The odds are 15 to 1 that Ted was at the party. Moreover, it is very likely that if Ted was at the party, Polly was also; in fact, the odds are 20 to 1. So, Ted and Polly were both at the party.

  8. The odds are 2 to 1 that Velasquez will defeat Lesnar in the semifinal. The odds are even that Mir will defeat Nelson in the semifinal. Therefore, Velasquez will meet Mir in the championship bout.

  9. The odds are 2 to 1 that Zeus exists. And the odds are 2 to 1 that wisdom is a virtue. "Zeus exists" is logically independent of "Wisdom is a virtue." Hence, Zeus exists and wisdom is a virtue.

  10. The odds are 9 to 1 that trees are real. And the odds are 0 to 1 that life is but a dream *given that* trees are real. So, trees are real and life is nothing but a dream.

PART F: Patterns Explore Bayes' theorem by answering the following questions.

  1. Suppose you are applying Bayes' theorem, and $P(H) = P(E/H) = P(E/\sim H)$. What is $P(H/E)$ in the following cases?
* a. $P(H) = 1/2$; $P(E/H) = 1/2$; $P(E/\sim H) = 1/2$
  b. $P(H) = 2/3$; $P(E/H) = 2/3$; $P(E/\sim H) = 2/3$
  c. $P(H) = 1/4$; $P(E/H) = 1/4$; $P(E/\sim H) = 1/4$

2. Suppose you are applying Bayes' theorem and the prior probability of the hypothesis is low, but P(E/H) and P(E/~H) are high and equal. What is P(H/E) in the following cases?

* a. P(H) = 1/5; P(E/H) = 9/10; P(E/~H) = 9/10
  b. P(H) = 1/3; P(E/H) = 7/8; P(E/~H) = 7/8
  c. P(H) = 3/8; P(E/H) = 3/4; P(E/~H) = 3/4

3. Suppose you are applying Bayes' theorem and the prior probability of the hypothesis is high, but P(E/H) is low and equal to P(E/~H). What is P(H/E) in the following cases?

* a. P(H) = 9/10; P(E/H) = 2/5; P(E/~H) = 2/5
  b. P(H) = 8/9; P(E/H) = 1/3; P(E/~H) = 1/3
  c. P(H) = 7/10; P(E/H) = 4/9; P(E/~H) = 4/9

4. Suppose you are applying Bayes' theorem and the prior probability of the hypothesis is 1/2, but P(E/H) is greater than P(E/~H). What is P(H/E) in the following cases? What is P(~H/E) in these cases?

* a. P(H) = 1/2; P(E/H) = 9/10; P(E/~H) = 3/5
  b. P(H) = 1/2; P(E/H) = 7/8; P(E/~H) = 3/4

5. Suppose you are applying Bayes' theorem and one of the probability values is 0. Specifically:

  a. Suppose the prior probability of the hypothesis is 0. Can P(E/H) be determined? [*Hint:* Applying the conditional rule, P(E/H) = P(H • E) divided by P(H).]

* b. Suppose P(H) is high, P(E/H) is 0, and P(E/~H) is not 0. For example, suppose P(H) = 9/10, P(E/H) = 0, and P(E/~H) = 1/10. What is P(H/E)? What is P(~H/E)?

  c. Suppose P(H) and P(E/H) are low, but P(E/~H) is 0. For example, suppose P(H) = 1/10, P(E/H) = 3/10, and P(E/~H) = 0. What is P(H/E)? What is P(~H/E)?

6. Suppose you are applying Bayes' theorem, and suppose P(H) and P(E/H) are both moderately high and P(E/~H) is a bit lower than P(E/H). What is P(H/E) in the following cases? What is P(~H/E)?

  a. P(H) = 7/10; P(E/H) = 7/10; P(E/~H) = 6/10
* b. P(H) = 5/7; P(E/H) = 5/7; P(E/~H) = 4/7

7. Suppose you are applying Bayes' theorem and the prior probability of the hypothesis H is slightly higher than that of its negation, but P(E/H) is slightly lower than P(E/~H). What is P(H/E) in the following cases? What is P(~H/E)?

  a. P(H) = 9/16; P(E/H) = 8/10; P(E/~H) = 9/10
  b. P(H) = 51/100; P(E/H) = 5/10; P(E/~H) = 6/10

PART G: Applying Bayes' Theorem The following exercises ask you to apply Bayes' theorem to a wide range of questions and issues. In a number of cases, the assignment of numerical values is deliberately contrived, for the sake of making a definite answer possible. But keep in mind that Bayes' theorem can sometimes be applied even when precise numerical values cannot be assigned.

* **1.** Bloggs is an impoverished college student working 40 hours a week. Due to the shortage of time, Bloggs prepares for only 40 percent of his exams. Bloggs passes 70 percent of the exams he prepares for. But he passes only 30 percent of the exams he does not prepare for. Furthermore, Bloggs passed his most recent exam. How probable is it that Bloggs prepared for his most recent exam?

  2. A veterinarian has diagnosed a dog as having either leukemia or severe anemia (but not both). Given the symptoms, 90 percent of dogs have severe anemia and 10 percent of dogs have leukemia. So, the vet initially surmises that the dog has severe anemia. Later, however, the vet conducts a test on the dog that turns out positive. Seventy percent of cases of leukemia yield a positive result when this test is applied, and 20 percent of cases of anemia yield a positive result. What is the probability that the dog has leukemia given the results of the test?

  3. Police detectives have determined that Smith and Jones are the only two possible murderers of McCann, and it is known that the murderer acted all by himself. (Thus, Smith and Jones are not both guilty of the murder.) Because Smith has a prior criminal record, Detective Wills initially gives odds of 5 to 3 that Smith is the murderer. However, while at the scene of the crime, Detective Wills finds the murder weapon, which has Jones's finger-prints on it *and not Smith's*. Detective Wills gives 9-to-1 odds that Jones's fingerprints are on the weapon *given that* Jones is the murderer; whereas Wills gives only 3-to-7 odds that Jones's fingerprints are on the weapon *given that* Smith is the murderer. (It is possible, but unlikely, that Smith somehow set Jones up.) Given Detective Wills's assessment of the odds, how likely is it that Jones is the murderer *given that* Jones's fingerprints are on the murder weapon? How likely is it that Smith is the murderer *given that* Jones's finger-prints are on the murder weapon?

* **4.** Valerie is trying to assess the evidence for the existence of a God who is all-powerful and perfectly good. Given her background evidence (e.g., she is aware of the cosmological and design arguments for God's existence), Valerie gives even odds that God exists. However, Valerie has recently heard of the so-called problem of evil. She finds it plausible to suppose that some of the suffering in the world, such as the suffering of animals, is not a necessary means to a greater good. Furthermore, Valerie is convinced that if God were all-powerful and perfectly good, then God would not permit any suffering unless it were a necessary means to a greater good. On reflection, Valerie gives only 1-to-3 odds that some unnecessary suffering occurs *given that* an all-powerful and perfectly good God exists. But she gives 2-to-1 odds that some unnecessary suffering occurs *given that* an all-powerful and perfectly

good God does *not* exist. Given Valerie's assignments of probability, what is the probability that God exists *given that* some unnecessary suffering occurs?

5. Nate is a sprinter at a college that hosts relatively few track meets. In fact, only 30 percent of Nate's races are at his own college. Nate wins 90 percent of the races held at his own college. But he wins only 40 percent of the races at other colleges. Nate won his last race. How likely is it that the race was at Nate's own college?

6. Sally claims to have telekinetic powers. She claims that she can cause a die to turn up any number she chooses. A fair die is produced, and Sally predicts that she will roll a six three times in a row. She proceeds to do just that. Our evidence and hypothesis are as follows:

   E: Sally rolls a six three times in a row (without cheating).

   H: Sally has telekinetic powers.

   Given that Sally has telekinetic powers, E is just the sort of thing we should expect. So, assume that $P(E/H) = 1$. But *prior* to considering E, we are understandably skeptical, giving odds of 1 to 9 that Sally has telekinetic powers. Assuming chance is the only alternative to Sally's alleged telekinetic powers, what is $P(E/\sim H)$? (*Hint:* You will need to use the restricted conjunction rule.) What is $P(H/E)$?

7. Suppose the police know that either Jones, Smith, or Dobbs stole the jewels. Furthermore, the police know that the thief acted all by himself. H_1 is "Jones stole the jewels," H_2 is "Smith stole the jewels," and H_3 is "Dobbs stole the jewels." The hypotheses are equally likely on the background evidence (e.g., the criminal records of the three suspects). Also, suppose the evidence at the crime scene allows us to assign these probabilities: $P(E/H_1) = 1/4$, $P(E/H_2) = 1/2$, and $P(E/H_3) = 3/4$. What is $P(H_1/E)$? $P(H_2/E)$? $P(H_3/E)$?

8. Chris thinks the prior probability that reincarnation occurs is low for two reasons. First, it is unclear what links any given soul with any given body (e.g., why does Jones's soul wind up in Smith's body?). Second, there seems to be no good answer to the question "How long has reincarnation been going on?" The usual answer is that the process is beginningless (infinite). However, this seems unlikely because, according to recent work in physics, the physical universe itself has been in existence for only 15–20 billion years—a finite period of time. (And, obviously, there were no physical bodies for souls to transmigrate to before the existence of matter.) For these reasons, Chris initially gives odds of only 1 to 3 that reincarnation occurs. But then Chris encounters new evidence in the form of a book about apparent past-life recall. (In the more interesting cases, a young child claims to be someone else, someone who lived and died in the surrounding area in the recent past. And in some of these cases, the child claims to remember the sort of thing that can be checked—for example, the location of some object—and his or her apparent memory turns out to be correct.) Chris becomes convinced that apparent past-life recall sometimes occurs and that in some cases the apparent

memories turn out to be correct. Chris realizes that the probability of accurate (apparent) past-life recall *given reincarnation* is very high. In fact, Chris offers 9-to-1 odds that accurate (apparent) past-life recall occurs *given reincarnation*. Chris finds it rather difficult to assess the probability of accurate, apparent past-life recall *given that reincarnation does not occur*. Chris judges that this depends on the probability of obtaining information about someone else's past life through some paranormal experience or through spiritism (mediumship). Chris is rather skeptical of these possibilities and, hence, gives only 2-to-3 odds that accurate (apparent) past-life recall occurs *if reincarnation doesn't occur*. Given Chris's probability estimates, what is the probability that reincarnation occurs given the evidence of accurate (apparent) past-life recall?

9. Suppose there is a fair lottery for which 1000 tickets have been sold. There will be only one winning ticket, and each ticket has a 1-in-1000 chance of being selected. Suppose Smith purchased exactly one ticket. What is the prior probability that Smith will win? Now, let our evidence and hypothesis be the following:

E: A reputable local newspaper, which makes a point of reporting lottery winners, carries a story reporting that Smith won the lottery.

H: Smith won the lottery.

P(E/H) is surely very high. That is, if Smith won, we would expect a reputable local newspaper (that makes a practice of reporting lottery winners) to report that Smith won. Thus, we give 9-to-1 odds that (E/H). However, P(E/~H) is surely quite low. How often does a newspaper report that someone won the lottery if he did not in fact win? Very seldom indeed. Accordingly, we give odds of 1 to 99 that (E/~H). What is P(H/E)?

10. Suppose that there are just three possible hypotheses that can account for E, the fact that I seem to see physical objects:

H_1: Physical objects exist, and my sensory experiences are produced by them.

H_2: There are no physical objects; I am simply experiencing a vivid dream.

H_3: There are no physical objects, and I am not dreaming, but a powerful demon is causing me to have hallucinations of physical objects.

Suppose I can somehow prove that $P(E/H_3)$ is less than $P(E/H_2)$ and that $P(E/H_2)$ is less than $P(E/H_1)$. Based on this information, can I rightly conclude that $P(H_1/E)$ is greater than $P(H_3/E)$? Why or why not?

NOTES

1. We have borrowed this label from Wesley Salmon, *Logic*, 3rd ed. (Englewood Cliffs, NJ: Prentice Hall, 1984), p. 97.
2. Our discussion of this common misconception is heavily indebted to Brian Skyrms, *Choice and Chance*, 3rd ed. (Belmont, CA: Wadsworth, 1986), pp. 13–15.

3. Anthony Flew, *Dictionary of Philosophy*, rev. ed. (New York: St. Martin's Press, 1979), p. 215.

4. *The Pleasure of Finding Things Out: The Best Short Works of Richard Feynman* (1999, pp. 141–149). *Pop quiz:* Does quoting Feynman on this point constitute an instance of the *ad verecundiam* fallacy? Why or why not?

5. Our discussion of the features of a good sample is heavily influenced by the discussion in Patrick Hurley, *A Concise Introduction to Logic*, 6th ed. (Belmont, CA: Wadsworth, 1997), pp. 548–552.

6. For an informative study of election polling, see Charles W. Roll, Jr., and Albert H. Cantril, *Polls: Their Use and Misuse in Politics* (New York: Basic Books, 1972).

7. Charles W. Roll, Jr., and Albert H. Cantril, *Polls: Their Use and Misuse in Politics* (New York: Basic Books, 1972), p. 67.

8. The illustration is borrowed from Roll and Cantril, *Polls*, p. 75.

9. See Kevin Hechtkopf, "Support for Gays in the Military Depends on the Question." CBSnews.com, February 11, 2010.

10. This example is borrowed from Salmon, *Logic*, p. 112. We have paraphrased freely.

11. Our account of Semmelweis's work borrows heavily from Carl G. Hempel, *Philosophy of Natural Science* (Englewood Cliffs, NJ: Prentice-Hall, 1966), pp. 3–6.

12. For an accessible discussion of the complexities involved in the confirmation of scientific hypotheses, see Del Ratzsch, *Philosophy of Science* (Downers Grove, IL: Inter-Varsity Press, 1986), pp. 41–96.

13. Our brief summary of criteria for good scientific hypotheses is indebted to the discussion in Irving M. Copi and Carl Cohen, *Introduction to Logic*, 9th ed. (Englewood Cliffs, NJ: Prentice-Hall, 1994), pp. 534–539.

14. This example is borrowed from Salmon, *Logic*, p. 134.

15. Our proof of Bayes' theorem follows that of Brian Skyrms, *Choice and Chance* (Belmont, CA: Wadsworth, 1986), p. 153.

16. If we wish to distinguish background evidence *b* from *e* (the "new" evidence or phenomenon to be explained), Bayes' theorem takes on a slightly more complicated appearance:

$$P[h/(e \bullet b)] = \frac{P(h/b) \times P[e/(h \bullet b)]}{\{P(h/b) \times P[e/(h \bullet b)]\} + \{P(\sim h/b) \times P[e/(\sim h \bullet b)]\}}$$

17. We are indebted to Stephen Minister (in conversation) for the proof to follow.

18. Perhaps the best-known example is Richard Swinburne, *The Existence of God* (New York: Oxford University Press, 1979).

Answer Key

CHAPTER 1

EXERCISE 1.1

Part A: Recognizing Statements

1. Statement
4. Statement
7. Neither
10. Statement

13. Statement
16. Sentence only
19. Statement

Part B: True or False?

1. False
4. True
7. False
10. False
13. True

16. False
19. True
22. False
25. False
28. True

Part C: Valid or Invalid?

1. Valid
4. Valid
7. Invalid

10. Invalid
13. Invalid

Part D: Soundness

1. Sound
4. Unsound. The argument is invalid.
7. Sound
10. Unsound. Valid, but the first premise is false.
13. Unsound. Valid, but the second premise is false.

EXERCISE 1.2

Part A: True or False?

1. True
4. False
7. False
10. True
13. True

16. True
19. True
22. True
25. True
28. False

Part B: Identify the Forms

        A   *B*

1. If the solution turns blue litmus paper red, then the solution contains acid.

        A   *B*

The solution turns blue litmus paper red. So, the solution contains acid.
    1. If A, then B.
    2. A.
So, 3. B.   *modus ponens*

       A   *B*   *B*

4. If Susan is a famous author, then she knows how to write. Moreover, Susan knows how to write.

       A

So, she is a famous author.
1. If A, then B.
2. B.

So, 3. A.   none

       A   *B*   *B*

7. Rilke is a dreamer if he is a poet. Therefore, Rilke is a poet.
1. If B, then A.

So, 2. B.   none

       A   *B*

10. If you study hard, you refine your communication skills.

             B   *C*

If you refine your communication skills, then your job opportunities increase.

       A   *C*

Hence, if you study hard, your job opportunities increase.
1. If A, then B.
2. If B, then C.

So, 3. If A, then C.   hypothetical syllogism

       A   *B*

13. Sam is wealthy if he has more than a billion dollars.

               not B   ***not A***

But Sam does not have more than a billion dollars. Therefore, Sam is not wealthy.
1. If B, then A.
2. Not B.

So, 3. Not A.   none

Part C: More Forms to Identify

       A   *B*   *A*   *B*

1. The sky is blue. The sky is cobalt blue only if it is blue. Hence, the sky is cobalt blue.
1. A.
2. If B, then A.

So, 3. B.   none

       not A   *B*

4. Eating meat is unhealthy if meat contains a lot of cholesterol.

           B   ***not A***

Meat does contain a lot of cholesterol. Therefore, eating meat is unhealthy.
1. If B, then not A.
2. B.

So, 3. not A.   *modus ponens*

       not A   ***not B***   ***not B***

7. If the zygote lacks a brain, then the zygote lacks a soul. If the zygote lacks a soul,

          C   ***not A***

then killing the zygote is permissible. So, if the zygote lacks a brain,

        C

then killing the zygote is permissible.
1. If not A, then not B.
2. If not B, then C.

So, 3. If not A, then C.   hypothetical syllogism

            A   *B*

10. Lying causes social discord. Hence, lying is wrong.

      1. A.

So,   2. B.   none

                A   *not A*

13. Either the animals used in research are a lot like humans, or they are not a lot like humans.

                  A   *C*

If the animals are a lot like humans, then experimenting on them is morally questionable.

                not A   *D*

If the animals are not a lot like humans, then experimenting on them is pointless.

                C   *D*

So, either experimenting on animals is morally questionable, or it is pointless.

      1. Either A or not A.

      2. If A, then C.

      3. If not A, then D.

So,   4. Either C or D.   constructive dilemma

Part D: Still More Forms to Identify

          A   *B*   *not B*

1. Overeating is foolish only if it causes disease. Overeating does not cause disease.

      not A

So, overeating is not foolish.

      1. If A, then B.

      2. Not B.

So,   3. Not A.   *modus tollens*

          A   *B*

4. You will win the chess tournament if you are very good at chess.

          not B   *not A*

Unfortunately, you are not very good at chess. Hence, you will not win the chess tournament.

      1. If B, then A.

      2. Not B.

So,   3. Not A.   none

          A   *B*

7. If God can arbitrarily decide what is morally right, then God can make cruelty right.

            not A

And if God cannot arbitrarily decide what is morally right,

            not D

then morality is not entirely in God's control.

            A

But either God can arbitrarily decide what is morally right,

            not A

or God cannot arbitrarily decide what is morally right.

          B   *not D*

Therefore, either God can make cruelty right, or morality is not entirely in God's control.

      1. If A, then B.

      2. If not A, then not C.

      3. Either A or not A.

So,   4. Either B or not C.   constructive dilemma

not A
10. The death penalty is inequitably applied to the poor and minorities.

not A
And given that the death penalty is inequitably applied to the poor and to

not B
minorities, it is unjust.

not B
Therefore, the death penalty is unjust.
  1. Not A.
  2. If not A, then not B.
So, 3. Not B.   *modus ponens*

A   B
13. Mercy killing is morally permissible only if it promotes a greater amount of happiness for everyone affected than the alternatives do.

A
And mercy killing does promote a greater amount of happiness for everyone affected than the alternatives do.

B
Therefore, mercy killing is morally permissible.
  1. If A, then B.
  2. B.
So, 3. A.   none

EXERCISE 1.3

Part A: Counterexamples

A   B   B
2. If Susan is a famous author, then she knows how to write. Moreover, Susan knows how to write.

A
So, she is a famous author.
  1. If A, then B.
  2. B.
So, 3. A.
     Counterexample: fallacy of affirming the consequent
       1. If the population of Nevada is more than 5 billion, then it is more than one thousand. well-known truth
       2. The population of Nevada is more than one thousand. well-known truth
So,   3. The population of Nevada is more than 5 billion. well-known falsehood

A   B   B
3. Rilke is a dreamer if he is a poet. Therefore, Rilke is a poet.
  1. If B, then A.
So, 2. B.
     Counterexample: (unnamed form)
       1. If the population of Nevada is more than 5 billion, then it is more than one thousand. well-known truth
So,   2. The population of Nevada is more than 5 billion. well-known falsehood

A   B
5. Sam is wealthy if he has more than a billion dollars.

not B   *not A*
But Sam does not have more than a billion dollars. Therefore, Sam is not wealthy.
  1. If B, then A.
  2. Not B.
So, 3. Not A.

Counterexample: fallacy of denying the antecedent:
1. If alligators are horses, then alligators are animals. well-known truth
2. Alligators are not horses. well-known truth
So, 3. Alligators are not animals. well-known falsehood

        A   B   A   B

8. The sky is blue. The sky is cobalt blue only if it is blue. Hence, the sky is cobalt blue.
1. A.
2. If B, then A.
So, 3. B.
Counterexample: fallacy of affirming the consequent (see (2), earlier)

        A   B

12. Lying causes social discord. Hence, lying is wrong.
1. A.
So, 2. B.
Counterexample: (unnamed form)
1. Trees exist. well-known truth
So, 2. Unicorns exist. well-known falsehood

        A   B

16. You will win the chess tournament if you are very good at chess.

        not B   *not A*

Unfortunately, you are not very good at chess. Hence, you will not win the chess tournament.
1. If B, then A.
2. Not B.
So, 3. Not A.
Counterexample: fallacy of denying the antecedent (see (5), earlier)

        A   B

19. Mercy killing is morally permissible only if it promotes a greater amount of happiness for everyone affected than the alternatives do.

        B

And mercy killing does promote a greater amount of happiness for everyone affected than the alternatives do.

        A

Therefore, mercy killing is morally permissible.
1. If A, then B.
2. B.
So, 3. A.
Counterexample: fallacy of affirming the consequent (see (2), earlier)

Part B: More Counterexamples

1. *Form:* No A are B. Some C are not B. So, some C are A.
Counterexample: No fish are cats. Some mammals are not cats. So, some mammals are fish.

4. *Form:* No A are B. Some C are B. So, no C are A.
Counterexample: No collies are cocker spaniels. Some dogs are cocker spaniels. So, no dogs are collies.

7. *Form:* Some A are B. All B are C. So, some C are not A.
Counterexample: Some animals are collies. All collies are dogs. So, some dogs are not animals.

10. *Form:* All A are B. Some A are not C. So, some C are not B.
Counterexample: All dogs are animals. Some dogs are not collies. So, some collies are not animals.

13. *Form:* All A are B. All C are B. So, all A are C.
Counterexample: All dogs are animals. All cats are animals. So, all dogs are cats.

16. *Form:* All A are B. No C is A. So, no C is B.
   Counterexample: Every cat is an animal. No dog is a cat. So, no dog is an animal.

19. *Form:* All A are B. No C is A. So, no C is B.
   Counterexample: All fish are animals. No dog is a fish. So, no dog is an animal.

EXERCISE 1.4

Part B: True or False?
1. False
4. False
7. False
10. False
13. False

Part C: Valid or Invalid? Strong or Weak?
1. Invalid and weak
4. Invalid but strong
7. Invalid and weak
10. Valid (therefore neither strong nor weak)
13. Invalid but strong
16. Invalid and weak
19. Invalid and weak

Part D: Cogency
1. Cogent.
4. Uncogent. Strong, but the premise is false (e.g., penguins and ostriches cannot fly).
7. Valid, and hence neither cogent nor uncogent.
10. The argument is weak and hence uncogent.

CHAPTER 2

EXERCISE 2.1

Part A: Arguments and Nonarguments
1. Nonargument (explanation).
4. Argument. *Conclusion:* Waging war is always wrong.
7. Argument. *Conclusion:* Pluto doesn't act much like the other planets.
10. Nonargument (explanation).
13. Nonargument (report).
16. Nonargument (illustration).
19. Nonargument (conditional).
22. Argument. *Conclusion:* The good don't always die young.
25. Argument. *Conclusion:* Stealing is wrong simply because society disapproves of it.

Part B: Constructing Arguments
1. It is morally permissible to experiment on nonhuman animals.
   Premises: If it is not morally permissible to experiment on nonhuman animals, then all new medical treatments must be tried out initially on human subjects. But surely not all new medical treatments must be tried out initially on human subjects.
4. Only violent criminals should be imprisoned.
   Premises: Sending people to prison tends to make them worse. And there are ways of controlling nonviolent criminals without sending them to prison.
7. Americans are too individualistic.
   Premises: Most Americans insist on using their own vehicles rather than using public transportation. And this pattern of behavior causes severe damage to the environment.

10. Beauty is in the eye of the beholder.
Premises: People often disagree about whether a given person or work of art is beautiful, whereas they seldom disagree about the shape or weight of an object.

13. It is wrong to misrepresent one's income on a tax form.
Premises: Lying is wrong, and misrepresenting one's income on a tax form is lying.

EXERCISE 2.2

Part A: Identifying Arguments

1. 1. The defendant is insane.
So, 2. The defendant is not guilty of murder.

4. 1. The UN Food and Agriculture Organization (FAO) reports that current food production can sustain world food needs even for the 8 billion people who are projected to inhabit the planet in 2030.
So, 2. All the world's farms currently produce enough food to make every person on the globe fat.

7. 1. Affirmative action involves giving a less qualified person the job.
    2. The most qualified person deserves the job.
So, 3. Affirmative action is unjust.

10. Not an argument.

13. Not an argument.

16. 1. Empirical data are scientific.
     2. Only what can in principle be shown false is scientific.
So, 3. Empirical data can in principle be shown false.

19. Not an argument.

Part B: Identifying Missing Premises

1. 1. Every woman has the right to do what she wants with her own body.
    2. Abortion is a use of one's own body.
So, 3. Every woman has the right to an abortion.

4. 1. Harry is the hero of the story.
    2. Heroes of stories are rarely killed early in books.
So, 3. Harry will not be killed at the beginning of book 2.

7. 1. There have been documented cases of an innocent person being wrongly convicted and executed.
    2. If so, then capital punishment is unjust.
So, 3. Capital punishment is unjust.
    4. Unjust forms of punishment should be abolished.
So, 5. Capital punishment should be abolished.

Or, more simply:

    1. There have been documented cases of an innocent person being wrongly convicted and executed.
    2. If so, then capital punishment should be abolished.
So, 3. Capital punishment should be abolished.

10. 1. I find this class very boring.
     2. Activities that we find boring are frequently too easy for us.
So, 3. This class is too easy for me.

Note that reversing the stated premise and conclusion, here, makes the passage read more like a nonargumentative statement.

13. 1. Well-behaved women rarely make history.
     2. If well-behaved women rarely make history, then I (a woman) should not behave myself.
So, 3. I should not behave myself.

Part C: More Identifying Arguments

1. Not an argument.

4.   1. Americans consume about 400 gallons of oil a year per citizen—about 17 percent of our nation's energy use—for agriculture, a close second to our vehicular use.

So, 2. Americans put almost as much fossil fuel into our refrigerators as our cars.

7.   1. If each culture should be judged only by its own moral standards, then no culture's moral standards should be criticized.

       2. Some cultures permit slavery, cannibalism, or the oppression of women.

So, 3. The moral standards of some cultures should be criticized. (from 2)

So, 4. It is not the case that each culture should be judged only by its own moral standards.

10. Not an argument.

13. 1. Deductive reasoning cannot have certainty about its premises.

       2. Inductive reasoning cannot have certainty about its conclusions.

So, 3. Absolute proof is something which the human being does not and cannot have.

16. 1. The civil disobedient withholds taxes or violates state laws knowing he is legally wrong but believing he is morally right.

       2. M. L. King led his followers in violation of state laws he believed were contrary to the federal Constitution.

       3. Supreme Court decisions generally upheld King's many actions.

So, 4. King should not be considered a true civil disobedient.

19. Not an argument.

Part D: Argument Forms and Well-Crafted Arguments

1.   1. H.

So, 2. If M, then L.

       3. M.

So, 4. L   2, 3, *modus ponens*

4.   1. If P, then C.

       2. If C, then F.

So, 3. If P, then F.   1, 2, hypothetical syllogism

       4. Not F.

So, 5. Not P.   3, 4, *modus tollens*

7.   1. Either E or A.

       2. Not W.

So, 3. Not A   2

So, 4. E.   1, 3, disjunctive syllogism

10. 1. If S, then C.

       2. If C, then A.

So, 3. If S, then A.   1, 2, hypothetical syllogism

       4. If A, then U.

So, 5. If S, then U.   3, 4, hypothetical syllogism

       6. If U, then W.

So, 7. If S, then W.   5, 6, hypothetical syllogism

EXERCISE 2.3

Note: Given the vagaries of the natural language, a certain amount of interpretation is required in some of the following exercises.

Part A: Argument Diagrams

1. [1][Photography makes representational art obsolete] because [2][no one, not even the best artist, can be more accurate than a camera.]

2

↓

1

4. While ¹[there is much wickedness in the world,] ²[there is also much good.] For ³[if there is evil, then there must be good,] since ⁴[good and evil are relative, like big and small.] And no one will deny that ⁵[evil exists.]

9. Despite the fact that ¹[contraception is regarded as a blessing by most Americans,] ²[using contraceptives is immoral.] For ³[whatever is unnatural is immoral] since ⁴[God created and controls nature.] And ⁵[contraception is unnatural] because ⁶[it interferes with nature.]

11. ¹[There is no life after death.] For ²[what's real is what you can see, hear, or touch.] And ³[you cannot see, hear, or touch life after death.] Furthermore, ⁴[life after death is possible only if humans have souls.] But ⁵[the notion of a soul belongs to a prescientific and outmoded view of the world.] And hence, ⁶[the belief in souls belongs to the realm of superstition.]

Note: (5) and (6) could alternatively be regarded as repetitious.

15. ¹[Violence as a way of achieving racial justice is both impractical and immoral.] ²[It is impractical] because ³[it is a descending spiral ending in destruction for all.] ⁴[The old law of an eye for an eye leaves everybody blind.] ⁵[It is immoral] because ⁶[it seeks to humiliate the opponent rather than win his understanding;] ⁷[it seeks to annihilate rather than to convert.] ⁸[Violence is immoral] because ⁹[it thrives on hatred rather than love.] ¹⁰[It destroys community and makes brotherhood impossible.]

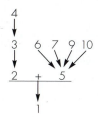

Note: The conclusion is a conjunction, so (2) and (5) must be understood to work together to support it.

Part B: More Argument Diagrams

1. [John and Robert Kennedy and Martin Luther King were, like them or not, this country's last true national leaders.] [None of John Kennedy's successors in the White House has enjoyed the consensus he built,] and [every one of them ran into trouble, of his own making, while in office.] In the same way, [none of this country's national spokespeople since Robert Kennedy and Dr. King has had the attention and respect they enjoyed.]

4. For a variety of reasons, [private colleges are in trouble.] First, [private colleges have repeatedly increased tuition well beyond the rate of inflation.] And [any business that increases prices in such a fashion is likely to run into trouble.] Second, [many people are beginning to question the value of higher education] since [a college degree no longer guarantees an attractive salary.] Third, rightly or wrongly, [the American public believes that colleges have not practiced good financial management,] and hence [the public thinks that tuition dollars often subsidize inefficiency.]

Note: (5) could well be understood simply to explain (4), rather than to argue for it.

10. While [colleges and universities have come under heavy criticism in the last decade,] [they will undoubtedly remain a vital force in American social life for generations to come.] For one thing, although [both the public and the media seem to have a thirst for stories about people who've gotten rich or famous with only a high school degree,] the fact remains that [a college or university degree is the surest way to increase one's social and occupational status.] For another, [college grads as a group indicate higher levels of satisfaction with their lives than do those with lesser educational attainments.] Finally, [you show me a nation with a weak system of higher education and I'll show you a nation with little power.] And [Americans will never willingly accept a position of relative powerlessness among the nations of the world.]

12. Not an argument; rather, a series of unsupported assertions, or exhortations.

14. [The only proof capable of being given that an object is visible is that people actually see it.] [The only proof that a sound is audible is that people hear it;] and [so of the other sources of our experience.] In like manner, I apprehend, [the sole evidence it is possible to produce that anything is desirable is that people do actually desire it.] Thus, [no reason can be given why the general happiness is desirable, except that each person . . . desires his own happiness.]

CHAPTER 3

EXERCISE 3.1: COGNITIVE MEANING AND EMOTIVE FORCE

1. 1. Terrorism in the Middle East is one of the greatest threats to world peace today.

So, 2. We should kill the leaders of each of the main terrorist groups.

4. 1. Since the introduction of welfare programs, this country has added many programs run by the federal government.

   2. Americans are opposed to a situation in which many programs are run by the federal government.

So, 3. We should eliminate welfare programs.

7. 1. Plato philosophized about a realm of ideas separate from physical reality.

   2. Aristotle developed the principles of logic.

   3. Descartes raised the possibility that we might be dreaming all the time.

   4. Kant took ordinary moral rules and reexpressed them in difficult technical terms.

So, 5. Philosophers have not done a lot for the world.

12. 1. The world is full of cruelty, poverty, starvation, and debilitating illness.

   2. Some people believe that a loving God controls the world.

So, 3. People believe what they want to believe regardless of the facts.

EXERCISE 3.2

Part A: Types of Definitions

1. D

4. E

7. C

10. E or F

13. F

Part B: Lexical Definitions

1. Unnecessarily negative

4. Unsuitable attribute: the conventional meaning is eight-sided figure.

7. Too narrow: leaves out triangles having sides that are unequal in length.

10. Figurative

13. Too narrow: leaves out lesbians.

16. Unsuitable attribute: the conventional meaning is having far more material possessions than most people. Also, too narrow because there are many people who do not possess as much money as Bill Gates or Donald Trump and yet would ordinarily be called wealthy.

19. Figurative: a visual or spatial metaphor is applied to the human mind or personality.

Part C: More Lexical Definitions

1. Circular

4. Figurative

7. OK

10. Unsuitable attribute: the conventional meaning is having a round shape.

13. Too narrow: leaves out lizards, turtles, crocodiles, and so on.

Part D: Precising Definitions

1. Too narrow because so many elderly persons are 92 or younger.

4. Too narrow, as many pacifists object not to the use of violence (e.g., think of police restraining an attacker) but specifically to killing (or lethal violence).

7. Too narrow, as it rules out teaching a form of evolution that is theologically neutral.

10. Too wide, as humans often assert what is false (because of ignorance) without intending to deceive anyone.

13. Too narrow, as a condition for mental competence should not be so restrictive (an IQ of 120 being relatively high).

Part E: Theoretical Definitions
4. E   **10.** F
7. A

EXERCISE 3.3

Part A: Equivocation
1. The equivocation is on "nothing." In the first premise, "nothing" means "no job at all," but in the second premise, it means something like "no end that humans seek."
4. The equivocation is on "lie." First, it means "intentionally tell a falsehood." Second, it means "to be prostrate on a surface."
7. The equivocation is on "miracles." Initially it means "wonders of science," and then later it means "divine interventions in the natural order."
10. The equivocation is on "nothing." Boiled down, the argument looks like this: When you choose not to exist, you choose nothing. But it makes no sense to prefer nothing to something. So, it makes no sense to prefer not to exist over being unhappy. In premise (1), "nothing" means "an end to existence." In premise (2), "nothing" means "nothing *whatsoever*," that is, no entity, state of mind, situation, and so on.

Part B: Merely Verbal Disputes and Persuasive Definitions
1. Merely verbal dispute. For Mr. Y "same person/man" means "someone who is unchanged in important characteristics." For Ms. X "same person/man" means "numerically identical person, man."
4. Persuasive definition. Unsuitable attribute: A more neutral (or less biased) description of the goals or values of the Republican Party is needed for a rational evaluation of the party as a whole.
7. Merely verbal dispute. Mr. X is using "local" to mean (perhaps) "grown within 400 miles of where it is sold" whereas Ms. Y is using "local" to mean "grown within the same state where it is sold." This can become more than a merely verbal dispute when significant amounts of value or emotion are invested in "eating local."
10. Merely verbal dispute. The scare quotes are the key. Ms. Y is saying that polygamy is *considered* right (i.e., regarded as morally permissible) by the members of some societies. Mr. X is making the entirely different claim that polygamy is not right, that is, not morally permissible.
13. Merely verbal dispute. For Ms. Y, "artist" means "a person who creates objects having beautiful form." For Mr. X, the forms must *depict* something.

Part C: Equivocation and Persuasive Definition
1. The definition of "self-serving act" is persuasive. A self-serving act is not merely one that accords with one's own motives; a self-serving act aims at selfish ends.
4. The definition of "psychiatrist" is persuasive. Psychiatrists do not merely talk with their patients; psychiatrists treat their patients.
7. Equivocation on "human." In premise (1), "human" means "biologically human," that is, an organism with genes of the type associated with *homo sapiens*. But in premise (4), "human" means "animal with higher faculties." (Fetuses presumably do not have such higher faculties.)

CHAPTER 4

Note: Many of the passages in these exercises contain very poor or unclear reasoning, and the logic of informal fallacies is not an exact science. Some interpretation is required, in some cases, to apply the fallacies discussed in this chapter. The student is encouraged to make the best possible use of the fallacies in analyzing these problems.

EXERCISE 4.1

Part A: Formal and Informal Fallacies

1. Argument against the person or *ad hominem* fallacy (abusive). "Ignorant" is the key word.

4. Appeal to the people or *ad populum* fallacy ("hot new thinkers" . . . "new wave in ethics").

7. Straw man ("seeking the power to kill anyone who has a serious illness"!).

10. Appeal to pity or *ad misericordiam* fallacy ("I stayed up all night," "I'll be put on . . . probation").

13. Appeal to force or *ad baculum* fallacy ("I can make good on that threat").

16. Argument against the person or *ad hominem* fallacy (abusive) ("immature and cold-hearted").

19. Argument against the person or *ad hominem* fallacy (circumstantial). The view is rejected because the person who holds it would benefit if more people held the belief.

22. Appeal to ignorance or *ad ignorantiam* fallacy ("nothing in his file to disprove that he's an eco-terrorist").

25. Appeal to the people or *ad populum* fallacy ("if you want to fit in around here"). This could also be read as a threat, so an *ad baculum* fallacy.

28. Appeal to ignorance or *ad ignorantiam* fallacy ("no one has succeeded in proving" the conjecture).

Part B: More Formal and Informal Fallacies

1. Straw man. No prochoice advocate would accept this description of his or her views.

4. Argument against the person or *ad hominem* fallacy (circumstantial). Persons who claim clairvoyant experiences stand to benefit by receiving lots of attention.

7. Appeal to ignorance or *ad ignorantiam* fallacy ("No one has ever shown . . .").

10. Not a fallacy.

15. Formal fallacy: No A are B. All B are C. So, no A are C. (Counterexample: No dogs are cats. All cats are animals. So, no dogs are animals.)

20. Straw man. The views of the evolutionist are being distorted here.

24. Appeal to the people or *ad populum* fallacy. (It's "what everyone else is doing.")

EXERCISE 4.2

Part A: Fallacies Involving Ambiguity

1. Amphiboly. We shall wear no clothes at all, or we shall wear no *distinctive* clothes?

4. Composition.

7. Division.

10. Equivocation. In premise (2), "reason to believe" means "something to gain by believing"; but in premise (3), "reason to believe" means "evidence in favor of the belief."

13. Not a fallacy.

16. Division.

19. Amphiboly. "All men are not losers" may mean either "not all men are losers" or "all men are nonlosers."

22. Composition.

25. Amphiboly. The sentence structure allows "fish" to be taken as either a verb or a noun.

28. Amphiboly. "That which can not-be at some time is not." Does this mean that those things that can fail to exist will all fail to exist at the same time (call it time "T")? Or does it mean that each thing that can fail to exist will fail to exist at some time or other? The inference drawn assumes the former interpretation, but the latter interpretation makes the first premise much more plausible.

31. Equivocation on "your home." In the premise, it means "the home of the driver who has been involved in an accident." In the conclusion, "your home" means "the home of the person being addressed."

34. Amphiboly. The previous employer presumably meant that *the recommendation* did not need to be qualified with statements indicating areas of concern about the applicant. The interviewer takes the previous employer's statement to mean that *the applicant* has no qualifications (experience, skills, etc.) needed to do the job.

EXERCISE 4.3

Part A: Identifying Fallacies

1. Appeal to unreliable authority or *ad verecundiam* fallacy. The president of General Motors is illegitimately assumed to be an authority on the country's religious and ethical moorings.

4. Appeal to unreliable authority or *ad verecundiam* fallacy. The unwarranted assumption is that tobacco companies are reliable authorities on the harmfulness of smoking.

7. False dilemma. The unwarranted assumption is that either men are superior to women or women are superior to men, which ignores the possibility that men and women may be equal in ability, moral standing, and so on.

10. Begging the question. The premise ("humans have the power to make choices") is merely another way of stating the conclusion ("humans have free will"); thus, the argument assumes the point to be proved.

13. Three fallacies. Composition ("each scene was excellent, so the whole play was excellent"). Appeal to the people or *ad populum* fallacy ("everybody who is anybody is raving about the play"). Begging the question: To say the play is superb is just another way of saying that it is excellent.

16. Complex question. The unwarranted assumption is that Harding was the best president of the first half of the twentieth century.

19. Appeal to unreliable authority or *ad verecundiam* fallacy. The unwarranted assumption is that Einstein, who *is* an authority on physics, is *also* an authority on morality.

22. False cause (slippery slope variety). The unwarranted assumption is that the various links in the alleged causal chain are all strong, when in fact they do not appear to be so.

25. False cause. The unwarranted assumption is that if A precedes B, A causes B.

28. Not a fallacy.

Part B: More Identifying Fallacies

1. Complex question. The unwarranted assumption is that being a good boy involves eating spinach.

4. Three fallacies. False dilemma: The unwarranted assumption is that one must favor either rehabilitation or deterrence (one might favor retribution or preventive detention instead). Argument against the person or *ad hominem* fallacy (abusive): "Silly" is an insult. Straw man: Rehabilitationists do not hold that hardened criminals can be cured so easily.

7. Appeal to unreliable authority or *ad verecundiam* fallacy. The unwarranted assumption is that psychology professors are authorities on the existence of God.

10. Complex question. The unwarranted assumption is that the world contains 10 times as much misery as happiness.

13. Appeal to unreliable authority or *ad verecundiam* fallacy. The unwarranted assumption is that sociology professors are authorities on what's just.

16. False dilemma. The unwarranted assumption is that "either I was hallucinating or he levitated." The possibility that I was tricked has been overlooked.

19. False dilemma: Either we intervene in all countries with wicked dictators or we intervene in none. There is a third alternative, namely, that we intervene in some (maybe those we can make a difference and do so without significant losses to our own troops) but not all.

22. Two fallacies. Appeal to unreliable authority or *ad verecundiam* fallacy: The unwarranted assumption is that chemistry professors are experts on the relation between language and logic. Appeal to the people or *ad populum* fallacy ("any intelligent person will agree that").

25. False dilemma: A third option is to think that abortion (and other acts) is neither right nor wrong, because such moral terms have no application. A fourth option, of course, is to be in doubt about the issue.

28. Four fallacies. Argument against the person or *ad hominem* fallacy (abusive); "logic choppers" is a put-down. Appeal to ignorance or *ad ignorantiam* fallacy (the philosophical arguments against time travel prove nothing, so time travel is possible). Begging the question: "it's possible because it can happen." Appeal to the people or *ad populum* fallacy ("just about everyone but philosophers thinks . . .").

31. Two fallacies. False dilemma: A given nation may choose from more than these two alternatives, given the complexity of foreign affairs. Appeal to the people (*ad populum* fallacy): Nobody wishes to be associated with terrorists.

34. Complex questions: Assumptions include that we are hated in the Muslim world, that it is our own government's actions that have caused the current terrorist threat, that we don't learn anything from our press, that our agencies are inept, and so forth.

CHAPTER 5

EXERCISE 5.1

Part A: Categorical Statements

Note: Answers are given in this order: name of form, subject term, predicate term, quantity, and quality.

1. **A,** hungry cannibals, dangerous people, universal, affirmative
4. **E,** green vegetables, minerals, universal, negative
7. **O,** poems, sonnets, particular, negative
10. **O,** numbers, odd numbers, particular, negative
13. **I,** celebrities, highly moral people, particular, affirmative
16. **E,** odd numbers, even numbers, universal, negative
19. **I,** art critics who like Picasso, snobs, particular, affirmative
22. **A,** individuals who lie frequently, deeply unhappy people, universal, affirmative
25. **E,** photons, objects visible to the naked eye, universal, negative
28. **O,** literature professors who love Tolstoy, good lecturers, particular, negative

Part B: Standard Forms

1. No human beings are beings who can swim across the Atlantic Ocean. (**E,** universal, negative)
4. Some persons are nerds. (**I,** particular, affirmative)
7. Some poems are not sonnets. (**O,** particular, negative)
10. **I,** particular, affirmative
13. Some animals that can fly are not birds. (**O,** particular, negative)
16. All Shawnees are persons who were skillful trackers. (**A,** universal, affirmative)
19. No people who are unlucky are happy persons. (**E,** universal, negative)
22. All lizards are reptiles. (**A,** universal, affirmative)
25. All birds are things that have feathers. (**A,** universal, affirmative)
28. Some paintings are not masterpieces. (**O,** particular, negative)
31. Some mountains are beautiful things. (**I,** particular, affirmative)
34. Some trees are ugly things. (**I,** particular, affirmative)
37. Some animals are vicious animals. (**I,** particular, affirmative)
40. All female siblings are sisters. (**A,** universal, affirmative)
43. Some living survivors of the Nazi prison camps are persons who were tortured. (**I,** particular, affirmative)
46. Some soldiers are persons who will be wounded. (**I,** particular, affirmative)
49. Some persons who choose not to fight are not cowards. (**O,** particular, negative)

EXERCISE 5.2

Part A: Logical Relationships

Note: Superalterns and subalterns are listed in the order in which they appear.

1. Contraries
4. Contradictories
7. Subaltern/superaltern

10. None. "Some odd numbers are numbers that can be divided by 2 (without remainder)" is necessarily false; hence, it cannot be true (subcontraries can both be true).
13. Subcontraries

Part B: Immediate Inferences
1. Valid
4. Valid
7. Valid
10. Valid

13. Invalid
16. Valid
19. Invalid

Part C: Generalizing
1. If the **A** statement is false: The **O** statement is true (corresponding **A** and **O** statements are contradictories). The truth value of the **E** and **I** statements is not guaranteed.
4. If the **O** statement is false: The **A** statement is true (corresponding **O** and **A** statements are contradictories), the **E** statement is false (because it implies the **O** statement), and the **I** statement is true (because corresponding **I** and **O** statements are subcontraries).

Part D: Standard Form
1.   1. No capitalists are heroes.
So, 2. Some capitalists are not heroes. Valid
4.   1. All positrons are things smaller than atoms.
So, 2. Some positrons are not things smaller than atoms. Invalid
7.   1. No acids are bases.
So, 2. All acids are bases. Invalid
10.   1. All persons who are kept awake for over a week are persons who will go crazy.
So, 2. All persons who will go crazy are persons who are kept awake for over a week. Invalid
13.   1. No persons who invented the airplane are persons who died flying an airplane.
So, 2. All persons who invented the airplane are persons who died flying an airplane. Invalid

EXERCISE 5.3

Part A: Term-Complements
1. No things that are not brown bears are nonherbivores.
4. Some entities that are not unhappy are not nonpeople.
7. No things that are not great women are nonmen.
10. Some metals are nonchemicals.

Part B: Conversion
1. No maggots are magnates. Valid
4. Some bombs are not explosives. Not in general valid
7. All copies are forgeries. Not in general valid
10. Some nontigers are leopards. Valid

Part C: Obversion
1. No shar-peis are nondogs.
4. Some heroes are nonmartyrs.
7. No colonels are objects not weighing at least 100 pounds.
10. All serigraphs are nonsculptures.

Part D: Contraposition
1. All nonpessimists are noncynics. Valid
4. Some dogs are not collies. Valid
7. All noncats are things that cannot run at more than 50 miles an hour. Valid
10. All guppies are things that are not great white sharks. Valid

Part E: Inferences from A Statements
1. Not guaranteed (converse)
4. T (contrapositive)

7. Not guaranteed (contrapositive of 2)
10. T (obverse of 3)
13. T (subaltern of the contrapositive)

Part F: Inferences from E Statements
1. T (obverse)
4. Not guaranteed (contrapositive)
7. F (contraries)
10. T (contraposition by limitation)
13. F (contradictory of the converse by limitation of the obverse)

Part G: Inferences from I Statements
1. T (converse)
4. Not guaranteed (contrapositive of 1)
7. Not guaranteed (contrapositive)
10. Not guaranteed
13. Not guaranteed

Part H: Inferences from O Statements
1. Not guaranteed (superaltern)
4. Not guaranteed (converse)
7. T (converse of 3)
10. Not guaranteed (converse of 5)
13. Not guaranteed (obverse of 6)

CHAPTER 6

EXERCISE 6.1
Part A: Standard Form
1.   1. All novels are books.
     2. Some works of art are books.
So, 3. Some works of art are novels.
4.   1. Some beautiful things are paintings.
     2. All sculptures are beautiful things.
So, 3. Some sculptures are not paintings.
7.   1. All sadists are mean persons.
     2. All art critics are mean persons.
So, 3. All art critics are sadists.
10. Already in standard form.
13. 1. No aspiring actors are saints.
     2. Some aspiring actors are not egoists.
So, 3. Some egoists are saints.

Part B: Mood and Figure
1. Second figure: **IAI** (not valid)
4. Third figure: **EOI** (not valid)
7. Second figure: **AII** (not valid)
10. First figure: **IAO** (not valid)
13. Second figure: **AAA** (not valid)

Part C: Putting Syllogisms into Standard Form
1.   1. All cowboys are persons who love horses.
     2. Some farmers are not persons who love horses.
So, 3. Some farmers are not cowboys. Second figure: **AOO** (valid)

4.   1.   No cowards are bull riders.
    2.   Some bull riders are fools.
So,   3.   Some fools are not cowards. Fourth figure: **EIO** (valid)
7.   1.   No cattle rustlers are good guys.
    2.   All cowboys in white outfits are good guys.
So,   3.   No cowboys in white outfits are cattle rustlers. Second figure: **EAE** (valid)
10.   1.   All bulls are animals that are hard to ride.
    2.   Some broncos are not bulls.
So,   3.   Some broncos are not animals that are hard to ride. First figure: **AOO** (invalid)
13.   1.   No trail bosses are hired hands.
    2.   Some ranchers are hired hands.
So,   3.   Some ranchers are trail bosses. Second figure: **EII** (invalid)

EXERCISE 6.2

Part A: Venn Diagrams and Standard Form

1.   Some ancient philosophers are persons who believed in the unreality of change.

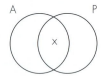

7.   No chlorofluorocarbons are things that are good for the ozone layer.

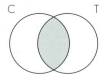

4.   All persons who deserve harsh treatment from the IRS are tax-dodgers.

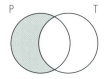

10.   No physical entities are spiritual entities.

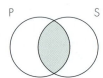

Part B: Venn Diagrams and Arguments

1.   Some chairs are not thrones. So, some thrones are not chairs.

INVALID

4.   Some married persons are persons who have attachment disorders. Thus, some persons who have attachment disorders are married persons.

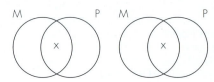

VALID

7. No elephants are beetles. Consequently, no nonbeetles are nonelephants.

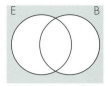

INVALID

Note regarding the diagram of the conclusion: The area of overlap between nonbeetles and nonelephants is the area outside BOTH circles; hence, the area outside both circles should be shaded.

10. Some wines are not merlots. Therefore, some nonmerlots are not nonwines.

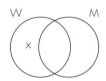

VALID

13. Some mammals are edentulous animals. Thus, all mammals are edentulous animals.

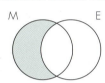

INVALID

EXERCISE 6.3

Part A: Argument Forms

1. 1. All M are P.
   2. Some M are not S.
So, 3. Some S are not P.

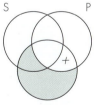

M   INVALID

4. 1. Some P are M.
   2. Some S are M.
So, 3. Some S are P.

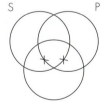

M   INVALID

7. 1. No P are M.
   2. Some M are S.
So, 3. Some S are P.

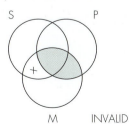

M   INVALID

10. 1. All M are P.
   2. No S are M.
So, 3. No S are P.

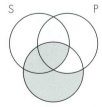

M   INVALID

Part B: Categorical Syllogisms

1. 1. All Athenians are Greeks.
2. Some humans are not Athenians.
So, 3. Some humans are not Greeks.

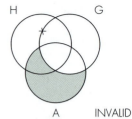

A   INVALID

4. 1. All liars are self-deceived persons.
2. All liars are wicked persons.
So, 3. All wicked persons are self-deceived persons.

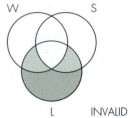

L   INVALID

7. 1. No human beings are omniscient beings.
2. Some divine beings are human beings.
So, 3. Some divine beings are not omniscient beings.

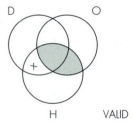

H   VALID

10. 1. All brain events are physical events.
2. No mental events are physical events.
So, 3. No mental events are brain events.

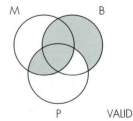

P   VALID

13. 1. All similarity statements are metaphorical statements.
2. All statements are similarity statements.
So, 3. All statements are metaphorical statements.

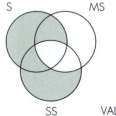

SS   VALID

16. 1. No acts foreknown by God are free acts.
     2. Some acts are acts foreknown by God.
So, 3. Some acts are not free acts.

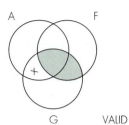

VALID

19. 1. All unhappy persons are persons who have inner conflicts.
     2. Some successful comedians are unhappy persons.
So, 3. Some successful comedians are persons who have inner conflicts.

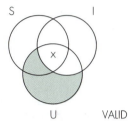

VALID

22. 1. No balalaikas are banjos.
     2. Some balalaikas are beautiful things.
So, 3. Some beautiful things are not banjos.

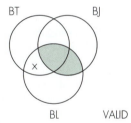

VALID

25. 1. All Saint Bernards are large dogs.
     2. Some large dogs are not brown dogs.
So, 3. Some brown dogs are not Saint Bernards.

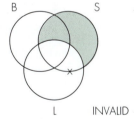

INVALID

EXERCISE 6.4

Part A: Argument Forms

1. 1. No M are P.
     2. All S are M.
So, 3. Some S are not P.

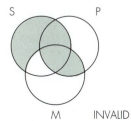

INVALID

4.   1.   All M are P.
    2.   All M are S.
    3.   At least one M exists.
So,   4.   Some S are P.

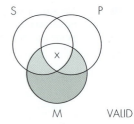

VALID

7.   1.   No S are P.
So,   2.   Some non-P are not non-S.

INVALID

10.   1.   No S are P.
     2.   At least one S exists.
So,   3.   Some non-P are not non-S.

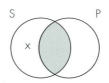

VALID

Part B: Testing Arguments

1.   1.   All persons who never make mistakes are
    admirable persons.
    2.   All ideal humans are persons who never
    make mistakes.
So,   3.   Some ideal humans are admirable persons.

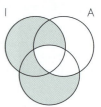

INVALID

4.   1.   All persons who advocate the use of
    overwhelming nuclear force are persons
    who lack moral sensibility.
    2.   All persons who advocate the use of
    overwhelming nuclear force are persons
    who should not serve as world leaders.
    3.   At least one person who advocates the use
    of overwhelming nuclear force exists.
So,   4.   Some persons who should not serve as world
    leaders are persons who lack moral sensibility.

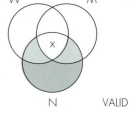

VALID

7.   1.   All sycophants are flatterers.
    2.   All flatterers are disgusting persons.
    3.   At least one flatterer exists.
So,   4.   Some disgusting persons are sycophants.

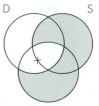

INVALID

10. 1. No members of the IRA are members of the IRS.
So, 2. It is false that all members of the IRA are members of the IRS.

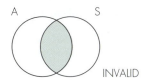

INVALID

13. 1. All scarlet things are red things.
So, 2. It is false that no scarlet things are red things.

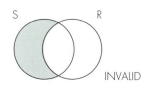

INVALID

19. 1. No kangaroos are karate experts.
So, 2. Some kangaroos are not karate experts.

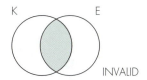

INVALID

EXERCISE 6.5

Part A: Enthymemes

1. 1. No certainties are propositions that should be rejected.
       2. All self-evident propositions are certainties.
So, 3. No self-evident propositions are propositions that should be rejected.

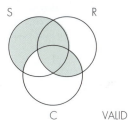

VALID

4. 1. All simple substances are indestructible entities.
       2. All atoms are simple substances.
So, 3. All atoms are indestructible entities.

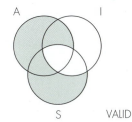

VALID

7. 1. All rational statements are scientific statements.
       2. No aesthetic judgments are scientific statements.
So, 3. No aesthetic judgments are rational statements.

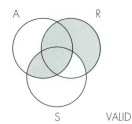

VALID

10. 1. All rational beliefs are beliefs that are proportioned to the available evidence.
     2. Some beliefs about aliens are not beliefs that are proportioned to the available evidence.
So, 3. Some beliefs about aliens are not rational beliefs.

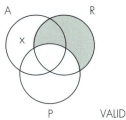

VALID

13. 1. All harmful traits are forms of laziness.
     2. All vices are harmful traits.
So, 3. All vices are forms of laziness.

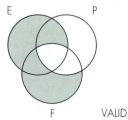

VALID

Part B: More Enthymemes

1. 1. All events that are foreseen by God are predetermined events.
     2. All events are events that are foreseen by God.
So, 3. All events are predetermined events.

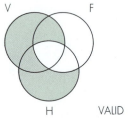

VALID

4. 1. No necessary events are events that can be avoided.
     2. All justly punished acts are events that can be avoided.
So, 3. No justly punished acts are necessary events.

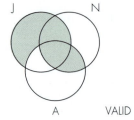

VALID

7. 1. All things that can be annihilated are things that can come apart.
     2. No things that have no parts are things that can come apart.
So, 3. No things that have no parts are things that can be annihilated.

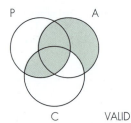

VALID

10.   1. All events are occurrences caused by a deity.
     2. All sins are events.
So, 3. All sins are occurrences caused by a deity.

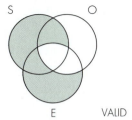

E   VALID

EXERCISE 6.6

Part A: Removing Term-Complements

1.   1. No M are P.
     2. All S are M.
So, 3. No S are P.

4.   1. All S are P.
     2. No P are C.
So, 3. No C are S.

7.   1. All M are P.
     2. All S are M.
So, 3. All S are P.

10.   1. Some S are M.
     2. All M are E.
So, 3. Some E are S.

Part B: Standard Form

1.   1. Some A are B.
     2. All B are C.   Sub 1: Some A are C.
     3. All C are D.
So, 4. Some D are A.

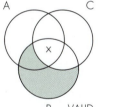 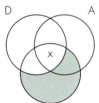

B   VALID   C   VALID

4.   1. No E are C.
     2. All D are E.   Sub 1: No D are C.
     3. All B are D.   Sub 2: No B are C.
     4. Some A are B.
So, 5. Some A are not C.

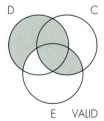 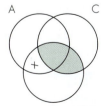

E   VALID   D   VALID   B   VALID

7. 1. All A are B.
    2. No C are B.   Sub 1: No C are A.
    3. Some D are not C.
So, 4. Some D are not A.

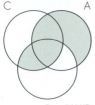

C   A   D   A

B VALID   C INVALID

This sorites is invalid.

10. 1. Some B are A.
     2. All B are C.   Sub 1: Some C are A.
     3. All C are D.
So, 4. Some D are A.

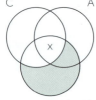

C   A   D   A

B VALID   C VALID

Part C: Sorites

1. 1. All A are T.
    2. No T are P.   Sub 1: No P are A.
    3. Some D are P.
So, 4. Some D are not A.

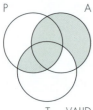

P   A   D   A

T VALID   P VALID

4. 1. All Z are D.
    2. All D are M.   Sub 1: All Z are M.
    3. No E are M.   Sub 2: No E are Z.
    4. Some P are E.

So, 5. Some P are not Z.

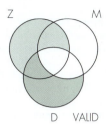 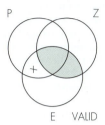

Z   M   E   Z   P   Z

D VALID   M VALID   E VALID

7. 1. All A are P.
     2. All P are R.   Sub 1: All A are R.
     3. Some F are not R.
So, 4. Some F are not A.

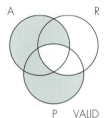 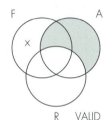

A   R   F   A

P VALID   R VALID

10. 1. All P are R.
      2. No B are R.   Sub 1: No B are P.
      3. All C are B.   Sub 2: No C are P.
      4. Some F are C.
So, 5. Some F are not P.

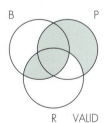 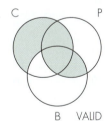 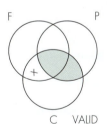

B   P   C   P   F   P

R VALID   B VALID   C VALID

EXERCISE 6.7

Part A: Forms

  1. **EEE.** Fourth figure. Violates Rule 4: invalid.
  4. **AAA.** Second figure. Violates Rule 2 (undistributed middle term): invalid.
  7. **AOO.** Second figure. Satisfies all five rules: valid.
10. **OOO.** Second figure. Violates Rules 3 (illicit major) and 4: invalid.
13. **OAO.** First figure. Violates Rule 2: invalid.
16. **AAI.** First figure. Violates Rule 5: invalid.
19. **III.** Third figure. Violates Rule 2: invalid.

Part B: Valid or Invalid?

1. Some M are P. No S are M. So, some S are not P. *Mood:* **IEO.** First figure. The syllogism violates Rule 3: invalid.

4. All P are M. No S are M. So, no S are P. *Mood:* **AEE.** Second figure. There is an equivocation on the word "animals." In the second premise, "animals" means "nonhuman animals." In the first premise, "animals" means (roughly) "living organisms capable of moving about." The syllogism thus violates Rule 1: invalid.

7. All M are P. All S are M. So, some S are P. *Mood:* **AAI.** First figure. Violates Rule 5: hence invalid on the modern view. But because it does not violate any other rules, it is valid on the traditional Aristotelian view.

10. Some M are not P. All S are M. So, some S are not P. *Mood:* **OAO.** First figure. The syllogism violates Rule 2: invalid.

CHAPTER 7

EXERCISE 7.1

Part A: Well-Formed Formulas?

1. Not a WFF. Missing a pair of parentheses.
4. Not a WFF. Missing a single parenthesis.
7. WFF.
10. WFF.
13. Not a WFF. Lowercase letters are not statement letters.
16. Not a WFF. Missing a pair of parentheses.
19. WFF.

Part B: Permissible Departures from Strict Grammar

1. Permissible.   **7.** Permissible.
4. Permissible.   **10.** Permissible.

Part C: Symbolizing

1. $C \lor R$
4. $M \to N$
7. $\sim R$
10. $\sim(B \lor S)$

13. $\sim S \to (J \lor T)$
16. $T \to D$
19. $(R \cdot \sim S) \cdot (\sim S \to \sim H)$

Part D: More Symbolizing

1. $S \to R$
4. $(W \lor F) \cdot \sim(W \cdot F)$

7. $B \to (F \to \sim P)$
10. $(B \to F) \to \sim B$

Part E: More Symbolizing

1. $D \to A$
4. $(M \to N) \cdot \sim N$
7. $\sim(O \to E)$

10. $[(R \cdot A) \to H] \cdot \sim R$
13. $(P \to S) \cdot \sim(S \to P)$

EXERCISE 7.2

Part A: True or False?

1. F
4. F
7. T
10. T
13. T

16. T
19. F
22. T
25. T

Part B: More True or False

1. T	**10.** T
4. T	**13.** T
7. T	

Part C: Assigning Truth Values

1. P true; Q false
4. A true; B false; C false
7. Y true; Z true
10. N true; P true
13. H true; J true; K true; L false

EXERCISE 7.3

Part A: Truth Tables

1.

A B	A ∨ B,	~A	∴ B	
T T	T	F	T	
T F	T	F	F	
F T	T	T	T	
F F	F	T	F	Valid

4.

P R	~P → ~R	∴ ~(P → R)		
T T	F T F	F	T	
T F	F T T	T	F	
F T	T F F	F	T	
F F	T T T	F	T	Invalid

7.

A B	A • B	∴ B	
T T	T	T	
T F	F	F	
F T	F	T	
F F	F	F	Valid

10.

F G	~F • ~G	∴ ~F ↔ ~G		
T T	F F F	F T F		
T F	F F T	F F T		
F T	T F F	T F F		
F F	T T T	T T T	Valid	

13.

D E C	D ↔ (E ∨ C),	~D	∴ ~C	
T T T	T T	F	F	
T T F	T T	F	T	
T F T	T T	F	F	
T F F	F F	F	T	
F T T	F T	T	F	
F T F	F T	T	T	
F F T	F T	T	F	
F F F	T F	T	T	Valid

16.

A B C	A → B, B → C		∴ A → C	
T T T	T	T	T	
T T F	T	F	F	
T F T	F	T	T	
T F F	F	T	F	
F T T	T	T	T	
F T F	T	F	T	
F F T	T	T	T	
F F F	T	T	T	Valid

19.

A B C	A ∨ B, A → C, B → C			∴ C	
T T T	T	T	T	T	
T T F	T	F	F	F	
T F T	T	T	T	T	
T F F	T	F	T	F	
F T T	T	T	T	T	
F T F	T	T	F	F	
F F T	F	T	T	T	
F F F	F	T	T	F	Valid

Part B: More Truth Tables

*1.

A B	A • ~B		∴ ~(A → B)		
T T	F F		F	T	
T F	T T		T	F	
F T	F F		F	T	
F F	F T		F	T	Valid

*4.

H K	~(H • K)		∴ ~H • ~K		
T T	F	T	F	F	F
T F	T	F	F	F	T
F T	T	F	T	F	F
F F	T	F	T	T	T	Invalid

*7.

A B	A	∴ (A ∨ B) • ~(A • B)				
T T	T	T	F F	T		
T F	T	T	T T	F		
F T	F	T	T T	F		
F F	F	F	F T	F	Invalid	

*10.

H J	~(H ↔ J)		∴ ~H ↔ ~J		
T T	F	T	F	T	F
T F	T	F	F	F	T
F T	T	F	T	F	F
F F	F	T	T	T	T	Invalid

Part C: English Arguments

1. A → ~E,   E ∴ ~A

A E	A → ~E,		E	∴ ~A	
T T	F	F	T	F	
T F	T	T	F	F	
F T	T	F	T	T	
F F	T	T	F	T	Valid

4. ~A ∨ W ∴ W → A

A W	~A ∨ W	∴ W → A	
T T	F T	T	
T F	F F	T	
F T	T T	F	
F F	T T	T	Invalid

7. V ↔ L, L → P, P → ~V ∴ ~L

V L P	V ↔ L,	L → P,	P → ~V	∴ ~L	
T T T	T	T	F F	F	
T T F	T	F	T F	F	
T F T	F	T	F F	T	
T F F	F	T	T F	T	
F T T	F	T	T T	F	
F T F	F	F	T T	F	
F F T	T	T	T T	T	
F F F	T	T	T T	T	Valid

EXERCISE 7.4

Part A: Abbreviated Truth Tables

1.

A B C	A → (B → C)	∴ B → C
F T F	F T T F F	T F F

4.

J K	J → ~K	∴ ~(J ↔ K)
F F	F T T F	F F T F

7.

S H U	~(S • H),	(~S • ~H) → ~U	∴ ~U
F T T	T F F T	T F F F T T F T	F T

10.

P Q R	(P ↔ ~Q) ↔ ~R,	R	∴ ~P
T T T	T F F T T F T	T	F T

13.

Z Y W	(Z • Y) → W	∴ Z → (Y • W)
T F T	T F F T T	T F F F T

16.

P Q R S	P → Q,	P → R,	Q ↔ R,	S,	S → R	∴ P • Q
F T T T	F T T	F T T	T T T	T	T T T	F F T

19.

Q S T U W	~(Q ∨ S),	~T ∨ S,	(U • W) → Q	∴ (~T • ~U) • W
F F F F F	T F F F	T F T F	F F F T F	T F T T F F F

Part B: More Abbreviated Truth Tables

1.

A B C D	~(A • B),	~A → C,	~B → D	∴ C • D
F T T F	T F F T	T F T T	F T T F	T F F

4.

V X Y	~(V • X) → ~Y	∴ ~(V • X) → Y
T F F	T T F F T T F	T T F F F F

7.

Z A B C	~(Z → A),	Z → B,	~A → C	∴ C • ~B
T F T T	T T F F	T T T	T F T T	T F F T

10.

H S Z P	H ∨ ~S,	H → Z,	~S → P	∴ P ↔ Z
F F F T	F T T F	F T F	T F T T	T F F

Part C: Still More Abbreviated Truth Tables

4.

A F D S X	~A → F,	A → D,	~D,	F → S	∴ S ∨ X
	T F / F	F T F	T F	F T F	F F F

10.

S R B P Q	~(S ∨ R),	B → (S ∨ R),	B ∨ P,	~Q ∨ B	∴ P • ~Q
	T F F F	T / F F F	T T F	F T T T	F F F T
	T F F F	T / F F F	T T F	T F T T	F F T F
	T F F F	T / F F F	T T T	F T T T	T F F T

14.

X Q Z T R	(X • Q) → (Z • ~T),	R • (T ∨ ~Z)	∴ (~X ∨ ~Q) • R
T T T T R	T T T T T T T F	F / F F F T	F T F F T F F
F F F T R	T T T T T T T F	F / F T F T	T F T T F F F
F F T T R	T T T T T T T F	F / F T F T	T F T F T F F
T F F T R	T T T T T T T F	F / F F F T	F T T T F F F
T T T T R	T T T T T T T F	T / F F F T	F T F F T F T

Part D: Valid or Invalid?

1.

A B	~A ∨ B	∴ A → B	
	F T / F	T F F	Valid

4.

A B C	A ∨ (B • C)	∴ (A • B) ∨ (A • C)	
F T T	F T T T T	F F T F F F T	Invalid

Part E: English Arguments

1. W → B ∴ ~W → ~B

W B	W → B	∴ ~W → ~B	
F T	F T T	T F F F T	Invalid

4. (W • H) → I, H • ~W ∴ ~I

W H I	(W • H) → I,	H • ~W	∴ ~I	
F T T	F T T T T	T T T F	F T	Invalid

7. S → (P → R), ~(S ∨ P) ∴ ~R

S P R	S → (P → R),	~(S ∨ P)	∴ ~R	
F F T	F T F T T	T F F F	F T	Invalid

EXERCISE 7.5

Part A: Tautologies, Contradictions, and Contingent Statements

1.

A B	~A → (A → B)
T T	F T T
T F	F T F
F T	T T T
F F	T T T tautology

4.

B A	B → (A → B)
T T	T T
T F	T T
F T	T F
F F	T T tautology

7.

P Q	P → (P → Q)
T T	T T
T F	F F
F T	T T
F F	T T contingent statement

10.

R S	(R • ~R) → S
T T	F F T
T F	F F T
F T	F T T
F F	F T T tautology

Part B: Logical Equivalence

1.

A B	~(A • B) ↔ (~A ∨ ~B)
T T	F T T F F F
T F	T F T F T T
F T	T F T T T F
F F	T F T T T T

4.

S U	(S → U) ↔ (~S ∨ U)
T T	T T F T
T F	F T F F
F T	T T T T
F F	T T T T

Part C: Logical Contradictoriness, Consistency, and Inconsistency

1.

A B	A • B ~(A ∨ B)
T T	T F T
T F	F F T
F T	F F T
F F	F T F logically inconsistent

4.

M	N	~M↔N		(~N•M)∨(M→~N)					
T	T	F	F	F	F	F	F	F	
T	F	F	T	T	T	T	T	T	
F	T	T	T	F	F	T	T	F	
F	F	T	F	T	F	T	T	T	logically consistent

7.

J	K	L	J•(K∨~L)			~K•(~L→~J)				
T	T	T	T	T F		F	F F	T F	
T	T	F	T	T T		F	F T	F F	
T	F	T	F	F F		T	T F	T F	
T	F	F	T	T T		T	F T	F F	
F	T	T	F	T F		F	F F	T T	
F	T	F	F	T T		F	F T	T T	
F	F	T	F	F F		T	T F	T T	
F	F	F	F	T T		T	T T	T T	logically inconsistent

Part D: English Arguments

1. G ∴ W → W

G	W	G ∴ W → W		
T	T	T	T	
T	F	T	T	
F	T	F	T	
F	F	F	T	Valid

And in fact every argument with a tautologous conclusion, as this one has, is automatically valid, since it is impossible for the conclusion to be false, and so it is impossible for the premises to be jointly true and the conclusion false.

4. P ↔ ~P ∴ E

P	E	P ↔ ~P		∴ E	
T	T	F F		T	
T	F	F F		F	
F	T	F F		T	
F	F	F F		F	Valid

Here again we have an argument with inconsistent premises, though in this case the inconsistency is an explicitly self-contradictory statement. The argument is valid by the same reasoning presented in the answer to number 2. Since the conclusion E can be any proposition whatever, this example shows that an argument with self-contradictory premises can validly yield any conclusion whatever.

CHAPTER 8

EXERCISE 8.1

Part A: Annotating

1.
1. F → G
2. G → H　　　　∴ F → H
3. F → H　　　　1, 2, HS

4. 1. H ∨ ~C
    2. H → ~B
    3. ~C → D
    4. (~B ∨ D) → (K • J)   ∴ J
    5. ~B ∨ D   1, 2, 3, CD
    6. K • J   4, 5, MP
    7. J   6, Simp

7. 1. ~(P • Q) ∨ R
    2. (~E • ~R) → (A • B)
    3. E → (P • Q)
    4. ~R   ∴ B ∨ (F • G)
    5. ~(P • Q)   1, 4, DS
    6. ~E   3, 5, MT
    7. ~E • ~R   4, 6, Conj
    8. A • B   2, 7, MP
    9. B   8, Simp
    10. B ∨ (F • G)   9, Add

10. 1. W → (X ∨ ~Y)
    2. ~~Y • W   ∴ X ∨ ~Z
    3. W   2, Simp
    4. X ∨ ~Y   1, 3, MP
    5. ~~Y   2, Simp
    6. X   4, 5, DS
    7. X ∨ ~Z   6, Add

Part B: Correct or Incorrect?

1. MT

4. CD

7. DS

10. Incorrect. The main connective of the premise is the arrow rather than the dot, so simplification cannot be applied.

13. Incorrect. To apply MT, we need both a conditional and the negation of its consequent as premises. And the negation of ~U is ~~U rather than U.

16. Incorrect. This is not CD. To have CD, the disjuncts of the disjunctive premise must be antecedents of the conditional premises.

19. Incorrect. To apply DS, we need a disjunctive premise and the negation of one of its disjuncts, but the first premise here is a conditional rather than a disjunction.

Part C: Proofs

1. 1. H → ~B
    2. D → B
    3. H   ∴ ~D
    4. ~B   1, 3, MP
    5. ~D   2, 4, MT

4. 1. ~A → F
    2. A → D
    3. ~D
    4. F → S   ∴ S ∨ X
    5. ~A   2, 3, MT
    6. F   1, 5, MP
    7. S   4, 6, MP
    8. S ∨ X   7, Add

7. 1. ~(S ∨ R)
2. B → (S ∨ R)
3. B ∨ P
4. ~Q ∨ B ∴ P • ~Q
5. ~B 1, 2, MT
6. P 3, 5, DS
7. ~Q 4, 5, DS
8. P • ~Q 6, 7, Conj

10. 1. (B • A) → C
2. ~D → (B • A)
3. ~C ∴ ~~D
4. ~(B • A) 1, 3, MT
5. ~~D 2, 4, MT

13. 1. (T → C) → ~F
2. S → C
3. T → S
4. F ∨ ~P ∴ ~P
5. T → C 2, 3, HS
6. ~F 1, 5, MP
7. ~P 4, 6, DS

16. 1. (E ∨ F) → ~G
2. ~H
3. H ∨ K
4. (K ∨ L) → E ∴ ~G
5. K 3, 2, DS
6. K ∨ L 5, Add
7. E 4, 6, MP
8. E ∨ F 7, Add
9. ~G 1, 8, MP

19. 1. ~~B
2. ~C → ~B
3. (~~C ∨ T) → P ∴ P
4. ~~C 2, 1, MT
5. ~~C ∨ T 4, Add
6. P 3, 5, MP

Part D: More Proofs

1. 1. P → Q
2. R → ~S
3. P ∨ R
4. (Q ∨ ~S) → (~T ∨ ~W)
5. ~~T ∴ ~W
6. Q ∨ ~S 3, 1, 2, CD
7. ~T ∨ ~W 4, 6, MP
8. ~W 7, 5, DS

4. 1. ~(R ∨ S)
2. ~(T • V) → (R ∨ S)
3. ~~(T • V) → W ∴ W ∨ ~R
4. ~~(T • V) 1, 2, MT
5. W 3, 4, MP
6. W ∨ ~R 5, Add

7. 1. ~F → J
 2. ~F ∨ ~G
 3. ~G → ~H
 4. (J ∨ ~H) → ~K
 5. ~L → ~K   ∴ ~~L
 6. J ∨ ~H   2, 1, 3, CD
 7. ~K   4, 6, MP
 8. ~~L   5, 7, MT

10. 1. ~A • ~C
 2. ~C → D
 3. (D • ~A) → (E → ~H)
 4. E • (~F → H)   ∴ ~~F
 5. ~C   1, Simp
 6. D   2, 5, MP
 7. ~A   1, Simp
 8. D • ~A   6, 7, Conj
 9. E → ~H   3, 8, MP
 10. E   4, Simp
 11. ~H   9, 10, MP
 12. ~F → H   4, Simp
 13. ~~F   12, 11, MT

13. 1. (Z • A) ∨ ~Y
 2. (Z • A) → U
 3. W ∨ ~U
 4. ~W   ∴ ~Y
 5. ~U   3, 4, DS
 6. ~(Z • A)   2, 5, MT
 7. ~Y   1, 6, DS

16. 1. (~M ∨ L) → (~A → B)
 2. ~S → T
 3. R → ~S
 4. ~M • J
 5. R ∨ ~A   ∴ T ∨ B
 6. R → T   3, 2, HS
 7. ~M   4, Simp
 8. ~M ∨ L   7, Add
 9. ~A → B   1, 8, MP
 10. T ∨ B   5, 6, 9, CD

19. 1. A ∨ D
 2. ~D
 3. (C ∨ A) → ~E   ∴ ~E
 4. A   1, 2, DS
 5. C ∨ A   4, Add
 6. ~E   3, 5, MP

22. 1. ~A
 2. [~A ∨ (B • C)] → (D → ~E)
 3. ~E → ~F
 4. (D → ~F) → G   ∴ (G • ~A) ∨ ~H
 5. ~A ∨ (B • C)   1, Add
 6. D → ~E   2, 5, MP
 7. D → ~F   6, 3, HS
 8. G   4, 7, MP
 9. G • ~A   8, 1, Conj
 10. (G • ~A) ∨ ~H   9, Add

25.   1. $(D \lor C) \rightarrow (F \lor H)$
   2. $(H \bullet G) \rightarrow (F \lor E)$
   3. $(D \lor B) \rightarrow (\sim F \rightarrow G)$
   4. $(F \lor D) \bullet (\sim F \bullet A)$ $\therefore E$
   5. $F \lor D$ 4, Simp
   6. $\sim F \bullet A$ 4, Simp
   7. $\sim F$ 6, Simp
   8. D 5, 7, DS
   9. $D \lor C$ 8, Add
   10. $F \lor H$ 1, 9, MP
   11. $D \lor B$ 8, Add
   12. $\sim F \rightarrow G$ 3, 11, MP
   13. G 12, 7, MP
   14. H 10, 7, DS
   15. $H \bullet G$ 13, 14, Conj
   16. $F \lor E$ 2, 15, MP
   17. E 16, 7, DS

Part E: English Arguments

1.   1. S
   2. $S \rightarrow U$
   3. $U \rightarrow A$
   4. $A \rightarrow K$ $\therefore K$
   5. $S \rightarrow A$ 2, 3, HS
   6. $S \rightarrow K$ 5, 4, HS
   7. K 6, 1, MP

4.   1. E
   2. $E \rightarrow (D \rightarrow C)$
   3. $(F \lor V) \rightarrow D$
   4. $S \rightarrow F$
   5. $A \bullet S$ $\therefore C$
   6. S 5, Simp
   7. F 4, 6, MP
   8. $F \lor V$ 7, Add
   9. D 3, 8, MP
   10. $D \rightarrow C$ 2, 1, MP
   11. C 10, 9, MP

7.   1. P
   2. $P \rightarrow A$
   3. $A \rightarrow (E \lor F)$
   4. $\sim E$ $\therefore F$
   5. $P \rightarrow (E \lor F)$ 2, 3, HS
   6. $E \lor F$ 5, 1, MP
   7. F 6, 4, DS

EXERCISE 8.2

Part A: Annotating

1.   1. $\sim\sim A \rightarrow B$ $\therefore A \rightarrow B$
   2. $A \rightarrow B$ 1, DN

4.   1. $\sim(E \lor D)$ $\therefore \sim D$
   2. $\sim E \bullet \sim D$ 1, DeM
   3. $\sim D$ 2, Simp

7. 1. [(P → Q) → R] • (~Q → ~P)   ∴ ~~R
    2. ~Q → ~P   1, Simp
    3. P → Q   2, Cont
    4. (P → Q) → R   1, Simp
    5. R   4, 3, MP
    6. ~~R   5, DN

10. 1. [~O → (~M → ~N)] • ~(N → M)   ∴ O
    2. ~O → (~M → ~N)   1, Simp
    3. ~(N → M)   1, Simp
    4. ~(~M → ~N)   3, Cont
    5. ~~O   2, 4, MT
    6. O   5, DN

13. 1. ~A   ∴ ~[(B • C) • A]
    2. ~(B • C) ∨ ~A   1, Add
    3. ~[(B • C) • A]   2, DeM

Part B: Correct or Incorrect?

1. DeM

4. DeM

7. Incorrect use of DeM. Correct sequence: from ~S ∨ T to ~S ∨ ~~T by DN; from ~S ∨ ~~T to ~(S • ~T) by DeM.

10. Cont

13. Com

16. As

19. DeM

Part C: Proofs

1. 1. ~(C • D)
    2. ~C → S
    3. ~D → T   ∴ S ∨ T
    4. ~C ∨ ~D   1, DeM
    5. S ∨ T   2, 3, 4, CD

4. 1. ~(~A ∨ B)   ∴ A
    2. ~~A • ~B   1, DeM
    3. A • ~B   2, DN
    4. A   3, Simp

7. 1. (A ∨ B) ∨ C
    2. ~A   ∴ C ∨ B
    3. A ∨ (B ∨ C)   1, As
    4. B ∨ C   2, 3, DS
    5. C ∨ B   4, Com

10. 1. F → (G • H)
    2. (H • G) → J   ∴ F → J
    3. (G • H) → J   2, Com
    4. F → J   1, 3, HS

13. 1. ~S → (T • U)
    2. (~S → X) → ~Z
    3. (U • T) → X   ∴ ~Z
    4. (T • U) → X   3, Com
    5. ~S → X   1, 4, HS
    6. ~Z   2, 5, MP

16. 1. (K ∨ P) ∨ X
         2. K → ~O
         3. (P ∨ X) → ~L   ∴ ~(O • L)
         4. K ∨ (P ∨ X)   1, As
         5. ~O ∨ ~L   2, 3, 4, CD
         6. ~(O • L)   5, DeM

19. 1. ~(L • M) → ~(N ∨ O)   ∴ (O ∨ N) → (M • L)
         2. ~(M • L) → ~(N ∨ O)   1, Com
         3. ~(M • L) → ~(O ∨ N)   2, Com
         4. (O ∨ N) → (M • L)   3, Cont

22. 1. ~(~P • Q)
         2. ~Q → R
         3. P → ~S   ∴ R ∨ ~S
         4. ~(~P • ~~Q)   1, DN
         5. ~~(P ∨ ~Q)   4, DeM
         6. P ∨ ~Q   5, DN
         7. ~S ∨ R   2, 3, 6, CD
         8. R ∨ ~S   7, Com

25. 1. ~B
         2. ~(C • B) → C
         3. ~F → ~C   ∴ F
         4. ~C ∨ ~B   1, Add
         5. ~(C • B)   4, DeM
         6. C   2, 5, MP
         7. ~~C   6, DN
         8. ~~F   3, 7, MT
         9. F   8, DN

Part D: Longer Proofs

1. 1. ~~T ∨ ~R
        2. ~(S ∨ ~R)
        3. (T • ~S) → ~Q
        4. W → Q   ∴ ~W
        5. ~S • ~~R   2, DeM
        6. ~~R   5, Simp
        7. ~~T   1, 6, DS
        8. T   7, DN
        9. ~S   5, Simp
        10. T • ~S   8, 9, Conj
        11. ~Q   3, 10, MP
        12. ~W   4, 11, MT

4. 1. B → E
        2. ~F ∨ G
        3. (B • C) • D
        4. (D • C) → F   ∴ E • G
        5. B • (C • D)   3, As
        6. B   5, Simp
        7. E   1, 6, MP
        8. C • D   5, Simp
        9. D • C   8, Com
        10. F   4, 9, MP
        11. ~~F   10, DN
        12. G   2, 11, DS
        13. E • G   7, 12, Conj

7. 1. ~(B • ~C)
2. ~B → D
3. C → ~E   ∴ ~E ∨ D
4. ~B ∨ ~~C   1, DeM
5. ~B ∨ C   4, DN
6. D ∨ ~E   5, 2, 3, CD
7. ~E ∨ D   6, Com

10. 1. ~A → ~B
2. D → E
3. (B → A) → (C ∨ D)
4. C → F   ∴ E ∨ F
5. B → A   1, Cont
6. C ∨ D   3, 5, MP
7. F ∨ E   2, 4, 6, CD
8. E ∨ F   7, Com

13. 1. ~[(M ∨ N) ∨ O]
2. (P • R) → N
3. ~P → T
4. ~R → S   ∴ T ∨ S
5. ~[(N ∨ M) ∨ O]   1, Com
6. ~[N ∨ (M ∨ O)]   5, As
7. ~N • ~(M ∨ O)   6, DeM
8. ~N   7, Simp
9. ~(P • R)   2, 8, MT
10. ~P ∨ ~R   9, DeM
11. T ∨ S   10, 3, 4, CD

16. 1. ~[(E • F) ∨ G]
2. (H ∨ ~E) → G   ∴ ~(F ∨ H)
3. ~(E • F) • ~G   1, DeM
4. ~G   3, Simp
5. ~(H ∨ ~E)   2, 4, MT
6. ~H • ~~E   5, DeM
7. ~(E • F)   3, Simp
8. ~E ∨ ~F   7, DeM
9. ~~E   6, Simp
10. ~F   8, 9, DS
11. ~H   6, Simp
12. ~F • ~H   10, 11, Conj
13. ~(F ∨ H)   12, DeM

19. 1. [(A • B) ∨ ~C] → (~X • ~Y)
2. ~(Y ∨ X) → Z
3. ~C ∨ (A • B)   ∴ ~~Z
4. (A • B) ∨ ~C   3, Com
5. ~X • ~Y   1, 4, MP
6. ~(X ∨ Y)   5, DeM
7. ~(Y ∨ X)   6, Com
8. Z   2, 7, MP
9. ~~Z   8, DN

22. 1. A ∨ (B ∨ C)
2. ~A • ~C   ∴ [(B ∨ C) • ~(A ∨ C)] • (A ∨ B)
3. ~A   2, Simp
4. B ∨ C   1, 3, DS
5. ~(A ∨ C)   2, DeM
6. (A ∨ B) ∨ C   1, As

7. ~C	2, Simp
8. A ∨ B	6, 7, DS
9. (B ∨ C) • ~(A ∨ C)	4, 5, Conj
10. [(B ∨ C) • ~(A ∨ C)] • (A ∨ B)	8, 9, Conj

25.

1. Z • Y	
2. T → X	
3. ~Y → ~S	
4. ~(X ∨ Y) ∨ ~Z	∴ ~(T ∨ S) • Y
5. Y	1, Simp
6. Z	1, Simp
7. ~~Z	6, DN
8. ~(X ∨ Y)	4, 7, DS
9. ~X • ~Y	8, DeM
10. ~X	9, Simp
11. ~Y	9, Simp
12. ~S	3, 11, MP
13. ~T	2, 10, MT
14. ~T • ~S	12, 13, Conj
15. ~(T ∨ S)	14, DeM
16. ~(T ∨ S) • Y	5, 15, Conj

EXERCISE 8.3

Part A: Annotating

1.

1. B ↔ E	∴ E → B
2. (B → E) • (E → B)	1, ME
3. E → B	2, Simp

4.

1. H → (J → ~H)	∴ H → ~J
2. H → (~~H → ~J)	1, Cont
3. (H • ~~H) → ~J	2, Ex
4. (H • H) → ~J	3, DN
5. H → ~J	4, Re

7.

1. M → ~N	∴ N → ~M
2. ~M ∨ ~N	1, MI
3. ~N ∨ ~M	2, Com
4. N → ~M	3, MI

10.

1. (U → U) ∨ (~U → U)	∴ ~U ∨ U
2. (~U ∨ U) ∨ (~U → U)	1, MI
3. (~U ∨ U) ∨ (~~U ∨ U)	2, MI
4. (~U ∨ U) ∨ (U ∨ U)	3, DN
5. (~U ∨ U) ∨ U	4, Re
6. ~U ∨ (U ∨ U)	5, As
7. ~U ∨ U	6, Re

13.

1. ~P → P	∴ ~P → Q
2. ~~P ∨ P	1, MI
3. ~~P ∨ ~~P	2, DN
4. ~~P	3, Re
5. ~~P ∨ Q	4, Add
6. ~P → Q	5, MI

Part B: Correct or Incorrect?

1. Correct (Re)
4. Correct (Dist)

7. Incorrect use of Dist. From the premise, by Dist, we get (K ∨ X) • (K ∨ R).
10. Incorrect. DS is an implicational rule and cannot be applied to part of a line.
13. Correct (Dist)
16. Correct (Dist)
19. Incorrect. Simplification is an implicational rule and may not be applied to part of a line.

Part C: Short Proofs

1. 1. ~M ∨ N   ∴ ~N → ~M
     2. M → N   1, MI
     3. ~N → ~M   2, Cont

4. 1. ~A ∨ ~A
     2. A ∨ P   ∴ P
     3. ~A   1, Re
     4. P   2, 3, DS

7. 1. (~J • K) → L
     2. ~J   ∴ ~L → ~K
     3. ~J → (K → L)   1, Ex
     4. K → L   3, 2, MP
     5. ~L → ~K   4, Cont

10. 1. ~R
     2. (R → S) → T   ∴ T
     3. (~R ∨ S) → T   2, MI
     4. ~R ∨ S   1, Add
     5. T   3, 4, MP

13. 1. E → H
     2. (E ∨ F) • (E ∨ G)
     3. (F • G) → H   ∴ H
     4. E ∨ (F • G)   2, Dist
     5. H ∨ H   4, 1, 3, CD
     6. H   5, Re

16. 1. ~~(R • S)
     2. T → (R → ~S)   ∴ ~T
     3. ~(~R ∨ ~S)   1, DeM
     4. ~(R → ~S)   3, MI
     5. ~T   2, 4, MT

19. 1. H ∨ H
     2. H ↔ ~J   ∴ ~J
     3. (H → ~J) • (~J → H) 2, ME
     4. H → ~J   3, Simp
     5. H   1, Re
     6. ~J   4, 5, MP

22. 1. P • Q   ∴ [(R ∨ P) • R] ∨ [(R ∨ P) • Q]
     2. R ∨ (P • Q)   1, Add
     3. (R ∨ P) • (R ∨ Q)   2, Dist
     4. [(R ∨ P) • R] ∨ [(R ∨ P) • Q]   3, Dist

25. 1. (A → B) ↔ C
     2. ~(A → B) ∨ ~C   ∴ ~C
     3. [(A → B) • C] ∨ [~(A → B) • ~C] 1, ME
     4. ~[(A → B) • C]   2, DeM
     5. ~(A → B) • ~C   3, 4, DS
     6. ~C   5, Simp

Part D: Longer Proofs

1.
1. $(Z \lor \sim Y) \bullet (Z \lor W)$
2. $Z \to \sim\sim U$
3. $\sim Y \to (W \to U)$ $\therefore U$
4. $Z \lor (\sim Y \bullet W)$ 1, Dist
5. $Z \to U$ 2, DN
6. $(\sim Y \bullet W) \to U$ 3, Ex
7. $U \lor U$ 4, 5, 6, CD
8. U 7, Re

4.
1. $\sim H \lor (G \lor F)$
2. $\sim F$
3. $S \to \sim(H \to G)$ $\therefore \sim S$
4. $(\sim H \lor G) \lor F$ 1, As
5. $\sim H \lor G$ 2, 4, DS
6. $H \to G$ 5, MI
7. $\sim\sim(H \to G)$ 6, DN
8. $\sim S$ 3, 7, MT

7.
1. $B \lor (C \bullet \sim D)$
2. $(D \to B) \leftrightarrow P$ $\therefore P$
3. $(B \lor C) \bullet (B \lor \sim D)$ 1, Dist
4. $[(D \to B) \to P] \bullet [P \to (D \to B)]$ 2, ME
5. $(D \to B) \to P$ 4, Simp
6. $B \lor \sim D$ 3, Simp
7. $\sim D \lor B$ 6, Com
8. $D \to B$ 7, MI
9. P 5, 8, MP

10.
1. $(B \bullet C) \to D$
2. B
3. $Q \to \sim(\sim C \lor D)$
4. $\sim Q \leftrightarrow T$ $\therefore T$
5. $B \to (C \to D)$ 1, Ex
6. $C \to D$ 5, 2, MP
7. $\sim C \lor D$ 6, MI
8. $\sim\sim(\sim C \lor D)$ 7, DN
9. $\sim Q$ 3, 8, MT
10. $(\sim Q \to T) \bullet (T \to \sim Q)$ 4, ME
11. $\sim Q \to T$ 10, Simp
12. T 11, 9, MP

Part E: English Arguments

1.
1. $P \to (N \lor S)$
2. $N \to (M \bullet F)$
3. $S \to E$
4. $P \bullet \sim F$ $\therefore E$
5. P 4, Simp
6. $N \lor S$ 1, 5, MP
7. $(M \bullet F) \lor E$ 6, 2, 3, CD
8. $\sim F$ 4, Simp
9. $\sim M \lor \sim F$ 8, Add
10. $\sim(M \bullet F)$ 9, DeM
11. E 7, 10, DS

4.
1. $S \lor (U \bullet P)$
2. $(S \lor U) \to R$ $\therefore R$

    3. (S ∨ U) • (S ∨ P)   1, Dist
    4. S ∨ U   3, Simp
    5. R   2, 4, MP

EXERCISE 8.4

Part A: Conditional Proofs

1.   1. Z → (~Y → X)
      2. Z → ~Y   ∴ Z → X
      3. Z   Assume (for CP)
      4. ~Y   2, 3, MP
      5. ~Y → X   1, 3, MP
      6. X   5, 4, MP
      7. Z → X   3–6, CP

4.   1. A → B
      2. A → C   ∴ A → (B • C)
      3. A   Assume (for CP)
      4. B   1, 3, MP
      5. C   2, 3, MP
      6. B • C   4, 5, Conj
      7. A → (B • C)   3–6, CP

7.   1. P   ∴ (P → Q) → Q
      2. P → Q   Assume (for CP)
      3. Q   2, 1, MP
      4. (P → Q) → Q   2–3, CP

10.   1. C → (~D → E)
      2. (D → ~D) → (E → G)   ∴ C → (~D → G)
      3. C   Assume (for CP)
      4. ~D → E   1, 3, MP
      5. (~D ∨ ~D) → (E → G)   2, MI
      6. ~D → (E → G)   5, Re
      7. ~D   Assume (for CP)
      8. E → G   6, 7, MP
      9. E   4, 7, MP
      10. G   8, 9, MP
      11. ~D → G   7–10, CP
      12. C → (~D → G)   3–11, CP

13.   1. (A ∨ N) → ~S
      2. M → [N → (S • T)]   ∴ ~(~M ∨ ~N) → (S • ~A)
      3. ~(~M ∨ ~N)   Assume (for CP)
      4. ~~M • ~~N   3, DeM
      5. ~~M   4, Simp
      6. M   5, DN
      7. N → (S • T)   2, 6, MP
      8. ~~N   4, Simp
      9. N   8, DN
      10. S • T   7, 9, MP
      11. S   10, Simp
      12. ~~S   11, DN
      13. ~(A ∨ N)   1, 12, MT
      14. ~A • ~N   13, DeM
      15. ~A   14, Simp
      16. S • ~A   11, 15, Conj
      17. ~(~M ∨ ~N) → (S • ~A)   3–16, CP

16. 1. A → (B → C)   ∴ (A → B) → (A → C)
    2. A → B   Assume (for CP)
    3. (A • B) → C   1, Ex
    4. A   Assume (for CP)
    5. B   2, 4, MP
    6. A • B   4, 5, Conj
    7. C   3, 6, MP
    8. A → C   4–7, CP
    9. (A → B) → (A → C)   2–8, CP

19. 1. A → (B • C)
    2. B → D
    3. C → ~D   ∴ A → X
    4. A   Assume (for CP)
    5. B • C   1, 4, MP
    6. B   5, Simp
    7. C   5, Simp
    8. D   2, 6, MP
    9. ~D   3, 7, MP
    10. D ∨ X   8, Add
    11. X   10, 9, DS
    12. A → X   4–11, CP

Part B: English Arguments

1. 1. ~V → (~I ∨ ~P)
    2. ~I → ~S
    3. ~P → ~S   ∴ ~V → ~S
    4. ~V   Assume (for CP)
    5. ~I ∨ ~P   1, 4, MP
    6. ~S ∨ ~S   5, 2, 3, CD
    7. ~S   6, Re
    8. ~V → ~S   4–7, CP

EXERCISE 8.5

Part A: Proofs

1. 1. A → B   ∴ ~(A • ~B)
    2. A • ~B   Assume (for RAA)
    3. A   2, Simp
    4. B   1, 3, MP
    5. ~B   2, Simp
    6. B • ~B   4, 5, Conj
    7. ~(A • ~B)   3–6, RAA

4. 1. (H ∨ R) • (H ∨ ~R)   ∴ H
    2. ~H   Assume (for RAA)
    3. H ∨ (R • ~R)   1, Dist
    4. R • ~R   3, 2, DS
    5. H   2–4, RAA

7. 1. Z → (X ∨ Y)
    2. X → ~W
    3. Y → ~W
    4. ~W → ~ Z   ∴ ~Z

5.	Z	Assume (for RAA)
6.	X ∨ Y	1, 5, MP
7.	~W ∨ ~W	6, 2, 3, CD
8.	~W	7, Re
9.	~Z	4, 8, MP
10.	Z • ~Z	5, 9, Conj
11.	~Z	5–10, RAA

10.
1.	~A • ~B	∴ A ↔ B
2.	~(A ↔ B)	Assume (for RAA)
3.	~[(A • B) ∨ (~A • ~B)]	2, ME
4.	~(A • B) • ~(~A • ~B)	3, DeM
5.	~(~A • ~B)	4, Simp
6.	(~A • ~B) • ~(~A • ~B)	1, 5, Conj
7.	A ↔ B	2–6, RAA

13.
1.	D → ~(A ∨ B)	
2.	~C → D	∴ A → C
3.	~(A → C)	Assume (for RAA)
4.	~(~A ∨ C)	3, MI
5.	~~A • ~C	4, DeM
6.	~C	5, Simp
7.	D	2, 6, MP
8.	~(A ∨ B)	1, 7, MP
9.	~A • ~B	8, DeM
10.	~A	9, Simp
11.	~~A	5, Simp
12.	~A • ~~A	10, 11, Conj
13.	A → C	3–12, RAA

16.
1.	W → (X ∨ G)	
2.	G → M	
3.	~M	∴ ~W ∨ X
4.	~(~W ∨ X)	Assume
5.	~~W • ~X	4, DeM
6.	~G	2, 3, MT
7.	~~W	5, Simp
8.	W	7, DN
9.	X ∨ G	1, 8, MP
10.	~X	5, Simp
11.	G	9, 10, DS
12.	G • ~G	11, 6, Conj
13.	~W ∨ X	4–12, RAA

19.
1.	~S → (T • U)	
2.	~R → ~(T ∨ U)	
3.	(T ↔ U) → (~~S • R)	∴ R • S
4.	~(R • S)	Assume (for RAA)
5.	(T ↔ U) → (S • R)	3, DN
6.	(T ↔ U) → (R • S)	5, Com
7.	~(T ↔ U)	6, 4, MT
8.	~R ∨ ~S	4, DeM
9.	~(T ∨ U) ∨ (T • U)	8, 2, 1, CD
10.	(T • U) ∨ ~(T ∨ U)	9, Com
11.	(T • U) ∨ (~T • ~U)	10, DeM
12.	T ↔ U	11, ME
13.	(T ↔ U) • ~(T ↔ U)	12, 7, Conj
14.	R • S	4–13, RAA

Part B: Valid or Invalid?

1.
1. $(F \rightarrow G) \rightarrow H$ $\therefore F \rightarrow (G \rightarrow H)$
2. F   Assume (for CP)
3. G   Assume (for CP)
4. ~H   Assume (for RAA)
5. ~$(F \rightarrow G)$ 1, 4, MT
6. ~$(\sim F \vee G)$ 5, MI
7. ~~F • ~G   6, DeM
8. ~G   7, Simp
9. G • ~G   3, 8, Conj
10. H   4–9, RAA
11. $G \rightarrow H$ 3–10, CP
12. $F \rightarrow (G \rightarrow H)$ 2–11, CP

4.

E	F	G	$(E \bullet F) \rightarrow G$	$\therefore F \rightarrow G$	
F	T	F	F F T T F	T F F	Invalid

Part C: English Arguments

1.
1. $R \rightarrow (T \vee P)$
2. $T \rightarrow (\sim L \vee C)$
3. $P \rightarrow (\sim L \vee W)$
4. R • (~C • ~W) $\therefore$ ~L
5. L   Assume (for RAA)
6. ~C • ~W   4, Simp
7. ~C   6, Simp
8. ~~L   5, DN
9. ~~L • ~C   8, 7, Conj
10. ~$(\sim L \vee C)$ 9, DeM
11. ~T   2, 10, MT
12. ~W   6, Simp
13. ~~L • ~W   8, 12, Conj
14. ~$(\sim L \vee W)$ 13, DeM
15. ~P   3, 14, MT
16. ~T • ~P   11, 15, Conj
17. ~$(T \vee P)$ 16, DeM
18. ~R   1, 17, MT
19. R   4, Simp
20. R • ~R   18, 19, Conj
21. ~L   5–20, RAA

EXERCISE 8.6

Part A: Theorems

1. $\therefore$ ~$(P \rightarrow Q) \rightarrow (P \bullet \sim Q)$
1. ~$(P \rightarrow Q)$ Assume (for CP)
2. ~$(\sim P \vee Q)$ 1, MI
3. ~~P • ~Q   2, DeM
4. P • ~Q   3, DN
5. ~$(P \rightarrow Q) \rightarrow (P \bullet \sim Q)$ 1–4, CP

4. $\therefore$ $(X \rightarrow Y) \rightarrow$ ~$(X \bullet \sim Y)$
1. $X \rightarrow Y$ Assume (for CP)
2. ~X ∨ Y   1, MI
3. ~X ∨ ~~Y   2, DN
4. ~$(X \bullet \sim Y)$ 3, DeM
5. $(X \rightarrow Y) \rightarrow$ ~$(X \bullet \sim Y)$ 1–4, CP

7.   ∴ K → [(K → L) → L]
```
 ┌── 1. K                          Assume (for CP)
 │ ┌─ 2. K → L                     Assume (for CP)
 │ │  3. L                         2, 1, MP
 │ └─ 4. (K → L) → L               2–3, CP
 └─── 5. K → [(K → L) → L]         1–4, CP
```

10.   ∴ (P • ~Q) → ~(P ↔ Q)
```
 ┌── 1. P • ~Q                     Assume (for CP)
 │ ┌─ 2. P ↔ Q                     Assume (for RAA)
 │ │  3. (P → Q) • (Q → P)         2, ME
 │ │  4. P                         1, Simp
 │ │  5. P → Q                     3, Simp
 │ │  6. Q                         5, 4, MP
 │ │  7. ~Q                        1, Simp
 │ └─ 8. Q • ~Q                    6, 7, Conj
 │    9. ~(P ↔ Q)                  2–8, RAA
 └── 10. (P • ~Q) → ~(P ↔ Q)       1–9, CP
```

Part B: Challenging Theorems

1.   ∴ (T → U) ∨ (U → T)
```
 ┌── 1. ~[(T → U) ∨ (U → T)]        Assume (for RAA)
 │   2. ~(T → U) • ~(U → T)         1, DeM
 │   3. ~(T → U)                    2, Simp
 │   4. ~(~T ∨ U)                   3, MI
 │   5. ~~T • ~U                    4, DeM
 │   6. T • ~U                      5, DN
 │   7. T                           6, Simp
 │   8. ~(U → T)                     2, Simp
 │   9. ~(~U ∨ T)                   8, MI
 │  10. ~~U • ~T                    9, DeM
 │  11. ~T                          10, Simp
 └─ 12. T • ~T                       7, 11, Conj
    13. (T → U) ∨ (U → T)           1–12, RAA
```

4.   ∴ [P ∨ (~P • Q)] ↔ (P ∨ Q)
```
 ┌── 1. P ∨ (~P • Q)               Assume (for CP)
 │ ┌─ 2. ~P                        Assume (for CP)
 │ │  3. ~P • Q                    1, 2, DS
 │ └─ 4. Q                         3, Simp
 │    5. ~P → Q                    2–4, CP
 │    6. ~~P ∨ Q                   5, MI
 │    7. P ∨ Q                     6, DN
 └──  8. [P ∨ (~P • Q)] → (P ∨ Q)  1–7, CP
 ┌──  9. P ∨ Q                     Assume (for CP)
 │ ┌─10. ~P                        Assume (for CP)
 │ │ 11. Q                         9, 10, DS
 │ └─12. ~P • Q                    11, 10, Conj
 │   13. ~P → (~P • Q)             10–12, CP
 │   14. ~~P ∨ (~P • Q)            13, MI
 └── 15. P ∨ (~P • Q)              14, DN
    16. (P ∨ Q) → [P ∨ (~P • Q)]   9–15, CP
    17. [(P ∨ (~P • Q)) → (P ∨ Q)] •
        [(P ∨ Q) → (P ∨ (~P • Q))]  8, 16, Conj
    18. (P ∨ (~P • Q)) ↔ (P ∨ Q)   17, ME
```

7.   ∴ [((L • M) ∨ (L • N)) ∨ ((P • M) ∨ (P • N))] → ((L ∨ P) • (M ∨ N))

1. [(L • M) ∨ (L • N)] ∨ [(P • M) ∨ (P • N)]   Assume (for CP)
2. [L • (M ∨ N)] ∨ [(P • M) ∨ (P • N)]   1, Dist
3. [L • (M ∨ N)] ∨ [P • (M ∨ N)]   2, Dist
4. ~[(L ∨ P) • (M ∨ N)]   Assume (for RAA)
5. ~(L ∨ P) ∨ ~(M ∨ N)   3, DeM
6. L • (M ∨ N)   Assume (for RAA)
7. M ∨ N   6, Simp
8. L   6, Simp
9. L ∨ P   8, Add
10. ~~(L ∨ P)   9, DN
11. ~(M ∨ N)   5, 10, DS
12. (M ∨ N) • ~(M ∨ N)   7, 11, Conj
13. ~[L • (M ∨ N)]   6–12, RAA
14. P • (M ∨ N)   3, 13, DS
15. P   14, Simp
16. M ∨ N   14, Simp
17. L ∨ P   15, Add
18. ~~(L ∨ P)   17, DN
19. ~(M ∨ N)   5, 18, DS
20. (M ∨ N) • ~(M ∨ N)   16, 19, Conj
21. (L ∨ P) • (M ∨ N)   4–20, RAA
22. [((L • M) ∨ (L • N)) ∨ ((P • M) ∨ (P • N))] →
    [(L ∨ P) • (M ∨ N)]   1–22, CP

10.   ∴[(A • B) ∨ (C • D)] → [((A ∨ C) • (A ∨ D)) • ((B ∨ C) • (B ∨ D))]

1. (A • B) ∨ (C • D)   Assume (for CP)
2. ~[((A ∨ C) • (A ∨ D)) • ((B ∨ C) • (B ∨ D))]   Assume (for RAA)
3. ~[(A ∨ C) • (A ∨ D)] ∨ ~[(B ∨ C) • (B ∨ D)]   2, DeM
4. [~(A ∨ C) ∨ ~(A ∨ D)] ∨ ~[(B ∨ C) • (B ∨ D)]   3, DeM
5. [~(A ∨ C) ∨ ~(A ∨ D)] ∨ [~(B ∨ C) ∨ ~(B ∨ D)]   4, DeM
6. [(~A • ~C) ∨ ~(A ∨ D)] ∨ [~(B ∨ C) ∨ ~(B ∨ D)]   5, DeM
7. [(~A • ~C) ∨ (~A • ~D)] ∨ [~(B ∨ C) ∨ ~(B ∨ D)]   6, DeM
8. [(~A • ~C) ∨ (~A • ~D)] ∨ [(~B • ~C) ∨ ~(B ∨ D)]   7, DeM
9. [(~A • ~C) ∨ (~A • ~D)] ∨ [(~B • ~C) ∨ (~B • ~D)]   8, DeM
10. [~A • (~C ∨ ~D)] ∨ [(~B • ~C) ∨ (~B • ~D)]   9, Dist
11. [~A • (~C ∨ ~D)] ∨ [~B • (~C ∨ ~D)]   10, Dist
12. [(~C ∨ ~D) • ~A] ∨ [(~B • (~C ∨ ~D)]   11, Com
13. [(~C ∨ ~D) • ~A] ∨ [(~C ∨ ~D) • ~B]   12, Com
14. (~C ∨ ~D) • (~A ∨ ~B)   13, Dist
15. ~(C • D) • (~A ∨ ~B)   14, DeM
16. ~(C • D) • ~(A • B)   15, DeM
17. ~(C • D)   16, Simp
18. ~(A • B)   16, Simp
19. A • B   1, 17, DS
20. (A • B) • ~(A • B)   19, 18, Conj
21. [(A ∨ C) • (A ∨ D)] • [(B ∨ C) • (B ∨ D)]   2–20, RAA
22. [(A • B) ∨ (C • D)] → [((A ∨ C) • (A ∨ D)) •
    ((B ∨ C) • (B ∨ D))]   1–21, CP

Part C: Corresponding Conditionals

1.   ∴ [(~A ∨ ~B) • B] → ~A

    | 1. (~A ∨ ~B) • B   Assume (for CP)
    | 2. ~A ∨ ~B   1, Simp
    | 3. B   1, Simp
    | 4. ~~B   3, DN
    | 5. ~A   2, 4, DS
       6. [(~A ∨ ~B) • B] → ~A   1–5, CP

CHAPTER 9

EXERCISE 9.1

Part A: Well-Formed Formulas?

1. WFF.
4. Not a WFF. The problem is that a is an individual constant rather than a variable. Quantifiers must contain variables. Note that (a)Ca is nonsense, like saying, "For all Adam, Adam is cold."
7. WFF.
10. WFF.
13. WFF.
16. Not a WFF. The problem is that b is an individual constant rather than a formula. Note that ~b is nonsense, like saying, "It is not the case that Bob."
19. WFF.
22. WFF.
25. WFF.

Part B: Free and Bound Variables

1. The x in Hx is bound by the quantifier; the y in Gy is free.
4. The z is Fz is bound by the (z) quantifier, as is the z in Gz; the x in Jx is free.
7. The x in (y)Pxy is bound by (x); the y in Pxy is bound by (y). The x in Qx is free.
10. The x in Bx is bound by (x); the y in Dy is bound by (y); the z in Ez is bound by (z).
13. The x in Lx is bound by the quantifier immediately to its left; the x in Nx is bound by the quantifier immediately to its left.

Part C: Symbolizing

1. (x)(Zx → ~Mx)
4. ~(x)(Mx → Kx)
7. (∃x)Rx
10. (∃x)(Mx • Hx)
13. (∃x)(Px • Gx) • (∃x)(Px • ~Gx)
16. (x)(Sx → Bx)
19. (∃x)(Ax • Sx)
22. (x)(Cx ↔ Px)
25. (x)[Hx → (Fx • Bx)]

Part D: More Symbolizing

1. (x)(Cx → Ax)
4. (x)(Lx → Wx)
7. (x)Ix
10. (x)(Rx → ~Wx)
13. (x)Mx → (x)~Px
16. (x)[(Px • Sx) → ~Hx]

19. (x)~Gx → (x)(Hx → ~Nx) or ~(∃x)Gx → (x)(Hx → ~Nx)
22. (x)[Cx → (Lx • Rx)]
25. (x)(Cx → Sx)

Part F: Challenging Translations

1. *In logicese:* For any x, if x is not equilateral, then it is not the case that x is both a rectangle and a square: (x)[~Ex → ~(Rx • Sx)]. In other words, for all x, if x is both a rectangle and a square, then it is equilateral: (x)[(Rx • Sx) → Ex].
4. (x)(Vx → Cx)
7. [(x)(Hx → Mx) • ~Ms] → ~Hs
10. (x)[(Fx • ~(Hx ∨ Mx)) → ~Rx]
13. [Db • (x)(Dx → Ax)] → Ab
16. (x)[(Px • (Hx • Sx)) → Cx]
19. (x)~Gx ∨ (∃x)Ex
22. (x)[Wx → ~(Kx ∨ Fx)]
25. (∃x)(Px • Cx) → Ck

EXERCISE 9.2

Part A: Demonstrating Invalidity

1.

Aa Ba	Aa → Ba ∴ Aa • Ba
F T	F T T F T F

4.

Ka Kb La Lb	(Ka ∨ Kb) → (La ∨ Lb) ∴ (Ka → La) • (Kb → Lb)
T F F T	T T F T F T T T F F F T T T

7.

Ha Hb Ja Jb	(Ha • Hb) → (~Ja • ~Jb) ∴ (Ja → ~Ha) • (Jb → ~Hb)
T F T T	T F T T F T F F T T F F T F T T T F

10.

Ra Rb Sa Sb	(Ra → Sa) ∨ (Rb → Sb) ∴ (Ra ∨ Rb) → (Sa ∨ Sb)
F T F F	F T F T T F F F T T F F F F

13.

Ad Bd	Ad → Bd, Bd ∴ Ad
F T	F T T T F

16.

Ma Mb Na Nb	(Ma → Na) • (Mb → Nb), Ma ∨ Mb ∴ Na • Nb
F T F T	F T F T T T T F T T F F T

19.

Aa Ab Ba Bb Ca Cb	(Aa • Ba) ∨ (Ab • Bb), (Ca • Ba) ∨ (Cb • Bb) ∴ (Aa • Ca) ∨ (Ab • Cb)
F T T T T F	F F T T T T T T T T T F F T F F T F T F F

22.

Aa Ba Bb Ab	~[(Aa → (Ba ∨ Bb)) • (Ab → (Ba ∨ Bb))] ∴ (Aa • Ab) → (Ba ∨ Bb)
T F F T	T T F F F F F T F F F F T T T F F F F

25.

Sa Sb Ra Rb	(Sa • Sb) → (Ra ∨ Rb) ∴ [Sa → (Ra ∨ Rb)] • [Sb → (Ra ∨ Rb)]
T F F F	T F F T F F F T F F F F F F T F F F

28.

Aa Ba Ab Bb	~[(Aa → Ba) • (Ab → Bb)] ∴ (Aa • Ab) → (Ba • Bb)
T F T F	T T F F F T F F T T T F F F F

Part B: English Arguments

1. (x)[(Sx • Lx) → Cx] ∴ (∃x)[(Sx • Lx) • Cx]

Sa La Ca	(Sa • La) → Ca ∴ (Sa • La) • Ca
F T T	F F T T T F F T F T

4. (x)(Sx → Gx), (∃x)(Bx • Gx) ∴ (∃x)(Bx • Sx)

Sa Ga Ba	Sa → Ga, Ba • Ga ∴ Ba • Sa
F T T	F T T T T T T F F

EXERCISE 9.3

Part A: Annotating

1.
  1. (x)(Rx → Tx)
  2. ~Tc   ∴ ~Rc
  3. Rc → Tc   1, UI
  4. ~Rc   2, 3, MT

4.
  1. Hn   ∴ (∃x)Hx
  2. (∃x)Hx   1, EG

7.
  1. (y)(Ry → Ny)
  2. ~Ng   ∴ (∃y)~Ry
  3. Rg → Ng   1, UI
  4. ~Rg   2, 3, MT
  5. (∃y)~Ry   4, EG

10.
  1. (∃y)Py → (z)(~Nz ∨ Oz)
  2. Pn
  3. ~Om   ∴ (∃x)~Nx
  4. (∃y)Py   2, EG
  5. (z)(~Nz ∨ Oz)   1, 4, MP
  6. ~Nm ∨ Om   5, UI
  7. ~Nm   3, 6, DS
  8. (∃x)~Nx   7, EG

13.
  1. (y)(Dy • Ey)   ∴ (y)Dy • (y)Ey
  2. Db • Eb   1, UI
  3. Db   2, Simp
  4. (y)Dy   3, UG
  5. Eb   2, Simp
  6. (y)Ey   5, UG
  7. (y)Dy • (y)Ey   4, 6, Conj

Part B: Correct or Incorrect?

1.
  1. (x)Ax → (x)Bx
  2. Aa → (x)Bx   1, UI   Incorrect. UI may *not* be applied to a part of a line.

4.
  1. (∃z)(Kz • Lz)
  2. (∃z)Kz   1, Simp   Incorrect. Simp may not be applied to a part of a line.

7.
  1. (x)(y)(My ↔ Nx)
  2. (y)(My ↔ Ny)   1, UI   Incorrect. (y)(My ↔ Ny) is not an instance of (x)(y)(My ↔ Nx) because the x in "Nx" is free in (y)(My ↔ Nx), but the y in "Ny" is not free in (y)(My ↔ Ny).

10. 1. $(x)(Bx \rightarrow (z)Cz)$
2. $(x)Bx$
3. $(z)Cz$ 1, 2, MP   Incorrect. To apply MP, we need a conditional on one line and its antecedent on another. Line (1) is not a conditional but a universally quantified statement.

13. 1. $(x)(Ax \lor Bx)$
2. $Aa \lor Ba$ 1, UI   Correct.
3. $(y)(Aa \lor By)$ 2, UG   Incorrect. The instantial constant has not been replaced uniformly.

PART C: Proofs

3. 1. $(y)(\sim Py \rightarrow \sim Ly)$
2. $Lc \lor Ld$ $\therefore Pd \lor Pc$
3. $\sim Pc \rightarrow \sim Lc$ 1, UI
4. $\sim Pd \rightarrow \sim Ld$ 1, UI
5. $Lc \rightarrow Pc$ 3, Cont
6. $Ld \rightarrow Pd$ 4, Cont
7. $Pc \lor Pd$ 2, 5, 6, CD
8. $Pd \lor Pc$ 7, Com

6. 1. $(x)(Ax \leftrightarrow \sim Ax)$ $\therefore Bc$
2. $Ac \leftrightarrow \sim Ac$ 1, UI
3. $(Ac \rightarrow \sim Ac) \bullet (\sim Ac \rightarrow Ac)$ 2, ME
4. $Ac \rightarrow \sim Ac$ 3, Simp
5. $\sim Ac \lor \sim Ac$ 4, MI
6. $\sim Ac$ 5, Re
7. $\sim Ac \rightarrow Ac$ 3, Simp
8. $\sim\sim Ac \lor Ac$ 7, MI
9. $Ac \lor Ac$ 8, DN
10. Ac 9, Re
11. $Ac \lor Bc$ 10, Add
12. Bc 11, 6, DS

9. 1. $(z)\sim(\sim(x)Jx \lor \sim Kz)$ $\therefore Jc \bullet Kc$
2. $\sim(\sim(x)Jx \lor \sim Kc)$ 1, UI
3. $\sim\sim(x)Jx \bullet \sim\sim Kc$ 2, DeM
4. $\sim\sim(x)Jx$ 3, Simp
5. $\sim\sim Kc$ 3, Simp
6. Kc 5, DN
7. $(x)Jx$ 4, DN
8. Jc 7, UI
9. $Jc \bullet Kc$ 8, 6, Conj

PART D: More Proofs

1. 1. $(x)(Fx \rightarrow \sim Gx)$
2. Fa $\therefore (\exists x)\sim Gx$
3. $Fa \rightarrow \sim Ga$ 1, UI
4. $\sim Ga$ 3, 2, MP
5. $(\exists x) \sim Gx$ 4, EG

5. 1. $(x)(Mx \rightarrow Ox)$
2. $\sim(Nc \lor \sim Md)$ $\therefore (\exists x)Ox$
3. $\sim Nc \bullet \sim\sim Md$ 2, DeM
4. $\sim\sim Md$ 3, Simp
5. Md 4, DN
6. $Md \rightarrow Od$ 1, UI

    7. Od   6, 5, MP
    8. (∃x)Ox   7, EG

9.   1. ~(z)Hz ∨ ((y)Gy ∨ ~(∃x)Fx)
      2. Fc
      3. Sc → ~((z)Hz → (y)Gy)   ∴ (∃z)~Sz
      4. [~(z)Hz ∨ (y)Gy] ∨ ~(∃x)Fx   1, As
      5. (∃x)Fx   2, EG
      6. ~~(∃x)Fx   5, DN
      7. ~(z)Hz ∨ (y)Gy   6, 4, DS
      8. (z)Hz → (y)Gy   7, MI
      9. ~~((z)Hz → (y)Gy)   8, DN
   10. ~Sc   9, 3, MT
   11. (∃z)~Sz   10, EG

PART E: Still More Proofs

2.   1. (x)(Dx → Lx)
      2. (∃x)Dx   ∴ (∃x)(Dx • Lx)
      3. Da   2, EI
      4. Da → La   1, UI
      5. La   4, 3, MP
      6. Da • La   3, 5, Conj
      7. (∃x)(Dx • Lx)   6, EG

6.   1. (z)[Uz → (Kz ∨ Sz)]
      2. (z)Uz
      3. (∃z)~Sz   ∴ (∃z)Kz
      4. ~Sa   3, EI
      5. Ua   2, UI
      6. Ua → (Ka ∨ Sa)   1, UI
      7. Ka ∨ Sa   5, 6, MP
      8. Ka   4, 7, DS
      9. ∃z(Kz)   8, EG

9.   1. (x)[Px → (∃y)Oy]
      2. (∃z)Pz   ∴ (∃y)Oy
      3. Pa   2, EI
      4. Pa → (∃y)Oy   1, UI
      5. (∃y)Oy   4, 3, MP

13. 1. (x)(Sx → Tx)
      2. (∃y)(Ry • ~Ty)   ∴ (∃z)(Rz • ~Sz)
      3. Rb • ~Tb   2, EI
      4. Sb → Tb   1, UI
      5. ~Tb   3, Simp
      6. ~Sb   4, 5, MT
      7. Rb   3, Simp
      8. Rb • ~Sb   7, 6, Conj
      9. (∃z)(Rz • ~Sz)   8, EG

17. 1. (x)[Bx → (Cx • Dx)]
      2. (∃x)Bx   ∴ (∃x)~(~Cx ∨ ~Dx)
      3. Bb   2, EI
      4. Bb → (Cb • Db)   1, UI
      5. Cb • Db   4, 3, MP
      6. ~~Cb • Db   5, DN
      7. ~~Cb • ~~Db   6, DN
      8. ~(~Cb ∨ ~Db)   7, DeM
      9. (∃x)~(~Cx ∨ ~Dx) 8, EG

PART F: Still More Proofs

2. 1. $(z)(Nz \rightarrow \sim Ez)$
2. $(z)(Sz \rightarrow Nz)$ $\therefore (z)(Sz \rightarrow \sim Ez)$
3. $Na \rightarrow \sim Ea$ 1, UI
4. $Sa \rightarrow Na$ 2, UI
5. $Sa \rightarrow \sim Ea$ 4, 3, HS
6. $(z)(Sz \rightarrow \sim Ez)$ 5, UG

5. 1. $(\exists y)Fy \rightarrow (y)My$
2. Fg $\therefore Mg$
3. $(\exists y)Fy$ 2, EG
4. $(y)My$ 1, 3, MP
5. Mg 4, UI

8. 1. $(x)[(Bx \vee Ax) \leftrightarrow Cx]$
2. $(x)\sim Cx$ $\therefore (x)(Ax \leftrightarrow Bx)$
3. $(Ba \vee Aa) \leftrightarrow Ca$ 1, UI
4. $[(Ba \vee Aa) \rightarrow Ca] \bullet [Ca \rightarrow (Ba \vee Aa)]$ 3, ME
5. $(Ba \vee Aa) \rightarrow Ca$ 4, Simp
6. $\sim Ca$ 2, UI
7. $\sim(Ba \vee Aa)$ 5, 6, MT
8. $\sim(Aa \vee Ba)$ 7, Com
9. $\sim Aa \bullet \sim Ba$ 8, DeM
10. $(Aa \bullet Ba) \vee (\sim Aa \bullet \sim Ba)$ 9, Add
11. $Aa \leftrightarrow Ba$ 10, ME
12. $(x)(Ax \leftrightarrow Bx)$ 11, UG

Part G: English Arguments

1. 1. $(x)(Ix \rightarrow Hx)$
2. $(x)(Cx \rightarrow \sim Hx)$ $\therefore (x)(Cx \rightarrow \sim Ix)$
3. $Ia \rightarrow Ha$ 1, UI
4. $Ca \rightarrow \sim Ha$ 2, UI
5. $\sim Ha \rightarrow \sim Ia$ 3, Cont
6. $Ca \rightarrow \sim Ia$ 4, 5, HS
7. $(x)(Cx \rightarrow \sim Ix)$ 5, UG

4. 1. Pg
2. $(x)(Px \rightarrow \sim\sim Rx)$ $\therefore Rg$
3. $Pg \rightarrow \sim\sim Rg$ 2, UI
4. $Pg \rightarrow Rg$ 3, DN
5. Rg 4, 1, MP

7. 1. $(x)[Px \rightarrow (Dx \leftrightarrow Sx)]$
2. $Sb \bullet \sim So$
3. $Pb \bullet Po$ $\therefore Db \bullet \sim Do$
4. $Pb \rightarrow (Db \leftrightarrow Sb)$ 1, UI
5. Pb 3, Simp
6. $Db \leftrightarrow Sb$ 4, 5, MP
7. $(Db \rightarrow Sb) \bullet (Sb \rightarrow Db)$ 6, ME
8. Sb 2, Simp
9. $Sb \rightarrow Db$ 7, Simp
10. Db 9, 8, MP
11. $Po \rightarrow (Do \leftrightarrow So)$ 1, UI
12. Po 3, Simp
13. $Do \leftrightarrow So$ 11, 12, MP
14. $(Do \rightarrow So) \bullet (So \rightarrow Do)$ 13, ME
15. $\sim So$ 2, Simp
16. $Do \rightarrow So$ 14, Simp

17. ~Do   16, 15, MT
18. Db • ~Do   10, 17, Conj

EXERCISE 9.4
Part A: Proofs

1. 1. (x)Ax → (x)Bx
    2. ~(x)Bx   ∴ (∃x)~Ax
    3. ~(x)Ax   1, 2, MT
    4. (∃x)~Ax   3, QN

4. 1. ~(∃x)~Gx   ∴ (x)Gx
    2. (x)~~Gx   1, QN
    3. (x)Gx   2, DN

7. 1. (x)(Nx → Ox)   ∴ ~(x)Ox → ~(x)Nx
    2. ~(x)Ox   Assume (for CP)
    3. (∃x)~Ox   2, QN
    4. ~Od   3, EI
    5. Nd → Od   1, UI
    6. ~Nd   5, 4, MT
    7. (∃x)~Nx   6, EG
    8. ~(x)Nx   7, QN
    9. ~(x)Ox → ~(x)Nx   2–8, CP

10. 1. (x)(Ax → ~Bx)
    2. (y)Ay   ∴ (z)~Bz
    3. ~(z)~Bz   Assume (for RAA)
    4. (∃z)~~Bz   3, QN
    5. ~~Bd   4, EI
    6. Bd   5, DN
    7. Ad → ~Bd   1, UI
    8. Ad   2, UI
    9. ~Bd   7, 8, MP
    10. Bd • ~Bd   6, 9, Conj
    11. (z)~Bz   3–10, RAA

(Note that, though in line (5) d is a constant introduced by EI, there are no subsequent applications of UG that depend on it.)

13. 1. (∃x)[Bx → (y)~Cy]
    2. ~(∃y)Cy → ~(∃z)Dz   ∴ (x)Bx → (z)~Dz
    3. (x)Bx   Assume (for CP)
    4. Ba → (y)~Cy   1, EI
    5. Ba   3, UI
    6. (y)~C   4, 5, MP
    7. ~(∃y)Cy   6, QN
    8. ~(∃z)Dz   2, 7, MP
    9. (z)~Dz   8, QN
    10. (x)Bx → (z)~Dz   3–9, CP

16. 1. ~(x)Mx ∨ (∃x)~Mx
    2. (∃x)Sx → (x)Mx
    3. Sb ∨ (x)~Px   ∴ ~Pa
    4. ~(x)Mx ∨ ~(x)Mx   1, QN
    5. ~(x)Mx   4, Re
    6. ~(∃x)Sx   2, 5, MT
    7. (x)~Sx   6, QN
    8. ~Sb   7, UI
    9. (x)~Px   3, 8, DS
    10. ~Pa   9, UI

19.
1. $(x)(Lx \leftrightarrow (y)My)$	$\therefore (x)Lx \lor (x)\sim Lx$
2. $\sim(x)Lx \lor (x)\sim Lx$	Assume (for RAA)
3. $\sim(x)Lx \bullet \sim(x)\sim Lx$	2, DeM
4. $\sim(x)Lx$	3, Simp
5. $(\exists x)\sim Lx$	4, QN
6. $\sim(x)\sim Lx$	3, Simp
7. $(\exists x)\sim\sim Lx$	6, QN
8. $(\exists x)Lx$	7, DN
9. La	8, EI
10. $La \leftrightarrow (y)My$	1, UI
11. $(La \rightarrow (y)My) \bullet ((y)My \rightarrow La)$	10, ME
12. $La \rightarrow (y)My$	11, Simp
13. $(y)My$	12, 9, MP
14. $\sim Lb$	5, EI
15. $Lb \leftrightarrow (y)My$	1, UI
16. $(Lb \rightarrow (y)My) \bullet ((y)My \rightarrow Lb)$	15, ME
17. $(y)My \rightarrow Lb$	16, Simp
18. $\sim(y)My$	14, 17, MT
19. $(y)My \bullet \sim(y)My$	13, 18, Conj
20. $(x)Lx \lor (x)\sim Lx$	2–19, RAA

Part B: More Proofs

1.
1. $(\exists x)Fx \rightarrow (\exists x)(Gx \bullet Hx)$	
2. $(\exists x)Hx \rightarrow (x)Jx$	$\therefore (x)(Fx \rightarrow Jx)$
3. Fa	Assume (for CP)
4. $(\exists x)Fx$	3, EG
5. $(\exists x)(Gx \bullet Hx)$	1, 4, MP
6. $Gb \bullet Hb$	5, EI
7. Hb	6, Simp
8. $(\exists x)Hx$	7, EG
9. $(x)Jx$	2, 8, MP
10. Ja	9, UI
11. $Fa \rightarrow Ja$	3–10, CP
12. $(x)(Fx \rightarrow Jx)$	11, UG

4.
1. $\sim(\exists x)Mx \rightarrow (\exists x)(Nx \bullet Px)$	
2. $(x)\sim Px$	$\therefore (\exists x)Mx$
3. $\sim(\exists x)Mx$	Assume (for RAA)
4. $(\exists x)(Nx \bullet Px)$	1, 3, MP
5. $Na \bullet Pa$	4, EI
6. $\sim Pa$	2, UI
7. Pa	5, Simp
8. $Pa \bullet \sim Pa$	7, 6, Conj
9. $(\exists x)Mx$	3–8, RAA

7.
1. $(x)(Cx \rightarrow Dx)$	
2. $\sim(\exists x)Cx \rightarrow (\exists x)Dx$	$\therefore \sim(x)\sim Dx$
3. $(x)\sim Dx$	Assume (for RAA)
4. $\sim(\exists x)Dx$	3, QN
5. $\sim\sim(\exists x)Cx$	2, 4, MT
6. $(\exists x)Cx$	5, DN
7. Ca	6, EI
8. $Ca \rightarrow Da$	1, UI
9. Da	8, 7, MP
10. $\sim Da$	3, UI
11. $Da \bullet \sim Da$	9, 10, Conj
12. $\sim(x)\sim Dx$	3–11, RAA

10.   1. (∃x)~Kx → ~(∃x)Dx
    2. ~(x)Kx
    3. Db ↔ Qa   ∴ ~Qa
    4. (∃x)~Kx   2, QN
    5. ~(∃x)Dx   1, 4, MP
    6. (x)~Dx   5, QN
    7. ~Db   6, UI
    8. (Db → Qa) • (Qa → Db)   3, ME
    9. Qa → Db   8, Simp
    10. ~Qa   9, 7, MT

13.   1. ~[(x)Ax → (∃x)Bx]
    2. (∃x)~Cx → (∃x)Bx
    3. (x)[(Ax • Cx) → Da]   ∴ Da
    4. ~[~(x)Ax ∨ (∃x)Bx]   1, MI
    5. ~~(x)Ax • ~(∃x)Bx   4, DeM
    6. ~(∃x)Bx   5, Simp
    7. ~(∃x)~Cx   2, 6, MT
    8. (x)Cx   7, QN
    9. ~~(x)Ax   5, Simp
    10. (x)Ax   9, DN
    11. Cd   8, UI
    12. Ad   10, UI
    13. Ad • Cd   11, 12, Conj
    14. (Ad • Cd) → Da   3, UI
    15. Da   13, 14, MP

16.   1. (x)[(Ax → ~Bx) ∨ Cb]
    2. ~(∃x)Cx
    3. (∃y)By   ∴ ~(y)Ay
    4. (Aa → ~Ba) ∨ Cb   1, UI
    5. (x)~Cx   2, QN
    6. ~Cb   5, UI
    7. Aa → ~Ba   4, 6, DS
    8. (x)(Ax → ~Bx)   7, UG
    9. Bd   3, EI
    10. ~~Bd   9, DN
    11. Ad → ~Bd   8, UI
    12. ~Ad   11, 10, MT
    13. (∃y)~Ay   12, EG
    14. ~(y)Ay   13, QN

19.   1. [~(x)(R • Px) → (R → ~(x)Px)] →
     (∃x)[Ax • (y)(~Ay ∨ ~By)]   ∴ ~(x)Bx
    2. ~(x)(R • Px)   Assume (for CP)
    3. R   Assume (for CP)
    4. (x)Px   Assume (for RAA)
    5. Pa   4, UI
    6. R • Pa   3, 5, Conj
    7. (x)(R • Px)   6, UG
    8. (x)(R • Px) • ~(x)(R • Px)   2, 7, Conj
    9. ~(x)Px   4–8, RAA
    10. R → ~(x)Px   3–9, CP
    11. ~(x)(R • Px) → (R → ~(x)Px)   2–10, CP
    12. (∃x)[Ax • (y)(~Ay ∨ ~By)]   1, 11, MP
    13. Ab • (y)(~Ay ∨ ~By)   12, EI
    14. Ab   13, Simp

15. (y)(~Ay ∨ ~By)	13, Simp
16. ~Ab ∨ ~Bb	15, UI
17. ~~Ab	14, DN
18. ~Bb	16, 17, DS
19. (∃x)~Bx	18, EG
20. ~(x)Bx	19, QN

Part C: Logical Equivalents

1.
1. (x)(Ax • Bx)	∴ (x)Ax • (x)Bx
2. Ad • Bd	1, UI
3. Ad	2, Simp
4. Bd	2, Simp
5. (x)Ax	3, UG
6. (x)Bx	4, UG
7. (x)Ax • (x)Bx	5, 6, Conj

4.
1. (∃x)Ax ∨ (∃x)Bx	∴ (∃x)(Ax ∨ Bx)
2. ~(∃x)(Ax ∨ Bx)	Assume (for RAA)
3. (x)~(Ax ∨ Bx)	2, QN
4. (x)(~Ax • ~Bx)	3, DeM
5. (∃x)Ax	Assume (for RAA)
6. Aa	5, EI
7. ~Aa • ~Ba	4, UI
8. ~Aa	7, Simp
9. Aa • ~Aa	6, 8, Conj
10. ~(∃x)Ax	5–9, RAA
11. (∃x)Bx	1, 10, DS
12. Bb	11, EI
13. ~Ab • ~Bb	4, UI
14. ~Bb	13, Simp
15. Bb • ~Bb	12, 14, Conj
16. (∃x)(Ax ∨ Bx)	2–15, RAA

7.
1. (x)(Ax → P)	∴ (∃x)Ax → P
2. (∃x)Ax	Assume (for CP)
3. Aa	2, EI
4. Aa → P	1, UI
5. P	4, 3, MP
6. (∃x)Ax → P	2–5, CP

Part D: English Arguments

1.
1. (x)(Tx → Dx)	
2. (∃x)[Tx • (Wx ∨ Cx)] → (∃x)(Tx • ~Dx)	∴ (x)(Tx → ~Cx)
3. Ta	Assume (for CP)
4. (x)(Tx → ~~Dx)	1, DN
5. (x)(~Tx ∨ ~~Dx)	4, MI
6. (x)~(Tx • ~Dx)	5, DeM
7. ~(∃x)(Tx • ~Dx)	6, QN
8. ~(∃x)[Tx • (Wx ∨ Cx)]	2, 7, MT
9. (x)~[Tx • (Wx ∨ Cx)]	8, QN
10. (x)[~Tx ∨ ~(Wx ∨ Cx)]	9, DeM
11. (x)[Tx → ~(Wx ∨ Cx)]	10, MI
12. (x)[Tx → (~Wx • ~Cx)]	11, DeM
13. Ta → (~Wa • ~Ca)	12, UI
14. ~Wa • ~Ca	13, 3, MP
15. ~Ca	14, Simp
16. Ta → ~Ca	3–15, CP
17. (x)(Tx → ~Cx)	16, UG

4.   1. (x)[Kx → (Wx ↔ Ex)]
    2. (x)(Px → Kx)
    3. (x)(Fx → Px)
    4. (x)(Px → Ex)   ∴ (x)(Fx → Wx)
    5. Fa   Assume (for CP)
    6. Fa → Pa   3, UI
    7. Pa → Ea   4, UI
    8. Pa   6, 5, MP
    9. Ea   7, 8, MP
   10. Pa → Ka   2, UI
   11. Ka   10, 8, MP
   12. Ka → (Wa ↔ Ea)   1, UI
   13. Wa ↔ Ea   12, 11, MP
   14. (Wa → Ea) • (Ea → Wa)   13, ME
   15. Ea → Wa   14, Simp
   16. Wa   15, 9, MP
   17. Fa → Wa   5–16, CP
   18. (x)(Fx → Wx)   17, UG

7.   1. (∃x)(Rx • Bx)
    2. (∃x)(Mx • Hx)
    3. (∃x)Rx → (x)[Hx → (Mx → Fx)]   ∴ (∃x)(Mx • Fx)
    4. Ra • Ba   1, EI
    5. Ra   4, Simp
    6. (∃x)Rx   5, EG
    7. (x)[Hx → (Mx → Fx)]   3, 6, MP
    8. Mb • Hb   2, EI
    9. Hb → (Mb → Fb)   7, UI
   10. Hb   8, Simp
   11. Mb → Fb   9, 10, MP
   12. Mb   8, Simp
   13. Fb   11, 12, MP
   14. Mb • Fb   12, 13, Conj
   15. (∃x)(Mx • Fx)   14, EG

EXERCISE 9.5

Part B: Symbolizing

  1. (x)~Lxx
  4. (∃x)[Fx • (y)(Py → Rxy)]
  7. (x)[Dx → ~(∃y)(Hy • Wxy)]
 10. (x)[(Ox • Px) → ~(∃y)((Oy • Wy) • Rxy)]
 13. (x)(Mx → ~Mxx)
 16. (x)(Mx → Axb)
 19. (x)[Sx → ~(y)(Py → (z)(Dz → Hxyz))]
 22. (x)(y)(z)[(Fxy • Fyz) → ~Fxz]
 25. (x)(y)(Nxy → Nyx)

Part D: More Symbolizing

  1. (∃x)[Px • (y)(Py → Axy)]
  4. (∃x)(Px • Lxx) • (∃y)(Py • ~Lyy)
  7. (x)(∃y)Cxy
 10. (x)~(∃y)Cxy

Part E: Ready for a Challenge?

  1. (∃x)(∃y)[(Px • Cy) • (Hxy • Exy)]
  4. (x)[(Mx • ~Ix) → (∃y)(Cy • Pxy)]
  7. (x)[(Px • (∃y)(Py • Hxy)) → Hxx]

10. (∃x)(∃y)[(Px • Myx) • Myj]
13. (∃x)[Tx • ~(∃y)(Ry • (∃y)(Pz • Lyzx))]
16. (x)[(Sx • Rx) → (y)(My → ~Gxy)]
19. (x)(y)[((Px • Py) • Mxy) → (∃z)(Pz • Wzxy)]

EXERCISE 9.6

Part A: Correct or Incorrect?

Note: Inferences are correct unless marked "incorrect."

1. 1. (x)(y)(Mx • Nxy)
    2. (y)(My • Nyy)   1, UI   Incorrect

4. 1. (x)[(∃y)Lxy → Kx]
    2. (∃y)Lby → Kb   1, UI

7. 1. Eab → Fab
    2. (x)(Exb → Fxb)   1, UG   Incorrect

10. 1. (∃x)(y)(Kyx ∨ ~Lxa)
    2. (y)(Kya ∨ ~Laa)   1, EI   Incorrect

13. 1. (x)[Sxb → (y)Rxy]
    2. Sbb → (y)Rby   1, UI

19. 1. ~Lnn
    2. (∃x)~Lxx   1, EG
    3. (∃x)~Lxn   1, EG
    4. (∃x)~Lnx   1, EG

22. 1. (∃x)Fxd
    2. Fad   1, EI
    3. (x)Fxd   2, UG   Incorrect

Part B: Proofs

1. 1. (x)(y)(Rxy → Ryx)
    2. Rab   ∴ Rba
    3. (y)(Ray → Rya)   1, UI
    4. Rab → Rba   3, UI
    5. Rba   4, 2, MP

4. 1. (y)(Bay ∨ Bya)   ∴ Baa
    2. Baa ∨ Baa   1, UI
    3. Baa   2, Re

7. 1. (∃x)[Hx • (y)(Hy → Lyx)]   ∴ (∃x)(Hx • Lxx)
    2. Ha • (y)(Hy → Lya)   1, EI
    3. Ha   2, Simp
    4. (y)(Hy → Lya)   2, Simp
    5. Ha → Laa   4, UI
    6. Laa   5, 3, MP
    7. Ha • Laa   3, 6, Conj
    8. (∃x)(Hx • Lxx)   7, EG

10. 1. ~(∃x)[Px • (∃y)(Py • Lxy)] ∴(x)[Px → (y)(Py → ~Lxy)]
    2. (x)~[Px • (∃y)(Py • Lxy)] 1, QN
    3. ~[Pa • (∃y)(Py • Lay)]   2, UI
    4. ~Pa ∨ ~(∃y)(Py • Lay) 3, DeM
    5. ~Pa ∨ (y)~(Py • Lay)   4, QN
    6. ~Pa ∨ (y)(~Py ∨ ~Lay) 5, DeM
    7. Pa → (y)(~Py ∨ ~Lay)   6, MI
    8. Pa → (y)(Py → ~Lay)   7, MI
    9. (x)[Px → (y)(Py → ~Lxy)] 8, UG

Part C: English Arguments

1. Ormazd is morally superior to Ahriman. For all x, for all y, if x is morally superior to y, then y is not morally superior to x. Hence, Ahriman is not morally superior to Ormazd. (o: Ormazd; a: Ahriman; Sxy: x is morally superior to y)

1. Soa
2. (x)(y)(Sxy → ~Syx)   ∴ ~Sao
3. (y)(Soy → ~Syo)   2, UI
4. Soa → ~Sao   3, UI
5. ~Sao   4, 1, MP

4. Any rational animal is of greater intrinsic value than any nonrational animal. Karen is a rational animal, but she is not of greater intrinsic value than George. So, if George is an animal, then he is rational. (Rx: x is rational; Ax: x is an animal; Gxy: x is of greater intrinsic value than y; k: Karen; g: George)

1. (x)[(Rx • Ax) → (y)[(~Ry • Ay) → Gxy]]
2. (Rk • Ak) • ~Gkg   ∴ Ag → Rg
3. (Rk • Ak) → (y)[(~Ry • Ay) → Gky]   1, UI
4. Rk • Ak   2, Simp
5. (y)[(~Ry • Ay) → Gky]   3, 4, MP
6. (~Rg • Ag) → Gkg   5, UI
7. ~Gkg   2, Simp
8. ~(~Rg • Ag)   6, 7, MT
9. ~~Rg ∨ ~Ag   8, DeM
10. ~Ag ∨ ~~Rg   9, Com
11. ~Ag ∨ Rg   10, DN
12. Ag → Rg   11, MI

10. There are sets. Hence, it is not the case that there is a set that contains all and only those sets that do not contain themselves. (Sx: x is a set; Cxy: x contains y)

1. (∃x)Sx   ∴ ~(∃x)[Sx • (y)(Sy → (Cxy ↔ ~Cyy))]
2. (∃x)[Sx • (y)(Sy → (Cxy ↔ ~Cyy))]   Assume (for RAA)
3. Sa • (y)[Sy → (Cay ↔ ~Cyy)]   2, EI
4. Sa   3, Simp
5. (y)[Sy → (Cay ↔ ~Cyy)]   3, Simp
6. Sa → (Caa ↔ ~Caa)   5, UI
7. Ca2 ↔ ~Caa   6, 4, MP
8. (Caa → ~Caa) • (~Caa → Caa)   7, ME
9. Caa → ~Caa   8, Simp
10. ~Caa ∨ ~Caa   9, MI
11. ~Caa   10, Re
12. ~Caa → Caa   8, Simp
13. Caa   12, 11, MP
14. Caa • ~Caa   13, 11, Conj
15. ~(∃x)[Sx • (y)(Sy → (Cxy ↔ ~Cyy))]   2–14, RAA

EXERCISE 9.7

Part A: Symbolizing

1. ~t = j
4. ~(∃x)~x = x
7. (x)x = x
10. (∃x)(∃y)(Px • Py • ~x = y • Ax • Ay)

Part B: More Symbolizing

1. (∃x)~x = x → (x)~Mx
4. (∃x)(∃y) [~x = y • (z)(z = x ∨ z = y)]
7. (∃x)(Px • Sxa • (y)[(Py • Sya) → x = y])
10. (Dk • Gk) • (x)[(Dx • ~x = k) → ~Gx]

EXERCISE 9.8

Part A: Proofs

1. 1. Na • ~Nb   ∴ ~a = b
     2. a = b   Assume (for RAA)
     3. Na • ~Na   1, 2, LL
     4. ~a = b   2–3, RAA

4. 1. c = d → e = g
     2. d = c
     3. Fg   ∴ Fe
     4. c = d   2, Sm
     5. e = g   1, 4, MP
     6. Fe   5, 3, LL

7. 1. (y)(Ay → By)
     2. Ab
     3. b = c   ∴ Bc
     4. Ab → Bb   1, UI
     5. Bb   4, 2, MP
     6. Bc   3, 5, LL

10.   1. (x)(Hx → Jx)
      2. (x)(Kx → Lx)
      3. Hd • Kc
      4. c = d   ∴ Jc • Ld
      5. Hd → Jd   1, UI
      6. Kc → Lc   2, UI
      7. Hd   3, Simp
      8. Jd   5, 7, MP
      9. Jc   4, 8, LL
    10. Kc   3, Simp
    11. Lc   6, 10, MP
    12. Ld   4, 11, LL
    13. Jc • Ld   9, 12, Conj

13.   1. (∃x)Hx
      2. (x)(y)[(Hx • Hy) → x = y]   ∴ (∃x)[Hx • (y)(Hy → x = y)]
      3. Ha   1, EI
      4. ~(∃x)[Hx • (y)(Hy → x = y)]   Assume (for RAA)
      5. (x)~[Hx • (y)(Hy → x = y)]   4, QN
      6. (x)[~Hx ∨ ~(y)(Hy → x = y)]   5, DeM
      7. ~Ha ∨ ~(y)(Hy → a = y)   6, UI
      8. ~~Ha   3, DN
      9. ~(y)(Hy → a = y)   7, 8, DS
    10. (∃y)~(Hy → a = y)   9, QN
    11. (∃y)~(~Hy ∨ a = y)   10, MI
    12. (∃y)(~~Hy • ~a = y)   11, DeM
    13. (∃y)(Hy • ~a = y)   12, DN
    14. Hb • ~a = b   13, EI
    15. (y)[(Ha • Hy) → a = y]   2, UI
    16. (Ha • Hb) → a = b   15, UI
    17. Hb   14, Simp
    18. Ha • Hb   3, 17, Conj
    19. a = b   16, 18, MP
    20. ~a = b   14, Simp
    21. a = b • ~a = b   19, 20, Conj
    22. (∃x)[Hx • (y)(Hy → x = y)]   4–21, RAA

16.
1. $(\exists x)([(Ax \bullet Bxa) \bullet (y)((Ay \bullet Bya) \to y = x)] \bullet Dxb)$
2. $Ac \bullet Bca$ $\therefore Dcb$
3. $[(Ad \bullet Bda) \bullet (y)((Ay \bullet Bya) \to y = d)] \bullet Ddb$ 1, EI
4. $(Ad \bullet Bda) \bullet (y)[(Ay \bullet Bya) \to y = d]$ 3, Simp
5. $Ad \bullet Bda$ 4, Simp
6. $(y)[(Ay \bullet Bya) \to y = d]$ 4, Simp
7. $(Ac \bullet Bca) \to c = d$ 6, UI
8. $c = d$ 7, 2, MP
9. Ddb 3, Simp
10. Dcb 8, 9, LL

Part B: English Arguments

1. No one antedates himself. Augustine antedates Boethius. Augustine and Boethius are both persons. Therefore, Augustine is not identical with Boethius. (Px: x is a person; Axy: x antedates y; a: Augustine; b: Boethius)

1. $(x)(Px \to {\sim}Axx)$
2. Aab
3. $Pa \bullet Pb$ $\therefore {\sim}a = b$
4. $a = b$ Assume (for RAA)
5. $Pa \to {\sim}Aaa$ 1, UI
6. Pa 3, Simp
7. ${\sim}Aaa$ 5, 6, MP
8. ${\sim}Aab$ 4, 7, LL
9. $Aab \bullet {\sim}Aab$ 2, 8, Conj
10. ${\sim}a = b$ 4–9, RAA

4. There are exactly two omniscient beings. Apollo is omniscient. We may infer that there is an omniscient being distinct from Apollo. (Ox: x is omniscient; a: Apollo)

1. $(\exists x)(\exists y)[(Ox \bullet Oy) \bullet {\sim}x = y] \bullet (x)(y)(z)$
   $[(Ox \bullet Oy \bullet Oz) \to (x = y \vee x = z \vee y = z)]$
2. Oa $\therefore (\exists x)(Ox \bullet {\sim}x = a)$
3. ${\sim}(\exists x)(Ox \bullet {\sim}x = a)$ Assume (for RAA)
4. $(x){\sim}(Ox \bullet {\sim}x = a)$ 3, QN
5. $(\exists x)(\exists y)[(Ox \bullet Oy) \bullet {\sim}x = y]$ 1, Simp
6. $(\exists y)[(Ob \bullet Oy) \bullet {\sim}b = y]$ 5, EI
7. $(Ob \bullet Od) \bullet {\sim}b = d$ 6, EI
8. $(x)({\sim}Ox \vee {\sim}{\sim}x = a)$ 4, DeM
9. $(x)({\sim}Ox \vee x = a)$ 8, DN
10. ${\sim}Ob \vee b = a$ 9, UI
11. $Ob \bullet Od$ 7, Simp
12. Ob 11, Simp
13. ${\sim}{\sim}Ob$ 12, DN
14. $b = a$ 10, 13, DS
15. ${\sim}b = d$ 7, Simp
16. ${\sim}a = d$ 14, 15, LL
17. ${\sim}Od \vee d = a$ 9, UI
18. Od 11, Simp
19. ${\sim}{\sim}Od$ 18, DN
20. $d = a$ 17, 19, DS
21. ${\sim}b = a$ 20, 15, LL
22. $b = a \bullet {\sim}b = a$ 14, 21, Conj
23. $(\exists x)(Ox \bullet {\sim}x = a)$ 3–22, RAA

CHAPTER 10

EXERCISE 10.1

Part A: True or False?

1.	T	**13.**	T
4.	T	**16.**	F
7.	T	**19.**	F
10.	F		

Part B: Identifying and Evaluating Statistical Syllogisms

1. Not a statistical syllogism. (In a statistical syllogism, the percentage is greater than 50 and less than 100.)

4. A statistical syllogism. Johnark is a U.S. senator and many senators oppose campaign reform, so there is a possible fallacy of incomplete evidence here.

7. A statistical syllogism. Goggans owns a coffeehouse, however, so it seems likely that he drinks coffee; so there is a possible fallacy of incomplete evidence here.

10. A statistical syllogism.

13. Not a statistical syllogism. (Unless taken as enthymematic, with a tacit assumption of the unstated premise that "most 65-year-old men do not make a living as professional boxers.")

EXERCISE 10.2

Part A: Identifying Inductive Arguments

1. Induction by enumeration.

4. Induction by enumeration. Sampling error: ±3 percent.

7. Argument from authority. Here the authority is an appropriate and reliable one.

10. Incorrect form. (This is an *ad verecundiam* fallacy.)

13. Induction by enumeration. Sampling error: ±2 percent.

16. Induction by enumeration. The sample is too small. (Sampling error will be greater than ±11 percent.)

19. Argument from authority. There is a fallacy of incomplete evidence here because the authorities (i.e., eyewitnesses) disagree about Black Coyote's role.

Part B: Analyzing and Evaluating Analogies

1. A is Mars; B is the earth; P is the property of being inhabited by living things. The reply indicates that being a heavenly body that orbits the sun is no guarantee of being inhabited by living things. We might add that Mars and the earth are dissimilar in relevant ways; for example, Mars is much colder than the earth and its atmosphere contains relatively little oxygen.

4. A is logic; B is whiskey; P is the property of being such that very large quantities should be avoided. The stated reply does not indicate a weakness in the argument, for even if logic does not contain alcohol, logic may nevertheless lose its beneficial effects when taken in very large quantities. (The same can be said about aspirin or vitamins.) The vagueness of the phrase "very large quantities" makes it difficult to evaluate the argument. What is a very large quantity of whiskey? Enough to cause drunkenness? Enough to impair one's judgment? Enough so that one is unable to walk? What is a very large quantity of logic? So much that one becomes mentally unbalanced—for example, unable to appreciate nonlogical aspects of life properly, such as the emotions? If so, then perhaps the argument is strong. But lovers of logic may rightly observe that very few people take logic in quantities of that magnitude, so the argument is seldom applicable.

10. A is a computer; B is a human brain; P is the property of being aware of one's own thoughts and feelings. The words "computer" and "brain" are used literally here. The stated reply does not seem to point to an important defect in the analogy. Metal, plastic, and brain tissue are all physical in nature. And metal and plastic can be structured so as to simulate *some* functions of the brain.

EXERCISE 10.3

Part A: Mill's Methods
1. Method of concomitant variation.
4. Method of agreement. A better hypothesis: Studying intensely for three hours increases the quality of Alonzo's performance on exams.
7. Joint method.
10. Method of agreement.
13. Joint method.
16. Joint method.
19. Joint method.
22. Method of residues.

Part B: Hypotheses
1. There seems to be no way to test the hypothesis, even though it has a certain measure of explanatory power (in the sense that if it were true, it might explain the observed behavior of the watch, depending on what one assumes about the demon's motives, means of operation, etc.). The notion of an invisible, unexorcisable demon is not clearly defined and may not be consistent with other well-established and perhaps simpler hypotheses.
4. The hypothesis appears to be low in explanatory power. Bees surely do not generate enough body heat to warm the atmosphere.
7. This hypothesis is inconsistent with well-established theories. Current physical theory holds that nothing starting from sub–light speeds can travel faster than the speed of light.

EXERCISE 10.4

Part A: Atomic Statements
1. $1/52$
4. $13/52 = 1/4$
7. $1/52$

Part B: Disjunctions
1. $13/52 + 13/52 = 26/52 = 1/2$
4. $1/52 + 13/52 = 14/52 = 7/26$
7. Alternatives not mutually exclusive. $26/52 + 4/52 – 2/52 = 28/52 = 7/13$

Part C: Conjunctions and Conditionals
1. $4/52 \times 4/51 = 16/2652 = 4/663$
4. $13/52 \times 12/51 = 156/2652 = 3/51$
7. $1/52 \times 0 = 0$

Part D: Various Compound Statements
1. $P(\sim G) = 1 – P(G) = 5/5 – 3/5 = 2/5$
4. $P(M \vee \sim M) = 1$ (tautology)
7. $P(M \bullet G) = P(M) \times P(G/M) = 3/10 \times 9/10 = 27/100$
10. $P[D \rightarrow (G \rightarrow D)] = 1$ (tautology)

Part E: The Strength of Arguments
1. $5/(5 + 1) = 5/6$ and $4/(4 + 1) = 4/5$. Using the restricted conjunction rule, the probability that Team A will play Team C in the semifinals is $5/6 \times 4/5 = 20/30 = 2/3$.
4. The events are independent, so the restricted conjunction rule applies:
P(2 on first throw and 2 on second throw) = P(2 on first throw) ×
P(2 on second throw) = $1/6 \times 1/6 = 1/36$
7. Using the general conjunction rule: P(Ted and Sue were both at the party) = P(Ted was at the party) × P(Sue was at the party given that Ted was at the party) = $15/(15 + 1) \times 20/(20 + 1) = 15/16 \times 20/21 = 25/28$

Part F: Patterns

1. a. $P(H/E) = \dfrac{1/2 \times 1/2}{[1/2 \times 1/2] + [1/2 \times 1/2]} = \dfrac{1/4}{1/4 + 1/4} = \dfrac{1/4}{2/4} = 1/4 \times 4/2 = 4/8 = 1/2$

2. a. $P(H/E) = \dfrac{1/5 \times 9/10}{[1/5 \times 9/10] + [4/5 \times 9/10]} = \dfrac{9/50}{9/50 + 36/50} = 9/45 = 1/5$

3. a. $P(H/E) = \dfrac{9/10 \times 2/5}{[9/10 \times 2/5] + [1/10 \times 2/5]} = \dfrac{18/50}{18/50 + 2/50} = 18/20 = 9/10$

4. a. $P(H/E) = \dfrac{1/2 \times 9/10}{[1/2 \times 9/10] + [1/2 \times 3/5]} = \dfrac{9/20}{9/20 + 3/10} = 9/15 = 3/5$

$P(\sim H/E) = \dfrac{1/2 \times 3/5}{[1/2 \times 3/5] + [1/2 \times 9/10]} = \dfrac{3/10}{3/10 + 9/20} = \dfrac{6/20}{6/20 + 9/20} = 6/15 = 2/5$

Is $P(\sim H/E) = 1 - P(H/E)$?   Yes

5. b. $P(H/E) = \dfrac{9/10 \times 0}{[9/10 \times 0] + [1/10 \times 1/10]} = 0$

$P(\sim H/E) = \dfrac{1/10 \times 1/10}{[1/10 \times 1/10] + [9/10 \times 0]} = 1$

In general, if $P(E/H) = 0$, then $P(H) \times P(E/H) = 0$, so that with its numerator zero, $P(H/E)$ will also be zero and $P(\sim H/E) = 1$.

6. b. $P(H/E) = \dfrac{5/7 \times 5/7}{[5/7 \times 5/7] + [2/7 \times 4/7]} = \dfrac{25/49}{25/49 + 8/49} = 25/33$

$P(\sim H/E) = \dfrac{2/7 \times 4/7}{[2/7 \times 4/7] + [5/7 \times 5/7]} = \dfrac{8/49}{8/49 + 25/49} = 8/33$

Is $P(\sim H/E) = 1 - P(H/E)$?   Yes

Part G: Applying Bayes' Theorem

1. P(Bloggs prepared) = .40 or 4/10
P(Bloggs passed *given* Bloggs prepared) = .70 or 7/10
P(Bloggs passed *given* Bloggs did not prepare) = .30 or 3/10

$$\dfrac{4/10 \times 7/10}{[4/10 \times 7/10] + [6/10 \times 3/10]} = \dfrac{28/100}{28/100 + 18/100} = \dfrac{28}{46} = \dfrac{14}{23}$$

4. P(God exists) = 1/2
P(some unnecessary suffering occurs *given that* an all-powerful and perfectly good God exists) = 1/(1 + 3) = 1/4
P(some unnecessary suffering occurs *given that* it is not the case that an all-powerful and perfectly good God exists) = 2/(2 + 1) = 2/3
P(God exists given some unnecessary suffering)

$$= \dfrac{1/2 \times 1/4}{[1/2 \times 1/4] + [1/2 \times 2/3]} = \dfrac{1/8}{1/8 + 2/6} = \dfrac{3/24}{3/24 + 8/24} = 3/11$$

Photo Credits

Glossary/Index

Bold words indicate glossary terms
Bold page numbers indicate the page on which the term is defined

proper subclass: class X is a proper subclass of class Y given that X is a
  subclass of Y but Y has members X
  lacks, **124**
propositions: truths or falsehoods that
  may or may not be expressed by a
  sentence, 107–**108**
  and arguments, 60
  and the suggestion that truth is conventional, 108–109
  and what enters into logical relations, 109

QN. *See* quantifier negation (QN)
quantifier: an expression used to indicate
  how many things have a given
  property, **415**
  existential, 418–420
  universal, 415–418
  See also quantifier negation (QN); scope
quantifier negation (QN): an inference
  rule, **460**–462

RAA. *See reductio ad absurdum* (RAA)
random sample: a sample in which each
  member of the population has an
  equal chance of being selected for
  observation, **514**–515
red herring fallacy (*ignoratio elenchi*):
  an argument in which the premises
  are logically unrelated to the conclusion, **159**–160
reductio ad absurdum **(RAA):** an inference rule, 397–402, 462–465
  See also indirect proof
Re. *See* redundancy (Re)
redundancy (Re): an inference rule, **379**
reflexive relation: a relation R such
  that: For all x (x bears R to x), **472**
relations, logic of. *See* logic of relations
repetition: a restatement of a premise or
  conclusion, perhaps with slightly
  altered wording, **76**
report: a set of statements intended to
  provide information about a situation, topic, or event, **64**

residues, method of. *See* method of residues
restricted conjunction rule: a rule of
  probability, **544**–555
restricted disjunction rule: a rule of
  probability, **538**–539
rhetorical elements: elements in an
  argument that increase its psychological persuasiveness without
  affecting its validity, strength,
  soundness, or cogency, 71, 75–**76**
  See also assurance; discount; hedge;
  repetition
rhetorical questions, 74, 81, 98, 291
Ross, James, 508
row in truth tables. *See* truth tables
rules of probability, 537–557
Russell, Bertrand, 508

Salmon, Wesley, 117, 145, 189, 277,
  556, 557
sample: a set of observed members of a
  population, **513**–514
  size of, 515–516
  See also random sample; sampling error
sampling error: the difference between
  the percentage of the sample that
  has the attribute in question and
  the percentage of the population
  that has it, **516**
scheme of abbreviation: an assignment
  of a distinct capital letter to an
  atomic statement, **280**–281, or an
  assignment of a distinct capital letter to a predicate, **415**
science
  precising definitions in, 121
  stipulative definitions in, 120
scientific reasoning, 522–536
  See also hypothesis; hypothetico-
  deductive method; confirming
  instance
scope: the shortest well-formed formula
  (WFF) immediately to the right of
  the quantifier, **422**–424
  See also well-formed formula (WFF)